The Questions on the Octateuch

On Genesis and Exodus

THE LIBRARY OF EARLY CHRISTIANITY

VOLUME 1

Theodoret of Cyrus
The Questions on the Octateuch

VOLUME 1

On Genesis and Exodus

Greek text revised by
JOHN F. PETRUCCIONE

English translation with
introduction and commentary by
†ROBERT C. HILL

The Catholic University of America Press
Washington, D.C.

Designed and typeset by Kachergis Book Design;
printed by Edwards Brothers

LIBRARY OF CONGRESS CATALOGING-IN-PUBLICATION DATA
Theodoret, Bishop of Cyrrhus.
[Quaestiones in Octateuchum. English & Greek.]
The questions on the Octateuch. On Genesis and Exodus /
Theodoret of Cyrus ; Greek text revised by John F. Petruccione ;
English translation with introduction and commentary by Robert
C. Hill.
p. cm. — (The library of early Christianity ; v. 1)
Includes bibliographical references and index.
ISBN 978-0-8132-1498-6 (cloth-vol 1 : alk. paper) — ISBN 978-0-
8132-1499-3 (paper-vol 1 : alk. paper) — ISBN 978-0-8132-1500-6
(cloth-vol 2 : alk. paper) — ISBN 978-0-8132-1501-3 (paper-vol 2 :
alk. paper)   1. Bible. O.T. Genesis—Criticism, interpretation, etc.
2. Bible. O.T. Exodus—Criticism, interpretation, etc.   I. Petruccione, John, 1950–   II. Hill, Robert C. (Robert Charles), 1931–
III. Title.   IV. Title: On Genesis and Exodus.   V. Series.
BR65.T753Q34 2007
222´.07—dc22   2007001312

CONTENTS OF VOLUME 1

ACKNOWLEDGMENTS

John F. Petruccione, Editorial Director
of the Library of Early Christianity

I am most grateful to Professor Robert C. Hill for choosing this nascent series for his fine translation of and commentary on Theodoret's *Questions on the Octateuch.* We had intended to print this work as the first volume of the LEC, but as the manuscript extended to a length greater than anticipated, Dr. McGonagle, Director of the CUA Press, and I decided to divide it between volumes one and two. We hope that we have consulted the interests of our readers by producing, rather than one very unwieldy and expensive tome, two books of manageable size and lower price.

Both Prof. Hill and I owe debts of gratitude to those who have advised and assisted us in this large project. Father Natalio Fernández Marcos has looked through lists of questions regarding *errata*, variant readings, and issues of punctuation. In addition, he has patiently answered numerous queries regarding the contents and *lacunae* of individual manuscripts. Dr. Françoise Petit has provided information regarding the source of passages erroneously attributed to Theodoret by the *Catena Nikephori.* Though I should have been able to locate all of these within her meticulous editions of the *Catenae* on Genesis and Exodus, she kindly replied to a request for direct assistance, thus rescuing me from my own confusions and sparing me some hours of searching.

I have frequently received assistance from my colleagues at the Catholic University of America. Drs. William McCarthy and Eustra-

Acknowledgments

tios Papaioannou (now of Brown University) entertained queries regarding Greek usage, and Dr. McCarthy also provided some useful bibliographical suggestions. I am especially indebted to Dr. Robert Caldwell, who devoted several evenings to discussing textual variants as well as issues of translation and punctuation. I am certain that his advice led me to better solutions on a number of points. My retired colleague, Dr. M. Scowcroft, has kindly provided information on the ms. Dublin, Trinity College, *D.1. 28.*

My research assistants have performed some very large tasks essential to the completeness and accuracy of this volume. Mr. Daryl Grissom has proofread the entire Greek text once and large sections of it a second time. Mrs. Rachel Gilbert has also assisted in the proofreading of both the Greek text and the "Introduction to the Greek Text." Throughout Mr. Brent Gilbert has been my primary assistant. After helping me compile the apparatus of ancient sources, he entered all the call-out letters in both the Greek text and the English translation. In addition, he proofread sections of the Greek text and all the textual notes, compiled the *Index scripturisticus,* and assisted in the compilation of the other indices. Indeed, his critical attention to myriad details has improved every aspect of this volume.

We have been particularly fortunate to have the editorial assistance of Susan Barnes. She has read the entire manuscript with her eagle's eye for inconsistencies, infelicities, and lack of clarity. In addition, her knowledge of both patristic literature and the Greek language has spared us the embarrassment, and the reader the confusion, that would have arisen from many a misstatement or inaccurate translation. Her contribution is thus that of scholarly reader as well as copy editor, functions seldom performed by the same person.

Finally, I wish to thank the many generous patrons who have contributed toward the endowment of this series. I am particularly grateful to my professional colleagues, the members of the North American Patristic Society, who have offered both moral and financial support. They have waited a long time for volume one.

Acknowledgments

Robert C. Hill

I am grateful to Dr. J. Petruccione, the Editorial Director of the Library of Early Christianity, and to Dr. D. McGonagle, Director of the CUA Press, for their decision to print this work in the first volumes of the LEC. It owes much to the painstaking attention of the Editorial Director.

ABBREVIATIONS

Abbreviations

Wis	Wisdom of Solomon
Sir	Wisdom of Jesus ben Sirach, Ecclesiasticus
Is	Isaiah
Jer	Jeremiah
Lam	Lamentations
Bar	Baruch
Ezek	Ezekiel
Dn	Daniel
Hos	Hosea
Jl	Joel
Am	Amos
Ob	Obadiah
Jon	Jonah
Mi	Micah
Na	Nahum
Hab	Habakkuk
Zep	Zephaniah
Hag	Haggai
Zec	Zechariah
Mal	Malachi
NT	New Testament
Mt	Matthew
Mk	Mark
Lk	Luke
Jn	John
Acts	Acts
Rom	The Epistle to the Romans
1–2Cor	The first and second Epistles to the Corinthians
Gal	The Epistle to the Galatians
Eph	The Epistle to the Ephesians
Phil	The Epistle to the Philippians
Col	The Epistle to the Colossians

Abbreviations

ANCIENT AUTHORS AND WORKS

Abbreviations

Abbreviations

Ier.	Thdt., *Commentarius in Ieremiam*
Ios.	Joshua
Iren.	Irenaeus Lugdunensis
Is.	Thdt., *Commentarius in Isaiam*
Iud.	Chrys., *Aduersus Iudaeos*
Iuln.	Cyr., *Contra Iulianum*
Iust.	Iustinus Martyr
Jos.	Josephus
Marc.	Tert., *Aduersus Marcionem*
Mi.	Thdt., *Commentarius in Michaeam*
Migr.	Ph., *De migratione Abrahami*
Or.	Origenes
or.	*oratio*
patm.	Thdt., *Epistulae, collectio patmensis*
pf.	*praefatio*
Ph.	Philo Iudaeus
Phot.	Photius Constantinopolitanus
Pl.	Plato
Placill.	Gr. Nyss., *Oratio funebris de Placilla*
Princ.	Or., *De principiis*
proem.	*proemium*
Proph. obscurit.	Chrys. *De prophetiarum obscuritate hom.* 1–2
Prouid.	Thdt., *Orationes de prouidentia*
Ps.	Thdt., *Commentarii in Psalmos*
Q. in Gen. (*Ex., Leu., Num., Deut., Ios., Iud., Ruth*)	Thdt., *Quaestiones in Genesin* (*Exodum, Leuiticum, Numeros, Deuteronomium, Iosuam, Iudices, Ruth*)
Quaest. et resp.	Thdt., *Quaestiones et responses ad orthodoxos*
Quaest. in oct.	Thdt., *Quaestiones in octateuchum*
Quaest. in Reg. et Par.	Diod. or Thdt., *Quaestiones in Reges et Paralipomena*
1–2 Reg.	libri 1–2 Regum = 1–2Kgs

Abbreviations

MODERN EDITIONS OF THE BIBLE, DICTIONARIES, SERIES, PERIODICALS

Abbreviations

Abbreviations

ThRes   Theological Resources
TLG   *Thesaurus linguae graecae* (stephanus.tlg.uci.edu)
TRE   *Theologische Realenzyklopädie*
VSen   Verba seniorum

OTHER ABBREVIATIONS

ad loc.   *ad locum* = on the aforementioned passage
ap. crit. *apparatus criticus* = the critical notes on the Greek text
ap. font. *apparatus fontium* = the apparatus of ancient sources

INTRODUCTION TO THEODORET'S
LIFE AND WORKS

1. THEODORET

Born about 393 in Antioch, Theodoret owed his name to grateful parents, who were responsible for his entering monastic life at an early age. Since his famous predecessors in that school, if we may use the term,[1] John Chrysostom and Theodore of Mopsuestia, both pupils of Diodore of Tarsus, had been appointed to episcopal responsibilities in Constantinople in 397 and in Mopsuestia in Cilicia in 392, they cannot have exercised much direct influence on Theodoret's formation. In 423 he was elected bishop of Cyrus, a city about 100 kilometers NE of Antioch, perhaps a "little backwater"[2] yet, as Theodoret tells us, a see with responsibility for eight hundred parishes.[3] Caught up in the theological turmoil in the wake of the council of Constantinople of 381, he represented the christological positions of the oriental bishops against that of Cyril of Alexandria and his party. His episcopal and civic duties did not prevent him from writing numerous dogmatic, apologetic, and historical works. In addition, he composed commentaries on Paul's letters and most

---

1. J. Quasten does speak (vol. 2, p. 121), in a local and corporate sense, of "the school of Antioch . . . founded by Lucian . . . in direct opposition to the excesses and fantasies of the allegorical method of Origen," but we prefer to use the term only of a fellowship of like-minded scholars joined by birth, geography, and scholarly principles, even if some members did exercise a magisterial role.

2. V. F.M. Young, *From Nicaea to Chalcedon*, p. 267, but on the evidence of *Ep.* 113, she also concedes (p. 268) the extent of Theodoret's pastoral responsibilities. All references to Theodoret's letters follow the edition of Y. Azéma.

3. V. *Ep.* 113 to Leo I.

of the Old Testament. The commentary on the Song of Songs began the series about the time of the council of Ephesus in 431; and in a letter written in 448 shortly before being deposed at the so-called Robber Council of Ephesus, he could make the claim to have produced expositions of "all the prophets, the psalter, and the apostle." [4] Theodoret was rapidly reinstated by Pope Leo and went on to play a leading role in the convention of the council of Chalcedon in 451. He died about 460. [5]

2. THE CIRCUMSTANCES OF COMPOSITION OF THE *QUESTIONS ON THE OCTATEUCH*

In this epistolary account of his biblical commentaries Theodoret does not mention any work on the Gospels, the Torah, or the Former Prophets. While he seems never to have attempted the first, in his later years, Theodoret did treat the second, and the work of the chronicler as well. He devoted two series of *Quaestiones* to obscure passages of the Octateuch (Genesis to Ruth) and of Kingdoms and Chronicles (1 Samuel through 2 Chronicles).[6] In both he claimed to be responding to a request from his coadjutor bishop Hypatius.[7] He admits to feeling the effects of illness, an admission not found elsewhere in his commentaries. As well, his remarks sometimes suggest a disillusioned veteran; he laments endemic problems of human society such as marital squabbling (*Q.* 30 on Gn) and frequent homicides (*ib. Q.* 43). In the opening of the commentary on Leviticus, he gives (*Q.* 1.1) an overview of his literary

4. *Ep.* 82, written to Eusebius of Ancyra.

5. For a more detailed account of Theodoret's life and works, *v.* J.-N. Guinot, "Theodoret von Kyrrhos," *TRE*, vol. 33, pp. 250–54.

6. N. Fernández Marcos and A. Sáenz-Badillos, *Theodoreti Cyrensis Quaestiones in octateuchum,* TECC, vol. 17 (Madrid 1979); N. Fernández Marcos and J.R. Busto Saiz, *Theodoreti Cyrensis Quaestiones in Reges et Paralipomena,* TECC, vol. 32 (Madrid 1984). The present edition and translation are based on the former.

7. It is possible, of course, that such opening remarks were more conventional than factual; *cf.* sec. 2 of the preface to Theodoret's commentary on the Song of Songs.

output: "writings against the Greeks and the heretics, and . . . the Persian magi, as well as . . . expositions of the Old Testament prophets and . . . commentaries on the epistles of the apostle." This includes the last of the Christian apologies, comparing Greek and Christian philosophy, a lost work against the Persian magi, a compendium of heresies from Simon Magus to Nestorius and Eutyches, and all his exegetical works on the books of the Old Testament and the epistles (κἀν ταῖς τῶν προφητῶν ἑρμηνείαις, καὶ τοῖς τῶν ἀποστολικῶν ἐπιστολῶν ὑπομνήμασιν), but not the Gospels, of the New.[8] The *Questions*, therefore, like a keystone, cap this remarkable edifice completed less than a decade before his death.

In the *Questions on the Octateuch,* Theodoret offers no comment on contemporary events apart from those odd melancholic remarks about social mores. We can glean the occasional insight into contemporary ecclesiastical life and practice from his discussions of the history of Israel and the institutions of Judaism. In *Q.* 109 on Genesis, which deals with Joseph's resuming the land of Egypt from all its citizens with the exception of the priests, the bishop comments wryly, "The priests of the true God do not enjoy this privilege." The issue of recompense for clerical services, dealt with in *Q.* 34 on Numbers, receives lengthy treatment by a cleric for whom it is apparently a burning issue. In Nm 10.7, which prescribes the summoning of the assembly by a trumpet blast, but one that is to be given in such a way as not to alarm the people, Theodoret sees a distinction akin to the differing degrees of explicitness of teaching imparted to the initiated and to the uninitiated in Christian communities.

Theodoret's readers evidently belong to the former category of the faithful.[9] He imagines that, in their Christian formation, they

8. G. Bardy ("La littérature patristique," *RB* 42 [1933]) finds in this statement more precise evidence for the actual date of the *Questions*. He claims (p. 220) that Theodoret's anti-heretical work (*Haereticarum fabularum compendium*) could not have been written before 453, but J.-N. Guinot (*L'Exégèse*) is less definite, placing the date (p. 63) of that work "about 453."

9. One wonders if Theodoret envisaged women among the readers of this or his other works. On rare occasions he makes remarks that the modern reader

may have encountered critics of this part of the Bible or been puzzled by apparent narrative or factual discrepancies. So he declares in his preface that he is intent on dealing with both sorts of problems: "Now, to begin with, you should know that not all inquirers share the same purpose. Some inquire irreverently, believing they find holy Scripture wanting, in some cases, not teaching right doctrine, in others, giving conflicting instructions. In contrast, others, longing to find an answer for their question, search because they love learning." Highlighting the ill-will of carping critics, Theodoret is thinking of Marcionites among others. But it is possible that he is also referring even to his fellow Antiochene commentators Diodore and Theodore, who may have had reservations about the canonicity of Ruth, a book for which there is no extant patristic commentary beyond these *Questions.*[10] As the commentator paraphrases the whole of this book, we may infer that many of his readers were not familiar with the text, despite its christologically significant appendix.[11] We shall examine below how sound an introduction to the Octateuch these readers received from Theodoret's three hundred and sixty-nine questions.[12]

3. THEODORET'S BIBLICAL TEXT

Theodoret read the Octateuch in his local Greek version. In an often-quoted passage of his letter to Sunnia and Fretela, Jerome had identified one of the different forms of the Greek Bible he knew to be current in his time as the "vulgate"; this recension, the one in use in Antioch-Constantinople, was also known as the "Lucianic text,"

---

might regard as sexist. For example, he sees (*Q.* 37.2 on Gn) no place for woman in any prelapsarian design, "since an immortal nature does not require the female." She owed her place to death and the need for procreation.

10. *V.* note 1 to *Q.* 2 on Ruth.

11. *V.* Mt. 1.3–5 and Lk 3.31–33, where the genealogy of Jesus includes the line from Boaz to David detailed in Ruth 4.18–22.

12. These are divided as follows : 112 on Gn, 72 on Ex, 38 on Lv, 51 on Nm, 46 on Dt, 20 on Jos, 28 on Jgs, 2 on Ruth.

for it was said to have been a revision of the Septuagint by Lucian of
Antioch, a scholar-priest of the third century.[13] The nature of Lucian's work has long been a topic of debate. [14] It was precisely because Theodoret's citations could help answer the question of
whether it is possible to identify a distinctively Lucianic or Antiochene text throughout the Octateuch that Natalio Fernández Marcos
and Angel Sáenz-Badillos decided to produce their critical edition.[15]
They concluded (1979) that a typically Antiochene text does emerge
in the last three books, if not in the Torah,[16] and in the revised edition of *The Septuagint in Context,* Fernández Marcos restated this
conclusion some twenty years later (2000). There he argued that, for
the books of Joshua–Ruth, one can identify a group of manuscripts
that agree with Theodoret's citations in a range of peculiar features
some of which predate Lucian while others are post-Hexaplaric. In
his discussion of these characteristics, which are found in different

13. *V. Ep.* 106.2: *admoneo, ut sciatis aliam esse editionem, quam Origenes et Cae-
sariensis Eusebius, omnesque Graeciae tractatores* Κοινήν, *id est,* "communem" *ap-
pellant, atque* "Vulgatam", *et a plerisque nunc* Λουκιάνειος *dicitur; v.* J. Labourt,
Saint Jérôme, Lettres.

14. P. Kahle (*The Cairo Genizah*), had argued (pp. 252–58) that there never was a
single original Greek translation of the Hebrew Scriptures. Instead several independent translations would have been assembled independently in different con-
texts as demanded by liturgical necessity, in a process parallel to the production of
the Aramaic targums. One of these Greek translations would have been made at
Antioch before the version that came to be known as the "Septuagint" was produced in Alexandria. This Antiochene version would have been revised by Lucian
with reference to Hebrew sources. Though Fernández Marcos admits (p. 22) that
the Septuagint is itself, not a translation, but a "collection of translations," he rejects
Kahle's theory of a number of independent Greek translations of the Hebrew Scriptures; *v. The Septuagint in Context,* pp. 54–57. For him, therefore, the question of the
Lucianic recension regards Lucian's alleged revision of the LXX rather than of another translation independently produced in Antioch.

15. *V.* N. Fernández Marcos, *The Septuagint in Context,* p. 229: "To remove this
difficulty [of determining the nature of the Lucianic recension of the Octateuch],
we decided to edit critically Theodoret's *Quaestiones in octateuchum*."

16. *V.* their edition of the *Quaest. in oct.,* pp. LX–LXII and N. Fernández Marcos, *The Septuagint in Context,* p. 229; also *cf.* p. LX of the edition, where they
seem prepared to recognize at least the traces of an Antiochene recension in some
texts of the book of Dt.

degrees in different books, he remains chary of attributing any to Lucian's intervention.[17] In addition, there are distinctive, if not typically Antiochene, readings in Theodoret's text of other books; I discuss some of the more significant in notes to the translation.[18]

The distinctiveness of the LXX *vis à vis* the Masoretic, the standard Hebrew text, is particularly evident in the books of Joshua and Judges. The former appears in a notably shorter form in the LXX and consequently in Theodoret's Antiochene text. In Judges, the Greek recensions are quite divergent among themselves. In the family of manuscripts associated with the *codex vaticanus* of the midfourth century, conventionally designated by the *siglum B,* this book appears in a recension in which the LXX was adapted to the form of the Hebrew text circulating in Palestine in the first century A.D. In manuscripts related to the British Library's *codex alexandrinus* of the fifth century, known as *A,* the Greek text closely resembles that of the LXX transcribed by the third-century scholar Origen in his *Hexapla.*[19] The Antiochene text used by Theodoret, closer throughout to *A* than to *B,* represents a third recension, which Fernández Marcos regards as the closest of the three to the translation of Judges originally incorporated into the LXX.[20] In the Antiochene recension as in the others, we occasionally find, as in the "Song of Deborah" (Jgs 5), the most archaic passage of the Hebrew Bible, mere transliterations of Hebrew words that proved too challenging for the translators.

17. N. Fernández Marcos, *The Septuagint in Context,* pp. 230–32.

18. The editors of the volumes dealing with the Octateuch in the *Ancient Christian Commentary on Scripture* under the general editorship of T.C. Oden (Downers Grove, Ill. 2001–) ought, therefore, to acknowledge the variety of Septuagintal forms used in their citations of the Greek fathers. They might also include reference to Diodore of Tarsus in their "Biographical Sketches," where Diodore's influential work on the Octateuch (*v.* note 35 below) is not cited, and Theodore is mistakenly listed as "founder of the Antiochene, or literalistic, school of exegesis."

19. *V.* K.G. O'Connell's "Greek Versions of the Old Testament," pp. 1095f. for a very brief account of the Greek uncial manuscripts and *ib.,* pp. 1094f. for a summary discussion of Origen's *Hexapla.*

20. *V. The Septuagint in Context,* pp. 94f. As the Göttingen Academy of Sciences has not yet published an edition of the book of Judges, Theodoret's citations of

Of course, like all the fathers except Jerome, Theodoret lacks the linguistic tools that would enable him to read the original text of the OT,[21] and whenever he deals with Hebrew terms, his efforts fall short. His text of Ex 22.28 reading, "You shall not revile gods," prompts an obvious question (51) about the plural. He could have solved the issue quite simply had he been able to comment on the Hebrew *'elohim,* here wrongly rendered in the plural by the LXX. Instead, he cites the more difficult case of Ps 82.1, where God is presented as presiding over the council of the gods of the nations. On the other hand, in his commentary on the Psalms, where Ex 22.28 is cited as parallel to Ps 82.1, he had insisted that in both cases "judges" are intended. Similarly, while discussing the significance of Passover for Jews and Christians (*Q.* 24.1 on Ex), he attempts to provide an accurate rendition of the Hebrew *pesach* (a term of doubtful etymology) based on the interpretations of a range of Jewish authorities: Philo, Theodotion, and the historian Josephus. He finds that their Greek translations of this term differ considerably, and being in no position to evaluate them, notes only that the event signifies the salvation of the firstborn of the Hebrews. His industry as an exegete is not matched by his linguistic skills.

Yet, Theodoret possesses philological resources to clarify an obscure text, though, in fact, he enlists their aid less frequently than in the subsequent series of *Questions* on Kings and Chronicles. First,

---

that book have been checked against Rahlfs' 1935 pocket edition of the Septuagint, which provides a transcription of both codices *A* and *B.* In my *ap. font.,* I do not specify which strand of the tradition offers a reading found in Theodoret's *Quaestt.* The reader should compare both the Greek texts provided by Rahlfs with that of Theodoret. For discussion of points of contact and difference between Theodoret's text and that offered by the *alexandrinus* and the *vaticanus* in the book of Judges, *v.* note 1 to *Q.* 4; n. 1 to *Q.* 8; n. 1 to *Q.* 9; n. 4 to *Q.* 12; n. 1 to *Q.* 19; n. 2 to *Q.* 22; and nn. 1f. to *Q.* 26.

21. Of the Antiochene fathers, only Theodore of Mopsuestia claimed some knowledge of Hebrew; on his limitations, *v.* my translation of *Theodore of Mopsuestia: Commentary on the Twelve Prophets,* p. 11 and note 40. As to Origen, H. Crouzel declares (p. 12): "Certainly it would be wrong to credit Origen with a knowledge of Hebrew like Jerome's, but he must have had enough to direct the compilation of the *Hexapla,* even if the actual work was done by some assistant."

though unfamiliar with Hebrew, Theodoret has the advantage of being a native speaker of Syriac, a dialect of Aramaic, and in some of his more formal commentaries he exploits this asset to advantage.[22] In this work, on the contrary, he invokes it only once (*Q*. 19 on Jgs): to throw light on the dialectal diversity in pronunciation of the Hebrew term *shibboleth* when Jephthah (Jgs 12.4–6) detects fugitives of Ephraim by their pronunciation of the initial sibilant.

More importantly, whether directly or through the citations of others, he had some information regarding other Greek translations of the Bible.[23] Thus, in *Q*. 38 on Leviticus, he is able to cite "some translators" who offer a different term for the monetary value of sacrificial animals stated in Lv 27.9–13. He mentions Aquila, Symmachus, and Theodotion by name.[24] When at Jgs 1.15 the Hebrew text reports that Caleb's daughter Achsah requested "irrigated land" for her husband, the LXX confuses that term with a similar one for "redemption." Unable to account for the confusion by reference to the original, Theodoret shrewdly turns to Symmachus for an alternative translation. At times, the commentator, always anxious to provide his readers with full information, goes to excess in citing these other versions. In *Q*. 1.4 on Leviticus, where the burnt offering of birds (1.17) figures in a long account of Jewish sacrifices, he remarks, "Now, for 'crop' (πρόλοβον) Theodotion put 'gullet' and Aquila 'feeder.' It receives the food and conveys it to the rest of the body; hence, the Septuagint calls it 'crop' (πρόλοβον) as it takes in (προσλαμβάνουσαν) the food." We suspect his readers would have regarded this anatomical detail, let alone the range of translations, as otiose.

22. *V.* P. Canivet, *Histoire d'une entreprise*, pp. 26f.

23. Guinot denies (pp. 181–83, 230–33, 250–52) that Theodoret had access either to Origen's *Hexapla* or to a copy of the recension of the LXX included in the *Hexapla*.

24. For Aquila, *v. Qq*. 22, 31, 41, 47, 51, 112.6 on Gn; 1 on Ex; 1, 22.2 on Lv; 8 on Dt; 10 on Jos; for Symmachus, *Qq*. 38 on Gn 23, 24.1; 23f., 30, 35 on Ex; 22.2 on Lv; 19, 44.2 on Nm; 8, 45.2 on Dt; 2.4 on Jos; 3, 8 on Jgs; for Theodotion, *Qq*. 24 on Gn; 1 on Lv; *v.* K.G. O'Connell, "Greek Versions of the Old Testament," for a brief introduction (p. 1094) to the versions of Aquila and Symmachus and the questions surrounding the identity of Theodotion.

4. THEODORET'S APPROACH TO SCRIPTURE

It is at the end of his life, of his episcopal ministry, and of two decades of exegetical work, or at least commentary,[25] that Theodoret comes to deal with the the Torah and the Former Prophets. Here, as elsewhere, we note his fundamental understanding of the inspired Word as a divine gesture of condescension to man, what Chrysostom had called συγκατάβασις and Origen συμπεριφορά.[26] In Q. 20 on Genesis dealing with the key notion of human beings created in God's "image" (1.26f.), before canvassing the views of his predecessors, Theodoret brusquely rejects those that present any anthropomorphic notion of God: "These simpletons fail to understand that the Lord God, when speaking to humans through humans, adjusts his language to the limitations of the listeners." The principle, of course, is vital for commentary, especially on this part of the Bible, if the commentator is not to adopt a fundamentalist stance.[27] Another principle basic to an Antiochene is recognition of the aim or intent (σκοπός) of Scripture and of individual books.[28] In accordance with this rule, he dismisses what he considers an "over-curious" question (Q. 3 on Gn) regarding the precise time of the creation of the angels: "I shall state what I believe is in keeping with the purpose of holy Scripture."

25. The distinction of J.N.D. Kelly (*Golden Mouth*, p. 94), is apposite: "Neither John, nor any Christian teacher for centuries to come, was properly equipped to carry out exegesis as we have come to understand it."

26. V. R.C. Hill, "On looking again at *synkatabasis,*" pp. 3–11 and B. Vawter, *Biblical Inspiration,* p. 40.

27. F.M. Young (*Biblical Exegesis*), attributes (pp. 170f.) the Antiochenes' emphasis on rhetorical aspects of biblical language to their education in rhetorical schools; John Chrysostom and probably Theodore of Mopsuestia, as well, were pupils of Libanius.

28. Young (*ib.,* pp. 183f.) points out that both the Alexandrians and the Antiochenes looked for the σκοπός of a scriptural passage. Origen and his followers had located this intent "at the level of the inspiring Spirit" so that "consistency lay . . . in the deeper spiritual realities to which the text referred," while the Antiochenes regarded the aim of a scriptural passage as that of the literary author and therefore tried to respect the consistency of wording and narrative development.

Though at this stage of his life he lacks the strength to complete a commentary on the full text of the Genesis through Ruth, Theodoret remains an Antiochene and is alert to detail in the verses cited by the questioner.[29] Precision (ἀκρίβεια) is a virtue not only in the sacred text but also in its commentator and reader, though the virtue can become a vice. Taking his cue from a question regarding Caleb's choice of Hebron for his inheritance (Q. 17 on Jos 14.13), the commentator launches into a digression to remove what might seem to be a chronological discrepancy in the years of wandering: the forty-five mentioned by Caleb in Jos 14.10 and the thirty-eight years of Dt 2.14. This is the sort of digression the genre tolerates.

Theodoret appreciates biblical imagery and is not loath to explicate it for his readers; he can also improve on the author's with effective imagery of his own. Responding to Q. 18 on Numbers, Theodoret first mentions the simile comparing Moses' relationship to the people to that of a mother nursing a babe (Nm 11.11f.). He then proceeds to the appointment of the seventy elders, who are to assist the lawgiver without diminishing his powers, and in his comment adduces both a striking image and a sacramental parallel (18.2): "Now, the sequence of events confirms that, by giving some to the seventy, God had not diminished Moses' grace, for he continued to perform the same functions and work wonders as he had done before. Just as, from a single taper, one can light countless others and, without diminishing it, share its light with the rest, so the God of the universe shared Moses' grace with the seventy without lessening the grace that had already been granted to him. We see this happening even today when countless people are baptized by one priest and receive the divine gift without diminishing the priest's grace, and great numbers are appointed by the high priests and receive priestly office without lessening the gift of the man who appointed them." After expounding the biblical metaphor of the suckling child, Theodoret

29. V. R.C. Hill, "*Akribeia*," pp. 32–36, where I argue that the term, though often rendered "accuracy," means rather "precision." The Antiochenes, though generally precise, are not always accurate in their treatment of scriptural detail.

supplies an equally effective simile of his own: the wick that lights other lamps, which he further develops with reference to the Christian rites of baptism and priestly ordination.

In this work, as ever, Theodoret shows himself "moderate" in his assessment of previous views.[30] Where no decisive factor is involved, he can leave his readers to make their own choice. After relaying from Diodore two explanations for Abraham's division of the victims sacrificed in the covenant rite of Gn 15.10f., he concludes (Q. 67), "I cite this view and the other for readers to take whichever strikes them as closer to the truth." In a similar manner, he sometimes expresses a commendable diffidence regarding his own interpretations. When the questioner presses him on that sensitive issue of the creation of the angels, he explicitly indicates that he can do no more than hazard an opinion on a question that does not admit of a conclusive answer (Q. 4.2 on Gn): "Now, I do not state this dogmatically, my view being that it is rash to speak dogmatically where holy Scripture does not make an explicit statement; rather, I have stated what I consider to be consistent with orthodox thought."

Again, as in other works, Theodoret sometimes evinces knowledge of the practices and beliefs of Judaism. In Q. 54 on Exodus he shows he is aware that the feasts of Pentecost and Tabernacles were originally agricultural but came to commemorate historical events. In the course of a long discussion of the tabernacle and its furnishings (ib. Q. 60), he speaks with understanding of the Jewish usage of the tetragrammaton (60.5).

Like his fellow Antiochenes, Theodoret desires principally that his readers understand the biblical text; only on occasion does he consider its ethical implications for daily life.[31] See, for example, his comment on Gn 6.5 ("Everyone's thoughts in his heart were focused on evil his whole life long"). On this verse that, as G. von Rad de-

---

30. It is G. Bardy who pays this compliment to Theodoret as commentator; v. "Interprétation," p. 582.

31. In his homilies Chrysostom evinces a more pastoral approach that constitutes an exception to this general practice of the Antiochenes.

clares, has "programmatic significance . . . for the entire Yahwistic primeval history," a moral comment is certainly not out of order.[32] In the lengthy response to Q. 1 on the animal sacrifices described in the opening chapters of Leviticus, he tentatively ventures into the ethical and parenetic: "I do not think I am out of order in remarking that those who offer themselves to God resemble the various animal victims. Those who embrace a life free of possessions and worries devote themselves wholly to the God of the universe and turn themselves into holocausts and whole victims; they put aside nothing for this life but transfer everything to the life eternal" (1.3). The commentator proceeds to compare other sacrifices to other Christian states of life.

We have observed that Theodoret, who may not have imagined that women would read his work, makes the occasional misogynist comment. His argument can also tend to the detriment of the women when he makes every effort to uphold the reputation of patriarchs and other male leaders. We might refer, for instance, to his defense of Abraham's conduct in the court of King Abimelech of Gerar (Q. 64)[33] and his justification of Abraham's treatment of Hagar (Q. 68).

5. THE SOURCES OF THEODORET'S EXEGESIS

Of course, the books of the Octateuch had long been studied and commented on by eastern Jews and Christians. Genesis had received the widest attention; its non-Antiochene interpreters included Philo, Origen, Didymus the Blind, Basil of Caesarea, Gregory of Nyssa, and Cyril of Alexandria. Philo had also written on Exodus; Origen on Exodus, Leviticus, Numbers, Joshua, and Judges; Cyril on Exodus, Leviticus, Numbers, and Deuteronomy; and Gregory of Nyssa

---

32. *Genesis,* p. 117.
33. In *hom.* 45.2 on Gn 20.2 Chrysostom adopts the same attitude to Abraham and Sarah.

on Exodus and Numbers.[34] Of the Antiochenes, Diodore of Tarsus had produced a series of questions on the Octateuch, and Chrysostom two sets of homilies on Genesis, while Theodore of Mopsuestia had commented on at least Genesis, and perhaps Exodus, Joshua, and Judges as well.[35] From the *Questions on the Octateuch,* J.-N. Guinot has collected forty-six cases where Theodoret apparently alluded to such works by the general form of reference, "There are those who say."[36] Having painstakingly sifted these allusions, he concludes that in the *Questions* on Genesis, Theodoret did make considerable direct use of at least Theodore's commentary and Chrysostom's homilies. But for the subsequent references to previous expositors and even for those to commentators on Genesis other than Theodore and Chrysostom, Theodoret, in the great majority of instances, drew from the questions composed by the early Antiochene exegete Diodore of Tarsus. Indeed, in books other than Genesis, Theodoret's allusions to previous exegetes are far fewer. The *Questions* on Exodus and Leviticus each contain only about half as many.[37] Very infrequent in the *Questions* on Numbers, Joshua, and Ruth, there are none at all in the *Questions* on Deuteronomy and Judges. Diodore had himself drawn from Eusebius of Emesa,[38] and though Guinot admits that Theodoret made some direct use of Eusebius, he argues from a collation of the available evidence that sim-

34. For Philo's exegesis of Gn, *v.* R. Marcus, *Philo, Questions and Answers on Genesis;* for Origen's exegesis of books of the Octateuch, *v.* Quasten, vol. 2, pp. 46, 51; for Didymus' commentary on Gn, *v.* P. Nautin and L. Doutreleau, *Didyme L'Aveugle sur la Genèse;* for Basil's *Hex., v.* Quasten, vol. 3, pp. 216–18; for Gregory's *Hom. opif., Expl. apol. in hex.,* and *V. Mos., v. ib.,* pp. 263–65; for Cyril's *Ador.* and *Glaph. Gn-Dt, v. ib.,* pp. 120f.

35. For Diodore's works, *v.* J. Deconinck, *Essai sur la chaîne, etc.;* for Chrysostom's *Hom. 9* and *Hom. 67 in Gn., v.* Quasten, vol. 3, p. 434; for Theodore's commentaries, whose extent remains unclear, *v.* Devreesse, *Essai,* pp. 25–27 and Guinot (*L'Exégèse,* note 79, p. 792), who regard only the work on Genesis as sufficiently attested, and *cf.* Quasten, vol. 3, pp. 403f.

36. *e.g., Q.* 29 on Gn: φασί τινες

37. Guinot catalogues (*L'Exégèse,* pp. 748–75) twenty allusions to earlier exegesis in the *Questions* on Gn, eleven in the *Questions* on Ex, eight in the *Questions* on Lv.

38. *V.* R. Devreesse, *Les anciens commentateurs, etc.*

ilarities between the expositions of Theodoret and Eusebius are usually to be explained by Diodore's mediation. Thus, Theodoret would have received much of this information at second, and some even at third, hand; only rarely, outside the *Questions* on Genesis, can he be credited with drawing from the work of any predecessor other than Diodore.[39]

6. THEODORET'S STYLE OF COMMENTARY: THE GENRE OF QUESTIONS

Imbued with such exegetical predispositions—some shared with other Antiochenes, others peculiar to himself—and relying on these sources, Theodoret undertakes the task of clarifying for his readers doubtful points (ζητήματα) of the Octateuch and rebutting criticisms of Scripture made by malicious adversaries. Experience has taught him that "careless reading of holy Scripture is the cause of error among ordinary people" (*Q.* 47.1 on Gn), and in the incident of the unauthorized offering of unholy fire by Nadab and Abihu (Lv 9.24–10.2) he finds a warning to avoid novelty. "These events teach us not to quench the Spirit but to rekindle the grace we have received, not to introduce anything foreign into holy Scripture but to be content with the teaching of the Spirit, and to abhor heretics, some of whom have combined their mythological fables with the divine oracles, while others have preferred their own unholy notions to the sense of Scripture" (*Q.* 9 on Lv). Thus, the commentator should aim at no more than to clarify the obscure as he promises to do in the preface to the entire work.[40] With God's help he will unveil the meaning (διάνοια) hidden in the text (γράμμα) just as Jesus had explained in more direct terms the statements expressed in riddling fashion (αἰνιγματωδῶς) in his parables.

In his wish to complete an exegetical project begun decades be-

---

39. Guinot (*L'Exégèse*), pp. 748–97, esp. 790–97.
40. He makes the same promise in his first commentary, that on the Song of Songs (on 8.12).

fore, Theodoret has chosen for comment on the Octateuch and Kingdoms and Chronicles a different genre, namely, that of Questions.[41] This genre would dispense the ailing scholar from commenting on the whole text. As we see in other examples, ancient and modern, it allows the author to restrict his attention to challenging passages that might puzzle the reader:[42] hence the terms τὰ ἄπορα and τὰ ζητούμενα traditionally included in the two titles.[43] In his preface to the *Questions on the Octateuch* Theodoret claims to be joining the ranks of those who have promised to solve apparent problems: τὰ δοκοῦντα εἶναι ζητήματα.[44] In the east, practitioners of this sort of exegesis included Philo, Eusebius, Theodoret, and, in the ninth century, Photius; in west, it was initiated by Jerome and Augustine and taken up by numerous medieval authors.

This was not an exclusively Christian genre. In fact, the earliest such works were devoted to the explication of the Homeric poems.[45] Sophists and rhetors as well as Stoics interested in casuistry and moral conundrums employed the format of question and answer.

41. Theodoret's work on Jeremiah may likewise show signs of a forced effort to round off his commentary on the prophetic corpus of the Bible. Though Guinot expresses doubt as to Theodoret's authorship of this work (*L'Exégèse*, note 34, p. 43 and p. 342), *v.* my outline of the manuscript tradition and the character of this commentary in the introduction to *Theodoret of Cyrus, Commentary on Jeremiah*.

42. On the other hand, from the treatment of 1–2 Chr, where Theodoret simply abandons question-and-answer form and settles for simple paraphrase, one could argue that his basic aim was commentary / paraphrase, and that he found it more taxing to recast the text into individual questions.

43. Though Fernández Marcos and Sáenz-Badillios print no title to their edition of the *Quaest. in oct.* (note 6 above), titles containing the term ἄπορα appear in at least several of the manuscripts as well as in the editions of Picot and Schulze; *v.* the *ap. crit. ad loc.* The term ζητήματα occurs in the introduction to the *Quaest. in oct*, and τὰ ζητούμενα in the title of the *Questions on Kingdoms and Chronicles* printed by Fernández Marcos and Busto Saiz (note 6 above).

44. The word "apparent" signals a necessary qualification that Jerome also makes in his *Pf. in hom. Origenis in Ez.*, where he says that Origen addressed *ea quae sibi videbantur obscura aut habere aliquid difficultatis; v.* M. Borret, *Origène, Homélies sur Ézéchiel.*

45. G. Bardy ("La littérature patristique," *RB* 41 [1932]) points out (p. 211) the very early use of this form by commentators on Homer, "the inexhaustible source of puzzles."

This format naturally found a place in academic instruction and would eventually provide the framework for catechisms.

The issues dealt with in the biblical treatises were chosen by the commentator or taken over from a predecessor. The questioner was merely a fictional device for the selection of texts to receive comment or of apparent discrepancies to be resolved. Many of Theodoret's questions deal with issues of detail, but others provide the impetus for an extensive essay. For example, the apparently ingenuous Q. 60 on Exodus, "Why did God command the construction of the tabernacle?" is the cue for a comprehensive account of the design and furnishings of the tabernacle and of the accoutrements of the priests described in Ex 25–29.[46]

At times, the questions reproduce criticism of the sacred text that calls for rebuttal. Such criticism might regard apparent contradictions of fact within Scripture. Why is Moses' father-in-law called Reuel in Nm 10.29 but Jethro in earlier passages (Q. 16 on Nm; cf. Ex. 3.1; 4.18 and 2.18 and Q. 4 on Jgs)? At other times, the criticism bears on the goodness, justice, and omniscience of the God of the Old Testament. How could the consumption of a morsel of illicit food merit the terrible punishment inflicted on Adam and Eve and their posterity (Q. 37 on Gn)? Should not God have prevented the slaughter of Jephthah's daughter (Q. 20 on Jgs)? In Q. 74 on Gn, Theodoret denies that God tested Abraham to learn whether or not he would obey his command to sacrifice Isaac. Sometimes, the criticism calls into question the morality of a biblical hero. Thus (Q. 73 on Gn), Theodoret defends Abraham from the charge of cruelty for driving off Hagar and the infant Ishmael, and Gideon (Q. 17 on Jgs) against the charge of introducing idol worship. As for Samson, if he did not observe the dietary restrictions of a nazirite, that was because these had become obsolete (Q. 22 on Jgs).

On occasion, the questions may strike a reader as trivial, as

46. Theodoret may here depend on Theodore of Mopsuestia. R. Devreesse suggests (*Essai*, p. 25, note 2) that Theodore included similar material in his commentary on the Epistle to the Hebrews.

though seeking to elicit insignificant information or posing a false conundrum. *Q.* 3 on Exodus asks how Pharaoh's daughter knew that baby Moses was a Hebrew. "Through circumcision," the commentator retorts, since he believes that the Egyptians learned this practice from the Hebrews (*Q.* 69 on Gn). *Q.* 100 on Genesis asks how Potiphar, a eunuch, had a wife.[47] One may suspect that other far-fetched questions are posed to introduce variety and entertainment. In *Q.* 59 on Genesis, Theodoret tries to identify the material used as mortar for the Tower of Babel. *Q.* 26 on Exodus—"What kind of wood was it that sweetened the water in Marah"—evinces the same interest in oddities of natural history. In *Q.* 45 on Exodus, after skipping without comment over the last seven commandments of the Decalogue, he pauses to consider what must have seemed a strange Hebrew law enjoining the piercing of the ear of a bondsman who chooses to abide with his master rather than go free.

Others seem calculated to provide an opportunity for commentary on present-day circumstances. The question (53 on Ex) "What is the meaning of 'You shall not appear before the Lord your God empty-handed?'" (Ex 23.15), receives an answer that suggests it was included for the ethical instruction of readers both in the world and in religious life: "When you go to worship the Lord God, offer gifts in accordance with your means. This verse teaches us, if we have money, to pray to God with the care of the needy, or, if we opt for a life of poverty, to approach God with a soul that is not empty of good things but wealthy in virtue." By and large, however, the questions address issues of substance that the commentator reckons among the puzzles of Scripture (ζητήματα), often because they were the subject of debate by his predecessors.[48]

Of course, given his limited philological and historical skills, Theodoret is often unable to settle these issues in a way that would please modern scholars. Unable to point to Hebrew usages or to the

---

47. In Gn 39.1, the LXX's εὐνοῦχος does not accurately render the Hebrew.
48. As we have seen, the work of Diodore would be Theodoret's principal source for these earlier debates; *v.* sec. 5 above.

redactional history of these complex documents, he often has recourse to little more than a process of rationalization. For example, when the questioner asks (*Q.* 93 on Gn), "Why did the angel wrestle with Jacob?" (32.34), the commentator, unaware of aetiologies lying behind the names Israel and Penuel, opines, "To give Jacob confidence when he was afraid of his brother. For the same reason he also yielded him the victory, as if to say, 'How can you fear a mere mortal after defeating me?'"

Nonetheless, one of Theodoret's great strengths is his willingness to provide the less advanced reader with a plethora of relevant and illuminating historical, linguistic, and cultural information. In this he is superior to Theodore. For instance, he goes to trouble to specify in his readers' terms the sum of money required by Lv 27.10 for the cash replacement of prescribed offerings (*Q.* 38 on Lv). As in his other works, he identifies geographical and topographical references. He can tell his reader that the town mentioned in Jgs 18.28 was once called Leshem and is "now called Paneas" (*Q.* 26 on Jgs). This sort of information made a narrative of the distant past more meaningful for his readers. As we have noted, it is particularly in the Octateuch that he can bring his extensive knowledge of Judaism to the fore.

A modern reader would naturally evaluate this genre by the degree to which it places the reader in touch with the key concerns of the text and its author(s). Are the items chosen of real significance? Are there regrettable omissions? Generally speaking, the questions allow comprehensive coverage of key issues in the Octateuch. There are only two questions on Ruth, but each receives lengthy responses. The first addresses the reasons for the composition of the work. It covers Ruth's place in the genealogy of Jesus (Mt 1.5) and thus, what Theodoret understands as the christological character of the book. If Theodoret does not discuss the lists of kings and allotments of land that bulk so large in the book of Joshua, it is probably in order to avoid wearying his readers.[49] On the other hand, he does not

---

49. In *Hom.* 2.2 *in Is. 6.1* (*in illud, Vidi dominum*), Chrysostom reports that some readers of Scripture, when reproached for skipping over chronological no-

shirk even Moses' blessings of the tribes of Israel (Dt 33), a poem that is obscure in the Hebrew and even more so in the LXX. It is also noticeable that texts that might seem sensational, such as the sun stopping in its course in Jos 10.12f., do not attract particular attention. Modern readers might well regret his delicate omission of the harrowing tale of the abuse of the Levite's concubine in Jgs 19.22–30.[50] Regrettably, in both Exodus and Deuteronomy he omits comment on the last seven commandments of the Decalogue. On balance, however, one would say that this genre allowed an ailing Theodoret to expound his position on the key questions facing a reader of the Octateuch.

7. THEODORET'S POSITION ON THE OCTATEUCH

Though Theodoret does not employ the term, we know that "Octateuch" was used in the early Church to designate the first eight books of the Bible.[51] The grouping is evidently customary for him, whereas a pentateuchal collection is not; he moves from Deuteronomy to Joshua without comment on Dt 34, which records the death of Moses and the mystery surrounding his tomb, and without remark on any change of authorship. In fact, unlike that of a modern work, his preface includes no general introductory treatment of the authorship or of the literary and theological unity of the *corpus* that he is about to introduce to his readers. This is true also of his commentary on the Pauline epistles. In this approach he differs from the more critical Diodore and his servile disciple Theodore. On occasion, he evinces exegetical concerns similar to those of Chrysostom, who viewed the Scriptures as a moralizing and hagiographical text.[52] Thus, though also admitting the christological import of Ruth,

---

tices or catalogues of names, would allege in self-justification, "This passage is just names and contains nothing of value"; *v.* J. Dumortier, *Homélies sur Ozias.*

50. *V.* P. Trible, *Texts of Terror,* pp. 65–91 and note 1 to *Q.* 27 on Jgs.

51. *V.* O. Eissfeldt, *The Old Testament,* p. 156. Nor does Theodoret speak of "Pentateuch" or "Torah."

52. *V.* R.C. Hill, "His Master's Voice," pp. 40–53.

Theodoret remarks that this book would be worthy of inclusion in the canon solely on the basis of its ethical teaching: "[T]his narrative is sufficient of itself to offer great benefit to those who know how to profit by it" (*Q.* 1.2).[53] Likewise, he interprets in a moralizing fashion passages where we find aetiological and doctrinal concerns, *e.g.* the name Gad, given to one of Jacob's sons in Gn 30.11 (*Q.* 88), Rachel's theft of the household gods in Gn 31.19 (*Q.* 91), and Tamar's ruse to secure a levirate marriage in Gn 38 (*Q.* 97).

Of course, neither Theodoret nor his contemporaries envisaged anything similar to the documentary hypothesis of the Pentateuch given classic form by Julius Wellhausen in the late nineteenth century.[54] Nonetheless, he presents Moses, the putative author of those books, in various literary roles: not only as lawgiver (νομοθέτης) and prophet (προφήτης), but also as historian (συγγραφεύς, *e.g.*, *Qq.* 1, 5, 9, 22 on Gn) or chronicler (ἱστοριογράφος, *Q.* 99 on Gn). Could the use of these latter terms, which can be applied to one who collects information from various sources or even composes a narrative on the basis of pre-existing materials, betray some inkling of multiple authorship for sections of Gn–Dt? Probably not. While this eastern commentator regards the distinctively anthropomorphic language used in what we now call "the Yahwistic history" as a potential stumbling block, he limits himself to dispelling possible misapprehensions as they arise. He denies that Moses could have seen God, as is claimed in Ex 33.16–23 (*Q.* 68 on Ex), or that the Lord and accompanying angels ate a meal in Abraham's tent (*Q.* 70 on Gn 18). In his discussion of the title "Deuteronomy," Theodoret rejects (*Q.* 1.1 on Dt) the notion that this could refer to a second law and, in

53. *Cf.* Chrys., *Hom.* 11.4 *in Gen.:* "The Holy Spirit has graciously left us a written account in holy Scripture of the biographies and way of life of all the saints so that we may learn that men who had the same nature as ourselves succeeded in performing virtuous deeds of every sort and not be slack in striving for virtue ourselves."

54. Wellhausen offered what became a very influential statement of this hypothesis in his *Prolegomena zur Geschichte Israels.* For a brief orientation to the different documentary strands combined to form the Pentateuch, *v., e.g.,* the introductions to the commentaries on Gn by E.A. Speiser and G. von Rad.

a literalistic manner, argues that the book "contains a summary of the legislation and the events of Exodus, Leviticus, and Numbers" for those who had grown up in the wilderness. Again, there are more curses than blessings in Dt 27f., not because of an interpolation or the impact of the exile on a Deuteronomistic editor, but because "for wicked servants promises of freedom are not so beneficial as threats of chastisement" (*Q.* 36). Balaam's changes of heart in Nm 22–24 are likewise not due to any difference in authorship (*Qq.* 39–44).

Therefore, it is not surprising that Theodoret evinces no awareness of the diverse concerns of the documentary strands subsumed into our present text. Like Chrysostom he regards Genesis 2.4–24 as a summary recapitulating the major topics of ch. 1 rather than as, what it is now known to be, an independent narrative of much earlier date. So, in his discussion of 2.4–6 (*Q.* 22), Theodoret tries to explain the source of the water that irrigated earth before the beginning of rainfall by harmonizing details of two discordant traditions: the earth was irrigated by "moisture and humidity left over from the division of the waters."[55] Only once does he explicitly admit that there is a cultic basis for the rulings in Leviticus; this is in *Q.* 21, where citing Lv 15.31 ("'You will make the children of Israel beware their uncleanness, and they will not die because of their uncleanness by defiling my tabernacle that is among them'") he points to the relationship between the state of uncleanness and exclusion from public worship. Elsewhere (*e.g., Qq.* 20, 27, 30, 32.2) he interprets these cultic regulations in an ethical sense. Furthermore, he does not grasp the ethical significance of the historical preface (Ex 20.2: "I am the Lord your God, who brought you out of the land of Egypt") to the apodictic commandments of the Decalogue.

---

55. Chrysostom thought that God had dictated this second narrative to underline the major points of ch. 1 and thus forestall the development of heresy in the Christian Church; *cf. Hom.* 12.2 *in Gen.* (on 2.4–6): "In his foreknowledge of the future, to prevent anyone born in subsequent generations from defying sacred Scripture and captiously setting his own notions against the dogmas of the Church, the Holy Spirit, after teaching us each step of the creation, here once more . . . goes over each detail to stop the unbridled tongue of people spoiling to display their impudence."

On the other hand, he is astute enough to recognize that the creation story is no eye-witness report but a later theological reflection that takes account of and refines earlier efforts from the ancient Near East. "Since the Egyptians used to worship the visible creation, and Israel, in their long association with them, had joined in this idolatry, he had to set out the facts of creation and explicitly teach them that it had a beginning of existence, and that the God of the universe was its Creator. Not that he passed over a treatment of the true doctrine of God (τῆς θεολογίας). The statement that heaven and earth and the other parts of the universe were created and the revelation that the God of the universe was their Creator provided a true doctrine of God sufficient for people of that time" (Q. 1 on Gn). When the questioner asks to whom the Creator addressed commands like "Let there be light" (Gn 1.3), Theodoret replies, "He was not commanding anyone else to create but summoning things not in existence, his will constituting a command" (Q. 9). This reply closely resembles that of his modern counterpart von Rad: "The idea of creation by the word preserves first of all the most radical essential distinction between Creator and creature." [56]

In fact, in numerous respects Theodoret's interpretations match those of modern scholars. In Q. 9 on Dt (12.8, 22), Theodoret expounds on the insistence on a central sanctuary; he has well understood the author's basic message: one God, one people, one temple. Likewise, at the close of Judges, Theodoret, surveying the structure of the book, notes, as do his modern counterparts, the function of the final five chapters as an epilogue to the presentation of the individual judges. [57] In the *Questions* on Genesis his discussions of the "signs" of 1.14 (Q. 15), the garment of skins in 3.21 (Q. 39), and the fate of Enoch in 5.24 (Q. 45), all *cruces interpretum*, are endorsed by modern scholars. [58]

Furthermore, in Joshua and Judges, he develops a limited docu-

---

56. *Genesis*, p. 51.
57. *V.* note 2 to Q. 27 on Jgs.
58. *V., e.g.*, von Rad, *Genesis*, pp. 56, 91, 71.

mentary hypothesis of his own. In Jos. 10.13 (*Q.* 14 *on Jos*), which refers to the hero's sovereign command to the sun, Theodoret's Antiochene recension of the LXX contained the question not found in other forms of the LXX: "Is this not written in the book that was found?" The phrase "that was found" renders a Hebrew reference to the book of *Jashar,* "the upright," an ancient anthology, as Theodoret, despite his poor translation, is able to surmise. Explicitly distinguishing between the historian (συγγραφεύς) and the protagonist Joshua (προφήτης), he rightly concludes, "the author of the book of Joshua lived in a subsequent age and drew his source material from that other book."[59] Similarly, from an apparent contradiction of fact, he infers a late date of composition for the book of Judges. At Jgs 1.8 it is said that the children of Judah took Jerusalem, whereas at 2Sm 5.6–9 we read that David captured Jebus, later re-named Jerusalem. Having compared these passages, Theodoret concludes (*Q.* 2 *on Jgs*), "I believe the composition of this book [Judges] is to be dated to a later period [*i.e.,* later than 2 Samuel]. In support, I note that the narrative refers to this city as 'Jerusalem'; previously named 'Jebus,' it was only later that it received this name." Only late in his exegetical career is Theodoret willing to acknowledge the complex processes that went into the formation of the biblical text.

8. THEODORET AS INTERPRETER OF THE OCTATEUCH

As primary attention to the literal meaning (τὸ ἱστορικόν) is typical of Antiochene biblical commentary even before Diodore,[60]

---

59. *Cf.* his comment (*Q.* 4 *in 2Reg.*) on the reference to the book of *Jashar* in 2Sm 1.18, where it is called "the book of *Right* (τοῦ εὐθοῦς)": "This is another indication that the narrative of Kings was composed from many prophetic sources." At the end of *Q.* 19.4 on Joshua (24.26) he may speak of "the history" (ἡ ἱστορία) rather than "the historian" (ὁ συγγραφεύς) precisely to avoid a question of authorship.

60. F.M. Young (*Biblical Exegesis*) discusses (pp. 163f.) Eustathius' earlier insistence on attending to "the coherence of narrative, both with itself and with the rest of scripture"; *cf.* R.C. Hill, *Reading the Old Testament,* pp. 135–39.

there is nothing new in Theodoret's insistence on searching for and adhering to the facts, especially in this part of the Bible. "[W]e should adhere to the facts of holy Scripture (τῇ τῆς θείας γραφῆς ἀληθείᾳ),"[61] he says in response to Q. 25 on Exodus (14.22), where he weighs various interpretations of the parting of the sea. And his interpretation of the plagues is straightforwardly literalist. Likewise, as is apparent from his response to Q. 32 about the serpent speaking to Eve, he takes the story of the Fall in Gn 3 as a narrative of historical fact. Though accepting the long-established view that the devil had adopted the guise of the serpent, he is not prepared to interpret the account as a theological reflection on the relationship between God and man. Yet, in Q. 40.1 on Ex, the commentator reminds his readers that those who attend to no more than "the face value of the text" (γυμνῷ . . . τῷ γράμματι) will not arrive at the full meaning of Scripture. There he argues that the Lord's threat to punish the children of idolaters to the fourth generation (Ex 20.5) requires interpretation by an inter-textual approach that draws on Ezekiel 18.

He assures his readers that a text may contain levels of meaning. When asked (Q. 26 on Gn) about the tree of life and the tree of the knowledge of good and evil, he insists that they are real trees, but that they also signify something further. "According to holy Scripture, they also sprouted from the ground, so they had a nature no different from that of other plants. Just as the tree of the cross was a tree and is called 'saving' because salvation is accomplished by faith in it, so these trees were products of the soil. By divine decree the one was called the 'tree of life,' the other, since the perception of sin occurred in connection with it, 'the tree of the knowledge of good and evil.' Adam was set a trial with regard to the latter, whereas the tree of life was proposed as his prize for keeping the commandment. Similarly, the patriarchs bestowed names on places and wells. They called one 'well of vision,' not because it granted the faculty of sight,

---

61. V. C. Schäublin, *Untersuchungen,* p. 170: "The appeal to 'reality,' ἀλήθεια, constitutes the perhaps definitive element of Antiochene 'historical' interpretation."

but because the Lord of the universe was seen near it, and another 'well of broad places,' because the people of Gerar, who had often fought over the other wells, did not interfere with those digging this one. Likewise, there was a 'well of the oath' because people used to swear oaths nearby. And the name 'Bethel' or 'House of God' was given to Luz, because that was where the Creator of the universe appeared to Jacob. There was a 'hill of witness,' not that the hill was alive, but because that was where they made treaties with one another. Likewise baptism is called 'living water,' not because the water of baptism has a different nature, but because, through that water, divine grace confers the gift of eternal life." The interpretation moves from the literal to the eschatological, spiritual, and sacramental.[62]

As he addresses octateuchal material, the commentator requires this hermeneutical range so that he may alternately endorse, disallow, or re-interpret the institutions and practices of Judaism. The prescriptions of Leviticus, in particular, call for this flexibility. In *Q.* 19 Theodoret moves from the priests' treatment of leprosy prescribed in 14.15–18 to contemporary Church practice regarding public sinners. "Furthermore, the cup of oil signifies spiritual ointment. The application of the oil to the right ear, hand, and foot suggests confining one's hearing to right words and one's hand and foot to right actions. The application to the head suggests the dedication of one's reason. But the person who remained leprous continued to dwell outside the camp, just as the sinner who remains unrepentant is expelled from the Church." This ready transposition sometimes involves Theodoret in the error of finding an ethical explanation for practices that were originally pragmatic and hygienic. For example, consider his comment (*Q.* 20) on the law (ch. 15) declaring sufferers of gonorrhea unclean: "I have already said that, through the physical, it gives instruction in moral, defects and conveys through the

---

62. Such hermeneutical breadth is at variance with the adherence shown by, *e.g.,* Theodore to the maxim, received through Diodore and Libanius and traditionally attributed to Aristarchus, of "clarifying Homer from Homer." In accordance with this, Antiochene interpreters tended to find the full meaning of OT texts within the OT; *v.* C. Schäublin (*Untersuchungen*), pp. 158–67.

former the gravity of the latter. If a naturally occurring discharge is unclean, lust must be all the more unlawful. Furthermore, this law teaches us to avoid associating with the immoral, for it pronounces unclean whoever approaches anyone with gonorrhea."

Both the cultic prescriptions and the heroic feats detailed in the Octateuch readily lend themselves to typological interpretations, of which even Antiochene commentators take frequent advantage. Christian liturgical practice had doubtless already adopted this way of reading the text. When a questioner asks about the priest's prescription of "two living clean birds and cedar wood and crimson yarn and hyssop" for the cleansing of a leper (Lv 14.4), Theodoret replies (Q. 19), "They present a type of the saving passion. As one was sacrificed, while the other was dipped in the blood of the sacrifice and released, so Christ the Lord was crucified for leprous humanity: the flesh undergoing death, the divinity appropriating the suffering of the humanity. And as the leper emerges glowing and cleansed when sprinkled with the blood of the slain bird mixed with pure water on a branch of cedar with hyssop and crimson yarn, so whoever believes in Christ the Savior and is purified in the water of most holy baptism casts off the stain of his sins. Now, cedar, an incorruptible wood, is symbolic of the impassible divinity; the crimson twine, of the humanity, composed of soul and body; and the hyssop, of the ardor and sweet fragrance of the most Holy Spirit. It is through these that the baptized are rid of the leprosy of the soul." This typological approach is so convenient for a pastoral commentator endeavoring to find the contemporary relevance of ancient Israelite texts that it can be sustained to the point of allegory. We may infer that this could give rise to uneasiness among his readers/ listeners, even when the word "allegory" was not used, since Theodoret feels it necessary to invoke (Q. 27 on Ex) the precedent for his exegesis supplied by Paul in 1Cor 10.2, 4:[63] "The old was a type of the

---

63. In *Hom.* 3.3 *in Is. 6.1* (*in illud, Vidi dominum*), Chrysostom reports that some in his congregation could not stomach the use of allegory. Citing Is 14.14 ("I will ascend above the heights of the clouds," *etc.*), a passage concerning a monarch

new, the Law of Moses a shadow, grace the body. As the Egyptians pursued the Hebrews, and, by crossing the Red Sea, the Hebrews were freed from the harsh domination of the Egyptians, the sea represents, in typological terms, the baptismal font, the cloud the Spirit, Moses Christ the Savior, the rod the cross, Pharaoh the devil, the Egyptians the demons, the manna the divine nourishment, and the water from the rock the saving blood." This is not the sort of allegory the Antiochenes attributed to Origen, because Theodoret still gives predominant attention to the literal sense, which is not subsumed into a spiritual interpretation.[64] Theodoret again quotes 1Cor 10 (v. 11) at the opening of his commentary on Joshua. There, presenting Moses and Joshua as types of Christ, he cites Gal 4.24, where Paul had used a participial form (ἀλληγορούμενα) related to the noun "allegory" to describe the exegetical technique by which he drew a parallel between Hagar and the earthly, and Sarah, and the heavenly, Jerusalem. Paul, Theodoret declares, "wrote this, not to deny the historical facts, but to compare the type to the reality." [65] He himself rejects that Alexandrian style of allegory in a pejorative reference (Q. 39 on Gn) to the allegorists' (ἀλληγορηταί) interpretation of the clothing of skins (Gn 3.21) as the human body.[66]

---

hostile to Israel, to show that the devil fell by incurring the sin of pride, he concedes, "Those who do not gladly accept allegories will reject our reference." Instead, to prove his point, he must cite 1Tm 3.6, a passage in which Paul explicitly speaks of the devil's pride; v. J. Dumortier (note 49 above). If in the *Quaest. in oct.* Theodoret seems to have unusually ready recourse to typology, and even allegory, it is partly because he is following the lead of his predecessors in this genre; v. Bardy ("La littérature patristique," *RB* 42 [1933]), pp. 224f.

64. In the prologue to his commentary on the Psalms, Diodore insists on beginning with a factual reading of the text (ἡ ἱστορία) and only then attempting to find the spiritual meaning (ἡ θεωρία); bypassing the former results not in θεωρία but in allegory (ἀλληγορία); cf. R.C. Hill, *Diodore of Tarsus*, pp. xxiv–xxx. Paul Ternant ("La θεωρία d'Antioche dans le cadre des sens de l'Écriture," *Bib.* 34 [1953]) comments (p. 137) that by θεωρία the Antiochenes understood their own position, and by ἀλληγορία that of their Alexandrian opponents.

65. V. note 1 to Q. 1 on Jos.

66. Theodoret may have known of the position advanced by Origen (*Cels.* 2.60f.) and Didymus (106–08) that, before its confinement in the material human body, the soul had made use of an immaterial, spiritual body; cf. 1Cor 15.44.

Nowhere else does he refer specifically to this style of interpretation.

Doubtless because of the liturgical practice of his church, Theodoret often finds christological significance in octateuchal texts. As we have noted, he believes that the canonicity of Ruth can be established by the position of this Moabite woman in the genealogy of Christ set out by the Gospel of Matthew. Encouraging hesitant Christians to read the Jewish Torah he declares (Q. 76 on Gn), "This race became the object of providential care, since this was the stock from which Christ the Lord, the only-begotten Son of God, was destined to be born according to the flesh." The ritual of the scapegoat (ἀποπομπαῖος) and the sacrificed goat, described in Leviticus 16.8–10, receives lengthy linguistic and theological clarification simply because of its perceived christological relevance (Q. 22.2 on Lv): "These two animals are also types of Christ the Lord, if they are taken, not as referring to two persons, but to two natures. Since it was impossible for Christ the Lord's mortality and immortality to be foreshadowed in one goat (the goat being only mortal), he necessarily ordered that both be offered so that the one sacrificed would prefigure the passibility of the flesh, and the one set free would manifest the impassibility of the divinity." [67]

9. THEOLOGICAL ISSUES IN THE
QUESTIONS ON THE OCTATEUCH

Perhaps because of the nature of the material, perhaps also because Theodoret seems to draw his knowledge of his predecessors' work, even that of the Alexandrians, from Diodore, the questions do not adopt a predominantly theological focus. Readers familiar with Theodoret's commentaries on Isaiah, Song of Songs, and Psalms will be struck by the different accent of this late work. Nonetheless, as we have seen, Theodoret frequently highlights the figure of Jesus, especially through typology.

67. *V.* note 2 to Q. 22 on Lv.

In this work, as in others,[68] his christological expressions are not always entirely felicitous. For example, in the questions on Joshua, Theodoret draws many typological parallels between the two personages, old and new, bearing the name Ἰησοῦς. So he declares that, as after the death of Moses, Joshua had led the Israelites into the promised land, Christ, "our Joshua," after the end of the Law, opened the Kingdom of Heaven to his holy people (*pf. Q.* on Jos).[69] But when asked (*Q. 25* on Nm) why Moses called Hosea "Joshua" when he sent him out as a spy (Nm 13.8, 16), Theodoret responds in a way that gives a less than adequate expression of the Incarnation: "Because he was a type of the true Joshua, who, to secure our salvation, imitated the disguise of the spies. As spies adopt the dress and language of the nations on which they are spying, so God the Word clad himself in human nature and adopted human language to secure our salvation."[70]

In this work he makes no consistent attempt to turn the Torah into a Christian text or to hunt for traces of Christian dogma. Rarely does he detect a suggestion of trinitarian terminology. The plural verb in Gn 1.26 ("Let us make the human being in our image and likeness") though actually no more than a royal plural or reflective of the plural form of the Hebrew word for God (*'elohim*) offers the commentator just such a suggestion (*Q. 19.1* on Gn): "But in a few cases, he uses plural forms to bring out the distinction of number of the persons of the Trinity (τῶν τῆς τριάδος προσώπων ἐμφαίνων τὸν ἀριθμόν). When he confused the languages, he did not say in the singular, 'I shall go down and confuse the languages,' but 'Come, let us go down and confuse their languages.'"[71] Similarly, Theodoret finds (*Q. 2* on Dt) a trinitarian reference in Dt 6.4, a text for which

---

68. *V.* R.C. Hill, *Theodoret of Cyrus, Commentary on the Song*, pp. 15f.

69. *V.* also *Qq.* 1f.

70. Theodoret was not aware that the Hebrew name has variants *Yehoshua, Yeshua,* and *Hoshea;* it appears in Greek as Ἰησοῦς.

71. E. Speiser (on Gn 11.7) translates the jussive in v. 7 with "Let me go down"; he remarks that "if it were not for the singular in vs. 5," the plural form in this verse "could also be interpreted as an allusion to Yahweh's celestial staff."

the NRSV offers four possible versions, and which the LXX renders as "Listen, Israel, our God is the Lord; the Lord is one."[72] He declares, "I have often remarked that the terms 'Lord' and 'God' refer to the divine nature, not to the distinction in persons, whereas 'Father,' 'Son,' and 'Holy Spirit' refer to the individual persons (τὸ ὄνομα τὸ Κύριος καὶ Θεός, τῆς θείας φύσεως, οὐ τῆς τῶν προσώπων διαιρέσεως δηλωτικά, ὁ δὲ πατήρ, καὶ ὁ υἱός, καὶ τὸ ἅγιον πνεῦμα τῶν ἰδιοτήτων σημαντικά). But the precise doctrine of God could not be presented to the Jews, who, imperfect as they were, would have found it a pretext for polytheism. Hence, in the Old Testament, the divine name is expressed in the singular but contains obscure hints of the Trinity. The verse, 'Your God is the Lord; the Lord is one,' as well as conveying the unity of being, also indicates the number of persons. Note that he used 'God' once and 'Lord' twice." While the commentator modestly concedes that the text offers only dark hints (αἰνίγματα) of trinitarian teaching, the final mathematical calculation will strike a modern reader as perversely contrived.

The angels seem to constitute a particular preoccupation of Theodoret's questioner. Three of the first four questions evince concerns that must have arisen among Christians due to the silence of Genesis on the creation of the angels. Theodoret has elsewhere acknowledged this high degree of contemporary interest and devotion while at the same time reporting the efforts of local Church councils to limit its liturgical expression.[73] Here, too, he moves in both directions. He seems to discourage what is of marginal importance (*Q*. 3 on Gn): "I regard this sort of question as over-curious; after all, what benefit could accrue from a knowledge of the exact moment of the creation of the angels?" Yet he also takes the issue seriously (*Q*. 2 on Gn): "I feel it is superfluous to go on at length about them; all the inspired Scripture is full of this doctrine." In *Q*. 41 on Nm, dis-

---

72. Ἄκουε Ἰσραὴλ· κύριος ὁ Θεὸς ἡμῶν κύριος εἷς ἐστι. Theodoret, however, reads "your (σοῦ) God," rather than "our (ἡμῶν) God."

73. *V.* Theodoret's commentary on Colossians (on 2.18).

pensing with further discussion, he simply reports that "some commentators" had identified Balaam's angel (22.22–35) as Michael, but in Q. 42.1 on Dt, he goes to some length to account for the reference to "God's angels" (32.43 LXX) at the close of Moses' song.

In the *Questions* on Genesis this Antiochene commentator always speaks of the fall of Adam and Eve in quite positive terms. Several focus on the narrative of ch. 3, some on details regarding the serpent (*Qq.* 31f., 34f.), other quite searching ones on the crime and the justice of the punishment (*Qq.* 37f.), but none on the question that preoccupies western moralists: the transmission of the sin to succeeding generations. Was it fair of God to offer Adam his blessings if these were to be forfeited (Q. 24)? Yes, Theodoret replies: "though foreknowing the fall, he made him share in his blessings. . . . [H]is intention was that Adam should experience the divine gifts, so that, when deprived of them, he would hate sin for stripping him of such wonderful blessings." Were human beings punished in anger (Q. 37)? Not at all. When considered within the whole of God's providential dispensation, the Fall proved to be a fortunate lapse, a *felix culpa,* regrettable but with positive consequences. "Thus the punishment is not the result of anger, but part of a divine plan of the greatest wisdom (οἰκονομία σοφίας μεγίστης). So that the human race would hate sin as the cause of death, after the transgression of the commandment, God, in his great wisdom, passed the sentence of death and in this way both ensured their hatred of sin and provided the race with the remedy of salvation, which, through the Incarnation of the Only-begotten, achieves the resurrection of the dead and immortality." With typical eastern optimism Theodoret concludes (Q. 40), "Indeed, death is healing, not punishment."

As is to be expected of one who shares the spiritual world-view of Antioch—scriptural, christological, and soteriological—Theodoret is occasionally ambiguous about the relationship between divine grace and human effort in the process of individual salvation. Although at the beginning of this commentary, after mentioning his own effort, he piously declares his reliance on God, he sometimes make statements that give priority to human effort. Commenting allegorically on the priest's offering of both the right thigh and breast of the ram in Ex 29.27, he explains (Q. 63), "faith does not suffice for salvation but requires works for perfection." Accent falls constantly on free will and moral accountability. God cannot be shown overriding the former; the latter must be upheld, even in defiance of the biblical text. Whether it be Pharaoh opposing the Exodus or the nations presuming to challenge the invading Israelites and thus meeting with extinction, the hardening of their hearts is attributed to the malice of those punished, a malice that God permits but does not cause. "God is responsible for good, not for evil. He indicates what we should do, turns us away from sin, does not force our choices but yields to our free will. Since God permits sin and, though he might, refuses to prevent it to avoid compelling any act by overwhelming force (for it is the voluntary aspect of virtuous action that is praiseworthy), Moses spoke of God's permission as responsibility" (Q. 37.1 on Dt).

10. THEODORET'S ACHIEVEMENT IN THE QUESTIONS ON THE OCTATEUCH

Taking on this task at the request of his coadjutor Hypatius at a time of failing health, Theodoret is conscious that he is reaching the end of his exegetical career. As he indicates in Q. 1.1 on Leviticus, he has already completed "expositions of the Old Testament prophets and . . . commentaries on the epistles of the apostle." One does not, however, sense grudging effort and enforced brevity, as though the *Questions* were not a labor of love like his other commentaries; he seems pleased to be nearing completion of his exegesis of well-nigh the whole of Scripture. And we are doubly pleased that the text is fully extant. Although the choice of genre rules out verse-by-verse comment, Theodoret has generally avoided the concomitant risks of omitting passages of major significance and settling for the sensational. Thankfully, his fictitious questioner has an eagle eye for even minor discrepancies. Theodoret's approach still evinces typically Antiochene precision, and, as ever, he tries to provide all information necessary for his reader's understanding of the text. He always seeks to achieve clarity and conciseness.

Though we are not surprised that Theodoret's conclusions do not always agree with those of his modern counterparts, we find throughout comments of great acuity. Convinced that the translation produced by the Seventy enjoyed the inspiration of the Spirit,[74] he is no more ready than his peers to submit it to searching criticism. And, like his predecessors, he is unfamiliar with Hebrew. On the other hand, from the beginning, he acknowledges that Genesis is a theological reflection as well as a factual narrative and devotes questions 19f. to the meaning of the key idea of "image and likeness" in the creation of man. He catches the significance of the sabbatical climax to chapter 1 even if he fails to note the significant differences in the second account of creation immediately following this climax.[75] He grasps the basic message of Deuteronomy and recognizes that the author of Joshua used an earlier source. Yet it is only in Joshua that he comes to acknowledge layers in a composite text; nowhere else does he realize that discrepancies of fact within a book or a chapter may reflect diversity of authorship. Though there are traces of literalism in his hermeneutic, he is also ready to admit that an adequate interpretation must sometimes go beyond the mere surface of the text; he prefers to interpret many passages eschatologically, christologically, spiritually, and/or sacramentally. He frequently has recourse to typology, less often to allegory. The ethical

74. Like his predecessors and contemporaries, Theodoret fully accepts the account of the origins of the LXX contained in the *Letter of Aristeas*. In the preface to his commentary on the Psalms (PG, vol. 80, col. 864), he argues that, since the translators enjoyed divine inspiration, the titles of the psalms must be accorded the same respect as the poetic text. This represents a tacit rejection of the position of Diodore, who had argued (*Comm. in ps., prol.*) that the titles were composed, not by the inspired authors, but by post-exilic compilers who assembled the dispersed psalms into one collection and excogitated the titles from an often erroneous conception of the meaning of the poems.

75. *V.* note 55 above.

tone of his work is typically Antiochene: the Fall, though real, is susceptible of positive assessment, and free will cannot be superseded even by the Almighty.

Though a work of his decline, the *Questions on the Octateuch* merit the praise that Photius in the ninth century conferred on Theodoret's biblical commentaries: "On the whole, he reached the top level of exegetes, and it would not be easy to find anyone better at elucidating obscure points."[76] The reader will turn eagerly to his next and final exegetical work, *The Questions on Kingdoms and Chronicles,* which begin with a like promise to make clear whatever requires elucidation.

11. THE IDENTIFICATION, TRANSLATION, AND PRESENTATION OF THEODORET'S QUOTATION OF SCRIPTURE [J. F. P.]

Our modern English versions of the Octateuch depend on the relatively late Masoretic Hebrew text.[77] As Theodoret read a Greek version current in Antioch that differed from other forms of the LXX and was translated from a Hebrew original in many respects different from the MT,[78] neither the *NRSV* nor any other English version, nor even the Greek texts read by other patristic commentators will correspond completely with the Bible that lay before Theodoret as he composed his *Questions.* When translating biblical passages, the primary concern has been to determine their meaning to Theodoret, interpreter of the Antiochene LXX, rather than to reproduce our current understanding of the Hebrew original. Unless

---

76. *Bibl., cod.* 203. Photius proceeds (*cod.* 204) to remark on the *Questions:* "I had an opportunity to read the explanation of the Octateuch by this same author of blessed memory; bearing a title appropriate to the work, it is called 'On questions regarding Scripture' (Εἰς τὰ ἄπορα . . . τῆς Γραφῆς). It contains comments also on the books of Samuel-Chronicles. This is an extremely useful work."

77. For a brief note on the Masoretic text, *v.* K.G. O'Connell, "Hebrew Text of the Old Testament," pp. 1089f.

78. *V.* sec. 3 above.

otherwise acknowledged, English renditions of biblical passages in the text and notes are those of the translator.

It is often difficult to determine whether Theodoret is quoting, paraphrasing, or simply alluding to the sacred text. In addition to the questions arising from the differences between his Greek Bible and more widely circulating recensions, there are those resulting from the exigencies of Greek grammar, which would sometimes force Theodoret to change the inflections of individual words in the course of a discussion. We define a quotation of the OT as a verbal correspondence with the Göttingen Septuagint, where this is available, or with Rahlfs' edition of 1935 for those books still unpublished by the Göttingen Academy, and a quotation of the NT as a verbal correspondence with the fourth edition of *The Greek New Testament,* edited by B. Aland *et al.*[79] Where Theodoret's text presents variants that consist of nothing more than differences of case endings, altered word order, the substitution of a close synonym for a word found, or the addition of a word or brief phrase not found in these editions, we have had to decide whether we thought he was quoting his Antiochene text or adjusting the wording to the context of his discussion. Where the former has seemed at least likely, we have adopted the italics of quotation, elsewhere, the ordinary roman font. Throughout we use points of suspension to note the absence of material appearing in our authorities. Of course, we do not pretend to know whether Theodoret is abbreviating his own biblical text or quoting it in full.

To the extent possible, we cite Theodoret's biblical references according to the chapter and verse of the *NRSV.* Yet in cases where his recension seems to have diverged markedly from (1) the MT and (2) more widespread forms of the LXX we follow the chapter and verse divisions of the LXX, rather than those of the *NRSV.* The parenthetical abbreviation "(LXX)" indicates that a verse or a portion of that verse is found in the Greek but not in the Hebrew,[80] the abbreviation

79. *V.* the section of the Bibliography entitled "Bible: Ancient Texts, Versions, Concordance, and Catenae."

80. We do not use this abbreviation to point out substantial differences of

"(LXX var.)" that the variation of Theodoret's text from that of our authorities for the LXX is quite substantial: either his text contains a significant word or phrase not in our standard version or presents a wording so different as to render the quotation difficult to recognize.[81] In the latter case, the reader may wish to consult the *apparatus criticus* of the Göttingen LXX for more information on the witnesses with whom Theodoret's text agrees against other recensions. We have used the abbreviation "(LXX var.)" also to mark a very few passages where Theodoret offers a form of words that more closely follows the MT than the LXX, even though the Göttingen editors have not taken these into their *apparatus criticus*.[82] The same principles govern the very rare deployment of the abbreviation "(NT var.)," where Theodoret presents a text substantially different from that of our authority.

The reader will frequently encounter in the English translation paraphrases of scriptural passages set off by quotation marks; as these are not direct quotations, the corresponding Greek has not been italicized.[83] This punctuation is meant to bring out an important rhetorical device, by which, to impress a word of command or exhortation more vividly on the imagination of his audience, Theodoret restates a direct address in what he regards as a more straightforward and forcible manner. In some cases he makes changes of

---

meaning between the MT and the LXX. *V., e.g.,* Jgs 1.14, where the MT reports that Achsah urged Othniel to ask Caleb for a field, and the LXX has the husband urge the wife to put the request. As the LXX does not add material not to be found in the MT, we do not mark this reference with "LXX." There are, as well, in the *Index scripturisticus* a few cases where we use "LXX" simply to indicate that an explanatory note quotes and discusses the Greek translation of a verse.

81. In the *Qq. on Jgs*, we use the abbreviation (LXX *B*) to mark quotations whose wording agrees with that of the *codex vaticanus* in a significant departure from that of the *codex alexandrinus; cf.* sec. 3 above.

82. *V. e.g.,* the discussion of his version of Jos 10.13 in note 1 to *Q.* 14 on Jos.

83. In the Greek text, italics mark (1) direct quotation of Scripture and (2) words or phrases that Theodoret wishes to highlight, and which may or may not be drawn from Scripture. For an example of the latter usage, *v. Q.* 11.1 on Gn: Ὁ δὲ πρότερος οὐρανὸς οὐκ ἐκλήθη *στερέωμα,* ἀλλ' *οὐρανὸς ἐξ ἀρχῆς* ὠνομάσθη.

subject (*e.g.,* from "the Lord" to "I") and inserts pronominal adjectives (*e.g.* "my" or "your") to intensify the dramatic effect. For a good example, compare the quotation and the subsequent paraphrase of Jgs 2.1–3 in *Q.* 7.1 on Jgs.

We have tried to make our documentation as full as possible. To help the reader draw detailed comparisons between scriptural text and commentary, we have indicated numerous references in addition to the direct quotations. Thus, for the *Questions on Genesis* alone our *apparatus* of ancient sources counts some 125 more citations than those noted by our most recent predecessors, and the vast majority of these are references.

We have not, however, attempted to list cross-references. Thus, where we believe that Theodoret is directing the reader to a NT passage that cites a Hebrew prophet, we cite only the former. Likewise, we do not cite the parallel passages for Gospel pericopes. Thus a reference to Mt 8.26f. should not be interpreted to mean that Theodoret must be referring to Matthew's, rather than Mark's or Luke's, account of the quelling of the storm.

Finally, we have regularly adapted proper nouns to the forms used in the *NRSV.* This was not possible in *Q.* 104 on Gn, where Theodoret offers a Greek transliteration of Joseph's Egyptian name that does not correspond with the Hebrew transliteration of the MT. Otherwise, all names will appear in the form most familiar to speakers of English.

INTRODUCTION
TO THE GREEK TEXT

J. F. P.

1. THIS EDITION AND ITS ANTECEDENTS

The present edition of Theodoret's *Quaest. in oct.* is only the fifth since the invention of movable type. The *editio princeps* appeared in 1558, the first more-or-less complete edition in 1642, and the first fully critical edition in 1979. Our own *editio minor* improves upon this last.

A. The *Editio princeps*

The complete text of the *Quaest.* became available in print in several steps. The first was the *editio princeps* of the French scholar J. Picot (Ioannes Picus).[1] In a note to the reader dated February 1, 1558, Picot explained that he had made use of a single very defective manuscript, whose purveyor he vaguely named as *Asulanus Venetus* (*Cum huius operis vnicum . . . exemplar Graecum ab Asulano Veneto nactus essem*).[2] As F. Petit has shown, this manuscript must have

---

1. Fernández Marcos and Sáenz-Badillos incorrectly refer to him (p. xxvii) as Pic. F. Petit reports (*Catenae*, vol. 2, p. xli, note 55) that she found a notice regarding Picot in J.P. Nicéron, *Mémoires pour servir à l'histoire des hommes illustres dans la république des lettres*. This mentions that he was a priest who employed his free time in producing Latin and French translations of Greek patristic texts and lists nine titles, including other editions, that appeared between 1556 and 1565, the year of his death. I have not been able to verify this information from the 12 volumes of Nicéron's work dated 1727 and the single supplementary volume from 1729 that are available at the Library of Congress.

2. Sirmond (*v.* sec. C below) reproduces Picot's remarks on the fourteenth unnumbered page following the frontispiece.

been brought to Paris by Giovanni Francesco d'Asola, the brother-in-law of the great Venetian printer of classical texts, Aldus Manutius. D'Asola's manuscript, probably purchased with numerous other Greek and Latin codices by the royal library at Fontainebleau in 1542, has not been recognized in any extant book.[3] If, as seems likely, it was used as printer's copy, it may well have been destroyed in the process of producing the printed edition. Nonetheless, in a piece of excellent philological detective work, Petit has been able to prove that the *asulanus* must have been a descendent of two other manuscripts, both still extant. For *Qq.* 2–67 on Gn, it must have reproduced the tradition preserved in Madrid, Bibl. Nac. *4710* (16th c.), and for the rest of the *Qq.* on Gn through *Q.* 20 on Jgs, that preserved in *Vat., gr. 631* (11th c. = *2c*). Thus, the *asulanus* was a late and derivative witness to the text.[4]

Worse, it was incomplete in two ways. For most of its text an apograph of the defective *2c,* and itself perhaps only a mangled copy of that, it lacked the general preface, *Q.* 1 on Gn, part of *Q.* 20 on Jgs, all of *Qq.* 21–28 on Jgs, and the two questions on Ruth.[5] Second, this branch of the tradition contains a recension of the *Qq.* on Gn 2–67 that is characterized by frequent abbreviation of the text.[6] Picot was able to restore the answer to the first *Q.* on Gn and the missing part of the twentieth on Jgs by reference to another royal manuscript containing a Greek exegetical chain.[7] He must have suspected that, even so, the work remained incomplete, because he noted that,

3. *V.* Petit, *Catenae,* vol. 2, p. xlii, note 56. Thus *asulanus venetus* was Picot's identification of the man who brought the manuscript to Fontainebleau, not his denomination of the manuscript itself, as Fernández Marcos and Sáenz-Badillos imply (p. xxvii): [Picus] "alude al 'asulano veneto,' no conocido, del que saca el texto." Nonetheless, I shall follow these editors and Petit (*e.g.,* the stemma, p. li), in applying this convenient label to Picot's manuscript.

4. Petit, *Catenae,* vol. 2, pp. xli–xlv, xlviiif., li, liii.

5. *Ibid.,* pp. xxxiii–xxxvii.

6. *v.* Petit, *Catenae,* vol. 2, pp. xxxi, lviii, note 107, and xcviiif.

7. Picot drew his supplements from the present Paris, Bibl. Nat. *gr. 130–132,* in which Theodoret's first question has been replaced by a citation of Gn 1.1; *v. ib.,* pp. xlii–xlv.

though entitled *Questions on the Octateuch,* in its present form, it offered comment only on the first seven books of the Old Testament.

Though shorter than it should have been, Picot's edition also contained interpolated passages belonging to fathers other than Theodoret. These, twelve in all, entered the tradition at a point earlier than the copying of the *asulanus,* whose scribe would have found them already intercalated among the *Questions on Gn* and unprovided with any indication of authorship or provenance.[8] The reader can find almost all of these in the eighteenth-century edition of J.L. Schulze, reprinted in vol. 80 of the PG.[9]

In addition to editing the Greek text, Picot produced a Latin translation for *Qq.* Gn 1–Jgs 20. Petit reports that, though bound together in the copy belonging to the Bibliothèque Nationale, text and translation each have a separate title page and pagination, an indication that they were meant to be published separately. Both, however, bear the same date and issue from the same press, that of Jacques du Puys (Iacobi Puteani).[10] Though Picot reported that he had seen a Latin translation of questions on later historical books (*in libros Regum*), his own was the earliest printed translation of the *Quaest. in oct.* and the sole translation available for most of that work until the publication of the present edition.[11]

B. Supplements to Picot's Text:
Gentien Hervet and David Hoeschel

The publication of those portions not printed by Picot would not be complete for the better part of a century. Almost fourteen years after the appearance of Picot's edition, Gentien Hervet (Gentianus Hervetus) published a Latin translation of the missing sections of Jgs and Ruth. In a note to the reader dated December 28,

8. *Ibid.,* pp. xxxv, xliii.
9. In Schulze's the edition, the first stands between *Qq.* 6 and 7 and the last between *Qq.* 57 and 58 on Gn.
10. *Catenae,* vol. 2, p. xli.
11. His translation was somewhat revised by Schulze; *v.* sec. D below.

1571, Hervet, then Canon of Rheims, recounts that while in attendance on Cardinal Charles of Lorraine at the Council of Trent (1562), he was offered the opportunity to purchase a Greek manuscript containing Anastasius Sinaita's work on the Hexaemeron and Theodoret's *Quaestiones*.[12] Upon examining the volume, he realized that it contained questions on the Octateuch not known to Picot as well as the *Questions* on 1Sm through 2Chr. In hopes of performing a service to the scholarly world, he purchased the volume from his meager personal funds and translated the missing *Q.* 21 on Jgs through Ruth and the *Questions on Kings and Chronicles* as well.[13]

Hervet never printed a Greek text for these materials. The *editio princeps* of most, though not all, of the missing *Quaest. in oct.* was provided by David Hoeschel (Hoeschelius) of Augsburg in his edition of Photius's *Bibliotheca*.[14] There, he supplied *Qq.* 21, 22, and about two thirds of *Q.* 27 on Jgs., and *Q.* 1 on Ruth. W. Gerhäuser, a colleague of A. Rahlfs, identified Hoeschel's source as the sixteenth-century manuscript Munich *gr. 47 (31)* whose lacunas correspond precisely with the limits of these partial supplements.[15]

---

12. For an account of Hervet (1499–1584), *v.* M. Ott, "Hervetus, Gentian," *The Catholic Encyclopedia*," vol. 7: *Greg.–Infal.* (New York 1910), p. 298. In his prefatory material, Sirmond (*v.* sec. C below) provides (*v.* the fourteenth unnumbered page following the frontispiece), as if in a complete and faithful transcript, a copy of the note attached by Hervetus to his translation of the *Questions on Kings and Chronicles*. But this is actually a summary; a more complete and apparently accurate transcript appears in *Beati Theodoreti episcopi cyrensis theologi vetustissimi, Opera omnia quae ad hunc diem latine versa sparsim extiterunt* (Cologne 1617), vol. 1, pp. 526f.

13. Hervet did not retranslate the material already dealt with by Picot. Later editions offering a Latin translation simply combine the work of Picot and Hervet.

14. At the Library of Congress I had access to Hoeschel's edition only as augmented with Latin translation and additional notes by Andreas Schottus of Antwerp: *Photii Myriobiblon, sive Bibliotheca librorum quos Photius Patriarcha constantinopolitanus legit et censuit, graece edidit Dauid Hoeschelius augustanus, et notis illustrauit. Latine uero reddidit et scholiis auxit Andreas Schottus antuerpianus* (Oliua Pauli Stephani 1612). Hoeschel's supplements to the Greek text of Picot are on pp. 53–56 of the "Notae D. H. ad Biblioth. Photii" = Cccc2r–v. His original edition of Photius was published in Augsburg in 1601; *v.* Fernández Marcos and Sáenz-Badillos, p. xxvii.

15. Fernández Marcos and Sáenz-Badillos are at the least misleading when they state (p. xxvii) that Hoeschel "completaría la parte que faltaba en la edición de [Pi-

C. Jacques Sirmond's Edition of 1642

It was not until 1642 that a more-or-less complete edition of *Quaest. in oct.* was finally published. This was the work of J. Sirmond, the Jesuit patristic scholar and confessor of Louis XIII. Sirmond had at his disposal a manuscript he described only as a complete and "outstanding witness of great age" (*exemplar . . . optimum uetustissimumque*). This provided him with the general preface, the correct form of the question to *Q.* 1 on Gn, and a full Greek text of all the *Qq.* that Hervet and Hoeschel had brought to light.[16] Thus he was able to print the *editio princeps* of the beginning (the general preface and the question of the first *Q.*) and the end of the work (*Qq.* 23–26 on Jgs, the last third of *Q.* 27, *Q.* 28, and *Q.* 2 on Ruth). Equally important, Sirmond's witness contained the longer recension of the entire work rather than the shortened form characteristic of the family from which the early part of Picot's *asulanus* was derived.[17] Rahlfs had identified this manuscript, received in the royal library some-

cot] algunos años más tarde" and that his edition "recoge las *Quaest.* desde la 21 *in Ju* hasta el final de *Rut* tal como se encontraban en los ff. 440v–442v del ms. *Munich, Bay. Staatsbibliothek Gr. 47*." For Gerhäuser's identification of Hoeschel's source, *v.* Rahlfs, *Verzeichnis*, pp. 151 and 380, note 1. His conclusion is open to some doubt. In a comparison of the readings and omissions reported for *31* in the *ap. crit.* of Fernández Marcos and Sáenz-Badillos with the text printed by Hoeschel, I noted the following discrepancies: l. 24, p. 304 ἐκδιητημένως *31* : ἐκδιαιτωμένως *Hoesch.* | l. 7, p. 306 τοῖς *31* : τῆς *Hoesch.* | l. 8, p. 312 μὲν γὰρ Θάμαρ καὶ ἡ Ῥαὰβ ἡ δέ *31* : μὲν Θάμαρ καὶ ἡ Ῥαὰβ καὶ ἡ Ῥοὺθ ἀλλόφυλοι. χανααναῖαι γὰρ ἡ Θάμαρ καὶ ἡ Ῥαάβ· ἡ δέ *Hoesch.* The last of these is very striking, yet it is equally striking that at ll. 13–15, p. 314, only *31* and Hoeschel's text agree in omitting καὶ τὴν–καὶ τρίτης. If the reports of the Madrid edition are entirely correct, it is possible that Hoeschel worked from either a brother of *31* or an apograph that carried the longer version of l. 8, p. 312 in a marginal addition. Or perhaps he supplemented the witness of *31* with that of some second manuscript. At l. 15, p. 314, where the Spanish editors print σοι, Hoeschel prints σου with the notation "*al.* τοι."

16. As Petit points out (*Catenae*, vol. 2, p. lviii, note 108), Sirmond never mentions, and was probably unacquainted with, Hoeschel's edition of the missing questions on Jgs and Ruth.

17. Sirmond declares that he has been able to use a manuscript that provided not only the preface and the questions missing at the end of Picot's edition *sed et alia passim multa pleniora vulgatis vel emendatiora; v.* Petit, *Catenae*, vol. 2, p. lviii.

time between 1558 and 1642, with the present Paris, Bibl. Nat. *gr. 842* (*37*).[18] But, noting that *37* differs from Sirmond's edition in contents, readings, and the numeration of the questions, Fernández Marcos has proven that it could not have served as his exemplar.[19]

In addition to filling in the lacunae of Picot's edition, Sirmond was able to distinguish between the text of Theodoret and the twelve adventitious quotations of other fathers that had entered the *Qq.* on Gn through the line represented by the *asulanus.* He retained almost all of these twelve texts, but, with the aid of information drawn from exegetical chains, succeeded in providing the correct attribution for most. In a few cases, he made attributions that have seemed plausible, if not provable, and which may have reposed on nothing but his historical and stylistic sense.[20]

Sirmond's text of the *Quaest. in oct.* appears in the first of the four volumes of his complete edition of the works of Theodoret. Some forty years after the publication of the complete edition, another Jesuit patristic scholar, Jean Garnier (Joannes Garnerius) published a volume known as the *Auctarium.*[21] Intended as a supplement to Sirmond's *Theodoreti episcopi Cyri Opera omnia*, it contains

18. *V.* Rahlfs, *Verzeichnis*, pp. 208 and 380, note 1.

19. In their edition, Fernández Marcos and Sáenz-Badillos had accepted (p. xix) Rahlfs' identification. For Fernández Marcos' negative conclusion, *v.* "La edición," p. 242, and *cf.* Petit, *Catenae*, vol. 2, p. lvi.

20. For more information on passages drawn from fathers other than Theodoret that Sirmond retained, dropped, or added, *v.* Petit, *Catenae*, vol. 2, pp. lviii–lxiv. On the general reliability of Sirmond's judgments, she remarks (p. lxv), "Les attributions précisées par Sirmond résistent donc fort bien à la critique. Si toutes ne sont pas également garanties, il est remarquable qu'aucune n'est controuvée." Given Sirmond's diligence in distinguishing these passages from the *Questions* of Theodoret, it is surprising that Fernández Marcos and Sáenz-Badillos aver (p. xxvii) that, as a consequence of his choice of manuscript, "durante siglos se atribuirían a Teodoreto comentarios que no son suyos"; *cf.* the similarly mistaken criticism in Fernández Marcos, "La edición," p. 236.

21. *Auctarium Theodoreti cyrensis episcopi* (Paris 1684); for the title and the place and date of publication, *v.* E.-H. Vollet, "Garnier (Jean)," *La Grande Encyclopédie* (Paris 1886–1902), vol. 18: "Franco-Gonon," pp. 541f. I have seen only the reprint in the PG. Fernández Marcos and Sáenz-Badillos speak (p. xxvii) inaccurately of "P. Garrier."

texts, some correctly others wrongly, attributed to Theodoret, along with critical essays on his works and doctrine. None of Garnier's additions to the text of Theodoret pertain to the *Quaest. in oct.*

D. Johann Ludwig Schulze's edition of 1769

In the accuracy and completeness of the Greek text, the subsequent edition of our work by the German Protestant scholar J.L. Schulze (1734–99) represented only a slight improvement over that of Sirmond.[22] Indeed, in his preface to the reader, Schulze confessed that he wished his own edition of Theodoret to be as close as possible to that of his predecessor.[23] Yet to check and supplement what he found in Sirmond's text of the *Quaest. in oct.*, Schulze was able to draw on a sixteenth-century manuscript, the present Munich, Bayer. Staatsbibl., *Cod. gr. 351* (32), then part of the collection belonging to the city of Augsburg.[24] From this he excerpted variant readings, which he usually recorded at the bottom of the page, but a review of even the very limited critical notes of the present *editio minor* will show that he sometimes preferred readings of this manuscript to those adopted by Sirmond.[25] Perhaps the most notable result of his

22. Schulze's edition of Theodoret is reprinted in PG, voll. 80–84; vol. 80 contains the *Quaest. in oct.*

23. *Ordinem librorum eumdem tenuimus, quem olim secutus est Jac. Sirmondus, cujus editioni nostram esse cupimus quam simillimam;* vol. 80, coll. 23f.

24. Schulze was much mistaken as to the age of this manuscript, which he described (*ib.*, coll. 25f.) as *chartaceus, sæculo xi, ut videtur, scriptus in fol.* He cited it as *cod. augustanus* or simply *cod.* As Petit shows (*Catenae*, vol. 2, pp. xxxviif., xlviii–liii) this manuscript draws its text of *Qq.* 2–71 on Gn from the still extant Madrid, Bibl. Nac. *4710* (16th c.) and that of the remainder of the *Qq.* on Gn through *Q.* 20 on Jgs from the still extant *Vat. gr. 631* (11th c.). As *32* is both the father (for *Qq.* 2–68 on Gn) and brother (for the remainder of the *Qq.* on Gn through *Q.* 20 on Jgs) of Picot's *asulanus* (*v.* Petit, *Catenae*, vol. 2, pp. xliif., li–liii), Schulze must have noted that it sometimes agreed with Picot's edition against that of Sirmond. If he ever paused to consider the relationship of his *codex augustanus* to Picot's *asulanus*, his mistaken notion as to the age of the former may have encouraged him to regard the two as independent witnesses.

25. *V., e.g.*, my critical notes for Gn 18 and 34; Lv 37; Dt 1 ($\dot{\eta}\mu\hat{\omega}\nu$ ... $\dot{\upsilon}\mu\hat{\alpha}_\varsigma$) and 44; and Jos 1. In *Qq.* 65, 91, and 112 on Gn he also corrected Sirmond's nonsensical κἄν to κἀν; *v.* note 53 below. Furthermore, Schulze implies (PG, vol. 80, coll. 25f.)

consultation of 32 was the admission of a brief question not included by either Picot or Sirmond.[26] Thus, in his edition of the *Quaest. in oct.*, Schulze did not, as has been repeatedly stated, merely reprint the Greek text of Sirmond.[27]

Schulze retained in his text, and with Sirmond's attributions, the adventitious passages derived from the tradition of Picot's *asulanus*. Indeed, following manuscript 32, Schulze reinstated a couple of excerpts ejected by the Jesuit editor. As he also retained another added by Sirmond, his edition provides convenient access to a goodly stock of comments by patristic exegetes prior to Theodoret on some important passages of Genesis.[28]

In addition, Schulze combed the recently published *Catena Nikephori* (1772–73) for passages of Theodoret unknown to his predecessors. This very rare work was then and remains today the only complete Greek chain on the Octateuch available in a printed text.[29] For

that he compared the readings of Hoeschel's and Sirmond's texts in Jgs 21f. and 27, and Ruth 1.

26. This is #94 on Gn in the edition of Fernández Marcos and Sáenz-Badillos. *V.* PG, vol. 80, col. 201 and note 99. Schulze was able to correct the very inaccurate text of this question offered in 32 by reference to the *Catena Nikephori*, which we shall discuss below.

27. For the identification of Schulze's text with that of Sirmond, *v. e.g.*, Devreesse (*Chaînes*, col. 1100): "le texte est celui de l'édition de Sirmond parue en 1642, auquel on a ajouté des notes et des variantes"; Fernández Marcos and Sáenz-Badillos (p. xxvii): "Schulze reproduce el texto de Sirmond, recogiendo a pie de página variantes"; P. Nautin (in his review of the edition of Fernández Marcos and Sáenz-Badillos *REG* 92 [1979], p. 581): "l'édition de Schulze . . . reprend simplement le texte de Sirmond."

28. *V.* Petit, *Catenae*, vol. 2, p. lviii, notes 110–12 and p. lxi. The passages of Gn for which Schulze presents comments of authors other than Theodoret include: 1.2 ("darkness covered the face of the deep"); 1.26 ("Let us make humankind in our image"); 1.26 ("and let them have dominion"); 2.2 ("and he rested on the seventh day"); 2.4–6 ("no plant of the field was yet in the earth . . . and there was no one to till the ground"); 2.8 ("the Lord God planted a garden in Eden"); 3.7f. ("they sewed fig leaves together . . . . They heard the sound of the Lord God walking"); 3.21f. (the tunics of skin); 3.24 (the Cherubim guarding Paradise with flaming sword); 9.18 ("Ham was the father of Canaan").

29. Petit (*Catenae*, vol. 1, p. xxx.) describes this work (*CPG* #C2) as "La seule chaîne grecque imprimée"; *v.* also "La Chaîne," vol. 1, pp. xxxivf. As it was published in Leipzig, Schulze refers to it as the *catena lipsiensis.*

the first two books, it relies solely on the eleventh-century Athens, Ἐθν. Βιβλ. *43*, which Petit describes as one of the worse representatives of a later interpolated strand of the *catena* for Gn and Ex and "particulièrement défectueux en ce qui regarde les lemmes." She concludes that the *Catena Nikephori* is of no value for the scientific study of the chains.[30] From this source, Schulze excerpted nine sizable passages, eight relative to Gn and one to Ex, which he printed in notes that have been reproduced at the bottom of the pages of vol. 80 of the PG.[31] In her editions of the chains on Genesis and Exodus, Petit has now published all this material with attributions to Theodoret's Antiochene predecessors.[32] Clearly, Schulze was too

30. *Catenae graecae*, vol. 1, pp. xxxf.

31. As the *Catena Nikephori* was published after the appearance of his first volume containing the *Quaest. in oct.*, Schulze included his excerpts in an appendix to the fifth volume, published in 1784. In his reissue of Schulze's edition, Migne inserted these as notes below the relevant section of text; *v.* PG, vol. 84, note *a* to coll. 11f. The first two (Ἀλλ' οὐκ ἐπὶ τοῦτο . . . ἔπεσθαι δὲ ἐκείνην and Ἔθος τοῖς ἀπατωμένοις . . . γίνεται ἐπίγνωσις) appeared in the *Catena Nikephori* between *Qq.* 33 and 34 on Gn; the third (Ποῖά εἰσι τὰ ἑπτα . . . ἐν πάσῃ τῇ γῇ) between *Qq.* 41 and 42; the fourth (Καὶ ἔζησε Θάρρα . . . εἰς τὴν Χάρραν ἐξῄεσαν) between *Qq.* 61 and 62; the fifth and sixth (Ἐδηλοῦντο μὲν . . . ὑποσχέσεις and Περὶ δὲ ἡλίου . . . λεγομένων ἀκρόασιν) at the end of *Q.* 66 (Schulze) = 67 (Fernández Marcos and Sáenz-Badillos); the seventh and eighth (Διατί οὐχ . . . εὐλογίας ἔτι and Ὁ Σύρος . . . εὐωδεστάτων) between *Qq.* 81 and 82 (Schulze) = 82 and 83 (Fernández Marcos and Sáenz-Badillos); and the ninth (Ἐπειδὴ ἴχνη . . . εἴη ἂν ἀμπωτισμός) at the end of the answer to *Q.* 25 on Ex.

32. Schulze's first excerpt = *La chaîne sur la Genèse*, vol. 1, frag. 377 (probably Theodore of Mopsuestia); Schulze's second = *La chaîne sur la Genèse*, vol. 1, frag. 378 (Didymus the Blind); Schulze's third excerpt = *Catenae*, vol. 2, frag. 128 (probably Diodore); Schulze's fourth excerpt = *Catenae*, vol. 2, frag. 174 (Diodore or Theodore of Mopsuestia); Schulze's fifth and sixth excerpts = *Catenae*, vol. 2, frag. 186 (perhaps Theodore of Mopsuestia); Schulze's seventh excerpt = *Catenae*, vol. 2, frag. 223 (probably Diodore); Schulze's eighth excerpt = *Catenae*, vol. 2, frag. 226 (Diodore); and Schulze's ninth excerpt = *La chaîne sur l'Exode*, vol. 2: *Coll. cois.*, frag. 11 (Diodore). Aware of Petit's work on the *Collectio coisliniana* and the chains, Fernández Marcos and Sáenz-Badillos decided not to offer a text of the passages assigned to Theodoret by the *Catena Nikephori* and inserted by Schulze into his notes. Despite their rejection of this material, the editors did not regard their edition as incomplete. I point this out only because English readers of Fernández Marcos' *The Septuagint in Context* may have been puzzled by the statement (p. 229): "we decided to edit critically Theodoret's *Quaestiones in octateuchum*, an edition with many chapters missing." The last phrase of the translation misrepresents

sanguine in his hope of reaping a bountiful harvest of supplements from the *Catena Nikephori*.[33]

In addition to checking and supplementing the Greek text of Sirmond, Schulze tried to improve both the annotation and the translation. In his identifications of scriptural passages, he provided, for the first time, not just the number of the chapter but also the verse. He made an effort, as well, to point out where Theodoret's biblical text departed from the more widely known LXX readings. Though he took over the translations of Picot and Hervet that he found in Sirmond, he added to and reworked these as he thought necessary.[34]

For scholars who understand its limitations, Schulze's edition will long retain a certain usefulness. Here, alongside of Theodoret's *Qq.*, one can read, albeit in a less than entirely satisfactory edition, the comments of other exegetes on a number of biblical passages that occasioned much debate in antiquity. In addition, Schulze provides both excerpts and variant readings from the *Catena Nikephori*, to which few will have direct access.[35] The Abbé Migne performed good service to the study of Theodoret by choosing this edition by a Protestant scholar for inclusion in his collection.

E. The First Critical Edition

The first truly critical edition of the *Quaest. in oct.*, that of N. Fernández Marcos and A. Sáenz-Badillos, was published only in

---

the words, "edición que por muchos capítulos se echaba de menos," where "capítulos" would be well rendered as "reasons," *i.e.*, "an edition that, for many reasons, was regarded as desirable"; *v. Introducción a las versiones griegas de la Biblia* (Madrid 1998), p. 233.

33. V. PG, vol. 80, coll. 11f.: *Largam enim esse hanc messem, intelligent omnes ex illis quae . . . attulimus.*

34. *Cum* [*Sirmondus*] *his . . . antiquioribus versionibus textum Græcum adjecerit, factum est ut hic illis non ubique responderet. Nunc enim plura, nunc pauciora, nunc vero longe alia in textu quam in versione erant expressa.* Schulze seems to refer primarily to such changes in the translation as were necessitated by the introduction of words to, or their elimination from, the Greek text.

35. A search of the listings in OCLC turned up only four copies in the United States, none in the Washington metropolitan area. I found no listing in the National Union Catalog.

1979, more than four hundred years after Picot's *editio princeps*. Drawing widely both on manuscripts that contain only Theodoret's *Questions* and those in which the *Questions* are embedded in a wealth of other patristic commentary, they undertook the massive task of collating completely thirty-one manuscripts, including twenty-six dating from the ninth through the fourteenth centuries, and inspecting for selected passages another fifteen, all *recentiores* from the fifteenth through the eighteenth centuries.[36] This edition is indispensable for any reader who wishes to see the full variety of manuscript readings and to form an idea of the relationships among the ancient witnesses.

Though they do not construct a complete stemma, the editors regard nineteen of the thirty-one fully collated manuscripts as sometimes or always representative of one of three classes: "*A*," "*B*," "*C*." The first two consist of manuscripts that contain only the text of Theodoret, the last of chain and chain-like texts.[37] All three groups are represented throughout the work but with more or fewer witnesses as one progresses from book to book.[38] There remain twelve manuscripts that they do not attempt to fit into any of these three classes.

Dividing the *A* group into several subgroups, a, a_1, and a_2, they seem almost unsure whether these are sufficiently similar to be regarded as a family. "*A,* más que un grupo homogéneo no es sino la fusión o coincidencia de estos tres subgrupos bien caracterizados." Nonetheless, they aver that, as a whole, *A* presents a text of good

36. Of course, these thirty-one contain very various amounts of text: ranging from a single question (*41*) to just a few questions (*18, 19, 26*), to the great majority of the text (*2c, 3, 5, 7, 8, 10, 11, 12, 14, 15, 24, 32, 35, 37, 51, 52*) to complete (*9*).

37. *V.* p. xxii. Though other manuscripts contain some interpolated comments from other patristic writers, the *C* group presents the text of Theodoret embedded in a wealth of extrinsic material. The editors describe the entire *C* group as that containing "los mss. propiamente catenáceos," but a further distinction is necessary; *v.* below.

38. For more information on the members of each group and the contents of each manuscript, *v.* the description of the manuscripts in the *Conspectus siglorum*.

quality, which merits primary attention in the establishment of the text.[39]

The *B* group is, in general, less ancient than the *A* or *C* but not derived from either. It is characterized by numerous errors typical of later texts. The editors declare that they have seldom adopted any readings peculiar to this class.[40]

Finally, the *C* group, is further subdivided into *c* and c_1. The first, including Paris, Bibl. Nat., *Coislinianus 113* of the ninth century, another codex of the tenth, and a third of the eleventh century, is the most ancient of all the subgroups. Here, Theodoret's *Questions* are presented in sequence, each followed by excerpts from other patristic authors, mostly representatives of the Antiochene school. Petit argues that the *c* codices should be regarded as sources, not of a chain, but of a dossier (the *Collectio coisliniana*) that was intended to present the *Questions* of Theodoret in the context of his sources.[41] This subgroup is characterized by a tendency to abbreviation, especially at the end of questions and answers. As we have seen, for more than half of the *Qq.* on Genesis (2–67) Picot's *asulanus* must have

---

39. *V.* p. xxiii: "Su calidad textual es por lo general elevada, y merece atención especialísima en la fijación del texto.

40. *V.* p. xxiv. In their "Siglas" one finds the following listing for this group: "B = 14, 24 (17, 30 desde *Le*)." Yet, as the description of *30* (Florence, Bibl. Medic. Laurent., *Plut. VI, 5*) states (p. xviii) that this ms. contains only some of the *Qq.* on Gn, the parenthetical qualification must refer only to *17* (Oxford, Bodl. Libr., *Barocci. 123*). In their discussion of *B* (p. xxiii) they strangely remark that they exclude *30* from this group despite its close affiliation with *14* and *24* in that portion of the work it contains. The listing in the "Siglas" is, thus, contradicted, in different ways, by both the description and the discussion, and the latter is, itself, incoherent. If *30* offers a text closely similar to that of *14* and *24*, it ought to be reckoned a part of the *B* group for the *Qq. on Gn.*

41. *Catenae*, vol. 2, p. xix; *cf.* also Fernández Marcos and Sáenz-Badillos, p. xxv. Petit's edition of the *Collectio coisliniana*, published seven years after the Madrid edition of Theodoret's *Quaest. in oct.*, is based upon many of the same manuscripts, which she describes and classifies with great care. Though her discussion is a model of philological precision and leads to clear and significant conclusions, her choice to adopt *sigla* different from those of her predecessors inevitably entails much confusion for the reader who tries to compare her treatment of the medieval tradition with that of Fernández Marcos and Sáenz-Badillos.

been a late descendant of this tradition. In contrast, the manuscripts of c_1, are true chains. In these, it is the biblical text, rather than the *Questions* of Theodoret, that constitutes the organizing principle of the collected material. The editors refer vaguely to numerous and recurrent agreements of c_1 with c.[42] Due to the antiquity of some of the representatives of the C group, Fernández Marcos and Sáenz-Badillos suggest that its peculiar readings may, on occasion, represent the original words of Theodoret corrupted or revised in the other branches. Clearly, they regard as most likely correct those variants supported by an agreement of A and C or of components of each.

The twelve manuscripts that do not fall within any one of these three families are regarded as of mixed character: as a group, more like A and C than B, and closer to A than C. Nonetheless, the largely complete Rome, Bibl. Angel., *Gr. 41 (4)* and Munich, Bayer. Staatsbibl., *Cod. gr. 47 (31)*, perhaps Hoeschel's exemplar, are said to offer a text very similar to that of family B, and Paris, Bibl. Nat. *Gr. 842 (37)*, once wrongly regarded as Sirmond's exemplar, a form of text rather like that of subgroup c.

Fernández Marcos and Sáenz-Badillos also remark on the affiliations of some of the *recentiores* that they consulted only at select passages.[43] Yet, as they do not indicate for what sections these were collated, the reader cannot know where the *recentiores* carried the reading of the text and can track their use only at the places where

---

42. *V.* Fernández Marcos and Sáenz-Badillos, p. xxv. Petit, though editing the passages representing the sources of Theodoret's *Questions*, rather than the *Questions* themselves, remarks (*Catenae*, vol. 2, pp. cxvif.) that the chains present a more complete text but one more frequently altered by deliberate scribal attempts at correction. On p. cxvi, she presents a stemma for the manuscripts of the *Collectio coisliniana*, in which one can see the c manuscripts (her *11, 12, 13* = Fernández Marcos and Sáenz-Badillos' *15, 3, 8*) contrasted with the c_1 manuscripts (her *31, 38, 39* = Fernández Marcos and Sáenz-Badillos' *53, 51, 52*).

43. *V.* p. xxiii on Rome, Bibl. Apost. Vat., *Pii II gr. 49 (21)*; Rome, Bibl. Apost. Vat., *Ottob. gr. 226 (23)*; Paris, Bibl. Nat., *Coisl. 16 (33)*; Naples, Bibl. Naz., *II B. 12 (36)*; p. xxiv on Florence, Bibl. Medic. Laurent., *Plut. V. 29 (29)*; Rome, Bibl. Apost. Vat., *Ottob. gr. 16 (22)*; Oxford, Bodl. Libr., *Barocci. 76 (27)*.

they are cited for a reading not adopted. It is, thus, impossible for a reader not in possession of the editors' collations to assess the value of any of these.

Indeed, the most serious defects of this critical edition are due precisely to such failures of transparency of method. It is of the essence of a scientific edition that other scholars be provided with information sufficient to reconstruct for each reading the rationale for the editor's preference. Given the large number of manuscripts, their very various contents, their many lacunas, and reprises, it was necessary to set at the head of each question or segment of text the list of available witnesses. Instead, the editors have provided four different sorts of indications in four different places to delimit the contents of their witnesses: the descriptions in the introduction; an elenchus at the beginning of each book, which apparently lists those manuscripts that contain at least the first question;[44] marginal signs in the body of the work to mark points where manuscripts end, fail, begin, or begin anew; and notices in the *apparatus* to the first line of questions that are omitted by one or more codices. As a result, the reader may have to consult several points of reference to identify the sources for any particular question.[45] And to assure himself that he is not missing any marginal signs of lacuna or reprise, he must constantly flip through many pages of text.

Furthermore, these scattered indications are incomplete. Thus, we are repeatedly told in the descriptions that a manuscript contains only a part of a question. Yet there is sometimes neither marginal sign nor note in the *apparatus* to indicate precisely where the text breaks off or begins.[46] At times, the various sources of information

44. This is my own surmise, based on the observation that only some of the manuscripts cited in the *ap. crit.* of any given book appear in the introductory elenchus of that book. The editors provide no explanation of the criteria for inclusion in or omission from these introductory lists.

45. In some cases, there will be only one sure indication that a ms. is available for a given question: a citation in the *ap. crit.* Of course, the absence of a ms. from the *apparatus* of a given question or from the list at any one reading is no indication that it does not carry the portion of text in question; *v.* pp. xxviiif.

46. We are told in the description (p. xv) that Patmos, Ἰωάννου τοῦ Θεολόγου,

are inconsistent[47] or even contradictory.[48] The result is that no reader not prepared to dedicate hours of checking and cross-checking can compile a list of those manuscripts actually available for each section of text.

The usefulness of this edition is further impaired by other omis-

---

10 (11) begins toward the end of *Q. 61* on Gn, but there is no marginal indication or note in the *ap. crit.* to indicate just where. The same problem arises also in connection with Patmos, Ἰωάννου τοῦ Θεολόγου, *264 (13:* Which lines of *Qq. 2* and *48* on Gn does this contain?); Paris, Bibl. Nat., *Gr. 5 (14:* Which lines of *Qq. 1, 32,* and *34* on Dt does this contain?); Oxford, Bodl. Libr., *Barocci. 216 (26b:* Which lines of *Qq. 2f.* on Gn does this contain?); Dublin, Trinity Coll., *D.1. 28 (41:* Which lines of *Q. 67* on Gn does this contain?); Rome, Bibl. Apost. Vat., *Vat. gr. 747 (52:* Which lines of *Q. 1* on Dt does this contain?).

47. It sometimes happens that a marginal sign of a lacuna is followed at some distance by another without any indication (*e.g.,* marginal sign, notice in the description, or note in the *ap. crit.*) of the intervening point of reprise. Thus, for Rome, Bibl. Apost. Vat., *Vat. gr. 747 (52)* a marginal sign of lacuna appears at the end of *Q. 32* on Lv and another at the end of *Q. 49* on Nm. As this ms. is not listed in the introductory elenchus for Nm, the reader will wonder if it contains any of *Qq. 33–38* on Lv and how much of *Qq. 1–49* on Nm. In other cases, a marginal sign of reprise is followed at some distance by another without any indication (marginal sign, notice in the description, or note in the *ap. crit.*) of the intervening lacuna. For Rome, Bibl. Vallicell., *E 63 (10),* a marginal indication of reprise in the middle of *Q. 7* on Gn is followed by another toward the end of the first third of *Q. 112.* The reader will wonder which *Qq.* between 7 and 112 this manuscript contains. As Fr. Fernández Marcos has pointed out to me, some of these confusions are due to the disordered presentation of the questions or even the dislocation of folios within a manuscript. For Florence, Bibl. Med. Laur., *Plut. VI. 5 (30)* the successive indications of a beginning at *Q. 13* on Gn and a reprise at *Q. 61,* though there is no intervening indication of lacuna, are due to the dislocation of folios 1–12 after folio 13; as it is now bound, this manuscript presents *Qq. 61–98* before 13–60.

48. According to the description (p. xiii), Florence, Bibl. Laur., *Plut. VI. 19 (1)* should contain *Qq. 3–8* on Nm, but there is a marginal sign indicating the beginning of the text at the head of the answer to *Q. 5.* Likewise, we are told (p. xviii) that Vienna, Österreich. Nat. Bibl., *Theol. Gr. 178 (19)* presents *Qq. 2f.* on Gn before passing on to the answer of *Q. 19,* yet a marginal note at the end of *Q. 5,* would indicate that this ms. contains also *Qq. 4* and *5,* a conclusion confirmed by repeated citations of *19* in the *ap. crit.* Again, the description of Patmos, Ἰωάννου τοῦ Θεολόγου, *264 (13)* omits mention of *Q. 11* on Gn, yet a marginal note at the head of *Q. 12* and references to *13* in the *ap. crit.* indicate that it does contain this question. Contrast also the description (p. xviii) of Patmos, Ἰωάννου τοῦ Θεολόγου, *767 (24)* with the marginal sign of lacuna at the end of *Q. 76* on Gn.

sions and questionable choices. First, when family alliances are dissolved by discordant readings, the editors cite the witnesses for the competing variants in the order of their numerical *sigla* rather than in that of their families.[49] The reader who wishes to check their conclusions regarding the affiliations of the manuscripts must mentally reassemble them in the order of their groups a, a_1, a_2, B, c, c_1, and the mixed class.[50] Second, in a handful of cases, the editors pay such deference to the majoritarian reading as to print nonsense[51] or Greek that, while meaningful, is so odd morphologically or stylistically, as to raise suspicion.[52] Third, their edition is rife with misprints. My list of *errata*, though restricted to the text of the *Quaest.*, will suggest the scope of the problem.[53]

Since the publication of this edition, F. Petit has advanced the study of both the most ancient and the most recent branches of the manuscript tradition. In the "Enquête philologique" introducing her edition of the *Collectio coisliniana*, where she discusses many of the manuscripts upon which the Madrid edition of the *Quaest. in oct.* is based, she demonstrates that two of the manuscripts used by Fernández Marcos and Sáenz-Badillos are apographs of still extant codices and thus of no value for constituting the text. That portion of Rome, Bibl. Apost. Vat., *gr. 631* containing *Qq.* 2–67 on Gn (*2b*) was copied from Madrid, Bibl. Nac., *4710*. This latter was also the source for *Qq.* 2–70 on Gn for Munich, Bayer. Staatsbibl., *gr. 351* (*32*), which drew the rest of its text from the early portion (tenth-eleventh centuries) of the Vatican's *gr. 631*.[54] In consequence, *2b* must be eject-

---

49. Thus, to pick an example at random, at line 18, p. 214 for the reading φησίν ἤ they list *B* 4 7 11 31 35 51. But according to their own division (pp. xxiii, xxvf.), *11* represents class a_2, *51* class c_1, and 4, 7, 31, and 35 are mixed and not to be assigned to any of the three families.

50. *Cf.* also note 40 above on their incoherent discussion of the *B* group.

51. *V.* my critical notes to *Qq.* 18 and 65 on Gn; 10 and 60 (τὴν κόχλον) on Ex; 1 (αὐτοὶ . . . ἠξίωσαν) on Dt; 19 on Jos (μὴ προσδοκήσητε . . . ἀπολαύσεσθαι); 8 and 12 on Jgs; and 2 on Ruth (τὸ δε . . . ἀοίδιμον, etc.).

52. *V.*, e.g., my critical notes to *Qq.* 17, 34, 51 (κρεοφαγεῖν), and 52 on Gn, and Q. 21 on Dt.

53. *V.* "Introduction to the Greek Text: Corrigenda to the Madrid Edition."

54. *V.* notes 24 and 41 above.

ed from class *c* and 32 from *a*. Though these conclusions entail changes in the evidence presented for many individual readings, they hardly shake the edifice of a text solidly constructed on such a broad foundation of medieval witnesses.

In conclusion, the edition of 1979 is the only fully critical edition of Theodoret's *Quaest. in oct.* It represents a major advance in our knowledge of the text and will long remain indispensable. Nonetheless, given its flaws of construction and presentation, it remains far from definitive.

F. This Edition

Though the largest contributions of our own edition will certainly consist in its interpretive apparatus—the introduction, the explanatory notes, and, above all, the translation—we believe that it also makes an advance on both the quality of the Greek text and the presentation of the ancient evidence. Indeed, I hope that this will be judged a competent *editio minor* to the *editio maior* of our prede-cessors. It does not offer a thoroughgoing revision. I have consulted only a few manuscripts and mostly just to determine their precise contents. Nor have I studied the entirety of the *apparatus criticus* of the Madrid edition. My goals have been (1) to avoid printing any Greek for which I can find no plausible translation or which, in comparison to the rest of Theodoret's corpus, displays anomalies so gross as to defy acceptance; (2) to rid the text of obvious errors; and (3) to set before the reader a *conspectus siglorum* and textual notes that list the ancient witnesses and the evidence for the variety of readings in a straightforward and easily comprehensible manner.

Given the length of this work, the total of textual notes, fewer than ninety, is very restricted. A careful reconsideration of all the readings adopted in the Madrid edition would probably raise numerous issues I have not considered. While some notes simply present variants that, though significant for one reason or another, have not been taken into the text, others offer some justification for a change I have thought necessary.[55] In fifty places, I have preferred a manuscript reading rejected by Fernández Marcos and Sáenz-Badillos[56] and in eleven more I have ventured to insert a conjecture.[57] Where the various possibilities would result in meanings substantially different, I have offered alternative translations that I hope will indicate what is at stake even to the Greekless reader. I have not, however, offered translations where I have made a change to what I regard as more plausible Greek usage or where I could make no sense of the rejected reading.

It goes without saying that I have eliminated the numerous misprints listed in the next section. Nevertheless, in the process of emending and repunctuating the Greek, I will have inadvertently introduced new errors of my own. I can only echo Schulze in begging learned readers to collect these and bring them to my attention so that we may eliminate them in a future reprinting.[58]

---

55. In my textual notes I can only repeat attributions explicitly stated by Fernández Marcos and Sáenz-Badillos, who, of course, excluded (*v.* the Madrid ed., pp. xxviiif.) from their apparatus phonetic variants such as etacisms and the addition of the epenthetic nu, sparsely attested errors obviously due to the misreading of an exemplar, and clearly wrong singular readings. Thus, the reader of either their edition or this edition cannot assume that the reading they adopted had the backing of all the manuscripts not listed as carrying something different. I arrange the variants in the order in which they decline from the truth, either because the sense of the reading becomes less appropriate or less clear or because something is changed or omitted that, in my opinion, points to the true reading.

56. *V.* the notes for the title, *Qq.* 4, 7, 17–20, 34, 48, 52, 54, 59 (ταῖς οἰκοδομίαις), 62 (ὁ περάτης), 65, 79, 99, and 112 (τὸν τῶν σικημιτῶν ἄδικον ὄλεθρον, δείκνυσι, and φησιν) on Gn; 10 (ἕτερα δὲ), 43, 60 (καταπέτασμα, καταπετάσματος, and τὴν κόχλον), 65 (ἐν ἐμοὶ and τοῖς υἱοῖς), and 66 on Ex; 1 (ἀποστολικῶν ἐπιστολῶν, μὴ, and φασιν), 22 (ἀπήλαυσε), 32, and 37 on Lv; 1 and 10 on Nm; 1 (αὐτοι . . . ἠξίωσαν and φιλικῶν) and 42 (first note) on Dt; 3 (περίτεμε and ἐπαγγελίαν), 19 (ἐξέτινεν) and 20 on Jos; 8 (τὸ . . . πειρᾶσαι, etc. and ἀσκῆσαι γὰρ, etc.), 11, 12, and 24 (θεραφίν and θεραφίν) on Jgs; and 2 (καὶ ἔσται ὄνομα, etc. and τὸ δε . . . ἀοίδιμον, etc.) on Ruth.

57. *V.* the notes for *Qq.* 51 (κρεοφαγεῖν) and 59 (ᾠκοδομῆσθαί) on Gn; 7, 10 (τούτῳ δὲ), 58, and 69 on Ex; 21 and 24 on Lv; 21 on Dt; 19 (μὴ προσδοκήσητε . . . ἀπολαύσεσθαι) on Jos; and 3 on Jgs. Schulze, without a note, prints ᾠκοδομῆσθαί in *Q.* 59 on Gn.; the others are my own suggestions, though some or all of them, straightforward as they are, may well be attested in the mss.

58. In an appeal to his *peritis lectoribus*, Schulze begs (PG, vol. 80, coll. 23f.) *ut*

Throughout I have tried to ensure that the reader can always assess the distribution of the manuscript evidence. For each question I provide the list of available manuscripts, which is itself based on the description of the manuscripts provided at the end of this essay. Both depend primarily on the information supplied in the edition of 1979 and on further clarifications graciously supplied by Father Natalio Fernández Marcos. Armed with the lists provided in this *editio minor,* the reader will now be able to read with much fuller comprehension the *apparatus criticus* of the *editio maior.*[59]

So that the reader may test for himself the consistency of the family alliances established by Fernández Marcos and Sáenz-Badillos, I have cited the manuscripts in the order of their classes, followed by the mixed manuscripts undivided by commas in the order of their numerical *sigla,* followed by the editors. Thus, if a single numbered manuscript set off by a comma appears anywhere before the mixed codices, that manuscript is the sole representative of its group to carry the reading in question.

I have reconfigured my predecessors' *Conspectus siglorum* to make it simpler and clearer. First, I restrict the use of class *sigla* to designate the agreement of at least two manuscripts. Thus, I have ejected the *siglum a* from the *Quaest. on Gn,* where *2a* and *2c* are the sole independent witnesses in sections that do not overlap. In Ex–Jgs *a* signifies the agreement of *2c* and *6,* but it is not used in Ruth, which is carried only by *6.* I have eliminated altogether the group a_p, since its membership, indicated as "5 and its congeners," seemed indeterminable.[60] Since all the congeners figure among *recentiores* consulted only for selected passages, no reader not in possession of the editors'

---

in rei litterariæ publicamque adeo utilitatem sua conferant consilia, si quid vel emendandum vel rectius disponendum esse videatur.

59. The introductory list contains all manuscripts that carry at least a part of the question. Readers studying the evidence for any given variant must check the left-hand margin for possible indications of points where the text breaks off or begins in any of those manuscripts. Despite my best efforts, some of these lists may need emendation; I shall be very grateful for all corrections or clarifications.

60. *V.* "Siglas": "5 (y sus afines)."

collations can know which manuscripts are involved at any one point. I have, therefore replaced a_1 with 5, the only manuscript whose readings can be certainly deduced from the editors' a_1. Consequently, in the listing of manuscripts in the *apparatus*, 5 will often stand between *a* and a_2, and the *siglum A* will mean the agreement of *a* (*2c* and *6*), 5, and a_2. Second, drawing the logical consequence from the close relationship of *30* with *14* and *24*, I employ the *siglum B* to refer to the agreement of *14*, *24*, and *30* in the *Quaest. on Gn.*[61] Third, taking stock of Petit's conclusions regarding *32* and *2b*, I have eliminated the former from class *a*, yet, in consideration of its importance for understanding the choices made by Schulze, I list it in parentheses among the mixed manuscripts for *Qq.* 1–70 on Gn and, from then on, after the *a* manuscripts. I have eliminated *2b* not only from class *c* but from the entire edition.

I have also intervened in the text to facilitate the understanding of both individual sentences and the development of discussions or arguments. I have repunctuated throughout with a system that, while observing the structure of the Greek periods, also takes into account norms generally accepted in modern English. This has resulted in hundreds of changes.[62] Most, though presupposing an un-

---

61. *Cf.* note 40 above.

62. My basic procedure has been: (1) to eliminate punctuation before conjunctions coördinating clauses unless these introduce a clause whose subject is different from that of the preceding coördinate clause, or the subject, though identical to that of the former clause, is repeated or restated in the second clause, or the clauses stand in a series of three or more; (2) to eliminate commas before subordinating conjunctions unless (a) the conjunction introduces a clause nestled within the main clause; (b) the conjunction introduces a clause that is resumptive or explanatory of a pronoun or phrase in the preceding main clause; (c) the conjunction introduces a causal clause or a clause with a causal nuance; (d) the conjunction introduces a non-restrictive relative clause; (3) to eliminate commas between verbs and clauses that play noun roles (subject, direct object, or predicate noun) in relation to those verbs; (4) to eliminate commas between two members of a pair of words, phrases, or clauses, but to introduce them to mark words, phrases, and clauses arranged in a series of three or more; (5) to introduce commas (a) between coördinate clauses in asyndeton or connected by particles rather than conjunctions, (b) after introductory adverbial clauses, (c) before and after subordinate clauses nestled within the main or another subordinate clause, and (d) before participial clauses

derstanding of Theodoret's periods that is the same or very similar to that of my predecessors, will, I hope, result in greater clarity. Many, however, reflect a substantially different understanding.[63] I have observed the same system for both Theodoret's words and his quotations of Scripture, since the two form a literary unity, and Theodoret has often adapted, abbreviated, or combined the latter for the purposes of his argument. Thus, though I have often adopted their punctuation, I have not tried to reproduce in any systematic way what I have found in either the Göttingen Septuagint or the most recent edition of *The Greek New Testament*.

The better to mark the argumentative stages in Theodoret's discussions, I have introduced paragraph divisions. As his replies often include brief notes on matters not germane to the questions, the paragraphing will help to isolate one topic from another and to signal the commentator's movement from one to another segment of the biblical text.[64] In addition, to facilitate scholarly reference and

---

that follow the main clause with no introductory conjunction; (6) to replace colons with commas to introduce direct quotations, unless (7) the quotation is epexegetic or explanatory of a previous statement (*e.g.*, the verb introducing the quotation governs a demonstrative pronoun or adverb, such as τοῦτο or οὕτως, or the quotation itself is interrupted by γάρ φησι), in which case colons replace commas; (8) to set off parenthetical remarks and additions within pairs of colons, rather than, as often in the Madrid edition, between a colon and a comma. In accord with rules one through four, I have eliminated many commas before and after conjunctions such as ὅτι, ἵνα, ὅπως, ὥστε, and καί, while, in accord with rules four and five, I have added many after καί or in places where there is no conjunction. In a partial exception to rule 3, I have retained or inserted commas before ὅτι when it serves as the equivalent of a mark of punctuation introducing a direct quotation.

63. *Cf., e.g.,* our very different punctuations in *Qq.* 112.1 on Gn (διὰ τὴν ἄκραν διεσπάρη τιμὴν ... ὡρισμένος πήχεων ἀριθμός); 112.4 on Gn (καὶ τὸ μὲν σῶμα ... τὴν περιβολὴν αὐτοῦ); 10 on Ex (πρὸς δὲ τούτοις ... οὐδὲν τῶν τοιούτων ἀκάθαρτον); 68 on Ex (ὡς ἐκείνην ἰδεῖν τὴν οὐσίαν ἀδύνατον—end); 1.6 on Lv (τοῖς μέντοι ὁλοκαυτώμασιν ἐπετίθετο ... τὰς ἡμετέρας προσφέρομεν προσευχάς); 27 on Lv (ὅτι γάρ, οὐ τὸ ἱμάτιον—end); 35 on Lv (ἐν ᾗ, φησίν, ... τὸ τῆς ἀφέσεως ἔτος); 34.2 on Dt (αἰνίττεται δὲ ... τῆς πολιορκίας τὰς συμφοράς); 44.2 on Dt (ἐφ' ὕδατος ἀντιλογίας—end); 2.2 on Jos (ὁ ἑβραίων Θεός.... τῷ λόγῳ σου τούτῳ); 17 on Jgs (ἐπειδὴ δὲ ὀργισθεὶς ὁ Θεὸς-end).

64. As Schulze points out (PG vol. 84, coll. 11f.), many of the questions seem to

quotation, I have introduced numerical subdivisions into every question that exceeds forty lines in the edition of Fernández Marcos and Sáenz-Badillos. Since I thought the beginnings of sections should always correspond with the paragraphing, the subdivisions occur at somewhat irregular intervals, usually equivalent to twenty-five to forty lines in their edition.

2. CORRIGENDA TO THE MADRID EDITION

I hope that this list may be of use in the preparation of a revision of the Madrid edition. In cases where errors have persisted from century to century, or an error in that can be traced to a careless use of an earlier edition, I list the editors: Sir. = Sirmond; Sch. = Schulze; F.M. = Fernández Marcos and Sáenz-Badillos. The line and page numbers refer only to the edition of F.M. I omit Picot's readings, to which I had only occasional access through Schulze's citations. As I have been able to consult Schulze's edition only as reprinted in the *Patrologia latina,* I may attribute to him errors due rather to the negligence of Migne.

Quaest. in Gen.: Pf. τοῦτο (l. 4, p. 3) : τοῦτό *Q.* 1 Θεόν (l. 14, p. 4) : -ὸν *Q.* 3 γάρ, φησί, *Sch.* : γάρ, φησί, (l. 6, p. 7) *F.M.* : γάρ φησι, | παραγγεῖλαι τισὶ (l. 17, p. 6) *Sir. F.M.* : -γεῖλαί τισι | καταφρονήσετε (l. 6f., p. 7) : -ητε | εἴρηκε (l. 12, p. 7) : εἴ- | ἔστησεν (l. 15, p. 7) : ἔσ- | οὔκ (l. 19, p. 7) : οὐκ *Q.* 4 ἤνεσαν (l. 21, p. 8) : ἤνεσάν | περήγαγεν (l. 1, p. 9) : παρ- | τοῦτα (l. 10, p. 9) : ταῦ- | τολμερὸν (l. 10, p. 9) : -μηρὸν | ὄντα (l. 13, p. 9) : ὄν- *Q.* 8 προσίειται (l. 24, p. 12) : -ίεται *Q.* 10 συγγραφεύς (l. 12, p. 13) : -ὺς *Q.* 11 γενηθήτο (l. 1, p. 14) : -τω | δήλοι (l. 3, p. 14) :

---

represent the later conflation of originally independent remarks on different verses; v. the preface to vol. 5, where, discussing the distribution of the *Quaest. in oct.* in the *Catena Nikephori,* he remarks, *intelleget Lector Quaestionum earum unam alteramve subinde ad plura capita et commata pertinere, multisque constare partibus, quae in Catena non sine improbo labore quæri et colligi potuerunt.*

-λοῖ Ι θεία (l. 23, p. 14) : ἡ θεία **Q.** 12 συνάχθη (l. 12, p. 15) : -ήχθη
Q. 15 ἐντεύθεν (l. 10, p. 17) : -εῦθεν Ι ἡμέρων (l. 12, p. 17) : -ῶν Ι
ἐντεύθεν (l. 22, p. 17) : -εῦθεν **Q.** 18 συμμαχιὰν (l. 6, p. 19) : -ίαν Ι
μωρίων (l. 12, p. 20) : μο- **Q.** 19 ἐστιν (l. 5, p. 22) *Sir. F.M.* : ἔ- Ι τὴν
(l. 24, p. 22) : τῆς **Q.** 20 προσεγορεύθη (l. 10, p. 26) : προση- **Q.** 21
ἑβδόμη (l. 13, p. 27) : -η **Q.** 26 γεράρων (ll. 9f., p. 30) : Γ-
Q. 29 Τιγρήτα (l. 3, p. 32) : Τί- **Q.** 32 παγίδα (l. 3, p. 34) : -ίδα
Q. 33 γύνη (l. 16, p. 34) : -νὴ **Q.** 34 συρόμενον (l. 6, p. 35) : συρόμενόν **Q.** 37 τᾶ (l. 13, p. 36) : τὰ Ι παλαία (l. 22, p. 36) : -ᾷ Ι
ἐκείνον (l. 18, p. 37) : -εῖνον Ι δεξαμένον (l. 21, p. 37) : -άμενον Ι
ἐξωκειλάντων (l. 1, p. 38) *Sir. Sch. F.M.* : ἐξο- Ι ἀθάνατο (l. 14, p. 38)
: -τος Ι ἀνθρώπων (l. 11, p. 39) : ἀνθρώ- **Q.** 40 πονηρὸν, (l. 13, p. 41)
Sir. Sch. F.M. : -όν, **Q.** 47 ἐπὶ (l. 22, p. 44) : ἐ- Ι ἡρμενευκέναι
(l. 24, p. 45) : ἡρμη- **Q.** 48 δυμιουργῆσαι (l. 2, p. 48) : δημι- Ι
τύφον (l. 3, p. 48) *Sir. Sch. F.M.* : τῦ- **Q.** 50 φύλη (l. 14, p. 48) : -λή
Q. 51 ἑαυτόν (l. 4, p. 50) : -τόν, **Q.** 53 Ὑπεδέξατο (l. 19, p. 51) :
Ὑπ- **Q.** 54 παντῶν (l. 17, p. 52) : πάν- **Q.** 57 πόρρω (l. 5, p. 54) :
-ρω **Q.** 58 προσέκει (l. 6, p. 55) : -ήκει **Q.** 60 κτήσις (l. 14, p. 56) :
κτῆ- **Q.** 62 Ἀλλὰ (l. 15, p. 57) : Ἀλλά Ι ἐμπαῖζειν (l. 5, p. 58) :
-παίζειν **Q.** 64 γραφή ὅτι (l. 15, p. 59) : -φὴ ὅτι Ι δικαιωσύνη
(l. 23, p. 59) : δικαιο- **Q.** 65 Μελχισεδὲχ (l. 15, p. 60) *Sir. Sch. F.M.* :
-δὲκ **Q.** 67 ποιεῖεσθαι (l. 3, p. 64) : ποιεῖσ- **Q.** 68 παιδοποΐας
(l. 11, p. 64) : -ίας **Q.** 69 τεσσάρακοντα (l. 7, p. 65) : -αράκοντα
Q. 71 ἐπεμέμψαιτο (l. 11, p. 66) *Sir. Sch. F.M.* : ἐπι- **Q.** 75 αὐτόν
(l. 4, p. 70) : -τὸν **Q.** 78 παρπόν (l. 22, p. 72) : κ- **Q.** 83 ἑρμενεία
(l. 9, p. 74) : ἑρμη- Ι τούτῳ (l. 6, p. 75) : Τού- Ι ἐκράτυνε (l. 13, p.
75) : ἐ- Ι δῷη (l. 15, p. 75) : δῴ- **Q.** 85 ἐλαίῳ (l. 25, p. 76) : ἐ- **Q.** 91
τοὐναντίο (l. 13, p. 80) : -τίον Ι ἀφεῖλε (l. 21, p. 80) : ἀφεῖλέ Ι
προσθήτω (l. 23, p. 80) *Sir. Sch. F.M.* : -έτω Ι κἂν *Sir.* : κἂν (l. 12, p.
81) *F.M.* : κὰν **Q.** 93 διὰ τοι (l. 18, p. 81) : διά τοι Ι φρινῆ (l. 20, p.
81) : φρον- **Q.** 97 σοφρωνοῦντα (l. 23, p. 83) : σωφρο- **Q.** 98 ὅτι
(l. 17, p. 84) : ὅ- **Q.** 99 ποιεῖ (l. 11, p. 85) *Sir. Sch. F.M.* : -ῇ **Q.** 104 τό
ψ- (l. 8, p. 87) : τὸ **Ψ**- **Q.** 105 ἐστι (l. 8, p. 88) *Sir. F.M.* : ἔ-
Q. 109 οἷον (l. 15, p. 89) : οἱοί **Q.** 110 Ἰωσήφ (l. 5, p. 90) : -ὴφ

Q. 111 ἡσθεὶς (l. 19, p. 90) : ἡσ- | Ἐφαῒμ (l. 24, p. 90) : Ἐφρ- **Q.** 112 ἐμνήσθε (l. 4, p. 92) : -θη | Ἰούδα (l. 6, p. 93) *Sir. Sch. F.M.* : -δᾳ | κἂν *Sir.* : κᾶν (l. 11, p. 93) *F.M.* : κἀν | χαραποιοὶ (l. 1, p. 96) : χαρο- **Quaest. in Ex.: Q.** 5 βατοῦ (l. 13, p. 101) : βά- | Θεός (l. 17, p. 101) : -ὸς | ὥσπερ δέ (l. 10, p. 102) : ὥσπερ δὲ | ἐφαίνων (l. 11, p. 102) : ἐμφ- **Q.** 6 παρθηνικὴν (l. 23, p. 102) : -θενικὴν **Q.** 11 ἀλιέας (l. 6, p. 105) : ἁ- **Q.** 12 φαρμακοῖς (l. 24, p. 107) *Sir. Sch. F.M.* : -μάκοις | φαρμακοὶ (l. 25, p. 107) *Sir. Sch. F.M.* : φάρ- | ξεραίνει (l. 20, p. 108) : ξη- **Q.** 14 βραδύγλωσσος (l. 4, p. 112) : -σσος **Q.** 24 δέ (l. 19, p. 119) : δέ, | κηλίδας (l. 27, p. 119) *Sir. Sch. F.M.* : κηλῖ- | ἑβραίοι (l. 3, p. 120) : -αῖοι **Q.** 25 εὑρεῖαν (l. 17, p. 121) *Sir. Sch. F.M.* : εὑ- **Q.** 30 Ἰώσηππος (l. 20, p. 123) : -ηπος **Q.** 35 ἔσεσθε (l. 12, p. 125) : -θέ **Q.** 39 γάρ (l. 17, p. 128) : γὰρ **Q.** 40 ἠμωδίασαν (l. 22, p. 129) : ἠ- | αἰμωδιάσουσιν (l. 25, p. 129) : αἰ- | κἂν (l. 9, p. 130) : κἀν **Q.** 48 μεμωρφωμένον (l. 10, p. 134) : μεμορ- **Q.** 57 ἡμέρων (l. 4, p. 138) : -ῶν **Q.** 58 Ὥς (l. 9, p. 138) : Ὡς **Q.** 60 εὖρος (l. 14, p. 140) : εὐ- | ἡμέρων (l. 26, p. 141) : -ῶν | ἐκδιαφόρων (l. 25, p. 142) : ἐκ δ- **Q.** 65 σφραγίδες (l. 9, p. 147) *Sir. Sch. F.M.* : -γῖδες **Q.** 66 διέγλυφεν (l. 12, p. 147) : -ψεν *(I suppose the impf. to be an error, rather than a conscious choice among variants; Sir. and Sch. both have the aor.)* **Q.** 67 Θεὸς, (l. 10, p. 148) : Θεὸς **Q.** 68 σκληρότητα (ll. 5f., p. 149) : -ρότητά | ἤτεσε (l. 12, p. 149) : ἤτη- **Q.** 69 ὅ τι (l. 4, p. 150) *Sch. F.M.* : ὅτι **Q.** 72 νουμενίᾳ (l. 16, p. 151) : -μηνίᾳ **Quaest. in Leu.: Q.** 1 εἴρεται (l. 2, p. 153) : εἴρη- | προφετῶν (l. 4, p. 153) : προφη- | ἑρμενείαις (l. 4, p. 153) : ἑρμη- | γεγενεμένα (ll. 10f., p. 153) : -ημένα | θυσίων (l. 14, p. 153) : -ῶν | γονορρύει (l. 18, p. 154) *Sir. Sch. F.M.* : -υεῖ | ὁλοκαύτωμα τε (l. 8, p. 155) : -καύτωμά τε | βομῷ (l. 13, p. 158) : βω- | ἑρμενευτὰς (l. 18, p. 158) : ἑρμη- **Q.** 11 ἀλλὰ (l. 12, p. 164) : ἄλλα | τοὺς ὄφεις (l. 24, p. 165) : τοὺς δὲ ὄφεις **Q.** 12 κλιβάνος (l. 21, p. 166) : -ους | ἐμπέσοντος (l. 23, p. 166) : -σόντος **Q.** 13 θνησιμαίον (l. 1, p. 167) : -μαῖον **Q.** 16 καλη (l. 14, p. 168) : -ῇ | μεδὴν (l. 16, p. 168) : μηδὲν **Q.** 18 πότε ... πότε (l. 1, p. 170) : ποτὲ ... ποτὲ | πότε (l. 6, p. 170) : ποτὲ **Q.** 19 κηλίδας (l. 22, p. 170) *Sir. Sch. F.M.* :

κηλῖ- **Q.** 21 τοιαύτοις (l. 10, p. 172) : -ταις **Q.** 22 τήν (l. 2,
p. 174) : τὴν | εἰσελελύθασι (l. 18, p. 175) : -ληλύθασι | τοὺ (l. 12,
p. 176) : -οῦ | πλεμμελημάτων (l. 16, p. 176) : πλη- | σκήνῃ (l. 20,
p. 176) : -νῇ **Q.** 24 εχει (l. 23, p. 178) : ἔ- **Q.** 25 μόλοχ (l. 13,
p. 179) : M- | μόλοχ (l. 17, p. 179) : M- **Q.** 27 ἀμπέλωνά (l. 7,
p. 180) : -πελῶνά **Q.** 28 οὐλας (l. 4, p. 181) Sch. F.M. : οὔ- **Q.** 30
ἀφείρεσιν (l. 6, p. 182) : ἀφαί- **Q.** 32 ἥνικα (l. 10, p. 183) : -ίκα |
φασί (l. 6, p. 184) : -σὶ **Q.** 33 συνῆφεν (l. 26, p. 184–l. 1, p. 185) :
-ψεν **Q.** 35 λεκεύει (l. 1, p. 186) : κελεύ- **Q.** 36 Ὤς (l. 21, p. 186) :
Ὡς **Q.** 37 πᾶσας (l. 3, p. 187) : πά- **Q.** 38 Ἰσμαὴλ, (l. 20, p.
188) Sir. Sch. F.M. : -ήλ, | δίδραχμον τινὲς (l. 12, p. 189) Sir. Sch.
F.M. : δίδραχμόν τινες **Quaest. in Num.: Q.** 3 ἀνατολὴ (l. 21,
p. 191) Sir. F.M. : Ἀ- | ἀρχοῦσαν (l. 10, p. 191) : -κοῦσαν **Q.** 4
Ἰσραὴλ. (l. 16, p. 192) Sir. F.M. : -ήλ. | λευῖται (l. 22, p. 192) Sir.
F.M. : -ῖται **Q.** 9 ἱλασμοῦ (ll. 22f., p. 195) : ἱ- **Q** 10 δῴη (l. 10, p.
197) : δῴη **Q.** 11 οὐ (l. 6, p. 198) : σὺ | ἡμέρων (l. 25, p. 198) : -ῶν |
κηλίδα (ll. 12f., p. 199) : κηλῖ- | τὸ, (l. 26, p. 199) Sir. Sch. F.M. : τὸ
Q. 13 γήρας (l. 3, p. 201) Sir. Sch. F.M. : γῆ- **Q.** 16 Διώνυμως
(l. 1, p. 203) : -ος **Q.** 18 ἤτησε (l. 10, p. 203) : ἤ- | ἐπιθεῖναι μοὶ
(l. 2, p. 204) : -θεῖναί μοι | σκηνήν (l. 17, p. 204) : -ὴν **Q.** 31
πᾶσας (l. 21, p. 211) : πά- **Q.** 33 δεμιουργεῖν (l. 6, p. 213) :
δημι- **Q.** 37 τό (l. 15, p. 216) : τὸ **Q.** 38 ὁμιώματι (l. 9, p. 217) :
ὁμοι- | κηλίδα (l. 14, p. 217) Sir. Sch. F.M. : κηλῖ- **Q.** 40 μὲν, (l. 4,
p. 218) Sch. F.M. : μέν, **Q.** 44 ἡ Γὼγ (l. 20, p. 222) Sir. Sch. F.M. :
ἢ Γὼγ **Q.** 45 λαὸν; (l. 24, p. 222) : -όν; **Q.** 46 τινί (l. 8, p. 223) :
-νὶ **Q.** 47 τί (l. 20, p. 224) : τι **Q.** 50 Ὅτι (l. 11, p. 225) : Ὅτι
Quaest. in Dt.: Q. 1 ἐριθμηθῆναι (l. 9, p. 227) : ἀ- | κα (l. 9, p. 229) :
καὶ | φιλιονεικούντων (l. 11, p. 229) : v. critical note, ad loc. |
ἐστὶν (l. 1, p. 230) : -τιν | ταῦτα φησίν (l. 25, p. 230) : ταῦτα,
φῆσίν **Q.** 2 ἁγιον (l. 7, p. 233) : ἅ- | ἅπας (l. 13, p. 233) : -αξ **Q.** 3
καὶπαῖδας (l. 18, p. 233) : καὶ π- **Q.** 7 τύφον (ll. 14f., p. 236) Sir.
Sch. F.M. : τῦ- | καίρω (l. 9, p. 237) : -ρῷ **Q.** 9 ἐνὶ (l. 1, p. 239) :
ἐ- **Q.** 12 φαρμακοὶ (l. 22, p. 240) Sir. Sch. F.M. : φάρ- | ἐκ (l. 10,
p. 241) : ἐξ | διδάσκει (l. 13, p. 241) Sir. Sch. F.M. : -η **Q.** 13 φοῖβον

(l. 1, p. 242) *Sir. F.M.* : Φ- | σίκερᾳ (l. 23, p. 242) *Sch. F.M.* : -α |
παντὶ ᾧ ἐπιθυμεῖ *Sir. Sch.* : παντὸς οὗ ἂν ἐπιθυμεῖ (l. 24, p.
242) *F.M.* : -ῇ | φαγῇ (l. 24, p. 242) *Sir. Sch. F.M.* : φά- | Ἰώσηππος
(l. 10, p. 243) *Sch. F.M.* : -ηπος **Q.** 15 ἑπτὰ (l. 19, p. 243) : ἑ- |
ἀποχρώντος (l. 21, p. 243) : -ως **Q.** 17 Ἐὰν φησὶ *Sch.* : Ἐὰν
φησί (l. 9, p. 244) *F.M.* : Ἐάν, φησί **Q.** 20 αληθές (l. 20, p. 245)
F.M. : ἀ- **Q.** 21 ἀφεῖνα (l. 22, p. 245) : -ναι **Q.** 22 πέσων (l. 7,
p. 246) : -ὼν **Q.** 25 δεδημιούργεται (l. 12, p. 247) : -γηται
Q. 29 Μαριαμ (l. 12, p. 249) : -ὰμ **Q.** 34 Ῥουβεὶν *Sch.* : Ῥουβὶν
(l. 22, p. 251) *F.M.* : -ὴν | αὐτὴν· (l. 1, p. 253) : -ήν· **Q.** 37
προμεθούμενος (l. 25, p. 255) : προμη- **Q.** 40 ουρανέ (l. 12,
p. 258) : οὐ- **Q.** 44 ἐκ Σινᾷ *Sir.* : ἐν Σινᾷ *Sch.* : ἐκ Σινᾷ (l. 20,
p. 262) *F.M.* : ἐκ -νᾷ | Ἰούδα (l. 16, p. 263) *Sir. Sch. F.M.* : -δᾳ | ὅτι
(l. 18, p. 263) : ὅ- | Πείρᾳ (l. 28, p. 263) : π- | Ἀντιλογίας (l. 1,
p. 264) : ἀ- | λόγια (l. 5, p. 264) : λόγιά | δὲ φησίν (l. 13, p. 264) :
δέ φησιν **Quaest. in Ios.:** intro. ἡμέρων (l. 10, p. 269) : -ῶν **Q.** 1
Μωϋσῇ (l. 1, p. 270) : -σῆ **Q.** 2 πεπιστεκυῖαν (ll. 6f., p. 271) :
πεπιστευ- | πότε (l. 14, p. 271) : πο- **Q.** 6 Μωϋσῇ (l. 1, p. 277) :
-σῆ **Q.** 12 ἅτε δὲ (l. 13, p. 279) : ἅτε δὴ **Q.** 13 μένος (l. 6, p. 280) :
μέσος | ἀπολεφθείς (ll. 6f., p. 280) : -ληφθείς **Q.** 17 ἔτη (l. 22,
p. 282) : ἔ- **Q.** 19 ἐὰν (l. 12, p. 284) *Sir. F.M.* : ἐάν **Quaest. in Iud.:**
Q. 1 κατορθωμένων (l. 7, p. 289) *Sir. Sch. F.M.* : κατω- | ἥττης
(l. 8, p. 289) : τῆς ἥττης **Q.** 2 πότε (l. 16, p. 289) : ποτὲ **Q.** 6
τοῦτο (l. 15, p. 291) : -τον **Q.** 7 κλαυθμῶνα (l. 12, p. 292) *Sir. Sch.*
F.M. : Κ- | εἰσακούσατε (l. 25, p. 292) : εἰση- | λαὸν (l. 27, p. 292)
Sir. Sch. F.M. : -όν | συνοχάς· *Sch.* : συνοχάς (l. 28, p. 292) *F.M.* :
-άς, | μου φησί (l. 1, p. 293) : μου, φησί **Q.** 9 υἱὸς ἦν *Sir. Sch.* :
υἱὸς (l. 2, p. 296) *F.M.* : -ός **Q.** 12 γύνη (l. 10, p. 297) : -νὴ **Q.** 13
κατεχούσων (l. 12, p. 299) : -ῶν | θεῖαν (l. 22, p. 299) : -ίαν **Q.** 17
σικημίταις (l. 26, p. 301) : -μίτας **Q.** 20 χρήζω (l. 21, p. 304)
Sch. F.M. : χρή- | τιμὴν (l. 22, p. 304) *Sir. F.M.* : -ήν **Q.** 21
ἐκδεδιητημένως (l. 24, p. 304) : -ητημένως **Q.** 22 δὲ (l. 21,
p. 305) : δέ | ὑπερφυεῖς (ll. 8f., p. 306) : ὑπ- **Q.** 24 τοιοῦτο
τρόπον (l. 3, p. 307) : τοιουτότροπόν **Q.** 25 ἀναμνησθητω (l. 23,

p. 307) : -ησθήτω | σκήνην (l. 3, p. 308) : -ὴν *Q.* 26 λευΐται *Sir.* : λευΐται (l. 23, p. 308) *Sch. F.M.* : -ῖται **Quaest. in Ruth: Q.** 1 συγγράψων (l. 3, p. 312) : -φων *(I suppose the fut. part. to be an error, rather than a conscious choice among variants; Sir. and Sch. both have the pres.)* **Q.** 2 γήνῃ (l. 16, p. 316) : -μῃ | τήν (l. 11, p. 317) : τὴν | γὰρ, φησὶ, *Sch.* : γάρ, φησί, (l. 17, p. 317) *F.M.* : γάρ φησι, | σπουδάξων (l. 19, p. 317) : -ζων | γυναῖκα (l. 21, p. 317) *Sir. F.M.* : -ναῖκά | 'Ισραὴλ (l. 23, p. 317) : -ήλ | 'Εφράθα (l. 24, p. 317) : -θά | 'Εφράθα (l. 3, p. 318) : -θά *(This name is always accented oxytone, though previous editors differ in regarding it as invariable or as susceptible of inflection.)*.

In a number of details, where editors have differed in their choices, Fernández Marcos and Sáenz-Badillos fail to observe consistency. In eight of ten occurrences they spell the name Ἰερεμίας with rough breathing, but in two (l. 9, p. 23 and l. 18, p. 94) with smooth, as in the listing of proper nouns provided at the end of the second vol. of Hatch and Redpath's concordance. In six of eight occurrences they accent Φαρές oxytone but in two (l. 25, p. 317 and l. 5, p. 318) print the paroxytone form preferred by Wevers (*v.* Gn 38.29). In seven of nine occurrences they accent Χαναάν oxytone, but in two (ll. 13 and 22, p. 55) paroxytone as does Wevers (*v.* Gn 9.18). In each case I have regularized according to the predominant practice of the Madrid edition.

Their spelling of forms of the verb γίνομαι / γίγν- is also inconsistent. In forty-three cases they adopt the former and in ten the latter. As in fifty-one of these fifty-three occurrences they simply reproduce Schulze's spelling, their variation cannot reflect the usage of the mss. The question of whether to retain or drop the gamma arises in only one of the two places (l. 10, p. 196) where they differ from Schulze's reading (γιγνόμενα F.M. : γιν- Sch.), and here they provide no note. As in hellenistic koine, the pronunciation -ν- had replaced the earlier Attic -γν- (*v., e.g.,* Mandilaris, sec. 158, pp. 89f.), I have adopted γίν- throughout.

Their treatment of the forms of θάλαττα is also problematic. They print forms in -σσ- wherever the noun appears in Theodoret's quotations of Scripture (twenty-four examples). Where Theodoret is speaking his own words, they print forms in -ττ- in sixteen places (variant readings in -σσ- are recorded at p. 143, l. 4 and 213, l. 6) and forms in -σσ- in seven others. See *e.g.*, ll. 5–7, p. 213, where one form in -ττ- (for which they list a variant in -σσ-) stands between two in -σσ-. Among recent editors, G.H. Ettlinger and Y. Azéma also allow forms of θάλασσα to jostle those of θάλαττα in Theodoret's direct speech; for the former *v. Eran.* p. 143, ll. 29f. and p. 157, ll. 3f., and for the latter, *ep.* 30 (*Collectio patmensis*), ll. 1 and 10. As Theodoret is unlikely to have intended such a variation of orthography in his own words, and the manuscript evidence, on the whole, suggests that he used θάλαττα when not quoting Scripture, I have changed these seven forms in -σσ- to the corresponding form in -ττ-. I find the same consistent division (θάλασσα in biblical quotations, θάλαττα in direct speech) in P. Canivet's edition of *Affect.*

In eight places Fernández Marcos and Sáenz-Badillos aspirate forms of the pronoun αὐτός used in a reflexive manner (l. 24, p. 93; l. 21, p. 106; ll. 1 and 4, p. 145; l. 11, p. 190; l. 7, p. 282 twice; l. 24, p. 313). Yet the aspirated pronunciation αὑ- had gone out of general usage before Theodoret's time, and later Greek relied on the reflexive forms with the prefixed ἑ-; *v.* F.T. Gignac, pp. 170f. As in three of these passages (l. 21, p. 106; 11, p. 190; and 24, p. 313) forms of ἑαυ- do have some attestation in the mss., the editors should have adopted these, not the simple forms. Indeed, their choice of just these eight places seems arbitrary, as they did not aspirate forms of αὐτός in such closely similar passages as [ὁ Φαραὼ] οὐκ ἂν αὐτοῦ τὴν γνώμην ἐνήλλαξε (l. 4, p. 107) or ἐβάρυνε ... τὴν καρδίαν αὐτοῦ (l. 9, p. 108). Furthermore, the unaspirated forms were not uncommonly used for the reflexive possessive even in Homeric and classical Greek; *v.* Kühner-Gerth, part 2, vol. 1, pp. 564f. Thus, given the obsolesence of the aspirated simple forms and the sparse representation of forms in ἑαυ-, I have thought best to change all eight pronouns to the unaspirated αὐ-. But see my critical notes for *Qq.* 12 on Ex and 1 on Nm, where the ms. evidence for a form with the prefixed ἐ- is substantial enough to raise doubts.

Finally, in some places they follow older conventions of word division observed by Sirmond and Schulze, yet in others the practice now current. In all appearances of the suffix -περ except that at l. 6, p. 8 (ὅτε περ), -περ is attached to the preceding syllable. *Cf.* also ἅ τε δὴ at l. 10, p. 16 with ἅτε δὴ in all other occurrences; διάτοι τοῦτο at ll. 11f., p. 117 with διά τοι τοῦτο in all other occurrences; ἤ τις at l. 18, p. 210 with ἤτις at both other occurences. Following both Sirmond and Schulze, they combine κατακράτος once (l. 19, p. 96) and divide κατὰ κράτος once (ll. 15f., p. 280); as a glance at the *TLG* indicates, the latter is the form preferred by modern editors even in texts of authors contemporary to and later than Theodoret. The combination γάρτοι appears only at l. 13, p. 238; for the division observed by modern editors, *v.* the examples assembled by Denniston, pp. 549f., esp. Her. 7.172.2: οὐ γάρ τοι προκατημένους τοσοῦτο πρὸ τῆς ἄλλης Ἑλλάδος μούνους πρὸ ὑμέων δεῖ ἀπολέσθαι. On the other hand, while it is their usual practice to print ὅταν and δήποτε, in several places they follow Sirmond and Schulze in printing ὅτ' ἂν (l. 21, p. 197; l. 12, p. 241; l. 11, p. 277), and in two places more modern usage in dividing δή ποτε (l. 1, p. 4 and l. 3, p. 5). In all these questions of word division, I have adopted the current practice.

BIBLIOGRAPHY

SECONDARY WORKS: DICTIONARIES, MONOGRAPHS, ESSAYS, ARTICLES, *ETC.*

Bardy, G., "Interprétation chez les pères," *DBS* 4 (1949), pp. 569–91

———, "La littérature patristique des '*Quaestiones et Responsiones*' sur l'écriture sainte," *RB* 41 (1932), pp. 210–36, 341–69, 515–37; 42 (1933), pp. 14–30, 211–29, 328–52

———, "Théodoret," *DThC*, vol. 15 (Paris 1946), pp. 299–325

Bindley, T.H., and F.W. Green, *The Oecumenical Documents of the Faith,* 4th ed. (London 1950)

Brown, F., S.R. Driver, and C.A. Briggs, *A Hebrew and English Lexicon of the Old Testament,* rev. ed. (Oxford 1951)

Brown, R.E., and R. North, "Biblical Geography," *NJBC,* pp. 1175–95

Canivet, P., *Histoire d'une entreprise apologétique au Ve siècle* (Paris 1957)

Chadwick, H., "The Relativity of Moral Codes: Rome and Persia in Late Antiquity," pp. 135–53 of *Early Christian Literature and the Classical Intellectual Tradition, in honorem Robert M. Grant,* ed. W.R. Schoedel and R.L. Wilken, ThH, vol. 53 (Paris 1979)

Crouzel, H., *Origen,* trans. A.S. Worrall (San Francisco 1989)

Dahood, M., "Ebla, Ugarit and the Old Testament," *Month* 239 (1978), pp. 271–76, 341–45

Denniston, J.D., *The Greek Particles,* 2nd ed. K.J. Dover (London, *etc.* 1950)

Devreesse, R., *Les anciens commentateurs grecs de l'Octateuch et des Rois, StT,* vol. 201 (Vatican City 1959)

———, "Chaînes exégétiques grecques," *DBS,* ed. L. Pirot, vol. 1: *Abdeh-Chronologie* (Paris 1928), coll. 1083–1233

Eissfeldt, O., *The Old Testament: An Introduction,* trans. P.R. Ackroyd (Oxford 1965)

Ellis, E.E., "A Note on First Corinthians 10 4," *JBL* 76 (1957), pp. 53–56

Fernández Marcos, N., "La edición de las *Quaestiones in Reges et Paralipomena* de Teodoreto," *Sef.* 40 (1980), pp. 235–53

———, *The Septuagint in Context: Introduction to the Greek Versions of the Bible,* trans. W.G.E. Watson (Boston, *etc.* 2000)

———, "Some Reflections on the Antiochian Text of the Septuagint," in *Studien zur Septuagint Robert Hanhart zu Ehren,* ed. D. Fraenkel, U. Quast, J.W. Wevers, *MSU* 20 (1990), pp. 219–29

Bibliography

Gignac, F.T., *A Grammar of the Greek Papyri of the Roman and Byzantine Periods,* vol. 2: *Morphology* = TDSA, vol. 55-2 (Milan 1981)

Guinot, J.N., *L'Exégèse de Théodoret de Cyr,* ThH, vol. 100 (Paris 1995)

_____, "Theodoret von Kyrrhos," *TRE,* vol. 33 (Berlin/New York 2002), pp. 250–54

Hill, R.C., "*Akribeia*: A Principle of Chrysostom's Exegesis," *Colloquium* 14 (1981), pp. 32–36

_____, "Chrysostom on the Obscurity of the Old Testament," *OCP* 67 (2001), pp. 371–83

_____, "His Master's Voice: Theodore of Mopsuestia on the Psalms," *HeyJ* 45 (2004), pp. 40–53

_____, "On Looking Again at *Synkatabasis,*" *Prudentia* 13 (1981), pp. 3–11

_____, "Orientale lumen: Western Biblical Scholarship's Unacknowledged Debt," in *Orientale Lumen Australasia-Oceania 2000: Proceedings,* ed. L. Cross (Melbourne 2001), pp. 157–72

_____, "Psalm 41 (42): A Classic Text for Antiochene Spirituality," *IThQ* 68 (2003), pp. 9–33

_____, *Reading the Old Testament in Antioch,* Bible in Ancient Christianity, vol. 5 (Leiden/Boston 2005)

_____, "Theodore of Mopsuestia, Interpreter of the Prophets," *SE* 40 (2001), pp. 107–29

_____, "Theodoret Wrestling with Romans," *StudP* 34 (2001), pp. 347–52

Kahle, P.E., *The Cairo Genizah,* 2nd ed. (Oxford 1959)

Keith, A.B., "Some Uses of the Future in Greek," *CQ* 6 (1912), pp. 121–26

Kelly, J.N.D., *Early Christian Doctrines,* 5th ed. (New York 1978)

_____, *Golden Mouth: The Story of John Chrysostom, Ascetic, Preacher, Bishop* (Ithaca, N.Y. 1995)

Kühner, R., and B. Gerth, *Ausführliche Grammatik der griechischen Sprache,* part 2: *Satzlehre,* vol. 1 (Hannover/Leipzig 1898)

Lampe, G.H.W., *The Cambridge History of the Bible,* vol. 2: *The West from the Fathers to the Reformation* (Cambridge 1969)

_____, *Patristic Greek Lexicon* (Oxford 1961)

Liddell, H.G., R. Scott, H.S. Jones, and R. McKenzie, *A Greek-English Lexicon,* 9th ed., *With a Supplement* (Oxford 1968)

Mandilaris, B.G., *The Verb in the Greek Non-Literary Papyri* (Athens 1973)

Martini, E., *Indici e Cataloghi,* part 19: *Catalogo di Manoscritti greci esistenti nelle biblioteche italiane,* vol. 2: *Catalogus codicum graecorum qui in bibliotheca vallicelliana Romae adseruantur* (Milan 1902)

McKenzie, J.L., *Dictionary of the Bible* (London/Dublin 1965)

O'Connell, K.G., "Greek Versions of the Old Testament," *NJBC,* pp. 1091–96

_____, "Hebrew Text of the Old Testament," *NJBC,* pp. 1085–91

Pásztori-Kupán, I., "Quotations of Theodoret's *De sancta et vivifica trinitate* in Euthymius Zigabenus' *Panoplia dogmatica,*" *Aug* 42 (2002), pp. 481–89

Quasten, J., *Patrology,* 3 voll. (Utrecht 1950)

Bibliography

Rahlfs, A., *Verzeichnis der griechischen Handschriften des Alten Testaments* (Berlin 1914)

Schäublin, C., "Diodor von Tarsus," *TRE*, vol. 8 (Berlin/New York 1981), pp. 763–67

———, *Untersuchungen zu Methode und Herkunft der antiochenischen Exegese,* Theoph., vol. 23 (Cologne/Bonn 1974)

Schwyzer, E., and A. Debrunner, *Griechische Grammatik,* vol. 2: *Syntax und syntaktische Stilistik* (Munich 1950)

Senior, D., "Aspects of NT Thought: The Miracles of Jesus," *NJBC*, pp. 1369–73

Stefani, A. de, *Etymologicum gudianum* (Leipzig 1909)

Ternant, P., "La Θεωρία d'Antioche dans le cadre des sens de l'Écriture," *Bib.* 34 (1953), pp. 135–58, 354–83, 456–86

Trible, P., *Texts of Terror: Literary-Feminist Readings of Biblical Narratives,* Overtures to Biblical Theology, vol. 13 (Philadelphia 1984)

Groningen, B.A. van, *Short Manual of Greek Palaeography,* 2nd ed. (Leiden 1955)

Vaux, R. de, *Ancient Israel: Its Life and Institutions,* trans. J. McHugh (London 1961)

Vawter, B., *Biblical Inspiration*, ThRes (London/Philadelphia 1972)

Weitzman, M.P., *The Syriac Version of the Old Testament* (Cambridge 1999)

Wellhausen, J., *Prolegomena zur Geschichte Israels,* 5th ed. (Berlin 1899)

Yadin, Y., *Hazor: The Rediscovery of a Great Citadel of the Bible* (New York 1975)

Yarnold, E., *The Awe-Inspiring Rites of Initiation: Baptismal Homilies of the Fourth Century* (Slough 1972)

Young, F.M., *Biblical Exegesis and the Formation of Christian Culture* (Cambridge 1997)

———, *From Nicaea to Chalcedon: A Guide to the Literature and Its Background* (Philadelphia 1983)

Zorell, F., *Lexicon hebraicum et aramaicum ueteris testamenti* (Rome 1963)

BIBLE: ANCIENT TEXTS, VERSIONS, CONCORDANCE, AND CATENAE

I. Ancient Texts and Versions

Masoretic Text (MT)

Kittel, R., K. Elliger, W. Rudolph, *et al., Biblia hebraica stuttgartensia* (Stuttgart 1967–77)

Septuagint (LXX)

Brenton, L.C.L., *The Septuagint with Apocrypha: Greek and English* (London 1851; rpt. Peabody, Mass. 1986)

Bibliography

Rahlfs, A., *Septuaginta: Id est Vetus Testamentum graece iuxta LXX interpretes* (Stuttgart 1935)

Wevers, J.W., *Genesis, Septuaginta*, vol. 1 (Göttingen 1974)

Wevers, J.W., and U. Quast, *Exodus, Septuaginta*, vol. 2.1 (Göttingen 1991)

Wevers, J.W., and U. Quast, *Leviticus, Septuaginta*, vol. 2.2 (Göttingen 1986)

Wevers, J.W., and U. Quast, *Numeri, Septuaginta*, vol. 3.1 (Göttingen 1982)

Wevers, J.W., and U. Quast, *Deuteronomium, Septuaginta*, vol. 3.2 (Göttingen 1977)

New Testament

Aland, B., *et al.*, *The Greek New Testament*, 4th ed. (Stuttgart 1994)

Vulgate

Weber, R., and R. Gryson, *Biblia sacra iuxta vulgatam versionem*, 4th ed. (Stuttgart 1994)

II. Concordance

Hatch, E., and H.A. Redpath, *A Concordance to the Septuagint and the Other Greek Versions of the Old Testament*, 2 voll. (Oxford 1897)

III. Catenae

Nikephoros Hieromonachos Theotokes, Σειρὰ ἑνὸς καὶ πεντήκοντα ὑπομνηματιστῶν εἰς τὴν ὀκτάτευχον καὶ τὰ τῶν βασιλειῶν, 2 voll. (Leipzig 1772–73)

Petit, F., *Catenae graecae in Genesim et in Exodum*, vol. 1: *Catena sinaitica*, CChr.SG, vol. 2 (Brepols/Turnhout 1977)

_____, *Catenae graecae in Genesim et in Exodum*, vol. 2: *Collectio Coisliniana in Genesim*, CChr.SG, vol. 15 (Brepols/Turnhout 1986)

_____, *La chaîne sur la Genèse: Édition intégrale*, TEG, voll. 1–4 (Louvain 1991–1996)

_____, *La chaîne sur l'Exode: Édition intégrale*, voll. 2: *Collectio coisliniana* and 3: *Fonds caténique ancien (Exode 1,1–15,21)*, TEG, vol. 10 (Louvain, etc. 2000)

BIBLE: MODERN TRANSLATION AND COMMENTARIES

I. Translation

Metzger, B.M., and R.E. Murphy, *The New Oxford Annotated Bible with the Apocryphal / Deuterocanonical Books* (New York 1991)

Bibliography

II. Commentaries

Entire Bible

Brown, R.E., *et al., New Jerome Biblical Commentary* (Englewood Cliffs, NJ 1990) = *NJBC*

Genesis

Clifford, R.J. and R.E. Murphy, "Genesis," *NJBC*, pp. 8–43

Rad, G. von, *Genesis*, trans. J.H. Marks, rev. ed., OTL (London 1972)

Speiser, E.A., *Genesis*, AncB, vol. 1 (Garden City, N.Y. 1964)

Exodus

Clifford, R.J., "Exodus," *NJBC*, pp. 44–60

Leviticus

Faley, R.J., "Leviticus," *NJBC*, pp. 61–79

Numbers

L'Heureux, C.E., "Numbers," *NJBC*, pp. 80–93

Deuteronomy

Blenkinsopp, J., "Deuteronomy," *NJBC*, pp. 94–109

Rad, G. von, *Deuteronomy, A Commentary*, trans. D. Barton (Philadelphia 1966)

Joshua, Judges, Ruth

Coogan, M.D., "Joshua," *NJBC*, pp. 110–31

Gray, J., *Joshua, Judges and Ruth*, NCBC (London 1967)

Laffey, A., "Ruth," *NJBC*, pp. 553–57

O'Connor, M., "Judges," *NJBC*, pp. 132–44

1–2 Samuel

Hertzberg, H.W., *I & II Samuel: A Commentary*, trans. J.S. Bowden (Philadelphia 1964)

Daniel

Hartman, L.F., and A.A. Di Lella, "Daniel," *NJBC*, pp. 406–20

Tobit

Nowell, I., "Tobit," *NJBC*, pp. 568–71

Psalms

Dahood, M., *Psalms*, 3 voll., AncB, voll. 16–17A (Garden City, N.Y. 1966–70)

Bibliography

Amos

Barré, M.L., "Amos," *NJBC*, pp. 209–16

Zechariah

Cody, A., "Haggai, Zecariah, Malachi," *NJBC*, pp. 349–59

Matthew

Albright, W.F., and C.S. Mann, *Matthew*, AncB, vol. 26 (Garden City, N.Y. 1971)

Viviano, B.T., "The Gospel According to St. Matthew," *NJBC*, pp. 630–74

Mark

Harrington, D.J., "Mark," *NJBC*, pp. 596–629

Luke

Fitzmyer, J., *The Gospel According to Luke I-IX*, AncB, vol. 28 (Garden City, N.Y. 1981)

John

Brown, R.E., *The Gospel According to John I-XII*, AncB, vol. 29 (Garden City, N.Y. 1966)

Perkins, P., "The Gospel According to John," *NJBC*, pp. 942–83

Galatians

Fitzmyer, J.A., "The Letter to the Galatians," *NJBC*, pp. 780–90

ANCIENT AUTHORS AND WORKS: TEXTS, TRANSLATION, COMMENTARIES

Augustine

Dekkers, E., and J. Fraipont, *Sancti Aurelii Augustini Enarrationes in Psalmos, Aurelii Augustini Opera*, part 10, vol. 1: *I-L*, CChr.SL, vol. 38 (Turnhout 1956)

Basil of Caesarea

Homilia in diuites

Courtonne, Y., *Saint Basile, Homélies sur la richesse* (Paris 1935)

Homiliae in hexaemeron

Giet, S., *Basile de Césarée, Homélies sur l'hexaéméron*, SC, vol. 26 bis (Paris 1968)

Bibliography

Clement of Alexandria

Le Boulluec, A., *Clément D'Alexandrie, Les Stromates, Stromate VII*, SC, vol. 428 (Paris 1997)

Didymus the Blind

Nautin, P., and L. Doutreleau, *Didyme L'Aveugle sur la Genèse*, SC, voll. 233 and 244 (Paris 1976–78)

Diodore of Tarsus

Quaestiones in octateuchum

Deconinck, J., *Essai sur la chaîne de l'Octateuch avec une édition des commentaires de Diodore de Tarse qui s'y trouvent contenus* (Paris 1912)

In Psalmos

Hill, R.C., *Diodore of Tarsus, Commentary on Psalms 1–51*, Writings of the Greco-Roman World, vol. 9 (Atlanta 2005)

Olivier, J.-M., *Diodori tarsensis Commentarii in psalmos*, vol. 1: *Commentarii in psalmos I-L*, CChr.SG, vol. 6 (Brepols/Turnhout 1980)

Eusebius of Caesarea

Heikel, I.A., *Eusebius Werke*, vol. 6: *Demonstratio euangelica*, GCS, vol. 23 (Leipzig 1913)

Gregory of Nyssa

Oratio funebris in Placillam imperatricem

Spira, A., *Gregorii Nysseni Opera*, vol. 9.1 (Leiden 1967)

Herodotus

Hude, C., *Herodoti Historiae*, vol. 2, 3rd ed. (Oxford 1927)

Hippolytus

Bonwetsch, G.N., and H. Achelis, *Hippolytus Werke*, vol. 1, pt. 2: *Hippolyt's kleinere exegetische und homiletische schriften*, GCS, vol. 1.2 (Leipzig 1897)

Jerome

Labourt, J., *Saint Jérôme, Lettres*, vol. 5: *Sancti Hieronymi Epistulae XCVI-CIX* (Paris 1955)

John Chrysostom

Opera omnia

Montfaucon, B. de, *Τοῦ ἐν ἁγίοις πατρὸς ἡμῶν Ἰωάννου ἀρχιεπ. Κωνσταντίνου πόλεως τοῦ Χρυσοστόμου τὰ εὑρισκόμενα πάντα.*

Bibliography

Sancti patris nostri Joannis Chrysostomi archiepiscopi Constantinopolitani opera omnia, 13 voll. (Paris 1718–38) = PG, voll. 47–64

Homiliae in Isaiam (in illud, Vidi dominum)
Dumortier, J., *Jean Chysostome, Homélies sur Ozias,* SC, vol. 277 (Paris 1981)

Josephus
Naber, S.A., *Flauii Iosephi Opera omnia,* voll. 1–4: *Antiquitates iudaeorum* (Leipzig 1888–93)

Origen
De Principiis
Crouzel, H., and M. Simonetti, *Origène, Traité des Principes,* vol. 4: (*Livres III et IV*) *Commentaire et fragments,* SC, vol. 269 (Paris 1980)

Homiliae in Ezechielem
Borret, M., *Origène, Homélies sur Ézéchiel,* SC, vol. 352 (Paris 1989)

Philo
Quaestiones et solutiones in Genesin
Marcus, R., *Philo, Questions and Answers on Genesis* (London/Cambridge, Mass. 1953)

De migratione Abrahami
Wendland, P., *Philonis alexandrini Opera quae supersunt,* vol. 2 (Berlin 1897)

The Suda
Adler, A., *Suidae Lexicon,* 5 voll. (Leipzig 1928–38) = *Lexicographi graeci,* vol. 1

Tertullian
Braun, R., *Tertullien, Contre Marcion,* vol. 2: *Livre II,* SC, vol. 368 (Paris 1991)

Theodore of Mopsuestia
Fragmenta in Genesin et Exodum
Devreesse, R., *Essai sur Théodore de Mopsueste, StT,* 141 (Vatican City 1948)
V. above (under *Catenae*) Nikephoros Hieromonachos Theotokes, Σειρὰ ἑνὸς, *etc.;* excerpted fragg. reprinted in PG, vol. 66, coll. 635–48

Bibliography

Commentarii in XII prophetas

Hill, R.C., *Theodore of Mopsuestia, Commentary on the Twelve Prophets,* FOTC, vol. 108 (Washington 2004)

Commentarii in Epistolas S. Pauli

Swete, H.B., *Theodori episcopi mopsuesteni in epistolas S. Pauli Commentarii,* vol. 1 (Cambridge 1880)

Theodoret

Opera omnia

Schulze, J.L., Θεοδωρήτου ἐπισκόπου Κύρου Ἅπαντα. *Theodoreti cyrensis episocopi opera omnia* (Halle 1769ff.) = PG, voll. 80–84

Sirmond, J., *Theodoreti episcopi Cyri Opera omnia in quatuor tomos distributa* (Paris 1642)

Quaestiones in octateuchum

Fernández Marcos, N., and A. Sáenz-Badillos, *Theodoreti Cyrensis Quaestiones in octateuchum,* TECC, vol. 17 (Madrid 1979)

Siquans, A., *Der Deuteronomiumkommentar des Theodorets von Kyros,* OBS, vol. 19 (Frankfurt am Main, *etc.* 2002)

Quaestiones in Reges et Paralipomena

Fernández Marcos, N., and J.R. Busto Saiz, *Theodoreti Cyrensis Quaestiones in Reges et Paralipomena,* TECC, vol. 32 (Madrid 1984)

Commentarii in Psalmos

Hill, R.C., *Theodoret of Cyrus, Commentary on the Psalms,* FOTC, voll. 101f. (Washington 2000–01)

Commentarii in Canticum canticorum

Hill, R.C., *Theodoret of Cyrus, Commentary on the Song of Songs,* Early Christian Studies, vol. 2 (Brisbane 2001)

[*Commentarii in Jeremiam*][1]

Hill, R.C., *Theodoret of Cyrus, Commentary on Jeremiah* (Boston 2004)

Commentarii in Epistolas S. Pauli

Hill, R.C., *Theodoret of Cyrus, Commentary on the Letters of St Paul* (Brookline, Mass. 2001)

---

1. This work is of dubious attribution.

Bibliography

Epistulae

Azéma, Y., *Théodoret de Cyr, Correspondance*, vol. 1: *Collectio patmensis, Epp. 1–52*, SC, vol. 40 (Paris 1955)

———, *Théodoret de Cyr, Correspondance*, vol. 2: *Collectio sirmondiana, Epp. 1–95*, SC, vol. 98 (Paris 1964)

———, *Théodoret de Cyr, Correspondance*, vol. 3: *Collectio sirmondiana, Epp. 96–147*, SC, vol. 111 (Paris 1965)

Eranistes

Ettlinger, G.H., *Theodoret of Cyrus, Eranistes* (Oxford 1975)

Graecarum affectionum curatio

Canivet, P., *Théodoret de Cyr, Thérapeutique des maladies helléniques*, SC, voll. 57, 57.2 (Paris 1958)

Historia religiosa

Canivet, P., and A. Leroy-Molinghen, *Théodoret de Cyr: Histoire des moines de Syrie*, SC, voll. 234 and 257 (Paris 1977, 1979)

Quaestiones et responsiones ad orthodoxos

Papadopoulos-Kerameus, A., Θεοδωρήτου ἐπισκόπου πόλεως Κύρρου πρὸς τὰς ἐπενεχθείσας αὐτῷ ἐπερωτήσεις παρά τινος τῶν ἐξ Αἰγύπτου ἐπισκόπων ἀποκρίσεις (St. Petersburg 1895)

CONSPECTUS SIGLORUM

J. F. P.

1. THE MANUSCRIPTS AND THEIR CONTENTS[1]
Abbreviations

1. Numbers accompanying abbreviated names of books of the Bible refer to the *Quaest. in oct.* Thus, "Gn 4–18" would indicate that a manuscript contains Theodoret's *Qq.* 4–18 on Gn, not chapters 4–18 of the biblical book.

2. An annotation of the form "38 (first line)" = the ms. contains the question of question 38 and the first line of the answer (*v., e.g.,* on *2a*)

3. An annotation of the form "Ex 2–54 (except question)" = the ms. contains the questions and answers of Ex 2–53, but only the answer of Ex 54 (*v., e.g.,* on *14*)

Class a

2: Rome, Biblioteca Apostolica Vaticana, *Vat. gr. 631* (11th c.)[2]

A composite of three different manuscripts united by one binding. Only the first contains the *Quaest. in oct.*, but, as this is in itself composite, each section is given its own *siglum:*

2a: Gn 4 (second half), 5–17, 18 (except last few lines of answer), 37 (except question, 37.1 and first third of 37.2), 38 (first line)

2c: Gn 67 (except question and first third of answer), 68–112; Ex; Lv; Nm; Dt; Jos; Jgs 1–19, 20 (first third)

These two, now separated from each other by the interposition of *2b* (*v.*

---

1. This list is based on information drawn from the introduction (pp. xi–xxvi), the marginal notes, and the *ap. crit.* of the edition of N. Fernández Marcos and A. Sáenz-Badillos, and further clarifications generously and patiently provided by Fr. Fernández Marcos in correspondence. It represents an attempt to specify which questions are available in a given manuscript, not the order in which they are actually found.

2. *Ibid.,* p. xiii and F. Petit, *Catenae,* vol. 2, pp. xxxiii–xxxvi.

class *c* below), are parts of the same book and were copied by the same hand.

6: Venice, Biblioteca Marciana, *Ms. gr. I. 33* = *977* (11th c.)

Ex 41 (except question and first line of answer), 42–72; Lv; Nm 1–26, 27 (except last couple of lines), 34 (except question and first third of answer), 35–51; Dt 1 (first third of 1.1 and last third of answer), 2–46; Jos; Jgs; Ruth

32: Munich, Bayerische Staatsbibliothek, *Cod. gr. 351* (16th c.)[3]

Gn 2–112; Ex; Lv; Nm; Dt; Jos; Jgs 1 (except question), 2–19, 20 (first third)

As the sections of this manuscript that contain the *Quaest. in oct.* are copied from other extant manuscripts, it has no value as a witness to the text; nonetheless it will be cited in this edition to illustrate its influence on Schulze's selection of readings.[4] It becomes representative of this group from Gn 71 on.

Class a$_1$

5: Florence, Biblioteca Medicea Laurenziana, *Plut. VI. 8* (13th–14th c.)

Gn 1–18, 19.1 (first quarter), 20 (except question and first half of answer), 21–45, 47–64, 66–112; Ex; Lv; Nm; Dt; Jos; Jgs; Ruth

Class a$_2$

11: Patmos, Ἰωάννου τοῦ Θεολόγου, *10* (11th c.)

Gn 62 (except question and first third of answer), 63–112; Ex; Lv; Nm; Dt; Jos; Jgs 5 (question only), 7 (except first half of 7.1), 8–19

12: Patmos, Ἰωάννου τοῦ Θεολόγου, *114* (10th–11th c.)

Gn 19–112; Ex; Lv; Nm; Dt; Jos; Jgs; Ruth

Class B

14: Paris, Bibliothèque Nationale, *Ancien fonds grec 5* (13th–14th c.)

Pf.; Gn 1–76; Ex 2–53, 54 (except question), 55–72; Lv; Nm 1–18, 19 (first half), 22 (last quarter), 23–32, 33 (twice), 34–51; Dt 1.2 (last few lines)–end, 2–31, 32 (last two lines), 33, 34 (except question, 34.1, and first third of 34.2), 35–46; Jos; Jgs 1–5, 6 (except last few lines), 7 (last fifth of 7.2), 8–28; Ruth

---

3. For the date, a century later than that indicated by Fernández Marcos and Sáenz-Badillos, *v.* F. Petit, *Catenae*, vol. 2, p. xxxiii, note 15.

4. *V.* F. Petit, *Catenae*, vol. 2, pp. xxxviif., li–liii. For the edition of J.L. Schulze, *v.* sec. 1.D of the "Introduction to the Greek Text."

The Manuscripts and Their Contents

17: Oxford, Bodleian Library, *Baroccianus 123* (13th c.)

Gn 58 (except question and first line and a half of answer), 59–76; Ex 2–53, 54 (except question), 55–72; Lv; Nm; Dt; Jos 16 (last third of answer), 17–20; Jgs 1–12, 13 (last third of answer), 17 (last couple of lines), 18–28; Ruth

This ms. will be cited with this group only from Lv on.

26a: Oxford, Bodleian Library, *Baroccianus 216* (12th–13th c.)

Jgs 13 (last third), 14–16, 17 (except last couple of lines of answer)

This is a leaf of *17* (f. 22) that has been bound with another portion of the *Quaest. in oct.* taken from a different book; *v.* the remarks on ms. *26b* listed among the unaffiliated mss.[5] As *17* and *26a* constitute just one source, I have not noted the spot in *Q.* 13 on Jgs, where *17* breaks off and *26a* begins nor that in *Q.* 17, where *26a* breaks off and *17* recommences. None of the text has been lost in the division of the codex.

24: Patmos, Ἰωάννου τοῦ Θεολόγου, *767* (14th c.)

Pf.; Gn 1–76; Ex 2–53, 54 (except question), 55–72; Lv 1–34, 35 (except question), 36–38; Nm 1–24, 31–51; Dt; Jos *pf.*–16, 17 (except question), 18–20; Jgs 1–17, 18 (first two thirds)

30: Florence, Biblioteca Medicea Laurenziana, *Plut. VI. 5* (12th c.)

Gn 13 (last few lines), 14–58, 59f. (both only partially legible), 61 (except question), 62–97, 98 (first third)

Class c

1: Florence, Biblioteca Medicea Laurenziana, *Plut. VI. 19* (11th c.)

Nm 3 (last quarter), 4–8, 12–22, 24–35; Dt 45f.; Jos; Jgs; Ruth

2b: Rome, Biblioteca Apostolica Vaticana, *Vat. gr. 631*

Pf. Gn 1–46 (question only), 47–66, 67 (question and first quarter of answer)

This section of the manuscript (*v.* on *2a* and *2c* in class *a* above) contains two texts both copied from Madrid, Biblioteca Nacional *4710*. The first, a transcription of Gn 2–67 was intercalated between *2a* and *2c* to supply the lacuna in the *Quaest. in Gn* in *2c*.[6] The second completed this supplement with the preface and *Q.* 1. As both sections are apographs of a surviving manuscript, *2b* will not be cited in this edition.[7]

5. N. Fernández Marcos and A. Sáenz-Badillos, p. xviii.
6. F. Petit, *Catenae*, vol. 2, p. xxxiv, note 20.
7. *Ibid.*, pp. xlviiif., lif., liv.

3: Florence, Biblioteca Medicea Laurenziana, *S. Marco 725* (9th c.)[8]
  Pf.; Gn 1–10, 11 (first few lines), 12–14, 15 (first sixth), 16–112; Ex 1–4,
  6–72; Lv; Nm; Dt; Jos; Jgs; Ruth

8: Munich, Bayerische Staatsbibliothek, *Cod. gr. 209* (10th c.)
  Pf.; Gn; Ex 1–4, 6–72; Lv; Nm; Dt; Jos; Jgs; Ruth

15: Paris, Bibliothèque Nationale, *Coislinianus 113* (9th–10th c.)[9]
  Pf.; Gn; Ex 1–4, 6–72; Lv; Nm; Dt; Jos; Jgs; Ruth

Class c_1

50: Munich, Bayerische Staatsbibliothek, *Cod. gr. 9* (11th c.)
  Pf.; Gn 1–5, 6 (except question), 7–19, 20 (except question), 21–37, 39–54,
  56–61, 63–69, 71–79, 81–101, 103–112; Ex 1–71, 72 (except question)

51: Rome, Biblioteca Apostolica Vaticana, *Vat. gr. 746* (11th-12th c.)
  Pf.; Gn 1 (except question), 2–14, 15 (first half), 18 (except first half of
  18.1), 19–33, 37–69, 71–74, 75 (except question), 77–79, 81–102, 104–112; Ex
  1f., 4, 6–18, 20–34, 37–46, 50, 52–54, 56, 61–63, 65, 67, 69–72; Lv 1, 3–5, 7–13,
  16–18, 20, 22f., 26–31, 36–38; Nm 1f., 4f., 7, 10, 12–14, 18–51; Dt 1–28, 30–39,
  41–46; Jos; Jgs 1–18, 21–28; Ruth

52: Rome, Biblioteca Apostolica Vaticana, *Vat. gr. 747* (11th c.)
  Pf.; Gn 1, 2 (except question), 3 (except question), 4 (except question),
  5–33, 37–41, 43–69, 71–73, 75 (except question), 77–79, 81–102, 104–112; Ex
  1–4, 6–18, 20–26, 28–38, 40–42, 44–46, 48–50, 52–67, 69–72; Lv 1, 3–32;
  Nm 5–49; Dt 2–6, 7.1 (first third), 9–46; Jos; Jgs; Ruth

53: Rome, Biblioteca Apostolica Vaticana, *Palat. gr. 203* (11th c.)
  Pf.; Gn 1–69, 71–75, 77–79, 81–103, 105–112; Ex 1–4, 6–18, 20–67, 69–72

Unaffiliated manuscripts

4: Rome, Biblioteca Angelica, *Gr. 41* (late 10th c.)
  Pf.; Gn 1–68, 69 (except last few lines of answer); Ex 40 (last fifth), 41–72;
  Lv; Nm; Dt 1–45, 46 (except last few lines of answer)

7: Vienna, Österreichische Nationalbibliothek, *Theol. gr. 153* (13th c.)
  Pf.; Gn 1–3 (except question), 4–112; Ex; Lv; Nm; Dt 1–44, 45 (except last
  couple of lines of answer); Jos; Jgs

---

8. For this date, which is different from that given by Fernández Marcos and
Sáenz-Badillos, *v.* F. Petit, *Catenae*, vol. 2, p. xxiii, note 16.
  9. *Ibid.*, p. xxi.

9: Rome, Biblioteca Vallicelliana, *B 25.1* (11th or 12th c.)

Complete

10: Rome, Biblioteca Vallicelliana, *E 63* (12th c. with later supplements)

In this ms., which has suffered the loss of the first two quaternios and of individual folios throughout, a hand of the 16th c. has replaced missing portions of the first fifteen questions on Gn.[10] Though the Madrid edition cites both the earlier and later portions by the same *siglum* (*10*), I have introduced the following distinction:

10 (12th c.): Gn. 3, 4 (question and first few lines of answer), 7.2–10, 11 (question only), 15 (last third), 16–32, 34–111, 112.1 (first sixth), 112.3 (last three fifths)–end; Ex; Lv 1–31, 32 (first half), 35 (except question and first 40 percent of answer), 36–38; Nm 1–14, 15 (except last couple of lines of answer), 19 (except question and first couple of lines of answer), 20–29 (twice), 30–51; Dt; Jos *pf.*–9, 10 (first half), 16 (except question and first half of answer), 17–20; Jgs; Ruth

10a (16th c.): Gn. 1f., 4 (except the question and first few lines of answer), 5f., 7 (question and first two lines of 7.1), 11 (answer only), 12–14, 15 (question and first two thirds of answer)

13: Patmos, Ἰωάννου τοῦ Θεολόγου, *264* (12th c.)

Pf.; Gn 1, 2 (except the question and first few lines and last third of answer), 3, 6–11, 15–20, 23–28, 30, 33, 48 (incomplete),[11] 49–66, 67 (first half), 69 (except question and first third of answer), 70–85, 87

17: *V.* the description of this ms. in class *B* above.

18: Vienna, Österreichische Nationalbibliothek, *Theol. gr. 173* (15th c.)

Pf.; Gn 1–19

19: Vienna, Österreichische Nationalbibliothek, *Theol. gr. 178* (15th c.)

Gn 2–5,[12] 19 (except question), 20–29

20: Venice, Biblioteca Marciana, *Ms. gr. I. 37 = 1341* (10th c.?)

Pf.; Gn 1–17, 19–30, 51, 56–62, 68, 70, 71 (except last few lines of answer)

---

10. E. Martini (#76) tentatively identifies the later hand as that of Andreas Darmarius.

11. Fr. Fernández Marcos informs me that this ms. recommences in the midst of Q. 48, somewhere in the area corresponding to PG, vol. 80, col. 152 B, thus somewhere between οὗτος ἐκ τῶν ῥαφαῖν and ἀλαζονείαν, its alternative spelling of which is noted in the Madrid edition (l. 3, p. 48).

12. I assume that the references to ms. *19* in the notes on l. 14, p. 13 (*Q.* 11 on Gn) of the Madrid edition must be mistakes, perhaps for "*9.*"

26b: Oxford, Bodleian Library, *Baroccianus 216* (12th–13th c.)

Pf.; Gn 1, 2 (first few lines), 3 (last few lines), 4, 5 (first couple of lines), 11 (second half), 12f., 14 (first couple of lines), 18 (except question and last two thirds of 18.2)[13]

Though these pages are bound with others containing questions on Jgs, the two portions of this ms. are drawn from different books; *v.* the remarks on *26a* in class *B* above.

31: Munich, Bayerische Staatsbibliothek, *Cod. gr. 47* (16th c.)

Ex 1 (except question), 2f., 5 (last few lines), 6–10, 11 (except question), 12 (through first half of 12.2 + one line in 12.4), 13f., 15 (except question), 16–26, 27 (except question), 28–33, 35f., 37 (except question), 38f., 41–62, 63 (except question), 64–68, 69 (except question), 70f., 72 (except question); Lv 1–4, 5 (except question), 6,[14] 9, 10 (except question), 11–16, 18–35, 36 (except question), 37f.; Nm 1–6, 8–16, 18–26, 27 (except question), 28–47; Dt 1–13, 14 (except question), 15f., 17 (except question), 18–23, 25, 27, 28 (except question), 29 (except question), 34, 35 (except question), 37 (except question), 38 (except question), 39, 41 (except question), 42–46; Jos *pf.*–1, 2 (except question and one fifth of 2.2), 5–10, 12–14, 16–18, 20; Jgs 1, 5–7, 8 (except question), 9, 12, 15f., 20–22, 27 (first three quarters); Ruth 1

32: *V.* the description of this ms. in class *a* above.

35: Paris, Bibliothèque Nationale, *Ancien fonds grec 841* (10th c.)

Gn 13 (except question), 14–112; Ex; Lv; Nm 1–28, 29 (first few lines), 34 (last 60 percent), 35–51; Dt; Jos; Jgs; Ruth

37: Paris, Bibliothèque Nationale, *Ancien fonds grec 842* (12th c.)

Gn 2–17, 18 (first third of 18.1), 19 (except question and first line of answer), 20–112; Ex 1–4, 6–28, 29 (except part of question and first couple of lines of answer), 30–72; Lv; Nm; Dt; Jos; Jgs; Ruth

41: Dublin, Trinity College, *D.1. 28* (15th–16th c.)

Gn 67 (except last five lines of answer)

---

13. This manuscript does not carry any of *Qq.* 6f. In the Madrid edition, the marginal sign of a lacuna in the middle of the second sentence of *Q.* 7 (p. 10) is a mistake. The lacuna at that point occurs in *10a*, not *26b*.

14. I assume that the references to ms. *31* in the notes on ll. 8 and 15, p. 162 (*Qq.* 7f. on Lv) of the Madrid edition must be mistakes.

Signs and Abbreviations

Manuscript Classes

a	in *Qq on* Gn		not used
	in *Qq. on* Ex–Jgs	=	the agreement of $2c$ and 6
	in *Qq. on* Ruth		not used
a_1	in *Qq. on* Gn–Ruth		replaced by "5"
a_2	in *Qq. on* Gn–Jgs	=	the agreement of 11 and 12
	in *Qq. on* Ruth		not used
A	in *Qq on* Gn	=	the agreement of $2c$, 5, and a_2
	in *Qq. on* Ex–Jgs	=	the agreement of a, 5, and a_2
	in *Qq. on* Ruth		not used
B	in *Qq. on* Gn	=	the agreement of 14, 24, 30
	in *Qq. on* Ex	=	the agreement of 14 and 24
	in *Qq. on* Lv–Jgs.	=	the agreement of 14, 17 (or $26a$), and 24
	in *Qq. on* Ruth	=	the agreement of 14 and 17
c	in *Qq. on* Gn–Lv	=	the agreement of 3, 8, and 15
	in *Qq. on* Nm–Ruth	=	the agreement of 1, 3, 8, and 15
c_1	in *Qq. on* Gn–Ex	=	the agreement of 50, 51, 52, and 53
	in *Qq. on* Lv–Ruth	=	the agreement of 51 and 52
C	in *Qq. on* Gn–Ruth	=	the agreement of c and c_1

Other Signs and Abbreviations

cod. A	*codex alexandrinus* (*V.* note 1 to *Q.* 4 on Jgs.)
cod. B	*codex vaticanus* (*V.* note 1 to *Q.* 4 on Jgs.)
codd.	*codices* = the reading of all the manuscripts
F.M.	N. Fernández Marcos and A. Sáenz-Badillos
F.P.	Françoise Petit
inc.	Marks manuscripts that are lacking something other than or more than just the initial query of a *Q.*
J.P.	conjectured by John Petruccione
om.	omit

Conspectus siglorum

Pic.	J. Picot
Q.	*Quaestio, i.e.* both the initial query and Theodoret's response
Sch.	J.L. Schulze[15]
Sir.	J. Sirmond
[32]	Citation within brackets indicates that a manuscript has no value as an independent witness.
‖	where a manuscript breaks off
│	where a manuscript begins after a lacuna
=	in the body of a textual note, introduces the translation of a rejected variant
*	marks manuscripts lacking the query that introduces the *Q.*
(Sch.)	An abbreviated name enclosed in parentheses indicates the scholar, other than Fernández Marcos and Sáenz-Badillos, who attests to a reading of a manuscript or an edition.[16]

15. *N.B.* in reff. to Schulze's edition, there are two different forms of citation: (1) "n. 28 to col. 277" indicates that the call-out number 28 appears next to the word or phrase of col. 277 that is illustrated or supplemented by reference to the *Catena Nikephori;* (2) "n. 99, col. 201" directs the reader to note 99, which stands below the excerpts from the *Catena Nikephori* in col. 201.

16. These parentheses are used repeatedly to attribute to Schulze reports of readings adopted by Picot. As I am informed by Mr. P. Goodman, a cataloguer at the Library of Congress, the national databases list only two copies of Picot's edition in the United States: one at Harvard and the other at the University of Chicago.

The Questions on the Octateuch

VOLUME 1
On Genesis and Exodus

ΘΕΟΔΩΡΗΤΟΥ ΕΙΣ ΤΑ ΑΠΟΡΑ ΤΗΣ ΘΕΙΑΣ ΓΡΑΦΗΣ ΚΑΤ' ΕΚΛΟΓΗΝ

Praefatio in Quaestiones in octateuchum

Καὶ ἄλλοι μὲν φιλομαθεῖς ἄνδρες ἐπηγγείλαντο διαλῦσαι
τῆς θείας γραφῆς τὰ δοκοῦντα εἶναι ζητήματα, καὶ τῶν μὲν
ἀναπτύξαι τὸν νοῦν, τῶν δὲ τὰς αἰτίας δηλῶσαι, καὶ
ἁπαξαπλῶς ἀποφῆναι σαφῆ τὰ τοῖς πολλοῖς οὐ τοιαῦτα
5 φαινόμενα. σὺ δὲ διαφερόντως, φίλτατε παίδων Ὑπάτιε, τοῦτό
με πρᾶξαι παρώτρυνας, πολλοῖς ὠφέλιμον ἔσεσθαι καὶ τόδε τὸ
σύγγραμμα λίαν ἰσχυρισάμενος. οὗ δὴ ἕνεκα καίτοι τοῦ
σώματος οὐκ εὖ μοι διακειμένου, τόνδε προειλόμην τὸν πόνον,
οὐκ ἐμαυτῷ γε θαρρῶν, ἀλλὰ τῷ ταῦθ' οὕτω συγγραφῆναι
10 προστεταχότι. αὐτοῦ γάρ ἐστιν ἐπιδεῖξαι τὴν ἐν τῷ γράμματι
κεκρυμμένην διάνοιαν· αὐτὸς γὰρ κἂν τοῖς ἱεροῖς εὐαγγελίοις

PRAEFATIO *14 24, C, 4 7 9 13 18 20 26b* = 16 mss.

Title Θεοδωρήτου εἰς τὰ ἄπορα τῆς θείας γραφῆς κατ' ἐκλογήν *15
(F.P.)* : Θεοδωρήτου εἰς τὰ ἄπορα τῆς θείας γραφῆς *3 (F.P.)* (-ρίτου
J.P.); *cf.* Photius, *Bibl. cod. 204 (Εἰς τὰ ἄπορα ... τῆς γραφῆς)* = *"Theodoret
on Questions regarding Holy Scripture"* : Τοῦ μακαρίου Θεοδωρήτου εἰς τὰ
ἄπορα τῆς θείας γραφῆς κατ' ἐκλογήν *8* (Θεοδορίτου, *F.P.) [32] (Sch.)* =
"St. Theodoret on Selected Questions regarding Holy Scripture" : Τοῦ μακαρίου
Θεοδωρήτου ἐπισκόπου Κύρου, εἰς τὰ ἄπορα τῆς θείας γραφῆς κατ'
ἐκλογήν *Sir.* (Θεοδορίτου) *Sch.* = *"St. Theodoret, Bishop of Cyr, on Selected
Questions regarding Holy Scripture"* : Θεοδωρίτου ἐπισκόπου Κύρου, εἰς τὰ
ζητούμενα καὶ ἀπορούμενα τῆς παλαιᾶς καὶ θείας γραφῆς *9 (J.P.)* =
*"Theodoret, Bishop of Cyr, on Issues and Questions of the Old Testament of Holy
Scripture"* : Θεοδωρήτου τοῦ ἐπισκόπου Κύρου, εἰς τὰ ζητούμενα ἄπορα
τῆς παλαιᾶς διαθήκης *4 (J.P.)* = *"Theodoret, Bishop of Cyr, on Disputed
Questions of the Old Testament"* : om. *F.M.*

THEODORET ON SELECTED QUESTIONS REGARDING HOLY SCRIPTURE

Preface

Previous scholars have promised to resolve apparent problems in holy Scripture by explicating the sense of some, indicating the background of others, and, in a word, clarifying whatever remains unclear to ordinary people.[1] And you, my dearest son, Hypatius,[2] above others have pressed me to undertake this task and insisted that the present work would be widely useful. Hence, although I am not in good health, I have undertaken this project, trusting not in myself, of course, but in the one who dictated this manner of composition for the Scriptures, as it belongs to him to bring to the fore the meaning concealed in the text.[3] He it was, after all, who in the sacred Gospels presented his teaching in parables and then provided the interpreta-

---

1. Theodoret refuses to concede that Scripture contains real problems. There is only a certain difficulty in dealing with these questions, which better informed people (φιλομαθεῖς) should be able to resolve.

2. In his *Dissertatio* on Theodoret's life and works, Schulze describes (PG, vol. 80, col. 53) Hypatius as an associate and assistant, perhaps a coadjutor, of Theodoret in his latter years.

3. For other places where Theodoret concedes his dependence on divine grace in his exegetical task; *v.* Thdt., *Ps.* 1–150 *proem.* and *Epp. Paul. proem.* Unearthing the sense hidden in the words (τὴν ἐν τῷ γράμματι διάνοιαν) is the commentator's job, for which he depends on the Spirit.

καὶ παραβολικῶς τὴν διδασκαλίαν προσέφερε καὶ τῶν
αἰνιγματωδῶς εἰρημένων ἐποιεῖτο τὴν ἑρμηνείαν.ᵃ παρ' αὐτοῦ
τοίνυν τῆς νοερᾶς ἀκτῖνος ἀντιβολήσας τυχεῖν, τῶν τοῦ
15 παναγίου πνεύματος ἀδύτων κατατολμῆσαι πειράσομαι.

Ἰστέον δὲ πρὸ τῶν ἄλλων ἁπάντων ὡς οὐχ ἅπαντες
σύμφωνον ἔχουσι τῆς ἐρωτήσεως τὸν σκοπόν, ἀλλ' οἱ μὲν
δυσσεβῶς ἐρωτῶσι, διελέγχειν οἰόμενοι τὴν θείαν γραφήν· νῦν
μέν, ὡς οὐκ ὀρθὰ παιδεύουσαν, νῦν δέ, ὡς ἐναντία
20 διδάσκουσαν· οἱ δὲ φιλομαθῶς ζητοῦσι καὶ ποθοῦσιν εὑρεῖν τὸ
ζητούμενον. κἀκείνων τοίνυν ἐμφράξομεν, σὺν θεῷ φάναι, τὰ
βλάσφημα στόματα, τῆς θείας ἐπιδεικνύντες γραφῆς καὶ τὴν
συμφωνίαν καὶ τὴν ἀρίστην διδασκαλίαν, καὶ τούτοις, ὡς οἷόν
τε, τῶν ἐπαπορουμένων τὴν λύσιν προσοίσομεν. ἀρχὴν δὲ
25 τούτων ποιήσομαι τῆς κτίσεως τὴν ἀρχήν· αὕτη γὰρ ἀρχὴ καὶ
προοίμιον τῆς θεοπνεύστου γραφῆς.

a. Mt 13.11–17

Preface

tion of what he had said in riddles.[4a] My appeal, therefore, shall be to gain illumination of the mind from him, so I may endeavor to penetrate the innermost sanctuary of the most Holy Spirit.[5]

Now, to begin with, you should know that not all inquirers share the same purpose. Some inquire irreverently, believing they find holy Scripture wanting: in some cases, not teaching right doctrine, in others, giving conflicting instructions. In contrast, others, longing to find an answer for their question, search because they love learning. Accordingly, it is my intention to stop the blasphemous mouths of the former, please God, by demonstrating the consistency of holy Scripture and the excellence of its teaching, and also, to the extent possible, provide the latter with solutions to their difficulties. I shall begin with the beginning of creation, which is the beginning and introduction of the inspired Scripture.

---

4. Though finding riddles primarily in the Old Testament, eastern commentators also regarded the Gospel parables (παραβολικῶς) as an oblique form of communication (αἰνιγματωδῶς); *cf.* Chrysostom's *Proph. obscurit.* (*CPG* #4420).

5. For Theodoret the task of scriptural commentary is an exalted, in fact, inspired, role. In the preface to his commentary on Song of Songs he speaks in very similar terms: "Exegesis of holy Scripture . . . requires a mind with wings that can behold the divine and will dare to enter the innermost sanctuary of the Spirit (κατατολμώσης τῶν ἀδύτων τοῦ Πνεύματος)."

QUAESTIONES IN GENESIN

I

Τί δή ποτε μὴ προτέταχε τῆς τῶν ὅλων δημιουργίας θεολογίαν ὁ συγγραφεύς;

Μετρεῖν εἴωθε τοῖς παιδευομένοις ἡ θεία γραφὴ μαθήματα καὶ τοῖς μὲν τελείοις προσφέρειν τὰ τέλεια, τοῖς ἀτελέσι δὲ
5 τὰ στοιχειώδη καὶ τῇ σφῶν δυνάμει συμβαίνοντα.ᵃ ἐπειδὴ τοίνυν αἰγύπτιοι τὴν ὁρωμένην κτίσιν ἐθεοποίουν, τούτοις δὲ συνδιάγων ἐπὶ πλεῖστον, ὁ Ἰσραὴλ ταύτης τῆς δυσσεβείας μετέλαχεν, ἀναγκαίως τὰ περὶ τῆς κτίσεως αὐτοῖς προσφέρει μαθήματα καὶ διδάσκει διαρρήδην ὅτι καὶ ἀρχὴν ἔσχε τοῦ
10 εἶναι καὶ ὅτι ποιητὴν ἔχει τὸν τῶν ὅλων Θεόν.ᵇ οὐ μὴν οὐδὲ τὸν τῆς θεολογίας παραλέλοιπε λόγον. τὸ γὰρ φάναι τὸν οὐρανόν, καὶ τὴν γῆν, καὶ τὰ ἄλλα ὅσα τῆς κτίσεως μόρια γενητὰ καὶ δεῖξαι τούτων δημιουργὸν τὸν τῶν ὅλων Θεὸν ἀρκοῦσαν τοῖς τότε θεολογίαν προσήνεγκε· τῶν μὲν γὰρ
15 ἐδήλωσε τὴν ἀρχήν, τοῦ δὲ εὑρεῖν οὐκ ἴσχυσε τὴν ἀρχήν. καὶ ἀΐδιον τοίνυν ἐγνωκὼς τὸν Θεὸν καὶ ποιητὴν τοῦ παντὸς ὀνομάσας καὶ ἀγαθὸν ποιητήν,ᶜ τῷ φυσιολογικῷ τὸ θεολογικὸν μάλα σοφῶς συνήρμοσεν.

Ἄλλως τε καὶ προμεμαθήκεσαν οἱ ταῦτα διδασκόμενοι τοῦ
20 Θεοῦ τὸ ἀΐδιον· ἀποσταλεὶς γὰρ εἰς Αἴγυπτον παρὰ τοῦ Θεοῦ τῶν ὅλων, ὁ θεσπέσιος Μωϋσῆς προσετάχθη τοῖς ὁμοφύλοις

---

1 5, 14 24, c, 50 51* 52 53, 4 7 9 10a 13 18 20 26b = 18 mss.

a. 1Cor 3.1f.   b. Gn 1.1   c. Gn 1.1, 4, 10, 12, 18, 21, 25, 31

ON GENESIS

I

Why did the author not first set down the true doctrine of God before relating the creation of the universe?[1]

Holy Scripture normally adapts the contents to the learners: to those who are mature proposing mature teachings, but to the immature the elements, in keeping with their capacity.[2a] Since the Egyptians used to worship the visible creation, and Israel, in their long association with them, had joined in this idolatry, he had to set out the facts of creation and explicitly teach them that it had a beginning of existence, and that the God of the universe was its Creator.[b] Not that he passed over a treatment of the true doctrine of God. The statement that heaven and earth and the other parts of the universe were created and the revelation that the God of the universe was their Creator provided a true doctrine of God sufficient for people of that time. Indeed, whereas he conveyed the beginning of created things, he was not capable of inquiring into God's beginning. Now, knowing God to be eternal, he very wisely associated the theological with the natural by referring to him as Creator of everything and a good Creator.[c]

Those he was teaching, however, had already learned of the eternity of God. When the divinely inspired Moses was sent into Egypt by God, he was commanded to say to his fellows, "He Who Is has

---

1. Though elsewhere (*e.g. Q.* 12 on Jgs) Theodoret applies to Moses, the putative author, the title used of the OT prophets (προφήτης), he here calls him "author" or "historian" (συγγραφεύς).

2. Chrysostom employs the noun συγκατάβασις to refer to God's conde-

εἰπεῖν, ὁ ὤν ἀπέσταλκέ με πρὸς ὑμᾶς·ᵈ τὸ δὲ ὁ ὤν τοῦ ἀϊδίου
δηλωτικόν. δῆλον δὲ τοῖς φιλομαθέσιν ὡς ἐκεῖνα πρὸ τούτων
ἐρρέθη· ἐκείνην γὰρ αὐτοῖς τὴν διδασκαλίαν ἔτι τὴν
25 Αἴγυπτον οἰκοῦσι προσήνεγκε, ταῦτα δὲ ἐν τῇ ἐρήμῳ
συνέγραφε.

II

Τί δή ποτε τῆς τῶν ἀγγέλων οὐκ ἐμνήσθη δημιουργίας;
Οὐδὲν στερρὸν εἶχον βέβαιον οἱ νομοαθετούμενοι· αὐτίκα
γοῦν, μετὰ πολλὰ καὶ ἄφραστα θαύματα, τὴν εἰκόνα τοῦ
μόσχου θεὸν ἀνηγόρευσαν.ᵃ οἱ δὲ τὰ τῶν κτηνῶν ἰνδάλματα
||26b   5   ῥᾳδίως οὕτω θεοποιήσαντες,|| τί οὐκ ἂν ἔδρασαν εἰ τῶν

d. Ex 3.14

II   5, 14 24, c, 50 51 52* 53, 4 7 9 10a 13(inc.) 18 19 20 26b(inc.) [32] 37 = 20 mss.
a. Ex 32.4

sent me to you."[3d] Now, "He Who Is" conveys eternity, and it will be obvious to the attentive that that statement was made before the teaching in this chapter. He taught them the former while they were still living in Egypt but composed this chapter in the wilderness.

11

Why did he not mention the creation of the angels?[1]

The people who were receiving the Law had no firm and stable basis; after all, immediately after many ineffable marvels, they hailed the image of the calf as a god.[2a] So if those people could so easily regard the likenesses of cattle as gods, what would they not have done,

----

scension in accommodating scriptural expression to the limitations of human readers/listeners. On the use of this term in his homilies on ch. 1 of Gn, *v.* R.C. Hill, "On looking again at *synkatabasis*."

3. Theodoret does not realize that the terms used to refer to God differ in the various Hebrew traditions that have been combined to create the present text of Gn and Ex; *v.* sec. 7 of the "Introduction to Theodoret's Life and Works." According to Ex 3.14, a verse belonging to the Elohist tradition (from Hebrew *'elohim*, "God"), God first revealed his name "Yahweh" to Moses, for "'I am who I am' is the name Yahweh transposed into the first person." In contrast, according to the Yahwist tradition in Gn 4.26, God had been invoked by the name "Yahweh" from the time of Adam. While Theodoret understands the use of the verb "to be" in the name of Ex 3.14 as a statement of God's eternal existence, R.J. Clifford regards the Hebrew as "probably the causative form, 'cause to be, create'"; *v.* "Exodus," on Ex 3.13–15.

1. This is the first of several questions regarding angels, which testify to theological debate about, and the interest in, angels in Theodoret's church. Chrysostom had raised the same point at the opening of the first of his eight early sermons on Genesis (*ser.* 1.2 *in Gen.*), to which Theodoret may have referred as he composed this question. In his commentary on Colossians (on 2.18), Theodoret shows some concern about the proliferation in Phrygia and Pisidia of the cult of the angels, especially Michael. In his belief that Scripture is "full of this doctrine" (*i.e.* regarding the angels), the commentator here has recourse to an ingenious rationalization; in fact, while angels appear throughout the Bible, there is little in the way of speculative angelology.

2. Chrysostom had adduced the same line of argument in *hom.* 2.2 *in Gen.*

ἀοράτων φύσεων τὴν γνῶσιν ἐδέξαντο; οὗ χάριν, μέχρι τῆς τοῦ Ἀβραὰμ τελειότητος, οὐδενὶ τῶν πάλαι ἀνθρώπων δι' ἀγγέλου ὁ τῶν ὅλων διελέχθη Θεός.

|13 |Ἐπὶ δὲ τῆς Ἄγαρ πρῶτον ἀγγέλου μνήμην ὁ θεσπέσιος ἐποιήσατο Μωϋσῆς,[b] καὶ μάλα εἰκότως· τύπος γὰρ ἡ Ἄγαρ τῆς παλαιᾶς διαθήκης κατὰ τὸν θεῖον ἀπόστολον. *τὸ γὰρ Ἄγαρ*, φησί, *Σινᾶ ὄρος ἐστὶν ἐν τῇ Ἀραβίᾳ, συστοιχεῖ δὲ τῇ νῦν Ἰερουσαλήμ.*[c] ἐπειδὴ τοίνυν δι' ἀγγέλων ὁ νόμος ἐδόθη· *διαταγείς*, γάρ φησι, *δι' ἀγγέλων ἐν χειρὶ μεσίτου*·[d] καὶ πάλιν, *εἰ γὰρ ὁ δι' ἀγγέλων λαληθεὶς λόγος ἐγένετο βέβαιος*·[e] καὶ μάλα προσφόρως ὁ τῶν ὅλων Θεὸς δι' ἀγγέλου καὶ τῆς δουλείας ἀνέμνησε καὶ τὰ περὶ τοῦ τεχθησομένου παιδὸς προηγόρευσεν.[f]

Ὅτι δὲ κτιστὴν ἔχουσι φύσιν καὶ ἄγγελοι, καὶ ἀρχάγγελοι, καὶ εἴ τι ἕτερόν ἐστιν ἀσώματον, πλὴν τῆς ἁγίας τριάδος, ἡ θεία σαφῶς ἡμᾶς διδάσκει γραφή. ὑμνεῖν γὰρ καὶ τούτοις Δαβὶδ παρακελεύεται ὁ προφήτης· *αἰνεῖτε* γὰρ *αὐτόν*, φησί, *πάντες οἱ ἄγγελοι αὐτοῦ, αἰνεῖτε αὐτόν, πᾶσαι αἱ δυνάμεις αὐτοῦ*·[g] καὶ τὴν αἰτίαν διδάσκων, ἐπήγαγεν, *ὅτι αὐτὸς εἶπε,*
||13 *καὶ ἐγενήθησαν,*|| *αὐτὸς ἐνετείλατο, καὶ ἐκτίσθησαν*·[h] καὶ πάλιν, ἐν ἑτέρῳ ψαλμῷ, *ὁ ποιῶν τοὺς ἀγγέλους αὐτοῦ πνεύματα καὶ τοὺς λειτουργοὺς αὐτοῦ πυρὸς φλόγα.*[i] καὶ οἱ τρεῖς μακάριοι παῖδες ἐν τῇ καμίνῳ τὸν θεῖον ὕμνον ὑφαίνοντες καὶ τὸ πανάριστον ἐκεῖνο καὶ λίαν ἁρμόδιον εἰρηκότες προοίμιον, *εὐλογεῖτε, πάντα τὰ ἔργα Κυρίου, τὸν Κύριον,* εὐθὺς ἐπήγαγον, *εὐλογεῖτε, ἄγγελοι Κυρίου, τὸν Κύριον,*[j] *πᾶσαι αἱ δυνάμεις Κυρίου, τὸν Κύριον.*[k] ἀλλὰ γὰρ παρέλκον οἶμαι περὶ τούτων μακρηγορεῖν· πᾶσα γὰρ ἡ θεόπνευστος γραφὴ τῆσδε τῆς διδασκαλίας ἀνάπλεως.

b. Gn 16.7 c. Gal 4.25 d. Gal 3.19 e. Heb 2.2 f. Gn 16.7–12
g. Ps 148.2 h. Ps 148.5 i. Ps 104.4 j. Dn 3.57f. (LXX) k. Dn 3.61 (LXX)

if they had acquired knowledge of powers of an invisible nature? This is why, up to the time of Abraham, a fully mature man, the God of the universe never communicated with the people of olden times by means of an angel.

The divinely inspired Moses first made mention of an angel in the case of Hagar,[b] and rightly so; Hagar was a type of the old covenant. According to the holy apostle, "Hagar is Mount Sinai in Arabia, and corresponds to the present Jerusalem."[c] So, as the Law was given through angels—"It was ordained through angels by a mediator";[d] and again, "If the message declared through angels was valid"[e]—it was also entirely appropriate for the God of the universe to employ an angel to speak of her slavery and to foretell the fate of the child that was to be born.[f]

Now, holy Scripture clearly teaches us that angels and archangels and anything else incorporeal—the Holy Trinity excepted—have a created nature. Thus, the prophet David commands them also to sing God's praise: "All you his angels, sing his praise; sing his praise, all you his powers."[g] And to convey the reason, he adds, "Because he spoke, and they were made; he gave orders, and they were created."[h] And again in another psalm: "He who makes his angels winds and his ministers a flaming fire."[i] Furthermore, the three blessed young men in the furnace composed their divinely inspired hymn and, beginning with a very fitting introduction, sang that excellent verse: "Bless the Lord, all you works of the Lord," and then, "Bless the Lord, angels of the Lord;[j] bless the Lord, all you powers of the Lord."[3k] In fact, I feel it is superfluous to go on at length about them; all the inspired Scripture is full of this doctrine.

3. For the Greek version of this passage of Dn, *v.* L.F. Hartman and A.A. Di Lella, "Daniel," on 3.24–90 and K.G. O'Connell, "Greek Versions of the Old Testament," p. 1094, and *cf.* the allusion to the same hymn at the end of Q. 7.

III

Προϋπάρχουσιν οὐρανοῦ καὶ γῆς ἄγγελοι, ἢ σὺν τούτοις
ἐγένοντο;

Περιττὰς μὲν ἐγὼ τὰς τοιαύτας ζητήσεις ὑπείληφα· τίς
γὰρ ὄνησις προσγενήσεται τοῖς ἐγνωκόσι τὸν τῆς τῶν
5 ἀγγέλων δημιουργίας καιρόν; οἶδα δὲ καὶ τὸν θεῖον ἀπόστολον
τῷ θαυμασίῳ Τιμοθέῳ παρεγγυῶντα, *παραγγεῖλαί τισι μὴ*
ἑτεροδιδασκαλεῖν μηδὲ προσέχειν μύθοις καὶ γενεαλογίαις
ἀπεράντοις.[a] ἐρῶ δὲ ὅμως ὅπερ συμβαίνειν ὑπείληφα τῷ σκοπῷ
τῆς θείας γραφῆς· ἀπερίγραφον μόνην ἐδιδάχθημεν εἶναι τὴν
10 θείαν φύσιν, ἅτε δὴ ἄκτιστον οὖσαν καὶ ἄναρχον καὶ ἀΐδιον,
τὰ δέ γε ἀρξάμενα τοῦ εἶναι περιγεγραμμένον ἔχει δηλονότι
τὸ εἶναι. οὐκοῦν, καὶ ἀσώματον λέγοντες εἶναι τῶν ἀγγέλων
τὴν φύσιν, περιγεγράφθαι φαμὲν αὐτῶν τὴν ὑπόστασιν. πῶς
γὰρ ἄν τις νοῆσαι *χιλίας χιλιάδας καὶ μυρίας μυριάδας,* κατὰ
15 τὸν θεῖον Δανιήλ,[b] μὴ ἕκαστον λογιζόμενος ἐν ἰδίᾳ εἶναι
περιγραφῇ;

Ἀλλ' ὅτι μὲν περιγεγραμμένην ἔχουσιν οἱ ἄγγελοι τὴν
οὐσίαν οὐδένα ἀντερεῖν οἶμαι. καὶ γὰρ τῶν ἀνθρώπων ἕκαστον
ὑφ' ἑνὸς ἔφη τετάχθαι κηδεμονίαν ὁ δεσπότης Χριστός·
20 *ὁρᾶτε,* γάρ φησι, *μὴ καταφρονήσητε ἑνὸς τῶν ἐλαχίστων* τῶν
πιστευόντων εἰς ἐμέ, *ὅτι οἱ ἄγγελοι αὐτῶν . . . διὰ παντὸς*
ὁρῶσι τὸ πρόσωπον τοῦ πατρός μου τοῦ ἐν οὐρανοῖς.[c] καὶ
ἑκάστῳ δὲ ἔθνει ἄγγελον ἐφεστάναι φησὶν ἡ θεία γραφή· ὁ

III 5, 14 24, c, 50 51 52* 53, 4 7* 9 10 13 18 19 20 26b(inc.) [32] 37 = 20 mss.
a. 1Tm 1.3f.   b. Dn 7.10   c. Mt 18.10 (NT var.)

III

Did the angels come into being before heaven and earth, or were they made along with them?

I regard this sort of question as over-curious; after all, what benefit could accrue from a knowledge of the exact moment of the creation of the angels? I am also aware that the holy apostle urges the admirable Timothy "to instruct certain people not to teach any different doctrine or give heed to mythological fables and endless genealogies."[1a] Yet I shall state what I believe is in keeping with the purpose of holy Scripture.[2] We were taught that the divine nature alone is uncircumscribed in that it is uncreated, without beginning, and eternal, whereas things that have had a beginning of existence clearly have limits to their existence. Therefore, even though we declare that the angels possess an incorporeal nature, we say that their substance is circumscribed. Indeed, how could anyone, in the words of the divinely inspired Daniel, form the notion of "thousands of thousands and myriads of myriads"[b] without understanding each one to exist within its own limits?

I believe, however, that no one contests that the angels have a being that is circumscribed. Christ the Lord said that each human being has been placed in the care of a single angel: "Be careful not to despise one of the least of those who believe in me, because their angels gaze constantly on the face of my Father in heaven."[c] Holy Scripture also says that an angel presides over each nation. The angel that conversed with the prophet Daniel mentioned a ruler of the

1. Though he wishes to convey the impression that such issues are trivial, Theodoret is aware that Origen (*Princ.* 3.5.3; *v.* H. Crouzel and M. Simonetti, vol. 4, note 13, pp. 105f.), Basil (*Hex.* 1.5), and Gregory Nazianzen (*Or.* 38.9f.) had placed the creation of the angels before that of heaven and earth, and that Theodore of Mopsuestia (in his commentary on Genesis; *v.* Devreesse, *Essai,* p. 8 and note 4) had rejected this view. Theodoret's argumentation follows closely the logic and the scriptural citations marshalled by Theodore; *v.* Guinot, *L'Exégèse,* pp. 749f.

2. Though qualifying this question as frivolous, Theodoret wishes to provide

γὰρ τῷ προφήτῃ Δανιὴλ προσδιαλεγόμενος ἄγγελος καὶ
25 ἄρχοντα περσῶν εἴρηκε,[d] καὶ ἄρχοντα ἑλλήνων,[e] καὶ Μιχαὴλ
τὸν ἄρχοντα τῶν ἰουδαίων.[f] καὶ Μωϋσῆς δὲ ὁ μέγας ἐν τῇ
ᾠδῇ φησιν, ὅτε διεμέριζεν ὁ Ὕψιστος ἔθνη, ὡς διέσπειρεν
υἱοὺς Ἀδάμ, ἔστησεν ὅρια ἐθνῶν κατὰ ἀριθμὸν ἀγγέλων Θεοῦ.[g]
εἰ τοίνυν ὁ μὲν τούτων, ὁ δὲ ἐκείνων ἄρχειν ἐτάχθη, ἕκαστος
30 δὲ τῶν ἀνθρώπων ὑπὸ τὴν ἑνὸς φροντίδα τελεῖ, εὔδηλον ὡς
περιγεγραμμένην ἔχουσι τὴν οὐσίαν.

Εἰ δὲ τοῦτο ἀληθές, ὥσπερ οὖν ἀληθές, τόπου ἄρα
|26b προσδέονται· Ιμόνον γὰρ τὸ θεῖον, ὡς ἀπερίγραφον, οὐκ ἐν
τόπῳ. εἰ δὲ τὸ περιγεγραμμένον ἐν τόπῳ, πῶς οἷόν τε
35 προϋπάρχειν οὐρανοῦ καὶ γῆς τοὺς ἀγγέλους; οὐ γὰρ ὄντος
τοῦ φέροντος, πῶς ἔνεστι τὸ φερόμενον εἶναι;

IV

Ἀλλά φασί τινες χρῆναι λέγειν προϋπάρχειν οὐρανοῦ καὶ
γῆς τοὺς ἀγγέλους· ἀγγέλων, γάρ φασι, οὐκ ὄντων, πῶς ὁ τῶν
ὅλων ὑμνεῖτο Θεός;[a]

(1) Ἀλλ' οἱ ταῦτα λέγοντες ἀγνοοῦσιν ὡς καὶ ἀνάρχους
5 αὐτοὺς καὶ ἀϊδίους οὗτος ὁ λόγος ποιεῖ· εἰ γὰρ ἐδεῖτο τῶν
ὑμνούντων ὁ τῶν ὅλων Θεός, ἀεὶ δὲ τούτους εἶχεν ὑμνοῦντας,

---

d. Dn 10.13, 20   e. Dn 10.20   f. Dn 10.21   g. Dt 32.8

IV 2a(inc.) 5, 14 24, c, 50 51 52* 53, 4 7 9 10(+ 10a) 18 19 20 26b [32] 37 = 20 mss.
l. 2 φασι 5, 14 24, 26b, Sir. Sch. (-ιν) : om.? J.P. : φησί F.M. = "he asks, 'how
was…?'" Cf. φασί τινες in the preceding clause. The verb might well be a
gloss, for the transposed order of 14 and 24 (οὐκ ὄντων φασί) suggests that its
place in the text was uncertain.
a. Jb 38.7

Persians,[d] a ruler of the Greeks,[e] and Michael the ruler of the Jews.[3][f] And in his song, the mighty Moses declares, "When the Most High divided the nations, when he dispersed the children of Adam, he set boundaries for nations according to the number of God's angels."[g] If, then, one was appointed to rule this group and another that, and each human being lives in the care of an angel, they clearly have a being that is circumscribed.

Now, if this is in fact true, and, of course it is, it follows that they require a place; only the divinity, uncircumscribed in being, does not occupy a place. But if what is circumscribed occupies a place, how could the angels have come into being before heaven and earth? If there was nothing to offer support, how could anything exist that needed to be supported?

IV

Yet, some commentators claim that the angels preëxisted heaven and earth, for "if there were no angels," they ask, "how was the God of the universe praised in song?"[a]

(1) Those who make this claim do not realize that it presents the angels as without beginning and without end. If the God of the universe needed singers of his praises and always had them singing his praises, it follows that the angels would be co-eternal with

----

an answer that will be in accord with the Antiochene exegetical practice of attempting to discern the general purport (ὁ σκοπός) of each passage of Scripture; thus he promises to provide what he takes to be the general sense of biblical passages dealing with angels (ὅπερ συμβαίνειν ὑπείληφα τῷ σκοπῷ τῆς θείας γραφῆς); v. sec. 4 of the "Introduction to Theodoret' s Life and Works."

3. Theodoret's argument recalls a passage in his commentary on Daniel (on 10.13), written some twenty-five years earlier; there Theodoret had cited together Dt 32.8 and Mt 18.10 to show that each individual enjoys the protection of a guardian angel while each nation lives under the guidance of a specially delegated archangel.

συναΐδιοι ἄρα οἱ ἄγγελοι τῷ τῶν ὅλων Θεῷ. εἰ δὲ οὐκ ἀεί, ἀλλ', ὅτεπερ ἠβουλήθη, τούτους ἐδημιούργησεν, ἦν ἄρα τις αἰὼν ἐν ᾧπερ τοὺς ὑμνοῦντας οὐκ εἶχεν ὁ τῶν ὅλων Θεός.

||10 |10a 10 οὐκοῦν οὐ δεῖται τῶν ὑμνούντων ὁ δεσπότης Θεός·|| ἀνενδεῆ γὰρ ἔχει τὴν φύσιν. δι' ἀγαθότητα δὲ μόνην καὶ ἀγγέλοις, καὶ ἀρχαγγέλοις, καὶ πάσῃ τῇ κτίσει τὸ εἶναι δεδώρηται.

Ποίαν δὲ καὶ λειτουργίαν εἶχον πρὸ τῆς κτίσεως ὄντες, οὐδενὸς ὄντος τοῦ τῆς τούτων ὠφελείας προσδεομένου; ὅτι
15 γὰρ εἰς τὴν τῶν ἀνθρώπων κηδεμονίαν ὑπουργοῦσι τῷ τῶν ὅλων Θεῷ μάρτυς ὁ θεῖος ἀπόστολος βοῶν, *οὐχὶ πάντες εἰσὶ λειτουργικὰ πνεύματα, εἰς διακονίαν ἀποστελλόμενα διὰ τοὺς μέλλοντας κληρονομεῖν σωτηρίαν;*[b] οὐκοῦν εὔδηλον ὡς ἡμεῖς μὲν τῆς ἐκείνων ἐπικουρίας δεόμεθα. ὁ δὲ Θεὸς ἥκιστα μέν
20 τινος ἐνδεής, ἄβυσσος δὲ ὢν ἀγαθότητος, ἠβουλήθη καὶ τοῖς μηδαμῇ μηδαμῶς οὖσι μεταδοῦναι τοῦ εἶναι.

|2a (2) [*Ἀλλὰ γὰρ οἱ προϋπάρχειν οὐρανοῦ καὶ γῆς τοὺς ἀγγέλους ἰσχυριζόμενοι ὡς ἰσχυρὸν ἡμῖν καὶ ἄμαχον προβάλλονται ἐκεῖνο τὸ παρὰ τοῦ Θεοῦ τῶν ὅλων πρὸς τὸν
25 Ἰὼβ εἰρημένον· *ὅτε ἐποίουν ἄστρα, ᾔνεσάν με ... πάντες ἄγγελοί μου.*[c] καὶ οὐ συνορῶσιν ὡς τῇ τετάρτῃ ἡμέρᾳ σὺν τῷ ἡλίῳ καὶ τῇ σελήνῃ τὰ ἄστρα παρήγαγεν ὁ τῶν ὅλων Θεός.[d] εἰκὸς δὲ τοὺς ἀγγέλους σὺν οὐρανῷ δημιουργηθῆναι καὶ γῇ ἵνα, καὶ τὸ φῶς ὁρῶντες ἐξ οὐδενὸς ὑποκειμένου
30 δημιουργούμενον,[e] καὶ τὸ στερέωμα ἐν μέσῳ τοῦ ὕδατος συμπηγνύμενον,[f] καὶ τὴν ὑγρὰν οὐσίαν χωριζομένην τῆς γῆς, καὶ τὴν γῆν ἅμα τῷ θείῳ λόγῳ παντοδαπῶς διακοσμουμένην βλαστήμασι, καὶ τ' ἄλλα πάντα πρὸς τὸ θεῖον γινόμενα βούλημα,[g] γνῶσι, δι' ὧν ὁρῶσιν, ὡς καὶ αὐτοὶ κτιστὴν ἔχουσι
35 τὴν φύσιν, παρ' αὐτοῦ τὸ εἶναι δεξάμενοι. καὶ γὰρ ὁ θεῖος ἀπόστολος τῷ κόσμῳ αὐτοὺς συζεύγνυσι, λέγων, *θέατρον ἐγενήθημεν τῷ κόσμῳ, καὶ ἀγγέλοις, καὶ ἀνθρώποις.*[h]

---

b. Heb 1.14   c. Jb 38.7   d. Gn 1.14–19   e. Gn 1.3   f. Gn 1.6
g. Gn 1.9–12   h. 1Cor 4.9

God.[1] If, on the other hand, they did not always exist, and he created them only when he wished, it follows that there was a time when the God of the universe did not have anyone singing his praises. The Lord God, therefore, does not need anyone to sing his praises, for he is by nature free of need. Instead, it was only out of his goodness that he conferred existence on angels, and archangels, and all of creation.

Furthermore, what service would they have rendered if they had existed before creation when there was no one in existence who needed their assistance? In fact, the holy apostle cries out that they minister to God by caring for human beings: "Are they not all ministering spirits sent on a mission of service for the sake of those who are due to inherit salvation?"[b] Thus, it is obvious that, whereas we need their assistance, God has no need of anyone, yet, being an abyss of goodness, he wanted to give a share of existence to those who did not exist at all.

(2) Nevertheless, those who insist that the angels preëxisted heaven and earth quote to us as a convincing and irrefutable proof text the statement that the God of the universe made to Job: "As I made the stars, all my angels sang my praises."[c] But this is to miss the fact that it was on the fourth day that God brought the stars into being along with the sun and the moon.[d] Now, the angels were probably created along with heaven and earth so that on seeing the light created from no preëxistent material,[e] the firmament fixed in the midst of the waters,[f] the water separated from the land, the earth beautified with all kinds of plants as soon as God spoke, and everything else made at God's discretion,[g] they might realize, through what they saw, that they also have a created nature and receive existence from him. The holy apostle, in fact, links them to the world in saying, "We have become a spectacle to the world, to angels, and to human beings."[h]

1. Epiphanius of Salamis (*haer.* 65.4.9–5.4) may have provided Theodoret with this further objection; *v.* Guinot, p. 750.

Ἐγὼ δὲ ταῦτα οὐκ ἀποφαινόμενος λέγω· τολμηρὸν γὰρ
ἀποφαντικῶς οἶμαι λέγειν περὶ ὧν ἡ θεία διαρρήδην οὐ λέγει
40 γραφή· ἀλλ' ὅπερ τοῖς εὐσεβέσι λογισμοῖς ἁρμόττειν ὑπέλαβον
εἴρηκα. ἐκεῖνο μέντοι ἀναγκαῖον εἰδέναι, ὡς ἅπαντα τὰ ὄντα,
πλὴν τῆς ἁγίας τριάδος, κτιστὴν ἔχει τὴν φύσιν.
συνομολογουμένου δὲ τούτου, τῷ τῆς εὐσεβείας οὐ λυμαίνεται
λόγῳ τὸ πρὸ οὐρανοῦ καὶ γῆς γεγενῆσθαι λέγειν τῶν ἀγγέλων
45 τοὺς δήμους. τὸ δὲ *λογομαχεῖν εἰς οὐδὲν χρήσιμον, ἐπὶ*
καταστροφῇ τῶν ἀκουόντων[i] ἀπαγορεύει διαρρήδην ὁ θεῖος
ἀπόστολος.

V

Εἰ ἦν ἡ γῆ, πῶς ἐγένετο; λέγει γὰρ ὁ συγγραφεύς, *ἡ δὲ γῆ*
ἦν.[a]

Ἠλίθιον καὶ ἄγαν ἀνόητον τὸ ἐρώτημα. ὁ γὰρ εἰπών, *ἐν*
||26b   *ἀρχῇ ἐποίησεν ὁ Θεὸς τὸν οὐρανὸν καὶ τὴν γῆν*,[b]|| οὐκ ἀΐδιον
5 ἔφη τὴν γῆν, ἀλλὰ μετὰ τὸν οὐρανόν, ἢ σὺν τῷ οὐρανῷ
δεξαμένην τὸ εἶναι. ἄλλως τε, οὐδὲ ἀπολύτως εἶπεν ὁ
συγγραφεύς, *ἡ δὲ γῆ ἦν*, ἀλλὰ τὸ ἑξῆς συναρμόσας, *ἡ δὲ γῆ*
ἦν ἀόρατος καὶ ἀκατασκεύαστος,[c] τοῦτ' ἔστιν, ἐγένετο μὲν
ὑπὸ τοῦ τῶν ὅλων Θεοῦ, ἔτι δὲ ἀόρατος ἦν, ἐπικειμένου τοῦ
10 ὕδατος, καὶ ἀκατασκεύαστος, μηδέπω κοσμηθεῖσα τῇ βλάστῃ
μηδὲ ἀνθήσασα λειμῶνας, καὶ ἄλση, καὶ λήϊα.

---

i. 2Tm 2.14

v *2a, 5, 14 24, C, 4 7 9 10a 18 19 20 26b(inc.) [32] 37* = 20 mss.

a. Gn 1.2   b. Gn 1.1   c. Gn 1.2

Now, I do not state this dogmatically, my view being that it is rash to speak dogmatically where holy Scripture does not make an explicit statement; rather, I have stated what I consider to be consistent with orthodox thought. Of course, we should all realize this fact: that everything in existence, with the exception of the Holy Trinity, has a created nature. If this is granted, the claim that the masses of angels were created before heaven and earth does not undermine the orthodox position. Yet the holy apostle clearly prohibits "disputation which does no good but only ruins those who are listening."[i]

V

If the earth was in existence, how did it come to be, since the historian says, "The earth was in existence"?[a]

This is a silly, foolish question. He who said, "In the beginning God made heaven and earth,"[b] did not say that the earth was eternal, but that it received its existence after, or along with, heaven. Furthermore, the historian did not simply say, "The earth was in existence," but connected it with what follows: "The earth was invisible and formless."[c] That is, though made by the God of the universe, it was invisible, because still covered by the water, and formless, because not yet arrayed with growth or sprouting meadows, groves, and crops.

VI

Οὐκ ἐδίδαξεν ἡμᾶς ὁ Μωϋσῆς ὅτι καὶ τὰ ὕδατα
ἐδημιούργησεν ὁ Θεός;

Καὶ μὴν εἰρηκώς, ἡ δὲ γῆ ἦν ἀόρατος καὶ ἀκατασκεύαστος,
καὶ σκότος ἐπάνω τῆς ἀβύσσου,ᵃ ἔδειξε μετὰ τῆς γῆς
5 δημιουργηθεῖσαν τῶν ὑδάτων τὴν φύσιν. καὶ περὶ τοῦ
σαββάτου δὲ νομοθετῶν, ὁ τῶν ὅλων Θεὸς οὕτως ἔφη· ἐξ
ἡμέρας ἐργᾷ, ... τῇ δὲ ἑβδόμῃ σάββατον, ἀνάπαυσις Κυρίῳ τῷ
Θεῷ σου· ... ἐν γὰρ ἐξ ἡμέραις ἐποίησε Κύριος ὁ Θεὸς τὸν
οὐρανόν, καὶ τὴν γῆν, καὶ τὴν θάλασσαν, καὶ πάντα τὰ ἐν
10 αὐτοῖς,ᵇ ὡς εἶναι δῆλον ὅτι πᾶν ὁτιοῦν ἐν τούτοις ὄν, ἢ
ὁρατὸν ἢ ἀόρατον, ἢ αἰσθητὸν ἢ νοητόν, πλὴν τῆς θείας
οὐσίας, κτιστὴν ἔχει τὴν φύσιν. καὶ ὁ θειότατος δὲ Δαβὶδ
εἰρηκώς, μακάριος οὗ ὁ Θεὸς Ἰακὼβ βοηθὸς αὐτοῦ, ἡ ἐλπὶς
αὐτοῦ ἐπὶ Κύριον τὸν Θεὸν αὐτοῦ, τὸν ποιήσαντα τὸν οὐρανόν,
15 καὶ τὴν γῆν, ἐπήγαγε, τὴν θάλασσαν, καὶ πάντα τὰ ἐν αὐτοῖς.ᶜ

VII

Εἰ τὸ φῶς ὁ Θεὸς ἐδημιούργησε, πῶς αὐτὸς τὸ σκότος
ἐποίησεν; ἐναντία γὰρ ταῦτα ἀλλήλοις.

(1) Ἐναντία μὲν ἀλλήλοις, ἀλλ' ἀναγκαῖα τοῖς ἀνθρώποις
ἀμφότερα. τὸ μὲν γὰρ πρὸς ἐργασίαν τε καὶ φιλοπονίαν
‖10a 5 συνεργεῖ τοῖς ἀνθρώποις,‖ καὶ ὑποδείκνυσι τὰ ὁρώμενα, καὶ
τὸν τούτων ποιητὴν ὑμνεῖσθαι παρασκευάζει· τὸ δὲ
διαναπαύει, καὶ νεουργεῖ τοὺς ἀνθρώπους, καὶ τὸν ἐκ τῆς
ἐργασίας ἐγγινόμενον διαλύει πόνον, καὶ τοὺς ἀνθρώπους μὲν

VI *2a, 5, 14 24, c, 50* 51 52 53, 4 7 9 10a 13 18 20 [32] 37 = 19 mss.*

a. Gn 1.2   b. Ex 20.9–11 (LXX var.)   c. Ps 146.5f.

VII *2a, 5, 14 24, C, 4 7 9 10a(+10 inc.) 13 18 20 [32] 37 = 19 mss.*

VI

Did Moses fail to teach us that God created the waters as well?

In fact, after saying, "The earth was invisible and formless, and darkness was over the deep,"[a] he showed that the waters, like the earth, have a nature that is created. The God of the universe spoke in similar terms also when legislating about the Sabbath: "Work on six days, but on the seventh there is to be a Sabbath, a rest, for the Lord your God; in six days the Lord God made heaven and earth, the sea, and all that is in them."[1b] So it is clear that, with the exception of the divine essence, whatever is in them, visible or invisible, material or spiritual, has a created nature. Indeed, after declaring, "Blessed is the one whose helper is the God of Jacob, whose hope is in the Lord his God, who made heaven and earth," the divinely inspired David proceeded to mention, "the sea, and all that is in them."[c]

VII

If God created the light, how could he have made the darkness, as these are opposed to each other?

(1) While they are opposed, they are both still necessary to human beings. One assists men with work and industry, brings visible things to their attention, and prompts them to sing the praises of their maker. The other gives rest and renewal and relieves the weariness caused by labor; it gathers people to their homes, and gives animals security in foraging. The holy David teaches us this quite ex-

---

1. While the more widely attested LXX form of this verse merely transliterates the Hebrew "Sabbath," ($\sigma\acute{\alpha}\beta\beta\alpha\tau\alpha$), Theodoret's Antiochene text glosses the transliteration with the term $\dot{\alpha}\nu\acute{\alpha}\pi\alpha\upsilon\sigma\iota\varsigma$ ("rest"); this textual peculiarity appears also in the quotations of Ex 20.10f. in Cyr., *Ador.* 7 (*ad loc.;* PG, vol. 68, col. 493C) and 16 (on Lv 1; *ib.,* col. 1012B); *v.* J.W. Wevers and U. Quast on Ex 20.10.

οἴκαδε συναγείρει, τοῖς δέ γε θηρίοις ἄδειαν παρέχει νομῆς.
10 καὶ τοῦτο σαφῶς ἡμᾶς ὁ θεῖος διδάσκει Δαβίδ· ἔθου, γάρ
φησι, σκότος, καὶ ἐγένετο νύξ. ἐν αὐτῇ διελεύσονται πάντα
τὰ θηρία τοῦ δρυμοῦ· σκύμνοι ὠρυόμενοι τοῦ ἀρπάσαι καὶ
ζητῆσαι παρὰ τῷ Θεῷ βρῶσιν αὐτοῖς. ἀνέτειλεν ὁ ἥλιος, καὶ
συνήχθησαν καὶ εἰς τὰς μάνδρας αὐτῶν κοιτασθήσονται.
15 ἐξελεύσεται ἄνθρωπος ἐπὶ τὸ ἔργον αὐτοῦ καὶ ἐπὶ τὴν
ἐργασίαν αὐτοῦ ἕως ἑσπέρας.ᵃ οὕτως ταῦτα εἰπών, τὴν τοῦ
ποιητοῦ θαυμάζει μεγαλουργίαν καί φησιν, ὡς ἐμεγαλύνθη τὰ
ἔργα σου, Κύριε· πάντα ἐν σοφίᾳ ἐποίησας.ᵇ

Ὅτι μὲν οὖν ἀναγκαῖον τὸ σκότος ἀκριβῶς μεμαθήκαμεν·
20 ὅτι δὲ οὐκ οὐσία τίς ἐστιν, ἀλλὰ πρᾶγμα συμβεβηκός,
καταμαθεῖν εὐπετές. οὐρανοῦ γὰρ καὶ γῆς ἐστιν ἀποσκίασμα.
διά τοι τοῦτο φροῦδον γίνεται, τοῦ φωτὸς ἀνίσχοντος. τὸ δὲ
φῶς οὐσία ἐστὶ καὶ ὑφέστηκε, καὶ δυόμενον ἀνίσχει, καὶ
ἀπιὸν ἐπανέρχεται. ὥσπερ γὰρ τὸ σῶμα τὸ ἡμέτερον οὐσία
25 τίς ἐστιν, ἡ δὲ διὰ τούτου ἀποτελουμένη σκιὰ συμβεβηκός
ἐστιν, οὐκ οὐσία, οὕτως ὁ οὐρανὸς καὶ ἡ γῆ, τὰ μέγιστα
σώματα, οὐσίαι εἰσὶ διάφοροι, ἡ δὲ ἐκ τούτων ἀποτελουμένη
σκιά, τοῦ φωτὸς οὐ παρόντος, ὀνομάζεται σκότος. εἰσελθὸν δὲ
|10 τὸ φῶς ἀφανίζει τὸ σκότος.

30 (2) Τοῦτο δὲ γνοίη τις ἂν καὶ ἑτέρωθεν· οἶκος γὰρ οὐκ
ἔχων φωταγωγούς, σκότους ἐστὶν ἀνάπλεως. εἰσκομισθείσης
δὲ λαμπάδος, φωτίζεται, οὐ τοῦ σκότους ἄλλοσε
μεταβαίνοντος· οὐ γὰρ ὑφέστηκεν, ἀνυπόστατον δὲ χρῆμά
ἐστιν· ἀλλὰ πάμπαν διολλυμένου τῇ τοῦ φωτὸς παρουσίᾳ· σκιὰ
35 γάρ ἐστι διὰ τῆς ὀροφῆς, καὶ τοῦ ἐδάφους, καὶ τῶν τοίχων
συνισταμένη, εἶτα ταῖς τοῦ φωτὸς διαλυομένη μαρμαρυγαῖς.
τοῦτο καθ' ἑκάστην ἡμέραν ὁρῶμεν ἐπιτελούμενον·
ὑποχωροῦντος γὰρ τοῦ φωτός, οὐρανοῦ καὶ γῆς ἡ σκιὰ τὸ
σκότος ἀποτελεῖ· ἀνίσχοντος δὲ πάλιν, διαλύεται τοῦτο.

---

l. 12 δρυμοῦ 2a, 5, 14 24, 4 7 9 13 18 20 : ἀγροῦ Sir. Sch. F.M. = "All the
beasts of the field." The reading δρυμοῦ is that of the majority of the mss. and
the *lectio difficilior*; it appears, apparently without variant, in the quotation of
Ps 104.20 in Q. 18.1 on Gn. and is the reading printed by Schulze in Thdt., *Ps.
ad loc.*

a. Ps 104.20–23   b. Ps 104.24

plicitly: "You put darkness in place, and night fell. All the beasts of the forest travel about in it: lion cubs roaring to hunt and to search for their food from God. The sun rose, and they gathered and will sleep in their lairs. Man will go to his work and his business until evening."[a] After saying this, he expressed admiration for the Creator's magnificence: "How magnificent are your works, O Lord! You made everything with your wisdom."[b]

Thus, we have precise knowledge of the necessity of darkness. And it is simple to grasp the truth that it is not a substance of some kind but only an accident, being a shadow cast by heaven and earth. This is why it vanishes when the light appears. Light, on the other hand, is and subsists as a substance; after setting, it rises, and after departing, it returns. In other words, just as our body is a substance, but the shadow created by the body is an accident, not a substance, so heaven and earth, the largest bodies, are substances of different kinds, but the shadow caused by them in the absence of light is called "darkness," and once the light enters, the darkness disappears.

(2) Other considerations lead to the same conclusion. A house with no windows is full of darkness, but when a lamp is brought in, it lights up—not that darkness has moved off elsewhere, for, being insubstantial, it does not subsist. Rather, it is completely dissolved with the coming of the light. After all, a shadow is caused by the roof, the floor, and the walls, and is dissipated by the beams of light. We see this occurring every day. When the light recedes, the shadow cast by heaven and earth brings darkness, and when the light rises again, the darkness is dissipated.

40 Οὐ τοίνυν ἀγένητος οὐσία τὸ σκότος, οὔτε μὴν γενητή τις
ὑπόστασις, ἀλλ' ἐκ τῶν γενητῶν συνισταμένη, χρῆσις
ἀναγκαία καὶ τοῦ Θεοῦ τὴν σοφίαν κηρύττουσα. αὐτίκα γοῦν ὁ
προφήτης τὸν τῶν ὅλων Θεὸν καὶ ἐντεῦθεν ὑμνεῖ· ὁ ποιήσας,
γάρ φησι, φῶς καὶ κατασκευάσας σκότος.ᶜ ἁρμοδίως δὲ ἄγαν
45 ἑκάτερα τέθεικεν· τὸ μὲν ποιήσας ἐπὶ τοῦ φωτός, τὸ δὲ
κατασκευάσας ἐπὶ τοῦ σκότους· συμβεβηκὸς γάρ ἐστι,
συνιστάμενον καὶ διαλυόμενον. καὶ οἱ τρισμακάριοι δὲ παῖδες,
πᾶσαν τὴν κτίσιν εἰς ὑμνῳδίαν καλέσαντες, τῇ ἡμέρᾳ τὴν
νύκτα συνέζευξαν καὶ φωτὶ τὸ σκότος συνήρμοσαν,ᵈ ἐπειδὴ
50 ταῖς τούτων διαδοχαῖς καὶ ὁ χρόνος μετρεῖται, καὶ ὁ τῶν
ἀνθρώπων συνίσταται βίος.

VIII

Ποῖον πνεῦμα ... ἐπεφέρετο ἐπάνω τοῦ ὕδατος;ᵃ

Τισὶ δοκεῖ τὸ πανάγιον πνεῦμα ζωογονοῦν τῶν ὑδάτων τὴν
φύσιν καὶ προδιαγράφον τὴν τοῦ βαπτίσματος χάριν.
ἀληθέστερον μέντοι ἐκεῖνον οἶμαι τὸν λόγον ὅτι πνεῦμα
5 ἐνταῦθα τὸν ἀέρα καλεῖ. εἰπὼν γὰρ ὅτι τὸν οὐρανὸν καὶ τὴν
γῆν ἐποίησε καὶ τῶν ὑδάτων διὰ τῆς ἀβύσσου μνησθείς,
ἀναγκαίως καὶ τοῦ ἀέρος ἐμνήσθη, ἐκ τῆς τοῦ ὕδατος
ἐπιφανείας μέχρι τοῦ οὐρανοῦ διήκοντος· ἀέρος γὰρ φύσις τὸ
τοῖς κάτω κειμένοις ἐπιφέρεσθαι σώμασι. μάλα δὲ ἁρμοδίως
10 τὸ ἐπεφέρετο καὶ οὐκ ἐπέκειτο εἴρηκε· τὸ γὰρ ἐπεφέρετο τὴν
κινητικὴν τοῦ ἀέρος οὐσίαν παρεδήλου.

Εἰ δέ τις τοῦτον οὐ προσίεται τὸν λόγον, ἐπειδὴ
γέγραπται, πνεῦμα Θεοῦ ἐπεφέρετο ἐπάνω τοῦ ὕδατος,
ἀκουσάτω τοῦ μακαρίου Δαβὶδ λέγοντος περὶ τοῦ Θεοῦ τῶν

---

c. Is 45.7   d. Dn 3.71f. (LXX)

VIII   2a, 5, 14 24, C, 4 7 9 10 13 18 20 [32] 37 = 19 mss.
a. Gn 1.2

Darkness, then, is neither an uncreated nor a created substance. Caused by created things, it is necessary and useful and proclaims God's wisdom. Indeed, the prophet regards this as yet another reason to praise the God of the universe: "I am he who created light and caused darkness."[c] He has mentioned each in a very appropriate way: "created" in the case of the light and "caused" in the case of the darkness, which is an accident that is brought about and dissipated. The three blessed young men also, in summoning creation to sing praise, linked night to day and joined the darkness to the light,[d] for in their mutual succession they allow the measurement of time and provide the composite elements of human life.

VIII

Which spirit "moved over the water"?[a]

Some commentators believe it was the most Holy Spirit vivifying the nature of the waters and foreshadowing the grace of baptism. But I think it more likely that by "spirit" he is here referring to the air. After declaring that God made heaven and earth and mentioning the waters by reference to "the deep," he logically goes on to mention as well the air, which extends from the water's surface to heaven, for air naturally moves over bodies lying under it.[1] Now, it was very apposite for him to say "moved over" and not "lying on": "moved" implying the kinetic character of the air.

Should you reject this view because Scripture says, "A spirit of God moved over the water," listen to blessed David speaking of the

1. Guinot lists (pp. 751f.) earlier allegorical interpretations of Gn 1.2 that equated the Spirit moving over the waters with the Holy Spirit. Diodore, Theodoret's model throughout the *Quaest. in oct.*, had been prepared to admit (Deconinck, frag. 4) that the spirit might be either the Holy Spirit or a wind. Given this and other differences between the interpretations of Theodoret and Diodore, Guinot suggests that our commentator may here have drawn from the lost work of

15 ὅλων, πνεύσει τὸ πνεῦμα αὐτοῦ, καὶ ῥυήσεται ὕδατα.ᵇ ὅτι δὲ
τὸν ἄνεμον οὕτως ἐκάλεσε δῆλόν ἐστι κἂν μὴ λέγω· Εὔρου γὰρ
ἢ Νότου πνέοντος, τὸ πεπηγὸς ὕδωρ διαλύεσθαι πέφυκεν.

IX

Τίνι λέγει ὁ Θεός, γενηθήτω φῶς,ᵃ καὶ γενηθήτω στερέωμα;ᵇ

Οὐκ ἄλλῳ τινὶ κελεύει δημιουργεῖν, ἀλλὰ τὰ μὴ ὄντα καλεῖ.
ἐνταῦθα δὲ πρόσταγμα τὸ βούλημα· πάντα, γάρ φησιν, ὅσα
ἠθέλησεν ὁ Θεός, ἐποίησεν.ᶜ εἰ δὲ καὶ φωνῇ τινι δημιουργῶν
5 ἐχρήσατο, δῆλον ὡς, οὐ τῶν ἀψύχων ἕνεκα στοιχείων, ἀλλὰ
τῶν ἀοράτων χάριν δυνάμεων, ἵνα γνῶσιν ὡς, αὐτοῦ
κελεύοντος, τὰ μὴ ὄντα συνίσταται.

X

Διὰ τί τέθεικεν ὁ συγγραφεὺς τὸ εἶδεν ὁ Θεὸς ... ὅτι
καλόν;ᵃ
Ἵνα πείσῃ τοὺς ἀχαρίστους μὴ ψέγειν ἅπερ ἡ θεία ψῆφος
ὀνομάζει καλά.

---

b. Ps 147.18

 IX 2a, 5, 14 24, C, 4 7 9 10 13 18 20 [32] 37 = 19 mss.
a. Gn 1.3   b. Gn 1.6   c. Ps 115.3

---

x 2a, 5, 14 24, C, 4 7 9 10 13 18 20 [32] 37 = 19 mss.
a. Gn 1.4

God of the universe: "He will breathe his spirit, and waters will flow."[b] The fact that this constitutes a reference to the wind is obvious and needs no comment of mine. In the natural course of events, frozen water melts when the east or south wind blows.

IX

To whom does God say, "Let there be light"[a] and "Let there be a firmament"?[b]

He was not commanding anyone else to create but summoning things not in existence, his will constituting a command. Scripture says, "God made everything he wished."[c] If, however, he also used speech in the act of creation, it was clearly not for the benefit of the lifeless elements but for the invisible powers, so that they might learn that, at his bidding, the non-existent comes into existence.

X

Why did the historian set down the statement: "God saw that it was good"?[a]

To persuade ungrateful people not to find fault with what God esteems good.[1]

Theodore of Mopsuestia, who might also have disputed the assertion that Gn 1.2 contains a prefiguration of baptism. No extant patristic commentary of this verse makes explicit reference to baptism.

1. Here and later (*e.g.,* Q. 18), Theodoret strangely passes up the opportunity to combat dualistic tendencies by highlighting the biblical author's insistence on the goodness of creation.

XI

||10   Εἰς οὐρανός, ἢ δύο εἰσίν;||

|10a   (1) ΙΤῆς θείας διδασκούσης γραφῆς ὡς *ἐν ἀρχῇ ἐποίησεν ὁ*
Θεὸς τὸν οὐρανὸν καὶ τὴν γῆν[a] εἶτα, μετὰ τὴν τοῦ φωτὸς
δημιουργίαν, ἐν τῇ δευτέρᾳ λεγούσης ἡμέρᾳ τὸ στερέωμα

||3   5 γεγενῆσθαι,|| πολλὴν ἡ ἐρώτησις τῶν πυνθανομένων ἐμφαίνει
τὴν ἄνοιαν. ἔδει γὰρ καὶ ἐκ τοῦ καιροῦ καὶ μέντοι καὶ ἐκ τοῦ
τρόπου τῆς δημιουργίας τὸ διάφορον γνῶναι· ὁ μὲν γὰρ πρὸ
τοῦ φωτός, ὁ δὲ μετὰ τὸ φῶς· καὶ ὁ μὲν οὐκ ἔκ τινος· ὁ δὲ ἐξ
ὑδάτων· *γενηθήτω,* γάρ φησι, *στερέωμα ἐν μέσῳ τοῦ ὕδατος*
10 *καὶ ἔστω διαχωρίζον ἀνὰ μέσον ὕδατος καὶ ὕδατος.*[b] εἶτα
εἰπὼν ὡς ὁ λόγος ἔργον ἐγένετο· τοῦτο γὰρ δηλοῖ τὸ *καὶ*
ἐγένετο οὕτως· διδάσκει καὶ πῶς ἐγένετο· *ἐποίησε,* γάρ
φησιν, *ὁ Θεὸς τὸ στερέωμα, καὶ διεχώρισεν ὁ Θεὸς ἀνὰ μέσον*
τοῦ ὕδατος ὃ ἦν ὑποκάτω τοῦ στερεώματος καὶ ἀνὰ μέσον τοῦ
15 *ὕδατος τοῦ ἐπάνω τοῦ στερεώματος, καὶ ἐκάλεσεν ὁ Θεὸς τὸ*
στερέωμα οὐρανόν.[c]

Ὁ δὲ πρότερος οὐρανὸς οὐκ ἐκλήθη *στερέωμα,* ἀλλ' *οὐρανὸς*
ἐξ ἀρχῆς ὠνομάσθη· οὗτος γὰρ ἐξ αὐτοῦ τοῦ πράγματος τὴν
προσηγορίαν ἐδέξατο. ἐπειδὴ γὰρ ἐκ τῆς ῥοώδους τῶν ὑδάτων
20 οὐσίας συνέστη, καὶ ἡ ῥυτὴ φύσις στεγανωτάτη γέγονε καὶ
στερέμνιος, προσηγορεύθη *στερέωμα.* εἶτα ὡς ἄνωθεν
ἐπικείμενος καὶ τοῦ προτέρου οὐρανοῦ τὴν χρείαν ἡμῖν
πληρῶν, *οὐρανὸς* προσωνομάσθη. διχῇ δὲ διεῖλε τῶν ὑδάτων
|26b   τὴν φύσιν ὁ τῶν ὅλων Θεός, καὶ τὰ μὲν ἄνωθεν Ιἐπιτέθεικε τῷ
25 στερεώματι, τὰ δὲ κάτω καταλέλοιπεν ἵνα τὰ μὲν ἄνωθεν
ἐπικείμενα τῇ τε ὑγρότητι καὶ ψυχρότητι μὴ συγχωρῇ τῷ
πυρὶ τῶν φωστήρων λωβᾶσθαι τὸ στερέωμα, τὰ δὲ κάτω

XI 2a, 5, 14 24, 3(inc.) 8 15, c*p*, 4 7 9 10(+10a) 13 18 20 26b(inc.) [32] 37 = 20 mss.
a. Gn 1.1   b. Gn 1.6   c. Gn 1.7f.

XI

Is there one heaven or two?

(1) Since holy Scripture teaches, "In the beginning God made heaven and earth,"[a] and then says that the firmament was made on the second day after the creation of light, the question betrays the foolishness of those who raise it. After all, from both the time and, indeed, the manner of creation one should grasp the difference. One heaven was created before the light, the other after; one from nothing else, the other from water. Scripture says, "Let a firmament be made in the midst of the water, and let it divide water from water."[b] Then, after saying that the word took effect, which is the meaning of, "And so it was," he conveys also how it came to be: "God made the firmament, and God separated the water that was under the firmament from the water that was above the firmament. And God called the firmament heaven."[c]

Now, from the very beginning, the first heaven was not called "firmament," but "heaven." The second got its name from the act of creation itself. Since it was composed of the fluid substance of the waters, and this liquid nature became quite firm and dense, it was called "firmament." Then, positioned on high, and meeting our need for the first heaven, it was given also the name "heaven." The God of the universe made a twofold division in the nature of the waters: some he placed above the firmament, and some he left below, the purpose being that what was placed above with its moisture and coolness would not permit the firmament to be damaged by the fire of the luminous bodies, while what remained below would sus-

The Questions on Genesis

μεμενηκότα διατρέφῃ τοῖς ἀτμοῖς τὸν ἀέρα διαυαινόμενον καὶ
ξηραινόμενον ὑπὸ τοῦ ἄνωθεν ἐπικειμένου πυρός.

30   (2) Τοιγαροῦν καὶ ὁ τῷ δευτέρῳ διαπιστῶν οὐρανῷ ἔξω
βαίνει τῆς εὐθείας ὁδοῦ, καὶ ὁ πλείους πειρώμενος ἀριθμεῖν
μύθοις ἕπεται, τῆς τοῦ θείου πνεύματος διδασκαλίας
καταφρονῶν. πληθυντικῶς δὲ ἡ θεία γραφὴ τοὺς οὐρανοὺς
ὀνομάζει, λέγουσα οἱ οὐρανοὶ τῶν οὐρανῶν,[d] ἐπειδὴ τῶν
35 ἑβραίων ἡ γλῶττα οὔτε τὸν οὐρανὸν οὔτε τὸ ὕδωρ οἶδεν ἑνικῶς
ὀνομάσαι. εὔροι δ' ἄν τις τοιαῦτα πολλὰ καὶ παρὰ τῇ ἑλλάδι
φωνῇ· Ἀθήναν γὰρ τὴν πόλιν οὐδεὶς ἑνικῶς ὀνομάζει, ἀλλ'
Ἀθήνας πληθυντικῶς, καὶ Δελφῶν πάλιν τὴν πόλιν οὐδεὶς
Δελφόν, ἀλλὰ Δελφοὺς πληθυντικῶς. οὐ τοίνυν ὡς πολλῶν
40 ὄντων οὐρανῶν, οὐρανοὺς οὐρανῶν ἡ θεία εἶπε γραφή, ἀλλὰ τὸ
ἰδίωμα φυλάξασα τῆς ἑβραΐδος φωνῆς, ἐπεὶ ἐν ἑτέρῳ ψαλμῷ
σαφέστερον ἡμᾶς τοῦτο διδάσκουσα καὶ παραλιποῦσα τὸ τῆς
γλώττης ἐκείνης ἰδίωμα, οὕτως ἔφη· ὁ οὐρανὸς τοῦ οὐρανοῦ τῷ
Κυρίῳ,[e] ὡς εἶναι δῆλον ὅτι, καθάπερ οὗτος ὁ οὐρανὸς ἡμῖν
45 ἐστιν ὄροφος, ἡ δὲ γῆ ἔδαφος, οὕτως ὁ ὁρώμενος οὐρανὸς
ὄροφον ἔχει τὸν ὑπερκείμενον οὐρανόν.

XII

Τί δή ποτε μίαν εἰπὼν τὴν τῶν ὑδάτων συναγωγήν, πολλὰς
μετὰ ταῦτα δηλοῖ; συνήχθη, γάρ φησι, τὸ ὕδωρ τὸ ὑποκάτω
τοῦ οὐρανοῦ εἰς τὰς συναγωγὰς αὐτῶν.[a]

Μία μέν ἐστι τῶν ὑδάτων συναγωγή· τὰ πελάγη γὰρ
5 ἀλλήλοις συνήρμοσται· τὰ μὲν κάτωθεν διά τινων ὑπογείων

---

d. Ps 148.4   e. Ps 115.16

XII 2a, 5, 14 24, C, 4 7 9 10a 18 20 26b [32] 37 = 19 mss.
a. Gn 1.9 (LXX)

tain with its mist the air parched and dried by the fire overhead.

(2) Consequently, those who refuse to accept the existence of the second heaven stray from the right path, while those who venture to enumerate more follow mythological fables and spurn the teaching of the Holy Spirit. Now, holy Scripture does speak in the plural of "the heavens": "The heavens of the heavens."[d] This is because the Hebrew language cannot speak in the singular of heaven or water. Greek provides many similar examples: no one calls the city "Athen" in the singular, but "Athens" in the plural; similarly, no one calls the city of the Delphians "Delphos," but "Delphi" in the plural. [1] Not that holy Scripture said "heavens of the heavens" as if there were many; it only observes the idiom of the Hebrew language. It teaches us this more clearly in another psalm, where, laying aside the idiom of that language, it declares: "The heaven of the heaven is the Lord's."[e] Thus we deduce that, just as this heaven is our roof, and the earth our floor, so that higher heaven provides the roof for the heaven we can see. [2]

Why, after mentioning one gathering together of the waters, does he later indicate many by saying, "The water under heaven was gathered together in its gatherings"?[a]

There is one gathering of waters, since the oceans mingle with

---

1. Theodoret had already dealt with this issue in his commentary on Ps 148.4; there, as here, he explains the plural form of the Hebrew term for "heaven" and cites the parallel example of plural forms of Greek place names; *cf.* Chrys., *hom.* 4.3 *in Gen* (on Gn 1.8).

2. Similarly, in his commentary on Ps 113.25 (113.24 LXX = 115.16 MT) Theodoret remarks: "[The Lord] dwells in heaven, not this visible one, but the one above it, which provides the roof for that lower heaven, which provides a roof for us."

πόρων, τὰ δὲ καὶ κατ' αὐτὴν τὴν ἐπιφάνειαν. πληθυντικῶς δὲ
πάλιν τὰς συναγωγὰς ὠνόμασεν, ἐπειδὴ ἄλλο μὲν τὸ Ἰνδικὸν
πέλαγος, ἄλλο δὲ τὸ Ποντικόν, καὶ τὸ Τυρρηνικὸν ἕτερον, καὶ
ἄλλη μὲν ἡ Προποντίς, ἄλλος δὲ ὁ Ἑλλήσποντος, καὶ ὁ
10 Αἰγαῖος ἕτερος, καὶ ἄλλος πάλιν ὁ Ἰώνιος κόλπος. ἔξωθεν δὲ
πάλιν ἐπίκειται τὸ μέγιστον πέλαγος, ὅ τινες μὲν
Ἀτλαντικόν, τινὲς δὲ Ὠκεανόν, ὀνομάζουσι. τούτου χάριν, ὡς
μὲν συνημμένην συναγωγὴν μίαν ὠνόμασεν, ὡς δὲ διῃρημένας,
συναγωγάς.

XIII

Τί δή ποτε τὰς οὐκ ἐδωδίμους βοτάνας βλαστῆσαι
προσέταξεν ὁ Θεός;[a]

Πολλὰ τῶν ἀλόγων ζῴων τὰ γένη· τὰ μὲν *θηρία, τὰ δὲ*
κτήνη προσαγορευόμενα, καὶ τὰ μὲν *ἑρπετά, τὰ δὲ πετεινά.*
5 τούτοις ἅπασι τροφὴν προηυτρέπισεν ὁ Θεὸς καὶ ταῦτα δὲ
τῆς τῶν ἀνθρώπων ἕνεκα πεποίηκε χρείας. αὐτίκα γοῦν καὶ δι'
ἡμᾶς αὐτά φησι διατρέφεσθαι· *τῷ ἐξανατέλλοντι, γάρ φησι,*
χόρτον τοῖς κτήνεσι καὶ χλόην τῇ δουλείᾳ τῶν ἀνθρώπων.[b] τὸ
τοίνυν τούτῳ ἄχρηστον ἐκείνῳ χρήσιμον, καὶ τὰ τοῖς
10 ἀνθρώποις οὐκ ἀναγκαῖα τοῖς δι' αὐτοῦ γεγενημένοις ἁρμόδια.

Πρὸς δὲ τούτοις προορῶν ὁ Θεὸς ὅτι καὶ πάθη
προσγενήσεται τοῖς ἀνθρώποις, ἅτε δὴ διὰ τὴν ἁμαρτίαν
δεξαμένοις τοῦ θανάτου τὸν ὅρον, οὐ μόνον ἐδωδίμους, ἀλλὰ
καὶ ἀλεξικάκους τῶν παθημάτων βοτάνας βλαστῆσαι τῇ γῇ
|30 15 προσέταξε. καὶ τοῦτο μάθοι τις ἂν ἰἀκριβέστερον παρὰ τῶν
τὴν ἰατρικὴν ἠσκημένων τέχνην, ὅτι καὶ τὰ δοκοῦντα εἶναι

XIII 2a, 5, 14 24 30(inc.), C, 4 7 9 10a 18 20 26b [32] 35* 37 = 21 mss.
a. Gn 1.11f. b. Ps 104.14

one another: some below the surface through subterranean channels, and others right on the surface. But he also spoke of "gatherings" in the plural, since the Indian Sea differs from the Black Sea, and the Adriatic. Likewise, the Propontis is different from the Hellespont, which is different from the Aegean, which is different from the Ionian. Furthermore, the largest sea, which some people call the "Atlantic," others the "Ocean," lies on the rim of the world. For this reason, he used the phrase "one gathering" for the connected body, and "gatherings" for the separated bodies.[1]

XIII

Why did God ordain the growth of inedible plants?[1a]

There are many kinds of irrational animals divided into the categories of "wild beasts," "cattle," "the reptiles," and "the birds." God made provision for the nourishment of all of these and created them to meet the needs of human beings. Indeed, Scripture says that they also receive nourishment for our sake: "He makes grass grow for the cattle, and crops for the service of man."[2b] So what is useless to the latter is useful for the former, and what is unnecessary for human beings fits the needs of creatures that were made for their use.

In addition, God foresaw the development of disease in the human race which, as a result of its sins, was to receive the sentence of death. So he ordered the earth to produce not only edible plants but also those that would repel sickness. Those versed in medical science could give you more detailed information about plants that, while

1. Antiochene congregations/readers, with their attention to detail (ἀκρίβεια), require an explanation of such apparent discrepancies. Theodoret, here, as elsewhere (cf. *Qq*. 5, 26 on Jgs), delights in providing geographical information.

___

1. *V. Gn* 1.11f., which do not actually speak of inedible plants.

2. In his comment on Ps 103.14 Theodoret declares: "Cattle also enjoy this providence because of their usefulness to man."

δηλητήρια παθῶν ἐστιν ἰατήρια· κεραννύμενα γὰρ ἑτέραις
βοτάναις, ἀλεξίκακα γίνεται καὶ ὑγείας παρεκτικά.

XIV

Τῶν φωστήρων δημιουργηθέντων, τί γέγονε τὸ πρότερον
φῶς;[a]

Ὁ δεσπότης Θεὸς καὶ ἐκ μὴ ὄντων ποιεῖ καὶ ἐξ ὄντων
δημιουργεῖ· τὸν μὲν γὰρ πρότερον οὐρανὸν ἐκ μὴ ὄντων
||26b   5 ἐδημιούργησε, τὸν|| δὲ δεύτερον ἐξ ὑδάτων ἐποίησεν.[b] οὕτω
τὴν γῆν μὴ οὖσαν παρήγαγεν, τὰ γένη δὲ τῶν δένδρων καὶ
τῶν σπερμάτων αὐτῇ βλαστῆσαι προσέταξεν.[c] καὶ τὸ φῶς
τοίνυν ἐδημιούργησεν ὡς ἠθέλησεν. ὥσπερ δὲ τῷ στερεώματι
διεῖλε τῶν ὑδάτων τὴν φύσιν, καὶ τὰ μὲν ἐπιτέθεικεν ἄνωθεν,
  10 τὰ δὲ κάτω καταλέλοιπεν, οὕτως ἐκεῖνο τὸ φῶς διελὼν ὡς
ἠθέλησεν, τοὺς φωστῆρας τοὺς μεγάλους καὶ τοὺς μικροὺς
κατεσκεύασεν.[d]

XV

Τί ἐστι τὸ *εἰς σημεῖα, καὶ εἰς καιρούς, καὶ εἰς ἐνιαυτούς,
καὶ εἰς ἡμέρας;*[a]

Ὁ ἥλιος, ἀνίσχων μὲν καὶ δυόμενος, τὰς ἡμέρας ποιεῖ, εἰς
δὲ τὰ νότια καὶ τὰ βόρεια μέρη διατρέχων, τὸν ἐνιαύσιον
  5 κύκλον ἀποτελεῖ. οὗτος καὶ τὰς τροπὰς ἐργάζεται, ἃς *καιροὺς*
ὠνόμασεν ἡ θεία γραφή· ἀπὸ γὰρ τοῦ ἰσημερινοῦ τόπου πρὸς
τὰ βόρεια μεταβαίνων, τὸ ἔαρ ποιεῖ· εἶτα ἐκεῖθεν ἐπανιὼν

---

xiv *2a, 5, B, C, 4 7 9 10a 18 20 26b(inc.) [32] 35 37* = 21 mss.
a. Gn 1.3, 14   b. Gn 1.1, 6   c. Gn 1.9–12   d. Gn 1.7, 16

---

xv *2a, 5, B, 3(inc.) 8 15, 50 51(inc.) 52 53, 4 7 9 10a(+10) 13 18 20 [32] 35 37* = 21 mss.
a. Gn 1.14

34

seeming harmful, actually cure disease. When mixed with others, they have curative properties and promote good health.

XIV

What happened to the original light when the lights of heaven were created?[a]

The Lord God creates from what does not yet exist and also fashions from what already exists. He created the first heaven from what did not exist and made the second from the waters.[b] Likewise, he produced the earth when it did not exist and ordered it to grow the different sorts of trees and seeds.[c] And so he created the light as he wished. Then, as he had divided the waters with the firmament and put some above and left others below, he divided that light as he wished in the fashioning of the greater and the lesser lights.[d]

XV

What is the meaning of the verse "For signs, and for times, for years, and for days"?[a]

In its rising and setting the sun makes the days and in covering its course to the south and the north completes the cycle of the year. It also produces the solstices, which holy Scripture calls "times." Crossing from the equator to the north, it causes the spring. Then,

||3 μέχρι τούτων τῶν ὅρων, τὴν θερινὴν‖ κατασκευάζει τροπήν·
προϊόντος δὲ αὐτοῦ ἐντεῦθεν ἐπὶ τὰ νότια, τὸ μετόπωρον
10 γίνεται· ἐπανιὼν δὲ αὖθις, τὸν χειμῶνα ποιεῖ. ἐκ δὲ τοῦ
δρόμου τῆς σελήνης τὸν τῶν μηνῶν μανθάνομεν ἀριθμόν· διὰ
τριάκοντα γὰρ ἡμερῶν, ἐξ ὡρῶν δεουσῶν, τὸν οἰκεῖον δρόμον
||51 πληροῖ. οὐ δὴ χάριν τὸν τῶν τοσούτων ἡμερῶν ἀριθμὸν‖ *μῆνα*
προσαγορεύομεν, ἐπειδὴ καὶ τὴν σελήνην ὀνομάζουσι *μήνην.*
15 Τὸ δὲ *εἰς σημεῖα* οὐ κατὰ τοὺς ἀνοήτους νοοῦμεν ἡμεῖς·
τὴν γὰρ τῆς γενεθλιαλογίας ματαιολογίαν οὐδὲ Πυθαγόρας,
οὐδὲ Σωκράτης, οὐδὲ Πλάτων, οὐδὲ οἱ στωϊκοὶ προσεδέξαντο.
εἰ δὲ οἱ τοῖς μύθοις ἐντεθραμμένοι τοῦδε τοῦ μύθου τὸ
δυσσεβὲς ἐβδελύξαντο, τίς ἂν τοῖς θείοις πιστεύων λόγοις
20 τῶν, οὐ δυσσεβῶν μόνον, ἀλλὰ καὶ λίαν ἀνοήτων ἀνάσχοιτο
λόγων; *σημεῖα* τοίνυν ἡ θεία καλεῖ γραφὴ τὸ εἰδέναι σπόρου
καιρόν, τοῦ φυτεῦσαι, τοῦ καθᾶραι, τοῦ ξύλα τεμεῖν εἰς
ναυπηγίαν καὶ οἰκοδομίαν ἐπιτήδεια. ἐντεῦθεν καὶ οἱ *ναυτιλίᾳ*
||10a |10 χρώμενοι μεμαθήκασι πότε μὲν‖ |ἀπᾶραι πότε δὲ καθορμίσαι
25 προσήκει τὸ σκάφος, καὶ πότε μὲν πετάσαι δεῖ τὸ ἱστίον
πότε δὲ καθελεῖν· ἡ πεῖρα γὰρ αὐτοὺς ἐξεπαίδευσε τὰς τῶν
ἀστέρων ἐπιτολάς τε καὶ δύσεις. πολλάκις δὲ καὶ ἡμεῖς
κομήτην, ἢ πωγωνίτην, ἢ δοκίδην ἰδόντες, ἢ πολεμίων ἔγνωμεν
προσβολήν, ἢ ἀκρίδος ἐμβολήν, ἢ κτηνῶν ἢ ἀνθρώπων φθοράν.
30 ταῦτα τοίνυν *σημεῖα* ἐκάλεσεν, οὐκ ἐκεῖνα τὰ πάσης ἀνοίας
καὶ δυσσεβείας μεστά.

XVI

Τί δή ποτε τὰ μὲν φυτὰ[a] πρὸ τῶν φωστήρων[b] ἐποίησε, τὰ
δὲ ζῷα μετὰ τούτους;[c]

xvi *2a, 5, B, C⁻⁵¹, 4 7 9 10 13 18 20 [32] 35 37* = 20 mss.
a. Gn 1.11f.   b. Gn 1.14f.   c. Gn 1.20–25

proceeding thence to these regions, it produces the summer solstice. Then as it proceeds to the south, autumn begins, and, as it returns to its point of departure, it causes the winter. We learn the number of the months from the course of the moon. It completes its course in twenty-nine days and eighteen hours. Hence, we give the name "month" to this number of days, since the moon is also called μήνη (mene).[1]

In our interpretation of the phrase "for signs," we do not follow the fools, whose idle astrological notions found no acceptance with Pythagoras, Socrates, Plato, or the Stoics. Now, if those raised on mythological fables abhorred this irreligious myth, what believer in the divine word could tolerate ideas that are not only irreligious but downright foolish? "Signs," then, is the term which holy Scripture uses for indications of the time for sowing, planting, winnowing, and cutting down trees for building ships and houses. From these, sailors have learned when to lift and when to cast anchor, when to unfurl and furl the sail, for experience has taught them the risings and settings of the stars. Furthermore, the observance of a comet, shooting star, or meteor has often informed us of an enemy attack, an invasion of locusts, or a plague on cattle or people. So this was the kind of "signs" meant by Scripture, not those figments of rank folly and irreligion.[2]

XVI

Why did God create the plants before,[a] and the animals after,[c] the heavenly lights?[b]

---

1. That is, the moon (σελήνη) is also called μήνη, a word similar in form and sound to μήν, the word for "month."

2. Theodoret recognizes that "signs" is the odd item in the series "signs, seasons, days, and years." His interpretation closely resembles that of von Rad (on

Ὀφθαλμοὺς ἔχει τὰ ζῷα καὶ τοῦ φωτὸς τὴν ὑπερβολὴν οὐκ
ἂν ἤνεγκε. τοῦτο δέ, διανεμηθὲν εἰς τοὺς μικροὺς καὶ
5 μεγάλους φωστῆρας, σύμμετρον τῇ ὄψει τῶν ζῴων ἀφίησιν
αἴγλην. τῶν δὲ φυτῶν ἡ φύσις αἰσθήσεως ἄμοιρος.

XVII

Τίνος χάριν τὰ μὲν φυτὰ οὐκ ηὐλόγησε,[a] τοῖς δὲ ζῴοις ἔφη,
αὐξάνεσθε, καὶ τὰ ἑξῆς;[b]

Τῶν λειμώνων, καὶ τῶν ληΐων, καὶ τῶν παντοδαπῶν βοτανῶν,
καὶ δένδρων, εὐθὺς ἐθελήσας, τὴν γῆν ἐπλήρωσεν ἅπασαν, τὰ
5 δέ γε ἄλογα ζῷα ἀνὰ δύο παρήγαγεν. εἰκότως τοίνυν αὐτοῖς
τὴν εὐλογίαν προσήνεγκεν ἵνα, διὰ τῆς πολυγονίας, τὰ μὲν
πελάγη, καὶ λίμνας, καὶ ποταμούς, τὰ δὲ τὸν ἀέρα, τὰ δὲ
πληρώσῃ τὴν γῆν.

XVIII

Διὰ τί τὰ θηρία καὶ τὰ ἑρπετὰ πεποίηκεν ὁ Θεός;[a]

(1) Δεῖται τὰ παιδία καὶ μορμολυκείων, καὶ ἱμάντων, καὶ
ῥάβδων· καὶ τοῖς μὲν αὐτὰ δεδιττόμεθα, τοῖς δὲ καὶ
παιδεύομεν· ἑκάτερα δὲ δρῶμεν, πᾶσαν αὐτοῖς εὐταξίαν
5 πραγματευόμενοι. ἐπειδὴ τοίνυν προῄδει ἡμᾶς ὁ δεσπότης
Θεὸς εἰς ῥαθυμίαν ἐκκλίνοντας, οἷον ἱμάντας τινὰς καὶ

xvii 2a, 5, B, C⁻⁵¹, 4 7 9 10 13 18 20 [32] 35 37 = 20 mss.

l. 4 καὶ δένδρων 2a, c, 50, 13 [32], Sir. Sch. : καί τε δένδρων F.M. For the
rarity and restricted usage of the collocation καί τε (epicism), v. Denniston,
pp. 529f. The *TLG* cites no other examples of καί τε in the works of Thdt.

a. Gn 1.12   b. Gn 1.22

xviii 2a(inc.), 5, B, c, 50 51(inc.) 52 53, 4 7 9 10 13 18 26b(inc.) [32] 35 37(inc.) = 21
mss.

a. Gn 1.24f.

Animals have eyes and could not have tolerated the excessively bright light. But when this was apportioned among the lesser and the greater lights, it emitted a brightness commensurate with the vision of the animals. Plants, in contrast, have no senses.

XVII

Why did he confer no blessing on the plants[a] yet say to the living beings, "Increase," and so on?[b]

He filled the whole earth with meadows, crops, and all kinds of plants and trees in a single act of will but brought forth the irrational animals in pairs. Accordingly, he bestowed a blessing on them, so that through their numerous offspring some might fill the oceans, lakes, and rivers, others the air, and others the land.

XVIII

Why did God make the wild beasts and the reptiles?[a]

(1) Children require bogey-men, straps, and sticks. We use the former to frighten, the latter to chastise, them, and in each case our goal is to instill orderly behavior. Now, foreseeing our inclination to indifference, the Lord God made provision for wild beasts so he could use them like straps and bogey-men to frighten us, draw us to

---

1.14–19): "'Signs' in Gn 1.14 are perhaps the sights in the heavenly vault which were not normal, as eclipses of the sun; in any case they were fixed astral points for regulating cult and work."

μορμολυκεῖα προκατεσκεύασε τὰ θηρία ἵνα, τούτοις ἡμᾶς
δεδιττόμενος, πρὸς ἑαυτὸν ἕλκῃ καὶ καλεῖν εἰς συμμαχίαν
παρασκευάζῃ. ἀλλ' ὥσπερ οἱ τέλειοι καὶ τῶν μορμολυκείων καὶ
10 ἱμάντων καταφρονοῦσιν, οὕτως οἱ τῆς ἀρετῆς τρόφιμοι τὰς
τῶν θηρίων οὐ δειμαίνουσι προσβολάς. καὶ γὰρ τῷ Ἀδὰμ πρὸ
τῆς ἁμαρτίας παρεστήκει τὰ θηρία, τὴν δουλείαν
ὁμολογοῦντα,[b] καὶ τῷ Νῶε πάλιν εἰς τὴν κιβωτὸν εἰσιόντι
||37   δίκην προβάτων καὶ λέων ἠκο||λούθει, καὶ πάρδαλις, καὶ τῶν
15 ἑρπετῶν τὰ πικρότατα,[c] καὶ τῷ Δανιὴλ παρεστήκεισαν οἱ
λέοντες, ὀρεγόμενοι μὲν τροφῆς, πελάσαι δὲ μὴ τολμῶντες·[d]
τοὺς γὰρ θεοειδεῖς τῆς θείας εἰκόνος ἑώρων ἐν αὐτῷ
χαρακτῆρας. οὕτως ἔχις τῇ τοῦ ἀποστόλου χειρὶ τοὺς ὀδόντας
ἐμβαλοῦσα καὶ τῆς ἁμαρτίας τὸ χαῦνον καὶ χαλαρὸν οὐχ
|51   20 εὑροῦσα, ἀπεπήδησε παραυτίκα καὶ κατὰ τῆς |πυρᾶς ἥλατο
ὥσπερ δίκας ἑαυτὴν εἰσπραττομένη, ὅτι τῷ μηδαμόθεν
προσήκοντι προσέβαλε σώματι.[e] ἡμεῖς δὲ τὰ θηρία δεδοίκαμεν,
ἐπειδὴ τῆς ἀρετῆς τὴν πολιτείαν οὐκ ἔχομεν. καὶ οὕτω δὲ
ῥαθυμούντων κηδόμενος, ὁ Θεὸς τοὺς ἐρημοτέρους ἐκείνοις
25 ἀπεκλήρωσε τόπους καὶ τὸν τῆς νυκτὸς αὐτοῖς καιρὸν
ἀπένειμεν εἰς διατροφήν· *ἐν αὐτῇ,* γάρ φησι, *διελεύσεται*
πάντα τὰ θηρία τοῦ δρυμοῦ·[f] τοῖς ἑρπετοῖς δὲ τοὺς ἐν τῇ γῇ
δέδωκε χηραμοὺς ὅπως, ἐν ἐκείνοις κρυπτόμενα, μὴ λυμαίνωσι
τῶν ἀνθρώπων τὸ γένος. ἵνα δὲ μή, παντάπασιν ἀλώβητοι
30 διαμένοντες, καταφρονῶμεν αὐτῶν ὡς βλάπτειν ἥκιστα
δυναμένων, ἔστιν ὅτε συγχωρεῖ δύο τινὰς ἢ τρεῖς ἐκ πολλῶν
μυριάδων ὁ σοφῶς τὰ καθ' ἡμᾶς πρυτανεύων ἢ ὑπὸ σκορπίων
κεντεῖσθαι ἢ ὑπὸ ὄφεων δάκνεσθαι ἵν' ἡμεῖς, ὡς δεδιότες μή
τι παραπλήσιον πάθοιμεν, εἰς ἐπικουρίαν καλῶμεν τὸν
35 πεποιηκότα Θεὸν καὶ ὑπὸ τῆς παναλκοῦς ἐκείνης προμηθείας
φρουρεῖσθαι παρακαλῶμεν. ἄλλως τε οὐδὲ ἐν τοῖς ἄλλοις ἡμῖν
ἄχρηστα τὰ θηρία· πολλὰ γὰρ καὶ ἐκ τούτων ἀλεξίκακα ἰατρῶν
παῖδες κατασκευάζουσι φάρμακα.

b. Gn 2.19f.   c. Gn 7.14–16   d. Dn 6.22   e. Acts 28.3–5   f. Ps 104.20

himself, and cause us to invoke his assistance.[1] But as adults feel scorn for bogey-men and straps, so Virtue's pupils have no fear of attack by wild beasts. Indeed, in acknowledgment of their subservient state, the wild animals waited on Adam before his sin.[b] Likewise, when Noah was boarding the ark, the lion, the leopard, and the most vicious of the reptiles followed him like sheep.[c] Lions attended on Daniel; though lunging for food, they dared not get too close,[d] since they recognized in him the godly stamp of the divine image. Though a viper fixed its fangs in the apostle's hand, not finding the loose and spongy consistency of sin, it immediately leapt away and threw itself into the fire as though punishing itself for assaulting a body it had no right to attack.[e] In contrast, our fear of the wild beasts is due to our failure to live virtuous lives. In his care for indifferent people, God set the wild beasts in deserted places and allotted them the night for foraging. Scripture says, "At night all the wild beasts of the forest will travel about."[f] He gave the reptiles hollows so they would hide away and not harm the human race. But to prevent us from going on free from injury and coming to scorn the creeping things as though they had no power to cause harm, every once in a while God, in his wise governance of our affairs, allows two or three people out of countless thousands to be stung by scorpions or bitten by snakes so we will dread suffering something similar, call on God the Creator for assistance, and entreat the protection of his all-powerful providence. Furthermore, the wild beasts are very useful in other ways as well, for they are the source of materials which the medical profession uses to prepare many a remedy against disease.[2]

---

1. Chrysostom's comment on Gn 1.24f. (*hom. 7.5 in Gen.*) confirms that the creation of wild animals and reptiles seemed to some to provide grounds for questioning God's goodness.

2. Chrysostom (*ib.*) had also made this point.

(2) Μηδεὶς τοίνυν, αὐτὸ καθ' ἑαυτὸ τὸ θηρίον ἐξετάζων,
40 ἐπιμεμφέσθω τῷ ποιητῇ ἀλλὰ τὴν χρείαν ἐπιζητείτω. ἐπεὶ καὶ
τὸ σῶμα τὸ ἀνθρώπινον πολλὴν ἔχει καὶ ὥραν, καὶ ἁρμονίαν,
καὶ τῶν μορίων τὴν χρείαν· ἀλλ' ἔχει καὶ κόρυζαν, καὶ
πτύελον, καὶ δυσώδη κόπρον ἐκκρινομένην. ἀλλ' οὐδεὶς εὖ
φρονῶν ἀπὸ τούτων διαβάλλει τὸ ζῷον· δίχα γὰρ τούτων
45 βιῶναι τῶν ἀδυνάτων. διὰ γὰρ τούτων ἀρδευόμενον τέθηλεν·
χρῄζει γὰρ καὶ φλέγματος, καὶ αἵματος, καὶ χολῆς ἑκατέρας.
ἀλλ' ὥσπερ διὰ τούτων συνέστηκεν, οὕτως καὶ διὰ τούτων
διόλλυται· ἑνὸς γὰρ τῶν εἰρημένων ἢ πλεονασμὸς ἢ ἔνδεια
διαλύει τὸ ζῷον. οὕτω πάλιν εἴ τις μίαν τῶν δακτύλων ἐκτέμῃ
50 σκυταλίδα, ὄψεται παντελῶς αὐτὴν ἄχρηστον, ἀλλὰ συνημμένη
‖26b πλείστην παρέχει τῷ‖ σώματι χρείαν.

Οὕτω τοίνυν καὶ ἡμᾶς προσήκει ποιεῖν, μὴ αὐτὸ καθ' ἑαυτὸ
ἕκαστον μέρος ἐξετάζειν τῆς κτίσεως, ἀλλὰ ζητεῖν εἰ τῷ
παντὶ χρήσιμον. ἐπεὶ καὶ τὸ πῦρ καυστικόν ἐστι καί, οὐ
55 μόνον σώματα διαφθείρει, ἀλλὰ καὶ οἴκους ἐμπίπρησι, καὶ
πλοῖα, καὶ λήϊα· ἀλλ' ὅμως ἕν ἐστι τῶν τεσσάρων στοιχείων
δι' ὧν τὰ πάντα συνήρμοσται, καὶ δίχα τούτου τὴν θνητὴν
φύσιν διαβιῶναι τῶν ἀδυνάτων. καὶ ὕδωρ ὡσαύτως ἐπικλύζει
τὴν γῆν, οἰκίας καταλύει, παμπόλλους τῶν ναυτιλλομένων
60 διόλλυσι, λυμαίνεται δὲ καὶ τοὺς ἀκαίρως καὶ ἀμέτρως πίνειν
ἀνεχομένους. ἀλλ' οὐδείς, μὴ κομιδῇ παραπαίων, ὀλέθριον τὸ
ὕδωρ ὠνόμασε· τοῦτο γὰρ καὶ τὴν γῆν ἄρδει καὶ τὰ φυτὰ
τρέφει, καὶ τὰ ἄλογα ζῷα, καὶ τῶν ἀνθρώπων τὴν φύσιν. οὕτω
τοίνυν καὶ τῶν ἄλλων ἕκαστον ἐξετάζομεν, μὴ αὐτὸ καθ' ἑαυτὸ
65 βασανίζοντες εἴ τε λυμαντικόν ἐστιν εἴ τε ὠφέλιμον, ἀλλ' εἰ
τῷ κοινῷ συντελεῖ τινα χρείαν.

Καὶ θηρία γὰρ αἰδεῖται μὲν τὸν ἄνθρωπον διὰ τὴν ἐξ ἀρχῆς
‖2a δοθεῖσαν αὐτῷ κατ' αὐτῶν ἐξουσίαν· ὡς παραβε‖βηκότος δὲ
τὸν θεῖον νόμον ἔστιν ὅτε καταφρονεῖ. καὶ γὰρ οἱ πονηροὶ
70 δοῦλοι διαπτύειν εἰώθασι τοὺς ἰθύνειν αὐτοὺς παρὰ τῶν

l. 53 ἐξετάζειν 2a, B⁻¹⁴, 50 53, 7 9 10 35, Sir. : ἐξετάζει Sch. F.M.

(2) So then, let no one find fault with its maker when examining a given wild beast in itself; instead, he should consider what use it might serve. Indeed, the human body, though possessing limbs endowed with great beauty, coördination, and utility, also has mucous, spittle, and malodorous excrement. But no one in his right mind criticizes the animal on this basis. Life would be impossible without these fluids, and by these the body is watered and flourishes, requiring, as it does, gall, blood, and both kinds of bile. As it needs these to grow, it is through them that it also deteriorates; excess or deficiency in any one of the aforementioned causes the dissolution of the living creature. Similarly, if you were to cut off a single joint of your fingers, you would find it completely useless, but when left in place, it does the body great service.

This is how we should judge: not focusing on each item of creation in isolation, but examining its usefulness to the whole. Fire, for example, can scorch, not only destroying bodies but also burning houses, ships, and crops, yet it is one of the four basic elements of which everything is composed, and mortal nature cannot survive without it. Similarly, water inundates the land, destroys houses, and is responsible for the death of great numbers of sailors. It also harms people who drink it at the wrong time or in excessive quantities, but no one who was not entirely mad ever categorized water as deadly. It irrigates the land and nourishes plants, brute beasts, and human beings. So, this is how we examine each of the other creatures; we do not look at it in isolation to see whether it is harmful or beneficial but consider whether it contributes somehow to the common good.

Indeed, even wild animals respect man because of the authority he was given over them at the beginning, though they occasionally scorn him for breaking God's law. It is a general rule that wicked slaves despise the supervisors to whom their masters have subjected

δεσποτῶν κεκελευσμένους ὅταν ἴδωσι διὰ πλημμελήματα
παρρησίας ἐστερημένους.

XIX

Τίνι ὁ Θεὸς εἴρηκε, *ποιήσωμεν ἄνθρωπον κατ' εἰκόνα
ἡμετέραν καὶ καθ' ὁμοίωσιν;*[a]

(1) Τινὲς μὲν τῶν δυσωνύμων αἱρετικῶν πρὸς τοὺς ἀγγέλους
|37 αὐτὸν εἰρηκέναι Ι καὶ τοὺς πονηροὺς δαίμονας ἔφασαν, οὐ
5 συνιέντες οἱ ἐμβρόντητοι τὸ *κατ' εἰκόνα ἡμετέραν.* Θεοῦ δέ,
καὶ ἀγγέλων, καὶ δαιμόνων οὔτε ἡ οὐσία οὔτε εἰκὼν ἡ αὐτή· ὁ
μὲν γὰρ ἀΐδιον ἔχει τὴν φύσιν, οἱ δὲ αὐτὸν ἔχουσι ποιητὴν
καὶ δημιουργόν, παρ' αὐτοῦ δεδεγμένοι τὸ εἶναι. οἱ δὲ
δαίμονες καὶ εἰς πονηρίαν ἑκόντες ἐτράπησαν· ἀνοίας τοίνυν
||5 10 ἐσχάτης τὸ μίαν ὑπο ΙΙλαβεῖν εἰκόνα τῶν πονηρῶν δαιμόνων καὶ
τοῦ πελάγους τῆς ἀγαθότητος.

Ἰουδαῖοι δὲ εἰς ἑτέραν ἐξώκειλαν παραφροσύνην· φασὶ
γὰρ πρὸς ἑαυτὸν εἰρηκέναι τὸν τῶν ὅλων Θεὸν τὸ
ποιήσωμεν ἄνθρωπον κατά τινα μίμησιν τῶν τὰς μεγάλας
15 πεπιστευμένων ἀρχάς. καὶ γὰρ ὕπαρχοι καὶ στρατηγοὶ
πληθυντικῶς εἰώθασι λέγειν τὸ *κελεύομεν,* καὶ *γράφομεν,* καὶ
προστάττομεν, καὶ ὅσα τοιαῦτα. καὶ οὐ συνεῖδον οἱ
παραπλῆγες ὡς ἑνικῶς τὰ πλεῖστα ὁ τῶν ὅλων λέγει Θεός·
καιρός, γάρ φησι, *παντὸς ἀνθρώπου ἥκει ἐναντίον μου,*[b] καί,
20 *ἐνεθυμήθην ὅτι ἐποίησα τὸν ἄνθρωπον,*[c] καί, *ἀπαλείψω τὸν
ἄνθρωπον,*[d] καί, *οὐκ ἔσονταί σοι θεοὶ ἕτεροι πλὴν ἐμοῦ,*[e] καί,
ἰδοὺ ἐγὼ ποιῶ καινὰ ἃ νῦν ἀνατέλλει,[f] καί, *ἀνοίξω ἐπὶ τῶν
ὀρέων πηγὰς καὶ ἐπὶ τῶν βουνῶν ποταμούς,*[g] καὶ ἐν πάσῃ δέ,
ὡς ἐπίπαν, τῇ θείᾳ γραφῇ ἑνικῶς ἔστιν ἀκοῦσαι τοῦ τῶν ὅλων

XIX 5(*inc.*), 12, B, C, 4 7 9 10 13 18 19* 20 [32] 35 37(*inc.*) = 22 mss.

a. Gn 1.26   b. Gn 6.13 (LXX)   c. Gn 6.6   d. Gn 6.7   e. Ex 20.3
f. Is 43.19   g. Is 41.18 (LXX var.)

them whenever they realize that, because of their failings, their supervisors can no longer exercise a free hand.

XIX

To whom did God say, "Let us make the human being in our image and likeness"?[a]

(1) Some ill-omened heretics have claimed that he was speaking to the angels and the wicked demons, but these madmen failed to understand the phrase "in our image."[1] God, the angels, and the demons do not share the same essence or image. His nature is eternal, whereas the others receive their existence from him, their Maker and Creator. The demons are those who, of their own accord, turned to evil. So, it is the height of folly to suppose that the wicked demons and the ocean of goodness have one and the same image.

Now, the Jews rushed headlong into a different delusion. They claim that, in imitation of those entrusted with important responsibilities, the God of the universe addresses himself in "Let us make the human being." After all, it is conventional for governors and generals to use the plural: "We order," "we write," "we command," and so forth.[2] Crazed, as they are, the Jews do not understand that the God of the universe generally speaks in the singular: "The time for all has come before my sight";[b] "I am angry that I created man";[c] "I shall blot out man";[d] "You shall have no other gods beside me";[e] "Lo, I am doing new things that are already taking effect";[f] and "I shall make springs gush forth on the mountains, and rivers on the hills."[g] In

1. Theodoret may be referring to the Gnostics who attributed the creation of the visible world to a subordinate power, the demiurge; *cf.* Iren., *Haer.* 1.5.2–5.6.

2. The first person plural verb form presents a *crux interpretum*. Seeing a reference to the Trinity, Theodoret rejects the Jewish notion of a simple royal plural. In contrast, Speiser, regarding (on 1.26) the question as "one of grammar alone, without a direct bearing on the meaning," takes the plural as due to the form of the

25 διαλεγομένου Θεοῦ. ὀλιγάκις δὲ πληθυντικῶς τὴν διάλεξιν
σχηματίζει, τῶν τῆς τριάδος προσώπων ἐμφαίνων τὸν ἀριθμόν·
καὶ γὰρ ἡνίκα τὰς γλώσσας συνέχεεν οὐχ ἑνικῶς εἶπε,
καταβήσομαι καὶ συγχεῶ τὰς γλώσσας, ἀλλὰ
δεῦτε, ... καταβάντες συγχέωμεν ... αὐτῶν τὰς γλώσσας.[h]

30 (2) Καὶ ἐνταῦθα τοίνυν, ἐπειδὴ τὸ λογικὸν διέπλαττε ζῷον,
ὃ μετὰ πολλὰς ἀνακαινίζειν ἤμελλε γενεάς, ταῖς τῆς ἁγίας
τριάδος ἐπικλήσεσι τελεσιουργῶν τὸ πανάγιον βάπτισμα,
μέλλων δημιουργεῖν τὴν ἐκεῖνα παραληψομένην τὰ μυστήρια
φύσιν, αἰνιγματωδῶς καὶ τὸ ταὐτὸν τῆς οὐσίας καὶ τὸν τῶν
35 προσώπων παρεδήλωσεν ἀριθμόν. τῷ φάναι μὲν γάρ, *εἶπεν ὁ*
Θεός, τὸ κοινὸν τῆς θείας δεδήλωκε φύσεως· ἐπαγαγὼν δὲ τὸ
ποιήσωμεν, ἐνέφηνε τῶν προσώπων τὸν ἀριθμόν. οὕτω πάλιν
ἑνικῶς μὲν εἰπών, *τὴν εἰκόνα*, τὸ ταὐτὸν τῆς φύσεως ἔδειξεν·
οὐ γὰρ εἶπε, κατ' εἰκόνας, ἀλλὰ *κατ' εἰκόνα*· ἡμετέραν δὲ
40 εἰρηκώς, τὸν τῶν ὑποστάσεων δεδήλωκεν ἀριθμόν. ἅπαντα γὰρ
προορῶν ὁ τῶν ὅλων Θεὸς ὡς ἤδη γεγενημένα τὰ μήπω
γενόμενα καὶ προθεωρῶν τὴν τοῦ μονογενοῦς σάρκωσίν, τε καὶ
ἐνανθρώπησιν, καὶ ὡς ταύτην τὴν φύσιν ἐκ παρθένου λήψεται,
καὶ οὕτως ἑαυτῷ συνάψει, τε καὶ ἑνώσει ὡς ἓν πρόσωπον Θεοῦ
45 τε καὶ ἀνθρώπου νοεῖσθαι, καὶ μίαν αὐτῷ προσκύνησιν παρὰ
τῆς κτίσεως ἁπάσης προσφέρεσθαι, μάλα εἰκότως καὶ αὐτὴν
τοῦ γένους τὴν κρηπῖδα τιμῆς μεγίστης ἠξίωσε. καὶ πρῶτον
βουλὴν τῆς δημιουργίας προτάξας ἵνα τοῦ δημιουργουμένου τὸ
λογικὸν προσημάνῃ, εἶτα τῶν προσώπων παραδηλώσας τὸν
50 ἀριθμὸν ἵνα τοὺς ὕμνους ὁ μέλλων προσφέρειν ἐπὶ τῆς γῆς
λάβῃ θεολογίας αἰνίγματα, καὶ οἱονεὶ αὐτουργὸς τῆς

l. 25 διαλεγομένου *24, 9 35, Sir. Sch.* : διαλεγόμενον *[32]* :
διαλεγουμένου *F.M.* While the *TLG* lists 167 attestations for διαλεγομ- and
προσδιαλεγομ- in other passages of the works of Theodoret, it offers only
three for the stem in -γουμ- for the entirety of Greek literature. In the *Quaest.*
in oct. alone there are seven other uses of the stem in -γομ- for none of which
does F.M. record a variant in -γουμ-. *Cf.* διαλεγόμενος in *Q.* 20 (l. 4, p. 24 of
the Madrid ed.).

h. Gn 11.7

short, throughout the whole of holy Scripture, one can hear God speaking in the singular. But in a few cases, he uses plural forms to bring out the distinction of number of the persons of the Trinity. When he confused the languages, he did not say in the singular, "I shall go down and confuse the languages," but "Come, let us go down and confuse their languages."[h]

(2) Here too, then, as he was forming the rational being, whom he would renew many generations later through the institution of most holy baptism with the invocation of the Holy Trinity—when he was on the point of creating the nature that would inherit that sacrament—he gave a riddling indication of both the identity of substance and the numerical distinction of persons. With "God said," he indicated the divine nature held in common, and adding, "Let us make," he revealed the numerical distinction of persons. Likewise, by saying "image" in the singular, he brought out the identity of nature. He did not say "images," but "image." Yet, when he said "our" he indicated the numerical distinction of the hypostases. Foreseeing what is not yet as already in existence and discerning in advance the enfleshment and Incarnation of the Only-begotten, his taking human nature from a virgin and joining and uniting it to himself, so that one person, both God and man would be acknowledged, to whom one adoration would be offered by all creation, it was entirely reasonable for the God of the universe to deem the foundation of the race worthy of the highest honor. First, taking previous counsel about his creation so as to signal in advance the rational character of the creature, then indicating the numerical distinction of the persons, so that he who was to offer hymns of praise on earth might grasp clues to the true doctrine of God, and then becoming, as it were, himself the very artisan of this moulding, he dis-

----

subject, God ('elohim). Unlike Speiser and like Theodoret, von Rad regards (on 1.26–28) the form as theologically meaningful, but his interpretation is closest to the first that Theodoret rejects: "The extraordinary . . . prevents one from referring God's image too directly to God the Lord. God includes himself among the heavenly beings and thereby conceals himself in this multiplicity."

διαπλάσεως γενόμενος, ἔδειξε τὴν πλείονα περὶ τόδε τὸ
πλάσμα φιλοστοργίαν. τοῦτο καὶ Ἰὼβ ὁ γενναῖος πρὸς αὐτὸν
βοᾷ, λέγων, *αἱ χεῖρές σου ἐποίησάν με καὶ ἔπλασάν με*·[i]
55 τούτοις ἐχρήσατο τοῖς λόγοις καὶ ὁ θεῖος Δαβίδ·[j] τοῦτο καὶ ὁ
τοῦ ἁγίου βαπτίσματος ἀξιούμενος γινώσκει σαφῶς, ὡς ὁ
πλάσας διέσωσε, καὶ ὁ σώσας διέπλασε· πρὸς δὲ τούτοις, καὶ
αὐτὸς ὁ δημιουργὸς καὶ διὰ Ἰερεμίου καὶ διὰ Ἡσαΐου φησίν
ὅτι, *ἡμεῖς ... πηλός, αὐτὸς δὲ πλάστης ἡμῶν.*[k] ἀλλ' οὔτε χεῖρας
60 ἔχειν τὸ θεῖον οὔτε δεῖσθαι βουλῆς τινος καὶ προθεωρίας
φαμὲν ἵνα, κατὰ τοὺς Πλάτωνος μύθους, πρὸς τὴν τῆς
ἐνθυμήσεως ἰδέαν κατασκευάσῃ τὸ ποίημα.[l] ἀλλὰ τούτων
ἕκαστον τὴν πλείονα τοῦ Θεοῦ περὶ τόδε τὸ ζῷον κηδεμονίαν
δηλοῖ.

XX

Τί ἐστι τὸ *κατ' εἰκόνα;*[a]

(1) Τινὲς τὸ ἀόρατον τῆς ψυχῆς *εἰκόνα Θεοῦ* κεκλήκασιν.
ἀλλ' οὐκ ἀληθῶς εἰρήκασιν· εἰ γὰρ εἰκὼν τοῦ Θεοῦ τῆς ψυχῆς
τὸ ἀόρατον, μᾶλλον ἂν εἰκόνες τοῦ Θεοῦ κληθεῖεν ἄγγελοι,
5 καὶ ἀρχάγγελοι, καὶ πᾶσαι αἱ ἀσώματοι καὶ ἅγιαι φύσεις, ἅτε
δὴ παντάπασι σωμάτων ἀπηλλαγμέναι καὶ ἀμιγὲς τὸ ἀόρατον
ἔχουσαι.

Τινὲς δὲ ὑπὸ πολλῆς εὐηθείας τὸ σῶμα τὸ ἀνθρώπινον *κατ'
εἰκόνα Θεοῦ* γεγενῆσθαί φασιν, ἐπειδὴ τῆς θείας λεγούσης
10 ἐπακούουσι γραφῆς, *ἄνοιξον ... τοὺς ὀφθαλμούς σου καὶ ἴδε*·

---

i. Jb 10.8   j. Ps 119.73   k. Is 64.8 (LXX var.)   l. Pl., *Ti.* 28a–29b

---

XX 5(*inc.*), 12, B, c, 50* 51 52 53, 4 7 9 10 13 19 20 [32] 35 37 = 21 mss.

ll. 5f ἅτε δὴ 12, 53, 4 19, *Sir.* : ἅτε δὲ *Sch. F.M.* In the *Quaest. in oct.* there
are fourteen more examples of ἅτε δὴ, but (with the exception of the apparent
misprint at l. 13, p. 279 of the Madrid ed.) no other example of ἅτε δὲ.
a. Gn 1.26f.

played his extraordinary affection for what he had formed. The noble Job cried to him in a loud voice, "Your hands made me and formed me."[i] And the divinely inspired David used the very same words,[j] and all who are accorded holy baptism know clearly that he who formed saved, and he who saved formed. In addition, the Creator himself declared through both Jeremiah and Isaiah, "We are clay, and he our potter."[k] Yet, we declare that the divinity had no hands nor any need of counsel or foresight in order, as Plato's stories would have it, to make his artifact match the plan of his design.[l] Instead, each of these details illustrates God's extraordinary care for this being.

XX

What is the meaning of "in the image"?[1a]

(1) Some commentators have referred the phrase "the image of God" to the invisibility of the soul;[2] but they are mistaken. If the invisibility of the soul constituted God's image, angels and archangels, along with all the incorporeal and holy natures, would with greater reason be called God's images. After all, they are completely free of bodies and possess an invisibility that is quite uncompromised.

Other superficial commentators claim that the human body was made in God's image, since they hear holy Scripture saying, "Open

1. In this question Theodoret painstakingly assembles a broad range of views from many predecessors. The phrase "in the image and likeness" continues to pose a challenge for modern commentators. For an interpretation based on materials discovered at the site of ancient Ebla (Tell Mardikh) in NW Syria in the mid-twentieth century, *v.* M. Dahood, "Ebla, Ugarit and the Old Testament" and *cf.* note 5 below.

2. As Guinot points out (p. 751), the first interpretation is that of the Alexandrian tradition generally; *v.* Or., *hom.* 1.13 *in Gen.* and Didym., *in Gen.* 57.

καί, κλῖνον ... τὸ οὖς σου καὶ ἄκουσον·ᵇ καί, ὠσφράνθη Κύριος
... ὀσμὴν εὐωδίας·ᶜ καί, τὸ ... στόμα Κυρίου ἐλάλησε ταῦταᵈ
καί, ἐν τῇ χειρὶ αὐτοῦ τὰ πέρατα τῆς γῆς,ᵉ καὶ ὅσα τοιαῦτα,
καὶ οὐ συνεῖδον οἱ ἄγαν ἠλίθιοι ὡς ἀνθρώποις δι' ἀνθρώπων
15 διαλεγόμενος, ὁ δεσπότης Θεὸς τῇ τῶν ἀκουόντων ἀσθενείᾳ
τοὺς λόγους μετρεῖ καί, ἐπειδὴ δι' ὀφθαλμῶν ὁρῶμεν ἡμεῖς,
τὴν ὀπτικὴν αὐτοῦ δύναμιν ὀφθαλμοὺς ὀνομάζει, καὶ αὖ πάλιν
τὴν ἀκουστικὴν ὦτα, ἐπειδὴ διὰ τούτων τῶν μορίων ἀκούομεν,
καὶ τὸ πρόσταγμα στόμα. ἔδει δὲ αὐτούς, μὴ τούτων μόνον
20 ἀκούειν τῶν λόγων, ἀλλὰ καὶ τῶν τὸ ἀπερίγραφον τοῦ Θεοῦ
διδασκόντων· ποῦ, γάρ φησι, πορευθῶ ἀπὸ τοῦ πνεύματός σου
καὶ ἀπὸ τοῦ προσώπου σου ποῦ φύγω; ἐὰν ἀναβῶ εἰς τὸν
οὐρανόν, σὺ ἐκεῖ εἶ· ἐὰν καταβῶ εἰς τὸν ᾅδην, πάρει, καὶ τὰ
ἑξῆς·ᶠ καὶ τῇ σαμαρείτιδι ὁ Κύριος ἔφη, πνεῦμα ὁ Θεός, καὶ
25 τοὺς προσκυνοῦντας αὐτὸν ἐν πνεύματι καὶ ἀληθείᾳ δεῖ
προσκυνεῖν.ᵍ εἰ δὲ πνεῦμα ὁ Θεός, ἁπλοῦς ἄρα, καὶ ἀσύνθετος,
καὶ ἀσχημάτιστος. ἀλλὰ γὰρ περιττὸν τοῦτον μηκύνειν τὸν
λόγον· δήλη γὰρ τούτων ἡ ἄνοια.

(2) Τὸ τοίνυν ποιήσωμεν ἄνθρωπον κατ' εἰκόνα ἡμετέραν
30 καὶ καθ' ὁμοίωσινʰ τινὲς τῶν διδασκάλων οὕτως ἐνόησαν· ὅτι
τὴν κτίσιν τὴν αἰσθητήν τε καὶ νοητὴν πεποιηκώς, ὁ τῶν
ὅλων Θεὸς τὸν ἄνθρωπον διέπλασεν ἔσχατον, οἷόν τινα εἰκόνα
ἑαυτοῦ ἐν μέσῳ τεθεικὼς τῶν ἀψύχων τε καὶ ἐμψύχων καὶ
αἰσθητῶν καὶ νοητῶν ἵνα τὰ μὲν ἄψυχά τε καὶ ἔμψυχα τούτῳ
35 προσφέρῃ, ὥσπερ τινὰ φόρον, τὴν χρείαν, αἱ δὲ νοηταὶ φύσεις
ἐν τῇ περὶ τοῦτον κηδεμονίᾳ τὴν περὶ τὸν πεποιηκότα
δεικνύωσιν εὔνοιαν. τοῦτο γὰρ καὶ ὁ θεῖος ἀπόστολος ἔφη·
οὐχὶ πάντες εἰσὶ λειτουργικὰ πνεύματα, εἰς διακονίαν
ἀποστελλόμενα διὰ τοὺς μέλλοντας κληρονομεῖν σωτηρίαν;ⁱ καὶ
40 ὁ Κύριος ἐν τοῖς εὐαγγελίοις, ὁρᾶτε μὴ καταφρονήσητε ἑνὸς
τῶν μικρῶν τούτων τῶν ἐλαχίστων· ἀμὴν γὰρ λέγω ὑμῖν ὅτι οἱ

---

b. 2Kgs 19.16   c. Gn 8.21   d. Is 1.20   e. Ps 95.4   f. Ps 139.7f.
g. Jn 4.24   h. Gn 1.26   i. Heb 1.14

your eyes and see, incline your ears and hear";[b] "The Lord smelt a sweet fragrance";[c] "The mouth of the Lord said this";[d] "In his hands are the ends of the earth,"[e] and similar statements. These simpletons fail to understand that the Lord God, when speaking to humans through humans, adjusts his language to the limitations of the listeners. Since we see with our eyes, he refers to his power of vision as "eyes." He refers to his power of hearing as "ears," since it is through these organs that we hear, and to his command as a "mouth."[3] But they should have paid attention not only to these words but also to those that teach of God's uncircumscribed nature: "Where am I to go from your Spirit, and where am I to flee from your face? If I ascend to heaven, you are there; if I descend to Hell, you are present" and so on.[f] Furthermore, the Lord said to the Samaritan woman, "God is spirit, and those who worship him must worship in spirit and in truth."[g] Now, if God is spirit, surely he is simple, without composition, and beyond representation. There is no point, however, in prolonging this argument, for their folly is obvious.

(2) Some commentators understand the verse, "Let us make the human being in our image and likeness,"[h] in the following manner: after completing the material and spiritual creation, the God of the universe formed man last and set him like an image of himself in the midst of the inanimate and the animate, the material and the spiritual, so that the inanimate and the animate might offer him their service as a kind of tribute, and the spiritual beings, by caring for him, might manifest their love for the Creator.[4] In fact, the holy apostle says, "Are they not all ministering spirits sent on a mission of service for the sake of those who are due to inherit salvation?"[i] And

3. The citations support the second interpretation, which as Guinot remarks (p. 751) was opposed by all Christian exegetes, Antiochene (*v.* Chrys. *hom.* 7.3f *in Gen.*) as well as Alexandrian (Or., *hom.* 1.13 *in Gen.* and Didym., *in Gen.* 56). It can be refuted, Theodoret proceeds to say, by a simple acknowledgment of the principle of συγκατάβασις, *i.e.,* God's gracious condescension to the limits of human understanding and language.

4. For the third interpretation, Guinot refers (p. 753) to Gr. Nyss., *Hom. opif.* 16.

ἄγγελοι αὐτῶν ... καθ' ἡμέραν ὁρῶσι τὸ πρόσωπον τοῦ πατρός
μου τοῦ ἐν οὐρανοῖς.[j]

Τινὲς δὲ κατ' εἰκόνα Θεοῦ κατὰ τὸ ἀρχικὸν γεγενῆσθαι τὸν
45 ἄνθρωπον ἔφασαν, τεκμηρίῳ κεχρημένοι σαφεστάτῳ τῷ τὸν
ποιητὴν ἐπαγαγεῖν, καὶ ἀρχέτωσαν τῶν ἰχθύων τῆς θαλάσσης,
καὶ τῶν πετεινῶν τοῦ οὐρανοῦ, καὶ τῶν κτηνῶν, καὶ πάσης τῆς
γῆς, καὶ πάντων τῶν ἑρπετῶν, τῶν ἑρπόντων ἐπὶ τῆς γῆς·[k]
ὥσπερ γὰρ αὐτὸς τῶν ὅλων ἔχει τὴν δεσποτείαν, οὕτω δέδωκε
50 τῷ ἀνθρώπῳ τῶν ἀλόγων ζῴων τὴν ἐξουσίαν.
Ἔστι δὲ καὶ ἄλλα εὑρεῖν ὡς ἀρχετύπου μιμήματα.
δημιουργεῖ γὰρ καὶ ἄνθρωπος κατὰ μίμησιν τοῦ πεποιηκότος
Θεοῦ καὶ οἰκίας, καὶ τείχη, καὶ πόλεις, καὶ λιμένας, καὶ ναῦς,
καὶ νεώρια, καὶ ἅρματα, καὶ ἕτερα μυρία οἷον οὐρανοῦ
55 ἐκτυπώματα καὶ ἡλίου, καὶ σελήνης, καὶ ἀστέρων ἰνδάλματα,
|5 Ικαὶ ἀνθρώπων καὶ ζῴων ἀλόγων εἰκόνας. ἀλλ' ἄπειρον τὸ τῆς
δημιουργίας διάφορον. ὁ μὲν γὰρ τῶν ὅλων Θεὸς καὶ ἐξ ὄντων
καὶ ἐκ μὴ ὄντων δημιουργεῖ καὶ δίχα πόνου καὶ χρόνου· ἅμα
γὰρ τῷ βουληθῆναι παράγει τὸ δόξαν. ἄνθρωπος δὲ δεῖται μὲν
60 ὕλης, δεῖται δὲ καὶ ὀργάνων, καὶ βουλῆς, καὶ ἐνθυμήσεων, καὶ
χρόνου, καὶ πόνου, καὶ τεχνῶν ἑτέρων εἰς τὴν τοῦ γενομένου
κατασκευήν· ὁ γὰρ οἰκοδόμος δεῖται χαλκέως, καὶ ὁ χαλκεὺς
μεταλλέως καὶ ἀνθρακέως, καὶ πάντες ὁμοῦ τῶν ὑλοτόμων, καὶ
οἱ ὑλοτόμοι τῶν φυτουργῶν τε καὶ γεωργῶν, καὶ οὕτως ἑκάστη
65 τέχνη παρὰ τῶν ἄλλων τεχνῶν τὴν οἰκείαν ἐρανίζεται χρείαν.
ἀλλὰ καὶ οὕτω δημιουργῶν, ὁ ἄνθρωπος μιμεῖται ἀμῇ γέ πη
τὸν ποιητὴν ὡς εἰκὼν τὸ ἀρχέτυπον. καὶ γὰρ ἡ εἰκὼν ἔχει τὰ
τοῦ ἀρχετύπου ἰνδάλματα, ἀλλὰ τὸ μὲν τῶν μορίων εἶδος ἔχει,
τὰς δὲ ἐνεργείας οὐκ ἔχει· ἐστέρηται γὰρ ψυχῆς, δι' ἧς
70 κινεῖται τὸ σῶμα.

j. Mt 18.10 (NT var.)   k. Gn 1.26

the Lord in the sacred Gospels warns, "Be careful not to despise one of the least of these little ones. Amen, I say to you, their angels day in and day out gaze on the face of my Father in heaven."[j]

Other commentators have claimed that humanity was made "in God's image" in the sense that it possesses the ability to rule. Their clearest proof text is the command subsequent to the act of creation: "and let them rule over the fish of the sea, the birds of heaven, the cattle, the whole earth, and all the reptiles crawling on the earth."[k] God, who enjoys lordship of all things, gave the human being authority over all irrational beings.[5]

In addition, one can discover other ways in which man imitates his archetype.[6] In imitation of the Creator, man also creates houses, walls, cities, harbors, ships, dockyards, chariots, and countless other things, including likenesses of heaven, representations of the sun, moon, and stars, and images of people and brute beasts. Nonetheless, the difference in creating is infinite. The God of the universe creates from both the existent and the non-existent, and, without effort or lapse of time, puts his intention into effect as soon he wills it. But a human being who sets out to make an object requires material, as well as tools, planning, consideration, time, effort, and the assistance of other trades. The builder requires a bronze smith, and the bronze smith a metallurgist and a charcoal maker, and all of these require woodcutters, while woodcutters require planters and farmers; every trade borrows what it needs from the others. Yet creating even in this fashion, the human being to some extent imitates the Creator as an image its archetype; the image has the external appearance of its archetype, but not its capacity for action, since it lacks the soul, which moves the body.

---

5. The fourth interpretation had been previously suggested by Didymus (*in Gen.* 57), Diodore (Deconinck, frag. 9), and Chrysostom (*hom.* 8.4, 9.2–5, 21.2, 23.5 *in Gen.*), but it is likely that Theodoret derived it from Diodore alone; *cf.* Guinot, p. 753. The Ebla tablets (*cf.* note 1 above) lend support to the notion of the human being acting as a deputy deity, for the word *dimutu,* occurring in their lists of deities, is akin to the Hebrew demuth = "likeness." Of course, Theodoret would not have known of this etymology.

6. For the next four suggestions regarding the meaning of "image," the human

Οὕτω πάλιν καὶ βασιλεύει ὁ ἄνθρωπος καὶ κρίνει κατὰ
μίμησιν τοῦ τῶν ὅλων Θεοῦ. ἀλλ' ὁ μὲν Θεὸς οὐ κατηγόρων, οὐ
μαρτύρων δεῖται δικάζων· οὕτω γὰρ καὶ τὸν Κάϊν κατέκρινεν
ὡς αὐτόπτης τοῦ μύσους γεγενημένος·[l] ὁ δὲ ἄνθρωπος κρίνων
75 καὶ μαρτύρων δεῖται καὶ κατηγόρων· ἀγνοεῖ γὰρ τὰ
γεγενημένα.

Οὕτω καὶ *Θεὸς* ὁ ἄνθρωπος ὠνομάσθη, ἐπειδὴ *εἰκὼν*
προσηγορεύθη *Θεοῦ· ἀνὴρ* ...*γάρ φησιν, οὐκ ὀφείλει*
κατακαλύπτεσθαι τὴν κεφαλήν, εἰκὼν καὶ δόξα Θεοῦ
80 *ὑπάρχων.*[m] ἀλλὰ πάλιν ὁ μὲν τῶν ὅλων Θεὸς φύσιν ἔχει θείαν,
οὐ προσηγορίαν ψιλήν· ὁ δὲ ἄνθρωπος, ὡς εἰκών, τοὔνομα ἔχει
μόνον, ἐστερημένος τοῦ πράγματος.

(3) Οὕτω τὸ ἀπερίγραφον ἀληθῶς μὲν καὶ κυρίως ἐστὶ τοῦ
τῶν ὅλων Θεοῦ· μιμεῖται δὲ οὕτω πως αὐτὸ καὶ ὁ νοῦς ὁ
85 ἀνθρώπινος. ἐν ἀκαρεῖ γὰρ περινοστεῖ καὶ τὰ ἑῷα, καὶ τὰ
ἑσπέρια, καὶ τὰ βόρεια, καὶ τὰ νότια, καὶ τὰ ἐπουράνια, καὶ
τὰ ὑποχθόνια, ἀλλ' οὐ τῇ οὐσίᾳ, μόνῃ δὲ τῇ τοῦ λογισμοῦ
φαντασίᾳ. ὁ δέ γε Θεὸς καὶ τῇ οὐσίᾳ, καὶ τῇ σοφίᾳ, καὶ τῇ
δυνάμει τὸ ἀπερίγραφον ἔχει.

90 Εὕροι δ' ἄν τις καὶ ἑτέραν μίμησιν ἀκριβεστέραν ἐν τῇ τοῦ
ἀνθρώπου πάλιν ψυχῇ. ἔχει γὰρ αὐτὴ καὶ τὸ λογικὸν καὶ τὸ
ζωτικὸν ἐν ἑαυτῇ, καὶ γεννᾷ μὲν ὁ νοῦς τὸν λόγον,
συμπρόεισι δὲ τῷ λόγῳ πνεῦμα, οὐ γεννώμενον καθάπερ ὁ
λόγος, συμπαρομαρτοῦν δὲ ἀεὶ τῷ λόγῳ, καὶ συμπροϊὸν
95 γεννωμένῳ. ἀλλὰ ταῦτα ὡς εἰκόνι πρόσεστι τῷ ἀνθρώπῳ, οὗ δὴ
χάριν καὶ ἀνυπόστατος ὁ λόγος ἐστὶ καὶ τὸ πνεῦμα. ἐπὶ δὲ
τῆς ἁγίας τριάδος τρεῖς νοοῦμεν τὰς ὑποστάσεις καὶ
ἀσυγχύτως ἡνωμένας καὶ καθ' ἑαυτὰς ὑφεστώσας. γεγέννηται
μὲν γὰρ πρὸ τῶν αἰώνων ἐκ τοῦ πατρὸς ὁ Θεὸς λόγος·
100 ἀχώριστος δέ ἐστι τοῦ γεννήσαντος· καὶ ἐκπορεύεται ἐκ τοῦ
Θεοῦ καὶ πατρὸς τὸ πανάγιον πνεῦμα, νοεῖται δὲ καὶ ἐν ἰδίᾳ

l. Gn 4.10   m. 1Cor 11.7

Likewise, humans reign and judge in imitation of the God of the universe. Yet, in judging, God has no need of witnesses for prosecution or defense, for it was as an eyewitness to the abominable crime that he condemned Cain.[1] In contrast, given his ignorance of the facts, when man sits in judgment, he needs witnesses for defense and prosecution.

Again, man has been called "God" inasmuch as he has been styled "image of God." Scripture declares, "A male does not need to cover his head, since he is the image and glory of God;"[m] but the God of the universe has the nature, not merely the title of divinity, while man, as an image, possesses only the name and lacks the reality.[7]

(3) Similarly, the property of being uncircumscribed belongs really and truly to the God of the universe, though the human mind imitates this to some extent. In a moment it surveys east and west, north and south, high and low—but not in actual presence, only through its mental powers of imagination. God, on the other hand, is uncircumscribed in his being, his wisdom, and his power.

Now, one might discover a further, more precise, resemblance in the human soul. This is both rational and vital. The mind begets the word, and with the word proceeds a breath, not begotten like the word, but always accompanying the word and proceeding with it when the word is begotten. But this is characteristic of the human being as a mere image. Hence, the word is without substance, as is the breath. In the Holy Trinity, by contrast, we understand three substances, united without confusion, and subsisting of themselves. God the Word has been begotten of the Father before the ages but is inseparable from the one who begat him, and the most Holy Spirit proceeds from the God and Father, and is also understood as an in-

----

being as builder, as judge, as possessor of wide-ranging vision, and as rational and vital being, Theodoret follows Theodore of Mopsuestia (Devreesse, *Essai*, pp. 13–15).

7. Like all writers of ancient Greek, Theodoret often uses the nouns "man" = "human being" (ἄνθρωπος) and "man" = "male" (ἀνήρ) interchangeably. None-

ὑποστάσει· πάντα, γάρ φησι, … ἐνεργεῖ τὸ ἓν καὶ τὸ αὐτὸ
πνεῦμα διαιροῦν ἰδίᾳ ἑκάστῳ καθὼς βούλεται.ⁿ ἀλλὰ περὶ
τούτου μηκύνειν τὸν λόγον οὐ δεῖ· μυρίας γὰρ ἔστιν εὑρεῖν
105 ἀποδείξεις τούτου παρὰ τῇ θείᾳ γραφῇ.

XXI

Τί δή ποτε διαφερόντως τὴν ἑβδόμην ἡμέραν εὐλόγησεν ὁ
Θεός;ᵃ

Ἑκάστη τῶν ἄλλων ἡμερῶν ἰδίαν τινὰ δημιουργίαν ἐδέξατο·
ἐπειδὴ τοίνυν μέχρι ταύτης σύμπασαν τὴν κτίσιν
5 ἐδημιούργησε, δέδωκεν, ἀντὶ δημιουργίας, τῇ ἑβδόμῃ ἡμέρᾳ
τὴν εὐλογίαν ἵνα μὴ μόνη παρὰ τὰς ἄλλας ἀγέραστος
διαμείνῃ. τὸ μέντοι *ἡγίασεν αὐτὴν* ἀντὶ τοῦ *ἀφώρισεν*
τέθεικε. πολλαχοῦ γὰρ οὕτω τοῦτο νοούμενον ἔστιν εὑρεῖν
παρὰ τῇ θείᾳ γραφῇ· καὶ γὰρ περὶ τῶν μήδων φησίν,
10 *ἡγιασμένοι εἰσί, καὶ ἐγὼ ἄγω αὐτούς,*ᵇ τουτέστιν, εἰς τοῦτο
ἀφωρισμένοι. ἄλλως τε καὶ ἰουδαίοις ταῦτα συγγράφων,
ἀναγκαίως τὸ *ἡγίασεν αὐτὴν* τέθεικεν ἵνα πλεῖον σέβας
ἀπονείμωσι τῷ σαββάτῳ· τοῦτο γὰρ καὶ νομοθετῶν ἔφη· ὅτι
ἐν … ἓξ ἡμέραις ἐποίησε Κύριος ὁ Θεός σου τὸν οὐρανὸν καὶ
15 *τὴν γῆν·*ᶜ *τῇ δὲ ἑβδόμῃ ἡμέρᾳ κατέπαυσεν ἀπὸ πάντων τῶν*
*ἔργων αὐτοῦ, ὧν ἐποίησεν … καὶ ἡγίασεν αὐτήν.*ᵈ

n. 1Cor 12.11

XXI 5, 12, B, C, 4 7 9 10 19 20 [32] 35 37 = 20 mss.

a. Gn 2.3   b. Is 13.3 (LXX var.)   c. Ex 20.11 (LXX var.)   d. Gn 2.2f.

dividual substance: "The one and same Spirit activates everything and allots to each one individually as he wishes."[8n] There is no need, however, to go on at length; one can find innumerable proofs of this doctrine in holy Scripture.

XXI

Why did God give the seventh day a special blessing?[a]

Each of the other days received its own act of creation. Therefore, since by this time he had finished making the whole of creation, he assigned the seventh day the blessing in place of an act of creation, so that it would have no less honor than the other days. He used the phrase "hallowed it" in the sense of "set it apart," a sense you can often find in holy Scripture. For example, it says of the Medes, "They are hallowed, and I lead them";[b] that is, "they are set aside for this purpose." As Moses was writing for the Jews, he made the essential addition, "He hallowed it," so they would accord the Sabbath a greater reverence. As you will recall, in his legislation for the Sabbath he declared, "In six days the Lord your God made heaven and earth,[c] but on the seventh day he rested from all the labors of his works and hallowed it."[1d]

----

theless, *v.* his comment on Ps 1.1 where he assures any women among his readers that the initial blessing of the "happy man" (μακάριος ἀνήρ) should not be understood as excluding women from the attainment of virtue.

8. In this comparison between the human production of word and breath and the begetting of "God the Word" by the Father and the procession of the Spirit from the Father alone, Theodoret applies to Trinitarian relationships terms that had been sanctioned at Chalcedon to describe the subsistence in the one person of Christ of both the divine and human natures: *cf.* his ἐπὶ δὲ τῆς ἁγίας τριάδος τρεῖς νοοῦμεν τὰς ὑποστάσεις, καὶ ἀσυγχύτως ἡνωμένας καὶ καθ' ἑαυτὰς ὑφεστώσας. γεγέννηται μὲν γὰρ πρὸ τῶν αἰώνων ἐκ τοῦ πατρὸς ὁ Θεὸς λόγος· ἀχώριστος δέ ἐστι τοῦ γεννήσαντος with the Chalcedonian ἕνα καὶ τὸν αὐτὸν [ὁμολογοῦμεν] Υἱόν, Κύριον μονογενῆ, ἐν δύο φύσεσιν ἀσυγχύτως, ἀτρέπτως, ἀδιαιρέτως, ἀχωρίστως γνωριζόμενον; *v.* T.H. Bindley and F.W. Green, p. 193.

1. Relating the seventh day to the previous six, Theodoret offers an accurate

XXII

Τί ἐστι πηγὴ δὲ ἀνέβαινεν ἐκ τῆς γῆς καὶ ἐπότιζε πᾶν τὸ πρόσωπον τῆς γῆς;[a]

Ἐν κεφαλαίῳ πάλιν ὁ συγγραφεὺς τὰ περὶ τῆς κτίσεως διηγήσατο καὶ ἐδίδαξεν ὅτι μὴ ὄντα τὰ στοιχεῖα παρήγαγεν ὁ
5 Θεός, καὶ ὅτι ταῦτα ἀπ' ἀλλήλων διεχώρισε, καὶ ὅτι ἕκαστον τούτων διεκόσμησεν ὡς ἠθέλησε, καὶ ὅτι, μήτε τοῦ ἀνθρώπου γεωργοῦντος τὴν γῆν, μήτε τῶν νεφῶν τὸν ὑετὸν ὠδινόντων, βεβλάστηκεν ὡς ὁ δημιουργήσας ἠθέλησεν, ἀρδείαν ἔχουσα τὴν μετὰ τὸν χωρισμὸν τῶν ὑδάτων ἐναπομείνασαν αὐτῇ
10 νοτίδα τε καὶ ἰκμάδα.[b] οὕτω γὰρ καὶ Ἀκύλας ἡρμήνευσε· καὶ ἐπιβλυσμὸς ἀνέβη ἐκ τῆς γῆς καὶ ἐπότισε πᾶν τὸ πρόσωπον τῆς χθονός.

XXIII

Εἰ ἐκ τοῦ θείου ἐμφυσήματος γέγονεν ἡ ψυχή,[a] ἐκ τῆς οὐσίας ἄρα τοῦ Θεοῦ ἐστιν ἡ ψυχή;

Ἀσεβείας ἐσχάτης καὶ βλασφημίας ἡ τοιαύτη ἔννοια· τῆς γὰρ δημιουργίας τὴν εὐκολίαν ἔδειξε διὰ τοῦτο ἡ θεία γραφή.
5 πρὸς δὲ τούτῳ καὶ τῆς ψυχῆς τὴν φύσιν αἰνίττεται· ὅτι πνεῦμά ἐστιν κτιστόν, ἀόρατόν τε καὶ νοερόν, τῆς τῶν σωμάτων ἀπηλλαγμένον παχύτητος. κἀκεῖνο δὲ χρὴ συνιδεῖν· ὅτι δεῖ πρότερον νοῆσαι πνεύμονα, καὶ τοὺς ἀποθλίβοντας τοῦτον μῦς καὶ συστέλλοντας, καὶ τὴν συμπεφυκυῖαν ἀρτηρίαν

XXII 5, 12, B, C, 4 7 9 10 19 20 [32] 35 37 = 20 mss.

a. Gn 2.6   b. Gn 2.4–6

XXIII 5, 12, B, C, 4 7 9 10 13 19 20 [32] 35 37 = 21 mss.

a. Gn 2.7

XXII

What is the meaning of "But a spring rose from the earth and watered all the face of the earth"?[a]

The historian has related the story of creation once again, this time in summary fashion, and taught that God produced the previously non-existent elements, that he separated them from one another, that he arrayed each of them as he wished, and that the earth produced plants in accordance with the will of the Creator, for it drew irrigation from the moisture and humidity left over from the division of the waters.[b] Aquila, in fact, gave this rendering: "A gushing water rose from the earth and watered the whole face of the land."[1]

XXIII

If the soul is derived from the breath of God,[a] must it not be a part of God's being?

Such an idea is a piece of the worst irreligion and blasphemy. Holy Scripture used this expression to bring out the ease of the creation. Moreover, it darkly suggests the nature of the soul: that it is a created spirit, invisible and spiritual, free of the materiality of bodies. You should also understand that this idea would require us first to imagine lungs, muscles to squeeze and contract them, a windpipe attached to the lungs, a palate, and last of all a mouth to breathe in

1. Chrysostom, emphasizing the dependence of life on God's command rather than on natural causes, had commented (*hom.* 12.2 *in Gen.*) on the apparent anomaly of crops growing without sun, rain, or human cultivation. He had accounted for the insertion of this second account of creation by explaining that the Spirit deliberately chose to emphasize important facts already mentioned in ch. 1 in order to forestall the later development of heresy; *v.* note 55 to the "Introduction to Theodoret' s Life and Works."

τῷ πνεύμονι, καὶ ὑπερῴαν, καὶ στόμα εἶθ' οὕτως δέξασθαι τὸ
ἐμφύσημα. εἰ δὲ τὸ θεῖον ἀσώματον, θεοπρεπῶς ἄρα καὶ τὸ
ἐμφύσημα νοητέον.

XXIV

Τί δή ποτε τὸν παράδεισον ἐφύτευσεν ὁ Θεός, μέλλων
εὐθὺς τὸν Ἀδὰμ διὰ τὴν ἁμαρτίαν ἐξορίζειν ἐκεῖθεν;[a]

Πρῶτον οὐκ ἀνέχεται ἐκ προγνώσεως κατακρῖναι ὁ
δεσπότης Θεός· διό, καὶ τὴν παράβασιν προορῶν, τῶν ἀγαθῶν
5 αὐτῷ μεταδέδωκεν. ἔπειτα καὶ γνῶναι αὐτὸν τὰς θείας δωρεὰς
ἠβουλήθη ἵνα, τούτων στερηθείς, μισήσῃ τὴν ἁμαρτίαν, ὡς
τοσούτων αὐτὸν γυμνώσασαν ἀγαθῶν. πρὸς δὲ τούτοις, ἔδει
τὸν δίκαιον ἀγωνοθέτην τοῖς τῆς ἀρετῆς ἀθληταῖς προθεῖναι
τῆς νίκης τὰ ἆθλα· οὗ δὴ χάριν καὶ περὶ τῆς τῶν οὐρανῶν
10 βασιλείας ἔφη, *δεῦτε, οἱ εὐλογημένοι τοῦ πατρός μου,*
κληρονομήσατε τὴν ἡτοιμασμένην ὑμῖν βασιλείαν ἀπὸ
καταβολῆς κόσμου.[b]

XXV

Τινὲς ἐν οὐρανῷ φασι τὸν παράδεισον εἶναι.

Τῆς θείας λεγούσης γραφῆς, *ἐξανέτειλεν ἔτι ὁ Θεὸς ἐκ τῆς*
γῆς πᾶν ξύλον ὡραῖον εἰς ὅρασιν καὶ καλὸν εἰς βρῶσιν,[a]
τολμηρὸν ἄγαν τὸ τοῖς οἰκείοις ἀκολουθεῖν λογισμοῖς
5 καταλιπόντας τὴν διδασκαλίαν τοῦ πνεύματος.

---

xxiv 5, 12, B, C, 4 7 9 10 13 19 20 [32] 35 37 = 21 mss.

a. Gn 2.8; 3.23   b. Mt 25.34

---

xxv 5, 12, B, C, 4 7 9 10 13 19 20 [32] 35 37 = 21 mss.

a. Gn 2.9

air.[1] But, if the divinity is incorporeal, surely his breath should also be thought of in a manner befitting God.

XXIV

Why did God plant the Garden of Paradise from which he would soon exclude Adam as a result of his sin?[a]

First, the Lord God does not countenance condemnation on the basis of foreknowledge. Hence, though foreknowing the fall, he made him share in his blessings. Next, his intention was that Adam should experience the divine gifts, so that, when deprived of them, he would hate sin for stripping him of such wonderful blessings. Also, the Righteous Arbiter had to set the prize of victory before the athletes of virtue. Thus, he said of the Kingdom of Heaven, "Come, you that are blessed by my Father, inherit the kingdom prepared for you from the foundation of the world."[1b]

XXV

Some commentators locate Paradise in heaven.

Since holy Scripture says, "God caused to grow up from the ground every tree that is beautiful to behold and good to eat,"[a] it is quite rash to abandon the teaching of the Spirit and follow one's own reasoning.[1]

---

1. Theodoret evinces an interest in anatomy also in his comment on the term "crop" = "gullet" in *Q.* 1.4 on Lv (on 1.17).

---

1. Theodoret presents the fall in largely positive terms; *v.* sec. 9 of the "Introduction to Theodoret's Life and Works."

---

1. Theodoret concisely disposes of the Alexandrian view (*v.* Or., *Sel. in Gen.* 29

XXVI

Τὸ ξύλον τῆς ζωῆς . . . καὶ τὸ ξύλον τοῦ εἰδέναι γνωστὸν
καλοῦ καὶ πονηροῦ[a] *νοητὰ χρὴ λέγειν ἢ αἰσθητά;*

Ἐκ τῆς γῆς βεβλαστηκέναι καὶ ταῦτα εἶπεν ἡ θεία γραφή·
οὐ τοίνυν ἑτέραν τινὰ φύσιν ἔχει παρὰ τὰ ἄλλα φυτά. ὥσπερ
5 γὰρ τὸ τοῦ σταυροῦ ξύλον *ξύλον ἐστὶ καὶ σωτήριον*
ὀνομάζεται διὰ τὴν ἐκ τῆς περὶ αὐτὸ πίστεως σωτηρίαν
προσγινομένην, οὕτω καὶ ταῦτα φυτὰ μέν ἐστιν ἐκ τῆς γῆς
βεβλαστηκότα, διὰ δὲ τὸν θεῖον ὅρον θάτερον αὐτῶν *ξύλον*
ζωῆς ὠνομάσθη, τὸ δὲ ἕτερον, διὰ τὸ περὶ αὐτὸ γενέσθαι τῆς
10 ἁμαρτίας τὴν αἴσθησιν, *ξύλον* ἐκλήθη *γνωστὸν καλοῦ καὶ*
πονηροῦ. καὶ περὶ τοῦτο μὲν ὁ ἀγὼν τῷ Ἀδὰμ προετέθη, τὸ δὲ
τῆς ζωῆς οἷόν τι ἔπαθλον προύκειτο τετηρηκότι τὴν ἐντολήν.
οὕτω καὶ οἱ πατριάρχαι καὶ χωρίοις καὶ φρέασι τὰς ἐπωνυμίας
ἐπέθηκαν. καὶ τὸ μὲν ἐκάλεσαν *φρέαρ ὁράσεως,*[b] οὐκ ἐπειδὴ
15 ὁρατικὴν δύναμιν ἐχαρίζετο, ἀλλ' ἐπειδὴ ὤφθη παρ' αὐτῷ τῶν
ὅλων ὁ Κύριος· καὶ *φρέαρ εὐρυχωρίας,*[c] ἐπειδή, περὶ τῶν ἄλλων
φρεάτων πολλάκις οἱ ἀπὸ Γεράρων διαμαχεσάμενοι, οὐκ
ἠνώχλησαν τοῖς τοῦτο κατεσκευακόσι τὸ φρέαρ· οὕτω *φρέαρ*
ὅρκου[d] διὰ τὸ παρ' αὐτῷ γεγενῆσθαι τοὺς ὅρκους. οὕτως ἡ
20 Λουζὰ *Βαιθὴλ* ὠνομάσθη, τουτέστιν *οἶκος Θεοῦ,*[e] ἐπειδὴ ὤφθη
τῷ Ἰακὼβ ἐν ἐκείνῳ γε τῷ χωρίῳ τῶν ὅλων ὁ ποιητής· καὶ
βουνὸς μάρτυς,[f] οὐκ ἐπειδὴ ἔμψυχος ἦν ὁ βουνός, ἀλλ' ὅτι ἐν
ἐκείνῳ τῷ χωρίῳ πρὸς ἀλλήλους ἐπεποίηντο τὰς συνθήκας.
οὕτως *ὕδωρ ζῶν*[g] καλεῖται τὸ βάπτισμα, οὐκ ἐπειδὴ φύσιν
25 ἑτέραν ἔχει τὸ τοῦ βαπτίσματος ὕδωρ, ἀλλ' ὅτι δι' ἐκείνου

---

xxvi 5, 12, B, C, 4 7 9 10 13 19 20 [32] 35 37 = 21 mss.

a. Gn 2.9   b. Gn 16.14   c. Gn 26.22   d. Gn 21.14, 31   e. Gn 28.19
f. Gn 31.47   g. Jn 4.10

XXVI

Should the tree of life and the tree of the knowledge of good and evil[a] be taken as spiritual or material?

According to holy Scripture, they also sprouted from the ground, so they had a nature no different from that of other plants. Just as the tree of the cross was a tree and is called "saving" because salvation is accomplished by faith in it, so these trees were products of the soil. By divine decree the one was called the "tree of life," the other, since the perception of sin occurred in connection with it, "the tree of the knowledge of good and evil."[1] Adam was set a trial with regard to the latter, whereas the tree of life was proposed as his prize for keeping the commandment. Similarly, the patriarchs bestowed names on places and wells. They called one "well of vision,"[b] not because it granted the faculty of sight, but because the Lord of the universe was seen near it, and another "well of broad places,"[c] because the people of Gerar, who had often fought over the other wells, did not interfere with those digging this one. Likewise, there was a "well of the oath"[d] because people used to swear oaths nearby. And the name "Bethel" or "House of God" was given to Luz,[e] because that was where the Creator of the universe appeared to Jacob. There was a "hill of witness,"[f] not that the hill was alive, but because that was where they made treaties with one another. Likewise baptism is called "living water,"[g] not because the water of baptism has a different nature, but because, through that water, divine grace con-

----
and Didym., *in Gen.* 107; *cf.* Guinot p. 754). Perhaps he was aware that Chrysostom had already condemned (*hom.* 13.3 *in Gen.*) this position as a product of philosophical arrogance. In his commentary on Genesis (*fragg. in Gen.* 2.8) Theodore of Mopsuestia had emphasised the physical reality of Paradise by discussing its location within the larger geographical unit of Eden, and in his comment on Gal 4.24 he had criticized those who, giving an allegorical interpretation of the garden, denied the historicity of the account of the Fall.

----

1. Theodoret evinces a balanced Antiochene recognition of levels of meaning:

τοῦ ὕδατος ἡ θεία χάρις τὴν αἰώνιον δωρεῖται ζωήν. οὕτω
ξύλον ζωῆς διὰ τὸν θεῖον ὅρον ἐκλήθη, καὶ ξύλον γνώσεως, διὰ
τὴν περὶ τοῦτο γεγενημένην αἴσθησιν τῆς ἁμαρτίας. οὐδέπω
γὰρ πεῖραν εἰληφότες τῆς ἁμαρτίας, εἶτα, τοῦ ἀπειρημένου
30 μετειληχότες καρποῦ, ὡς παραβεβηκότες τὴν ἐντολήν, τὰς
τοῦ συνειδότος ἀκίδας ἐδέξαντο.

XXVII

Οὐκοῦν εἶχον τὴν γνῶσιν τοῦ ἀγαθοῦ καὶ τοῦ κακοῦ πρὸ
τῆς τοῦ ἀπειρημένου καρποῦ μεταλήψεως;
Καὶ πῶς οἷόν τε ἦν τοὺς λόγῳ τετιμημένους καὶ κατ'
εἰκόνα θείαν γεγενημένους οὐκ ἔχειν διάκρισιν ἀγαθοῦ καὶ
5 κακοῦ; πῶς δ' ἂν αὐτοῖς ἐτεθείκει νόμον τῆς δικαιοσύνης ἡ
ἄβυσσος, ταύτην οὐκ ἔχουσιν ἐν τῇ φύσει τὴν γνῶσιν, μηδὲ
γινώσκουσιν ὡς ἀγαθὸν μὲν τὸ φυλάξαι τὴν ἐντολήν, ὀλέθριον
δὲ τὸ παραβῆναι; εἶχον οὖν ἄρα τὴν γνῶσιν· τὴν δὲ πεῖραν
προσέλαβον ὕστερον.

XXVIII

Πῶς οὖν μετὰ τὴν βρῶσιν ἔγνωσαν ὅτι γυμνοὶ ἦσαν; πρὸ
γὰρ τῆς βρώσεως ταύτην οὐκ εἶχον τὴν αἴσθησιν.[a]
Οὐδὲ τὰ κομιδῇ νέα παιδία ἐρυθριᾶν πέφυκε τῆς ἐσθῆτος
γεγυμνωμένα. κατὰ βραχὺ δέ, τοῦ σώματος αὐξανομένου, καὶ
5 τοῦ νοῦ λοιπὸν ἀρχομένου τὴν οἰκείαν φύσιν ἐπιδεικνύναι,
οὐκέτι λοιπὸν φορητὴ τοῖς μειρακίοις ἡ γύμνωσις, ἀλλ'

---

xxvii 5, 12, B, C, 4 7 9 10 13 19 20 [32] 35 37 = 21 mss.

xxviii 5, 12, B, C, 4 7 9 10 13 19 20 [32] 35 37 = 21 mss.
a. Gn 3.7

fers the gift of eternal life. Thus, the "tree of life" received its name from the divine decree and the "tree of knowledge" from the sense of sin gained in connection with it. To that point, they had no experience of sin, but afterwards, when they had partaken of the forbidden fruit, they suffered the pangs of conscience for breaking the commandment.

XXVII

So they did possess the knowledge of good and evil before partaking of the forbidden fruit?

How could those endowed with reason and made in the divine image be unable to distinguish good and evil? How could the Depths of Righteousness impose a law on those who were naturally unprovided with this knowledge and unaware that it was good to keep the commandment and fatal to break it? So it follows that they had the knowledge, and what they gained later was experience.[1]

XXVIII

So how was it that, after eating, they knew they were naked? After all, they had no such knowledge before eating.[a]

Nor do infants possess any natural shame of their nakedness. Soon, however, as the body develops, and the mind begins to reveal its natural properties, youngsters can no longer tolerate nakedness.

---

the trees are real trees, but they signify something further. Not surprisingly, the bishop illustrates his exegesis with a sacramental analogy: the water of baptism, though real water, has become as well the vehicle of salvation; *v.* sec. 8 of the "Introduction to Theodoret' s Life and Works."

1. Chrysostom had responded (*hom.* 16.6 *in Gen.*) equally vigorously—and at characteristically greater length—to this questioning of divine justice.

ἐρυθριῶσι καὶ περιβάλλονται, κἄν τις ἀφέληται τὴν ἐσθῆτα,
ταῖς χερσὶ τὰ παιδογόνα καλύπτουσι μόρια. πολλῶν δὲ καὶ τὸ
ἔθος ἀφαιρεῖται ταύτην τὴν αἰσχύνην. καὶ γὰρ οἱ ναῦται,
10 γυμνοὶ πλέοντες, καὶ οἱ λουόμενοι, γυμνοὶ ὑπ' ἀλλήλων
ὁρώμενοι, ταύτην ἐνταῦθα τὴν αἰσχύνην οὐκ ἔχουσιν· ἐὰν δέ
τις ἔξω τῶν βαλανείων γυμνὸς ᾖ, λίαν ἐρυθριᾷ. οὕτω καὶ οἱ
περὶ τὸν Ἀδάμ, εὐθὺς μὲν διαπλασθέντες, οἷα δὴ νήπιοι, καὶ
εὐθυγενεῖς, καὶ τῆς ἁμαρτίας ἀμύητοι, οὐκ ᾐσχύνοντο δίχα
15 περιβολαίων διάγοντες· μετὰ δὲ τὴν πεῖραν, τοῖς φύλλοις ἔνια
τοῦ σώματος συνεκάλυψαν μόρια.

XXIX

Πῶς ἐκ τοῦ παραδείσου φησὶν ὁ Μωϋσῆς τὸν Τίγρητα
ἐξιέναι καὶ τὸν Εὐφράτην, οὓς φασί τινες ἐκ τῶν ὀρῶν
ἀναβλύζειν τῆς Ἀρμενίας;[a]

Ἔστιν ἰδεῖν καὶ ἄλλους ποταμοὺς ἑτέρωθεν μὲν ἐξιόντας,
5 ἔπειτα δὲ εἰς τὴν γῆν διά τινων καταδύσεων χωροῦντας, καὶ
πάλιν ἄνωθεν ἀναβλύζοντας. τοῦτο καὶ ἐπὶ τούτων γεγένηται
τῶν ποταμῶν· ἐξίασι μὲν γὰρ ἐκεῖθεν ὥς φησιν ἡ θεία γραφή,
εἶτα, διά τινων ὑπογείων διιόντες πόρων, ἑτέρας ἀρχὰς
ἐνταῦθα λαμβάνουσι.

10 Τοῦτο δὲ οὐ μάτην οὕτως ᾠκονόμησεν ὁ τῶν ὅλων Θεός,
ἀλλὰ τὴν περιττὴν τῶν ἀνθρώπων πολυπραγμοσύνην ἐκκόπτων·
εἰ γὰρ δῆλος ἦν αὐτῶν ἅπας ὁ πόρος, ἐπειράθησαν μὲν ἄν
τινες, παρὰ τὰς τούτων ὄχθας ὁδεύοντες, τὸ τοῦ παραδείσου
κατοπτεῦσαι χωρίον· διημάρτανον δὲ τοῦ ποθουμένου καὶ τῷ
15 μήκει τῆς ὁδοιπορίας κοπτόμενοι, καὶ τῇ σπάνει τῶν
ἀναγκαίων διαφθειρόμενοι, καὶ νῦν μὲν εἰς δυσχωρίας, νῦν δὲ
εἰς ἐρημίας ἐμπίπτοντες, ἔστι δὲ ὅτε καὶ ἀπηνέσι καὶ

XXIX 5, 12, B, C, 4 7 9 10 19 20 [32] 35 37 = 20 mss.
a. Gn 2.10, 14

They feel shame and put on clothes, and even if someone removes their clothing, they cover their genitalia with their hands. Nonetheless, many people lose this shame through force of habit. Mariners go naked while sailing, and bathers feel no shame when exposed to one another's view. But if someone emerges naked from the baths, he is quite embarrassed. Just so, soon after being created, Adam and his partner, like newborn babes and innocent of sin, were not ashamed to go about without clothing, but after experiencing sin, they covered some parts of their bodies with leaves.[1]

XXIX

How is it that Moses says the Tigris and the Euphrates flow out of Paradise though some commentators claim they rise in the mountains of Armenia?[a]

We can observe other rivers emerging at one point, then going into the earth through channels, and once more coming to the surface. This is the case with these rivers as well. Rising at that point indicated by holy Scripture, they then travel though underground passages and there take a different outlet.

Now, it was not without purpose that the God of the universe arranged this; he wanted to put a stop to man's pointless prying. After all, if the whole course of these rivers had been visible, some people would have tried to follow their banks and spy out the site of Paradise. But they would have been disappointed in this wish: tired out by the length of the journey and wasted with hunger and some-

---

1. Theodoret here develops a point he may have felt Chrysostom treated (*hom.* 16.5 *in Gen.*) too briefly.

βαρβάροις ἀνθρώποις περιπίπτοντες. καὶ τούτων τοίνυν
προμηθούμενος, ὁ φιλοικτίρμων Θεὸς ἀδήλους αὐτῶν τοὺς
20 πόρους ἀπέφηνεν.

XXX

Τί δή ποτε ἀπὸ τῆς πλευρᾶς τοῦ Ἀδὰμ τὴν γυναῖκα
διέπλασεν;[a]

Εἰς ὁμόνοιαν ἠβουλήθη τὰ γένη συναγαγεῖν ὁ τῆς φύσεως
ποιητής. τούτου χάριν τὸν μὲν Ἀδὰμ ἀπὸ τῆς γῆς διέπλασεν,
5 ἐκ δὲ τοῦ Ἀδὰμ τὴν γυναῖκα ἵνα καὶ τὸ ταὐτὸν ἐπιδείξῃ τῆς
φύσεως καὶ φυσικήν τινα φιλοστοργίαν αὐτοῖς περὶ ἀλλήλους
ἐμφύσῃ. εἰ γάρ, καὶ τούτων οὕτω γεγενημένων, καὶ ἄνδρες
γυναιξὶ διαμάχονται, καὶ γυναῖκες ἀνδράσιν, τί οὐκ ἂν
ἔδρασαν εἰ ἑτέρωθέν ποθεν τὴν γυναῖκα διέπλασε;

10 Σοφῶς οὖν ἄρα καὶ διεῖλε καὶ πάλιν συνήρμοσεν· ὁ γὰρ
γάμος εἰς ἓν συνάγει τὰ γένη· *ἔσονται γάρ*, φησιν, *οἱ δύο εἰς*
σάρκα μίαν.[b] καὶ ὅτι τοῦτο ἀληθὲς μαρτυρεῖ τὸ γενόμενον·
διὰ γὰρ τῆς γαμικῆς ὁμιλίας εἷς ἐξ ἀμφοῖν βλαστάνει καρπός,
ἐκ μὲν τούτου σπειρόμενος, ἐκ δὲ ταύτης τρεφόμενος,
15 τελεσιουργούμενος δὲ ὑπὸ τοῦ τῆς φύσεως δημιουργοῦ.

---

xxx 5, 12, B, C, 4 7 9 10 13 20 [32] 35 37 = 20 mss.

a. Gn 2.21f.   b. Gn 2.24

times ending up in impassable places, in the wilderness, or even falling victim to fierce savages. Accordingly, in his care for man, the compassionate God hid the course of these rivers.[1]

XXX

Why did he form the woman from the side of Adam?[a]

It was the will of the Creator of the order of nature to bring the sexes together in harmony. Therefore, he formed Adam from the earth, and the woman from Adam, to demonstrate the identity of nature and to instill in them a natural affection for each other. If even after this, husbands fight with wives, and wives with husbands, what would they not have done if he had formed the woman from some other source?

He showed his wisdom not only in dividing, but also in reuniting, them, for marriage combines the sexes into one. Scripture says, remember, "The two will become one flesh."[1b] The truth of this is confirmed by experience. Through marital intercourse one fruit sprouts up from both, its seed coming from him, its nourishment from her, with the Creator of nature bringing it to full term.

---

1. Here again, Theodoret follows his Antiochene predecessors in insisting that the biblical narrative describes a real garden that could be located in the material world; cf. Q. 25 and note 1.

---

1. Theodoret here reveals some disillusionment with what he observes of the relations between the sexes. Unlike Theodore of Mopsuestia (Devreesse, *Essai*, pp. 19f. and note 3), he does not take occasion from the creation of woman (2.20–22) to highlight the biblical author's understanding of the essential identity of the human nature bestowed upon both man and woman. Failing to derive any theologically significant doctrine from vv. 23f., he concludes that procreation, even in the absence of harmonious coëxistence, fulfils the Creator's plan.

XXXI

Εἰ φρόνιμος ὁ ὄφις,[a] καὶ ἐπαινούμενος· μόριον γὰρ ἡ φρόνησις ἀρετῆς.

Πολλὰ τῶν ὀνομάτων ὁμωνύμως προφέρεται· καὶ γὰρ τὰ εἴδωλα τῶν ἐθνῶν θεοὺς ὠνομάκασι, τοῦτο δέ γε ἀκριβέστερον
5 περὶ τοῦ ἐν ἐκείνῳ ἐνεργήσαντος εἴρηται δαίμονος. ἀμαθῶς δὲ οἱ ἀνόητοι καὶ τοὺς περὶ τοὺς μύθους ἐσχολακότας *σοφοὺς* προσηγόρευσαν· οὕτω καὶ ἡ θεία λέγει γραφή· *ἐξελέξατο ὁ Θεὸς τὰ μωρὰ τοῦ κόσμου ἵνα καταισχύνῃ τοὺς σοφούς·*[b] καὶ πάλιν, *ποῦ σοφός·*[c] καὶ διὰ τοῦ προφήτου, *σοφοί εἰσι τοῦ*
10 *κακοποιῆσαι.*[d] τοιγάρτοι κἀνταῦθα *φρόνιμον* τὸν ὄφιν ὡς *πανοῦργον* ὠνόμασεν. οὕτω γὰρ καὶ ὁ Ἀκύλας ἡρμήνευσεν· *καὶ ὁ ὄφις ἦν πανοῦργος ἀπὸ παντὸς ζῴου τῆς χώρας, οὗ ἐποίησεν Κύριος ὁ Θεός.*[e]

XXXII

Ἄλογος ὢν ὁ ὄφις, πῶς διελέχθη τῇ Εὔᾳ;[a]

Ὄργανον ἦν αὐτὸς τοῦ τῆς ἀληθείας ἐχθροῦ. καὶ τοῦτο δεδήλωκεν ὁ Κύριος ἐν τοῖς θείοις εὐαγγελίοις· εἰρηκὼς γὰρ τοῖς ἰουδαίοις, *ὑμεῖς ἐκ τοῦ πατρὸς ὑμῶν τοῦ διαβόλου ἐστέ,*
5 ἐπήγαγεν, *ἐκεῖνος ἀνθρωποκτόνος ἦν ἀπ' ἀρχῆς.*[b] οὗτος τοίνυν διὰ τοῦ ὄφεως διελέχθη τῇ Εὔᾳ. ἐπειδὴ γὰρ τῶν ἀλόγων ἁπάντων παρὰ τοῦ Θεοῦ τῶν ὅλων τὴν ἡγεμονίαν εἰλήφεισαν,

---

xxxi 5, 12, B, C, 4 7 9 10 [32] 35 37 = 18 mss.

a. Gn 3.1   b.1Cor 1.27   c. 1Cor 1.20   d. Jer 4.22   e. Gn 3.1

---

xxxii 5, 12, B, C, 4 7 9 10 [32] 35 37 = 18 mss.

a. Gn 3.1–5   b. Jn 8.44

XXXI

If the serpent was described as "prudent,"[a] that was a title of commendation, for prudence is one of the virtues.[1]

Many terms have an ambiguous connotation. People call the images of the nations "gods," whereas this word is more precisely applied to the demon active in the image. And in their ignorance, fools refer to those versed in mythological fables as "wise." Thus holy Scripture says, "God chose the foolish things of the world to confound the wise";[b] and again, "Where is the wise man?";[c] and, through the prophet, "They are wise in wrongdoing."[d] Thus, in this case, it called the serpent "prudent" because he is crafty. Indeed, Aquila rendered: "The serpent was craftier than any other land animal created by the Lord God."[e]

XXXII

How was it that the serpent, though lacking reason, talked to Eve?[a]

He was an instrument of the enemy of truth. The Lord also indicated this in the holy Gospels when he declared to the Jews, "You are from your father the devil" and added, "He was a murderer from the beginning."[1b] So it was he who spoke to Eve through the serpent. You see, since the God of the universe had given them control of all the irrational creatures, the devil set a trap for her through one of

---

1. While the *NRSV* uses the adjective "crafty" to describe the serpent, the LXX offers the superlative of the more positive epithet "prudent" or "sagacious" (φρο-νιμώτατος).

---

1. Chrysostom (*hom.* 16.1: τούτῳ ὥσπερ ὀργάνῳ τινὶ χρώμενος) and Theodore of Mopsuestia (Devreesse, *Essai*, p. 20 and note 2) had also explained

δι' ἑνὸς αὐτῇ τῶν ὑπηκόων τὴν παγίδα προσήνεγκε,
πιθανωτέραν οὕτω τὴν ἀπάτην κατασκευάζων. ὅτι δὲ καὶ
10 αὐτόν, τὸν διὰ τοῦ ὄφεως ἐνεργήσαντα, *ὄφιν* ἡ θεία
προσαγορεύει γραφὴ μάρτυς Ἡσαΐας ὁ προφήτης βοῶν, *τῇ*
ἡμέρᾳ ἐκείνῃ ἐπάξει ὁ Θεὸς τὴν μάχαιραν αὐτοῦ τὴν
ἁγίαν . . ., τὴν μεγάλην, καὶ τὴν ἰσχυρὰν ἐπὶ τὸν δράκοντα
τὸν ὄφιν, τὸν σκολιὸν καὶ ἰσχυρόν, ἐπὶ τὸν δράκοντα τὸν ὄφιν,
15 *τὸν φεύγοντα, τὸν ἐν τῇ θαλάσσῃ.*[c] καὶ ὁ Κύριος δὲ τοῖς
ἱεροῖς εἴρηκε μαθηταῖς, *ἰδοὺ δέδωκα ὑμῖν τὴν ἐξουσίαν τοῦ*
πατεῖν ἐπάνω ὄφεων, καὶ σκορπίων, καὶ ἐπὶ πᾶσαν τὴν
δύναμιν τοῦ ἐχθροῦ.[d]

XXXIII

Τί ἐστι *διηνοίχθησαν οἱ ὀφθαλμοὶ τῶν δύο;*[a]
Ὅτι καὶ πρὸ τῆς βρώσεως οὐ μεμυκότας εἶχον τοὺς
ὀφθαλμοὺς δῆλον τοῖς προσέχειν ἐθέλουσι· πῶς γὰρ εἶδεν ἡ
γυνὴ τὸ ξύλον, ὅτι καλὸν εἰς βρῶσιν, καὶ ἀρεστὸν τοῖς
5 ὀφθαλμοῖς ἰδεῖν, καὶ ὡραῖόν ἐστι τοῦ κατανοῆσαι εἰ μὴ
ἀνεῳγότας εἶχον τοὺς ὀφθαλμούς; οὐκοῦν τὴν μετὰ τὴν
ἁμαρτίαν αἴσθησιν οὕτω κέκληκεν ἡ θεία γραφή· εὐθὺς γὰρ
μετὰ τὴν ἁμαρτίαν κεντᾶται τὸ συνειδός.

---

c. Is 27.1 (LXX var.)   d. Lk 10.19

XXXIII 5, 12, B, C, 4 7 9 13 [32] 35 37 = 18 mss.
a. Gn 3.7

their subjects and thus presented a more plausible deception. The prophet Isaiah who cries out, "On that day God will strike with his holy, mighty, strong sword the dragon, the serpent twisted and strong, the dragon, the serpent fleeing in the sea,"[c] confirms that holy Scripture calls "serpent" the one who was at work in the serpent.[2] Moreover, the Lord declared to the sacred disciples, "Lo, I have given you power to walk on serpents and scorpions and on all the might of the foe."[d]

XXXIII

What is the meaning of "The eyes of both were opened"?[a]

Anyone who is paying attention can see that, even before eating, their eyes were not closed. After all, unless her eyes were open, how did the woman see that "the tree was good for eating, pleasant to behold, and attractive to contemplate"? Thus, we conclude that holy Scripture was referring to a sensation that followed the sin; immediately after the sin, they felt the pang of conscience.

----

that the devil employed the body of the serpent to communicate with Eve. No Antiochene commentator was prepared to regard any aspect of this narrative as less than entirely historical.

2. Theodoret's Antiochene recension of Isaiah differs significantly from the septuagintal form that is more widely attested: Τῇ ἡμέρᾳ ἐκείνῃ ἐπάξει ὁ Θεὸς τὴν μάχαιραν τὴν ἁγίαν καὶ τὴν μεγάλην καὶ τὴν ἰσχυρὰν ἐπὶ τὸν δράκοντα ὄφιν φεύγοντα, ἐπὶ τὸν δράκοντα ὄφιν σκολιόν, καὶ ἀνελεῖ τὸν δράκοντα.

XXXIV

Τί δή ποτε, τοῦ διαβόλου τὴν ἀπάτην προσενεγκόντος, ὁ ὄφις κολάζεται;[a]

Κυρίως μὲν τὴν ἀρὰν τῷ ἐνεργήσαντι προσενήνοχεν ὁ Θεός. ὄφις γὰρ κἀκεῖνος ὠνόμασται, οὐ ταύτην παρὰ τοῦ
5   Θεοῦ τῶν ὅλων τὴν φύσιν δεξάμενος· ἀγαθὸς γὰρ ἐκτίσθη καὶ ταῖς ἀσωμάτοις συνεδημιουργήθη δυνάμεσιν. ἐπειδὴ δὲ ἑκὼν εἰς πονηρίαν ἀπέκλινε, καὶ τῆς τιμῆς, ἧς ἐξ ἀρχῆς ἔλαχεν, ἐστερήθη καὶ εἰς τὴν γῆν ἀπερρίφη.

Καὶ αὐτὸ δὲ τὸ ζῷον εἰς ὄνησιν τῶν ἀνθρώπων ἐδέξατο τὴν
10   ἀράν. ὁρῶντες γὰρ τὸν ὄφιν ἐπὶ τῆς γῆς συρόμενόν τε καὶ ἰλυσπώμενον, τῆς ἀρχαίας ἀρᾶς ἀναμιμνησκόμεθα καὶ μανθάνομεν ὡς ἡλίκων πρόξενος ἡ ἁμαρτία κακῶν, οὐ μόνον τοῖς ταύτην ἐνεργοῦσιν, ἀλλὰ καὶ τοῖς ὑπουργοῦσι. καὶ αὐτὸς μὲν ὁ ὄφις οὐδεμίαν ἐντεῦθεν δέχεται βλάβην, οὕτω βαδίζειν
15   πεφυκώς· ἐν τῇ φύσει γὰρ ἔχει τὸ τοιόνδε τῆς κινήσεως εἶδος· οὐδὲν δὲ τῶν φυσικῶν φορτικὸν εἶναι δοκεῖ. ὁ δὲ ἄνθρωπος πολλὴν ἐντεῦθεν ὠφέλειαν καρποῦται.

XXXIV   5, 12, B, c, 50 53, 4 7 9 10 [32] 35 37 = 16 mss.

l. 11 ἰλυσπώμενον 53 (J.P.), 4 (J.P.) 9 (J.P.) 10 (J.P.), Sir. : ηλισπομενον B⁻²⁴, 7 : ἰλυσσώμενον Sch. F.M. Cf. Q. 13 on Lv (τὰ ἐπὶ τῆς κοιλίας ἰλυσπώμενα). The minuscule ligatures for σπ and σσ are easily confused; *cf.* van Groningen, p. 44. The reading with -σπ- is certainly carried by 53, 4, 9, and 10. The *TLG* offers no other attestation for forms of ἰλυσσάομαι, and the *PGL* only one (Areth. *Apoc.* 67 = PG, vol. 106, col. 777B). But this, the participle ἰλυττώμενα, is actually written with rough breathing. I suspect it is no more than an error for ἰλυσπώμενα.

a. Gn 3.14f.

XXXIV

Why was the serpent punished when it was the devil who was responsible for the deception?[a]

Properly speaking, God inflicted the curse on the one who brought about the action, who was also called "serpent," though that was not the nature he had received from the God of the universe. For he was created good and made along with the incorporeal powers. But since he willingly took the path of evil, he forfeited the dignity accorded him in the beginning and was cast down to earth.[1]

The animal itself also became the object of the curse for the benefit of humanity. When we see the serpent crawling and slithering on the ground, we remember the original curse and understand the extent of the evil caused by sin, not only to those who commit it but also to those who assist them. As it was born to move in this fashion, the serpent has received no harm from the curse. This is its natural kind of movement, and there is no burden in a natural characteristic. Furthermore, man draws from this a great benefit of his own.

1. In his comment on Gn 3.14 (*hom.* 17.6 *in Gen.*), Chrysostom poses the same question and responds in similar terms.

XXXV

Διὰ τί δὲ τὸν ὄφιν ἐδημιούργησεν ὁ Θεός, ὄργανον αὐτὸν
προειδὼς τῆς πονηρίας ἐσόμενον;

Τοῦτο ἄν τις εἴποι καὶ περὶ τοῦ ἀνθρώπου· προήδει γὰρ ὡς
καὶ αὐτὸς τὴν ἐντολὴν παραβήσεται. ἄλλως τε ῥάδιον ἦν τῷ
5 διαβόλῳ καὶ δι' ἑτέρου θηρίου τὴν ἀπάτην προσενεγκεῖν.

XXXVI

Διὰ τί δὲ τὸν διάβολον ἐποίησεν, εἰδὼς τοιοῦτον ἐσόμενον;

Ὁ Θεὸς πᾶσαν τῶν ἀσωμάτων τὴν φύσιν ἐδημιούργησε,
λογικὴν αὐτὴν καὶ ἀθάνατον ἀποφήνας· τοῦ λογικοῦ δὲ τὸ
αὐτεξούσιον ἴδιον· τούτων δὲ οἱ μὲν τὴν περὶ τὸν ποιητὴν
5 ἐφύλαξαν εὔνοιαν, οἱ δὲ εἰς πονηρίαν ἀπέκλιναν. τοῦτο δὲ καὶ
ἐπὶ τῶν ἀνθρώπων ἔστιν εὑρεῖν· οἱ μὲν γάρ εἰσι τῆς ἀρετῆς
ἐρασταί, οἱ δὲ τῆς κακίας ἐργάται.

Εἰ τοίνυν μέμφεταί τις τῇ τῶν πονηρῶν δημιουργίᾳ,
ἀποστερεῖ ἄρα τῶν τῆς νίκης βραβείων τοὺς τῆς ἀρετῆς
10 ἀθλητάς· εἰ γάρ, μὴ ἐν τῇ αἱρέσει τῆς γνώμης εἶχον τὸν
πόθον τῆς ἀρετῆς, ἀλλὰ ἐμπεφυκὸς τὸ ἄτρεπτον, ἔλαθον ἂν οἱ
ἀξιόνικοι τῆς εὐσεβείας ἀγωνισταί. ἐπειδὴ δὲ τὴν αἵρεσιν τῶν
ἀγαθῶν καὶ τῶν ἐναντίων ἔχει ἡ γνώμη, δικαίως καὶ οὗτοι
τυγχάνουσι τῶν νικηφόρων στεφάνων, κἀκεῖνοι δίκας
15 τιννύουσιν ὑπὲρ ὧν κατὰ γνώμην ἐξήμαρτον.

---

xxxv 5, 12, B, c, 50 53, 4 7 9 10 [32] 35 37 = 16 mss.

xxxvi 5, 12, B, c, 50 53, 4 7 9 10 [32] 35 37 = 16 mss.

XXXV

Why did God create the serpent when he knew in advance that it would become an instrument of wickedness?

You could raise the same question about human beings. He knew in advance that they too would break the commandment. Anyway, it would have been easy for the devil to accomplish the deception through some other animal.

XXXVI

Why did God create the devil when he knew what he would be like?

God created the entirety of incorporeal existence, which he made rational and immortal. Now, free will is proper to the rational being. While some maintained their loyalty to the Creator, others fell away into evil. The same is true of human beings: some are lovers of virtue, others, workers of wickedness.

If you find fault in the creation of the wicked, you also rob the athletes of virtue of their prize of victory. For had they been naturally changeless, with no passion for virtue when engaged in the exercise of free will, the victorious champions of goodness would have gone unsung. But since free will exercises a choice between good and evil, they were rightly awarded the victors' crowns, while the others pay the penalty for the sins they committed through their free will.[1]

---

1. This question evokes a response, based not on a reference to Scripture, but on a favorite moral principle of the Antiochenes: the necessity of free will for human beings and other rational creatures; *cf. Q.* 1.1 on Dt and note 1.

XXXVII

Ἀγαθὸν τὸν Θεὸν ὀνομάζοντες, πῶς αὐτῷ περιάπτετε
τοσαύτην ἀποτομίαν; ὠμότητος γὰρ καὶ ἀπηνίας τὸ διὰ
βρῶσιν ὀλίγην τοσαύτην ἐπενεγκεῖν τιμωρίαν, οὐ τοῖς
ἡμαρτηκόσι μόνον, ἀλλὰ καὶ τοῖς ἐξ ἐκείνων βεβλαστηκόσι.ᵃ

5 (1) Πρῶτον πεπεῖσθαι προσήκει τοὺς εὐσεβεῖν
προαιρουμένους ὡς πᾶν ὁτιοῦν ὑπὸ τοῦ Θεοῦ τῶν ὅλων
γινόμενον ἢ κελευόμενον καὶ ὅσιον, καὶ δίκαιον, καὶ ἀγαθόν,
καὶ φιλάνθρωπον· εἰ γὰρ ταῦτα πάντα ἔχειν αὐτὸν
ὁμολογοῦμεν, καὶ τὰ ὑπ' αὐτοῦ οἰκονομούμενά τε καὶ
10 προστατόμενα χρὴ τοιαῦτα εἶναι νομίζειν. ἔπειτα εἰδέναι
δεῖ ὡς πᾶς νόμος, κἂν περὶ σμικρῶν τινων διαγορεύῃ, τὴν
ἴσην ἔχει δύναμιν τῷ τὰ μέγιστα κελεύοντι ποιεῖν ἢ
ἀπαγορεύοντι δρᾶν, καὶ διαφερόντως πᾶς θεῖος νόμος. αὐτίκα
γοῦν ὁ περιτέμνεσθαι κελεύων—οὐδεμίαν παραβαινόμενος τῷ
15 πέλας ἐργάζεται βλάβην, ἀλλ' ὅμως ὁ νομοθέτης φησὶν ὅτι,
*πᾶς ἀπερίτμητος ἄρσην, ὃς οὐ περιτμηθήσεται... τῇ ἡμέρᾳ τῇ
ὀγδόῃ, ἐξολοθρευθήσεται*ᵇ καί, ἣν ὥρισε τοῖς ἀνδροφόνοις καὶ
τοῖς μοιχοῖς τιμωρίαν, ταύτην καὶ τούτῳ ἐκλήρωσεν.

Ἐπειδὴ δὲ εἰκὸς τοὺς δυσωνύμους αἱρετικοὺς ἄντικρυς τῇ
20 παλαιᾷ πολεμοῦντας γραφῇ καὶ τοῦδε κατηγορῆσαι τοῦ νόμου,
ἐκ τῆς εὐαγγελικῆς νομοθεσίας τὰς ἀποδείξεις ποιήσομαι·
εὑρίσκομεν γὰρ ἐν ἐκείνοις τοῖς νόμοις τὸν λάγνως ὁρῶντα
γύναιον μοιχείας κρινόμενον·ᶜ καὶ τὸν εἰκῇ ὀργιζόμενον,
ἔνοχον ὄντα τῇ κρίσει· τὸν δὲ *ῥακὰ* τὸν ἀδελφὸν ὀνομάζοντα,
25 γραφῆς πάλιν ὑπεύθυνον· τὸν δὲ *μωρὸν* ἀποκαλοῦντα, τῆς
γεέννης ἄξιον·ᵈ καὶ τὸν ὀμνύντα, κἂν ἀληθεύων ὀμνύῃ, τῆς
διαβολικῆς ὄντα συμμορίας.ᵉ Τί δή ποτε τοίνυν τοῦτον μὲν

---

xxxvii 2a(inc.), 5, 12, B, C, 4 7 9 10 [32] 35 37 = 19 mss.

a. Gn 3.14–19   b. Gn 17.14   c. Mt 5.28   d. Mt 5.22   e. Mt 5.37

XXXVII

How can you call God good and yet attribute so much severity to him? Only someone harsh and cruel would inflict, for just a little food, such an awful penalty on both the sinners and their descendants as well.[a]

(1) First, those who choose virtue must be convinced that every single act or command of the God of the universe is holy, just, kind, and loving. If we confess that he is all these things, we must also believe that his designs and commands are of the same character. Next, we must acknowledge that every law, even one prescribing minutiae, has force equal to one requiring performance of, or abstinence from, the most important things. This is especially true of every divine law. For example, in the case of the law prescribing circumcision, the transgressor does no harm to his neighbor, yet the Lawgiver says, "Every uncircumcised male who has not been circumcised on the eighth day will be destroyed."[b] Thus, he assigns this person the punishment allotted to murderers and adulterers.

Yet, since the ill-omened heretics who openly dispute the Old Testament are likely to criticize this law, I shall make my point from the Gospel legislation. In these laws we find that the man who merely looks at a woman lustfully is condemned for adultery,[c] the one who becomes angry without provocation is regarded as guilty of a crime, the one who speaks contemptuously of his brother is said to be liable to prosecution, while the one who calls him a fool is condemned to hell,[d] and he who swears, even if swearing the truth, is relegated to the devil.[1e] So why do they call this Lawgiver good, but

1. Throughout this response Theodoret counters pejorative attitudes toward the ethical teaching of the Old Testament; this is a task he had foreseen in the preface. He argues that both OT and NT teachings are from God, though the latter are more developed.

ἀγαθὸν ὀνομάζουσιν, ἀπηνῆ δὲ τὸν τῆς παλαιᾶς νομοθέτην;
ταῦτα γὰρ ἐκείνων κατὰ τὸν τούτων ὅρον ὠμότερα. ἀλλὰ τῆς
30 ἐκείνων ταῦτα βλασφημίας τολμᾶν· ἡμεῖς δὲ κἀκείνους καὶ
τούτους τοὺς νόμους ἑνὸς ἴσμεν Θεοῦ. τὸ δὲ διάφορον ἡ τῶν
νομοθετουμένων ποιότης εἰργάσατο· οἷα γὰρ σοφὸς
διδάσκαλος, τοῖς μὲν ἀτελέσι τὰ ἀτελῆ, τοῖς δὲ τελείοις τὰ
τέλεια προσενήνοχε.ᶠ

35 (2) Πρὸς δὲ τούτοις σκοπητέον καὶ τοῦτο, ὡς τοῖς πρώτοις
παραβαίνουσι τοὺς νόμους ἐπιφέρονται δίχα συγγνώμης
τιμωρίαι ὥστε τοὺς ἄλλους, ὁρῶντας τὴν κόλασιν, μὴ τολμᾶν
τὴν παράβασιν. τοῦτο καὶ ἐπὶ τῆς τοῦ σαββάτου νομοθεσίας
ἐγένετο· τὸν γὰρ ἐν σαββάτῳ τὰ ξύλα συλλέξαι τετολμηκότα
40 καὶ πρῶτον τὸν περὶ τούτου παραβεβηκότα νόμον ἅπας
κατέλευσεν ὁ λαός, τοῦ Θεοῦ τοῦτο προστεταχότος, ἵνα,
αὐτουργοὶ τῆς τιμωρίας γενόμενοι, φρίττωσι τὴν παρανομίαν,
ὡς τὴν τιμωρίαν ἐπάγουσαν.ᵍ χρόνῳ δὲ ὕστερον, πολλῶν τὸν
περὶ τοῦ σαββάτου παραβεβηκότων νόμον, μακροθύμως ὁ
45 νομοθέτης ἤνεγκε τὴν παράβασιν. οὕτω τὸν Κάϊν πρῶτον
πεφονευκότα ταῖς ἀνηκέστοις ὑπέβαλε τιμωρίαις ἵνα τοὺς ἐπ'
ἐκείνου καὶ μετ' ἐκεῖνον γεγενημένους δεδίξηται τὰ
παραπλήσια μὴ τολμᾶν.ʰ πολλῶν δὲ ὕστερον ἀνδροφόνων
γεγενημένων, οὐ παραυτίκα τὰς τιμωρίας ἐπήγαγεν.

50 Ἔδει τοίνυν καὶ τὸν Ἀδὰμ πρῶτον δεξάμενον νόμον καὶ
νόμον κουφότατον· τῶν παντοδαπῶν γὰρ αὐτῷ καρπῶν
ἐδεδώκει τὴν ἀφθονίαν, ἑνὸς δὲ μόνου τὴν ἐδωδὴν
ἀπηγορεύκει·ⁱ δοῦναι δίκην τοῦ πλημμελήματος εἰς ὠφέλειαν
|2a τοῦ γένους. ἰεὶ δὲ δυσόργητος ὤν, ὡς ὁ δυσώνυμος ἔφη
55 Μαρκίων, διὰ βρῶσιν ὀλίγην τὴν τοῦ θανάτου τιμωρίαν
ἐπήνεγκε, πῶς ἁπάντων ἀνθρώπων εἰς ἀσέβειαν καὶ
παρανομίαν ἐσχάτην ἐξοκειλάντων, οὐ πανωλεθρίαν ἐπήνεγκεν,
ἀλλὰ τὸν υἱὸν ἔδωκεν καὶ τὴν διὰ σταυροῦ καὶ πάθους
ἐδωρήσατο σωτηρίαν;

---

f. 1Cor 3.1f.   g. Nm 15.32–36   h. Gn 4.11–14   i. Gn 2.16f.

the giver of the old law harsh, when the penalties of the new law, by their own reckoning, are more severe than those of the old? Their temerity is a form of blasphemy. But we are aware that both the old law and the new come from the one God. The difference lies in the character of those who receive the law. A wise teacher, after all, proposes less developed teaching to immature people and more developed to the mature.[f]

(2) Furthermore, we should consider that punishment is inflicted without mitigation on those who are the first to transgress, so that, on seeing the punishment, others will not dare the same. This happened in the case of the Sabbath. The people as a whole stoned the man who was the first to break the law by presuming to collect wood on the Sabbath. God gave this command so that, after themselves exacting the punishment, they would fear transgression for the punishment it entailed.[g] Later, however, when many people had broken the law about the Sabbath, the Lawgiver in his long-suffering put up with the transgression. Similarly, he inflicted an irremediable punishment on Cain, the first murderer, so as to render his contemporaries and descendants fearful of committing similar crimes.[h] But later, after the commission of many other murders, he did not inflict an immediate punishment.

Therefore, Adam also had to pay the penalty for his sin for the benefit of the race.[2] He had received the first law, and a very light one at that. While he was regaled with an abundance of fruits of all kinds, the eating of one alone was forbidden.[i] But if an ill-tempered creator inflicted the punishment of death for just a little food, as the ill-omened Marcion claims, how is it that, with all humanity rushing headlong into the worst wickedness and sin, he did not inflict universal ruin but gave his Son and bestowed the gift of salvation through cross and passion?

2. Theodoret never speaks of original sin or the transmission to posterity of the guilt for Adam's sin (*cf.* also *Q.* 43). He deplores the Fall as an event that resulted in death for the human race but rejoices in the divine plan (οἰκονομίας μυστήριον), which, through the sacrifice of Christ, reverses death through resurrection.

60 Καὶ ταῦτα λέγω πρὸς τοὺς οἰομένους ὀργῇ τινι ταῦτα
δεδρακέναι τὸν τῶν ὅλων Θεὸν καὶ ἀγνοοῦντας τὸ τῆς
οἰκονομίας μυστήριον. δῆλον γὰρ οἶμαι τοῖς τὰ θεῖα
πεπαιδευμένοις ὡς οὐδὲν ἐκ μεταμελείας ποιεῖν εἴωθε ὁ τῶν
ὅλων Θεός· τοῦτο γὰρ δὴ τὸ πάθος ἴδιον τῶν τρεπτὴν ἐχόντων
65 τὴν φύσιν, καὶ νῦν μὲν τούτοις, νῦν δὲ ἐκείνοις, ἀρεσκομένων,
καὶ τὸ μέλλον ἔσεσθαι παντάπασιν ἀγνοούντων. ὁ δὲ τῶν ὅλων
Θεὸς ἄτρεπτον μὲν ἔχει τὴν φύσιν, οἶδε δὲ ὡς ἤδη
γεγενημένα τὰ μήπω γεγενημένα. αὐτίκα γοῦν καὶ τὰ κατὰ
τὸν Ἀδὰμ προορῶν καὶ προγινώσκων, ὡς θνητὸς γενήσεται,
70 τὴν ἐντολὴν παραβάς, τοιαύτην αὐτοῦ καὶ τὴν φύσιν
προκατεσκεύασεν· εἰς ἄρρεν γὰρ καὶ θῆλυ τοῦ σώματος
ἐσχημάτισε τὴν διάπλασιν.ʲ τῶν δὲ θνητῶν καὶ παιδοποιίας
δεομένων εἰς τὴν τοῦ γένους διαμονὴν ἡ τοιαύτη τῶν
σωμάτων κατασκευή· ἡ γὰρ ἀθάνατος φύσις οὐ δεῖται τοῦ
75 θήλεος. τούτου χάριν ὁ ποιητὴς ὁμοῦ τὸν τῶν ἀσωμάτων
παρήγαγεν ἀριθμόν, τῶν δὲ θνητῶν ζῴων ἀνὰ δύο καθ' ἕκαστον
ἐδημιούργησε γένος, ἄρσεν καὶ θῆλυ, καὶ τῆς αὐξήσεως αὐτοῖς
τὴν εὐλογίαν ἐπήνεγκεν· *αὐξάνεσθε,* γάρ φησιν, *καὶ
πληθύνεσθε.*ᵏ οὕτω καὶ τὸν ἄνθρωπον διέπλασεν ἄρσεν καὶ θῆλυ
80 καὶ τὴν αὐτὴν αὐτοῖς ἔδωκεν εὐλογίαν· *αὐξάνεσθε, καὶ
πληθύνεσθε, καὶ πληρώσατε τὴν γῆν, καὶ κατακυριεύσατε
αὐτῆς.*ˡ ταῦτα τοίνυν προορῶν, ὁ τῶν ὅλων Θεός, οὐ μόνον
αὐτοὺς οὕτω διέπλασεν, ἀλλὰ καὶ τὸν ἐπὶ τῆς βρώσεως αὐτοῖς
δέδωκε *νόμον· ἰδού,* γάρ φησι, *δέδωκα ὑμῖν πάντα χόρτον*
85 *σπόριμον σπεῖρον σπέρμα, ὅ ἐστιν ἐπάνω πάσης τῆς γῆς, καὶ
πᾶν ξύλον, ὃ ἔχει ἐν ἑαυτῷ καρπὸν σπέρματος σπόριμον· ὑμῖν
ἔσται εἰς βρῶσιν, καὶ πᾶσι τοῖς θηρίοις τῆς γῆς, καὶ πᾶσι
τοῖς πετεινοῖς τοῦ οὐρανοῦ, καὶ παντὶ ἑρπετῷ ἕρποντι ἐπὶ τῆς
γῆς, ὃ ἔχει ἐν ἑαυτῷ ψυχὴν ζωῆς. καὶ πάντα χόρτον χλωρὸν*
90 *ὑμῖν δέδωκα εἰς βρῶσιν.*ᵐ ταῦτα γὰρ πρὸ τῆς ἐντολῆς πρὸς

l. 90 *ὑμῖν* Sir. Sch. F.M. : om. 51 52, 7 = "'I have given every green plant for
food.'"

j. Gn 1.27   k. Gn 1.22   l. Gn 1.28   m. Gn 1.29f. (LXX var.)

Furthermore, to those who, in their ignorance of the mystery of the divine plan, hold that the God of the universe acted in a burst of anger, I submit the following. I believe it is clear to anyone versed in religion that God does nothing on the basis of second thoughts. This weakness is typical of those with a changeable nature, opting at one time for this, at another for that, and completely ignorant of the future. The God of the universe, by contrast, is unchangeable by nature and knows what has yet to happen as though it had already happened. For example, because he foresaw Adam's behavior and foreknew that he would break the commandment and become liable to death, he prepared in advance this physical constitution; that is, he arranged their bodily make-up as male and female.[j] Their bodies were so constituted in view of their being mortal and requiring procreation for the continuance of the race, since an immortal nature does not require the female. Thus, the Creator produced all at once the complete number of the beings that have no body but made each race of mortal beings in couples, male and female, and bestowed on them the blessing of increase: "Increase and multiply."[k] Thus he created humanity both male and female and gave them the blessing: "Increase, multiply, fill the earth and dominate it."[l] The God of the universe exhibited his foresight not only in the creation of humanity as male and female, but also in giving them the law about their food: "Lo, I have given you every plant upon all the earth bearing seed fit for sowing and every tree containing fruit with seed fit for sowing; these will be your food and the food of all the beasts of the earth, all the birds of heaven, and every reptile creeping on the earth, which has the spirit of life in it. I have given you every green plant for food."[3m] Now, the God of the universe said this to

3. It is difficult to know just how Theodoret would have divided the clauses of this quotation. The appearance here of the phrase ὑμῖν δέδωκα (I have given you) seems to necessitate the introduction of a stop after ζωῆς and the beginning of a new sentence with καί. Yet, as the critical note indicates, several manuscripts omit the pronoun ὑμῖν. Furthermore, when Theodoret once more quotes this passage in Q. 51, both pronoun and verb are omitted, and we must regard everything from βρῶσιν to ζωῆς as a parenthesis and construe καὶ πάντα χόρτον as direct object

τὸν Ἀδὰμ ὁ τῶν ὅλων ἔφη Θεός· θνητῶν δὲ ἡ βρῶσις· ἀθάνατος γὰρ φύσις οὐ δεῖται τροφῆς. καὶ τοῦτο διδάσκων, ὁ Κύριος ἔφη ὅτι, μετὰ τὴν ἀνάστασιν *οὔτε γαμοῦσιν, οὔτε γαμίσκονται, ἀλλ᾽ εἰσὶν ὡς ἄγγελοι ἐν τοῖς οὐρανοῖς.*[n]

95 (3) Οὐ τοίνυν ὀργῆς ἡ τιμωρία, ἀλλ᾽ οἰκονομία σοφίας μεγίστης. ἵνα γὰρ μισῇ τὴν ἁμαρτίαν τῶν ἀνθρώπων τὸ γένος, ὡς αἰτίαν θανάτου γεγενημένην, μετὰ τὴν παράβασιν τῆς ἐντολῆς ἐπιφέρει τοῦ θανάτου τὴν ψῆφον ὁ πάνσοφος· τούτῳ μὲν τὸ περὶ τὴν ἁμαρτίαν μηχανώμενος μῖσος, προευτρεπίζων
100 δὲ τῷ γένει τῆς σωτηρίας τὸ φάρμακον, τὸ διὰ τῆς τοῦ μονογενοῦς ἐνανθρωπήσεως τὴν ἐκ νεκρῶν ἀνάστασιν καὶ τὴν ἀθανασίαν πραγματευσάμενον. τί δὲ ἀπηνὲς ἡ ἀπόφασις ἔχει, *γῆ εἶ καὶ εἰς γῆν ἀπελεύσῃ;*[o] ἀπὸ γῆς σε, φησίν, ἔπλασα καὶ εἰς ἀμείνω πολλῷ μετεσκεύασα φύσιν· ἐπειδὴ δὲ φυλάξαι μου
105 τὴν ἐντολὴν οὐκ ἐθέλησας, πρὸς τὴν προτέραν ἐπάνελθε φύσιν.

Ἀνθ᾽ ὅτου δὲ σμικρὸν εἶναι δοκεῖ τὸ ἁμάρτημα; πάντων αὐτῷ τῶν φυτῶν ἐδεδώκει τὴν ἐξουσίαν, ἑνὸς δὲ μόνου τὴν ἐδωδὴν ἀπηγόρευκει. ὁ δέ, τὰ ἄλλα πάντα καταλιπών, τοῦτον
110 καὶ πρῶτον καὶ μόνον ἐτρύγησε τὸν καρπόν· τοῦτο γὰρ αὐτῷ καὶ ὁ δεσπότης Θεὸς ἐμέμψατο· *τίς, γάρ φησιν, ἀνήγγειλέ σοι ὅτι γυμνὸς εἶ εἰ μὴ ἀπὸ τοῦ ξύλου, οὗ ἐνετειλάμην σοι τούτου μόνου μὴ φαγεῖν, ἀπ᾽ αὐτοῦ ἔφαγες;*[p] δεδήλωκε δὲ τοῦτο καὶ ὁ διάβολος δι᾽ ὧν ἔφη τῇ Εὔᾳ· *τί ὅτι εἶπεν ὁ Θεός,*
115 *οὐ μὴ φάγητε ἀπὸ παντὸς ξύλου, τοῦ ἐν τῷ παραδείσῳ;*[q] εἰ δὲ εἶδεν ἐδηδοκότας, οὐκ ἂν ᾠήθη περὶ πάντων αὐτοὺς τῶν δένδρων εἰληφέναι τὴν ἐντολήν. οὐ σμικρὰ τοιγαροῦν ἡ παράβασις· πρώτου γὰρ μετέλαβον οὗ μόνου μὴ μετασχεῖν ἐκελεύσθησαν.

---

n. Mt 22.30   o. Gn 3.19   p. Gn 3.11   q. Gn 3.1

Adam before the commandment, and food is for mortals; beings naturally immortal have no need of food. The Lord also taught this when he said, "After the resurrection they neither marry nor are given in marriage but are like angels in heaven."[n]

(3) Thus the punishment is not the result of anger, but part of a divine plan of the greatest wisdom. So that the human race would hate sin as the cause of death, after the transgression of the commandment, God, in his great wisdom, passed the sentence of death and in this way both ensured their hatred of sin and provided the race with the remedy of salvation, which, through the Incarnation of the Only-begotten, achieves the resurrection of the dead and immortality. What is the harshness in the sentence, "Earth you are, and to earth you will return"?[o] He is saying, "I formed you out of earth and transformed you to a far better condition, but since you were not prepared to keep my commandment, return to your former condition."

Surely the sin does not seem slight? He gave him authority over all the plants and forbade him to eat just one. But Adam, passing over all the others, sank his teeth into this fruit first and into this one alone. The Lord God held him accountable for this: "Who told you that you were naked, unless you have eaten from the only tree I commanded you not to eat?"[p] This is clear also from what the devil said to Eve: "Why did God tell you not to eat from every tree in the garden?"[q] Had he known that they had already eaten, he would not have imagined that the commandment enjoined on them applied to all the trees. Thus, the transgression was not slight; they ate first of that one thing of which they were forbidden to partake.

----

of δέδωκα, the second word of the quotation. In either case, man and animals are grouped together. Here, if we should omit the difficult pronoun, the passage would first devote two independent clauses to man's nourishment and then a third to that of the beasts: "Lo, I have given you every plant upon all the earth bearing seed fit for sowing and every tree containing fruit with seed fit for sowing; these will be your food. And to all the beasts of the earth, all the birds of heaven, and every reptile creeping on the earth, which has the spirit of life in it, I have given every green plant for food."

XXXVIII

Τίνος ἔνεκα τοῦ Θεοῦ εἰρηκότος, ᾗ δ' ἂν ἡμέρᾳ φάγῃ ἀπὸ τοῦ ξύλου, θανάτῳ ἀποθανῇ,[a] οὐκ εὐθὺς ἀπέθανε, τὴν ἐντολὴν παραβάς;

'Εναντία αὕτη κατηγορία· πρὸ βραχέος γὰρ ἀπηνῆ τὸν
||2a 5 Θεὸν|| ἀποκαλοῦντες, νῦν αὐτοῦ φιλανθρωπίαν κατηγορεῖτε.
ὑμνεῖν δὲ μᾶλλον ἐχρῆν ἀλλ' οὐ κατηγορεῖν τῆς ἀγαθότητος
τοῦ Θεοῦ· εἴωθε γὰρ μείζονα μὲν ἀπειλεῖν, ἐλάττους δὲ τῶν
ἀπειλῶν τὰς τιμωρίας ἐπάγειν, καὶ τοῦτο πολλαχῇ ἔστιν
εὑρεῖν παρὰ τῇ θείᾳ γραφῇ. ἐνταῦθα μέντοι τὸν τῆς
10 θνητότητος ὅρον ὠνόμασε θάνατον· οὕτω γὰρ καὶ ὁ Σύμμαχος
ἡρμήνευσεν· ᾗ δ' ἂν ἡμέρᾳ φάγῃ ἀπὸ τοῦ ξύλου, θνητὸς ἔσῃ·
μετὰ γὰρ δὴ τὴν θείαν ἀπόφασιν καθ' ἑκάστην, ὡς ἔπος
εἰπεῖν, ἡμέραν τὸν θάνατον προσεδέχετο. οὕτως οἱ
πεπιστευκότες τῷ δεσπότῃ Χριστῷ, καὶ σφαττόμενοι, ζῶσι,
15 προσμένοντες τὴν ἀνάστασιν καὶ τὴν τῶν οὐρανῶν βασιλείαν·
τῇ γὰρ ἐλπίδι ἐσώθημεν.[b]

XXXIX

Τοὺς χιτῶνας τοὺς δερματίνους τί νοητέον;[a]

Οἱ μὲν ἀλληγορηταὶ τὴν θνητὴν σάρκα φασὶ τὰ δέρματα,
ἄλλοι δέ τινες ἀπὸ φλοιῶν δένδρων τούτους κατεσκευάσθαι
εἰρήκασιν. ἐγὼ δέ γε οὐδέτερον τούτων προσίεμαι· τὸ μὲν γὰρ
5 περίεργον, τὸ δὲ ἄγαν μυθῶδες· τῆς γὰρ θείας γραφῆς καὶ

---

xxxviii 2a(inc.), 5, 12, B, C⁻⁵⁰, 4 7 9 10 [32] 35 37 = 18 mss.
a. Gn 2.17   b. Rom 8.24

---

xxxix 5, 12, B, C, 4 7 9 10 [32] 35 37 = 18 mss.
a. Gn 3.21

XXXVIII

Why was it that though God had said, "The day you eat from the tree you will certainly die,"[a] Adam did not immediately die on breaking the commandment?

This charge is the exact opposite of the former. Just a moment ago you accused God of harshness, now you charge him with mercy. Instead of criticizing God's goodness, you should sing his praises. It is usually the case that his threats are more severe than the punishments he actually inflicts, as you can find in many places in holy Scripture. In this case, however, by "death" he referred to the sentence of mortality. Hence, Symmachus translated, "On the day you eat from the tree you will be mortal."[1] After the divine sentence, they had, so to speak, death to look forward to each day. Similarly, those who believe in Christ the Lord, even if put to death, live in the expectation of the resurrection and the Kingdom of Heaven, "for we were saved in hope."[b]

XXXIX

How are we to understand the clothing of skins?[a]

Allegorizing commentators have claimed that the skins were mortal flesh, others that they were made from the bark of trees.[1] But I adopt neither of these views; the latter is merely inquisitive, the

---

1. In this work, perhaps because of the question and answer format, Theodoret makes relatively few references to Aquila, Symmachus, and Theodotion, the three who were traditionally credited with editing Greek versions substantially different from that attributed to the seventy; *v.* sec. 3 of the "Introduction to Theodoret' s Life and Works."

---

1. This detail (Gn 3.21) has excited the interest of both ancients and moderns. As Guinot points out (pp. 755f.), Theodoret rejects first the Alexandrian allegorical

πρὸ τῆς ψυχῆς τὸ σῶμα διαπεπλάσθαι φησάσης, πῶς οὐ
μυθῶδες τὸ λέγειν μετὰ τὴν παράβασιν τῆς ἐντολῆς σάρκα
αὐτοὺς εἰληφέναι θνητήν; τὸ δέ γε πολυπραγμονεῖν πόθεν τῷ
Θεῷ δέρματα καὶ διὰ τοῦτο καινὸν εἶδος περιβολαίων ἐπινοεῖν
10 περιττὸν εἶναί μοι δοκεῖ. χρὴ τοίνυν στέργειν τὰ γεγραμμένα,
καὶ εἰδέναι ὡς οὐδὲν ἄπορον τῷ τῶν ὅλων δημιουργῷ, καὶ
θαυμάζειν αὐτοῦ τὴν ἄπειρον ἀγαθότητα, ὅτι καὶ
παραβεβηκότων ἐπιμελεῖται καὶ δεηθέντων περιβολαίων οὐ
περιεῖδε γυμνούς.

XL

Τί ἐστι τὸ *ἰδοὺ γέγονεν Ἀδὰμ ὡς εἷς ἐξ ἡμῶν;*[a]

Ἐπειδὴ ὁ διάβολος εἶπεν, *ἔσεσθε ὡς θεοὶ γινώσκοντες
καλὸν καὶ πονηρόν,*[b] ἐδέξατο δὲ τοῦ θανάτου τὸν ὅρον, τὴν
ἐντολὴν παραβάς, εἰρωνικῶς τοῦτο εἴρηκεν ὁ τῶν ὅλων Θεός,
5 δεικνὺς τῆς διαβολικῆς ἐπαγγελίας τὸ ψεῦδος. μεταλαβεῖν δὲ
αὐτὸν τοῦ καρποῦ τοῦ ξύλου τῆς ζωῆς διεκώλυσεν, οὐ φθονῶν
αὐτῷ τῆς ἀθανάτου ζωῆς, ἀλλὰ τῆς ἁμαρτίας ἐπέχων τὸν
δρόμον. ἰατρεία τοίνυν ὁ θάνατος, οὐ τιμωρία· ἐπέχει γὰρ τῆς

---

xl 5, 12, B, C, 4 7 9 10 [32] 35 37 = 18 mss.
a. Gn 3.22   b. Gn 3.5

former too much of a mythological fable. Since holy Scripture says that the body was formed even before the soul, how can this claim that the man and woman took mortal flesh only after the transgression of the commandment amount to anything but a fable? And it strikes me as futile to pry into the way God came by skins and to imagine a novel form of clothing. We should be content with the text, acknowledge that there is no task beyond the Creator of the universe, and admire the unlimited goodness of God who, taking care for sinners, did not overlook their need for clothing when they were naked.[2]

XL

What is the meaning of the verse "Lo, Adam has become like one of us?"[a]

Though the devil had declared, "You will be like gods, knowing good and evil,"[b] Adam incurred the sentence of death for breaking the commandment. So the God of the universe said this ironically to bring out the lie in the devil's promise.[1] Now, God had forbidden Adam to partake of the fruit of the tree of life, not because he begrudged him eternal life, but to check the course of sin. Indeed, death is healing, not punishment, for it checks the onset of sin: "He

---

interpretation (*v.* Or., *Sel. in Gen.* 29; Didym., *In Gen.* 106) and then the ingenious suggestion of Theodore of Mopsuestia (*fragg. in Gen.* on 3.22 LXX = 3.21 MT).

2. In his expression of admiration for the kindliness of providence Theodoret agrees with Diodore (Deconinck, frag. 17). Similarly, von Rad remarks (on 3.21): "[I]t is an act of marked significance. For the first time we see the Creator as the preserver!"

---

1. Theodoret's questioner rightly notes that Gn 3.22 seems to affirm the devil's promise in v. 5. The modern commentator Speiser suggests (pp. 26f.) that the biblical author may have derived, either directly or indirectly, the notion of wisdom rivalling that of the gods from a passage of the Gilgamesh Epic but concludes that we have no "way of knowing how the [Hebrew] author himself interpreted these notions."

ἁμαρτίας τὴν ὁρμήν· ὁ γὰρ ἀποθανών, φησί, δεδικαίωται ἀπὸ
10 τῆς ἁμαρτίας.ᶜ καταντικρὺ δὲ αὐτὸν τοῦ παραδείσου διάγειν
προσέταξεν ἵνα, τῆς ἀλύπου βιοτῆς εἰς μνήμην ἐρχόμενος,
μισῇ τὴν ἁμαρτίαν ὡς πρόξενον τῆς ἐπιπόνου ζωῆς.

XLI

Εἰ ἐλυπήθη ὁ Κάϊν, μὴ δεχθέντων τῶν παρ' αὐτοῦ
προσενεχθέντων, δῆλον ὅτι μετεμελήθη· τῶν γὰρ
μεταμελουμένων ἡ λύπη.ᵃ

Ἡνίασεν αὐτόν, οὐχ ἡ αὐτοῦ πλημμέλεια, ἀλλ' ἡ τοῦ
5 ἀδελφοῦ εὐπραξία. τοῦτο γὰρ καὶ ὁ Ἀκύλας ἠνίξατο· ἔφη δὲ
οὕτως· καὶ ὀργίλον τῷ Κάϊν σφόδρα, καὶ ἔπεσε τὸ πρόσωπον
αὐτοῦ. καὶ εἶπε Κύριος πρὸς Κάϊν, εἰς τί ὀργίλον σοι;ᵇ

XLII

Ποῖον σημεῖον ἔθετο τῷ Κάϊν ὁ Θεός;ᵃ
Αὐτὸς ὁ τοῦ Θεοῦ ὅρος σημεῖον ἦν, κωλύων αὐτὸν
ἀναιρεθῆναι. καὶ αὐτὸς δὲ τῶν μελῶν ὁ κλόνος ἐπίσημον αὐτὸν
καὶ δῆλον εἰργάζετο.

c. Rom 6.7

---

xli 5, 12, B, C, 4 7 9 10 [32] 35 37 = 18 mss.
a. Gn 4.5   b. Gn 4.5f. (LXX var.)

---

xlii 5, 12, B, C⁻⁵², 4 7 9 10 [32] 35 37 = 17 mss.
a. Gn 4.15

who has died has been acquitted of sin."[2c] He ordered him to live directly opposite the garden so that he would remember his trouble-free existence and hate sin for causing his life of hardship.

XLI

If Cain was grieved when his offerings were not received, he had clearly repented, since grief is a mark of remorse.[a]

It was not his sin that grieved him, but his brother's success, as Aquila also implies in his translation: "Cain was very angry, and his face fell. The Lord said to Cain, What is the reason for your anger?"[b]

XLII

What kind of sign did God put on Cain?[a]
God's judgment was itself a sign, which protected him from being killed. In addition, the shaking of his limbs was enough to mark him out.[1]

2. Here, as in *Qq.* 24 and 37, Theodoret advances a positive interpretation of the Fall and its consequences.

---

1. Chrysostom also takes (*hom.* 19.5 *in Gen.*) the mark of Cain (Gn 4.15) to consist in bodily tremors. Speiser thinks (on 4.15) rather of "protective signs, usually placed on the forehead" such as that in Ezek 9.4 and 6; von Rad (on 4.15f.) of a "tattoo."

The Questions on Genesis

XLIII

Τίνα ὁ Κάϊν ἔσχε γυναῖκα;[a]

Δῆλον ὅτι τὴν ἀδελφήν. οὐκ ἦν δὲ τοῦτο τηνικαῦτα κατηγορία, οὐδενὸς ἀπαγορεύοντος νόμου, ἄλλως τε οὐδὲ οἷόν τε ἦν ἄλλως αὐξηθῆναι τὸ γένος. ἠβουλήθη δὲ ὁ Θεὸς ἐξ ἑνὸς
5 ἀνδρὸς καὶ μιᾶς γυναικὸς ἅπαντα συστῆσαι τῶν ἀνθρώπων τὰ ἔθνη· πρῶτον ἵνα τὸ ταὐτὸν τῆς φύσεως γινώσκωσιν, ὡς ἐξ ἑνὸς ζεύγους βεβλαστηκότες, ἔπειτα καὶ εἰς ὁμόνοιαν συνάπτωνται, ὡς ἐκ μιᾶς ῥίζης ἠνθηκότες. εἰ γάρ, καὶ τούτων παρὰ τοῦ Θεοῦ τῶν ὅλων πρυτανευθέντων, μυρίαι τολμῶνται
10 σφαγαί, τί οὐκ ἂν ἔδρασαν εἰ ἐκ διαφόρων βεβλαστηκέναι πατέρων ᾠήθησαν; τούτου χάριν ἕνα μὲν ἐκ τῆς γῆς διέπλασεν ἄνδρα,[b] ἐκ δὲ τούτου μίαν ἐδημιούργησε γυναῖκα,[c] ἐκ δὲ τούτων πᾶσαν τὴν οἰκουμένην τοῦ γένους ἐπλήρωσε. διὰ τήνδε τοίνυν τὴν αἰτίαν συνεχώρησεν ἐν ἀρχῇ τῶν ἀδελφῶν
15 τὴν ἐπιμιξίαν· ἐπειδὴ δὲ ηὐξήθη τὸ γένος, ὡς παράνομον τοῦτον ἀπαγορεύει τὸν γάμον.[d] διά τοι τοῦτο σὺν τῷ Νῶε καὶ τοῖς υἱέσι καὶ τὰς ἐκείνων γυναῖκας διέσωσεν ἐν τῇ κιβωτῷ[e] ἵνα ταῖς ἀνεψιαῖς οἱ ἐκείνων συναφθῶσι παῖδες.

XLIV

Τίνας ἀνεῖλεν ὁ Λάμεχ;[a]

Οὐ δύο, καθά τινες ὑπειλήφασιν, οὐδὲ τὸν Κάϊν ὡς ἕτεροι μεμυθολογήκασιν, ἀλλ' ἕνα καὶ τοῦτον νέον· ἄνδρα, γάρ φησιν,

---

XLIII 5, 12, B, C, 4 7 9 10 [32] 35 37 = 18 mss.

a. Gn 4.17   b. Gn 2.7   c. Gn 2.21f.   d. Lv 18.9   e. Gn 7.7, 13

XLIV 5, 12, B, C, 4 7 9 10 [32] 35 37 = 18 mss.

a. Gn 4.23f.

XLIII

Whom did Cain marry?[a]

His sister, of course. At the time, this was not an offense, no law forbidding it, especially since there was no other way to provide for the increase of the race.[1] God willed that all the nations of humanity be brought into being from one man and one woman: first, so that springing from one couple, they would perceive that they all possessed the same basic nature; second, so that growing from one root, they would be joined in harmony.[2] If even after the God of the universe arranged things like this, they dare to commit countless murders, what would they stop at if they thought themselves descended from different parents? Therefore, he formed one man from the earth,[b] created one woman from him,[c] and filled the whole world with their offspring. To achieve this goal, he allowed intercourse of brother and sister in the beginning, but when the race had increased, he made this kind of marriage unlawful.[d] Hence, in the ark along with Noah and his sons he saved also the wives of his sons,[e] so that the boys could be married to their cousins.

XLIV

Whom did Lamech kill?[a]

Not two people, as some commentators suppose, nor Cain, a tale invented by others, but one, a young man. The text says, note, "I

---

1. The question of the identity of Cain's wife in Gn 4.17 is a familiar conundrum. Theodoret follows Chrysostom (*hom.* 20.1 *in Gen.*) in identifying her as Cain's sister and defending the arrangement as unavoidable.

2. Though affirming that all of humanity had to derive from a single stock, Theodoret does not cite a factor that would have seemed important to Augustine, *viz.* the necessity for the transmission of original sin through natural genera-

ἀπέκτεινα εἰς τραῦμα ἐμοὶ καὶ νεανίσκον εἰς μώλωπα ἐμοί,[b]
5 τουτέστιν, ἄνδρα νέαν ἄγοντα τὴν ἡλικίαν. διέφυγε μέντοι
τὴν τιμωρίαν διὰ τὴν τῆς ἁμαρτίας ὁμολογίαν καί, καθ'
ἑαυτοῦ τὴν ψῆφον ἐξενεγκών, τὴν θείαν διεκώλυσε ψῆφον.

XLV

Ποῦ μετατέθεικε τὸν Ἐνὼχ ὁ τῶν ὅλων Θεός;[a]

Οὐ δεῖ ζητεῖν τὰ σεσιγημένα, στέργειν δὲ προσήκει τὰ
γεγραμμένα. ἐγὼ δὲ οἶμαι τοῦτο πεποιηκέναι τὸν τῶν ὅλων
Θεὸν εἰς ψυχαγωγίαν τῶν τῆς ἀρετῆς ἀθλητῶν. ἐπειδὴ γὰρ ὁ
5 Ἄβελ, πρῶτος γεγονὼς τῆς δικαιοσύνης καρπός, πρόωρός τε
καὶ πρόρριζος ἐξεκόπη,[b] ἐλπὶς δὲ τῆς ἀναστάσεως οὐδέπω
τοὺς ἀνθρώπους ἐψυχαγώγει, μετέθηκεν εὐαρεστήσαντα τὸν
Ἐνὼχ ὁ τῶν ὅλων Θεὸς[c] καὶ τῆς τῶν θνητῶν ἐχώρισε βιοτῆς
ἵνα ἕκαστος τῶν εὐσεβεῖν προαιρουμένων λογίζηται, οἷα δὴ

b. Gn 4.23

---

xlv 5, 12, B, C, 4 7 9 10 *[32]* 35 37 = 18 mss.

a. Gn 5.24   b. Gn 4.8   c. Gn 5.22, 24

killed a man as a wound to myself and a youth as a bruise to myself";[b] that is, a man in his youth. Yet he escaped punishment by confessing the sin, and, by delivering sentence on himself, headed off the divine verdict.[1]

XLV

To what place did God remove Enoch?[a]

We should not pry into secrets but be grateful for what is written. Nonetheless, my view is that the God of the universe did this for the encouragement of the athletes of virtue. Since Abel, the first fruit of righteousness, was cut down in his prime without leaving offspring,[b] and people could not yet draw encouragement from the hope of the resurrection, the God of the universe took Enoch, who was pleasing to him,[c] to another place and set him apart from the life of mortals.[1] His purpose was that everyone who chooses a life of

---

tion. He locates the effects of the fall primarily in the weakening of human nature, which can still resist sin. V. his commentary on Ps 51.5 = 50.7 LXX (PG, vol. 80, col. 1244 B-C): "We learn from all these passages [i.e., from Ps 51.5; Gn 8.21; Rm 5.12], not that the power of sin is built into human nature—for if that were the case, we would not be liable to punishment—but that our nature is inclined to slip and fall, as it is undermined by the passions. Nonetheless, rationality prevails when supported by our efforts" (νικᾷ δὲ ὅμως ἡ γνώμη, πόνοις συνεργοῖς κεχρημένη). Compare this with Augustine's remark (*Enarr. in Ps.* 50, sec. 10) on the same verse: "No one is born without trailing along with him the punishment [i.e., for Adam's sin] and the guilt that merits that punishment (*Nemo nascitur nisi trahens poenam, trahens meritum poenae*)." For a discussion of Antiochene teaching on original sin and its transmission, v. R.C. Hill, *Reading the Old Testament*, pp. 177–82 and *cf.* note 2 to Q. 37 above.

---

1. Though "as a wound to myself and . . . as a bruise to myself" (εἰς τραῦμα ἐμοὶ and εἰς μώλωπα ἐμοί); represent Hebrew phrases meaning "for wounding me" and "for striking me," Theodoret apparently understands the preposition εἰς in the sense of "bringing about" or "causing" and the pronoun ἐμοὶ as reflexive: "to cause a wound, to cause a bruise to myself." Thus, he concludes that Lamech himself acknowledged that he deserved punishment for killing the young man. *Cf.* Brenton's translation of 4.23.

---

1. The fate of Enoch in Gn 5.24 is intriguing, a predictable topic for a ques-

10 λόγῳ τετιμημένος, ὡς ὁ τοῦτον τετιμηκὼς ἀγέραστον οὐκ
ἐάσει τὸν Ἄβελ, ἅτε δὴ δίκαιος ὢν καὶ δικαίως ἰθύνων τὰ
σύμπαντα. τούτου δὴ χάριν, τὸν μὲν παρεῖδεν ἀναιρούμενον,
τὸν δὲ μετατέθεικεν ἵνα τῇ ἀναρρήσει τῇ τούτου μηνύσῃ τὴν
ἐσομένην ἀνάστασιν· ὁ γὰρ κατὰ τόνδε τὸν βίον τῶν τῆς
15 ἀρετῆς μὴ τετυχηκὼς ἀντιδόσεων, δῆλον ὡς ἐν ἑτέρῳ τούτων
ἀπολαύσεται βίῳ.

XLVI

Τί δή ποτε, τοῦ Ἀδὰμ ἡμαρτηκότος, Ἄβελ ὁ δίκαιος
ἐτελεύτησε πρῶτος;[a]
Σαθρὸν ἠβουλήθη γενέσθαι τὸν τοῦ θανάτου θεμέλιον. εἰ
γὰρ Ἀδὰμ πρότερος ἐτελεύτησεν, ἔσχεν ἂν ἐκεῖνος ἰσχυρὰν
5 τὴν κρηπῖδα, πρῶτον νεκρὸν τὸν ἡμαρτηκότα δεξάμενος.
ἐπειδὴ δὲ τὸν ἀδίκως ἀνῃρημένον ἐδέξατο πρῶτον, σφαλερὸν
τὸ θεμέλιον ἔχει.

XLVII

Τίνας *υἱοὺς τοῦ Θεοῦ* κέκληκεν ὁ Μωϋσῆς;[a]
(1) Ἐμβρόντητοί τινες καὶ ἄγαν ἠλίθιοι ἀγγέλους τούτους
ὑπέλαβον, τῆς οἰκείας ἴσως ἀκολασίας ἀπολογίαν σχήσειν
ἡγούμενοι εἰ τῶν ἀγγέλων τοιαῦτα κατηγοροῖεν. ἔδει δὲ
5 αὐτοὺς ἀκοῦσαι τοῦ Θεοῦ τῶν ὅλων λέγοντος, *οὐ μὴ*
καταμείνῃ τὸ πνεῦμά μου ἐν τοῖς ἀνθρώποις τούτοις εἰς τὸν

XLVI 12, B, C, 4 7 9 10 [32] 35 37 = 17 mss.
a. Gn 4.8

XLVII 5, 12, B, C, 4 7 9 10 [32] 35 37 = 18 mss.
a. Gn 6.2

virtue might be able to use his inborn reason to deduce that after honoring this man, God, both righteous and governing everything righteously, would not let Abel go without a reward. Therefore, though he had permitted the murder of Abel, he took Enoch to another place so that, by the message proclaimed regarding the latter, he might suggest the resurrection that was to come. For it is obvious that anyone who fails to receive a reward for virtue in this life will enjoy it in the next.

XLVI

Why was it that, though Adam sinned, the righteous Abel was the first to die?[a]

God wanted Death's foundation to be unsound. If Adam had been the first to die, Death would have established a strong base by taking the sinner as his first victim. But since he first took the man unjustly slain, his foundation is insecure.

XLVII

Whom did Moses call the "sons of God"?[a]

(1) Some mad fools have assumed they were angels, perhaps in the belief that they might have some excuse for their own intemperate behavior if they could level such charges against angels. But, they should have given due attention to the words of the God of the universe—"My spirit shall not abide in these men forever, for they are

---

tion. Von Rad (on 5.22–24) agrees with Theodoret in seeing a hint here at "otherworldly spheres of existence."

αἰῶνα, διὰ τὸ εἶναι αὐτοὺς σάρκας· ἔσονται δὲ αἱ ἡμέραι
αὐτῶν ἕκατον εἴκοσι ἔτη,[b] καὶ συνιδεῖν ἐντεῦθεν ὡς οὔτε
σάρκας ἔχει τῶν ἀσωμάτων ἡ φύσις οὔτε χρόνῳ ῥητῷ
10 περιωρισμένην ἔχουσι τὴν ζωήν· ἀθάνατοι γὰρ ἐκτίσθησαν.
καὶ τὰ ἑξῆς δὲ τὴν αὐτὴν ἔχει διάνοιαν· ἰδών..., γάρ φησι,
*Κύριος ὁ Θεὸς ὅτι ἐπληθύνθησαν αἱ κακίαι τῶν ἀνθρώπων ἐπὶ
τῆς γῆς, καὶ πᾶς τις διανοεῖται ἐν τῇ καρδίᾳ αὐτοῦ ἐπιμελῶς
ἐπὶ τὰ πονηρὰ πάσας τὰς ἡμέρας, καὶ ἐνεθυμήθη ὁ Θεὸς ὅτι*
15 *ἐποίησε τὸν ἄνθρωπον ἐπὶ τῆς γῆς.*...*καὶ εἶπεν ὁ Θεός,
ἀπαλείψω τὸν ἄνθρωπον, ὃν ἐποίησα, ἀπὸ προσώπου τῆς γῆς,
ἀπὸ ἀνθρώπου ἕως κτήνους καὶ ἀπὸ ἑρπετῶν ἕως πετεινῶν τοῦ
οὐρανοῦ, ὅτι ἐνεθυμήθην ὅτι ἐποίησα αὐτούς*[c] καὶ τῷ Νῶε
πάλιν ἔφη, *καιρὸς παντὸς ἀνθρώπου ἥκει ἐναντίον μου, ὅτι*
20 *ἐπλήσθη ἡ γῆ ἀδικίας ἀπ' αὐτῶν· καὶ ἰδοὺ καταφθείρω αὐτοὺς
καὶ τὴν γῆν.*[d]

Ταῦτα δὲ πάντα ἀνθρώπους εἶναι δηλοῖ τοὺς τὸν
παράνομον βίον ἠγαπηκότας. εἰ δὲ ἄγγελοι ταῖς τῶν
ἀνθρώπων ἐπεμίγησαν θυγατράσιν, ἠδίκηνται μὲν οἱ ἄνθρωποι
25 παρὰ τῶν ἀγγέλων· βίᾳ γὰρ δηλονότι τὰς τούτων θυγατέρας
διέφθειραν. ἠδίκηνται δὲ καὶ παρὰ τοῦ πεποιηκότος Θεοῦ,
ὑπὲρ ἀγγέλων λελαγνευκότων αὐτοὶ κολαζόμενοι. ἀλλὰ ταῦτα
οὐδὲ αὐτὸν οἶμαι φάναι τολμῆσαι τὸν τοῦ ψεύδους πατέρα·[e]
διὰ πολλῶν γὰρ ἐδίδαξεν ἡ θεία γραφὴ καὶ ἀνθρώπους
30 ἡμαρτηκέναι καὶ κατ' ἀνθρώπων ἐξενηνέχθαι τὴν θείαν ψῆφον.

(2) Ποιεῖ δὲ τοῖς πολλοῖς τὴν ἄγνοιαν τὸ παρέργως
ἀναγινώσκειν τὴν θείαν γραφήν. εἰρηκὼς γὰρ ὁ συγγραφεὺς
ὅπως ἐκ μὲν τοῦ Ἀδὰμ ὁ Σὴθ ἐγεννήθη,[f] ἐκ δὲ τοῦ Σὴθ ὁ
Ἐνώς, προσέθηκεν, *οὗτος ἤλπισεν ἐπικαλεῖσθαι τὸ ὄνομα*
35 *Κυρίου τοῦ Θεοῦ.*[g] ὁ δὲ Ἀκύλας οὕτως τοῦτο ἡρμήνευσεν· *τότε
ἤρχθη τοῦ καλεῖν ἐν ὀνόματι Κυρίου.* αἰνίττεται δὲ ὁ λόγος
ὡς διὰ τὴν εὐσέβειαν οὗτος πρῶτος τῆς θείας προσηγορίας
τετύχηκε καὶ ὑπὸ τῶν συγγενῶν ὠνομάσθη Θεός· ὅθεν οἱ ἐκ

b. Gn 6.3   c. Gn 6.5–7   d. Gn 6.13 (LXX)   e. Jn 8.44   f. Gn 4.25
g. Gn 4.26

flesh; their life-span will be one hundred and twenty years"[b]—and reflected that incorporeal beings have no flesh, and that, as they were created immortal, their lives are not limited to a set span. The following words also prove this: "The Lord God saw that the evil deeds of men were multiplied on earth, and everyone's thoughts in his heart were focused on evil his whole life long, and God regretted that he had made man on earth. God said, I shall wipe out the man that I made from the face of the earth, and cattle as well as men, and serpents, and birds of heaven as well, because I regret that I made them."[c] And to Noah he said, "The time of every man has come before me, because it is their fault that the land is filled with iniquity. Lo, I am destroying them and the earth as well."[1d]

Now, all this points to human beings and to those who were fond of a lawless life. If the angels had had relations with the daughters of man, humans would have been wronged by the angels, since, of course, the angels would have raped their daughters. Furthermore, they would have been wronged by God the Creator who punished them for the lascivious behavior of the angels. I do not believe that even the father of falsehood would dare to make any such claim.[e] After all, it is the consistent teaching of Scripture that men are sinners and men the recipients of the divine condemnation.

(2) Yet careless reading of holy Scripture is the cause of error among ordinary people. For after saying that Seth was born of Adam,[f] and Enosh of Seth, the historian added, "He hoped to be called the name of the Lord God."[g] Now, Aquila renders this: "That was the time when a beginning was made of calling on the name of the Lord," but this verse expresses in riddling form the idea that,

1. Like Chrysostom, Theodoret rejects the Alexandrian interpretation equating "the sons of God" with angels; *v.* Didym., *in Gen.* 151f. and *cf.* Guinot, p. 757. In fact, he seems to build his own interpretation on the foundation of the strong antithesis that Chrysostom had drawn (*hom.* 22.3) between the family of Cain (= "the sons of man") and that of Seth (= "the sons of God").

τούτου φύντες *υἱοὶ Θεοῦ* ἐχρημάτιζον ὥσπερ δὴ καὶ ἡμεῖς ἐκ
40 τῆς τοῦ δεσπότου Χριστοῦ προσηγορίας *χριστιανοὶ*
καλούμεθα.

Εἰ δέ τις ταύτην οὐ δέχεται τὴν διάνοιαν διὰ τὸ τὸν
Ἀκύλαν οὕτως ἡρμηνευκέναι, ἀκουσάτω τοῦ Θεοῦ διὰ Δαβὶδ
τοῦ προφήτου λέγοντος, *ἐγὼ εἶπα, θεοί ἐστε, καὶ υἱοὶ*
45 *Ὑψίστου πάντες* [h] καί, *ὁ Θεὸς ἔστη ἐν συναγωγῇ θεῶν, ἐν*
μέσῳ δὲ θεοὺς διακρινεῖ. [i] οὕτω δὲ ὀνομάζει τοὺς ἄρχοντας, ὡς
δηλοῖ τὰ ἑξῆς· *ἕως πότε κρίνετε ἀδικίαν καὶ πρόσωπα*
ἁμαρτωλῶν λαμβάνετε;... κρίνατε ὀρφανῷ καὶ πτωχῷ,
ταπεινὸν καὶ πένητα δικαιώσατε, καὶ τὰ ἑξῆς· [j] καὶ αὖθις,
50 *Θεὸς θεῶν Κύριος ἐλάλησε καὶ ἐκάλεσε τὴν γῆν,* [k] τούτων
αὐτῶν, δηλονότι, τῶν χάριτι τῆς προσηγορίας ταύτης
ἠξιωμένων· οὕτω καὶ ὁ νομοθέτης ἔφη, *θεοὺς οὐ κακολογήσεις*
καὶ ἄρχοντας τοῦ λαοῦ σου οὐκ ἐρεῖς κακῶς. [l]

(3) Κἀκεῖνοι τοίνυν, ὡς εὐσεβεῖς, ὠνομάσθησαν *υἱοὶ τοῦ*
55 *Θεοῦ·* κεχώριστο γὰρ τοῦ Σὴθ τὸ γένος καὶ οὐκ ἐπεμίγνυτο
τοῖς ἐκ τοῦ Κάϊν διὰ τὴν ἐπενεχθεῖσαν αὐτῷ παρὰ τοῦ Θεοῦ
τῶν ὅλων ἀράν. ἀλλὰ χρόνου συχνοῦ διελθόντος· μετὰ πλείονα
γὰρ ἢ δισχίλια ἔτη τὸν κατακλυσμὸν ἐπήγαγεν ὁ Θεός· [m]
εὐειδεῖς θεασάμενοι τῆς τοῦ Κάϊν συγγενείας τὰς θυγατέρας
60 καὶ καταθελχθέντες, ὡς εἰκός, τοῖς παρ' αὐτῶν ἐπινοηθεῖσι
μουσικοῖς ὀργάνοις· ὁ γὰρ Ἰουβὰλ ἐξ αὐτῶν ἀνθήσας
ψαλτήριον καὶ κιθάραν κατέδειξεν· [n] ἐπεμίγησαν αὐταῖς καὶ
διέφθειραν τὴν οἰκείαν εὐγένειαν. καὶ τὰ αὐτὰ τοῖς
ἰσραηλίταις ὑπέμειναν, οἵ, ταῖς τῶν μαδιανιτῶν θυγατράσι
65 μιγέντες, καὶ τῆς ἐκείνων δυσσεβείας μετέσχον καὶ θεήλατον

---

h. Ps 82.6   i. Ps 82.1   j. Ps 82.2f.   k. Ps 50.1   l. Ex 22.28
m. Gn 7.11   n. Gn 4.21

thanks to his virtue, this man was the first to hit upon the divine name and was called "God" by his kindred. Hence, his offspring were styled "sons of God," just as we are called "Christians" from the Lord's title "Christ".[2]

If you do not accept this interpretation on account of Aquila's version, listen to God speaking through the prophet David: "I said, You are gods, and all of you sons of the Most High";[h] and "God has taken his place in an assembly of gods; in their midst, he will judge gods."[i] This is the title he gives to rulers, as indicated by what follows: "How long will you deliver unjust judgments and take the part of sinners? Judge in favor of orphan and poor, give justice to the lowly and needy" and so on;[j] and again, "The Lord God of gods spoke and summoned the earth,"[k] that is, the Lord God of those who had been accorded this title. Hence, the lawgiver said, "You shall not revile gods or malign rulers of your people."[l]

(3) Thus, those ancient men were called "sons of God" because of their virtue. Indeed, the family of Seth lived apart and did not mingle with Cain's family because of the curse laid on him by the God of the universe. But after the passage of a long period of time (it was more than two thousand years later that God brought on the flood),[m] they found the daughters of Cain's line comely, and, perhaps attracted by the musical instruments they had invented (Jubal, one of their race, introduced the harp and lyre),[3n] the descendants of Seth intermarried with them and contaminated their own lineage. Thus, they suffered the same fate as the Israelites who had relations with the daughters of the Midianites, participated in their idolatry,

---

2. Theodoret's identification of the sons of God rests on two errors: a mistranslation presented by his Bible and his own mistaken understanding of the LXX. In 4.26 the LXX, confusing two similar Hebrew forms, wrongly renders as "hoped" (ἤλπισεν) a verb actually meaning "to begin." Theodoret compounds the confusion by interpreting the following ἐπικαλεῖσθαι as a passive meaning "to be called" or "to be surnamed" rather than a middle meaning "to call upon" or "invoke."

3. Theodoret regards the separate genealogies of chs. 4 and 5 as indicating the

τιμωρίαν ἐδέξαντο.° περὶ τούτων καὶ ὁ θεῖος ἔφη Δαβίδ, *καὶ*
ἐμίγησαν ἐν τοῖς ἔθνεσι, καὶ ἔμαθον τὰ ἔργα αὐτῶν, καὶ
*ἐδούλευσαν τοῖς γλυπτοῖς αὐτῶν.*ᵖ οὕτως οἱ ἐκ τοῦ Σὴθ τὸ
γένος κατάγοντες πάλαι μέν, ὡς ἀρετῆς ἐπιμελούμενοι, *υἱοὶ*
70 *Θεοῦ* ἐχρημάτιζον· ὑπὸ δὲ τῆς ὥρας τῶν ἀνοσίων γυναικῶν
δελεασθέντες, συνέχεαν μὲν διακεκριμένα τὰ γένη, καρπὸν δὲ
κληρονομίας τὴν πανωλεθρίαν ἐδέξαντο.

Ἐκεῖνο μέντοι ἐπισημήνασθαι χρή, ὡς, οὐχ ἁπλῶς αὐτῶν
ἁμαρτίαν ὁ θεῖος λόγος κατηγορεῖ, ἀλλὰ τὴν μετ' ἐπιμελείας
75 καὶ σπουδῆς παρανομίαν. τοῦτο γὰρ δηλοῖ τὸ *πᾶς τις*
διανοεῖται ἐν τῇ καρδίᾳ αὐτοῦ ἐπιμελῶς ἐπὶ τὰ πονηρὰ πάσας
τὰς ἡμέρας.�q οἱ μὲν γὰρ δυσχεραίνοντες τῆς ἁμαρτίας τὴν
προσβολήν, ἡττώμενοι δὲ διὰ τὴν τοῦ νοῦ ῥαθυμίαν τῇ
πονηρίᾳ, εἶθ' ὕστερον ἀλγοῦντες καὶ στένοντες, ἔχουσί τινα
80 μετρίαν ἁμῇ γέ πῃ παραίτησιν· οἱ δὲ εἰς ἀκολασίαν καὶ
πονηρίαν παντάπασιν ἀποκλίνοντες καὶ δοῦλον τῶν παθῶν τὸν
λογισμὸν ἀποφαίνοντες ὥστε καὶ προσεπινοεῖν ἑτέρας κακίας
ἰδέας καὶ τοῦτο, οὐχ ἅπαξ ἢ δίς, ἀλλὰ παρὰ πάντα τὸν βίον,
ποίας ἄξιοι συγγνώμης; ποία δὲ κόλασις οὐ σμικρὰ τοῖς οὕτω
85 σφᾶς αὐτοὺς ἐκδεδωκόσιν εἰς ὄλεθρον;

XLVIII

Τίνας καλεῖ *γίγαντας* ἡ θεία γραφή;ᵃ
Τινές φασι τοὺς ἔτη πολλὰ βεβιωκότας, τινὲς δὲ τοὺς
θεομισεῖς καὶ ἀντιθέους ἀνθρώπους. οἱ δὲ ταῦτα οὕτω
νενοηκότες οὔ φασι τούτους μείζονα τῶν ἄλλων ἀνθρώπων
5 σώματα ἐσχηκέναι. ἐγὼ δὲ ὅταν ἀκούσω τῆς θείας γραφῆς

---

o. Nm 25.1–9   p. Ps 106.35f.   q. Gn 6.5

XLVIII *5, 12, B, C, 4 7 9 10 13(inc.) [32] 35 37* = 19 mss.
a. Gn 6.4

and received retribution from heaven.[o] The divinely inspired David said of them: "They mingled with the nations, learned their practices, and served their idols."[p] Likewise the descendants of Seth, though formerly attentive to virtue and styled "sons of God," were seduced by the charm of the unholy women, mingled races once kept apart, and thus inherited utter ruin.

Of course, we should observe that the divine word blames not simply their sin but the wholehearted zeal of their lawlessness. That is the meaning of "Everyone's thoughts in his heart were focused on evil his whole life long."[q] Some people, though disgusted at the first attack of sin, make no serious effort to oppose it and are overcome by wickedness but later evince profound grief. These have some slight excuse. But others, who are wholeheartedly inclined to intemperance and vice, and whose mind is so enslaved to passion as to excogitate new forms of wickedness, not once or twice, but all their life—what pardon do they deserve? What punishment could possibly be severe enough for people who have surrendered themselves to ruination?

XLVIII

Whom does holy Scripture call "giants"?[a]

Some commentators have claimed that the giants were people who lived to a great age; others that they were people who hated and opposed God. Those who hold these opinions deny that they were bigger than other people. But I am persuaded that there were men

separation of the races of Seth and Cain. In fact, as R.J. Clifford and R.E. Murphy point out (p. 13) the two lists, deriving from different strands of tradition, actually contain the same names or variants of the same name: "Cain/Kenan; Enoch/ Enoch; Irad/Jared; Mehuyael/Mahalalel; Methushael/Methusalah; Lamech/ Lamech." The reader will note that in 5.1–32 the LXX's calculations of the ages of the patriarchs are often at variance with those of the MT.

λεγούσης περὶ τοῦ Ἐνάκ, ὅτι ἀπόγονος ἦν τῶν γιγάντων·[b] καὶ
περὶ τοῦ Ὢγ ὅτι, ἡ κλίνη αὐτοῦ ἦν σιδηρᾶ... ἐννέα πήχεων
τὸ μῆκος..., καὶ τεσσάρων πήχεων τὸ εὖρος καὶ ὅτι οὗτος ἐκ
τῶν ῥαφαῖν ὑπελείφθη·[c] καὶ τῶν κατασκόπων διηγουμένων ὅτι,
10 ἦμεν ἐνώπιον αὐτῶν ὡσεὶ ἀκρίδες·[d] καὶ τοῦ Θεοῦ βεβαιοῦντος
τοὺς λόγους καὶ λέγοντος ὅτι, παραδέδωκά σοι τὸν ἀμορραῖον,
οὗ τὸ ὕψος ἦν ὡς κέδρου, καὶ ἰσχυρὸς ἦν ὡς δρῦς·[e] καὶ περὶ
τοῦ Γολιὰδ ὅτι, τεσσάρων πήχεων καὶ σπιθαμῆς τὸ μῆκος
εἶχεν,[f] ἡγοῦμαι γεγενῆσθαι τινὰς παμμεγέθεις ἀνθρώπους, τοῦ
15 Θεοῦ καὶ τοῦτο σοφῶς πρυτανεύσαντος ἵνα γνῶσιν ὡς, οὐκ
ἀσθενῶν, ὁ δημιουργὸς τοσοῦτον τοῖς ἀνθρώποις ἀπένειμε
μέτρον· ῥάδιον γὰρ ἦν αὐτῷ καὶ μείζους δημιουργῆσαι· ἀλλὰ
τὸν τῦφον ἐκκόπτων καὶ τὴν ἀλαζονείαν κωλύων, μέγιστα τοῖς
ἀνθρώποις οὐκ ἔδωκε σώματα. εἰ γὰρ ἐν σμικροῖς σώμασιν,
20 οὐ κατ' ἀλλήλων μόνον, ἀλλὰ καὶ κατ' αὐτοῦ μεγαλαυχοῦσι τοῦ
ποιητοῦ, τί οὐκ ἂν ἔδρασαν εἰ μεγίστων σωμάτων μετέλαχον;

XLIX

Διὰ τί πολὺν χρόνον ἔζων οἱ παλαιοί;[a]

Ὥστε αὐξηθῆναι τὸ γένος τῷ πλείονι χρόνῳ. διὰ τοῦτο καὶ
πολλαῖς συνήπτοντο γυναιξίν. αὐτίκα γοῦν καὶ μετὰ τὸν
κατακλυσμὸν μέχρι τῶν πατριαρχῶν, μακρόβιοι ἦσαν. ἐπειδὴ
5 δὲ τὴν οἰκουμένην ἐπλήρωσαν, ἠλαττώθη λοιπὸν ὁ τῶν ἐτῶν
ἀριθμός.[b]

l. 20 οὐ ... μόνον ... ἀλλὰ καὶ B[-30], 4 7 9 13 35 : οὐ ... μόνον ... ἀλλὰ 12, 30
: οὐ ... ἀλλὰ καὶ 5, 51 52, 10 : οὐ ... ἀλλὰ Sir. Sch. F.M. = "they do not develop
self-importance toward one another but toward the Creator himself." In the Quaest.
in oct. there are forty-nine other examples of οὐ ... μόνον ... ἀλλὰ καὶ, but
none of either οὐ ... μόνον ... ἀλλὰ or οὐ ... ἀλλὰ καὶ. The obvious sense of
the alternative preferred by previous editors is quite inappropriate to the context.

b. Dt 2.10, 21; 9.2   c. Dt 3.11   d. Nm 13.33   e. Am 2.9   f. 1Sm 17.4

XLIX 5, 12, B, C, 4 7 9 10 13 [32] 35 37 = 19 mss.

a. Gn 5   b. Gn 6.3

of extraordinary size when I hear holy Scripture say of Anak that "he was a descendant of the giants";[b] that Og had "a bed of iron, nine cubits long and four cubits wide," and that "he was a survivor of the Rephaim";[c] that the spies reported, "we were like grasshoppers to them";[d] that God declared, "I have surrendered to you the Amorite, tall as a cedar and strong as an oak";[e] and when I hear that Goliath "was four cubits and a span tall,"[1f] And I imagine that, in his wisdom, God decided to create the giants so that it would be understood that men were allotted their present stature, not out of any weakness of the Creator, who might easily have fashioned bigger people, but rather because he chose to deny them huge bodies in order to repress their arrogance and conceit. Even with small frames, they develop self-importance not only toward one another but also toward the Creator himself. Just imagine how they would have behaved if they had received huge bodies!

XLIX

Why did people of old live for such a long time?[a]

So that the race would grow in numbers thanks to the longer lifespan. This is also the reason they had many wives. Indeed, from the flood up to the time of the patriarchs, they had long lives, but when they had populated the world, the number of their years was shortened.[1b]

---

1. In his interpretation of the giants (Gn 6.4), Theodoret rejects two opinions, the first favored by Diodore (Deconinck, frag. 20), the second by Origen (*Cels.* 4.92), to accept a position previously endorsed by Chrysostom (*hom.* 22.4 *in Gen.*); *v.* Guinot, p. 758).

---

1. Theodoret does not moralize about the effects of the Fall and the subsequent moral deterioration of the human race.

L

Τί δή ποτε τῷ κατακλυσμῷ τὰ τῶν ἀνθρώπων πλήθη διέφθειρεν;[a]

(1) Ἐξαλεῖψαι τοῦ Κάϊν τὸ γένος ἠθέλησεν· ἀνεμίγη δὲ αὐτῷ καὶ τῶν εὐσεβῶν ἡ φυλή· διὸ καὶ τῆς τιμωρίας μετέσχηκεν.

5 ἀρχὴν δέ τινα καινοῦ βίου ποιήσασθαι βουληθείς, τὸν Νῶε καὶ τοὺς ἐκείνου παῖδας σὺν ταῖς γυναιξὶ διετήρησεν,[b] εὐσεβῆ τε ὄντα καὶ δίκαιον, ἐκ τῆς τῶν εὐσεβῶν συγγενείας βλαστήσαντα, καὶ τὴν τῆς παρανομίας ἐπιμιξίαν μισήσαντα.[c]

Οὐ μήν, ὥς τινές φασιν, ὀργῇ τινι ταῦτα καὶ μεταμελείᾳ

10 πεποίηκε· ταῦτα γάρ τοι ἀνθρώπινα πάθη, ἡ δὲ θεία φύσις ἐλευθέρα παθῶν. ἄλλως τε ἡ μεταμέλεια τοῖς μετὰ τὴν πεῖραν μανθάνουσι τῶν πραγμάτων τὴν φύσιν κατάλληλος· ἀγνοοῦντες γὰρ τὸ ἐσόμενον, προβουλεύονται· εἶτα τῇ πείρᾳ μανθάνοντες ὡς οὐκ ὀρθῶς ἐβουλεύσαντο, μεταμέλονται. ὁ δὲ

15 Θεὸς οὕτως ὁρᾷ τὰ μετὰ πολλὰς ἐσόμενα γενεὰς ὡς ἤδη γεγενημένα· ὡς προορῶν τοίνυν καὶ προγινώσκων, οὕτως ἅπαντα πρυτανεύει. τί δή ποτε τοίνυν μεταμελεῖται, ἅπαντα πρὸς τὴν πρόγνωσιν τὴν οἰκείαν οἰκονομῶν; οὐκοῦν, ἐπὶ Θεοῦ, μεταμέλεια οἰκονομίας μεταβολή· *μεταμεμέλημαι*, φησὶν ὅτι,

20 *κέχρικα τὸν Σαοὺλ εἰς βασιλέα*,[d] ἀντὶ τοῦ· ἐδοκίμασα μὲν παῦσαι τοῦτον, ἕτερον δὲ χειροτονῆσαι. οὕτω κἀνταῦθα, *ἐνεθυμήθην ὅτι ἐποίησα τὸν ἄνθρωπον*,[e] ἐδοκίμασα διολέσαι τῶν ἀνθρώπων τὸ γένος. ἀλλὰ φιλάνθρωπος ὤν, σπέρμα τὸν Νῶε τῇ φύσει τετήρηκεν.

25 (2) Ἐπειδὴ δὲ καὶ τῶν ἀλόγων τὰ γένη τῆς τῶν ἀνθρώπων ἕνεκα δεδημιούργηται χρείας, καὶ ταῦτα τοῖς ἀνθρώποις συνδιεφθάρη, πλὴν τῶν ἐν τῇ κιβωτῷ σὺν τῷ Νῶε διασωθέντων·

L 5, 12, B, C, 4 7 9 10 13 [32] 35 37 = 19 mss.

a. Gn 6.21–23   b. Gn 8.18   c. Gn 6.9   d. 1Sm 15.11 (LXX var.)
e. Gn 6.7

Question L

Why was the bulk of the human race wiped out by the flood?[a]

(1) His intention was to annihilate Cain's line, but since the tribe of the virtuous had intermarried with Cain's line, it was also involved in the punishment. Wanting to make a beginning of a new way of life, he preserved Noah and his sons along with their wives,[b] for Noah was good and righteous, one who had come from the line of the virtuous men and shunned intercourse with lawlessness.[c]

He did this, not, as some commentators claim, out of anger or on second thoughts, as these are, of course, human states, from which the divine nature is free. Second thoughts are typical of those who learn how things really stand only after experience: they make their plans in ignorance of the future, but later, in the light of experience, realizing that their decision was wrong, have second thoughts. By contrast, God sees what will happen many generations in the future as if it had already happened; it is with foresight and foreknowledge that he governs the universe. Why, then, would he have second thoughts when he plans everything in accord with his own foreknowledge? In God's case, therefore, a second thought is a change in the plan of salvation: "I have second thoughts about anointing Saul king"[d] is equivalent to "I have decided to depose him and appoint someone else." Similarly, in this case: "I regret making the human being,"[e] means "I have decided to destroy humanity." But being merciful, he preserved Noah as seed for the race.

(2) And since the species of irrational animals had been created for man's use, they were destroyed along with the human race ex-

ἐκέλευσε γὰρ ὁ δεσπότης Θεὸς ἀνὰ δύο μὲν ἐξ ἑκάστου
γένους τῶν δοκούντων ἀκαθάρτων διασωθῆναι, ἀνὰ ἑπτὰ δὲ
30 τῶν καθαρῶν.ᶠ ἐπειδὴ γὰρ ἤμελλε συγχωρεῖν τοῖς ἀνθρώποις
μεταλαμβάνειν κρεῶν,ᵍ ἤμελλον δὲ καὶ θυσίας αὐτῷ προσφέρειν
τῆς εὐσεβείας οἱ τρόφιμοι, πλείονα τὰ καθαρὰ φυλαχθῆναι
προσέταξε· τὰς μὲν τρεῖς συζυγίας εἰς τὴν αὔξησιν τοῦ
γένους, τὸ δὲ ἓν τὸ περιττὸν εἰς θυσίαν. εὐθὺς γὰρ ὁ Νῶε,
35 μετὰ τὴν παῦλαν τῆς τιμωρίας, θυσίαν τῷ Θεῷ χαριστήριον
προσενήνοχεν· ἀπὸ πάντων, φησί, τῶν κτηνῶν τῶν καθαρῶν καὶ
ἀπὸ πάντων τῶν πετεινῶν τῶν καθαρῶν,ʰ ὡς εἶναι δῆλον ὅτι
τούτουγε χάριν ἀνὰ ἑπτὰ προσέταξεν ἐξ ἑκάστου γένους τῶν
καθαρῶν εἰς τὴν κιβωτὸν εἰσαχθῆναι, ἵνα, τὸ ἓν ζῷον ἐξ ἑκάστου
40 γένους ὁ Νῶε προσφέρων, μὴ διαφθείρῃ τὰς συζυγίας.

LI

Τί ἤσθιεν ἐν τῇ κιβωτῷ τὰ θηρία;

Δῆλον ὅτι χιλόν τε καὶ σπέρματα. ἔφη γὰρ πρὸς αὐτὸν ὁ
Θεός, σὺ δὲ λήψῃ σεαυτῷ ἀπὸ πάντων τῶν βρωμάτων, ὧν
ἔδεσθε, καὶ συνάξεις πρὸς ἑαυτόν, καὶ ἔσται σοὶ καὶ ἐκείνοις
5 φαγεῖν.ᵃ ἐξ ἀρχῆς δὲ ὁ Θεὸς οὐ κρεοφαγεῖν ἐνομοθέτησε τοῖς
ἀνθρώποις· ἰδού, γὰρ ἔφη, δέδωκα ὑμῖν πάντα χόρτον σπόριμον

---

f. Gn 7.2f.   g. Gn 9.2f.   h. Gn 8.20

LI   5, 12, B, C, 4 7 9 10 13 20 [32] 35 37 = 20 mss.

ll. 5f.   ἐξ ἀρχῆς … ἀνθρώποις F.M. : ταὐτὸ δε καὶ τοῖς ἀνθρώποις
ἐσθίειν ἐνομοθέτησεν C, [32] 37, Sir. Sch. = "The divine law enjoined that the
animals should have the same food as human beings."

l. 5   κρεοφαγεῖν J.P. : κρέον φαγεῖν F.M. : τοῦτο φαγεῖν 5. While the
TLG lists ten attestations of κρεοφαγεῖν, the form κρέον is elsewhere attested
only in the *Suda* (Adler 2378) and the *Et. gud.* (*ad* κρεῖον), in each case only to
provide a term intermediary between κρέας = meat and κρεῖον = meat tray.

a. Gn 6.21

cept for those kept alive on the ark along with Noah. The Lord God, remember, ordered that there be preserved two of each species of animals considered unclean and seven of the clean.[f] Since he meant to permit humanity to consume meat,[g] and the virtuous were to offer him sacrifices, he gave orders for the preservation of more clean animals: namely, three pairs for natural increase and the one left over for sacrificing. Immediately after the cessation of the punishment, Noah made an offering of thanksgiving to God "from all the clean animals and all the clean birds."[1h] This shows that he ordered seven of each of the clean animals to be taken aboard the ark, so that in offering a single animal from each species, Noah would not destroy the pairs.

LI

What did the animals eat while aboard the ark?

Fodder and seeds, of course. God said to him, "You will take for yourself of all the foods you eat and store it up for yourself, and it will serve as food for you and them."[a] In the beginning, God's law did not countenance the human consumption of flesh: "Lo, I have given you every plant upon all the earth bearing seed fit for sowing

1. As Theodoret had not adverted to difference in authorship in creation stories and genealogies, so he does not highlight the discrepancies in the numbers of animals taken aboard the ark in 6.19f. and 7.2f.

σπεῖρον σπέρμα, ὅ ἐστιν ἐπάνω πάσης τῆς γῆς, καὶ πᾶν ξύλον,
ὃ ἔχει ἐν ἑαυτῷ καρπὸν σπέρματος σπόριμον· ὑμῖν ἔσται εἰς
βρῶσιν καὶ πᾶσι τοῖς θηρίοις τῆς γῆς, καὶ πᾶσι τοῖς πετεινοῖς
10 τοῦ οὐρανοῦ, καὶ παντὶ ἑρπετῷ ἕρποντι ἐπὶ τῆς γῆς, ὃ ἔχει ἐν
ἑαυτῷ ψυχὴν ζωῆς· καὶ πάντα χόρτον χλωρὸν εἰς βρῶσιν,[b] ὡς
εἶναι δῆλον ὅτι καὶ οἱ ἄνθρωποι καὶ τὰ ζῷα κρεωφαγίας
ἀπείχοντο, τροφὴν δὲ εἶχον τοὺς ἀπὸ γῆς φυομένους καρπούς.
τὸ δὲ σπεῖρον σπέρμα, σπερμαῖνον σπέρμα ὁ Ἀκύλας
15 ἡρμήνευσεν.

LII

Πῶς νοητέον τὸ ἐμνήσθη Κύριος τοῦ Νῶε;[a]

Προσφόρως τοῖς ἀνθρώποις ἡ θεία γραφὴ διαλέγεται καί,
ὡς ἀκούειν δύνανται, μετασχηματίζει τοὺς λόγους. ὥσπερ
τοίνυν ἐπὶ Θεοῦ ἡ μεταμέλεια οἰκονομίας ἐστὶ διαφορά·
5 μεταμεμέλημαι γὰρ ὅτι κέχρικα τὸν Σαοὺλ εἰς βασιλέα[b] ἀντὶ
τοῦ· ἐδοκίμασα ἄλλον ἀντ' αὐτοῦ καταστῆσαι. οὕτω καὶ
ἐνταῦθα νοητέον ἐνεθυμήθην ὅτι ἐποίησα τὸν ἄνθρωπον[c] ἀντὶ
τοῦ· ἐδοκίμασα αὐτοῖς πανωλεθρίαν ἐπαγαγεῖν. καὶ τοῦτο
τοίνυν τὸ ἐμνήσθη ὁ Θεὸς τοῦ Νῶε, οὐ προτέραν λήθην
10 αἰνίττεται, ἀλλὰ τὴν ἄρρητον αὐτοῦ φιλανθρωπίαν δηλοῖ, ὅτι
διὰ τὴν περὶ ἐκεῖνον φιλοστοργίαν προσέταξεν ὡς τάχιστα
καταποθῆναι τὸ ἄπειρον ἐκεῖνο καὶ ἀμέτρητον ὕδωρ. δήλην δὲ

b. Gn 1.29f.

LII 5, 12, B, C, 4 7 9 10 13 [32] 35 37 = 19 mss.

l. 8 αὐτοῖς πανωλεθρίαν ἐπαγαγεῖν B⁻²⁴, c₁, 4 37 : εἰς αὐτοὺς
πανωλεθρίαν ἐπαγαγεῖν 24, 8, 13, Sir. Sch. : αὐτοὺς πανωλεθρίαν
ἐπαγαγεῖν F.M. Theodoret regularly combines ἐπάγειν + direct object with
the dative. In the *Quaest. in oct.* there is no other example of either ἐπάγειν +
direct object + εἰς + accusative or of ἐπάγειν + double accusative.

a. Gn 8.1   b. 1Sm 15.11 (LXX var.)   c. Gn 6.6

and every tree containing fruit with seed fit for sowing; these will be your food. And to all the beasts of the earth, all the birds of heaven, and every reptile creeping on the earth, which has the spirit of life in it, I have given every green plant for food."[1b] So we may infer that humans as well as animals abstained from eating meat and got their nourishment from the produce of the earth. Aquila renders "bearing seed" as "procreating seed."

LII

How should we understand the verse "The Lord remembered Noah"?[a]

Holy Scripture speaks in a manner suited to human beings and frames its expressions so we may receive them. So just as in God's case second thoughts represent a change in the plan of salvation—"I have second thoughts about anointing Saul king"[b] in the sense, "I have decided to put someone else in his place"—so here "I regret making humanity,"[c] is to be taken to mean "I have decided to wipe them out." Accordingly, the verse, "God remembered Noah," does not imply previous forgetfulness but indicates his ineffable loving-kindness in giving instructions, out of his affection for Noah, for that vast, immeasurable quantity of water to be swallowed up as quickly as possible. Indicating his unspeakable goodness, Moses

1. *Cf.* note 3 to *Q.* 37.

αὐτοῦ ποιῶν τὴν ἄφραστον ἀγαθότητα, προστέθεικεν ὅτι, *καὶ*
πάντων τῶν κτηνῶν, καὶ πάντων τῶν πετεινῶν, καὶ πάντων
15 *τῶν ἑρπετῶν, ὅσα ἦν μετ' αὐτοῦ ἐν τῇ κιβωτῷ.*[d] ἡμῶν δὲ χάριν
καὶ ταῦτα προμηθείας ἠξίωσεν· τοῦτο γὰρ καὶ ὁ μέγας Δαβὶδ
βοᾷ· *ὁ ἐξανατέλλων χόρτον τοῖς κτήνεσι καὶ χλόην τῇ δουλείᾳ*
τῶν ἀνθρώπων·[e] καὶ πάλιν, *ἀνθρώπους καὶ κτήνη σώσεις, Κύριε·*[f]
δι' ἡμᾶς γὰρ καὶ τῶν ἡμετέρων ἐπιμελεῖται.

LIII

Τί ἐστιν *ὠσφράνθη Κύριος . . . ὀσμὴν εὐωδίας;*[a]

Ὑπεδέξατο τοῦ Νῶε τὸ εὔγνωμον, οὐ τῇ κνίσσῃ τερφθείς·
ὀστῶν γὰρ καιομένων οὐδὲν δυσωδέστερον· ἀλλὰ τοῦ
προσενηνοχότος ἐπαινέσας τὴν γνώμην. οὐ γὰρ σωματικὰ ἔχει
5 μόρια ἵνα καὶ ῥῖνας αὐτῷ περιθῶμεν· διὰ ῥινῶν γὰρ ἡ
ὄσφρησις. ἀμείβεται οὖν αὐτὸν τῇ εὐλογίᾳ, καί, ἐπειδὴ
σπέρμα τοῦ γένους ἦν, καὶ ῥίζα τῆς φύσεως, καὶ δεύτερος
Ἀδάμ, δίδωσιν αὐτῷ τὴν εὐλογίαν, ἧς ἐκεῖνος εὐθὺς
διαπλασθεὶς ἀπολελαύκει· *αὐξάνεσθε, καὶ πληθύνεσθε, καὶ*
10 *πληρώσατε τὴν γῆν, καὶ κατακυριεύσατε αὐτῆς· καὶ ὁ φόβος*
ὑμῶν καὶ ὁ τρόμος ὑμῶν ἔσται ἐπὶ πᾶσι τοῖς θηρίοις τῆς γῆς,
καὶ ἐπὶ πάντα τὰ πετεινὰ τοῦ οὐρανοῦ, καὶ ἐπὶ πάντα τὰ
κινούμενα ἐπὶ τῆς γῆς, καὶ ἐπὶ πάντας τοὺς ἰχθύας τῆς
θαλάσσης, ἃ ὑπὸ χεῖρα ὑμῖν δέδωκα.[b] καὶ ὁ λόγος ἔργον
15 γέγονε· δέδιε γὰρ ἅπαντα καὶ αὐτὴν τὴν τοῦ ἀνθρώπου σκιὰν
καὶ τὰ νηκτά, καὶ τὰ χερσαῖα, καὶ τὰ πτηνά. εἶτα τὸν περὶ
τῆς κρεωφαγίας αὐτῷ δέδωκε νόμον, ὡς λαχάνων τῶν κρεῶν
ἀπολαύειν κελεύσας.[c]

d. Gn 8.1   e. Ps 104.14   f. Ps 36.6

LIII 5, 12, B, C, 4 7 9 10 13 [32] 35 37 = 19 mss.

a. Gn 8.21   b. Gn 9.1f.   c. Gn 9.3

adds, "and God remembered all the cattle, all the birds, and all the reptiles that were with him in the ark."[d] It was for our sake that he regarded them worthy of his providence. Thus, the mighty David also proclaims: "He makes grass grow for the cattle and crops for the service of man";[e] and again, "Lord, you will save men and cattle."[f] For our sake, he cares also for our possessions.

LIII

What is the meaning of "The Lord smelled a pleasing odor"?[1a]

This indicates God's kindliness toward Noah—not that he was pleased with the smell. Nothing smells worse than burning bones, but God commended the attitude of the offerer. God has no body divided into parts that we should imagine him with a nose, for smell comes through the nose. So he rewarded Noah with the blessing, and since he was the seed of the race, the root of human nature, and a second Adam, God gave him the blessing which the first Adam had received immediately after his creation: "Increase, multiply, fill the earth, and subdue it. Fear of you and dread of you will be upon all the beasts of the earth, upon all the birds of heaven, upon everything that moves on the earth, and upon all the fish of the sea; I have put them under your control."[b] The word took effect. All things were in dread even of man's shadow: those that swim, those on land, those that fly. Then delivering the law about the eating of flesh, he commanded Noah to consume flesh as well as vegetables.[2c]

1. An Antiochene commentator could not pass over this "striking and daring statement, even for Old Testament anthropomorphism" (von Rad, on 8.21f.).

2. Since this remark serves as a link to the next question, it looks likely that the commentator is here selecting the questions to raise issues on which he wishes to comment; often the questioner seems no more than a mere fiction.

The Questions on Genesis

LIV

Τίνος χάριν ἀπαγορεύει τοῦ αἵματος τὴν μετάληψιν;[a]
Σαφέστερον ἐδίδαξεν ἐν τῷ νόμῳ· ὅπερ γάρ ἐστι, φησίν,
ἀνθρώπῳ ψυχή, τοῦτο τοῖς ἀλόγοις τὸ αἷμα.[b] δίχα τοίνυν τοῦ
αἵματος τῶν κρεῶν μεταλαμβάνων, ὡς λαχάνων δήπουθεν
5 μεταλήψῃ· ἄψυχον γὰρ τὸ λάχανον· εἰ δὲ μετὰ τοῦ αἵματος
μεταλάβοις, ψυχὴν ἐσθίεις. διὸ δὴ καὶ ἐνταῦθα ἔφη, πλὴν κρέας
ἐν αἵματι ψυχῆς οὐκ ἔδεσθε· καὶ γὰρ τὸ ὑμέτερον αἷμα τῶν
ψυχῶν ὑμῶν ἐκζητήσω, ἐκ χειρὸς πάντων τῶν θηρίων ἐκζητήσω
αὐτό, ... ἐκ χειρὸς ἀνθρώπου, ἀδελφοῦ αὐτοῦ, ἐκζητήσω τὴν
10 ψυχὴν αὐτοῦ.[c] ἐνταῦθα αἰνίττεται τὴν ἀνάστασιν, οὐχ ὡς τὰ
θηρία παράξων εἰς τὸ κριτήριον καὶ δίκας τῆς ἀνθρωποφαγίας
εἰσπραξόμενος, ἀλλ' ὡς τὰ ὑπὸ τούτων καταναλωθέντα σώματα
συνάξων τε καὶ ἀναστήσων. ἐν γὰρ τῇ χειρὶ αὐτοῦ τὰ πέρατα
τῆς γῆς,[d] καὶ ῥάδιον αὐτῷ πάντοθεν συναγαγεῖν τὸ ἡμέτερον
15 σῶμα. ἐνταῦθα μὲν οὖν αἰνιγματωδῶς τοῦτο δεδήλωκε, διὰ δὲ
Ἰεζεκιὴλ σαφέστερον ἐκήρυξε τὴν ἀνάστασιν.[e]

LV

Διὰ τί δὲ ὅλως τὴν κρεωφαγίαν ἐνομοθέτησεν;[a]
Εὐθὺς δημιουργήσας τὸν ἄνθρωπον, τῆς γῆς αὐτῷ τοὺς
καρποὺς ἐδωρήσατο, ἀπὸ σπερμάτων καὶ δένδρων βιοτεύειν
κελεύσας.[b] μετὰ δὲ τὸν κατακλυσμόν, πλείονα φιλοτιμεῖται

LIV 5, 12, B, C, 4 7 9 10 13 [32] 35 37 = 19 mss.

l. 12 εἰσπραξόμενος B, 3 8, c_1, 4 7 9 37 : πραξόμενος 5 : εἰσπραξάμενος
Sir. Sch. F.M. The future, more widely attested than the aorist, seems clearly
required by the context: cf. παράξων . . . συνάξων . . . ἀναστήσων.

a. Gn 9.4   b. Lv 17.14   c. Gn 9.4f.   d. Ps 95.4   e. Ezek 37.1–14

LV 5, 12, B, C^{-50}, 4 7 9 10 13 [32] 35 37 = 18 mss.

a. Gn 9.3   b. Gn 1.29

LIV

Why did he forbid the consumption of the blood?[a]

His teaching was clearer in the Law: "As is the life for man, so is blood for the brute beasts."[b] When you eat meat without blood, you eat it like vegetables, as vegetables are lifeless. Whereas if you were to eat it with the blood, you would eat the life. Hence, he said here, too, "Only, you shall not eat flesh with the blood of life. I shall require an account of the blood of your lives; from the hand of all the beasts I shall require it, and from the hand of a man's brother I shall require an account of his life."[c] Here he hints at the resurrection—not that he intends to bring wild animals to judgment and call them to account for killing people. Rather he will assemble the bodies they have consumed and raise them up. After all, "In his hand are the ends of the earth,"[d] and he can easily assemble our body from all quarters. This passage has only obscure hints of the resurrection, which he proclaimed quite clearly through Ezekiel.[1e]

LV

Why did he legislate at all about the eating of meat?[a]

Immediately after creating man, he made him a gift of the fruits of the earth and commanded him to live off seeds and trees.[b] After the flood, however, he regaled him with a wider provision and com-

---

1. Such eschatological interpretations are rare in this, largely literalist, commentary.

5 τροφήν, καὶ πετεινά, καὶ νηκτά, καὶ χερσαῖα ζῷα θύειν τε καὶ
ἐσθίειν κελεύσας, πάθει πάθος ἐξελαύνων καὶ τῷ ἐλάττονι
θεραπεύων τὸ μεῖζον· προορῶν γὰρ ὁ Θεὸς ὅτι ταῦτα πάντα
θεοποιήσουσιν οἱ εἰς ἐσχάτην ἀλογίαν ἐκπεπτωκότες,
συγχωρεῖ τὴν βρῶσιν ἵνα τὴν ἀσέβειαν παύσῃ· ἀβελτηρίας γὰρ
10 ἐσχάτης τὸ ἐσθιόμενον προσκυνεῖν. διά τοι τοῦτο τὰ μὲν
ἀκάθαρτα τῶν ζῴων λέγει, τὰ δὲ καθαρά, ἵνα, τὰ μὲν ὡς
ἀκάθαρτα βδελυττόμενοι, μὴ θεοποιῶσι, τὰ δὲ μὴ προσκυνῶσιν
ἐσθιόμενα.

LVI

Τίνος ἕνεκα μὴ ἐμέμφθη Νῶε, μέθῃ περιπεσών;[a]
Ἀπειρίας ἦν, οὐκ ἀκρασίας, τὸ πάθος· πρῶτος γὰρ
ἀνθρώπων ἀποθλίψας τὸν τῆς ἀμπέλου καρπὸν καὶ ἀγνοῶν, οὐ
μόνον τὸ πόσον τῆς πόσεως, ἀλλὰ καὶ τὸν τρόπον τῆς
5 μεταλήψεως, ὅτι δεῖ κεράσαι πρότερον, εἶθ' οὕτω πιεῖν, τὸν
κάρον ὑπέμεινε. καινὸν δὲ οὐδὲν πέπονθε γυμνωθείς· καὶ γὰρ
νῦν τινες γυμνοῦνται καθεύδοντες, ἀφαιρουμένου τοῦ ὕπνου
τὴν αἴσθησιν. τῷ ὕπνῳ δὲ ἡ μέθη προσγινομένη, πιθανωτέραν
τῆς γυμνώσεως τὴν ἀπολογίαν ποιεῖ.

LVII

Τοῦ νόμου μηδέπω τεθέντος ὃς διαγορεύει τιμᾶν τὸν
πατέρα καὶ τὴν μητέρα,[a] πῶς ὁ Χὰμ ὡς πατραλοίας κρίνεται;[b]
Τῇ φύσει τοὺς ἀναγκαίους ἐντέθεικε νόμους ὁ ποιητής·

LVI 5, 12, B, C, 4 7 9 10 13 20 [32] 35 37 = 20 mss.
a. Gn 9.20f.

LVII 5, 12, B, C, 4 7 9 10 13 20 [32] 35 37 = 20 mss.
a. Ex 20.12   b. Gn 9.25–27

manded him to slaughter and eat animals that fly, swim, and live on land. In this way, he purposed to drive out one passion with another and cure a greater ailment with a lesser. That is to say, as God foresaw that people would succumb to the worst folly and make gods of all these things, he allowed them to eat animals to put a stop to idolatry, since only the worst fools will worship what they eat. Indeed, he spoke of some animals as unclean and others as clean, so that men would not make gods of the unclean, which they loathed, nor worship the clean, which they ate.

LVI

Why did Noah incur no blame for succumbing to drunkenness?[a]

What happened to Noah was the result of inexperience, not intemperance. He was the first to crush the fruit of the vine and was unaware of both the amount to drink and of the way to imbibe—that is, that one must dilute the wine before drinking it—so he fell into torpor. His nakedness was hardly odd. Today as well people go to sleep naked, as sleep robs them of awareness. And when sleep is accompanied by intoxication, there is an even more plausible excuse for nakedness.[1]

LVII

If the law requiring honor of father and mother had not yet been promulgated,[a] why was Ham condemned as a parricide?[b]

The Creator placed the necessary laws in human nature itself.

---

1. As Speiser remarks (p. 62), the story of Noah's drunkenness (Gn 9.20–27) is "actually aimed at Canaan and, by extension, at the Canaanites," rather than at Noah himself; Theodoret, who does not recognize this aetiological issue, is concerned to defend the patriarch from the charge of immorality. He does not address the curse of Canaan until *Q.* 58.

οὕτω τὸν Κάϊν κατέκρινεν, ἐπειδήπερ αὐτὸν ἡ φύσις
5 ἐδίδασκεν ὡς ὁ φόνος παράνομος. αὐτίκα γοῦν δόλῳ
χρησάμενος συνεργῷ, πόρρω τῶν γεγεννηκότων ἀπαγαγών,
ἀνεῖλε τὸν ἀδελφὸν καί, τοῦ Θεοῦ πυνθανομένου, ποῦ...
Ἄβελ ὁ ἀδελφός σου; ἠρνήθη·[c] δῆλον δὲ ὡς ἐπιστάμενος ὅτι
κακὸν τὸ γεγενημένον ἠρνήθη τὸ τολμηθέν. ἐλεγχθεὶς δὲ ὑπὸ
10 τοῦ δικαίου κριτοῦ, ὡμολόγησεν ὑπὲρ συγγνώμην ἡμαρτηκέναι·
μείζων, γάρ φησιν, ἡ ἁμαρτία μου τοῦ ἀφεθῆναί με.[d] καὶ
μέντοι καὶ ὁ Ἀδάμ, τῆς θείας ἐπιφανείας αἰσθόμενος,
ἐπειράθη λαθεῖν, ὡς εἰδὼς ὅτι δὴ τὸ κλέπτειν κακόν.[e]

Οὕτω καὶ ὁ Χὰμ τὴν τοῦ πατραλοίου κατηγορίαν ἐδέξατο,
15 ὡς παραβὰς τὸν τῆς φύσεως νόμον. ὅτι γὰρ καὶ τὸ γεραίρειν
τοὺς γεγεννηκότας ἡ φύσις ἐδίδασκε μαρτυροῦσιν οἱ τοῦ Χὰμ
ἀδελφοί, οἵ, τοῦ πατρὸς τὸ πάθος παρ' ἐκείνου μεμαθηκότες,
μετὰ πολλῆς αἰδοῦς συνεκάλυψαν τὸν πατέρα, εἰς τοὐπίσω
βαδίζοντες ὡς ἂν ἥκιστα ἴδοιεν ὅθεν σπαρέντες ἐβλάστησαν.[f]
20 τοιγάρτοι μάλα εἰκότως καὶ τοῦ πατρὸς τὴν εὐλογίαν
ἐδρέψαντο.

LVIII

Τί δή ποτε τοῦ Χὰμ ἐπταικότος, ὁ ἐκείνου παῖς ἐδέξατο
τὴν ἀράν;[a]

Κοινῇ πάντες μετὰ τὴν τοῦ κατακλυσμοῦ παῦλαν τῆς θείας
|17 μετέλαχον εὐλογίας· τολμηρὸν τοίνυν ὑ|πέλαβεν ὁ Νῶε
5 ἐπαγαγεῖν ἀρὰν τῷ τῆς θείας εὐλογίας μετειληχότι· τούτου
χάριν τῷ ἐκείνου παιδὶ περιτέθεικε τὴν ἀράν. ἔχει δὲ καὶ ἡ
τιμωρία τὸ δίκαιον· ἐπειδὴ γάρ, υἱὸς ὤν, ἐξήμαρτεν εἰς
πατέρα, διὰ τῆς τοῦ παιδὸς ἀρᾶς δέχεται τιμωρίαν. πρὸς δὲ

---

c. Gn 4.9   d. Gn 4.13   e. Gn 3.8   f. Gn 9.22f.

LVIII 5, 12, B, C, 4 7 9 10 13 17(inc.) 20 [32] 35 37 = 21 mss.
a. Gn 9.25–27

Thus, he condemned Cain, since nature had taught him that murder was unlawful. Indeed, employing a ruse, Cain led his brother far away from his parents and killed him. When God asked, "Where is your brother Abel?" he denied what he had done.[c] So, we conclude that he denied committing the deed because he understood he had done wrong. When censured by the righteous judge, he confessed he had committed a sin too great for pardon: "My sin is too grave for forgiveness."[d] Adam is another example; sensing the divine presence, he tried to hide, for he knew that stealing was wrong.[e]

Thus, Ham was charged with parricide for transgressing the natural law. The behavior of Ham's brothers confirms that nature herself had inculcated respect for parents; after learning from Ham of their father's condition, they displayed great respect in going in backwards to cover their father so there would be no chance of seeing the organ of their own sowing and generation.[f] Thus, it was right and proper that they should receive their father's blessing.

LVIII

As the fault was Ham's, why was his son the object of the curse?[a]

After the flood, everyone shared alike in the divine blessing. Therefore, Noah, judging it rash to heap curses on one who was a recipient of divine blessing, imposed the curse on that man's son. And the punishment was justified; since as son Ham had sinned against his father, he received retribution through the curse on his own son. A further point to take into consideration is that if Ham personally had been the object of the curse, the punishment would

The Questions on Genesis

τούτοις σκοπητέον κἀκεῖνο, ὡς εἰ αὐτὸς ὁ Χὰμ ἐδέξατο τὴν
10 ἀράν, εἰς ὅλον ἂν διέβη τὸ γένος ἡ τιμωρία· εἰς δὲ τὸν
νεώτατον υἱὸν τὴν παιδείαν παρέπεμψε.

Καὶ τοῦτο δὲ εἰδέναι προσήκει, ὡς πρόρρησίς ἐστιν, οὐκ
ἀρά, τοῦ δικαίου τὰ ῥήματα. ἐπειδὴ γὰρ ἔμελλεν ὁ Ἰσραήλ, ἐκ
τοῦ Σὴμ κατάγων τὸ γένος, τῆς Παλαιστίνης παραλαμβάνειν
15 τὴν δεσποτείαν· ταύτην δὲ πάλαι ᾤκουν οἱ ἐκ τοῦ Χαναὰν
βεβλαστηκότες· εἰς ἀρὰν σχηματίζει τὴν πρόρρησιν,
προαγορεύων μὲν τὰ ἐσόμενα, δεδιττόμενος δὲ τοὺς ὕστερον
ἐσομένους μὴ πλημμελεῖν εἰς γονέας. καὶ τοῦτο σαφῶς ἡμᾶς
ἡ τοῦ Σὴμ εὐλογία διδάσκει· εὐλογητός, γάρ φησι, Κύριος ὁ
20 Θεὸς τοῦ Σήμ, καὶ ἔσται Χαναὰν παῖς αὐτοῦ·[b] οὐ γὰρ τοῖς δύο
τοῦτον ὑπέταξεν, ἀλλὰ μόνῳ τῷ Σήμ. καὶ τοῦ μὲν Ἰάφεθ τὴν
πολυγονίαν προείρηκε, τοῦ δὲ Σὴμ τὴν εὐσέβειαν· τὸν γὰρ
Θεὸν ἐν τοῖς σκηνώμασι τοῦ Σὴμ κατοικήσειν προείρηκε.

Κατῴκησε δὲ ἐν τοῖς ἐκ τοῦ Σὴμ πατριάρχαις καὶ ἐν τοῖς
25 ἐκ τούτων βεβλαστηκόσι προφήταις, καὶ ἐν τῇ σκηνῇ
πρότερον καὶ ἐν Ἱεροσολύμοις ὕστερον. ἀκριβὲς δὲ τέλος
ἔσχηκεν ἡ προφητεία τὸ τῆς οἰκονομίας μυστήριον ὅτε αὐτὸς
ὁ Θεὸς λόγος, ὁ τοῦ Θεοῦ καὶ πατρὸς μονογενὴς υἱός,
ἐσαρκώθη, καὶ ἐνηνθρώπησε, καὶ ναὸν ἑαυτοῦ προσηγόρευσεν[c]
30 ἣν ἐκ σπέρματος Δαβὶδ καὶ Ἀβραὰμ ἔλαβε σάρκα·[d] ἐκ τοῦ Σὴμ
γὰρ καὶ οὗτοι κατῆγον τὸ γένος. ἡ δὲ τοῦ Χαναὰν δουλεία ἐν
τοῖς γαβαωνίταις τὸ τέλος ἐδέξατο.[e]

LIX

Τὴν ἄσφαλτόν τινες τῶν διδασκάλων ἄσβεστον ἔφασαν
εἶναι.[a]

b. Gn 9.26   c. Jn 2.19–21   d. Mt 1.1   e. Jos 9.3–27

LIX 5, 12, B, C, 4 7 9 10 13 17 20 [32] 35 37 = 21 mss.

a. Gn 11.3

have passed to the race as a whole, whereas it was on the youngest son that Noah inflicted the chastisement.

You should also realize that the righteous man's words were prophecy, not curse. Since Israel was destined to descend from Shem and take possession of Palestine, which the descendants of Canaan had long occupied, he presented the prophecy as a curse so as both to foretell the future and discourage subsequent generations from sinning against their parents. For this we have the explicit testimony of the blessing of Shem, for he says, "Blessed be the Lord, the God of Shem, and Canaan will be his servant."[1b] He subjected Canaan not to the two of them but only to Shem. In Japheth's case he foretold many descendants, but in Shem's, virtue, since he predicted that God would dwell in the tents of Shem.

It is true that, first in the tent and later in Jerusalem, he did dwell among the patriarchs from the line of Shem and among the prophets descended from them. Yet, the prophecy received its exact fulfillment in the mystery of the Incarnation when God the Word in person, the only-begotten Son of God the Father, took on flesh, and became man, and referred to the body he had taken from the stock of David and Abraham[d] (they too being descended from Shem) as his temple.[c] The servitude of Canaan, on the other hand, was fulfilled in the case of the Gibeonites.[2e]

LIX

Some commentators have claimed that the bitumen was unslaked lime.[a]

1. In 9.26, one would expect the blessing to fall on Shem, rather than on Shem's God, and the translators of the *NRSV*, accepting an emendation of the MT, render "Blessed by the Lord my God be Shem"; both von Rad (on 9.24–27) and Speiser (on 9.26) accept the reading of the MT, which has the support of the LXX.

2. *V. Q.* 13 on Jos.

Ἀγνοοῦντες, ὡς εἰκός, τὰς ἐν τῇ Ἀσσυρίᾳ πηγάς, ᾠήθησαν ἀσβέστῳ τὸν πύργον ᾠκοδομῆσθαι. ἀκριβῶς δὲ παρὰ τῶν
5 ἐκεῖθεν ἀφικομένων μεμάθηκα ὡς εἰσὶ πηγαὶ ταύτην ἀναβλύζουσαι τὴν ὕλην μεθ' ὕδατος, καὶ ὅτι, ταῖς οἰκοδομίαις συνυφαίνοντες, ἐπὶ ταύτης τὴν ὠπτημένην συνετίθεσαν πλίνθον. οὕτω τὸν πύργον ἐκεῖνον ᾠκοδομῆσθαί φασι, καὶ οἱ αὐτόπται τούτου καὶ διορύξαι τι μέρος ἰσχυρίσαντο καὶ
10 ἀκριβῶς διαγνῶναι ὡς ἄσφαλτος ταῖς ὠπτημέναις ὑπέστρωται πλίνθοις. ἄλλως τε καὶ λίθων εἶναι σπάνιν ἐν τῇ Ἀσσυρίᾳ φασί, καὶ διὰ τοῦτο ταῖς πλίνθοις ἀντὶ λίθων κεχρῆσθαι. λίθων δὲ δίχα πῶς ἂν γένοιτο ἄσβεστος;

LX

Ποία γλῶσσα ἀρχαιοτέρα;[a]

Δηλοῖ τὰ ὀνόματα· Ἀδὰμ γάρ, καὶ Κάϊν, και Ἄβελ, καὶ Νῶε τῆς Σύρων ἴδια γλώττης· *ἀδαμθὰ* γὰρ τὴν ἐρυθρὰν γῆν ἔθος τοῖς σύροις καλεῖν. Ἀδὰμ τοίνυν ἢ ὁ *γήϊνος* ἢ ὁ *χοϊκὸς*
5 ἑρμηνεύεται,[b] καὶ Κάϊν *κτῆσις·* τοῦτο δὲ ὑμνῶν ὁ Ἀδὰμ

---

l. 2 ᾠκοδομῆσθαι *Sch.* : οἰκοδομεῖσθαι *B, 15, 4 7 17* : ᾠκοδομεῖσθαι *Sir. F.M.* For the perfect infinitive governed by an aorist, *cf.* Eus., *D. e.* 8.2.64 (οὗτοι μὲν τεσσαράκοντα καὶ ἓξ ἔτεσιν ᾠκοδομῆσθαι τὸν ναὸν ἔφασαν). While the *TLG* provides eighteen attestations of the form ᾠκοδομῆσθαι, ᾠκοδομεῖσθαι, clearly an error of etacism, is listed only for this passage.

l. 6 ταῖς οἰκοδομίαις *15, c₁, Sir. Sch.* : ταῖς ἐν ὕδασι οἰκοδομίαις *F.M.* = *"the people apply this to each layer of the buildings they construct on the water and then lay the baked brick on top"*: τὰς ἐν ὕδασι οἰκοδομίας *12, 7 10* = *"as they construct their buildings on the water, the people lay the baked brick on top of it (i.e., the bitumen)."* Construction with brick, *i.e.*, baked mud, in or over water, seems quite implausible; *cf.*, *e.g.*, Caesar, *Civ.* 2.10 on the use of water to destroy brick.

LX 5, 12, B, C, 4 7 9 10 13 17 20 [32] 35 37 = 21 mss.

a. Gn 11.6   b. Gn 2.7

They probably thought the tower was built with unslaked lime because they did not know about the springs in Assyria. But from travelers who have been there I have gathered circumstantial information to the effect that there are springs, which, along with their water, pour forth bitumen, and that the people apply this to each layer of their constructions and then lay the baked brick on top. This, so they claim, is how the tower was built, and eyewitnesses, who have managed to break off a piece, have come to the definite conclusion that bitumen was laid on the baked bricks. Indeed, as my informants indicate that there is a shortage of stone in Assyria—hence, people there build with bricks rather than stone—it is hard to see how there could be any unslaked lime without stone.[1]

LX

Which is the most ancient language?[a]

The names give the clue; Adam, Cain, Abel, and Noah belong to Syriac. Speakers of Syriac normally refer to red earth as "adamtha," so Adam means "earthly" or "made of dust";[b] Cain "acquisition," for when he sang God's praises, Adam said, "Thanks to God I have ac-

---

1. Though the story of the Tower was "the keystone to the Yahwistic primeval history" (von Rad, p. 152), Theodoret selects for comment no more than this detail, which testifies to his interest in natural history. He may be contradicting an opinion of Eusebius of Emesa repeated by Diodore, *v.* Petit, *La chaîne,* vol. 2, frag. 838 and *cf.* Petit, *Catenae,* vol. 2, frag. 166.

εἴρηκεν, ἐκτησάμην ἄνθρωπον διὰ τοῦ Θεοῦ᾿ᶜ καὶ Ἄβελ
πένθος· πρῶτος γὰρ οὗτος ὤφθη νεκρὸς καὶ πρῶτος τοῖς
γεγεννηκόσι προὐξένησε πένθος·ᵈ καὶ Νῶε ἀνάπαυσις.ᵉ

LXI

Ἡ οὖν ἑβραία πόθεν ἤρξατο;

Οἶμαι αὐτὴν ἱερὰν εἶναι φωνήν· ὥσπερ γὰρ ἐν τοῖς
ἑλληνικοῖς ναοῖς ἴδιοί τινες ἦσαν χαρακτῆρες γραμμάτων, οὓς
ἱερατικοὺς προσηγόρευον, οὕτω διὰ τοῦ Μωϋσέως ὁ τῶν ὅλων
5 Θεὸς ταύτην ἔδωκε τὴν γλῶτταν, διδακτὴν οὖσαν, οὐ φυσικήν.
τοιγάρτοι τῶν ἄλλων ἁπάντων κατὰ τὴν τῶν ἐθνῶν ἐν οἷς ἂν
γεννηθῶσι φθεγγομένων φωνήν, καὶ τῶν μὲν ἐν Ἰταλίᾳ
τικτομένων τῇ ἰταλῶν κεχρημένων, τῶν δὲ ἐν τῇ Ἑλλάδι τῇ
ἑλλήνων, καὶ τῶν ἐν Περσίδι τῇ περσῶν, καὶ τῶν ἐν Αἰγύπτῳ
10 τῇ αἰγυπτίων, τὰ ἑβραίων παιδία οὐ τῇ ἑβραίᾳ ἔστιν εὑρεῖν
εὐθὺς κεχρημένα φωνῇ, ἀλλὰ τῇ ἐκείνων παρ' οἷς ἐγεννήθησαν.
εἶτα, μειράκια γενόμενα, διδάσκεται τῶν γραμμάτων τοὺς
χαρακτῆρας, μανθάνει δὲ διὰ τῶν γραμμάτων τὴν θείαν
γραφήν, τῇ ἑβραῗδι γεγραμμένην φωνῇ. οἶμαι δὲ τοῦτο
15 αἰνίττεσθαι καὶ τὸν μακάριον Δαβὶδ ἐν τῷ ὀγδοηκοστῷ ψαλμῷ·
γλῶσσαν ἣν οὐκ ἔγνω ἤκουσεν.ᵃ

---

c. Gn 4.1   d. Gn 4.25   e. Gn 5.29

LXI 5, 12, 14 24 30*, C, 4 7 9 10 13 17 20 [32] 35 37 = 21 mss.
a. Ps 81.5

quired a man";[c] Abel "grief," since his was the first death ever seen and he was the first to cause his parents pain;[d] and Noah "rest."[1e]

LXI

So what was the origin of Hebrew?

I believe that Hebrew is a sacred tongue. As in the pagan temples there were special signs called "hieratic," so, through Moses, the God of the universe imparted this language, which comes, not from nature, but from instruction. Indeed, other peoples speak the language of the nations in which they have been born, those raised in Italy using that of the Italians, those in Greece that of the Greeks, those in Persia that of the Persians, and those in Egypt that of the Egyptians. Likewise, we observe the children of the Hebrews using initially, not Hebrew, but the language of the people among whom they have been born. Then in their teens they are taught the alphabet of the written language, and, through the written word, gain knowledge of holy Scripture, which is written in Hebrew. I believe blessed David also hints at this in the eighty-first psalm: "He heard a language which he did not know."[1a]

---

1. When Theodoret, a native speaker of Syriac, relies on his knowledge of this dialect of Aramaic to make direct use of the Hebrew text, he sometimes misinterprets the etymologies of the biblical authors. Here his grasp of Syriac does not prevent his confusing similar Hebrew terms for "red," "man," and "earth" and accepting unreliable etymologies for the names Cain, Abel, and Noah.

---

1. Theodoret seems to be referring to Jews of his acquaintance who had learned Hebrew in preparation for a Bar Mitzvah. In his earlier commentary on the Psalms, he had explained the "language" or "tongue" of 80.6 LXX (81.5 MT) as referring to the divine voice, which Israel had never heard until God conferred the Law during their trek through the wilderness.

LXII

Ἀλλά τινές φασιν ἀπὸ τοῦ ″Εβερ ἑβραίαν κεκλῆσθαι τὴν γλῶσσαν· ἐκεῖνον γὰρ μόνον ἐν τῇ προτέρᾳ μεῖναι φωνῇ, καὶ ἐκεῖθεν ἑβραίους ὀνομασθῆναι.[a]

Ἐγὼ δὲ οἶμαι ἑβραίους ὀνομασθῆναι ἐκ τοῦ τὸν πατριάρχην

5 Ἀβραὰμ ἀπὸ τῆς χαλδαίων χώρας εἰς τὴν Παλαιστίνην ἐλθεῖν, τὸν Εὐφράτην ποταμὸν διαβάντα· ἑβρα γὰρ τῇ σύρων φωνῇ ὁ περάτης ὀνομάζεται. οὕτω δὲ καὶ αὐτὸς ἐκαλεῖτο, καὶ μάρτυς ἡ θεία γραφή· μετὰ γὰρ τὴν τοῦ Λὼτ αἰχμαλωσίαν ἐλθών τις, φησίν, ἀπήγγειλεν Ἀβραὰμ τῷ περάτῃ.[b] τοῦτο δὲ

|11 10 παρὰ τῷ ἑβραίῳ κείμενον εὗρον ἑβρει· Ἰτὸ δὲ ἑβρει ἐξελληνιζόμενον ἑβραῖος γίνεται· καὶ γὰρ ἐν ἐκείνῳ τῷ χωρίῳ, ἔνθα ἡ αἰγυπτία περὶ τοῦ Ἰωσὴφ ἔφη, εἰσήγαγες ἡμῖν παῖδα ἑβραῖον ἐμπαίζειν ἡμῖν,[c] παρὰ τῷ ἑβραίῳ ἑβρει κεῖται.

Εἰ δὲ ἐκ τοῦ ″Εβερ ἑβραῖοι καλοῦνται, οὐ μόνους ἐχρῆν

15 τούτους οὕτω προσαγορεύεσθαι· πολλὰ γὰρ ἔθνη ἐκ τοῦ ″Εβερ κατάγει τὸ γένος, καί, ἵνα τοὺς ἄλλους πάντας παρῶ, ἐκ τούτου εἰσὶν ἰσμαηλῖται, καὶ οἱ ἀπὸ τῆς Χεττούρας, καὶ ἰδουμαῖοι, καὶ ἀμαληκῖται, καὶ μωαβῖται, καὶ ἀμμανῖται, καὶ οἱ τὰς Κάρρας οἰκοῦντες· ἐκ τοῦ γὰρ Ναχὼρ καὶ τοῦ Λάβαν

LXII 5, 11(*inc.*) 12, B, C⁻⁵⁰, 4 7 9 10 13 17 20 [32] 35 37 = 21 mss.

l. 7 ὁ περάτης C⁻⁵⁰, [32] 37, Sir. Sch. : διάβασις F.M. = "for 'hebra' in *Syriac means* 'crossing'" : ἡ διάβασις 12, 30, 7 9 13 20 35 : om. 5. N.B. the following οὕτω δὲ ... γὰρ, which look forward to the term περάτῃ in the following quotation of Gn 14.13, and *cf.* Ph., *Migr.* 20 (περάτης γὰρ ὁ Ἑβραῖος ἑρμηνεύεται) and F. Petit, *La chaîne*, vol. 3, frag. 922.

l. 9 Ἀβραὰμ Sir. Sch. F.M. : Ἀβρὰμ (?) J.P. It is difficult to believe that such a precise scholar as Thdt. would not have adverted to the premature use of this form of the name, not conferred by God until 17.5. Nonetheless, as F.M. reports no variants in the spelling either here or in the quotation of 12.20 in the next question, and as Wevers cites more than isolated support for Ἀβραὰμ at 12.20, I have left it unchanged; *cf.* the critical note on *Q.* 63.

a. Gn 10.21, 24f.;11.14–16   b. Gn 14.13   c. Gn 39.14

LXII[1]

But some commentators have claimed that the language is called "Hebrew" after Heber, because he alone continued to use the original language, and that the "Hebrews" were named from him.[a]

I rather think that the Hebrews received their name from the fact that the patriarch Abraham came from the land of the Chaldeans into Palestine by crossing the Euphrates, for "hebra" is the Syriac term for an emigrant. Holy Scripture witnesses that he was called by this name. For after Lot was captured, someone came and "reported to Abraham the emigrant (περάτῃ)."[b] I find the word "perates" expressed in the Hebrew as "hebrei," which, when translated into Greek, becomes "Hebraios."[2] Indeed, in the passage where the Egyptian woman says of Joseph, "You brought us a Hebrew slave to insult us,"[c] "hebrei" occurs in the Hebrew.

If, on the other hand, they are called Hebrews after Heber, they should not be the only ones to have this name, for many nations are descended from Heber. I shall not try to produce a complete list, but the Israelites come from him, as well as those born of Keturah, the Idumeans, the Amalekites, the Moabites, the Ammonites, and the people who live in Haran, the descendants of Nahor and Laban.

1. In the editions of J. Sirmond and J.L. Schulze, this question forms part of the previous; thus, in their numeration, all questions from 62–93 bear a number lower by one; *cf.* note 1 on *Q.* 94. My numeration here and to the end of the work follows that of Fernández Marcos and Sáenz-Badillos.

2. The Greek terms διαβάντα and διάβασις, the first a participle, the second a noun, both derive from the verb διαβαίνειν "to cross"; περάτης or "emigrant" derives from περαίνω, another verb meaning "to cross." Theodoret correctly detects the semantic similarity of the Syriac *hebra,* the Hebrew *hebri,* and the Greek περάτης. Somewhat similarly, Chrysostom had seen (*hom.* 35.3 *in Gen*) in the use of περάτης in Gn 14.13 an etymological pun on the name "Abraham," which he wrongly understood to be derived from '*br* "to cross," the root of *hebri.*

20 τὸ γένος κατάγουσιν. ἀλλ' οὐδεὶς τούτων τῇ ἑβραΐδι χρῆται
φωνῇ. ἀλλὰ περὶ τούτου ζυγομαχεῖν περιττόν· οὐδὲν γὰρ τῷ
λόγῳ τῆς εὐσεβείας λυμαίνεται, κἄν τε τοῦτο, κἄν τε ἐκεῖνο
δεξώμεθα.

LXIII

Τινές φασι τῇ Σάρρᾳ μιγῆναι τὸν Φαραώ.[a]

Ποίας οὖν κηδεμονίας ἀπήλαυσεν Ἀβραὰμ παρὰ τοῦ τῶν
ὅλων Θεοῦ, εἰ περιεῖδεν αὐτοῦ μοιχευομένην τὴν γαμετήν; τί
δή ποτε δὲ καὶ ἤτασεν ἐτασμοῖς μεγάλοις καὶ πονηροῖς τὸν
5 Φαραὼ καὶ ἅπαντα τὸν οἶκον αὐτοῦ[b] εἰ μὴ κωλῦσαι τὴν
παράνομον ἠβούλετο συναφήν; καὶ αὐτὸς δὲ ὁ Φαραὼ τὴν
ἄγνοιαν εἰς ἀπολογίαν προβάλλεται, καὶ μέμφεται τῷ Ἀβραὰμ
ἀδελφὴν κεκληκότι τὴν γαμετήν, καὶ διδάσκει ὡς, οὐχ ὑβρίσαι
αὐτήν, ἀλλὰ γῆμαι βουλόμενος ἔλαβε· *τί τοῦτο, γάρ φησιν,*
10 *ἐποίησάς μοι ... ὅτι γυνή σού ἐστιν; ἵνα τί εἶπας ... ἀδελφή*
μού ἐστι; καὶ ἔλαβον αὐτὴν ἐμαυτῷ εἰς γυναῖκα. καὶ νῦν ἰδοὺ
ἡ γυνή σου ἐναντίον σου· λαβὼν ἀπότρεχε.[c] καὶ οὐ μόνον
εἶπεν, ἀλλὰ καὶ ἔπραξε, καὶ παντοδαπῆς κηδεμονίας ἠξίωσεν·
ἐνετείλατο, γάρ φησι, Φαραὼ ἀνδράσι περὶ τοῦ Ἀβραὰμ
15 *συμπροπέμψαι αὐτόν, καὶ τὴν γυναῖκα αὐτοῦ, καὶ πάντα ὅσα*
ἦν αὐτῷ.[d] δῆλον τοίνυν ὡς, εὐθὺς ἁρπασθείσης τῆς Σάρρας,
ἐπέδησε τῇ νόσῳ τὸν Φαραὼ τῶν ὅλων ὁ πρύτανις, ἡ δὲ νόσος
τὴν ὄρεξιν ἤμβλυνεν, καί, τῶν δικτύων εἴσω τὴν θήραν ἔχων, ὁ
θηρευτὴς οὐκ ἀπήλαυσε τῆς ἄγρας· ἡ γὰρ νόσος ἐκώλυσε.

LXIII 5, a₂, B, C, 4 7 9 10 13 17 [32] 35 37 = 21 mss.

l. 14 Ἀβραὰμ v. the critical note to l. 9 of the previous question.

a. Gn 12.10–20   b. Gn 12.17   c. Gn 12.18f.   d. Gn 12.20

None of these uses the Hebrew language. No point, however, in squabbling over this: no harm is done to religion, whichever opinion we adopt.[3]

LXIII

Some commentators have claimed that Pharaoh had relations with Sarah.[a]

What kind of care would Abraham have received from the God of the universe if God had allowed his spouse to be defiled in an adulterous relationship? Why would he have put Pharaoh and all his household to the test with severe and painful trials[b] unless his intention was to prevent the unlawful union? Pharaoh himself alleged ignorance as an excuse and blamed Abraham for saying his spouse was his sister, and this shows that he took Sarah, not to violate, but to marry, her: "Why did you do this to me, as she is your wife? Why did you say, 'She is my sister?' And so I took her for my wife! Now, lo, here is your wife before you; take her and be off."[c] He not only spoke but acted on his words and then honored him with every mark of respect: "Pharaoh gave his men instructions regarding Abraham, to accompany him, his wife, and all his possessions."[1d] We can, therefore, conclude that, as soon as Sarah was snatched away, he who governs the world restrained Pharaoh with an ailment, and this blunted his desire; though the prey was already in his toils, the hunter, prevented by the ailment, could not enjoy his catch.

---

3. Exhibiting the moderation for which Bardy has praised him ("Interprétation," p. 582), Theodoret finally concedes that such details are not vital to what is, after all, a pastoral commentary; cf. note 30 to the "Introduction to Theodoret's Life and Works" and the last two sentences of Q. 67.

---

1. Guinot (p. 760) is unable to identify the source of the contrary and understandable view cited in the question. Chrysostom (*hom.* 32.7 *in Gen.*), like Theodoret, emphasises the role of God's providence in protecting Sarah.

LXIV

Καὶ τίνος ἕνεκεν ἐνταῦθα μὲν ἐσίγησεν ἡ γραφὴ τὸ
φυλαχθῆναι τὴν Σάρραν ἀλώβητον,ᵃ ἐν δὲ τῷ κατὰ τὸν
Ἀβιμέλεχ διηγήματι σαφῶς τοῦτο δεδήλωκε;ᵇ

῎Εμελλεν ἡ Σάρρα τηνικαῦτα τίκτειν τὸν Ἰσαάκ.ᶜ ἵνα τοίνυν
5 μὴ ὕποπτον γένηται τὸ σπέρμα τοῦ Ἀβραάμ, σαφῶς ἐκεῖ
δεδήλωκεν ἡ θεία γραφὴ ὅτι οὐχ ἥψατο αὐτῆς ὁ Ἀβιμέλεχ.

Καὶ ἐντεῦθεν μέντοι κἀκεῖθεν ἰστέον ὡς καὶ τοὺς
βαρβάρους ἡ φύσις ἐδίδαξεν ὅτι πονηρὸν ἡ μοιχεία καὶ
τιμωρίας ἄξιον. καὶ γὰρ ὁ Φαραὼ τοῦτο δεδήλωκεν,
10 ἐπιμεμψάμενος τῷ Ἀβραάμ,ᵈ καὶ ὁ Ἀβιμέλεχ πρὸς τὸν τῶν
ὅλων ἔφη Θεόν, *Κύριε, ἔθνος ἀγνοοῦν καὶ δίκαιον ἀποκτενεῖς;*
οὐκ αὐτός μοι εἶπεν ὅτι ἀδελφή μού ἐστι, καὶ αὐτή μοι εἶπεν,
ἀδελφός μού ἐστιν; ἐν καρδίᾳ καθαρᾷ καὶ ἐν δικαιοσύνῃ
*χειρῶν ἐποίησα τοῦτο.*ᵉ τέθεικε δὲ ὁ συγγραφεὺς καὶ τοῦ Θεοῦ
15 τὴν ἀπόκρισιν· *εἶπε...,* γάρ φησιν, *ὁ Θεὸς τῷ Ἀβιμέλεχ καθ'*
ὕπνον, κἀγὼ ἔγνων ὅτι ἐν καθαρᾷ καρδίᾳ ἐποίησας τοῦτο καὶ
ἐφεισάμην... σου τοῦ μὴ ἅψασθαι αὐτῆς, τοῦ μὴ
ἁμαρτεῖν... εἰς ἐμέ· ἕνεκεν τούτου οὐκ ἀφῆκά σε ἅψασθαι
αὐτῆς. νῦν οὖν ἀπόδος τὴν γυναῖκα τῷ ἀνθρώπῳ, ὅτι προφήτης
20 *ἐστὶ καὶ προσεύξεται περὶ σοῦ, καὶ σωθήσῃ σὺ καὶ πᾶς ὁ*
*οἶκός σου. εἰ δὲ μὴ ἀποδίδως, γνῶθι ὅτι ἀποθανῇ σύ.*ᶠ

Διδάσκει δὲ ἡμᾶς ὁ θεῖος λόγος ὅτι τῆς δικαιοσύνης τοὺς
ἐραστὰς πλημμελεῖν ἐξ ἀγνοίας μέλλοντας οὐκ ἐᾷ· δῆλον
τοίνυν ὡς καὶ τὸν Φαραὼ κεκώλυκεν ἁμαρτεῖν, ὡς ἀδελφὴν τοῦ
25 Ἀβραὰμ νόμῳ γάμου τὴν Σάρραν εἰληφότα. ἐπειδὴ δὲ κρείττων
ἦν, ὡς εἰκός, ὁ Ἀβιμέλεχ τοῦ Φαραώ, ἐκεῖνον μὲν διὰ
παιδείας τὴν παρανομίαν ἐδίδαξεν, τούτῳ δὲ καὶ τῆς αἰκίας
καὶ τοῦ πλημμελήματος οὐκ ἔδωκεν αὐτὸς τὴν συγχώρησιν

LXIV   5, a_2, B, C, 4 7 9 10 13 17 [32] 35 37 = 21 mss.

a. Gn 12.10–20   b. Gn 20.4   c. Gn 21.1–3   d. Gn 12.18f.   e. Gn 20.4f.
f. Gn 20.6f.

LXIV

Why, then, does Scripture here make no mention of Sarah's protection from harm[a] while it states this explicitly in the passage regarding Abimelech?[b]

Sarah was then on the point of giving birth to Isaac.[c] To forestall any doubt of Abraham's paternity of the child, in that passage, holy Scripture explicitly stated that Abimelech did not lay a hand on her.

From this incident and the other we should realize that nature teaches even savages that adultery is wicked and deserving of punishment. After all, Pharaoh indicated this when he reproached Abraham.[d] And Abimelech said to the God of the universe, "Lord, will you slaughter an ignorant and righteous people? Did he not say to me, 'She is my sister,' and did she not say to me, 'He is my brother'? I did this with a clear conscience and with unstained hands."[e] The historian also cited God's reply: "God said to Abimelech in a dream, I too am aware that you did this with a clear conscience, and I prevented you from touching her so you would not sin against me; that is why I did not allow you to touch her. So now give his wife back to her husband, because he is a prophet and will pray for you, and you will be saved, you and all your household. But if you do not give her back, know that you will die."[f]

The divine word teaches us that he restrains the lovers of virtue when they are about to sin through ignorance. Thus, we may conclude that he also prevented Pharaoh from sinning after he had taken Sarah for lawful marriage under the impression she was Abraham's sister. Abimelech was evidently a better man than Pharaoh. God taught Pharaoh about his transgression by punishing him. In the case of Abimelech, though not himself pardoning the outrage

ἀλλὰ τὸν ἠδικημένον αἰτῆσαι ταύτην ἀνέμεινεν, ἐπιφανείας
30   τε ἡμέρως ἠξίωσε, καὶ λόγοις ἠπίοις ἐπέδειξε τὴν
τετολμημένην παρανομίαν.

LXV

Ὁ Μελχισεδὲκ πόθεν κατῆγε τὸ γένος;[a]

Τοῦ θεσπεσίου λέγοντος Παύλου, ἀπάτωρ, ἀμήτωρ,
ἀγενεαλόγητος,[b] τίς ἂν γνοίη τὸ ἀληθές; εἰκὸς δὲ αὐτὸν ἐκ
τῶν ἐθνῶν ἐκείνων εἶναι, τῶν τὴν Παλαιστίνην οἰκούντων·
5   ἐκείνων γὰρ καὶ βασιλεὺς καὶ ἱερεὺς ἐτύγχανεν ὤν, ἱερεὺς δὲ
τοῦ τῶν ὅλων Θεοῦ· ἦν..., γάρ φησιν, ἱερεὺς τοῦ θεοῦ τοῦ
ὑψίστου.[c] ὅθεν αὐτῷ καὶ Ἀβραὰμ ὁ πατριάρχης προσενήνοχε
τὰς τῶν λαφύρων δεκάτας καί, δίκαιος ὢν καὶ τοῦ Θεοῦ φίλος,
παρ' ἐκείνου τὴν εὐλογίαν καρποῦται.[d] τῆς γὰρ δεσποτικῆς
10 εἶχεν ἱερωσύνης τὸν τύπον·[e] διὸ δὴ καὶ ἄρτους τῷ Ἀβραὰμ καὶ
οἶνον ἀντέδωκεν, ὡς τοιαῦτα τυχὸν προσφέρειν εἰωθὼς τῷ τῶν
ὅλων Θεῷ·[f] ἔδει γὰρ κἂν τούτῳ δειχθῆναι τὸν τύπον.

---

l. 31 παρανομίαν. *Sir. F.M.* : παρανομίαν. εἶπε δὲ Ἀβιμέλεχ τῷ Ἀβράμ·
τί ἐνιδὼν ἐποίησας τὸ ῥῆμα τοῦτο; εἶπε δὲ Ἀβράμ· εἶπον γάρ, μήποτε
οὐκ ἔστιν θεοσέβεια ἐν τῷ τόπῳ τούτῳ, ἐμέ τε ἀποκτενοῦσιν ἕνεκεν
τῆς γυναικός μου. καὶ γὰρ ἀληθῶς ἀδελφή μού ἐστιν ἐκ πατρὸς ἀλλ'
οὐκ ἐκ μητρός· καὶ γὰρ ἀληθῶς ἀδελφή μου· θυγάτηρ πατρὸς μού ἐστιν,
πλὴν οὐ θυγάτηρ μητρός μου (Gn 20.10–12 LXX var.) added at end of quest. in
C, [32] (with some variants), Sch. (ἀλλ' οὐκ ἐκ μητρός· καὶ γὰρ ἀληθῶς οὐ
θυγάτηρ μητρός μου) = "the transgression he had committed. 'Then Abimelech
asked Abraham, "What was your purpose in doing this?" And Abraham replied, "I
thought, 'Most likely there is no fear of God in this place and they will kill me for
my wife.' In fact, she really is my sister from the same father but not from the same
mother. In fact, she is my sister, daughter of my father, but not of my mother.""

LXV a₂, B, C, 4 7 9 10 13 17 [32] 35 37 = 20 mss.

l. 13 κἂν τούτῳ 11, 7 9 10 17 35, Sch. : κἂν τούτῳ Sir. : κἂν τοῦτο F.M. For
κἂν τούτῳ, cf. Q. 91 (ἵνα τὴν ἀλήθειαν κἂν τούτῳ σκιαγραφήσῃ) and for the
same confusion of κἂν and κἂν, cf. F.M., l. 12, p. 81 and l. 11, p. 93.

a. Gn 14.18   b. Heb 7.3   c. Gn 14.18   d. Gn 14.19f.   e. Heb. 7.1
f. Gn 14.18

and the sin and though leaving it to the wronged man to beg pardon on Abimelech's behalf, God kindly accorded him a vision and pointed out in mild words the transgression he had committed.[1]

LXV

What was Melchizedek's ancestry?[a]

Since the divinely inspired Paul says, "Without father, without mother, without a family tree,"[b] who could know for sure? He probably belonged to those nations that inhabited Palestine, and while their king and priest both, he was also a priest of the God of the universe. Scripture says, "He was a priest of God the Most High."[c] Hence, the patriarch offered him a tenth of the spoils and, being a righteous man, a friend of God's, Abraham gained his blessing.[d] In fact, Melchizedek provided a type of the kingly priesthood.[e] Thus, he gave Abraham in return both bread and wine, things he was perhaps in the habit of offering to the God of the universe,[f] for the type had to be made manifest in this as well.[1]

---

1. Theodoret apparently compares the cases of Abimelech (Gn 20) and Pharaoh (Gn 12.10–17) in order to engage in further reflection on the idea of natural law; *cf. Q. 57.*

---

1. Guided by Heb 7.3f., Theodoret sees Melchizedek as a type of Christ as well as a priest of "God Most High." He is, of course, unaware of the Canaanite origins of this latter term and the unique character of this chapter, whose international setting and unusual style and vocabulary set it apart from all the "established sources of Genesis"; *v.* Speiser, p. 105. Though Theodoret commends Abraham as "righteous," he does not follow Chrysostom (*hom. 35.5 in Gen.*) in pointing out that the noun "righteousness" (zedek) constitutes the second half of Melchizedek's name.

LXVI

Πῶς Ἀβραὰμ πιστὸς ὀνομάζεται,[a] εἰρηκὼς τῷ Θεῷ, κατὰ τί γνώσομαι τοῦτο, ὅτι κληρονομήσω αὐτήν;[b]

Τὸ κατὰ τί γνώσομαι τοῦτο, οὐκ ἀπιστοῦντός ἐστιν, ἀλλὰ μαθεῖν ποθοῦντος τῆς κληρονομίας τὸν τρόπον. ἐπειδὴ γὰρ
5 ἑώρα πλήθη μυρία τὴν Παλαιστίνην οἰκοῦντα, μαθεῖν ἠβουλήθη τίνι τρόπῳ παραλήψεται τῆς γῆς ἐκείνης τὴν δεσποτείαν· πολέμου νόμῳ, δίχα πολέμου, ζώντων ἐκείνων, ἀναιρουμένων, ἐξελαυνομένων. τούτου χάριν μετὰ τὴν θυσίαν ὁ τῶν ὅλων ἔφη Θεός, γινώσκων γνώσῃ ὅτι πάροικον ἔσται τὸ σπέρμα σου ἐν
10 γῇ οὐκ ἰδίᾳ, καὶ δουλώσουσιν αὐτούς, καὶ κακώσουσιν αὐτούς, καὶ ταπεινώσουσιν ... ἔτη τετρακόσια. τὸ δὲ ἔθνος ᾧ ἐὰν δουλεύσωσι κρινῶ ἐγώ· μετὰ δὲ ταῦτα ἐξελεύσονται ὧδε μετὰ ἀποσκευῆς πολλῆς. σὺ δὲ ἀπελεύσει πρὸς τοὺς πατέρας σου ἐν εἰρήνῃ, τραφεὶς ἐν γήρει καλῷ. τετάρτῃ δὲ γενεᾷ
15 ἀποστραφήσονται ὧδε· οὔπω γὰρ ἀναπεπλήρωνται αἱ ἁμαρτίαι τῶν ἀμορραίων ἕως τοῦ νῦν.[c]

Ἐκ τῆς θείας ἀποκρίσεως ἔστι γνῶναι τὸν τρόπον τῆς ἐρωτήσεως. ἐπειδὴ γὰρ εἶπε, κατὰ τί γνώσομαι ὅτι κληρονομήσω αὐτήν, ἐδιδάχθη ὅσον μὲν παροικήσουσι χρόνον,
20 καὶ ὅπως ταλαιπωρήσουσιν, ὅσης τε ἀξιωθήσονται προμηθείας· τῶν μὲν πολεμήσειν ἐθελόντων αὐτοῖς κολασθησομένων, τούτων δὲ τὰ ἐκείνων καρπωσαμένων· καὶ ὅτι, τούτων αὐτὸς οὐδεμίαν πεῖραν λαβών, ἐν εἰρήνῃ καταλύσει τὸν βίον.

Ἐδίδαξε δὲ καὶ τῆς ἀναβολῆς τὴν αἰτίαν ἵνα μή τις
25 τοπάσῃ διὰ τὸ πλῆθος τῶν ἐνοικούντων μὴ δυνηθῆναι τὸν δεσπότην Θεὸν τῆς γῆς αὐτοῖς ἐκείνης παραδοῦναι τὴν

LXVI A⁻²ᶜ, B, C, 4 7 9 10 13 17 [32] 35 37 = 21 mss.
a. Cf. Rom 4.2–5.   b. Gn 15.8   c. Gn 15.13–16

LXVI

How can Abraham be called "faithful"[a] when he asked God, "How am I to know that I shall inherit the land?"[b]

The question, "How am I to know?" comes not from one who lacks belief but from one anxious to learn the manner of inheritance. Since he saw the countless hordes occupying Palestine, he wanted to know how he was to take possession of that land: by fighting or without fighting, leaving them alive, killing them, or driving them out. Therefore, after the sacrifice, the God of the universe declared, "You will know this for certain: Your offspring will be aliens in a land that is not theirs. They will enslave, afflict, and oppress them for four hundred years. But I shall bring judgment on the nation to whom they are enslaved, and afterwards they will escape to this place with many possessions. But you will go to your fathers in peace, nourished to a fine old age. [1] They will return here in the fourth generation; at present, the sins of the Amorites are not yet complete."[c]

We can determine the manner of the enquiry from God's reply. After asking, "How am I to know that I shall inherit it?" he was informed of the duration of their time as aliens; the way they would suffer; the degree of providential assistance they would receive when those bent on warring against them would be punished, and they would enter into the enjoyment of their property; and, last of all, that he himself would experience none of this but end his life in peace.

He also informed him of the reason for the delay, in case anyone should think that the Lord God could not give them control of the land because it was so thickly populated. He declared, "At present,

---

1. For "nourished," τραφείς, the reading of Theodoret's text of Genesis, other forms of the LXX read "buried," ταφείς; this is the meaning of the Hebrew.

δεσποτείαν. ἔφη δὲ οὕτως· *οὔπω γὰρ ἀναπεπλήρωνται αἱ* *ἁμαρτίαι τῶν ἀμορραίων ἕως τοῦ νῦν.* οὐδέπω, φησίν, ἄξια πανωλεθρίας δεδράκασιν, οὐ χρὴ δὲ πρὸ τῆς ἁμαρτίας ἐκ
30 προγνώσεως ἐπενεχθῆναι τὴν τιμωρίαν. ὅτι δὲ εἶχον κατ' ἐκεῖνον τὸν καιρὸν εὐσεβεῖς δῆλον ἐκ τοῦ Μελχισεδέκ, καὶ τοῦ Ἀβιμέλεχ, καὶ τῶν τὴν Χεβρὼν οἰκούντων· καὶ γὰρ ἐκεῖνοι πολλῆς τὸν πατριάρχην θεραπείας ἠξίωσαν, καὶ ἔστιν ἀκοῦσαι αὐτῶν βοώντων, *βασιλεὺς εἶ σὺ παρὰ Θεοῦ ἐν ἡμῖν· ἐν τοῖς*
35 *ἐκλεκτοῖς μνημείοις ἡμῶν θάψον τὸν νεκρόν σου.*[d]

LXVII

Διὰ τί δὲ τυθῆναι προσέταξε *δάμαλιν τριετίζουσαν . . . καὶ* *κριὸν τριετίζοντα,* καὶ τὰ ἑξῆς;[a]

Αἰνίγματα ταῦτα ἦν τῶν τῷ γένει συμβησομένων. τοιγάρτοι μετὰ τὰς θυσίας ἐπήγαγε, *γινώσκων γνώσῃ ὅτι*
5 *πάροικον ἔσται τὸ σπέρμα σου ἐν γῇ οὐκ ἰδίᾳ*[b] καὶ προσέθηκε, *τετάρτῃ δὲ γενεᾷ ἀποστραφήσονται ὧδε.*[c] διὰ τοῦτο τρία τῶν καθαρῶν τετραπόδων καὶ ἕκαστον τριετὲς τυθῆναι προσέταξε εἰς δήλωσιν τῶν τριῶν γενεῶν αἳ παροικοῦσαι διατελέσουσιν. ἡ δὲ τρυγὼν τὴν γενεὰν ἐκείνην
|2c 10 ἐνέφηνε, τὴν οἱονεὶ ἀποπτᾶσαν μὲν καὶ ἐξελθοῦσαν |ἐξ Αἰγύπτου, ἐν δὲ τῇ ἐρήμῳ κατασκηνώσασαν· φιλέρημον γὰρ τόδε τὸ ὄρνεον. ἡ δέ γε περιστερὰ τὴν ἄλλην γενεὰν παρεδήλου, ἢ τὴν ἐπηγγελμένην ἀπελάμβανε γῆν· ἥμερον γὰρ τὸ ζῷον καὶ ταῖς οἰκίαις ἐμφιλοχωροῦν. διά τοι τοῦτο τὰ μὲν
15 οὐ διεῖλεν, ὡς τὴν τῆς δουλείας ἀπαλλαγὴν αἰνιττόμενα, τὰ δὲ τετράποδα διεῖλεν, ἐπειδὴ τὴν ἐν Αἰγύπτῳ κακουχίαν
||13 ἐσήμαινε.[d] τὰ δέ γε|| ἐφιπτάμενα τοῖς διχοτομήμασιν ὄρνεα,

---

d. Gn 23.6

LXVII 2c(*inc.*), 5, a₂, B, C, 4 7 9 10 13(*inc.*) 17 [32] 35 37 41(*inc.*) = 23 mss.

a. Gn 15.9   b. Gn 15.13   c. Gn 15.16   d. Gn 15.9f.

the sins of the Amorites are not yet complete"; that is, "they have not yet committed sins deserving utter ruin, and punishment should not be imposed before the sin on the basis of foreknowledge." Now, we conclude from the cases of Melchizedek, Abimelech, and the inhabitants of Hebron that, at that time, there were religious people among them. Indeed, the latter showed the patriarch great deference, and we hear them crying out, "You are a king among us sent by God. Bury your dead in the choicest of our burial places."[d]

LXVII

Why did God order the sacrifice of a three-year-old heifer, a three-year-old ram, *etc.*?[a]

These are obscure hints of what would happen to the race. Indeed, after the sacrifices, he went on, "You will know for certain that your offspring will be aliens in a land that is not theirs";[b] and he added, "They will return here in the fourth generation."[c] Hence, he ordered sacrifice of three of the clean quadrupeds, each of which was three years old, as an indication of the three generations that would live as aliens. The turtle-dove revealed the generation that left Egypt on wings, as it were, and camped in the wilderness, that bird being fond of the wilderness. And the pigeon hinted at the next generation that took possession of the promised land, for the pigeon is a tame creature that likes to nest in houses.[1] He did not divide the birds, as they symbolized liberation from slavery, while he did divide the quadrupeds, which signified their ill-treatment in Egypt.[d]

---

1. Perhaps under Alexandrian influence, Theodoret takes the details of the ritual as αἰνίγματα, obscure hints of deeper realities, and develops an allegorical interpretation. Furthermore, he sees Abraham as a type of a later leader of the people of promise. The modern commentator Speiser, rather than adopting an intertextual approach, interprets (on 15.9) the covenant rite by reference to the practice of the Amorites as revealed in the Mari documents.

ἄπερ ὁ πατριάρχης ἐκ τῶν ἱερείων ἐξήλαυνε, τὴν φονικὴν τῶν
αἰγυπτίων προηνίττετο γνώμην,ᵉ ἣν ἄπρακτον ἀπέφηνεν ὁ
20 δεσπότης Θεός, τὰς πρὸς τὸν Ἀβραὰμ ἐμπεδῶν ὑποσχέσεις·
ὥσπερ γὰρ ἐν τῷ τύπῳ τοὺς σαρκοβόρους ὄρνεις ἐξήλαυνεν
Ἀβραάμ, οὕτως ἡ τιμὴ τοῦ Ἀβραὰμ τοὺς αἰγυπτίους ἐκόλασε.
τὸ δὲ περὶ ἡλίου δυσμὰς ὀφθῆναι τὸν καπνιζόμενον κλίβανον
καὶ τὰς τοῦ πυρὸς λαμπάδας ἐδήλου μὲν καὶ τὸ δεχθῆναι τὰ
25 θύματα,ᶠ προεσήμαινε δὲ καὶ τὴν παρὰ τὸ τέλος τοῦ
προρρηθέντος χρόνου ἐσομένην ἐπιφάνειαν τοῦ τῶν ὅλων
Θεοῦ· διὰ πυρὸς γὰρ ἐπεφάνη καὶ Μωϋσῇ τῷ νομοθέτῃᵍ καὶ
||41   μετὰ ταῦτα παντὶ τῷ λαῷ.ʰ|| ἐδίδασκε δὲ πρὸς τούτοις καὶ ὅτι
ταῦτα ὕστερον νομοθετήσει τὰ ζῷα προσφέρεσθαι.ⁱ
30   Τινὲς δέ φασιν ὅτι βεβαίαν δεῖξαι βουλόμενος τὴν
ὑπόσχεσιν, ὁ Θεὸς κατὰ τὸ κρατοῦν ἔθος ἐποιήσατο τὰς
συνθήκας· εἰώθασι γάρ, ὥς φασι, διχῇ τὰ ἱερεῖα διαιροῦντες,
οὕτω ποιεῖσθαι τοὺς ὅρκους. ἐγὼ δὲ καὶ ταῦτα κἀκεῖνα
τέθεικα ἵνα τὸ δοκοῦν ἀληθέστερον οἱ ἐντυγχάνοντες
35   δέξωνται.

LXVIII

Πολλοὶ τῶν ἀκολάστων ἀφορμὴν εἰς λαγνείαν λαμβάνουσι
τὸν πατριάρχην Ἀβραὰμ παλλακὴν ἐσχηκέναι.ᵃ
    Ἕκαστον τῶν πραττομένων ἐκ τοῦ σκοποῦ κρίνεται τῶν
διαπραττομένων. οὕτω τοίνυν καὶ τὰ κατὰ τὴν Ἅγαρ
5 σκοπήσωμεν, κἂν ἐπιθυμίᾳ δεδουλευκότα τὸν πατριάρχην
ἴδωμεν, νεμεσητὸν τὸ πρᾶγμα καλέσωμεν. εἰ δὲ τῆς ὁμοζύγου
τῆς φύσεως ἐπιδειξάσης τὸ πάθος, καὶ τὸν ποιητὴν ἄγονον

e. Gn 15.11   f. Gn 15.17   g. Ex 3.2–6   h. Ex 19.16–18
i. V., e.g., Lv 1.10–17; Nm 19.1–3.

LXVIII A, B, C, 4 7 9 10 17 20 [32] 35 37 = 22 mss.
a. Gn 16.1–4

The birds that flew onto the divided carcasses, and which the patriarch drove off from the offerings, presaged the murderous intention of the Egyptians,[e] which the Lord God brought to naught in his guarantee of the promises to Abraham. As Abraham drove off the scavengers in the type, so it was God's regard for Abraham that led to the punishment of the Egyptians. The vision at sunset of the smoking pan and the fiery torches showed the acceptance of the offerings[f] and foreshadowed the appearance of the God of the universe that would occur at the end of the prophesied time, for he appeared in fire to Moses the lawgiver[g] and later to all the people.[h] In addition, it taught that, at some later date, God would prescribe the offering of these animals.[i]

Now, some commentators have held that, in his wish to bring out the reliability of the promise, he made the treaty according to the prevailing practice, since people normally divided victims in two (so they claim) to take an oath. I cite this view and the other for readers to take whichever strikes them as closer to the truth.

LXVIII

As an excuse for their own lust many licentious people adduce the example of the patriarch Abraham, who kept a concubine.[a]

Every act is to be judged according to the intention of those who perform it. Therefore, let us consider the case of Hagar, and if we should see the patriarch in thrall to lust, we shall brand his conduct as reprehensible. But if his wife pointed out her natural infirmity, admitted that the Creator had made her barren, revealed her own

δεδημιουργηκέναι τὴν μήτραν εἰρηκυίας, καὶ τῆς παιδοποιίας
δηλωσάσης τὸν πόθον, καὶ τούτου χάριν ἱκετευσάσης ὁμιλῆσαι
10 τῇ Ἄγαρ, ἵνα αὐτῇ παιδίον ἐκεῖθεν ἐπινοήσῃ, τί ἐξήμαρτεν
Ἀβραάμ, οὔτε τῆς φύσεως οὔτε νόμου τινὸς ἐγγράφου
τηνικαῦτα τὴν πολυγαμίαν κωλύοντος, τῆς δὲ ὁμοζύγου
στερίφης μὲν οὔσης, λιπαρησάσης δὲ τὸν ἄνδρα τῇ παιδίσκῃ
μιγῆναι, οὐχ ἵνα ἡδυπαθείᾳ δουλεύσῃ, ἀλλ' ὅπως αὐτὸς μὲν
15 φύσει, αὐτὴ δὲ θέσει, παίδων κληθῶσι γεννήτορες;

Ὅτι γὰρ κρείττων ἦν αἰσχρᾶς ἡδονῆς ὁ θεῖος ἐκεῖνος
ἀνήρ, οὐ μόνον ταῦτα, ἀλλὰ καὶ τὰ ἑξῆς μαρτυρεῖ. ἐπειδὴ γὰρ
ἐγκύμων ἡ Ἄγαρ γενομένη μεγαλαυχίας πρόφασιν ἔσχε τὴν
κύησιν καὶ κατὰ τῆς δεσποίνης ἐλύττησεν, ἐδυσχέραινε μὲν ἡ
20 Σάρρα καὶ τοῦ πατριάρχου κατεβόησεν οὐκ ὀρθῶς.[b] ὁ δὲ μάλα
ἠπίως τὴν παροινίαν δεξάμενος, ἐξέδωκεν αὐτῇ τὴν παιδίσκην
εἰς τιμωρίαν, οὐδὲ τεχθῆναι προσμείνας τὸ κυοφορούμενον
βρέφος· *ἰδού, γάρ φησιν, ἡ παιδίσκη σου ἐν ταῖς χερσί σου·
χρῶ αὐτῇ ὡς ἐάν σοι ἀρεστὸν ᾖ.*[c]

LXIX

Τί δή ποτε περιτμηθῆναι αὐτὸν προσέταξεν ὁ Θεός;[a]

Προειπὼν τὴν παροικίαν,[b] φυλακήν τινα μηχανᾶται τῇ
εὐσεβείᾳ ἵνα, τοῖς δυσσεβέσιν ἀνθρώποις ἀναμιγέντες, μὴ
διαφθείρωσι τὴν εὐγένειαν, ἀλλ' εἰς τὸ σημεῖον ὁρῶντες,
5 ἄσβεστον τοῦ δεδωκότος τοῦτο τὴν μνήμην φυλάττωσι. καὶ
ὅτι τοῦτό ἐστιν ἀληθὲς ἡ ἔρημος μάρτυς· τεσσαράκοντα γὰρ
χρόνους ἐν αὐτῇ διατρίψαντες, περιττὴν ἐνόμιζον τὴν
περιτομήν, τῶν ἐθνῶν κεχωρισμένοι καὶ καθ' ἑαυτοὺς
πολιτευόμενοι. ἡνίκα δὲ λοιπὸν εἰς τὴν ἐπηγγελμένην

b. Gn 16.4f.   c. Gn 16.6

LXIX *A, B, C, 4(inc.) 7 9 10 13(inc.) 17 [32] 35 37 = 22 mss.*

a. Gn 17.9–14   b. Gn 15.13

desire for a child, and implored him to have relations with Hagar so that she might reckon that woman's child as her own, what sin did Abraham commit? Neither nature nor any law promulgated at that time forbade polygamy, and his wife was barren and importuned her husband to have intercourse with the servant girl, not so that he would become a slave to lust, but so they could be called parents, he naturally, and she by adoption.

Moreover, what happens next confirms that that holy man was proof against dishonorable pleasure. As you recall, when Hagar conceived, she made her pregnancy a ground for boasting and behaved insolently towards her mistress Sarah, who became upset and unjustly complained against the patriarch.[b] But he took her unreasonable behavior very patiently and handed the servant girl over to her for punishment without even waiting for the birth of the child in her womb: "See," he said, "the servant girl is in your hands. Treat her as you please."[1c]

LXIX

Why did God order Abraham to be circumcised?[a]

When he foretold the exile,[b] he devised a protection for their religion so that, when mingling with pagans, they would not contaminate their noble descent, but rather, looking to the sign, keep an undying memory of the one who had conferred it. The account of their wanderings confirms this. They spent forty years in the wilderness and thought circumcision pointless, since they were cut off from the nations and living a life apart. But when they later entered the promised land, the God of the universe ordered Joshua son of

1. Theodoret, taking the line of interpretation already suggested by Chrysostom (*hom.* 38.4 *in Gen.*), regards the central issue in 16.1–6 as the morality of Abraham's conduct. As he points out, the attack against Abraham is anachronistic, because the patriarchs lived in a society that countenanced polygamy. While his behavior was entirely reasonable, that of his wife and maidservant was flawed by outbursts of

|13

10 εἰσήγοντο γῆν, τηνικαῦτα πάλιν ὁ τῶν ὅλων Θεὸς Ἰησοῦ τῷ
τοῦ Ναυῆ Ιπροσέταξε περιτεμεῖν ἅπαντας καὶ οὕτω τῆς γῆς
παραδοῦναι τὴν δεσποτείαν·ᶜ ἔμελλον γὰρ ἔθνεσιν ἀλλοφύλοις
πελάζειν, οὗ δὴ χάριν ἀναγκαίως τῆς σφραγῖδος ἐδέοντο, τῆς
ἀπὸ τῶν ἀλλογενῶν αὐτοὺς χωριζούσης ἐθνῶν.

15 Εἰ δὲ μέγα φρονοῦσιν ἐπὶ τῇ περιτομῇ ἰουδαῖοι, μαθέτωσαν
ὡς οὐ μόνος ὁ πατριάρχης περιετμήθη, ἀλλὰ καὶ Ἰσμαὴλ ὁ
ἡμίδουλος, καὶ οἱ οἰκογενεῖς οἰκέται, καὶ οἱ ἀργυρώνητοι,ᵈ καὶ
οἱ ἰδουμαῖοι,ᵉ καὶ οἱ ἀπὸ τῆς Χεττούρας·ᶠ ἔμαθον δὲ ἐκ τῶν
ἰσραηλιτῶν καὶ αἰγύπτιοι περιτέμνεσθαι.ᵍ οὐ τοίνυν ἡ
20 περιτομὴ δικαίους ἐργάζεται· οὗτοι γὰρ ἅπαντες ὡς
δυσσεβεῖς ὑπὸ τῆς θείας κατηγοροῦνται γραφῆς. οὐκοῦν οὐδὲ

||4 τὸν|| Ἀβραὰμ ἡ περιτομὴ ἐδικαίωσεν, ἀλλ' ἡ μὲν πίστις
ἀπέφηνε δίκαιον,ʰ λαμπρότερον δὲ ἡ ἀρετὴ κατεσκεύασεν. ἡ
δὲ περιτομὴ σημεῖον ἐδόθη τῆς πίστεως.

---

c. Jos 5.2–7   d. Gn 17.24–27   e. Jer 9.25f.   f. Gn 25.1–4   g. Jer 9.25f.
h. Gn 15.6

Nun to circumcise all the men before handing over ownership of the land.[1c] They were destined to come into close proximity with the gentiles and hence were in need of a seal that would distinguish them from peoples of foreign lineage.

Now, if Jews make so much of their circumcision, they should learn that it was not only the patriarch who was circumcised but also Ishmael, a half-slave, as well as the homeborn slaves, the purchased slaves,[d] the Idumeans,[e] and the offspring of Keturah.[f] Even the Egyptians learned circumcision from the Israelites.[g] And circumcision did not have the effect of making them righteous, since holy Scripture condemns all these peoples as godless. Therefore, it was not circumcision that justified Abraham; faith made him righteous,[h] and virtue rendered him still more illustrious. Circumcision was given as a sign of faith.[2]

---

selfish emotion. Yet this defense of Abraham is equally anachronistic, as it is concerned to make Abraham's conduct conform, as much as possible, to a Christian ideal of a much later era. Speiser (p. 119) highlights rather the skill of the Hebrew storyteller who, after concentrating on the broader issue of the successor to Abraham in ch. 15, in this episode focuses on the individuals with their conflicting rights, desires, and emotions. He adduces (pp. 119–21) parallels from Mesopotamian legal documents for the provision of a concubine for the purpose of producing children in cases where the wife should prove barren.

---

1. Theodoret rightly notes that, according to the biblical narrative, circumcision was overlooked in the wilderness years and reinstituted by Joshua. Nevertheless, he does not see that the account of God's original decree in Gn 17.9–14, which seems to emphasize the value of circumcision as a sign in the days of Abraham, was actually informed by the concerns of priestly authors writing during the Exile when national symbols of identity were lacking; *v.* von Rad, *ad loc.*

2. Though always ready to concede Jewish privileges in the era of the old dispensation, Theodoret follows Paul's argument in Rom 2f. and promotes faith over circumcision as the key factor in achieving righteousness. In a way typical of the Antiochenes, he also emphasises virtuous behavior. The issue of circumcision will be raised again in *Q.* 3 on Ex.

LXX

Ἡ θεία λέγει γραφὴ ὅτι ἔφαγον οἱ ἄγγελοι ἐν τῇ σκηνῇ τοῦ Ἀβραάμ.[a]

Καὶ ἡ αὐτὴ λέγει γραφὴ ὅτι ἄνδρας εἶδεν Ἀβραάμ.[b] εἰ τοίνυν γυμνῷ προσεκτέον τῷ γράμματι, ἄνδρες, οὐκ ἄγγελοι,
5 ἔφαγον. εἰ δὲ τὸν νοῦν ἀναπτύσσωμεν, ὡς ὤφθησαν, ἔφαγον· ὥσπερ γάρ, ἀσώματον ἔχοντες φύσιν καὶ αὐτοὶ καὶ ὁ τούτων δεσπότης, σώματα ἔχειν ἔδοξαν· οὕτως γὰρ ἑωράθησαν· οὕτως ἐσθίοντες ὤφθησαν, οὐ στόματι καὶ γαστρὶ τὴν τροφὴν προσενεγκόντες· οὔτε γὰρ εἶχον σώματα· ἀναλώσαντες δὲ
10 αὐτὴν ὡς ἠθέλησαν. ἀνοίας γὰρ ἐσχάτης τὸ πολυπραγμονῆσαι τῶν ἀρρήτων τὸν τρόπον.

LXXI

Διὰ τί ὁ Λὼτ οὐκ ἐνεκλήθη, ταῖς θυγατράσι μιγείς;[a]

Ἐπειδὴ τοῖς ἐξ ἀγνοίας πλημμελουμένοις καὶ οἱ ἄνθρωποι συγγινώσκειν εἰώθασιν. οὐ τοίνυν οὐδὲ τῷ Λὼτ ἐπιμέμψαιτο ἄν τις δικαίως τῆς μίξεως ἕνεκα· ἠγνόει γὰρ τὸ πραττόμενον.
5 τὸ δὲ τῆς μέθης ἔχει τινὰ μέμψιν κεκραμένην συγγνώμῃ· ἀδημονῶν γὰρ κομιδῇ καὶ ἀλύων, ὡς πάντων ὁμοῦ τῶν ὄντων γεγυμνωμένος καὶ πρὸς τοῖς ἄλλοις ἅπασι καὶ αὐτῆς τῆς ὁμοζύγου,[b] ἠνέσχετο τῶν θυγατέρων τὸν οἶνον προσφερουσῶν

LXX A, B, C⁻⁵⁰, 7 9 10 13 17 20 [32] 35 37 = 21 mss.

a. Gn 18.8   b. Gn 18.2

LXXI A [32], B, C, 7 9 10 13 17 20(inc.) 35 37 = 22 mss.

a. Gn 19.30–38   b. Gn 19.26

LXX

Holy Scripture declares that angels ate in Abraham's tent.[a]

The same passage of Scripture says that Abraham had a vision of men.[b] If we must attend to the mere letter of the text, it was men, not angels, who ate. But if we are to unfold the meaning, they ate in the same form in which they had appeared. In other words, as they were incorporeal beings—they and their Lord—and yet seemed to have bodies (for that is how they appeared), so they seemed to eat. Not that they put food into their mouths and stomachs, for they were incorporeal. Rather, they consumed it as they wished. Only the worst fool would try to pry further into the ways and means of a holy mystery.[1]

LXXI

Why did Lot incur no censure for having relations with his daughters?[a]

Because people normally make allowances for those who transgress in ignorance. So you would not be right to blame Lot for this intercourse, as he was unaware of what he was doing. The fact of intoxication involves some blame tempered with pardon. Severely distressed and beside himself after losing everything all at once, especially his wife,[b] he did not resist when his daughters brought him

1. Theodoret employs this question to resolve two difficulties. First, there is the identity of Abraham's guests. In Gn 18.1f., the LXX recounts that God appeared to Abraham and then mentions three men (ἄνδρες); two of these become angels (ἄγγελοι) in 19.1. Second, these naturally incorporeal beings are seen to take food. Theodoret's treatment of the second issue is very similar to Theodore of Mopsuestia's explanation of how the angelic visitants partook of Lot's hospitality in 19.3 (*Fragg. in Gen., ad loc.*); the question had exercised the ingenuity of Jewish as well as Christian expositors (*v.* von Rad, on 18.6–8) and Theodoret will take it up again in *Q.* 20.2 on Jgs.

περαιτέρω τῆς χρείας, ἅτε δὴ τὸ μὲν κατασκευαζόμενον
10 ἀγνοῶν, ψυχαγωγίαν δὲ καὶ παραμυθίαν τὸ δρώμενον
ὑποπτεύων.

Ἐκεῖναι δὲ παντάπασίν εἰσιν κατηγορίας ἀθῷοι·
θεασάμεναι γὰρ τὰς μὲν τέσσαρας πόλεις καὶ τὰς κώμας
ἁπάσας ἐμπρησθείσας τῷ ὑετῷ τοῦ πυρός, τοὺς δὲ τὴν Σηγὼρ
15 οἰκοῦντας καταποθέντας·ᶜ τοῦτο γὰρ σημαίνει καὶ τοὔνομα·
κατάποσις γὰρ ἡ Σηγὼρ ἑρμηνεύεται· ἐνόμισαν ἄρδην
ἀπολωλέναι τῶν ἀνθρώπων τὴν φύσιν.ᵈ καὶ τὴν κατέχουσαν
ἐρημίαν ὁρῶσαι καὶ τοῦ γήρως προθεωρήσασαι τὴν ἀσθένειαν,
ἠβουλήθησαν ἐπινοῆσαι καὶ σπέρμα τῷ γένει καὶ ἑαυταῖς
||20 20 ψυχαγωγίαν τινά.|| τούτῳ χρησάμεναι τῷ λογισμῷ καὶ οὐκ
ἐπιθυμίᾳ δουλεύσασαι, τὸν μὲν οἶνον ἔλαβον συνεργόν,
ἔκλεψαν δὲ τῇ πλείονι πόσει τοῦ γεγεννηκότος τὴν αἴσθησιν,
ἀπέφηναν δὲ τὸν πατέρα σπορέα.

LXXII

Τί δή ποτε ὁ Θεὸς οὐκ ἐκώλυσε τὴν παράνομον μίξιν;ᵃ
Προεώρα τὴν τοῦ γένους ἀσέβειαν· μωαβῖται μὲν γὰρ
ἐδούλευον τῷ Χαμῶς, τῷ δὲ Μελχὼμ ἀμμανῖται.ᵇ ἵνα οὖν μή,
ὡς συγγενέσιν ἐπιμιγνύμενοι τούτοις, οἱ ἰσραηλῖται
5 μετάσχωσι τῆς ἀσεβείας, οὐκ ἐκώλυσε τὸν παράνομον γάμον
ὅπως ταύτῃ γοῦν αὐτοὺς μυσαροὺς ἀποφήνῃ καὶ βδελυκτοὺς
ἰουδαίοις. δηλοῖ δὲ τοῦτο καὶ ὁ τῶν ὅλων Θεός, διὰ Μωϋσέως
τοῦ νομοθέτου διαγορεύων, *ἀμμανίτης καὶ μωαβίτης οὐκ*
εἰσελεύσεται εἰς ἐκκλησίαν Κυρίου ἕως δεκάτης γενεᾶς καὶ
10 *ἕως εἰς τὸν αἰῶνα.*ᶜ

c. Gn 19.24f.   d. Gn 19.31

lxxii   A *[32]*, B, C, 7 9 10 13 17 35 37 = 21 mss.

a. Gn 19.30–38   b. Gn 19.37f.; *v., e.g.,* Nm 21.29; 1Kgs 11.5   c. Dt 23.3

more wine than necessary. He was ignorant of their scheme and presumed they were trying to comfort and console him.[1]

They, as well, were entirely beyond accusation. Having seen the four cities and all the towns incinerated by the rain of fire, and all the inhabitants of Segor swallowed up[c] (this is the import of the name, for "Segor" means "swallowing up."),[2] they presumed that the whole human race had perished.[d] Seeing the desolation everywhere and observing the old man's debility, they formed the intention of continuing the race and giving themselves some comfort. With this plan in mind, and not because they were enthralled to lust, they enlisted the help of the wine to beguile their parent's senses with excessive drink and thus brought their father to beget children.

LXXII

Why did God not intervene to prevent the unlawful intercourse?[a]

He foresaw the idolatry of their offspring, for the Moabites served Chemosh and the Ammonites Moloch.[b] Thus, he did not prevent the unlawful union to make them defiled and abominable in the eyes of the Jews, so the Israelites would not intermarry with these kindred peoples and participate in their idolatry. The God of the universe revealed his intention when he declared through Moses the lawgiver, "Neither Ammonite nor Moabite shall enter the assembly of the Lord to the tenth generation and forever."[c]

1. An incident (Gn 19.30–38) originally intended to provide a discreditable aetiology for the Moabites and Ammonites is for Theodoret primarily a moral conundrum. Here, as in his commentary on the Song of Songs, he deals with sexual issues in a manner free of prudery. To his credit, he explains this passage in such a way that, in the words of his modern counterpart Speiser (p. 145), "All of this adds up to praise rather than blame."

2. The Hebrew name of the town is Zoar, which in 19.22 is explained by popular

LXXIII

Ὠμὸν ἄγαν εἶναι δοκεῖ τὸ νέον ὄντα τὸν Ἰσμαὴλ
ἐξελαθῆναι τῆς πατρικῆς οἰκίας μετὰ μόνης τῆς μητρὸς καὶ
τοῦ ἀσκοῦ τοῦ ὕδατος.[a]

Καὶ τοῦτο ἄντικρυς δείκνυσι τὴν τοῦ Ἀβραὰμ ἀρετήν. τῆς
5 μὲν γὰρ Σάρρας εἰρηκυίας, *ἔκβαλε τὴν παιδίσκην . . . καὶ τὸν*
υἱὸν αὐτῆς,[b] οὐχ ὑπήκουσε· τοῦ δὲ Θεοῦ κελεύσαντος, εὐθὺς
τῷ λόγῳ τὸ ἔργον ἐπέθηκε, καὶ ταῦτα φιλοστόργως περὶ τὸν
Ἰσμαὴλ διακείμενος. καὶ γὰρ ἡνίκα τὴν ἐκ τῆς Σάρρας
παιδοποιίαν ὁ Θεὸς ἐπηγγείλατο, αὐτὸς ἔφη, *Ἰσμαὴλ οὗτος*
10 *ζήτω ἐναντίον σου*[c] ἀλλ' ὅμως, καὶ στέργων κομιδῇ τὸ
παιδίον, πεποίηκεν ὅπερ ὁ δεσπότης προσέταξεν. οὕτω δὲ
ταῖς θείαις ἐπαγγελίαις πεπίστευκεν ὅτι, οὐ παῖδας, οὐ
παιδίσκας, οὐ χρυσόν, οὐκ ἄργυρον δεδωκώς, ἀπέλυσε τῆς
οἰκίας τὸ παιδίον, ἀλλ' ἄρτους ὀλίγους, καὶ ἀσκὸν ὕδατος, καὶ
15 τὴν μητέρα· ᾔδει γὰρ ὡς ἀψευδὴς ἡ τοῦ προστεταχότος
ὑπόσχεσις.

Ὑπέσχετο δὲ αὐτῷ ὁ Θεὸς εἰς ἔθνος μέγα ποιήσειν αὐτόν,
ἅτε δὴ τῆς αὐτοῦ γεωργίας ἠξιωμένον.[d] ὃ δὴ καὶ πεπλήρωκεν·
ἅμα γὰρ ἔκλαυσε τὸ παιδίον, πόματος ἐφιέμενον, καὶ ἄγγελος
20 θεόθεν ἀποσταλεὶς φρέαρ ὑπέδειξε ποτίμου ὕδατος πλῆρες.[e]
ὅτι δὲ καὶ τῆς παιδοποιίας τὸ πλῆθος δέδωκεν, ὡς ὑπέσχετο,
μαρτυρεῖ τὰ ὁρώμενα· ἀπὸ γὰρ τῶν ὅρων Αἰγύπτου μέχρι
Βαβυλῶνος τοῦδε τοῦ γένους ἡ ἔρημος πλήρης.

Ὁ μέντοι Ἀβραὰμ καὶ τοῖς τόποις ἐκ τῆς εὐσεβείας
25 ἐπιτέθεικε τὰ ὀνόματα· φυτεύσας γὰρ ἄρουραν ἐπὶ τῷ φρέατι
τοῦ ὅρκου, ἐπεκαλέσατο τὸ ὄνομα τοῦ τόπου ἐκείνου *Θεὸς*
αἰώνιος.[f]

LXXIII A [32], B, C, 7 9 10 13 17 35 37 = 21 mss.

a. Gn 21.14   b. Gn 21.10   c. Gn 17.18   d. Gn 21.13   e. Gn 21.15–19
f. Gn 21.33

LXXIII

The expulsion of Ishmael as a child from his father's home with just his mother and a flask of water seems very harsh.[a]

On the contrary, it brings out Abraham's virtue. He did not obey Sarah when she told him to "throw out the servant girl and her son."[b] But when God gave the order, he immediately put that word into effect, despite his fondness for Ishmael. Indeed, when God promised that Sarah would have a child, he said, "May Ishmael here live in your sight."[c] Yet, though he loved the child, he did what the Lord commanded. Now, this was how he expressed his trust in the divine promises: he sent the child away without servants, maidservants, gold, or silver, but with just a few loaves, a flask of water, and his mother, for he knew he could trust the promise of the one who had laid this order upon him.

God had promised to make a mighty nation of Ishmael, one whom he deemed worthy of his care.[d] And he did just that. As soon as the child, in his longing to drink, burst into tears, an angel sent by God showed him a well full of drinking water.[e] Now, the evidence confirms that he also gave him a vast number of offspring; the desert is full of this race from the borders of Egypt to Babylon.

Note how Abraham's toponyms reflected his piety. After planting a field at the well of the oath, he named the place "God Eternal."[f]

----
etymology as "the little" town. The septuagintal rendition Σηγώρ is the transliteration of a Hebrew stem meaning "to close up" or "to close in"; it is at 14.2 that the LXX offer the alternative name Βάλακ, a transliteration of the Hebrew stem "to swallow up." Theodoret is not in a position to critique the Hebrew etymologies of his sources.

LXXIV

Εἰ πάντα ὁ Θεὸς προγινώσκει, τίνος χάριν τὸν Ἀβραὰμ
ἐπείρασε;[a]

Οὐχ ἵνα αὐτὸς ἅπερ ἠπίστατο μάθῃ, ἀλλ' ἵνα τοὺς
ἀγνοοῦντας διδάξῃ ὡς μάλα δικαίως τὸν πατριάρχην ἠγάπησε.

5 τούτου χάριν ἐν τρισὶν ἡμέραις καὶ τοσαύταις νυξὶ τὸν θεῖον
ἐβασάνιζε πόθον·[b] μέσος γὰρ ὢν ὁ πατριάρχης φύσεώς τε καὶ
πίστεως καὶ νυττόμενος ἑκατέρωθεν, ἔδωκε τῇ πίστει τὰ
νικητήρια. ὁ δὲ Θεός, δείξας αὐτοῦ τὴν εὐσέβειαν, τὴν θυσίαν
ἐκώλυσεν.[c]

10 Ὁ γὰρ καὶ τὰς τῶν ἀλόγων ἀπαγορεύων θυσίας, πῶς ἂν
τοιαύτης ἱερουργίας ἠνέσχετο; τοῦτο γὰρ ἰουδαίων κατηγορῶν
διετέλεσε καὶ διὰ μὲν Δαβὶδ τοῦ προφήτου βοᾷ, *ἔθυσαν τοὺς*
υἱοὺς αὐτῶν καὶ τὰς θυγατέρας αὐτῶν τοῖς δαιμονίοις καὶ
ἐξέχεαν αἷμα ἀθῷον, αἷμα υἱῶν αὐτῶν καὶ θυγατέρων, ὧν
15 *ἔθυσαν τοῖς γλυπτοῖς Χαναάν·*[d] διὰ δὲ τοῦ Ἰεζεκιήλ, *καὶ*
ἔλαβες τοὺς υἱούς σου καὶ τὰς θυγατέρας σου, οὓς ἐγέννησάς
μοι,[e] *καὶ προσήνεγκας αὐτοὺς τοῖς ἐρασταῖς σου·* εἶτα
δεικνὺς τὴν τῆς ἀτοπίας ὑπερβολήν, ἐπήγαγε τοῦτο· *παρὰ*
πᾶσαν τὴν πορνείαν σου.[f] ὁ τοίνυν τῶν ταῦτα τολμώντων
20 κατηγορῶν πῶς ἂν αὐτὸς ἠνέσχετο δέξασθαι παῖδα μονογενῆ,
παρὰ πατρὸς προσφερόμενον;

Ἀλλὰ γὰρ ταῦτα σκιὰ ἦν τῆς ὑπὲρ ἡμῶν γεγενημένης
οἰκονομίας. ὑπὲρ γὰρ τῆς οἰκουμένης τὸν ἀγαπητὸν υἱὸν ὁ
πατὴρ προσενήνοχε·[g] τύπος γὰρ τῆς μὲν θεότητος ὁ Ἰσαάκ,
25 τῆς δὲ ἀνθρωπότητος ὁ κριός. καὶ αὐτὸς δὲ ὁ χρόνος ἰσάριθ-
μος· τρεῖς γὰρ ἡμέραι καὶ τρεῖς νύκτες καὶ ἐνταῦθα κἀκεῖ.

---

lxxiv A *[32]*, B, C, *7 9 10 13 17 35 37* = 21 mss.

a. Gn 22.1–14   b. Gn 22.4   c. Gn 22.10–12   d. Ps 106.37f.
e. Ezek 16.20   f. Ezek 16.22   g. Cf. Mt 3.17.

LXXIV

If God knows everything in advance, why did he put Abraham to the test?[a]

Not to learn what he already knew, but to teach the ignorant that he had good reason to love the patriarch. That was why he tested his love of God for three days and nights.[b] The patriarch, torn between nature and faith and pulled both ways, decided in favor of faith. Having brought out his devotion, God stopped the sacrifice.[c]

After all, how could he who forbade sacrifices of brute beasts have tolerated such a rite? In fact, this is a charge he often laid against the Jews, as, for example, when he proclaimed through the prophet David, "They sacrificed their sons and their daughters to the demons and poured out innocent blood, blood of their sons and daughters, whom they sacrificed to the idols of Canaan";[d] and also through Ezekiel, "You took your sons and your daughters, whom you bore me,[e] and offered them to your lovers." Then to bring out the depth of their wickedness, he added, "This is worse than all your licentiousness."[f] If he laid charges against people who committed this crime, how could he have accepted a father's offering of his only-begotten son?

No, this was a shadow of the divine plan implemented for our benefit; for the sake of the world, the Father offered his beloved Son.[g] Isaac was a type of the divinity, the ram of the humanity. The actual time was also of equal length: three days and three nights in both cases.

The Questions on Genesis

LXXV

Τί ἐστι θὲς τὴν χεῖρά σου ἐπὶ τὸν μηρόν μου;[a]

(1) Ἐπὶ γάμον ἀπέστελλεν τῶν οἰκετῶν τὸν ἡγούμενον, ἐπάρατον μὲν ἐπιστάμενος τοῦ Χαναὰν τὸ γένος,[b] εὐλογίας δὲ ἠξιωμένην τὴν οἰκείαν συγγένειαν.[c] ἐπειδὴ τοίνυν ἐν τῷ
5 σπέρματι καὶ τὴν εὐλογίαν καὶ τὴν τῶν ἀγαθῶν ἐπαγγελίαν ἐδέξατο, ἐκεῖ θεῖναι τὸν παῖδα τὴν χεῖρα προσέταξεν, ἔνθα καὶ τῆς πίστεως τὸ σημεῖον ἐδέξατο· πιστεύσας γὰρ ταῖς θείαις ἐπαγγελίαις, ἔλαβε τῆς περιτομῆς τὴν σφραγῖδα.[d] ἐκεῖ δὲ θεῖναι τὴν χεῖρα προσέταξεν ἵνα, καὶ τῆς θείας
10 ἐπαγγελίας καὶ τῆς περιτομῆς μεμνημένος, ἀλλοφύλῳ γάμῳ τὴν δεσποτικὴν εὐγένειαν μὴ λωβήσηται. ἰστέον δὲ ὡς ἡ μὲν χεὶρ ὑπὸ τὸν μηρὸν ἐτέθη, ὁ δὲ ὅρκος κατὰ τοῦ Θεοῦ τῶν ὅλων ἐγένετο· ἐξορκίζω σε, γὰρ ἔφη, Κύριον τὸν Θεὸν τοῦ οὐρανοῦ... καὶ τῆς γῆς ἵνα μὴ λάβῃς γυναῖκα τῷ υἱῷ μου
15 Ἰσαὰκ ἀπὸ τῶν θυγατέρων τῶν χαναναίων, μεθ' ὧν ἐγὼ οἰκῶ ἐν αὐτοῖς, καὶ τὰ ἑξῆς.[e]

Σοφωτάτη δὲ ἄγαν καὶ τοῦ παιδὸς ἡ ἐρώτησις. δείσας γὰρ τὸν ὅρκον, δήλους αὐτῷ γενέσθαι παρεκάλει τοῦ γάμου τοὺς ὅρους· εἰ, γάρ φησι, μὴ ἔλοιτο ἐνταῦθα ἐλθεῖν ἡ μνηστευομένη
20 κόρη ἀλλὰ πρὸς αὐτὴν ἀπελθεῖν τὸν μνηστῆρα κελεύει, προστάττεις τὸν υἱὸν εἰς ἐκεῖνο τὸ ἔθνος ἐπανελθεῖν; ἀλλ' ὁ πατριάρχης Ἀβραάμ, εἰδὼς ὡς ἐκεῖθεν μὲν αὐτὸν ἡ θεία κλῆσις ἐξήγαγε,[f] περὶ δὲ τοῦ γάμου νόμον οὐκ ἐδέξατο θεῖον· αὐτὸς δέ, ὡς εὐσεβείᾳ συντεθραμμένος, ἠθέλησεν ἐκ τῆς συγγενικῆς
25 οἰκίας τῷ παιδὶ κατεγγυῆσαι γυναῖκα· ἐκεῖνο μὲν ἀπαγορεύει γενέσθαι, ἄτε δὴ θείῳ νόμῳ κεκωλυμένον, τοῦτο δὲ τῇ θείᾳ ἐγχειρίζει κηδεμονίᾳ. ταύτῃ θαρρήσας, ὁ παῖς ἐξεδήμησεν.

LXXV A [32], B, c, 50 51* 52* 53, 7 9 10 13 17 35 37 = 21 mss.

a. Gn 24.2   b. Gn 9.25   c. Gn 12.2f.   d. Gn 17.10–14   e. Gn 24.3
f. Gn 12.1

LXXV

What is the meaning of "Put your hand on my thigh"?[a]

(1) He sent his head servant to arrange a marriage, as he knew that the race of Canaan was under a curse,[b] and his own kindred had been granted a blessing.[c] So, since in his seed he had received both the blessing and the promise of good things, he ordered the servant to put his hand in the place where he had also received the sign of faith. Remember that when he had believed in the divine promise, he was given the seal of circumcision.[d] He ordered him to place his hand there so that, mindful of the divine promise and circumcision, he would not besmirch his master's nobility with a foreign marriage. Now, you should understand that he placed his hand under the thigh, but he was made to swear by the God of the universe: "I adjure you by the Lord, the God of heaven and earth, not to get a wife for my son Isaac from the daughters of the Canaanites among whom I live" and so on.[e]

The servant's question was a very wise one. In awe of his oath, he required a clear statement of the conditions of the marriage: "If the betrothed maiden should not choose to come here but ask the suitor to come to her, is it your instruction that your son go back to that nation?" The patriarch Abraham knew that the divine summons had brought him out from there,[f] yet he had not received a divine directive regarding the marriage. Nevertheless, as one who had been nourished in right religion, he wanted to betroth to his son a woman from his family line. So he forbade Isaac's return as something prohibited by God's law, but entrusted his betrothal to divine providence.[1] And with trust in providence the servant took his leave.

---

1. Abraham forbade the marriage of Isaac to a Canaanite woman but entrusted to the guidance of God the ways and means of Isaac's marriage to a bride from his own family line.

The Questions on Genesis

(2) Ἐκείνην δὲ τὴν εὐχὴν οὐ συμβολικῶς προσενήνοχεν, ὥς τινες τῶν ἄγαν ἠλιθίων ὑπέλαβον, ἀλλ', ἐπειδὴ τὸν Θεὸν
30 συνεργὸν ἔλαβε τῆς μνηστείας, σημεῖά τινα αὐτῷ δειχθῆναι παρεκάλει, δι' ὧν ἠβούλετο γνῶναι εἰ ἀρέσκουσα τῷ Θεῷ ἡ μνηστεία. τὸ δὲ σημεῖον ἦν, οὐχ ὥρα σώματος, οὐδὲ περιφάνεια γένους, οὐδὲ ἄλλο τι τῶν δοκούντων λαμπρῶν, ἀλλὰ φιλοξενία, καὶ φιλοφροσύνη, καὶ ἠπιότης φρονήματος·
35 ἔσται, γάρ φησιν, ἡ παρθένος ᾗ ἂν ἐγὼ εἴπω, ἐπίκλινόν μοι τὴν ὑδρίαν σου ἵνα πίω, καὶ εἴπῃ μοι, πίε, κύριε, καὶ τὰς καμήλους σου ποτιῶ ἕως ἂν παύσωνται πίνουσαι, ταύτην ἡτοίμασας τῷ παιδί σου Ἰσαάκ, καὶ ἐν τούτῳ γνώσομαι ὅτι ἐποίησας ἔλεον μετὰ τοῦ κυρίου μου Ἀβραάμ.[g] ἐπειδὴ γὰρ
40 τούτοις ἐκοσμεῖτο τοῖς πλεονεκτήμασι διαφερόντως ὁ πατριάρχης, ἠβουλήθη καὶ τὴν νύμφην συμβαίνειν τῷ τρόπῳ τοῦ κηδεστοῦ ἵνα μὴ ἔριν τινὰ καὶ φιλονεικίαν ὁ σκοπὸς ὁ ἐναντίος ἐργάσηται.

Ὅτι δὲ οὐ συμβολικὰ ταῦτα ἦν ἀλλὰ πίστεως καὶ εὐσεβείας
45 δηλωτικά, πρῶτον διδάσκει τὸ σπουδαῖον τῆς προσευχῆς, ἔπειτα τὸ προσμένειν αὐτὸν τὴν βουλὴν τοῦ Θεοῦ. τοῦτο γὰρ ἡ θεία διδάσκει γραφή· ὁ δὲ ἄνθρωπος κατεμάνθανεν αὐτὴν καὶ παρεσιώπα τοῦ γνῶναι εἰ εὐώδωκε Κύριος τὴν ὁδὸν αὐτοῦ ἢ οὔ[h] ἐκείνης γὰρ τὸ ὕδωρ ἀρυομένης καὶ ταῖς καμήλοις
50 προσφερούσης τὸ νᾶμα, ἀνέμενεν οὗτος ἰδεῖν εἰ πάσαις παρέχει τὴν χρείαν κατὰ τὴν αἴτησιν. πιουσῶν δὲ τῶν καμήλων, εὐθὺς προσενήνοχε τῆς μνηστείας τὰ σύμβολα. γνοὺς δὲ τὸ γένος καὶ τὴν δεσποτικὴν συγγένειαν,[i] εὐδοκήσας, φησίν, ὁ ἄνθρωπος προσεκύνησε τῷ Κυρίῳ καὶ
55 εἶπεν, εὐλογητὸς Κύριος ὁ Θεὸς τοῦ κυρίου μου Ἀβραάμ, ὃς οὐκ ἐγκατέλιπε τὴν δικαιοσύνην αὐτοῦ καὶ τὸν ἔλεον αὐτοῦ ἀπὸ τοῦ κυρίου μου, κἀμὲ ἐν ὁδῷ ἤγαγε Κύριος εἰς τὸν οἶκον τοῦ ἀδελφοῦ τοῦ κυρίου μου.[j] καὶ πᾶσα δὲ αὐτοῦ ἡ διάλεξις τὸ εὐσεβὲς κηρύττει τῆς γνώμης καὶ μέντοι καί, μετὰ τὴν

---

g. Gn 24.14   h. Gn 24.21   i. Gn 24.22–24   j. Gn 24.27

(2) Now, it was not in any figurative sense, as some commentators have quite foolishly imagined, that the servant offered his prayer. Since he had chosen God to help him in the betrothal, he requested that he be shown signs by which he might know if the betrothal was pleasing to God.[2] The sign was not bodily charm or famous lineage or anything betokening superficial notoriety, but hospitality, friendliness, and a kindly manner: "She will be the maiden to whom I say, 'Lower your water jar for me to drink,' and who says, 'Drink, sir, and I shall water your camels until they stop drinking'; this is the one you have prepared for your servant Isaac. By this I shall know that you have had mercy on my master Abraham."[g] You see, knowing the patriarch was particularly gifted with these qualities, he wanted the bride to be suited to the ways of her father-in-law so that no difference of values would give rise to strife and contention.

The fact that these events were not an allegory but indicative of faith and devotion emerges first from the earnestness of the prayer and then from his patient attendance upon the will of God. Holy Scripture tells us that "the fellow watched her in silence to learn if the Lord had prospered his journey or not."[h] When she was drawing the water and bringing drink for the camels, he waited to see if she would provide for all of them as requested. Once the camels had drunk, he proffered the tokens of betrothal. When he discovered her family and her relationship to his master's family,[i] the fellow was grateful, as the text says, and, bowing down to the Lord, declared, "Blessed be the Lord, the God of my master Abraham, who has not forsaken his righteousness and his mercy to my master. The Lord has led me as well on my way to the house of my master's brother."[j] The whole of his speech proclaimed his piety, and after that speech, he

---

2. Origen (*hom.* 10.2 *in Gen.*) had regarded the servant as a representative of prophecy and his prayer as a revelation of the need of the soul for spiritual refreshment from the teaching of Scripture; *v.* Guinot, p. 761 and *cf.* Philo, *Quaest. in Gen.* 191.

60 διάλεξιν, τὸν αὐτὸν σημαίνει σκοπόν· συνθεμένων γὰρ τῶν τὴν
κόρην γεγεννηκότων τῷ γάμῳ, εὐθὺς αὐτὸς *προσεκύνησε τῷ*
Κυρίῳ.[k] καὶ τὰ ἐξῆς δὲ τῆς αὐτῆς ἔχεται διανοίας· *μὴ*
κατέχετε γάρ με, φησί, *καὶ Κύριος εὐώδωσε τὴν ὁδόν μου.*[l]

LXXVI

Διὰ τί τῶν πατριαρχῶν αἱ γυναῖκες στεῖραι; καὶ γὰρ Σάρρα
στεῖρα,[a] καὶ Ῥεβέκκα ὡσαύτως,[b] καὶ ἡ Ῥαχήλ,[c] καὶ μέντοι καὶ
ἡ Λεία· *ἰδών . . . ,* γάρ φησι, *Κύριος ὅτι μισεῖται ἡ Λεία,*
ἀνέῳξε τὴν μήτραν αὐτῆς.[d]

5 Τὸ ἰσραηλιτικὸν συστῆσαι γένος βουληθείς, ὁ Θεὸς
δείκνυσιν, οὐ κατὰ φύσεως ἀκολουθίαν, ἀλλὰ κατὰ τὴν τῆς
χάριτος φιλοτιμίαν τὴν πολυγονίαν δεξάμενον. ταύτης δὲ τῆς
κηδεμονίας ἐκεῖνο τὸ γένος τετύχηκεν, ἐπειδήπερ ὁ δεσπότης
Χριστός, ὁ μονογενὴς τοῦ Θεοῦ υἱός, ἐκεῖθεν ἔμελλε κατὰ
10 σάρκα βλαστήσειν.

LXXVII

Διὰ τίνος μαθεῖν ἠθέλησεν ἡ Ῥεβέκκα τὰ περὶ τῶν
κυοφορουμένων παιδίων;[a]
Τινές φασι πρὸς τὸν Μελχισεδὲκ αὐτὴν ἀπεληλυθέναι, ἅτε
δὴ καὶ ἀρχιερέα ὄντα τοῦ Θεοῦ τοῦ ὑψίστου, καὶ ἐπίσημον ἐν
5 εὐσεβείᾳ, καὶ λίαν περιφανῆ. ἐπειδὴ δὲ εἰώθεισαν οἱ

k. Gn 24.26   l. Gn 24.56

LXXVI A *[32]*, B, c, 50, 7 9 10 13 17 35 37 = 18 mss.

a. Gn 16.1   b. Gn 25.21   c. Gn 29.31   d. Gn 29.31

LXXVII A *[32]*, 30, C, 7 9 10 13 35 37 = 18 mss.

a. Gn 25.22f.

revealed the same mindset. Once the maiden's parents had agreed to the marriage, he immediately "worshiped the Lord." [k] And his subsequent words evinced the same spirit: "Do not delay me, for the Lord has prospered my journey."[l]

LXXVI

Why were the wives of the patriarchs barren? Sarah was barren,[a] as were Rebekah,[b] and Rachel,[c] and Leah as well. Indeed, Scripture says, "When the Lord saw that Leah was hated, he opened her womb."[d]

As he willed the development of the Israelite race, God highlights, not natural increase, but the growth in numbers resulting from grace liberally bestowed. This race became the object of providential care, since this was the stock from which Christ the Lord, the only-begotten Son of God, was destined to be born according to the flesh.[1]

LXXVII

From whom did Rebekah intend to learn about the children in her womb?[a]

Some commentators have claimed that she went to Melchizedek, since he was high priest of God the Most High, conspicuous for piety, and very famous.[1] But given that the patriarchs normally

---

1. In his review of the patriarchal history, Theodoret's choice of questions often reflects moral concerns while he passes without comment over issues of theological significance, such as Abraham's calling to a foreign land. In this question, however, Theodoret offers a christological interpretation of the barrenness of the patriarchs' wives.

---

1. Without trying to identify him any further, Chrysostom says (*hom.* 50.1 *in Gen.*) only that Rebekah went to "the priest, the servant of God" (τὸν ἱερέα τὸν τοῦ θεοῦ θεραπεύτην).

πατριάρχαι καὶ θυσιαστήρια τῷ Θεῷ κατασκευάζειν ἐν οἷς
ἐσκήνουν χωρίοις, εἰκὸς παρ' ἐν τούτων αὐτὴν ἀπελθοῦσαν
ἱκετεῦσαι τὸν ὅλων Θεὸν καὶ γνωρίσαι τὰ συμβησόμενα.

LXXVIII

Διὰ τί κωλύει τὸν Ἰσαὰκ ὁ Θεὸς εἰς τὴν Αἴγυπτον
ἐκδημῆσαι, τοῦ λιμοῦ τοῦτο πρᾶξαι καταναγκάζοντος;[a]
   Τὴν οἰκείαν σοφίαν τε καὶ κηδεμονίαν διὰ πάντων δηλοῖ ὁ
δεσπότης Θεός. καὶ γὰρ τὸν πατριάρχην Ἀβραάμ, οὐχ ὡς
5 ἀπορῶν ἐν τῇ Παλαιστίνῃ διαθρέψαι, συνεχώρησεν εἰς τὴν
Αἴγυπτον ἀπελθεῖν[b] ἀλλ' ἵνα τοῖς αἰγυπτίοις ἐπιδείξῃ τοῦ
ἀνδρὸς τὴν εὐσέβειαν καὶ ζηλῶσαι προτρέψῃ τοῦ πατριάρχου
τὴν ἀρετήν. τὸν δὲ Ἰσαὰκ αὐτοῦ μεῖναι προσέταξε καὶ τῇ τῶν
ἀναγκαίων αὐτὸν περιέκλυσεν ἀφθονίᾳ, δεικνὺς ὡς καὶ τῷ
10 πατρὶ ταῦτα παρασχεῖν οἷός τε ἦν ἃ καὶ αὐτῷ ἔδωκε
φιλοτίμως· πάντων γὰρ ἐν ἐνδείᾳ ὄντων καὶ σπάνει τῶν
ἀναγκαίων, καὶ τῆς γῆς ἀγόνου γεγενημένης, αὐτὸς σπείρας
πολύχουν ἔλαβε τὸν καρπόν.[c]

LXXIX

Τίνος ἕνεκεν ὁ Ἰσαὰκ τῷ Ἠσαῦ δοῦναι τὴν εὐλογίαν
ἠβούλετο;[a]
   Κατὰ τὸν νόμον τῆς φύσεως· πρωτότοκος γὰρ ἦν,[b] οἱ δὲ
πρωτότοκοι καὶ πρῶτοι καὶ διπλῆν ἐλάμβανον μοῖραν.[c] ηὔξησε
5 δὲ καὶ ἡ θεραπεία τὸ φίλτρον· ἡ γὰρ θήρα αὐτοῦ βρῶσις

LXXVIII A [32], 30, C, 7 9 10 13 35 37 = 18 mss.
a. Gn 26.1f.   b. Gn 12.10   c. Gn 26.12

LXXIX A [32], 30, C, 7 9 10 13 35 37 = 18 mss.
a. Gn 27.1–4   b. Gn 25.25   c. Dt 21.17

erected altars to God wherever they encamped, it was probably at one of those altars that she prayed to the God of the universe and gained her knowledge of the future.

LXXVIII

Why did God prevent Isaac from departing for Egypt when he was being driven to this by famine?[a]

In everything the Lord God reveals his wise providence. He had allowed the patriarch Abraham to leave for Egypt,[b] not because he had no way to feed him in Palestine, but to show the Egyptians Abraham's devotion and to encourage them to imitate the patriarch's virtue. But he ordered Isaac to stay put and showered him with an abundance of food to show that he could have provided also to his father the things he gave so generously to him. When everyone was in need because of the famine and the infertility of the land, Isaac sowed and gathered a plentiful harvest.[c]

LXXIX

Why did Isaac intend to give his blessing to Esau?[a]

This was according to the law of nature. Esau was the firstborn,[b] and the firstborn had first place and received a double portion.[c] Esau's attendance on his father also increased his affection: "For the

αὐτῷ.[d] ἱκανὴ δὲ ἡ θεραπεία καὶ τοὺς ὠμοτάτους μειλίχεσθαι,
μή τί γε δὴ πατέρα καὶ πατέρα φιλόστοργον. εὕροι δ' ἄν τις
καὶ τὸν θεῖον ἀπόστολον πλείσταις ὅσαις εὐλογίαις τοὺς
τεθεραπευκότας αὐτὸν ἀμειψάμενον.[e]

LXXX

Πόθεν ἡ Ῥεβέκκα τεθάρρηκεν ὅτι δὴ τεύξεται τῆς εὐλογίας
ὁ Ἰακὼβ καὶ οὕτω τεθάρρηκεν ὡς εἰπεῖν, *ἐπ' ἐμὲ ἡ κατάρα*
σου, τέκνον· μόνον ἐπάκουσον τῆς φωνῆς μου;[a]
Προεγνώκει παρὰ τοῦ θεοῦ τῶν ὅλων ὅτι *ὁ μείζων δουλεύσει*
5 *τῷ ἐλάσσονι.*[b] ἐκείνη τῇ προρρήσει πιστεύουσα, πάντα
ἐκίνησεν πόρον ὥστε τὸν Ἰακὼβ τὴν πατρικὴν εὐλογίαν λαβεῖν.

LXXXI

Τί δή ποτε τῷ Ἰσαὰκ τὸ βούλημα τὸ οἰκεῖον οὐκ
ἀπεκάλυψεν ὁ θεός;
 Ἵνα ἐναργὴς γένηται ἡ τοῦ θεοῦ περὶ τὸν Ἰακὼβ κηδεμονία.

l. 7 μή τί γε δὴ *15, c₁, Sir.* (μήτι) *Sch.* (μήτι) : μή πού γε δὴ *13* : εἴ που
γε δὴ *Pic.* (εἴπου, *Sch.*) *F.M.* = "if a parent, especially a doting parent." For the
rather common collocation μή τί γε δή, *cf.* Thdt., *H. rel. vita* 23.2 (οὓς καὶ
ἀριθμῆσαι μόνον οὐκ εὐπετές, μή τί γε δὴ τὸν ἑκάστου βίον
συγγράψαι). The reading of *13* is also possible; *cf.* Ps. 23.5 (Πᾶσαι γὰρ τῶν
ἀνθρώπων αἱ δικαιοσύναι, οὐδὲν πρὸς τὰς ἤδη δεδομένας ὑπὸ τοῦ Θεοῦ
δωρεὰς ἀποχρῶσι, μήπου γε δὴ πρὸς τὰς ἐσομένας). In contrast, the
doubt expressed by the εἴ in εἴ πού γε δὴ is quite inappropriate to the
context. Furthermore, this collocation is unexampled elsewhere among all the
works now comprised within the *TLG*.

d. Gn 25.28   e. *V., e.g.,* Phil 4.15–19.

---

lxxx *A [32], 30, c, 7 9 10 13 35 37* = 14 mss.

a. Gn 27.13   b. Gn 25.23

---

lxxxi *A [32], 30, C, 7 9 10 13 35 37* = 18 mss.

game he caught was his food."[d] Such attendance can soften very cruel people, not to mention a parent, especially a doting parent. One might also cite the example of the holy apostle who showered his blessings on those who had taken care of him.[e]

LXXX

How could Rebekah be so confident that Jacob would be given the blessing, in fact, so confident as to say, "On me your curse, son, only hearken to my voice"?[a]

Thanks to the God of the universe, she knew in advance that "the elder would serve the younger."[b] Trusting in that prediction, she took every step to ensure that Jacob would receive his father's blessing.

LXXXI

Why did God not reveal his wishes to Isaac?

To make God's care for Jacob entirely clear. Isaac's insistence on

δείκνυσι δὲ τοῦτο τὸ μὲν Ἰσαὰκ ἐσπουδακέναι τὸν Ἡσαῦ
5 εὐλογῆσαι, τὴν δὲ θείαν χάριν, καὶ παρὰ γνώμην τοῦ Ἰσαάκ,
ἐπὶ τὸν Ἰακὼβ ἑλκῦσαι τὴν εὐλογίαν. τοῦτο δὲ καὶ αὐτὸς
συνῆκεν ὁ Ἰσαάκ, ὡς γὰρ πάντα πόρον ἐκίνησε, καὶ ἀπέστειλε
τὸν Ἡσαῦ ἐπι τὴν θήραν,ᵃ καί, τοῦ Ἰακὼβ τὴν τροφὴν
προσενηνοχότος,ᵇ πολλάκις ἤρετο εἰ αὐτὸς εἴη Ἡσαῦ ὁ
10 πρωτότοκος,ᶜ καί, οὐ μόνον ἤρετο, ἀλλὰ καὶ τὰς χεῖρας τῷ
σώματι προσενήνοχεν.ᵈ εἶτα, τοῦ Ἡσαῦ εἰσεληλυθότος, τὸ
γεγενημένον καταπλαγείς, οὐκ ἐχαλέπηνεν ὡς παρὰ παιδὸς
ἐξαπατηθείς, ἀλλὰ τὸ θεῖον ἔγνω σκοπόν, καὶ ἣν ἔδωκεν
ἐβεβαίωσεν εὐλογίαν.ᵉ

LXXXII

Εἶτα οὐ δοκεῖ ἐψεῦσθαι ὁ Ἰακὼβ εἰπών, *ἐγώ εἰμι Ἡσαῦ ὁ
πρωτότοκός σου;*ᵃ
Πριάμενος ἦν τὰ τῶν πρωτοτοκίων πρεσβεῖα· ἀληθεύων
τοιγαροῦν ἑαυτὸν ἀπεκάλει πρωτότοκον.ᵇ

LXXXIII

Τίς δὲ τῆς εὐλογίας ἡ ἑρμηνεία;ᵃ
Ἔμελλεν ἐξ αὐτοῦ κατὰ σάρκα βλαστήσειν ὁ δεσπότης
Χριστός,ᵇ ἡ τῶν ἐθνῶν προσδοκία, ὁ τῆς οἰκουμένης ἀπάσης
καὶ σωτὴρ καὶ δεσπότης. ταῦτα προορῶν, ὁ πατριάρχης φησίν,

---

a. Gn 27.3f.   b. Gn 27.18f.   c. Gn 27.24   d. Gn 27.22   e. Gn 27.33

LXXXII A *[32], 30, C, 7 9 10 13 35 37* = 18 mss.

a. Gn 27.19   b. Gn 25.29–34

LXXXIII A *[32], 30, C, 7 9 10 13 35 37* = 18 mss.

a. Gn 27.27–29   b. Mt 1.1

blessing Esau brings this out, for the divine grace drew the blessing onto Jacob against Isaac's wishes. Even Isaac himself realized this, for he knew how he had done everything possible: he had sent Esau hunting[a] and then asked repeatedly,[c] when Jacob offered him the food,[b] if he was Esau his firstborn. Indeed, he not only questioned, but even put his hands on, Jacob,[d] and then, when Esau came in and expressed his astonishment at what had happened, Isaac was not angry at the deceit perpetrated by his son, but, recognizing the divine purpose, confirmed the blessing he had just imparted.[1e]

LXXXII

Does it not seem that Jacob lied in saying, "I am Esau your first-born"?[a]

He had paid for the privileges of the firstborn, so he could truthfully call himself the firstborn.[b]

LXXXIII

What is the meaning of the blessing?[a]

Christ the Lord, the expectation of the nations, the Savior and Lord of the whole world, was to draw his bodily descent from Jacob.[b] Foreseeing this, the patriarch declared, "Lo, the smell of my son is

---

1. Here Theodoret abandons the ethical viewpoint to which we have just pointed (note 1 to Q. 76) and almost seems to endorse Speiser's position (p. 211): "[I]t goes without saying that the task of the interpreter is not to justify or sit in judgment, to condone or condemn, but only to inquire what the given source means in terms of its own context and background." Like Chrysostom (*hom.* 53.2 *in Gen.; cf.* B. De Montfaucon's note 1, col. 473, PG, vol. 54), he saw the transference of the blessing to Jacob as a mystery. It was part of the divine plan he discerned also in the barrenness of the patriarch's wives. But as the following question reveals, Theodoret feels compelled to address the moral dimension.

5 ἰδοὺ ὀσμὴ τοῦ υἱοῦ μου ὡς ὀσμὴ ἀγροῦ πλήρους, ὃν εὐλόγησε
Κύριος.ᶜ ὅτι δὲ πολλάκις ἀγρὸν τὸν κόσμον ἡ θεία καλεῖ
γραφὴ μάρτυς ὁ Κύριος ἐν τοῖς ἱεροῖς εὐαγγελίοις, τὴν
παραβολὴν ἑρμηνεύων· ἀγρός, γάρ φησιν, ἔστιν ὁ κόσμος· ὁ δὲ
σπείρων τὸ καλὸν σπέρμα ἐστὶν ὁ υἱὸς τοῦ ἀνθρώπου.ᵈ ὅρα
10 τοιγαροῦν ἐν τῷ Ἰακὼβ τῆς οἰκουμένης ἁπάσης τὴν σωτηρίαν.

Διὸ ἐπεύχεται αὐτῷ τοῦ οὐρανοῦ τὴν δρόσον καὶ τῆς γῆς
τὴν πιότητα,ᵉ ἃ, κατὰ μὲν τὸ πρόχειρον καὶ ἐπιπόλαιον τοῦ
γράμματος νόημα, δηλοῖ τὴν ἄνωθεν χάριν καὶ τῶν ἀπὸ γῆς
ἀγαθῶν τὴν ἀφθονίαν, κατὰ δὲ τὴν τοῦ ἀγροῦ ἑρμηνείαν,
15 αἰνίττεται τοῦ δεσπότου Χριστοῦ, διὰ τῆς δρόσου μὲν τὴν
θεότητα, διὰ δὲ τῆς πιότητος τῆς γῆς τὴν ἐξ ἡμῶν
ἀνθρωπότητα. καὶ γὰρ ὁ μακάριος Δαβὶδ ταῦτα προαγορεύων
ἔφη, καταβήσεται ὡς ὑετὸς ἐπὶ πόκον καὶ ὡσεὶ σταγόνες
στάζουσαι ἐπὶ τὴν γῆν·ᶠ ὥσπερ γὰρ ἡ δρόσος ἀοράτως μὲν
20 κάτεισι, κάτω δὲ συνισταμένη γίνεται δήλη, οὕτως, ἀόρατος
ὢν ὁ Θεὸς λόγος, διὰ τῆς σαρκὸς ἐπὶ γῆς ὤφθη, καὶ τοῖς
ἀνθρώποις συνανεστράφη, καὶ ἐφανερώθη ἐν σαρκί,ᵍ κατὰ τὸν
θεῖον ἀπόστολον. καὶ ὁ σῖτος δὲ καὶ ὁ οἶνος τῶν θείων ἐστὶ
μυστηρίων αἴνιγμα.

25 Τούτῳ συμφωνεῖ τῷ λόγω καὶ τὰ ἑξῆς· καὶ δουλευσάτωσάν
σοι ἔθνηʰ πάντα, γάρ φησιν, τὰ ἔθνη δουλεύσουσιν αὐτῷ, ἢ
φησιν ὁ θεῖος Δαβίδ, καὶ προσκυνήσουσιν οἱ ἄρχοντες·
βασιλεῖς, γάρ φησι, Θαρσεὶς καὶ . . . νῆσοι δῶρα προσοίσουσι·
βασιλεῖς ἀράβων καὶ Σαβὰ δῶρα προσάξουσι, καὶ
30 προσκυνήσουσιν αὐτῷ πάντες οἱ βασιλεῖς τῆς γῆς.ⁱ ταύτην
ἐκράτυνε τὴν εὐλογίαν καὶ ἡνίκα αὐτὸν εἰς τὴν
Μεσοποταμίαν ἐξέπεμψεν· ἔσῃ, γάρ φησιν, εἰς συναγωγὰς
ἐθνῶν, καὶ δῴη σοι Κύριος τὴν εὐλογίαν Ἀβραὰμ τοῦ πατρός
σου.ʲ τίς δὲ ἡ εὐλογία ῥάδιον τῷ βουλομένῳ καταμαθεῖν· τῷ
35 γὰρ Ἀβραὰμ ὁ τῶν ὅλων ἔφη Θεός, ἐν τῷ σπέρματί σου
εὐλογηθήσεται πάντα τὰ ἔθνη τῆς γῆς.ᵏ

c. Gn 27.27   d. Mt 13.37f.   e. Gn 27.28   f. Ps 72.6   g. 1Tm 3.16
h. Gn 27.29   i. Ps 72.10f.   j. Gn 28.3f.   k. Gn 22.18

like the smell of an abundant field, which the Lord has blessed."c
Now, as we can see from his interpretation of the Gospel parable, the
Lord himself is a witness that holy Scripture often refers to the world
as a "field": "The field is the world, and the sower of the good seed is
the Son of Man."d In Jacob, therefore, we should recognize the salvation of the whole world.

Hence, he prays for him to enjoy the dew of heaven and the fat-
ness of the earth.e While, in the obvious and superficial understanding, this means grace from on high and abundance of good things
from earth, in our interpretation of the field it hints at Christ the
Lord: the dew referring to his divinity and the richness of the earth
to his humanity, which comes from us. In fact, foretelling this, the
blessed David declared, "He will come down like rain upon a fleece
and like drops falling on the earth."f Just as dew descends invisibly,
and gathers, and becomes visible on the ground, so God the Word,
though invisible, was seen on earth through the flesh, held converse
with human beings, and in the words of the holy apostle "was revealed in flesh."g "The grain and the wine" constitute an oblique reference to the sacred Eucharist.[1]

What follows is also consistent with this interpretation: "Let nations serve you."h Now, the divinely inspired David says, "All the nations will serve him, and their rulers will bow down. The kings of
Tarshish and the isles will offer gifts. Kings of Arabia and Seba will
bring gifts, and all the kings of the earth will bow down to him."i
Furthermore, Isaac enhanced this blessing when he saw Jacob off to
Mesopotamia: "You will become gatherings of nations, and may the
Lord give you the blessing of Abraham your father."j Whoever desires may easily learn the content of that blessing: the God of the
universe said to Abraham, "In your offspring all the nations of the
earth will be blessed."k

1. Theodoret employs a comprehensively intertextual interpretation of the patriarchal blessing, in which he interweaves Ps 72.6, the dominical saying from
the Gospel, and the hymn of 1Tm 3.16 to develop levels of meaning referring to
christological and even eucharistic mysteries that go "beyond the obvious and

The Questions on Genesis

LXXXIV

Τί δή ποτε τοσαύτας εὐλογίας λαβών, ὁ Ἰακὼβ
ἀποδιδράσκει τὸν ἀδελφὸν καὶ μόνος ἀποδημεῖ, τῶν ἀναγκαίων
ἐστερημένος;[a]

Ἐναργέστερον ἐν ταῖς δοκούσαις κακοπραγίαις ἡ τοῦ Θεοῦ
5 κηδεμονία δηλοῦται· οἱ γὰρ ἐν εὐκληρίᾳ ὄντες οὐχ οὕτως
ἴσασιν ὅσων ἀγαθῶν ἀπολαύουσι. τούτου χάριν ἀποδιδράσκει
καὶ μόνος ἀποδημεῖ, ἵνα, μετὰ πολλῆς περιουσίας ἐπανελθών,
καὶ αὐτὸς γνῷ ὅση τοῦ Θεοῦ τῶν ὅλων ἡ προμήθεια καὶ τοὺς
ἄλλους διδάξῃ.

10 Ταύτην αὐτῷ τὴν κηδεμονίαν παραυτίκα διὰ τῆς
ἐπιφανείας ἐδήλωσεν. ἐπέδειξε μὲν γὰρ αὐτῷ κλίμακα μέχρις
αὐτοῦ διϊκνουμένην τοῦ οὐρανοῦ, τοὺς δὲ ἁγίους ἀγγέλους
ἀνιόντας καὶ κατιόντας· αὐτὸς δέ, ἄνωθεν ἐφεστώς,
παρεθάρρυνέ τε καὶ τὸ δέος ἐξήλασεν.[b] ἐδήλουν δὲ οἱ ἄγγελοι
15 τὴν θείαν διακονίαν· περὶ τούτων γὰρ καὶ ὁ μακάριος ἔφη
Παῦλος, *οὐχὶ πάντες εἰσὶ λειτουργικὰ πνεύματα, εἰς*
διακονίαν ἀποστελλόμενα διὰ τοὺς μέλλοντας κληρονομεῖν
σωτηρίαν;[c] τούτων δὲ ἕκαστον ἱκανὸν ἦν θάρσος ἐνθεῖναι τῷ
πατριάρχῃ· διδάσκεται γὰρ ὡς οὐδὲν ἀτημέλητον οὐδὲ
20 ἀκηδεμόνευτον παρὰ τῷ τῶν ὅλων Θεῷ, ἀλλ' αὐτὸς ἅπαντα
πρυτανεύει, διακόνοις χρώμενος τοῖς ἁγίοις ἀγγέλοις.

Ἔδωκε δὲ αὐτῷ καὶ τὴν εὐλογίαν ἣν καὶ τῷ πατρὶ καὶ τῷ
προπάτορι ἐδεδώκει περί τε τῆς τοῦ σπέρματος πολυγονίας
καὶ περὶ τοῦ τῆς οἰκουμένης δεσπότου· *ἐνευλογηθήσονται, γάρ*
25 φησιν, *ἐν τῷ σπέρματί σου πᾶσαι αἱ φυλαὶ τῆς γῆς.*[d] εἶτα
ὑπισχνεῖται αὐτῷ καὶ τὴν ἐν τοῖς προκειμένοις κηδεμονίαν·
ἰδού, γάρ φησι, μετὰ σοῦ εἰμι διαφυλάσσων σε ἐν τῇ ὁδῷ, ... οὗ
ἐὰν πορευθῇς, καὶ ἀποστρέψω σε εἰς τὴν γῆν ταύτην, ὅτι οὐ
μή σε ἐγκαταλίπω ἕως τοῦ ποιῆσαί με πάντα ὅσα ἐλάλησα.[e]

LXXXIV A [32], 30, C, 7 9 10 13 35 37 = 18 mss.

a. Gn 27.41–28.5   b. Gn 28.12f.   c. Heb 1.14   d. Gn 28.14   e. Gn 28.15 (LXX var.)

LXXXIV

After receiving such great blessings, why did Jacob flee his broth-er and go off by himself, completely unprovided for?[a]

Divine providence manifests itself all the more strikingly in seeming misfortunes; in prosperity people are not aware of all the good things they enjoy. Therefore, he took to his heels and went off by himself so that, on returning in affluence, he might realize the greatness of the providence of the God of the universe and teach this to others.

God immediately manifested this care by appearing to him. He showed him a ladder reaching as far as heaven and the holy angels ascending and descending, while God himself, standing on high, en-couraged him and drove away his fear.[b] Now, the angels were clearly performing service to God, for as St. Paul said, "Are they not all ministering spirits sent on a mission of service for the sake of those who are due to inherit salvation?"[c] Every detail of this vision was sufficient to instill confidence in the patriarch, for it taught him that God does not leave anyone outside his care and providence but gov-erns the universe with the holy angels as his ministers.

Then God conferred on Jacob as well the blessing he had given to his father and grandfather regarding both numerous offspring and the Lord of the world: "In your offspring all the tribes of the earth will be blessed."[d] Then, he promised him his care even for the fu-ture: "See, I am with you to protect you in whatever path you travel and shall bring you back to this land, because I shall not abandon you before bringing all my promises to accomplishment."[e]

---

surface meaning of the text." In the sentence beginning "What follows," *etc.* (Τούτῳ . . . τὰ ἑξῆς), he apparently means that the rest of the blessing (Gn 27.29) follows logically on the prophecy of the Incarnation that he has discerned in both the blessing and the Psalm.

LXXXV

Διὰ τί τὸν λίθον ἀλείφει ὁ Ἰακώβ;[a]

Οἷς εἶχε τὸν μεγαλόδωρον ἠμείψατο Κύριον· ὀρθώσας γὰρ τὸν λίθον, ὃν ὑπέθηκε τῇ κεφαλῇ, κατέχεεν αὐτοῦ ἔλαιον.

Τοῦτο δὲ καὶ νῦν ἔστιν εὑρεῖν παρὰ πολλῶν γυναίων τῷ
5 Κυρίῳ πεπιστευκότων γινόμενον· εἰώθασι γὰρ ἐν τοῖς θείοις σηκοῖς ἐλαίῳ χρίειν τὰς τῶν ἀνακτόρων κιγκλίδας καὶ τῶν ἁγίων μαρτύρων τὰς θήκας. δηλοῖ δὲ τοῦτο τῆς ψυχῆς τὴν εὐγένειαν. δέχεται δὲ καὶ τὰ σμικρὰ ὁ φιλάνθρωπος Κύριος, ἀποδεχόμενος τὸν τοῦ γινομένου σκοπόν.

LXXXVI

Πολλοὶ πρόφασιν ἀκολασίας ποιοῦνται τὸ τέτταρας ἐσχηκέναι γυναῖκας τὸν Ἰακώβ.[a]

Τὸν σκοπὸν ἑκάστου τῶν γινομένων ἐξετάζειν προσήκει· οὕτω γὰρ κρίνοντες, εὑρήσομεν καὶ Ἰακὼβ τὸν πατριάρχην τὴν
5 μὲν Ῥαχὴλ μνηστευσάμενον μόνην, παρὰ γνώμην δὲ συναφθέντα τῇ Λείᾳ. παραυτίκα γοῦν τῆς ἀπάτης αἰσθόμενος, καὶ ἐδυσχέρανε καὶ τοῦ κηδεστοῦ κατεβόησε.[b] τῇ δὲ Βαλλᾷ, οὐ διὰ φιληδονίαν, ἀλλὰ διὰ τὴν τῆς ὁμοζύγου παραμυθίαν ἐμίγη· τῆς γὰρ Ῥαχὴλ διὰ τὴν ἀπαιδίαν ἀνιωμένης καὶ ἀνοήτως
10 λεγούσης, *δός μοι τέκνα· εἰ δὲ μή γε, ἀποθανοῦμαι,*[c] ἐπέπληξε μὲν εὐσεβῶς ὁ πατριάρχης καὶ ἔδειξε τὸν τῆς φύσεως

LXXXV A *[32]*, *30*, C, *7 9 10 13 35 37* = 18 mss.

a. Gn 28.18

LXXXVI A *[32]*, *30*, C, *7 9 10 35 37* = 17 mss.

a. Gn 29.21–30; 30.1–9   b. Gn 29.25   c. Gn 30.1

LXXXV

Why did Jacob pour oil on the stone?[a]

This was how he made a return to the munificent Lord from his own possessions. Setting up the stone, which he had put under his head, he poured oil on it.

Even today you can observe a very similar practice among many Christian women. In God's chapels they often anoint with oil both the latticed gates of the shrines and the tombs of the holy martyrs, and this is an indication of their nobility of soul. Appreciating the intention behind the act, the loving Lord welcomes even insignificant gifts.[1]

LXXXVI

As a pretext for their own lust, many people allege the example of Jacob who had four wives.[a]

We should examine the purpose of every act. If we judge by this standard, we shall find that the patriarch Jacob, though betrothed only to Rachel, was joined to Leah against his will. Indeed, as soon as he recognized the deception, he became angry and expostulated with his father-in-law.[b] He had intercourse with Bilhah, not for pleasure's sake, but with a view to comforting his spouse. Rachel was distressed at her childlessness and unreasonably demanded, "Give me children; otherwise, I shall die."[c] The patriarch piously rebuked her and explained who is nature's Creator, and that, not marriage, but

---

1. Theodoret does not grasp the biblical author's interest in providing aetiologies for sacred sites such as Bethel. It is perhaps the similarity of Jacob's action to the devotional practice of his church that prompts the question.

ποιητὴν καὶ ὅτι, οὐ γάμος ἐστὶ παίδων δημιουργός, ἀλλ' ὁ τοῦ
γάμου νομοθέτης Θεός· ἔφη γὰρ πρὸς αὐτήν, μὴ ἀντὶ Θεοῦ
σοί εἰμι ἐγώ, ὃς ἐστέρησέ σε καρπὸν κοιλίας·ᵈ ψυχαγωγῶν δὲ
15 ὅμως αὐτήν, ἠνέσχετο τῆς αἰτήσεως. ᾔτησε αὐτὸν τῇ
παιδίσκῃ μιγῆναι ἵνα τὸ ἐξ αὐτῆς φυόμενον οἰκεῖον
ἀποκαλέσῃ παιδίον.ᵉ τοῦτο καὶ ἐπὶ τῆς Ζέλφας ἐγένετο· πάλιν
γὰρ ἡ Λεία, παυσαμένη τοῦ τίκτειν, ἠντιβόλησεν αὐτὸν εἰς
ἐκείνην σπεῖραι τὴν ἄρουραν.ᶠ ταῦτα φιληδονίαν μὲν οὐδεμίαν
20 αἰνίττεται, τὴν δὲ τοῦ ἀνδρὸς ἐπιείκειαν δείκνυσι καὶ ὅπως
τὰς γυναῖκας θεραπεύειν ἐσπούδαζε.

Πρὸς δὲ τούτῳ κἀκεῖνο σκοπητέον, ὅτι νόμος οὐδεὶς
τηνικαῦτα ἦν τὴν πολυγαμίαν κωλύων καὶ ὡς τρισολβίους
ὑπελάμβανον τότε τοὺς πολλῶν παίδων γινομένους πατέρας.
25 καὶ ὅτι τοῦτό ἐστιν ἀληθὲς αἱ θεῖαι μαρτυροῦσιν ἐπαγγελίαι·
τῷ γὰρ Ἀβραὰμ ὁ τῶν ὅλων ἔφη Θεός, ἀνάβλεψον εἰς τὸν
οὐρανὸν καὶ ἴδε τοὺς ἀστέρας εἰ δυνήσῃ ἐξαριθμῆσαι αὐτούς·
καὶ ἐπήγαγεν, οὕτως ἔσται τὸ σπέρμα σουˢᵍ καί, ὡς ἡ ἄμμος ἡ
παρὰ τὸ χεῖλος τῆς θαλάσσης,ʰ ἥτις οὐκ ἐξαριθμηθήσεται ἀπὸ
30 τοῦ πλήθους.ⁱ οὐκ ἂν δὲ αὐτῷ ταύτην ἔδωκε τὴν ὑπόσχεσιν εἰ
μὴ τὴν πολυγονίαν μέγιστον ἐνόμιζεν ἀγαθόν.

LXXXVII

Τίνος δὲ χάριν αἱ γυναῖκες ἐζηλοτύπουν ἀλλήλας;ᵃ
Ἀτελεῖς ἦσαν καὶ δυσσεβοῦς ἀνδρὸς θυγατέρες, τὰ ξόανα
θεοὺς ὀνομάζοντος. τούτου ἕνεκεν νομοθετῶν, ὁ Θεὸς τὸν
τοιοῦτον ἀπαγορεύει γάμον· οὐ λήψῃ, γάρ φησι, γυναῖκα ἐπ'
5 ἀδελφῇ αὐτῆς ἀντίζηλον αὐτῆς.ᵇ

---

d. Gn 30.2   e. Gn 30.3   f. Gn 30.9   g. Gn 15.5   h. Gn 22.17   i. Gn 16.10

lxxxvii A [32], 30, C, 7 9 10 13 35 37 = 18 mss.

a. Gn 30.1   b. Lv 18.18

God, the legislator of marriage, creates children. Indeed, he replied, "Certainly, you do not regard me as in the position of God, the one who deprived you of the fruit of the womb?"[d] Nevertheless, to console her, he did not refuse her request. She had asked him to have intercourse with Bilhah so she could count the child born of her maidservant as her own.[e] The same thing happened with Zilpah; Leah in turn ceased bearing children and begged him to sow seed in that furrow.[1f] This is in no way suggestive of lust but rather shows the husband's reasonableness and solicitous care for his wives.

Furthermore, we should also consider that, at that time, there was no law forbidding polygamy, and people regarded fathers with many children as especially blessed, a fact that is apparent from the divine promises. Thus, the God of the universe said to Abraham, "Look up to heaven and see if you can count the stars," and added, "Thus will be your offspring,"[g] and "like the sand on the seashore,"[h] "whose vast number cannot be counted."[i] Now, God would not have made this promise unless he regarded many children as a very great good.

LXXXVII

Why were the wives jealous of each other?[a]

They were ignorant of religious truth, the daughters of a pagan, who had idols for his gods. Hence, when he gave the Law, God forbade such a marriage: "You will not marry a woman as a rival to her sister."[1b]

---

1. Theodoret not only understands biblical imagery but can also imitate biblical language in figures of his own; *cf.* the image of the dowry agreement in Q. 68 on Ex.

---

1. According to R.J. Faley ("Leviticus," p. 73), Lv 18.18 is usually understood as "an anti-incest law forbidding simultaneous marriage with two sisters." At the beginning of the second sentence, the connective "Hence" (τούτου ἕνεκεν) appar-

LXXXVIII

Διὰ τί ἡ γραφὴ μέμνηται τύχης;

Ἴδια τῆς γραφῆς τὰ τοῦ πνεύματος λόγια, αἱ θεῖαι διατάξεις, τῶν εὐσεβῶν ἀνθρώπων τὰ ῥήματα· τὰ δὲ ἄλλα ἱστορικῶς λέγει. χρὴ τοίνυν, μὴ μόνον προσέχειν τῷ λόγῳ,
5 ἀλλὰ καὶ τῷ προσώπῳ τοῦ λέγοντος· τὸ τοίνυν εὐτύχηκα,[a] οὐ τοῦ Ἰακώβ ἐστι ῥῆμα, ἀλλὰ τῆς Λείας γυναικός, ὡς ἔφην, ἐν δυσσεβείᾳ τραφείσης καὶ κατὰ βραχὺ τὰ θεῖα παιδευομένης. οὕτω καὶ ὁ ταύτης πατὴρ ἔφη τὸ οἰωνισάμην,[b] ἀλλ' ὁ θεῖος ἀπαγορεύει νόμος τοῖς οἰωνοῖς κεχρῆσθαι. μηδεὶς τοίνυν τοὺς
10 τοιούτους λόγους τῆς θείας εἶναι νομιζέτω γραφῆς· τὰ γὰρ παρὰ τῶν οὐκ εὐσεβῶν εἰρημένα τίθησιν ὁ συγγραφεύς, ἅτε δὴ ἱστορίαν συγγράφων. οὕτω τέθεικεν ὁ θειότατος Μωϋσῆς καὶ τοῦ Φαραὼ τὸν βλάσφημον λόγον· οὐκ οἶδα τὸν Κύριον καὶ τὸν Ἰσραὴλ οὐκ ἐξαποστέλλω·[c] ἀλλ' οὐ τοῦ θείου πνεύματος οὗτος
15 ὁ λόγος ἀλλὰ τοῦ δυσσεβοῦς βασιλέως. οὕτω πάλιν ἀκούομεν τοῦ Σεναχηρεὶμ λέγοντος, μή σε ἀπατάτω ὁ Θεός σου, ἐφ' ᾧ σὺ πέποιθας ἐπ' αὐτῷ, λέγων ὅτι ῥύσεται Κύριος τὴν Ἱερουσαλὴμ ἐκ χειρός μου,[d] ἀλλ', οὐ βλασφημεῖν ἐντεῦθεν μανθάνομεν, ἀλλὰ βλασφημίας κατηγορεῖν.

LXXXVIII A *[32]*, 30, C, 7 9 10 35 37 = 17 mss.

l. 5 εὐτύχηκα *F.M.* : εὐτύχημα a₂, 30, *Sir. Sch.* = "'A piece of luck!'" *Cf. Q.* 99 (ηὐ-) and Wevers, *ap. crit.* on Gn 30.11.

a. Gn 30.11 (LXX var.)   b. Gn 30.27   c. Ex 5.2   d. Is 37.10; 2Kgs 19.10

LXXXVIII

Why does Scripture mention good luck?

The distinctive features of Scripture are the oracles of the Spirit, God's laws, and the teachings of the devout; the rest is historical narration. So one must take into account not only what is said but also who says it. Now, the expression "I'm in luck!"[1a] was not Jacob's but Leah's, a woman, as I remarked, raised in idolatry and only briefly schooled in religion. Similarly, her father declared, "I would take omens,"[b] whereas God's Law forbids recourse to omens. So no one should imagine that such words are those of holy Scripture; the author sets down the words of pagans, because he is writing history. Moses, though a holy man, recorded the blasphemous remark of Pharaoh: "I do not know the Lord, and I do not intend to release Israel,"[c] a statement that comes not from the divine Spirit but from the impious king. Again, we hear Sennacherib saying, "Do not let your God in whom you trust deceive you when he says that the Lord will rescue Jerusalem from my hand."[d] From this we learn, not to blaspheme, but to condemn blasphemy.

----
ently refers to the rivalry mentioned in the question rather than to the previous statement regarding the religious ignorance of Rachel and Leah.

---

1. Theodoret, who has missed the etymologies connected with the names of Jacob's other sons, here fails to grasp the relationship between the name "Asher" and the Hebrew adjective "happy" and that between the verb εὐτύχηκα ("I am in luck") and "Gad." Developing an ethical interpretation, he condemns Leah's happy exclamation in 30.11 as also Laban's reference to divination in v. 27, apparently for calling into question the reliability of Providence. Though Leah and her father did not deliberately oppose God, their remarks seem to him as reprehensible as those made by God's avowed enemies, the Pharaoh of the Exodus (Ex 5.2) and Sennacherib (2Kgs 19.10). To empty all references to luck or fortune of theological content, Theodoret emphasizes that they are recorded, not as divine revelation, but only as the thoughts of the human personages. Thus, in this question, he refers to the author of Genesis not as "blessed Moses" (cf. Q. 98), or "prophet" (προφήτης; cf. Q.12.3 on Exodus), but as "historian" συγγραφεύς; cf. also Q. 99, which deals with another mention of good luck, and where Theodoret again describes the biblical author as an historian (ἱστοριογράφος).

LXXXIX

Ἀλλὰ καὶ αὐτὸς ὁ Ἰακὼβ ἔφη τῷ Λάβαν, *εὐλόγησέ σε*
Κύριος ἐπὶ τῷ ποδί μου.[a]

Δήλη τοῦ ῥητοῦ διάνοια· *πόδα* γὰρ τὴν παρουσίαν ἐκάλεσεν
ἀντὶ τοῦ· διὰ τῆς ἐμῆς παρουσίας καὶ τῆς ἐμῆς κηδεμονίας,
5 τῶν θεοσδότων ἀπήλαυσας ἀγαθῶν. εἰς γὰρ τὴν ἐμὴν
εὐσέβειαν ἀφορῶν, ὁ Θεὸς τὰ ἐγχειρισθέντα μοι παρὰ σοῦ
πάσης εὐλογίας ἠξίωσεν.

XC

Τίνος ἕνεκεν τὰς ῥάβδους λεπίσας, πίνουσιν παρέθηκε τοῖς
προβάτοις;[a]

Ὥσπερ ἠγάγετο μὲν παιδοποιῆσαι ποθῶν, οὐκ ἐν τῷ γάμῳ
δὲ εἶχε τὴν ἐλπίδα τῆς παιδοποιίας, ἀλλ' ἐν τῷ τοῦ γάμου
5 νομοθέτῃ θεῷ, οὕτω καὶ τὰς ῥάβδους ἐλέπισεν, οὐ ταύταις
θαρρῶν, ἀλλὰ τὴν θείαν ἐπικουρίαν προσμένων. ὅθεν καὶ τῆς
θείας ἐπιφανείας τετύχηκε καὶ λέγοντος ἤκουσεν, *ἀνάβλεψον*
τοῖς ὀφθαλμοῖς σου καὶ ἴδε τοὺς τράγους καὶ τοὺς κριοὺς
ἀναβαίνοντας ἐπὶ ... τὰς αἶγας· διαλεύκους, καὶ ποικίλους, καὶ
10 *σποδοειδεῖς ῥαντούς· ἑώρακα γὰρ ὅσα σοι Λάβαν ποιεῖ. ἐγώ*
εἰμι ὁ Θεός, ὁ ὀφθείς σοι ἐν τόπῳ Θεοῦ, οὗ ἤλειψάς μοι ἐκεῖ
στήλην, καὶ ηὔξω μοι ἐκεῖ εὐχήν.[b] ἐπειδὴ γὰρ τὰ φαιὰ καὶ τὰ
ποικίλα τοῖς υἱέσι τοῦ Λάβαν ἐνεχειρίσθη, καὶ τριῶν ἡμερῶν
ὁδὸν ἀφεστήκεσαν ἐκεῖναι τούτων αἱ ποίμναι,[c] δείκνυσιν αὐτῷ

LXXXIX A *[32]*, *30*, C, *7 9 10 35 37* = 17 mss.
a. Gn 30.30

XC A *[32]*, *30*, C, *7 9 10 35 37* = 17 mss.
a. Gn 30.37–39   b. Gn 31.12f.   c. Gn 30.35f.

LXXXIX

But Jacob himself declared to Laban, "The Lord has blessed you at my foot."[1a]

The sense of the expression is clear: by "foot" he meant his coming. In other words, "through my coming and my care you have enjoyed God-given bounty. Observing my devotion, God deemed what you had assigned me worthy of his blessing."

XC

Why did he peel the rods and place them in front of the sheep at the water troughs?[a]

When he desired children, he married while resting his hope of children, not in marriage, but in God, who had established marriage. So too he peeled the rods, not relying on them, but awaiting God's assistance. Hence, he was accorded the vision of God and heard him say, "Lift up your eyes and see that the goats and rams mounting the she-goats are white and speckled, ashen and mottled. For I have seen all that Laban is doing to you. I am the God who appeared to you in the place of God, where you anointed a pillar to me and made a vow to me."[b] Since the grey and speckled ones had been turned over to Laban's sons, and their flocks were separated by a distance of three days,[c] the champion of the wronged gave him this vision of speckled

1. At Gn 30.30 the LXX offers a literal rendition of the Hebrew, which Theodoret correctly interprets for his questioner, who is imagined to have understood the expression as blasphemous or at least indelicate; *cf.* Is 6.2, where the same Hebrew word is a euphemism for genitalia, and note 1 on *Q.* 14 on Ex.

15 τῶν ἀδικουμένων ὁ πρόμαχος ποικίλους κριοὺς καὶ τράγους
ὀχεύοντας ἵνα τῇ πείρᾳ μάθῃ πόσης ἀπολαύουσι προμηθείας
οἱ τεθαρρηκότες τῷ τῶν ὅλων Θεῷ.

Ἐπισημήνασθαι δὲ προσήκει ὡς, ἄγγελον εἰρηκὼς τὸν ἄνω
ὀφθέντα, ἔδειξεν τὸν αὐτὸν καὶ Θεόν· *ἐγὼ γάρ εἰμι, φησίν, ὁ*
20 *Θεὸς ὁ ὀφθείς σοι ἐν τῇ ὁδῷ.* εἶδε δὲ ἀγγέλους μὲν ἀνιόντας
καὶ κατιόντας διὰ τῆς κλίμακος, τὸν δὲ Κύριον ἄνω
ἐστηριγμένον. τοῦτον ἐνταῦθα καὶ *ἄγγελον* ὠνόμασε καὶ *Θεόν·*
Θεὸν μὲν ὡς τοῦτο τὴν φύσιν ὄντα, *ἄγγελον* δὲ ἵνα γνῶμεν
ὡς, οὐχ ὁ πατήρ ἐστιν ὁ ὀφθείς, ἀλλ' ὁ μονογενὴς υἱός. τίνος
25 γὰρ ἄγγελος ὁ πατήρ; ὁ δὲ υἱὸς καὶ Θεὸς καὶ *μεγάλης βουλῆς*
ἄγγελος·[d] αὐτὸς γὰρ ἡμῖν ἀπήγγειλε τοῦ πατρὸς τὰ μυστήρια·
ἃ γὰρ ἤκουσα, φησί, παρὰ τοῦ πατρός μου ἐγνώρισα ὑμῖν.[e]
οὕτω τὸν κεκληκότα τὸν Ἀβραὰμ καὶ *ἄγγελον*[f] ὠνόμασε καὶ
Θεόν.[g]

XCI

Τίς ὁ σκοπὸς τῆς τῶν εἰδώλων κλοπῆς;[a]

Τινὲς ἔφασαν ἔτι διακειμένην περὶ αὐτά, τὴν Ῥαχὴλ
κεκλοφέναι αὐτά· ἐγὼ δὲ τοὐναντίον ὑπολαμβάνω, ὅτι, καὶ τὸν
πατέρα τῆς δεισιδαιμονίας ἐλευθερῶσαι βουλομένη, σεσύληκεν
5 αὐτά. τὸ γὰρ εὐσεβὲς αὐτῆς ἡ θεία διδάσκει γραφή·
ἐμνήσθη..., γάρ φησιν, ὁ Θεὸς ... Ῥαχήλ, καὶ ἐπήκουσεν
αὐτῆς ὁ Θεός, καὶ ἀνέῳξεν αὐτῆς τὴν μήτραν·[b] ἀκούσασα γὰρ
παρὰ τοῦ Ἰακώβ, *μὴ ἀντὶ Θεοῦ σοι ἐγώ εἰμι, ὃς ἐστέρησέν σε*
καρπὸν κοιλίας;[c] δῆλον ὅτι σπουδαιοτέραν τῷ Θεῷ
10 προσενήνοχε προσευχὴν καὶ ἐτετυχήκει τῆς αἰτήσεως. καὶ
μέντοι καὶ τεκοῦσα, δεδήλωκε τὴν εὐσέβειαν· *εἶπε..., γάρ*

d. Is 9.6   e. Jn 15.15   f. Gn 22.11   g. Gn 22.1

xci A [32], 30, C, 7 9 10 35 37 = 17 mss.

a. Gn 31.19   b. Gn 30.22   c. Gn 30.2

rams and goats mounting, so that Jacob would learn from his own experience the degree of providence enjoyed by those who trust in the God of the universe.

Now, note that after reporting that an angel had appeared from above, Jacob indicated that this was none other than God himself: "I am God, who appeared to you on the way." He had seen angels ascending and descending the ladder and God set firm at the top, whom he here called both "angel" and "God": "God" as to his nature, and "angel" so we would know that it was not the Father who appeared to him but the only-begotten Son. While the Father does not serve as anyone's messenger,[1] the Son is both God and "angel of great counsel."[d] It was he who announced to us the mysteries of the Father: "All I have heard from my Father I have revealed to you."[e] Likewise, the one who called out to Abraham is referred to as both "angel"[f] and "God."[g]

XCI

What was the point of stealing the images?[a]

Some commentators have claimed that Rachel stole the images because she was still attached to them. My impression is the opposite: that she carried them off because she wanted to free her father of superstition. Indeed, holy Scripture informs us of her piety: "God remembered Rachel; God hearkened to her and opened her womb."[1b] So she must have listened to Jacob's words—"Certainly, you do not regard me as in the position of God, the one who deprived you of the fruit of the womb?"[c]—and offered a more ardent prayer to God, who granted her request. Then, on giving birth, she displayed her piety

1. The Greek word ἄγγελος means both "angel" and "messenger"; *cf. Q.* 5 on Ex.

1. Both Chrysostom (*hom.* 57.4 *in Gen.*) and Theodoret display ethical concerns in their interpretation of this event. It is Chrysostom's position that Theodoret rejects at the beginning of his response.

φησι, Ῥαχήλ, ἀφεῖλέ μου ὁ Θεὸς τὸ ὄνειδος. καὶ ἐκάλεσε τὸ
ὄνομα αὐτοῦ Ἰωσήφ, λέγουσα, προσθέτω μοι ὁ Θεὸς υἱὸν
ἕτερον.ᵈ πῶς τοίνυν, ταύτην ἔχουσα περὶ τὸν Θεὸν τὴν
15 διάθεσιν, τοῖς οὐκ οὖσι θεοῖς δουλεύειν ἠνείχετο;

Ἐγὼ δὲ οἶμαι καὶ ἕτερον ἐντεῦθεν προδηλοῦσθαι. τύπον γὰρ
εἶχεν ὁ Ἰακὼβ τοῦ τῶν ὅλων Θεοῦ· δύο γὰρ καὶ ὁ Θεὸς ἔσχε
λαούς· τὸν μὲν πρεσβύτερον, κάλυμμα ἔχοντα ἐπὶ τὴν καρδίαν,ᵉ
τὸν δὲ νεώτερον, τὸ τῆς πίστεως περικείμενον κάλλος· καὶ ὁ
20 Ἰακὼβ δύο γυναῖκας· τὴν μὲν Λείαν, ἀσθενεῖς ἔχουσαν
ὀφθαλμούς, τὴν δὲ Ῥαχήλ, καλὴν τῷ εἴδει καὶ ὡραίαν τῇ ὄψει
σφόδρα,ᶠ καὶ πολύπαιδα μὲν τὴν πρεσβυτέραν, στερίφην δὲ τὴν
νεωτέραν. καὶ γὰρ ἡ ἐξ ἐθνῶν ἐκκλησία στεῖρα ἦν πάλαι ἀλλ'
ἐγένετο μετὰ ταῦτα πολύπαις· εὐφράνθητι, γάρ φησι, στεῖρα ἡ
25 οὐ τίκτουσα· ῥῆξον καὶ βόησον, ἡ οὐκ ὠδίνουσα, ὅτι πολλὰ τὰ
τέκνα τῆς ἐρήμου μᾶλλον ἢ τῆς ἐχούσης τὸν ἄνδρα.ᵍ ἐπειδὴ
τοίνυν ἡ ἐκκλησία, τῷ σωτῆρι πεπιστευκυῖα Θεῷ, τὴν
προγονικὴν πρόρριζον ἀνέσπασε πλάνην, τύπος δὲ ταύτης
ἐτύγχανεν οὖσα, ἡ Ῥαχὴλ κέκλοφε τὰ εἴδωλα τοῦ πατρὸς ἵνα
30 τὴν ἀλήθειαν κἂν τούτῳ σκιαγραφήσῃ.

XCII

Τί ἐστιν ὤμοσεν Ἰακὼβ κατὰ τοῦ φόβου τοῦ πατρὸς αὐτοῦ
Ἰσαάκ;ᵃ

Φόβον τοῦ Ἰσαὰκ τὴν εὐσέβειαν ἐκάλεσε, τουτέστι τὸν
Θεὸν οὗ τὸν φόβον ἐν τῇ ψυχῇ περιέφερεν.

---

d. Gn 30.23f.   e. 2Cor 3.14f.   f. Gn 29.17f.   g. Is 54.1

xcii A [32], 30, C, 7 9 10 35 37 = 17 mss.

a. Gn 31.53

once more: "Rachel declared, 'God has taken away my reproach,' and she called him 'Joseph,' saying, 'May God grant me yet another son.'"[d] Now, if she had this disposition towards God, how could she have tolerated slavery to false gods?

In my view, however, there is also something more foreshadowed in this event. Jacob was a type of the God of the universe, for God had two peoples: the elder with a veil over its heart,[2e] the younger clad in the beauty of faith. And Jacob had two wives: Leah with weak eyes and Rachel shapely and very fair to behold,[f] the elder having many children and the younger barren. Now, the Church of the nations was once barren but later had many children: "Rejoice, you who are barren and have no children; cry out, you who have no birth pangs, because she who is without a husband has more children than she who is married."[g] Thus, as the Church, believing in God the Savior, has uprooted the ancestral error, and Rachel was a type of the Church, she stole her father's images to foreshadow the reality in this as well.

XCII

What is the meaning of "Jacob swore by the fear of his father Isaac"?[a]

By "Fear of Isaac" he referred to his piety; that is, "Fear of Isaac" signifies God, fear of whom was lodged in his soul.

2. Theodoret now looks beyond the interpretation of his fellow Antiochene Chrysostom to an allegory developed by the Alexandrian Cyril (*Glaph. Gen.* 5). Building upon the septuagintal description (Gn. 29.17) of Leah's eyes as "weak" (ἀσθενεῖς) rather than "tender" or "lovely" (other possible translations of the Hebrew adjective *racoth*), which is itself due to a popular etymology connecting the name "Leah" to a Hebrew stem meaning "to be weary," Cyril had taken the unattractive Leah as prefiguring the Jewish people, and the lovely Rachel as prefiguring the Christian (gentile) Church. In Theodoret's terminology Rachel is a foreshadowing (σκιαγραφήσῃ) of the Church, the reality (ἀλήθειαν); *cf.* Guinot, p. 762.

XCIII

Τίνος ἕνεκα παλαίει τῷ Ἰακὼβ ὁ ἄγγελος;[a]

Δεδιότι τὸν ἀδελφὸν θάρσος ἐντίθησι. διά τοι τοῦτο καὶ
τῆς νίκης αὐτῷ παρεχώρησε, μονονουχὶ λέγων, ἐμὲ νενίκηκας
καὶ ἄνθρωπον δέδοικας; ἵνα δὲ μὴ μέγα φρονῇ, δόξας
5 νενικηκέναι Θεόν, τῇ ἁφῇ τοῦ μηροῦ τὸ ἐθελούσιον τῆς ἥττης
ἐδήλωσε· τῇ γὰρ ἁφῇ τὴν νάρκην εἰργάσατο. γνοὺς δὲ τοῦ
ἐπιφανέντος τὴν δύναμιν, τὴν εὐλογίαν αἰτεῖ. ὁ δὲ καὶ τὴν
αἴτησιν δίδωσι[b] καὶ τὴν προσηγορίαν ἀμείβει· *οὐκέτι, γάρ*
φησι, κληθήσεται τὸ ὄνομά σου Ἰακώβ, ἀλλ᾽ Ἰσραὴλ ἔσται τὸ
10 *ὄνομά σου, ὅτι ἐνίσχυσας μετὰ Θεοῦ καὶ μετὰ ἀνθρώπων*
δυνατὸς ἔσῃ.[c] ἔδειξε δὲ καὶ τὴν αἰτίαν τῆς νίκης· μὴ δείσῃς,
γάρ φησιν, ἄνθρωπον, ἐμοῦ σοι τῆς νίκης παραχωρήσαντος.
διέμεινε δὲ καὶ μετὰ τὴν ἐγρήγορσιν ὁ μηρὸς ναρκῶν τε καὶ
ὑποσκάζων ἵνα, μὴ φαντασίαν ὑπολάβῃ τὴν ὄψιν, ἀλλ᾽
15 ἀκριβέστερον γνῷ τοῦ ἐνυπνίου τὸ ἀληθές. διὰ τοῦτο καὶ
ἐρωτήσας τίνα προσηγορίαν ἔχει, οὐ μόνον διαμαρτάνει τῆς
αἰτήσεως, ἀλλὰ καὶ ἐπιπλήττεται, ὡς ὑπερβὰς τὰ μέτρα τῆς
φύσεως· ἵνα τί, γάρ φησι, ...*ἐρωτᾷς τὸ ὄνομά μου; καὶ τοῦτο*
θαυμαστόν.[d]

20 Ἐπισημαντέον δὲ κἀνταῦθα ὡς τὸν αὐτὸν καὶ *ἄνθρωπον*
ἐκάλεσε καὶ Θεόν· *ἐνίσχυσας,* γὰρ ἔφη, *μετὰ Θεοῦ. ...καὶ*
ἐκάλεσε ... τὸ ὄνομα τοῦ τόπου ἐκείνου Εἶδος Θεοῦ· εἶδον γὰρ
Θεὸν πρόσωπον πρὸς πρόσωπον, καὶ ἐσώθη μου ἡ ψυχή·[e] καὶ
πάλιν, *ἀνέτειλεν δὲ αὐτῷ ὁ ἥλιος ἡνίκα παρῆλθε τὸ Εἶδος τοῦ*
25 *Θεοῦ.*[f] διὰ τούτων δὲ πάντων μανθάνομεν ὡς ὁ μονογενὴς υἱὸς
καὶ Θεὸς ἐπεφάνη κἀνταῦθα τῷ Ἰακώβ.

xciii A [32], 30, C, 7 9 10 35 37 = 17 mss.

a. Gn 32.24–32   b. Gn 32.25–29   c. Gn 32.28   d. Gn 32.29 (LXX var.)
e. Gn 32.28, 30   f. Gn 32.31

XCIII

Why did the angel wrestle with Jacob?[a]

To give Jacob confidence when he was afraid of his brother. For the same reason he also yielded him the victory, as if to say, "How can you fear a mere mortal after defeating me?" But to prevent Jacob from becoming conceited at thinking he had defeated God, he touched his thigh to indicate that he allowed himself to be bested, for at his touch, the thigh became numb. Then Jacob recognized the power of the one who had appeared to him and requested his blessing. The angel granted his request[b] and gave him a new name: "You will no longer be called Jacob; your name will be Israel, because you have prevailed against God and will be powerful against men."[c] He also brought out the reason for the victory: "Do not fear, man, now that I have yielded you the victory." Even after he awoke, the thigh remained numb and lame so that he would not think he had only imagined the vision but recognize with complete clarity the reality of the dream. Thus, he not only failed to get an answer but received a rebuke for exceeding the limits of nature when he asked the angel his name: "Why do you ask my name? It inspires awe."[1d]

Now, we should note that, here as well, the same being is called both "man" and "God": "You prevailed against God"; "and he named that place 'Face of God,' 'for I saw God face to face, and my life was preserved'";[e] and again, "The sun rose upon him as he passed Face of God."[f] Hence, we conclude that the only-begotten Son and God appeared to Jacob here as well.[2]

1. Theodoret's, but not Chrysostom's text of 32.29 (*hom.* 58.3 *in Gen.*), contained the sparsely attested clause, καὶ τοῦτο θαυμαστόν ("It inspires awe"); *v.* J.W. Wevers, *Genesis, ad loc.* J.L. Schulze's suggestion (note 96 to Q. 92) that the additional clause might be a gloss is inconsistent with the appearance of the fuller version of 32.29 also in Theodoret's comment on Ps 8.2 LXX (8.1 MT). Both Chrysostom and Theodoret agree that the angel warns Jacob against trespassing on forbidden territory.

2. Again (*cf.* note 1 to Q. 88), Theodoret misses the aetiologies of central impor-

The Questions on Genesis

XCIV

Τί ἐστιν οὗτός ἐστιν ὁ Ἀϊνὰν ὃς εὗρεν τὸν Ἰαμὴν ἐν τῇ ἐρήμῳ ὅτε ἔνεμεν τὰ ὑποζύγια Σεβεγών, τοῦ πατρὸς αὐτοῦ;[a]

Ὁ Σύρος λέγει πηγὴν αὐτὸν εὑρηκέναι· ἡ γὰρ πηγὴ αἰνὰ καλεῖται τῇ Σύρων φωνῇ.

XCV

Ὁ Ἰὼβ πόθεν κατάγει τὸ γένος;

Ἀπὸ τοῦ Ἡσαῦ. τοῦτο γὰρ καὶ ἡ κατ' αὐτὸν ἱστορία διδάσκει· ἄνθρωπος... γὰρ ἦν, φησίν, ἐν χώρᾳ τῇ Αὐσίτιδι.[a] δεδήλωκε δὲ τοῦτο καὶ ὁ μακάριος Μωϋσῆς· τῶν γὰρ ἐκ τοῦ
5 Ἡσαῦ βεβασιλευκότων τὰς διαδοχὰς συγγράφων, οὕτως ἔφη· ἀπέθανε δὲ Βαλάκ, καὶ ἐβασίλευσεν ἀντ' αὐτοῦ Ἰωβὰβ υἱὸς Ζαρὰ ἐκ Βοσόρας.[b] συμφωνεῖ δὲ ταῦτα τῇ τοῦ Ἰὼβ ἱστορίᾳ.

xciv A [32], 30, C, 7 9 10 35 37 = 17 mss.

This question was not printed by Sir. : It was transcribed from cod. 32 and placed, without number, between Qq. 92 and 93 by Sch., who remarks (n. 99, col. 201), "Dubitatur autem, sintne haec Theodoreti, an potius Diodori" ("It is unclear whether this should be attributed to Theodoret or Diodore").

a. Gn 36.24

xcv A [32], 30, C, 7 9 10 35 37 = 17 mss.

a. Jb 1.1   b. Gn 36.33

XCIV[1]

What is the meaning of "He is the Anah who found the Iamin in the wilderness when he pastured the cattle of his father Zibeon"?[a]

The Syriac says he found a spring, for "Anah" is the Syriac for "spring."[2]

XCV

What was Job's ancestry?

From Esau, as indicated in the book of Job: "There was a man in the land of Uz."[a] The blessed Moses also explained this. Listing the kings who succeeded Esau, he declared, "Bela died, and Jobab son of Zerah of Bozrah reigned in his place."[1b] This notice is quite consistent with the story of Job.

----
tance to the ancient Hebrew narrator: the origin of the names Israel and Penuel and of the dietary taboo on the sciatic muscle; *v.* R.J. Clifford and R.E. Murphy, p. 34. In contrast, Theodoret is concerned primarily with what he regards as a Trinitarian issue: *i.e.,* the relationship to God of Jacob's mysterious opponent. Here, as in *Q.* 90, he follows the long-established tradition of attributing to the Son the theophanies of the OT; *cf.* J.N.D. Kelly, *Early Christian Doctrines,* pp. 96f and note 1 to *Q.* 5 on Jos.

1. In the editions of Sirmond and Schulze, all questions from 94 through 112 bear a number lower by two; *v.* the critical note to this question and note 1 on *Q.* 62.

2. In Gn 36.24 the LXX's Iamin ('Ιαμὴν) is merely a transliteration of the Hebrew. Theodoret's explanation is unsatisfactory, for as an unknown scholiast pointed out, Anah ('Αϊνὰν) should not mean "spring," because it is Anah who discovers Iamin, not Iamin who discovers Anah. Theodoret may have misunderstood a remark of Diodore's to the effect that Iamin is a Hebrew noun meaning "water" and that the verse would thus mean that Anah had discovered a spring in the desert; *v.* Deconinck, frag. 88.1. As Speiser (*ad loc.*) indicates, the Hebrew term is itself obscure and gave rise to the most various interpretations in the ancient versions. He takes it to be a corruption of the common noun for "water": "The discovery of water in the desert would be sufficient cause for astonishment."

1. In his earlier commentary on Ezekiel, Theodoret had not made this connec-

XCVI

Διὰ τί ἐφθόνησαν τῷ Ἰωσὴφ οἱ ἀδελφοὶ αὐτοῦ;[a]
Ἠγαπᾶτο παρὰ τοῦ πατρὸς καὶ ὡς ὀψίγονος, καὶ ὡς τῆς
Ῥαχὴλ υἱός, καὶ ὡς ἀρετῇ διαπρέπων· ἐβάσκαινον τοίνυν,
ὁρῶντες αὐτὸν προτιμώμενον. καὶ πρῶτον μὲν ἐπειράθησαν
5 κακῶς αὐτὸν παρὰ τῷ πατρὶ διαθεῖναι, πολλαῖς κατ' αὐτοῦ
λοιδορίαις χρησάμενοι· τοῦ σκοποῦ δὲ διαμαρτόντες, ἀνελεῖν
ἠβουλήθησαν· εἶτα, συμβουλευθέντες, ἀπέδοντο.[b] τὸ δὲ τῶν
δραγμάτων ὄναρ[c] προσημαίνει τὴν διὰ τῶν πυρῶν γεγενημένην
προσκύνησιν· σιτοδοχίας γὰρ χάριν εἰς τὴν Αἴγυπτον
10 εἰσελθόντες,[d] κατὰ τὴν πρόρρησιν προσεκύνησαν.[e]

XCVII

Τί δή ποτε ἡ Θάμαρ, ἑταιρικὸν σχῆμα περιθεμένη, τὸν
κηδεστὴν ἐξηπάτησεν;[a]
Περιφανὲς ἄγαν ἐγεγόνει τοῦ Ἀβραὰμ τὸ γένος δι' ἣν
εἶχεν εὐσέβειαν. τοῦτο ἡ Θάμαρ εἰδυῖα, σπουδὴν ἔσχεν ἐξ
5 ἐκείνου παιδοποιῆσαι τοῦ γένους. ἐπειδὴ τοίνυν αὐτὴν ὁ
κηδεστὴς οὐ κατηγγύησε τῷ νεωτάτῳ παιδί, δείσας μὴ τοῖς
ἀδελφοῖς παραπλησίως καὶ αὐτὸς τελευτήσῃ, ἠναγκάσθη
κλέψαι τῆς παιδοποιίας τὰς ἀφορμάς, ἐπειδὴ προφανῶς
λαβεῖν αὐτὰς ἐκωλύετο.[b] πρὸς δὲ τούτῳ καὶ ἐλέγχει τὸν
10 κηδεστήν, ὡς, αὐτὸν μὲν οὐ σωφρονοῦντα, αὐτὴν δὲ σωφρονεῖν
ἀναγκάζοντα.[c] τοῦτο δὲ κἀκεῖνος κρίνων ἐδήλωσε· κύουσαν μὲν
γὰρ αὐτὴν μεμαθηκώς, κατεψηφίσατο θάνατον, γνοὺς δὲ ὅθεν

---

xcvi A [32], 30, C, 7 9 10 35 37 = 17 mss.

a. Gn 37.4, 11   b. Gn 37.19–28   c. Gn 37.6f.   d. Gn 42.1–3   e. Gn 42.6

---

xcvii A [32], 30, C, 7 9 10 35 37 = 17 mss.

a. Gn 38.13–19   b. Gn 38.6–11   c. Gn 38.25

XCVI

Why did his brothers envy Joseph?[a]

His father loved him because he was a son of his old age, Rachel's son, and outstanding in virtue. So, seeing him given pride of place, his brothers became jealous. At first, in their effort to set their father against Joseph, they had recourse to frequent slander, but when they failed to achieve their purpose, they decided to do away with him and then agreed to sell him.[b] The dream of the sheaves[c] foreshadowed the obeisance they made to him for the wheat, since it was for grain supplies that they went to Egypt[d] and bowed down to Joseph just as he had foretold.[e]

XCVII

Why did Tamar disguise herself as a prostitute to deceive her father-in-law?[a]

Abraham's descendants had become very famous for their virtue. Aware of this, Tamar was eager to bear children from this stock. Since her father-in-law did not betroth her to his youngest son for fear he might die as had his brothers, she was forced to snatch an opportunity of conceiving a child when prevented from doing this openly.[b] Moreover, she upbraided her father-in-law for obliging her to continence when he was not continent himself.[c] He, too, indicated as much in his verdict. For when he learned that she was preg-

---

tion between the Jobab of Gn 36.33 and the protagonist of the book of Job; *v. in Ezech.* on 14.14, 20.

ἐκύησε, τὴν μὲν ἀθῷον ἀπέφηνεν, ἑαυτὸν δὲ κατέκρινε·
δεδικαίωται, γὰρ ἔφη, Θάμαρ ἢ ἐγώ, οὗ εἴνεκεν οὐ δέδωκα
15 αὐτὴν Σηλὼμ τῷ υἱῷ μου.[d] ὅτι δὲ παιδοποιίας χάριν, καὶ οὐ
φιληδονίας, τοῦτο ἡ Θάμαρ ἐμηχανήσατο τὰ μετὰ ταῦτα
δηλοῖ· οὐκ ἔτι γάρ, οὔτε τῷ Ἰούδᾳ οὔτε ἄλλῳ συνήφθη τινι·
ἠρκέσθη δὲ μήτηρ κληθῆναι τῶν ἐξ ἐκείνου βεβλαστηκότων τοῦ
σπέρματος.[e]

XCVIII

Τίνος ἦν μήνυμα τὰ κατὰ τὸν Ζαρὰ καὶ τὸν Φαρές;[a]
Τῶν δύο λαῶν· ὁ Φαρὲς τῶν ἰουδαίων, καὶ ὁ Ζαρὰ τῶν ἐξ
ἐθνῶν πεπιστευκότων. καὶ γὰρ πρὸ τοῦ νόμου ἦσαν πολλοὶ τῆς
εὐσεβείας τρόφιμοι κατὰ πίστιν, οὐ κατὰ νόμον,
5 πολιτευόμενοι· διὰ τοῦτο ὁ Ζαρὰ προεξήνεγκε τὴν χεῖρα, τὴν
πρὸ τοῦ νόμου πολιτείαν δεικνύς. τὸ δὲ κόκκινον σπαρτίον
μήνυμα ἦν τῶν παλαιῶν θυσιῶν· καὶ γὰρ ἐκεῖνοι θυσίαις τὸν
Θεὸν ἱλεύοντο· καὶ Ἄβελ,[b] καὶ Ἐνώχ,[c] καὶ Νῶε,[d] καὶ
Μελχισεδέκ,[e] καὶ Ἀβραάμ,[f] καὶ Ἰσαάκ,[g] καὶ Ἰακώβ.[h] εἶτα,
10 ἐκείνου τὴν χεῖρα συστείλαντος, ἐξῆλθεν ὁ Φαρές· μέσος γὰρ
ὁ νόμος τῶν πρὸ νόμου καὶ μετὰ νόμον. διὸ καὶ ὁ μακάριος
λέγει Παῦλος, *νόμος δὲ παρεισῆλθε,*[i] διδάσκων ὅτι καὶ πρὸ τοῦ
νόμου κατὰ πίστιν ἐδικαιοῦντο, καὶ μετὰ τὸν νόμον ἡ χάρις
διέλαμψε.
15 Καὶ ὁ Κύριος δὲ κατὰ σάρκα ἐκ τοῦ Φαρὲς ἐβλάστησεν· *ὧν,*
γάρ φησιν, οἱ πατέρες καὶ ἐξ ὧν ὁ Χριστός, τὸ κατὰ σάρκα, ὁ
ὢν ἐπὶ πάντων Θεός·[j] καὶ ἐν τῇ πρὸς ἑβραίους, *πρόδηλον γὰρ*

||30

---

d. Gn 38.26   e. Gn 38.26

---

xcviii A [32], 30(inc.), C, 7 9 10 35 37 = 17 mss.

a. Gn 38.27–30   b. Gn 4.4   c. Cf. Gn 5.22.   d. Gn 8.20   e. Gn 14.18
f. Gn 15.9–11   g. Gn 26.25   h. Gn 28.18   i. Rom 5.20   j. Rom 9.5

nant, he sentenced her to death, but, on realizing how she became pregnant, declared her innocent and condemned himself: "Tamar is more in the right than I, since I did not give her to my son Shelah."[d] Now, the sequel indicates that Tamar resorted to this ruse to conceive a child and not for pleasure. Indeed, she had no further relations with Judah or anyone else and was content to be known as the mother of the children sprung from his line. [1e]

XCVIII

What is the symbolical point of the story about Zerah and Perez?[a]

It has to do with two peoples: Perez referring to the believers descended from the Jews, and Zerah to those descended from the gentiles. Before the Law, there were many virtuous men who lived by faith rather than the Law. Thus, Zerah thrust his hand out first to point to the way of life before the Law. The crimson thread referred to the sacrifices of old, for the ancients Abel,[b] Enoch,[c] Noah,[d] Melchizedek,[e] Abraham,[f] Isaac,[g] and Jacob[h] all appeased God with sacrifices. Then, when he withdrew his hand, Perez came out, for the Law came between those before the Law and those after the Law. Hence, St. Paul says, "But the Law slipped in,"[i] to teach us that, even before the Law, there was justification by faith, and, after the Law, grace shone forth.

Now, the Lord was descended from Perez according to the flesh: "To them belong the patriarchs, and from them, according to the flesh, came the Christ, who is God over all";[j] and in the Epistle to the

1. Theodoret, neglecting the bearing of this story on the institution of levirate marriage, focuses entirely on its moral import. Von Rad (on 38.25–30) agrees with Theodoret in concluding that Tamar receives the approbation of the biblical author: "Tamar, in spite of her action which borders on a crime, is the one justified in the end. Judah states it at the climax of the story."

ὅτι ἐξ Ἰούδα ἀνατέταλκεν ὁ Κύριος ἡμῶν Ἰησοῦς Χριστός.[k]
τοῦτο καὶ ὁ μακάριος Ματθαῖος, τὴν γενεαλογίαν συγγράφων,
20 ἐδίδαξε.[l] τοῦτο μέντοι τὸ διήγημα τέθεικεν ὁ μακάριος
Μωϋσῆς, διδάσκων ἰουδαίους ὡς τοῦ Δαβὶδ τὸ πολυθρύλλητον
γένος ἐκ γυναικῶν ἀλλοφύλων συνέστη ἵνα μὴ κατὰ τῶν ἐξ
ἐθνῶν πεπιστευκότων ἀλαζονεύωνται, ὡς ἀκήρατον φυλάξαντες
τὴν εὐγένειαν.

XCIX

Θῶμεν τὴν Λείαν, ὡς ἀτελῆ κατὰ τὴν εὐσέβειαν, εἰρηκέναι
τὸ ηὐτύχηκα,[a] πῶς ὁ ἱστοριογράφος, τὰ κατὰ τὸν Ἰωσὴφ
συγγράφων, εἶπε τὸ ἦν ἀνὴρ ἐπιτυγχάνων;[b]

Ἀνάγνωθι τὸ προτεταγμένον ῥητὸν καὶ εὑρήσεις τὴν λύσιν.
5 εἰπὼν γάρ, ἦν Κύριος μετὰ Ἰωσήφ, ἐπήγαγε, καὶ ἦν ἀνὴρ
ἐπιτυγχάνων, καὶ προσέθεικε, καὶ ἐγένετο ἐν τῷ οἴκῳ παρὰ
τῷ κυρίῳ τῷ αἰγυπτίῳ. ᾔδει δὲ ὁ κύριος αὐτοῦ ὅτι Κύριος μετ'
αὐτοῦ καὶ ὅσα ἂν ποιῇ, Κύριος εὐοδοῖ.[c] οὐκοῦν εἰς ἅπαντα
ἐπετύγχανεν, ἐπειδὴ Κύριος ἦν μετ' αὐτοῦ· αὐτὸς γὰρ εὐώδου
10 τὰ παρ' αὐτοῦ γινόμενα. τοῦτο, καὶ τὰ κατὰ τὸ δεσμωτήριον
διηγούμενος, ἔφη· πάντα γὰρ ἦν, φησί, διὰ χειρὸς Ἰωσήφ, διὰ
τὸ τὸν Κύριον μετ' αὐτοῦ εἶναι, καὶ ὅσα αὐτὸς ἐποίει, Κύριος
εὐώδου ἐν ταῖς χερσὶν αὐτοῦ.[d]

---

k. Heb 7.14   l. Mt 1.3

---

xcix A [32], C, 7 9 10 35 37 = 16 mss.

l. 10 τὰ κατὰ τὸ δεσμωτήριον a_2, c^{-3}, 51 52, 7 9 35 : τὰ κατὰ
δεσμωτήριον Sir. Sch. F.M. The TLG offers no other example of the phrase τὰ
κατὰ δεσμωτήριον among the works it now contains; cf. Chrys., hom. 43.1 in
Acta ap. (ἔνθα τὰ κατὰ τὸ δεσμωτήριον ἐγένετο), which supports the
widely attested reading here adopted.

a. Gn 30.11 (LXX var.)   b. Gn 39.2   c. Gn 39.2f.   d. Gn 39.23

Hebrews: "For it is evident that our Lord Jesus Christ was descended from Judah."[k] St. Matthew taught the same thing in his genealogy.[l] Indeed, blessed Moses composed this account to teach the Jews that the celebrated line of David was derived from foreign women, so they could not lord it over the believers from the nations and claim they had kept their own noble line uncontaminated.

XCIX

Granted that Leah said, "I am in luck,"[a] because she was ignorant of religion, what did the historian mean when he remarked of Joseph: "He was a fortunate man"?[b]

Read the preceding sentence, and you will find the solution. Having said, "The Lord was with Joseph," he went on, "and he was a fortunate man," and proceeded, "He was in the house of his Egyptian master, and his master realized that the Lord was with him, and the Lord caused all he did to prosper."[c] So he was fortunate in everything because the Lord was with him; the Lord caused everything he did to prosper. And, describing what happened in the prison, Moses said "Everything was done by the hand of Joseph, since the Lord was with him, and everything he did the Lord caused to prosper in his hands."[d]

C

Πῶς, εὐνοῦχος ὤν, ὁ ἀρχιμάγειρος γυναῖκα εἶχεν;[a]
Μάλιστα μὲν οὖν καὶ τοὺς εὐνούχους καὶ τοὺς ἐκτομίας
ὁμωνύμως καλοῦσιν. οὐδὲν δὲ ἦν ἀπεικός, καὶ εὐνοῦχον ὄντα,
γυναῖκα ἔχειν ἐν τῇ οἰκίᾳ, τῶν ἔνδον ἐπιμελουμένην
5 πραγμάτων.

CI

Τίνος ἔνεκεν, χρόνου τοσούτου παρεληλυθότος, οὔτε Ἰωσὴφ
τῷ πατρὶ τὴν δουλείαν ἐγνώρισεν, οὔτε ὁ Θεὸς δι'
ἀποκαλύψεως ἐδήλωσε τοῦτο τῷ Ἰακώβ;
Ἔδει κατὰ τὴν πρόρρησιν, τὴν πρὸς τὸν Ἀβραὰμ
5 γεγενημένην, τὸν Ἰακὼβ μετὰ τῶν παίδων καὶ τῶν ἐκγόνων
εἰς τὴν Αἴγυπτον κατελθεῖν.[a] εἰ δὲ τὰ κατὰ τὸν Ἰωσὴφ
ἐγνώκει, πάντως ἂν αὐτόν, λύτρα πεπομφώς, ἐπανήγαγε.
τούτου χάριν αὐτὸν ἀθυμοῦντα παρεῖδεν[b] ἵνα καὶ τὴν
οἰκονομίαν πληρώσῃ καὶ θυμηρεστέραν αὐτῷ μετὰ ταῦτα τὴν
10 ζωὴν καταστήσῃ. καὶ αὐτὸς δὲ ὁ Ἰωσὴφ τοῦ Θεοῦ τὴν
οἰκονομίαν διδάσκει τοὺς ἀδελφούς· εἰς γὰρ ζωήν, φησίν,
ἀπέσταλκέ με ὁ Θεὸς ἔμπροσθεν ὑμῶν[c] τοῦ διαθρέψαι λαὸν
πολύν.[d] καὶ ὁ Δαβὶδ ταῦτά φησι· καὶ ἐκάλεσε λιμὸν ἐπὶ τὴν
γῆν, πᾶν στήριγμα ἄρτου συνέτριψεν. ἀπέστειλεν ἔμπροσθεν
15 αὐτῶν ἄνθρωπον· εἰς δοῦλον ἐπράθη Ἰωσήφ, καὶ τὰ ἑξῆς.[e]

---

c A [32], C, 7 9 10 35 37 = 16 mss.
a. Gn 39.1

---

cı A [32], C, 7 9 10 35 37 = 16 mss.
a. Gn 15.13–16   b. Gn 37.34f.   c. Gn 45.5   d. Gn 50.20   e. Ps 105.16f.

C

How is it that the chief steward, a eunuch, had a wife?[a]

The terms "eunuch" and "castrated male" are frequently employed to mean more than one thing. But it was not unusual even for one who was truly a eunuch to have a wife in his house to attend to domestic affairs.[1]

CI

Why, despite the lapse of so much time, did Joseph not notify his father of his enslavement, or God make this known to Jacob through a special revelation?

For the fulfillment of the prophecy made to Abraham, Jacob had to go down to Egypt with his sons and their children.[a] But, if he had known about Joseph, he would definitely have paid a ransom and brought him back. Hence, to fulfil his providential purpose and make Jacob's subsequent life happier, God overlooked his grief.[b] Joseph himself informed his brothers of God's plan: "It was for life that God sent me before you,[c] to feed a numerous people."[d] Likewise David declared, "He summoned famine upon the land; he broke every staff of bread; he sent a man ahead of them; Joseph was sold as a slave" and so on.[e]

---

1. Theodoret regards the question as merely inquisitive and disposes of it briefly. The LXX uses two different terms to refers to Potiphar as a "eunuch" at 37.36 (σπάδων) and 39.1 (εὐνοῦχος); the Hebrew in both cases is *siri'm*, "eunuch" or as Speiser translates (pp. 289, 301; *cf.* on 37.36), "courtier." The first translator of Theodoret's *Quaest. in oct.*, the sixteenth-century scholar Jean Picot (*v.* sec. 1.A. of the "Introduction to the Greek Text"), quite plausibly rendered the first sentence of this answer: *Ut plurimum quidem eunuchos et excisos sub eodem nomine uocant* ("The terms 'eunuch' and 'castrated male' are frequently employed synonymously"). The difficulty lies in determining the sense in which Theodoret has used the adverb ὁμωνύμως; *cf. Q.* 33 on Lv: καὶ θεὸν μὲν ὁμωνύμως ἐκάλεσε τὸν ψευδώνομον.

Εἰ δὲ ὁ πατριάρχης τοῦ παιδὸς τὴν δουλείαν ἐγνώκει,
πάντως ἂν αὐτὸν ἐλυτρώσατο· λυτρωθεὶς δέ, οὐκ ἂν
δεσμωτήριον ᾤκησεν·[f] εἰ δὲ μὴ τοῦτο ἐγεγόνει, οὐκ ἂν τοὺς
ὀνείρους τοῖς οἰκέταις ἐκείνοις ἡρμήνευσεν·[g] μὴ ἑρμηνεύσας
20 δέ, γνώριμος οὐκ ἂν ἐγεγόνει τῷ Φαραώ· γνώριμος δὲ μὴ
γενόμενος, οὐκ ἂν τὴν διὰ τῶν ὀνείρων ἐσαφήνισε πρόρρησιν·
τοῦτο δὲ μὴ δεδρακώς, οὐκ ἂν ἐπιστεύθη τῆς Αἰγύπτου τὰς
ἡνίας·[h] τῆς Αἰγύπτου δὲ μὴ παραλαβὼν τὴν ἀρχήν, οὐκ ἂν τὸν
πατριάρχην μετὰ τοῦ γένους ἤγαγεν εἰς τὴν Αἴγυπτον.[i] ἐκ
25 τοῦ τέλους οὖν γίνεται δῆλος τῆς θείας οἰκονομίας ὁ σκοπός.

CII

Οὐκοῦν οὐκ ἐξήμαρτον οἱ ἀδελφοί, οἰκονομίᾳ
ὑπουργήσαντες θείᾳ;

Τὸ μὲν ἐκείνων ἔργον βασκανίας καὶ φθόνου·[a] σοφὸς δὲ ὤν,
ὁ Θεὸς τῇ πονηρίᾳ τῇ ἐκείνων εἰς τοὐναντίον ἐχρήσατο· δι'
5 ὧν γὰρ ἐπειράθησαν κωλῦσαι τῶν ὀνείρων τὴν ἔκβασιν, διὰ
τούτων ἐπιτέθεικε τοῖς ὀνείροις τὸ τέλος.[b]

CIII

Τίνος χάριν εὐθὺς ὀφθεῖσι τοῖς ἀδελφοῖς ὠμότερον
προσηνέχθη;[a]

f. Gn 39.20   g. Gn 40.9–19   h. Gn 41.9–45   i. Gn 46.5–7

CII A *[32]*, C⁻⁵⁰, *7 9 10 35 37* = 15 mss.

a. Gn 37.4, 11   b. Gn 45.5–8

CIII A *[32]*, c, *50 53, 7 9 10 35 37* = 14 mss.

a. Gn 42.7

If the patriarch had known of his son's enslavement, he would definitely have ransomed him. If he had ransomed him, Joseph would not have been imprisoned.[f] And if that had not happened, he would not have interpreted their dreams to the servants.[g] And if Joseph had not interpreted their dreams, he would not have become known to Pharaoh. And if he had not become known to Pharaoh, he would not have explained the prophecy contained in his dreams. And if he had not done that, he would not have been entrusted with the reins of the government of Egypt.[h] And if Joseph had not been given control of Egypt, he would not have brought the patriarch down to Egypt with his family.[i] Thus, it is from the outcome that the purpose of the divine plan becomes clear.

CII

Are we to conclude that the brothers committed no sin, since they were serving the divine plan?

Though they acted out of malice and envy,[a] God in his wisdom used their wickedness to the opposite effect; he employed their very efforts to obstruct the outcome of the dreams to bring them to fulfillment.[b]

CIII

Why did Joseph deal so severely with his brothers when he first saw them?[a]

Μεμνημένος τῶν εἰς αὐτὸν γεγενημένων καὶ τὸν Βενιαμὶν
οὐκ ἰδών,[b] ὑπετόπασε κἀκεῖνον ταῦτα παρ' αὐτῶν πεπονθέναι.
5 ἐπειδὴ δὲ ζῶντα τὸν ἀδελφὸν εἶδε,[c] καὶ συγγνώμης καὶ
παντοδαποῦς κηδεμονίας ἠξίωσε.[d]

CIV

Τίνα ἑρμηνείαν ἔχει τὸ *Ψομιθὸμ φανέχ;*[a]
Τῶν ἀπορρήτων ἑρμηνευτὴν αὐτὸν κέκληκεν, ὡς τοὺς
ὀνείρους διασαφήσαντα.

CV

Τίνος ἕνεκεν τὸν δεύτερον, καὶ οὐ τὸν πρῶτον, τῶν
ἀδελφῶν καθειρχθῆναι προσέταξεν;[a]
Ἐγνώκει τοῦ Ῥουβὴν τὸν σκοπὸν καὶ ἤδει σαφῶς ὁπόσους
ὑπὲρ αὐτοῦ πρὸς τοὺς ἀδελφοὺς ἐποιήσατο λόγους καὶ ὅσην
5 ὑπὲρ τῆς αὐτοῦ σωτηρίας εἰσενηνόχει σπουδήν.[b] ἐπειδὴ τοίνυν
οὐ συνήργησεν ὁ Συμεὼν τῷ Ῥουβήν, μάλα δικαίως αὐτὸν
καθειρχθῆναι προσέταξεν ἀλλ', ἐκδεδημηκότων τῶν ἀδελφῶν,
πάσης αὐτὸν θεραπείας ἠξίωσε.
Τούτων μέντοι γινομένων, ἡσυχίαν ἄγειν τὸ συνειδὸς οὐκ
10 ἠνείχετο, ἀλλὰ τῆς γεγενημένης εἰς τὸν ἀδελφὸν παρανομίας
ἀνέμνησεν· εἶπε, γάρ φησιν, *ἕκαστος πρὸς τὸν ἀδελφὸν αὐτοῦ,*
ναί· ἐν ἁμαρτίαις γάρ ἐσμεν περὶ τοῦ ἀδελφοῦ ἡμῶν, ὅτι
ὑπερείδομεν τὴν θλῖψιν τῆς ψυχῆς αὐτοῦ, ὅτε κατεδέετο

b. Gn 42.4   c. Gn 43.16   d. Gn 45.9–15

civ   A *[32]*, C^{-53}, 7 9 10 35 37 = 16 mss.

a. Gn 41.45

cv   A *[32]*, C, 7 9 10 35 37 = 16 mss.

a. Gn 42.24   b. Gn 37.21f.

Remembering his own experience and not seeing Benjamin,[b] he suspected that he had suffered the same fate at their hands. But when he saw his brother alive,[c] he decided they deserved pardon and his every consideration.[d]

CIV

What is the meaning of Psomithom Phanech?[a]

He called him "explainer of mysteries" since he had elucidated the meaning of the dreams.[1]

CV

Why did he order the imprisonment of the second, rather than the eldest, of the brothers?[a]

He knew Reuben's intentions and was well aware of the plea he had made to his brothers on his behalf and of the great effort he had made to save him.[b] So since Simeon had not supported Reuben, Joseph was quite justified in ordering him to be imprisoned; yet when his brothers departed, he accorded him every attention.

After this, however, their conscience refused to rest and reminded them of the crime they had committed against their brother: "Each said to his brother, 'To be sure, we are guilty of sin towards our brother, for we disregarded his distress of soul when he pled with us and we did not hearken to him.' Therefore, all this distress

---

1. "Psomithom Phanech" is a transliteration of the form of the name (Ψομιθὸμ φανέχ) offered by Theodoret; the more widely attested LXX form is Ψονθομφαν-ήχ (Psonthomphanech); v. J.W. Wevers ad Gn 41.45. In contrast, the MT offers a form transliterated as Zaphenath-paneah, which, according to Speiser, probably represents the Egyptian for "God speaks: he lives"; v. note e, p. 311 and on 41.45. Jerome had offered, "Savior of the world" (Salvatorem mundi). Theodoret's readers would not be in a position to gainsay his version, which lacks linguistic foundation.

ἡμῶν, καὶ οὐκ εἰσηκούσαμεν αὐτοῦ. ἕνεκεν τούτου ἐπῆλθεν ἐφ'
15 ἡμᾶς ἡ θλῖψις αὕτη.ᶜ καὶ ὁ Ῥουβὴν δὲ εἰς καιρὸν ἐπάγει τὸν
ἔλεγχον· εἶπε, γάρ φησιν, αὐτοῖς, οὐκ ἐλάλησα ὑμῖν, λέγων,
μὴ ἀδικήσητε τὸ παιδάριον; καὶ οὐκ εἰσηκούσατέ μου. καὶ
ἰδοὺ τὸ αἷμα αὐτοῦ ἐκζητεῖται.ᵈ ἐντεῦθεν ἔστι γνῶναι σαφῶς
τὸ ἀκλινὲς τοῦ συνειδότος κριτήριον· τῆς γὰρ πρὸ δύο καὶ
20 εἴκοσι ἐτῶν γεγενημένης ἀναμιμνήσκει παρανομίας.

CVI

Διὰ τί τῷ Ῥουβὴν οὐκ ἐθάρρησε δοῦναι τὸν Βενιαμὶν ὁ
πατήρ;ᵃ

Ὕποπτος ἦν αὐτῷ διὰ τὴν παράνομον συνουσίαν καὶ τῆς
εὐνῆς παροινίαν,ᵇ ἠγνόει δὲ καὶ ὅσην ὑπὲρ τοῦ Ἰωσὴφ
5 εἰσενηνόχει σπουδήν.ᶜ

CVII

Τί ἐστιν οἰωνισμῷ οἰωνίζεται ἐν αὐτῷ;ᵃ

Αὐξῆσαι τῆς δοκούσης κλοπῆς τὸ ἔγκλημα βουληθέντες,
μαντείας ὄργανον τὸ ποτήριον ὀνομάζουσι. τοῦτο δὲ καὶ
αὐτὸς ἔφη Ἰωσήφ· οὐκ οἴδατε ὅτι οἰωνισμῷ οἰωνιεῖται
5 ἄνθρωπος οἷος ἐγώ;ᵇ ταῦτα δὲ ἔλεγεν, οὐ μαντείᾳ καὶ οἰωνοῖς

---

c. Gn 42.21   d. Gn 42.22

---
cvi A [32], C, 7 9 10 35 37 = 16 mss.

a. Gn 42.36–38   b. Gn 35.22   c. Gn 37.21f.

---
cvii A [32], C, 7 9 10 35 37 = 16 mss.

a. Gn 44.5   b. Gn 44.15

has come upon us."[c] And Reuben brought a timely charge against them: "He said to them, 'Did I not tell you, "Do no wrong to the child," and did you hearken to me? Lo, an account is required of his blood.'"[d] From this we can form a clear idea of the unswerving judgment of conscience, which reminded them of the crime they had committed twenty-two years before.[1]

CVI

Why was his father afraid to hand Benjamin over to Reuben?[a]

Jacob was suspicious of Reuben after his drunken violation of his bed.[b] Furthermore, he was unaware of all the effort Reuben had made on behalf of Joseph.[c]

CVII

What is the meaning of "he practices augury with it"?[a]

To add to the seriousness of the accusation for the alleged theft, they called the cup an instrument of divination. In fact, Joseph himself declared: "Are you unaware that a man of my station will practice augury?"[1b] Now, he said this, not because he was practicing div-

---

1. This passage exemplifies Theodoret's concern with precise chronology. He probably arrived at this calculation through a comparison of the data in 37.2 (Joseph was seventeen when sold into slavery.); 41.46 (He was thirty when raised to power.); 41.53 (The seven years of plenty had passed.); and 45.6 (It was then the second year of the famine.); thus 13 + 7 + 2 = 22. Of course, such a precise reckoning is possible only for a reader who ignores the different strands of tradition combined to form this narrative. Speiser attributes the chronological notice of 37.2 to the Yahwistic (p. 287), that of 41.46 to the Priestly (p. 309 and *ad loc.*), that of 41.53 to the Elohistic (p. 309), and that of 45.6 to the Yahwistic source (p. 336); *v.* also his introduction to the narrative, pp. 292–94.

---

1. Theodoret, who avoids the obvious sense of Joseph's remark, is trying to

κεχρημένος, ἀλλὰ πρὸς τὴν προκειμένην ὑπόθεσιν σχηματίζων
τοὺς λόγους. ἄξιον δὲ αὐτοῦ θαυμάσαι τῶν λόγων τὸ ἀκριβές·
οὐδὲ ἀδελφοὺς γὰρ ὑποκρινόμενος, ἠνέσχετο ἑαυτῷ τὸν
οἰωνισμὸν περιθεῖναι, ἀλλ' ἄλλῳ τινὶ τὴν αὐτὴν πεπιστευμένῳ
10 ἀρχήν· οὐ γὰρ εἶπεν, οἰωνίζομαι, ἀλλ' *οἰωνισμῷ οἰωνιεῖται*
ἄνθρωπος οἷος ἐγώ.

CVIII

Τί δή ποτε τὸ κατὰ τὸ κόνδυ κατεσκεύασε δρᾶμα;[a]
Βασανίσαι τῶν ἀδελφῶν ἠβουλήθη τὴν γνώμην καὶ γνῶναι
σαφῶς εἰ τῷ Βενιαμὶν συκοφαντουμένῳ συναγωνίζονται. διά
τοι τοῦτο καὶ εἰς τὸν ἐκείνου σάκκον τὸ κόνδυ κατέκρυψεν.
5 ἐπειδὴ δέ, οὐχ ἁπλῶς συνηγοροῦντας, ἀλλὰ καὶ
ὑπερμαχοῦντας ἐθεάσατο,[b] ῥίψας τὸ προσωπεῖον, τὸ ἀδελφικὸν
ἐπέδειξε πρόσωπον.[c] ἐκείνων δὲ καταπτηξάντων καὶ μονονουχὶ
χάναι αὐτοῖς βουληθέντων τὴν γῆν, αὐτὸς παραθαρρύνει
λέγων, *νῦν οὖν μὴ φοβεῖσθε, μηδὲ σκληρὸν ὑμῖν φανήτω ὅτι*
10 *ἀπέδοσθέ με ὧδε· εἰς γὰρ ζωὴν ἀπέσταλκέ με ὁ Θεὸς*
ἔμπροσθεν ὑμῶν.[d] μάλα δὲ χαριέντως καὶ προπέμπων αὐτούς,
παρήνεσεν· *μὴ ὀργίζεσθε,* γάρ φησιν, *ἐν τῇ ὁδῷ*[e] ἀντὶ τοῦ· μὴ
τοιαῦτα δράσητε οἷα εἰς ἐμὲ τετολμήκατε.

CIX

Τί δή ποτε καὶ τὴν γῆν τῶν αἰγυπτίων καὶ τὰ κτήνη
προσεπόρισε τῷ βασιλεῖ;[a]

cviii A *[32]*, C, 7 9 10 35 37 = 16 mss.

a. Gn 44.1–5   b. Gn 44.14–34   c. Gn 45.3   d. Gn 45.5   e. Gn 45.24

cix A *[32]*, C, 7 9 10 35 37 = 16 mss.

a. Gn 47.20f.

ination and augury, but to adapt his words to the role he had assumed. We must admire his precise choice of words. Even when putting on this act for his brothers, he was unwilling to attribute divination to himself and applied the attribution to another man in the same position. Note, he did not say, "I practice augury," but "a man of my position will practice augury."

CVIII

Why did he stage the incident of the cup?[a]

He wanted to test his brothers' intentions and find out whether they would take Benjamin's side when he was unjustly accused; therefore, he hid the cup in his sack. But when he saw them not simply pleading for, but even championing, him,[b] he cast off his mask and revealed the face of a brother.[c] As they cowered, all but wishing the earth would swallow them up, he spoke words of comfort: "Do not be afraid now, nor think it was cruel to sell me here. God has sent me before you on a mission of life."[d] He sent them on their way quite graciously with the recommendation, "Do not quarrel on the way,"[e] that is, "Do not commit any crime like the one you committed against me."

CIX

Why did he acquire the Egyptians' land and cattle for the king?[a]

---

acquit the patriarch of any imputation of pagan belief or practice; *cf.* his defense of Moses, whom he takes to be author of Genesis, in *Qq.* 88 and 99 and of Gideon in *Q.* 17 on Jgs.

Οὔτε τὰ κτήνη θρέψαι οἷοί τε ἦσαν ἐν σιτοδείᾳ καὶ
σπανοσιτίᾳ οὔτε σπεῖραι τὴν γῆν. ταῦτα τοίνυν λαβὼν ἐν τῷ
5 καιρῷ τοῦ λιμοῦ, ὕστερον ἀποδέδωκε, τῆς προσόδου τὸ
πέμπτον εἰσφέρειν νομοθετήσας ἵνα ἐν ταῖς ἐνδείαις
ἀποκειμένας ἔχωσι τὰς τῆς ζωῆς ἀφορμάς. εἰς θεραπείαν δὲ
τοῦ βασιλέως τὴν ἱερατικὴν γῆν ἀτελῆ καταλέλοιπε μόνην.[b]
ταύτης δὲ τῆς τιμῆς οἱ τοῦ Θεοῦ τοῦ ὄντος οὐκ ἀπολαύουσιν
10 ἱερεῖς· τοσοῦτον οἱ δυσσεβεῖς τοῖς οὐκ οὖσι θεοῖς ἀπένεμον
σέβας.

CX

Διὰ τί ὁ Ἰακὼβ εἰς τὴν Χεβρὼν τὸ σῶμα αὐτοῦ ταφῆναι
κελεύει;[a]

Οὐ τάφου φροντίζων, ὥς τινες ὑπειλήφασιν, ἀλλὰ τὸ γένος
ψυχαγωγῶν καὶ διδάσκων ὡς ἅπαντας αὐτοὺς ὁ δεσπότης
5 Θεὸς μεταστήσει τῆς Αἰγύπτου καὶ τὴν ἐπηγγελμένην αὐτοῖς
ἀποδώσει γῆν. τοῦτον δὲ σαφέστερον ὁ Ἰωσὴφ τὸν λόγον
ἀπέφηνε· τελευτῶν γὰρ οὕτως ἔφη· ἐγὼ ἀποθνήσκω. ἐπισκοπῇ
δὲ ἐπισκέψεται ὑμᾶς ὁ Θεὸς καὶ ἀνάξει ὑμᾶς ἐκ τῆς γῆς
ταύτης εἰς τὴν γῆν ἣν ὤμοσεν ὁ Θεὸς τοῖς πατράσιν ἡμῶν, τῷ
10 Ἀβραάμ, καὶ Ἰσαάκ, καὶ Ἰακώβ. καὶ ὤρκισεν Ἰωσὴφ τοὺς υἱοὺς
Ἰσραήλ, λέγων, ἐν τῇ ἐπισκοπῇ ᾗ ἐπισκέψεται ὑμᾶς ὁ Θεὸς
καὶ συνανοίσετε τὰ ὀστᾶ μου ἐντεῦθεν μεθ' ὑμῶν·[b] ὡς εἶναι
δῆλον ὅτι κἀκεῖνος καὶ οὗτος, τὴν ἐπάνοδον προαγορεύοντες,
τὰ περὶ τῆς ταφῆς ἐνετείλαντο.

b. Gn 47.22

---

cx A [32], C, 7 9 10 35 37 = 16 mss.
a. Gn 49.29f.   b. Gn 50.24f.

Due to the famine and dearth of grain, they were unable to feed their cattle or sow the soil. So he took them over during the famine and later returned them after legislating a tax of a fifth of their income to provide stockpiles of supplies for times of shortage. Out of respect for the king, he exempted only the priests' land.[b] The priests of the true God do not enjoy this privilege—such being the veneration that pagans accorded their false gods.[1]

CX

Why did Jacob give directions for the burial of his body in Hebron?[a]

Despite the opinions of some commentators, he was concerned, not with his own burial, but with persuading and teaching his family that the Lord God would set them free from Egypt and give them the promised land. And in his own last moments, Joseph indicated this more explicitly when he said, "'I am dying, but God will surely visit you and bring you up from this land into the land that God swore to our fathers, Abraham, Isaac and Jacob.' And Joseph adjured the sons of Israel in the words, 'When God visits you, as he surely will, you will take my bones away with you.'"[b] Thus, we conclude that both Jacob and Joseph gave instructions for their burial as a way of foretelling the return.[1]

1. In ch. 47 Joseph implements the economic plan he had outlined when interpreting Pharaoh's dream (41.25–36). The result was the enslavement of the Egyptian people, not, as Theodoret maintains, the eventual restoration of cattle and land. Despite some modern commentators "who have found in this report of the enslavement of the Egyptian peasant shocking proof of Joseph's inhumanity," Speiser argues (p. 353) that, given the socio-economic conditions of the New Kingdom, it is likely that, at the time, such changes would have seemed "constructive."

1. Theodoret uses Joseph's instructions in Gn 50.24f. to clarify Jacob's arrangements for burial in Hebron (49.29f.), where Abraham had purchased land and a cave as a family tomb (23.19f.). Theodoret's argument seems implicitly to criticize

CXI

Τί ἐστι *προσεκύνησεν Ἰσραὴλ ἐπὶ τὸ ἄκρον τῆς ῥάβδου αὐτοῦ;*[a]

Καὶ πρεσβύτης ὢν καὶ ἀσθενῶς διακείμενος, ἐπὶ τῆς κλίνης κατέκειτο, γνοὺς δὲ τοῦ παιδὸς τὴν παρουσίαν,
5 ἐξαναστὰς ἐκαθέσθη, βακτηρίᾳ δὲ κεχρημένος ἐπεστηρίζετο αὐτῇ, τοῦ μὲν ἄκρου ταύτης ἐπειλημμένος τῇ δεξιᾷ, ἐπικείμενον δὲ τὸ πρόσωπον ἔχων· ἡσθεὶς τοίνυν ἐπ' αὐτῷ καὶ τῇ τῆς ταφῆς ἐπαγγελίᾳ, προσεκύνησεν, ἐπικλίνας τῇ ῥάβδῳ τὴν κεφαλήν. καὶ πρῶτον μὲν τὸ τοῦ Ἰωσὴφ ἐνύπνιον τὸ
10 πέρας ἐδέξατο· εἶδε γὰρ τὸν ἥλιον, καὶ τὴν σελήνην, καὶ ἕνδεκα ἀστέρας προσκυνοῦντας αὐτῷ.[b]

Πρὸς δὲ τούτοις προαγορεύει καὶ τῆς Ἐφραῒμ φυλῆς τὴν βασιλείαν καὶ τῶν δέκα φυλῶν τὴν ὑποταγήν. ταῦτα γὰρ καὶ ὁ θεῖος ἀπόστολος ἔφη· *πίστει Ἰακὼβ ... ἕκαστον τῶν υἱῶν*
15 *Ἰωσὴφ εὐλόγησε καὶ προσεκύνησεν ἐπὶ τὸ ἄκρον τῆς ῥάβδου αὐτοῦ.*[c] δέδωκε δὲ αὐτῷ καὶ κλῆρον διπλοῦν· *Ἐφραΐμ, γάρ* φησι, *καὶ Μανασσῆς ὡς Ῥουβὴν καὶ Συμεὼν ἔσονταί μοι.*[d] προφητικῶς δὲ προτέταχε τοῦ Μανασσῆ τὸν Ἐφραΐμ· καὶ γὰρ τοῦ Ἰωσὴφ ὡς πρωτοτόκῳ τῷ Μανασσῆ τὰ πρεσβεῖα
20 φυλάξαντος καὶ κατὰ τάξιν ἑκάτερον στήσαντος, ἐναλλάξας ὁ πατριάρχης τὰς χεῖρας, ἐπιτέθεικε τῷ νεωτέρῳ τὴν δεξιάν, τὴν εὐώνυμον δὲ τῷ πρεσβυτέρῳ. εἶτα νομίσας ὁ Ἰωσὴφ ἐξ ἀγνοίας δεδρακέναι τοῦτο τὸν Ἰακώβ, καὶ τοπάσας τοῦ πάθους εἶναι τῶν ὀφθαλμῶν τὴν αἰτίαν, καὶ εἰρηκώς, *οὐχ*
25 *οὕτως, πάτερ· οὗτος γάρ ἐστιν ὁ πρεσβύτερος,*[e] ἤκουσεν, *οἶδα, τέκνον, οἶδα· καὶ οὗτος ἔσται εἰς λαόν, καὶ οὗτος ὑψωθήσεται, ἀλλ' ὁ ἀδελφὸς αὐτοῦ ὁ νεώτερος μείζων αὐτοῦ ἔσται.*[f]

---

cxi A [32], C, 7 9 10 35 37 = 16 mss.

a. Gn 47.31   b. Gn 37.9   c. Heb 11.21   d. Gn 48.5   e. Gn 48.18
f. Gn 48.19

CXI

What is the meaning of "Israel bowed down on the tip of his rod"?[a]

An old man and infirm, he was lying in bed. Aware of his son's arrival, he sat up; he used a staff to support himself, taking its tip in his right hand and resting his head on it. Pleased with Joseph and the promise of burial, Jacob bowed down, bending his head to the rod.[1] Consequently, Joseph's dream was fulfilled, in which he saw the sun, the moon, and eleven stars bowing down to him.[b]

In addition, Jacob foretold the reign of the tribe of Ephraim and the subjection of the ten tribes. As the holy apostle said, "By faith Jacob blessed each of the sons of Joseph and bowed down on the tip of his rod."[c] Now, he gave him a double inheritance: "Ephraim and Manasseh, like Reuben and Simeon, will be mine."[d] In his prophetic speech Jacob put Ephraim ahead of Manasseh. Though Joseph kept the privileges of the elder for Manasseh his firstborn and put each in order, the patriarch crossed his arms and placed his right hand on the younger and his left on the elder. Then, Joseph thinking that Jacob, due to his poor eyesight, had committed an inadvertent mistake, said, "Not that way, father; this one is the elder,"[e] and heard the reply, "I know, son, I know; he will also become a people, and he will also be elevated, but his younger brother will be greater than him."[f]

----

an undue concern for the place of burial; *cf.* Chrysostom's criticism of Christians who desired prominent tombs in sec. 6 of his *Exp. in* Ps. 48.12 LXX (49.11 MT).

1. In Gn 47.31 the consonantal text of the Hebrew contains *mṭṭh*, which could be pointed to mean either "bed" or "staff." The LXX chose the latter alternative, the Masoretes, Aquila, and Symmachus the former.

Ἐπισημαντέον δὲ ὅτι πανταχοῦ τῶν πρωτοτόκων οἱ μετ'
αὐτοὺς προτιμῶνται· καὶ γὰρ τοῦ Κάϊν προεκρίθη ὁ Ἄβελ,[g]
30 καὶ τοῦ Ἰάφεθ ὁ Σήμ, δεύτερος ὤν· ἀδελφός, γάρ φησιν, Ἰάφεθ
τοῦ μείζονος·[h] καὶ τοῦ Ἰσμαὴλ ὁ Ἰσαάκ,[i] καὶ τοῦ Ἡσαῦ ὁ
Ἰακώβ,[j] καὶ τοῦ Ῥουβὴν καὶ Ἰούδα ὁ Ἰωσήφ,[k] καὶ τοῦ
Μανασσῆ ὁ Ἐφραΐμ.[l] τοῦτο καὶ ἐν τοῖς μετὰ ταῦτα εὕροι τις
ἄν· καὶ γὰρ τοῦ Ἀαρὼν ὁ Μωϋσῆς προετάχθη,[m] καὶ Δαβίδ,
35 νεώτατος ὤν, τῶν ἑπτὰ ἀδελφῶν.[n]

Ὁ μέντοι πατριάρχης Ἰακὼβ ἐδίδαξε διὰ τῆς προρρήσεως
τῆς ταφῆς τὴν αἰτίαν· ἰδού, γάρ φησιν, ἐγὼ ἀποθνήσκω, καὶ
ἔσται ὁ Θεὸς μεθ' ὑμῶν καὶ ἀποστρέψει ὑμᾶς...εἰς τὴν γῆν
τῶν πατέρων ἡμῶν.[o]

CXII

Πῶς εὐλογῆσαι λέγεται τοὺς παῖδας ὁ Ἰακώβ, ἐνίοις
ἐπαρασάμενος;

(1) Οὔτε ἀραί εἰσιν, οὔτε εὐλογίαι, ἀλλὰ προρρήσεις οἱ
τελευταῖοι τοῦ πατριάρχου λόγοι· συνάχθητε, γάρ φησιν, ἵνα
5 ἀπαγγείλω ὑμῖν τί ἀπαντήσεται ὑμῖν ἐπ' ἐσχάτων τῶν
ἡμερῶν.[a] ἐμνήσθη δὲ καὶ τῶν παρ' ἐνίων γεγενημένων, οὐκ
ἐπειδὴ δίκας οἱ παῖδες εἰσεπράττοντο τῶν πατρικῶν
ἁμαρτημάτων, ἀλλὰ σχηματίζων εἰς ἀρὰν καὶ εὐλογίαν τοὺς
λόγους εἰς κοινὴν τῶν ἐντευξομένων ὠφέλειαν. καὶ τῷ μὲν
‖10 10 Ῥουβὴν αὐθάδειαν‖ ἐπιμέμφεται, καὶ θρασύτητα, καὶ τὴν εἰς
τὴν πατρῴαν εὐνὴν παροινίαν.[b] οὗ δὴ χάριν ὀλίγους αὐτοῦ
γεγενῆσθαι τοὺς ἀπογόνους προλέγει· τοῦτο γὰρ δηλοῖ τὸ ὡς
ὕδωρ μὴ ἐκζέσῃς[c] ἀντὶ τοῦ· μὴ θερμανθείης εἰς πολυγονίαν.

---

g. Gn 4.1–5   h. Gn 10.21   i. Gn 21.12   j. Gn 25.23   k. Gn 37.4
l. Gn 48.20   m. 1Chr 6.3   n. 1Sm 16.6–13   o. Gn 48.21

CXII A *[32]*, C, *7 9 10(inc.) 35 37* = 16 mss.

a. Gn 49.1   b. Gn 35.22   c. Gn 49.4

Question CXII

Note that throughout Scripture the later born are ranked ahead of the firstborn: Abel was given preference to Cain,[g] and Shem, though second, to Japheth—"brother of Japheth, the elder,"[h] as Scripture says[2]—Isaac to Ishmael,[i] Jacob to Esau,[j] Joseph to Reuben and Judah,[k] and Ephraim to Manasseh.[l] And there are more examples in subsequent generations: Moses was ranked ahead of Aaron,[m] and David, though the youngest, ahead of his seven brothers.[n]

Now, the patriarch Jacob conveyed the reason for his burial in the following prophecy: "Lo, I am dying; God will be with you and will bring you back to the land of your fathers."[o]

CXII

Why is Jacob said to have blessed his sons though he actually cursed some of them?[1]

(1) The dying words of the patriarch are neither curses nor blessings, but prophecies: "Gather round and I shall tell you what will happen to you in the last days."[a] He also mentions some of the things they did, not because the children were to pay the penalty for their fathers' sins, but to present his words in the form of curse and blessing with a view to the general benefit of future readers. Upbraiding Reuben for willful audacity and his drunken defilement of his father's bed,[b] he predicted that his offspring would be few. This is the meaning of "May you not bubble up like water";[c] that is, "May

2. At Gn 10.1 both the Hebrew and the LXX present the order Shem, Ham, Japheth, but in 10.21, where the Hebrew speaks of "Shem . . . the elder brother of Japheth," the LXX reverses the order: τῷ Σὴμ . . . ἀδελφῷ Ἰάφεθ τοῦ μείζονος.

1. On the pretext of a single question, Theodoret now begins to comment on a passage generally known as "The Testament of Jacob" (v. R.J. Clifford and R.E. Murphy on Gn 49.1–28); he rightly insists that these are prophecies, even if modern scholarship would date them to a period later than the patriarchs.

The Questions on Genesis

νεμεσᾷ δὲ καὶ τῷ Συμεὼν καὶ τῷ Λευί, τὸν τῶν σικημιτῶν
15 ἄδικον ὄλεθρον ὀδυρόμενος,ᵈ καὶ εὔχεται μηδεμίαν κοινωνίαν
εἰς τὴν παρανομίαν ἔχειν ἐκείνην. ἐπαρᾶται μέντοι, οὐκ
αὐτοῖς, ἀλλὰ τοῖς πονηροῖς αὐτῶν πάθεσι· τῇ ὀργῇ, τῇ μήνιδι.
ἐπιθυμίαν δὲ τὴν ὀργὴν ἐκάλεσεν· ἐκ ταύτης γὰρ καὶ ἡ ὀργὴ
τὴν ἐτυμολογίαν ἔχει· ὀρέγεται γὰρ ὁ ὀργιζόμενος ἀμύνασθαι
20 τὸν ἐχθρόν. καὶ αὕτη δὲ ἡ τιμωρία πρόρρησις ἦν· διαμεριῶ
γὰρ αὐτούς, φησίν, ἐν Ἰακὼβ καὶ διασπερῶ αὐτοὺς ἐν Ἰσραήλ.ᵉ
ἀλλ' ἡ τοῦ Λευὶ φυλὴ διὰ τὴν ἄκραν διεσπάρη τιμήν· ὥστε
γὰρ ἑκάστῃ φυλῇ συνεῖναι λευίτας καὶ ἱερέας, καὶ τὴν παρ'
αὐτῶν ὠφέλειαν καρποῦσθαι, οὐκ ἔλαβον ἴδιον κλῆρον, ἀλλ' ἐν
25 ἑκάστῃ φυλῇ τινες αὐτοῖς ἀπενεμήθησαν πόλεις καὶ τῆς
προαστείου γῆς ὡρισμένος πήχεων ἀριθμός.ᶠ καὶ ἡ τοῦ Συμεὼν
δὲ φυλὴ οὐκ εἶχε κλῆρον κεχωρισμένον ἀλλά, κατὰ τὴν τοῦ
πατριάρχου πρόρρησιν, μεταξὺ τῶν ἄλλων διεσπάρη φυλῶν.ᵍ

Τοῦ δὲ Ἰούδα πολλοὺς ἐπαίνους διέξεισιν· Ἰούδα, σὲ
30 αἰνέσαισαν οἱ ἀδελφοί σου· αἱ χεῖρές σου ἐπὶ νώτου τῶν
ἐχθρῶν σου· προσκυνήσουσί σοι οἱ υἱοὶ τοῦ πατρός σου.
σκύμνος λέοντος Ἰούδα· ἐκ βλαστοῦ, υἱέ μου, ἀνέβης·
ἀναπεσὼν ἐκοιμήθης ὡς λέων καὶ ὡς σκύμνος. τίς ἐγερεῖ
αὐτόν;ʰ ἀλλὰ τούτων οὐδὲν τῷ Ἰούδᾳ ἁρμόττει ἀλλ' ἢ τῇ ἐκ
35 τούτου βλαστησάσῃ φυλῇ· βασιλικὴ γὰρ ἦν αὕτη, πρώτου μὲν
τοῦ Δαβὶδ βασιλεύσαντος, εἶτα τῶν ἐξ ἐκείνου. καὶ πασῶν δὲ
τῶν ἄλλων φυλῶν ἦν δυνατωτάτη· καὶ γὰρ ἡνίκα Δαβὶδ ὁ
βασιλεὺς ἀριθμηθῆναι προσέταξε τὸν λαόν,ⁱ τετρακοσίας τοῦ
Ἰούδα χιλιάδας εὗρε, τῶν δὲ ἄλλων φυλῶν ἐννακοσίας,ʲ καὶ
40 μέντοι κἂν τῇ ἐρήμῳ διαριθμηθέντες, πλείους ὤφθησαν τῶν
ἄλλων φυλῶν.ᵏ

ll. 14f. τὸν τῶν σικημιτῶν ἄδικον ὄλεθρον a₂, c⁻³, 37 : τῶν τῶν
σικημιτῶν ἄδικον ὄλεθρον 2c [32], 5 : τῶν σικημιτῶν ἄδικον τὸν ὄλεθρον
3 : τῶν σικημιτῶν ἄδικον ὄλεθρον Sir. Sch. F.M.

d. Gn 34.25–31   e. Gn 49.7   f. Nm 35.1–8   g. Jos 19.1   h. Gn 49.8f.
i. 2Sm 24.1f.   j. 2Sm 24.9

you not grow warm to produce numerous children." He expressed his anger against Simeon and Levi as well, and, distressed at their unlawful slaughter of the Shechemites,[d] prayed to have no share in their transgression. Nonetheless, he cursed, not them, but their wicked passions: their wrath, their frenzy. He referred to their wrath as "desire," since the word "wrath" is derived from desire, for an angry man desires to take vengeance on his foe.[2] And this punishment of theirs was also a prophecy: "I shall divide them in Jacob and scatter them in Israel."[e] Yet it was on account of its exalted position that the tribe of Levi was scattered, the result being that Levites and priests were associated with every tribe and received support from them. Though they received no inheritance of their own, some cities and a fixed amount of land in the suburbs were allotted to them in every tribe.[f] The tribe of Simeon also received no separate allotment. Instead, according to the patriarch's prophecy, it was scattered among the other tribes.[g]

Then he related the many commendations of Judah: "Judah, may your brothers praise you! Your hands will be on the back of your foes. Your father's sons will bow down to you. Judah is a lion's cub; from a shoot you have risen up, my son; you have lain down and rested like a lion and like a cub. Who will rouse him?"[h] None of this, however, is applicable to Judah—only to the tribe descended from him. It was a royal tribe—David was the first king and was succeeded by his descendants—and of all the tribes it was the most powerful. For example, when King David ordered a census of the nation,[i] he found Judah to number 400,000 and the other tribes 900,000,[3j] and even in the census conducted in the desert they were found to be more numerous than the other tribes.[k]

2. Theodoret derives ὀργή (wrath) from ὀρέγομαι, " stretch out for" or "yearn for." This etymology is not linguistically sound.

3. These, the numbers in Theodoret's Antiochene text, differ from those in other forms of the LXX and the MT, where the figures are 500,000 and 800,000.

(2) Ἀλλὰ τὸ ἀκριβὲς τῆς προρρήσεως τὴν ἔκβασιν ἔλαβεν ἐπὶ τοῦ δεσπότου Χριστοῦ, ὃς ἐκ βλαστοῦ ἀνέτειλε κατὰ τὸν πατριάρχην Ἰακὼβ καὶ κατὰ τὸν προφήτην Ἡσαΐαν· ἐξῆλθε
45 *ῥάβδος ἐκ τῆς ῥίζης Ἰεσσαί, καὶ ἄνθος ἐκ τῆς ῥίζης ἀνέβη.*[l] αὐτῷ δὲ καὶ τὸ *ἀναπεσὼν* ἐκοιμήθη *ὡς λέων* ἁρμόττει καὶ *ὡς σκύμνος λέοντος·*[m] ὥσπερ γὰρ ὁ λέων, καὶ καθεύδων, ἐστι φοβερός, οὕτως ὁ δεσποτικὸς θάνατος φοβερὸς καὶ τῷ θανάτῳ καὶ διαβόλῳ γεγένηται. *λέοντα* δὲ αὐτὸν καὶ *σκύμνον* κέκληκε
50 λέοντος ὡς βασιλέα καὶ βασιλέως υἱὸν καὶ Θεὸν καὶ Θεοῦ υἱόν· καί, κατὰ τὸ ἀνθρώπινον γάρ, ἐκ τοῦ Δαβὶδ ἐβλάστησε καί, ὡς Θεός, πρὸ τῶν αἰώνων ἐκ τοῦ πατρὸς ἐγεννήθη. καὶ τὸ *τίς ἐγερεῖ αὐτόν;* τὴν ἄφατον αὐτοῦ δείκνυσι δύναμιν· αὐτὸς γὰρ ἑαυτὸν ἀνέστησε κατὰ τὴν αὐτοῦ πρόρρησιν· *λύσατε τὸν*
55 *ναὸν τοῦτον, καὶ ἐν τρισὶν ἡμέραις ἐγερῶ αὐτόν.*[n]

(3) Προαγορεύει καὶ τῆς ἐπιφανείας αὐτοῦ τὸν καιρόν· *οὐκ ἐκλείψει ἄρχων ἐξ Ἰούδα, καὶ ἡγούμενος ἐκ τῶν μηρῶν αὐτοῦ ἕως ἂν ἔλθῃ ᾧ ἀπόκειται, καὶ αὐτὸς προσδοκία ἐθνῶν.*[o] τοῦτο τῆς τοῦ Κυρίου παρουσίας σημεῖον σαφέστατον· ἐξέλιπον γὰρ
60 τῶν ἰουδαίων, οὐχ οἱ βασιλεῖς μόνον, ἀλλὰ καὶ οἱ ἀρχιερεῖς καὶ οἱ προφῆται ὥστε δειχθῆναι τὸ τῆς προρρήσεως τέλος· τοῦ γὰρ σωτῆρος ἡμῶν τίκτεσθαι μέλλοντος, ἀλλόφυλοι αὐτῶν ἐκράτησαν βασιλεῖς[p] ἵνα ὁ αἰώνιος δειχθῇ βασιλεύς, ἡ τῶν ἐθνῶν προσδοκία, κατὰ τὴν δοθεῖσαν παρὰ τοῦ Θεοῦ τῶν ὅλων
65 τοῖς πατριάρχαις ἐπαγγελίαν· καὶ γὰρ καὶ τῷ Ἀβραάμ, καὶ τῷ Ἰσαάκ, καὶ τῷ Ἰακὼβ ὑπέσχετο ὁ τῶν ὅλων Θεὸς ἐν τῷ σπέρματι αὐτῶν εὐλογήσειν πάντα τὰ ἔθνη τῆς γῆς.[q] τοῦτο ἐνταῦθα παρεδήλωσε, τὸν Ἰούδαν εὐλογῶν, ὁ Ἰακὼβ ὁ πατριάρχης· *οὐκ ἐκλείψει ἄρχων ἐξ Ἰούδα, καὶ ἡγούμενος ἐκ*
70 *τῶν μηρῶν αὐτοῦ ἕως ἂν ἔλθῃ ᾧ ἀπόκειται, καὶ αὐτὸς προσδοκία ἐθνῶν.*[r]

k. Nm 1.26f.; 26.22   l. Is 11.1   m. Gn 49.9   n. Jn 2.19   o. Gn 49.10
p. *Cf.* Lk 2.1f.

(2) Yet the precise sense of this prophecy received its fulfillment in Christ the Lord, who sprang up from a shoot of Judah according to the words of the patriarch Jacob and the prophet Isaiah: "A rod came out of the root of Jesse, and a flower rose up from its root."[l] The verse, "He lay down and rested like a lion and like a lion's cub,"[m] also refers to Christ. As the lion is fearsome even while asleep, so the Lord's death proved fearsome both to Death and to the devil. Now, he referred to him as "a lion" and as "a lion's cub" since he is a king and a king's son, God and Son of God. According to his humanity, he was descended from David, and as God, he was born of the Father before the ages. The verse, "Who will rouse him?" reveals his ineffable power, for he raised himself in fulfillment of his own prophecy: "Destroy this temple, and in three days I shall raise it up."[n]

(3) Jacob also foretold the time of his coming: "There will not fail a ruler from Judah, nor a leader from his thighs until he comes for whom it is laid up, he the expectation of nations."[o] This was the clearest sign of the Lord's coming. Not only the kings of the Jews, but also their chief priests and prophets had come to an end, as the fulfillment of the prophecy demanded. In fact, at the time of our Savior's birth, they were ruled by foreign kings,[p] so the eternal king, the "expectation of the nations," might be revealed according to the promise given to the patriarchs by the God of the universe. Indeed God promised Abraham, Isaac, and Jacob that he would bless all the nations of the earth in their offspring.[q] The patriarch Jacob hinted at the same idea in his blessing of Judah: "There will not fail a ruler from Judah, nor a leader from his thighs until he comes for whom it is laid up, he the expectation of nations."[r]

The Questions on Genesis

Εἶτα δείκνυσι τὸν ἐξ ἐθνῶν καὶ ἰουδαίων συστάντα λαόν· δεσμεύων πρὸς ἄμπελον τὸν πῶλον αὐτοῦ καὶ τῇ ἕλικι τῆς ἀμπέλου τὸν πῶλον τῆς ὄνου αὐτοῦ.[s] ὅτι δὲ ἄμπελος ὁ Ἰσραὴλ

75 ὠνομάζετο ἅπαντες οἱ προφῆται διδάσκουσι· καὶ γὰρ Δαβὶδ φησιν, ἄμπελον ἐξ Αἰγύπτου μετῆρας, καὶ τὰ ἑξῆς·[t] καὶ ὁ Ἡσαΐας, ἀμπελὼν ἐγενήθη τῷ ἠγαπημένῳ ἐν κέρατι, ἐν τόπῳ

|10 |πίονι·[u] καὶ διὰ τοῦ Ἱερεμίου ὁ τῶν ὅλων ἔφη Θεός, ἐγὼ δὲ ἐφύτευσά σε ἄμπελον καρποφόρον, πᾶσαν ἀληθινήν·[v] καὶ διὰ

80 τοῦ νομοθέτου, ἐκ γὰρ ἀμπέλου Σοδόμων ἡ ἄμπελος αὐτῶν·[w] καὶ ὁ Κύριος ἐν τοῖς ἱεροῖς εὐαγγελίοις, ἄνθρωπός τις ἐφύτευσεν ἀμπελῶνα, καὶ ἐξέδοτο αὐτὸν γεωργοῖς, καὶ ἀπεδήμησεν.[x] πῶλον δὲ τὸν ἐξ ἐθνῶν ὀνομάζει λαὸν ὡς ἀδάμαστον ὄντα καὶ πωλοδάμνην οὐκ ἐσχηκότα· τοῦτο γὰρ καὶ

85 ὁ Κύριος ἠνίξατο τοῖς ἀποστόλοις προστετάχὼς εἰς τὴν κατέναντι κώμην[y] ἀπελθεῖν καὶ λῦσαι τὴν ὄνον τὴν δεδεμένην καὶ τὸν ταύτης πῶλον,[z] ἐφ' ὅν, φησίν, οὐδείς... ἀνθρώπων ἐκάθισεν·[aa] οὔτε γὰρ πατριάρχης, οὔτε νομοθέτης, οὔτε προφήτης τῆς τῶν ἐθνῶν ἐφρόντισε σωτηρίας. οἱ δὲ θεῖοι

90 ἀπόστολοι, προσταχθέντες μαθητεῦσαι πάντα τὰ ἔθνη καὶ βαπτίσαι εἰς τὸ ὄνομα τοῦ Πατρός, καὶ τοῦ Υἱοῦ, καὶ τοῦ ἁγίου Πνεύματος,[bb] ἔλυσαν μὲν τὴν ὄνον· τουτέστι τῶν ἀνθρώπων τὴν φύσιν, τὴν δεδεμένην ταῖς τῆς ἁμαρτίας σειραῖς· ἔλυσαν δὲ καὶ τὸν πῶλον, τὸν ἐκ ταύτης

---

q. Gn 12.3; 26.4; 28.14   r. Gn 49.10

l. 72 δείκνυσι 3, c₁, 9 37 : δεικνὺς Sir. Sch. F.M. = "Next, revealing that there would be a people formed from both the gentiles and the Jews, . . ." Unless we should read φησί after δεσμεύων (v. next note), a finite verb here seems more likely than a participle; cf. 112.4 (Εἶτα δείκνυσι τὴν ἀπὸ τοῦ πάθους γενησομένην εὐθυμίαν).

l. 73 δεσμεύων Sir. Sch. F.M. : δεσμεύων, φησί, 5 = "Next, he revealed that there would be a people formed from both the gentiles and the Jews, saying, . . ." Cf. Q. 74 on Gn (εἶτα δεικνὺς τὴν τῆς ἀτοπίας ὑπερβολήν, ἐπήγαγε τοῦτο) and Q. 17 on Jgs (εἶτα, τεταραγμένους τοὺς πολεμίους ἰδὼν καὶ τὴν νίκην δεδηλωμένην, συνάγαγε, φησί, τὸ ἐφούδ).

s. Gn 49.11   t. Ps 80.8   u. Is 5.1   v. Jer 2.21   w. Dt 32.32   x. Lk 20.9
y. Lk 19.30   z. Mt 21.2   aa. Mk 11.2; Lk 19.30   bb. Mt 28.19

210

Next, he revealed that there would be a people formed from both the gentiles and the Jews: "Binding his foal to the vine and his ass's foal to the tendril of the vine."[s] We learn from all the prophets that Israel is called a "vine." David says, "You transplanted a vine from Egypt" and so on,[t] and Isaiah, "My beloved had a vineyard on a hill in a fertile spot."[u] Through Jeremiah the God of the universe says, "I planted you as a fruitful vine, entirely right,"[v] and through the lawgiver, "Their vine is from the vine of Sodom."[w] And the Lord in the sacred Gospels says, "A man planted a vineyard, let it out to tenant farmers, and went away."[x] He called the gentiles a "foal" since they were untamed and had no one to tame them. The Lord alluded to the same idea in his command to the apostles: "Go into the town opposite,[y] untie the tethered ass and its foal,[z] which no one has ridden."[aa] Now, no patriarch, lawgiver, or prophet had shown an interest in the salvation of the nations. It was the holy apostles who received the order to teach all the nations and baptize them in the name of the Father, the Son, and the Holy Spirit.[bb] They untied the ass (that is, human nature shackled with the cords of sin) as well as the foal (the people descended from it) and, placing their garments

95 βεβλαστηκότα λαόν, καί, ἐπιθέντες αὐτῷ τὰ ἑαυτῶν ἱμάτια·^{cc}
τουτέστι τὴν χάριν ἧς ἔτυχον· ὅσοι γὰρ εἰς Χριστὸν
ἐβαπτίσθησαν, Χριστὸν ἐνεδύσαντο·^{dd} καὶ εὐήνιον ἀπέφηναν
τὸν ἀδάμαστον πῶλον, καὶ ἐπεκάθισαν αὐτῷ τὸν δεσπότην, καὶ
προσέδησαν αὐτὸν τῇ ἀμπέλῳ, τουτέστιν ἑαυτοῖς. ἐξ ἰουδαίων
100 γὰρ οἱ ἀπόστολοι καί, οὐ μόνον αὐτοί, ἀλλὰ καὶ οἱ
ἑβδομήκοντα μαθηταί,^{ee} καὶ οἱ τρισχίλιοι οὓς κατὰ ταὐτὸν
ἐσαγήνευσε τῶν ἀποστόλων ὁ πρῶτος,^{ff} καὶ οἱ πεντακισχίλιοι,^{gg}
καὶ αἱ πολλαὶ μυριάδες περὶ ὧν ὁ τρισμακάριος Ἰάκωβος τῷ
θειοτάτῳ διελέχθη Παύλῳ.^{hh} οὐ μόνον τοίνυν τοῖς ἀποστόλοις
105 συνήφθησαν οἱ πεπιστευκότες, ἀλλὰ καὶ τοῖς τῶν ἀποστόλων
μαθηταῖς· καί, τοῦτο προορῶν, ὁ πατριάρχης ἔφη, *δεσμεύων*
πρὸς ἄμπελον τὸν πῶλον αὐτοῦ καὶ τῇ ἕλικι τῆς ἀμπέλου τὸν
*πῶλον τῆς ὄνου αὐτοῦ.*ⁱⁱ

(4) Εἶτα καὶ τὸ πάθος προλέγει· *πλυνεῖ ἐν οἴνῳ τὴν στολὴν*
110 *αὐτοῦ καὶ ἐν αἵματι σταφυλῆς τὴν περιβολὴν αὐτοῦ·*
χαροποιοὶ οἱ ὀφθαλμοὶ αὐτοῦ ἀπὸ οἴνου, καὶ λευκοὶ οἱ ὀδόντες
αὐτοῦ ἢ γάλα.^{jj} καὶ τὸ μὲν σῶμα αὐτοῦ στολὴν ὀνομάζει, τὸ
δὲ αἷμα *οἶνον.* ἐπειδὴ καὶ τὸν μυστικὸν οἶνον *αἷμα* κέκληκεν ὁ
δεσπότης, ἀκούομεν δὲ καὶ τοῦ εὐαγγελιστοῦ Ἰωάννου
115 διδάσκοντος ὥς, τοῦ στρατιώτου νύξαντος αὐτοῦ τὴν πλευράν,
ἐξῆλθεν αἷμα καὶ ὕδωρ·^{kk} οὗτοι δὲ οἱ κρουνοὶ διὰ τοῦ σώματος
κατερρύησαν· διὰ τοῦτό φησιν ὁ πατριάρχης, *πλυνεῖ ἐν οἴνῳ*
τὴν στολὴν αὐτοῦ καὶ ἐν αἵματι σταφυλῆς τὴν περιβολὴν
αὐτοῦ.^{ll}

120 Εἶτα δείκνυσι τὴν ἀπὸ τοῦ πάθους γενησομένην εὐθυμίαν·
χαροποιοὶ οἱ ὀφθαλμοὶ αὐτοῦ ἀπὸ οἴνου·^{mm} εὐφροσύνη γὰρ
τῆς οἰκουμένης τὸ σωτήριον πάθος. ὅτι δὲ οὕτω τὸ πάθος
ἐκάλεσε μάρτυς αὐτὸς ὁ Κύριος λέγων, *πάτερ...*, *εἰ*
δυνατόν..., *παρελθέτω τὸ ποτήριον τοῦτο ἀπ' ἐμοῦ·*ⁿⁿ οὕτω
125 καὶ τοῖς υἱοῖς ἔφη Ζεβεδαίου, *δύνασθε πιεῖν τὸ ποτήριον ὃ*

cc. Mt 21.6f.   dd. Gal 3.27   ee. Lk 10.1   ff. Acts 2.41   gg. Acts 4.4
hh. Acts 21.20   ii. Gn 49.11   jj. Gn 49.11f.   kk. Jn 19.34   ll. Gn 49.11
mm. Gn 49.12   nn. Mt 26.39

on it[cc] (the grace they had received, for "All who have been baptized in Christ have put on Christ"[dd]), they made the untamed foal obedient to the rein, set the Lord on it, and secured it to the vine, that is, to themselves. As you recall, the apostles were Jews by birth, and not only they but also the seventy disciples,[ee] the three thousand, whom the first of the apostles netted on a single occasion,[ff] the five thousand,[gg] and the countless others of whom James, the thrice blessed, spoke to St. Paul.[hh] Thus, the believers were joined not only to the apostles but also to the disciples of the apostles. Foreseeing this, the patriarch said, "Binding his ass to the vine, and his ass's foal to the tendril of the vine."[ii]

(4) Next, he foretold the passion: "He will wash his clothing in wine and his attire in the blood of the grape. His eyes are more sparkling than wine, his teeth whiter than milk."[jj] He called his body "clothing" and his blood "wine." Since the Lord also used the term "blood" of the eucharistic wine, and we hear the evangelist John relate that when the soldier pierced his side, there flowed forth blood and water[kk] (these springs streamed through his body), the patriarch said, "He will wash his clothing in wine and his attire in the blood of the grape."[4][ll]

Next he revealed the joy that would result from the passion: "His eyes are more sparkling than wine."[mm] The saving passion means joy for the world. The Lord confirmed that Jacob was here referring to his passion when he said, "Father, if possible, let this cup pass me by."[nn] Likewise, he had said to the sons of Zebedee, "Are you able to

4. Even Theodore of Mopsuestia had taken 49.11f. in a messianic sense; *v. Fragg. in Gen.* (on vv. 11f.) and Devreesse, *StT* vol. 141, p. 25).

ἐγὼ μέλλω πίνειν;ᵒᵒ τὸ τοίνυν χαροποιὸν τῶν ὀφθαλμῶν τὴν
μετὰ τὸ πάθος εὐφροσύνην δηλοῖ· μετὰ γὰρ τὸ πάθος καὶ τὴν
ἀνάστασιν εἰς πᾶσαν ἀπεστάλησαν τὴν οἰκουμένην οἱ
μαθηταί, τὴν σωτηρίαν προσφέροντες τοῖς πιστεύουσι. τῆς δὲ
130 γε διδασκαλίας τὸ διειδὲς καὶ τὸ διαφανὲς λευκοτάτοις
ὀδοῦσιν ἀπείκασεν· λευκοί, γάρ φησιν, οἱ ὀδόντες αὐτοῦ ἢ
γάλα.ᵖᵖ τοσαῦτα προείρηκεν ὁ πατριάρχης, εὐλογῶν τὸν
Ἰούδαν.

Τοῦ δὲ Ζαβουλὼν προεῖπε τὴν παράλιον οἴκησιν,�qq τοῦ δὲ
135 Ἰσσάχαρ τὴν γηπονίαν,ʳʳ τοῦ δὲ Δάν, κατὰ μέν τινας, τὰ ὑπὸ
τοῦ Σαμψὼν γεγενημένα· ἐκ ταύτης γὰρ ἦν τῆς φυλῆς,ˢˢ
συνηριθμήθη δὲ καὶ τοῖς κριταῖς,ᵗᵗ καὶ διὰ τοῦτό φησιν, Δὰν
κρινεῖ τὸν ἑαυτοῦ λαὸν ὡσεὶ καὶ μία φυλὴ ἐν Ἰσραήλ.ᵘᵘ ἔνιοι
δέ φασι τὰ κατὰ τὴν Λάϊσαν, τὴν νῦν Πανεάδα καλουμένην,
140 προαγορεῦσαι· ἐξαπίνης γάρ τινες ἀπὸ ταύτης ὁρμώμενοι τῆς
φυλῆς, ταύτῃ προσβαλόντες τῇ πόλει, εἷλόν τε κατὰ κράτος,
καὶ ᾤκησαν, καὶ τὴν οἰκείαν αὐτῇ προσηγορίαν ἐπέθηκαν· Δὰν
γὰρ αὐτὴν ἐκάλεσαν.ᵛᵛ

(5) Ἐγὼ δὲ οἶμαι τὸ θεῖον Πνεῦμα, τὰ κατὰ τὸν σωτῆρα
145 τὸν ἡμέτερον διὰ τοῦ πατριάρχου προθεσπίσαν, καὶ τὰ κατὰ
τὸν ἀντίχριστον διὰ ταύτης εἰπεῖν τῆς προρρήσεως. σφόδρα
δὲ αὐτῷ καὶ τὰ γεγραμμένα ἁρμόττει· Δάν, γάρ φησι, κρινεῖ
τὸν ἑαυτοῦ λαὸν ὡσεὶ καὶ μία φυλὴ ἐν Ἰσραήλ.ʷʷ ὥσπερ, γάρ
φησιν, ἐκ τῆς Ἰούδα φυλῆς ὁ Σωτὴρ καὶ Κύριος ἡμῶν
150 βλαστήσας, διασώσει τὴν οἰκουμένην, οὕτως ἐκ τῆς τοῦ Δὰν
φυλῆς ὄφις ὀλέθριος ἐξελεύσεται· τοῦτο γὰρ λέγει· καὶ
γενηθήτω Δὰν ὄφις ἐφ' ὁδοῦ, ἐγκαθήμενος ἐπὶ τρίβου, δάκνων
πτέρναν ἵππου, καὶ πεσεῖται ὁ ἱππεὺς εἰς τὰ ὀπίσω, τὴν
σωτηρίαν περιμένων Κυρίου.ˣˣ ἐπειδὴ γάρ, ἀπάταις

---

l. 137 φησιν 11, 7, Sir. Sch. : φησιν ἔφη F.M. = "Hence the statement, he
said, . . ."

oo. Mt 20.22   pp. Gn 49.12   qq. Gn 49.13   rr. Gn 49.14f.   ss. Jgs 13.2
tt. Jgs 16.31   uu. Gn 49.16   vv. Jos 19.47f.   ww. Gn 49.16   xx. Gn 49.17f.

drink the cup that I am about to drink?"[oo] So the sparkling of the eyes suggests the joy after the passion. After the passion and the resurrection, the disciples were sent into the whole world to bring salvation to believers. He likened the perfect clarity of their teaching to gleaming white teeth: "His teeth are whiter than milk."[pp] These were the prophecies pronounced by the patriarch in the blessing of Judah.

He also foretold a coastal settlement for Zebulun,[qq] farming for Issachar,[rr] and for Dan, according to some commentators, the deeds of Samson, who was from this tribe[ss] and was numbered among the judges.[tt] Hence the statement, "Dan will judge his people as one tribe in Israel."[uu] On the other hand, several commentators have maintained that this was a prediction of the fate of Leshem, now called Paneas. Some men from that tribe made a sudden advance on this city, attacked it, took it by force, occupied it, and gave it their own name, calling it "Dan." [5][vv]

(5) My own view is that the divine Spirit, who had prophesied through the patriarch regarding our Savior, spoke in this prophecy about the Antichrist. This passage fits him quite well: "Dan will judge his people as one tribe in Israel."[ww] That is, just as our Savior and Lord, descended from the tribe of Judah, will save the world, so the deadly serpent will emerge from the tribe of Dan. This is the meaning of "Let Dan become a serpent in the way, lying on the path to bite a horse's heel, and the rider will fall backwards, awaiting the Lord's salvation."[xx] Since, with every possible means of deception, he tries to decoy people and hunt them to the death, he is likened to a

5. Theodoret probably drew from Diodore the first two interpretations, both historically based, of the oracle regarding Dan. As Guinot notes (p. 763), a fragment containing the second (Deconinck, frag. 58) is still extant.

155 παντοδαπαῖς κεχρημένος, πειρᾶται τοὺς φενακιζομένους
ἀγρεύειν εἰς ὄλεθρον, ὄφει τινὶ αὐτὸν ἀπεικάζει παρά τινα
τρίβον φωλεύοντι καὶ τοῖς παριοῦσι λυμαινομένῳ. ἵππον δὲ
οἶμαι καλεῖν αὐτὸν τὸ σῶμα, ἐπιβάτην δὲ τὴν ψυχήν· τὸ δὲ
εἰς τοὐπίσω πεσεῖν, τουτέστιν ὕπτιον κεῖσθαι, τὸν θάνατον
160 παραδηλοῖ· τοιοῦτο γὰρ τῶν τεθνεώτων τὸ σχῆμα. διὰ δὲ τῆς
πτέρνης τὴν ἀπάτην ᾐνίξατο. ἐπειδὴ γὰρ τοὺς μὲν ἐξαπατᾷ,
τοῖς δὲ παγχαλέπας ἐπιφέρει κολάσεις, διὰ τοῦ ἵππου τὸ
σῶμα δεδήλωκεν, οὗ δακνομένου καὶ διαφθειρομένου, ὁ
θάνατος γίνεται, τοὺς τῆς ἐλπίδος τοῖς ὑπομένουσι κομίζων
165 καρπούς· καρπὸς δὲ τῆς τοιαύτης ἐλπίδος ἡ σωτηρία.

Προλέγει καὶ τῷ Γὰδ τὰς ἐσομένας αὐτῷ παρὰ τῶν
ληστρικῶν ἐφόδων ἐπιβουλάς· τοῦτο γὰρ λέγει· *πειρατήριον*
πειρατεύσει αὐτόν· προαγορεύει δὲ καὶ τὴν ἐσομένην αὐτοῦ
νίκην· καὶ *αὐτός . . . ,* γάρ φησι, *πειρατεύσει αὐτὸν κατὰ*
170 *πόδας·*[yy] ὡσαύτως δὲ καὶ τοῦ Ἀσὴρ τὴν σιτοφόρον χώραν καὶ
τοῦ Νεφθαλεὶμ τὴν εἰς πλῆθος ἐπίδοσιν· τοῦτο γὰρ ἔφη·
στέλεχος ἀνειμένον ἐπιδιδοὺς ἐν τῷ γεννήματι κάλλος.[zz]

(6) Εἶτα τοῦ Ἰωσὴφ τὸν φθόνον καὶ τὰς παντοδαπὰς
ἐπιδείξας ἐπιβουλάς, τὴν θείαν ὑμνεῖ κηδεμονίαν, δι' ἧς τοὺς
175 πεπολεμηκότας νενίκηκε· *συνετρίβη,* γάρ φησι, *μετὰ κράτους*
τὰ τόξα αὐτῶν, καὶ ἐξελύθη νεῦρα βραχιόνων χειρῶν αὐτῶν διὰ
χεῖρα δυνατοῦ Ἰακώβ. ἐκεῖθεν ὁ κατισχύσας Ἰσραὴλ παρὰ
Θεοῦ τοῦ πατρός σου· καὶ ἐβοήθησέ σοι ὁ Θεὸς ὁ ἐμὸς καὶ
εὐλόγησέ σε εὐλογίαν οὐρανοῦ ἄνωθεν καὶ εὐλογίαν γῆς
180 *ἐχούσης πάντα. ἕνεκεν εὐλογίας μασθῶν καὶ μήτρας, εὐλογίας*
πατρός σου καὶ μητρός σου, ὑπερίσχυσας ὑπὲρ εὐλογίας ὀρέων
μονίμων καὶ ἐπιθυμίας θινῶν αἰωνίων. ἔσονται ἐπὶ κεφαλῆς
Ἰωσὴφ καὶ ἐπὶ κορυφῆς ὧν ἡγήσατο ἀδελφῶν.[aaa] διὰ πάντων δὲ
τούτων ὕμνησε τὸν οἰκεῖον Θεόν, ὃς καὶ αὐτὸν κρείττονα τοῦ

---

yy. Gn 49.19   zz. Gn 49.21   aaa. Gn 49.24–26

serpent lurking by the path and attacking the passers-by. In my view, the "horse" signifies the body, the "rider" the soul, and "falling backwards"—that is, lying on one's back—death, since this is the posture of death. The mention of the "heel" hints at deception. Since the Antichrist deceives some and afflicts others with inhuman chastisements, the "horse" suggests the body, because bitten and disabled, it dies, though death brings the fruit of hope to those who persevere, the fruit of this hope being salvation.

Jacob also told Gad that he would one day suffer the inroads of raiders. This is the meaning of "A nest of pirates will plunder him." He also foretold his future victory: "He will plunder him in close pursuit."[yy] Likewise, he prophesied the grain-rich country of Asher and Naphtali's growth in numbers; this is the meaning of "A branch coming forth yields beauty in its bud."[6zz]

(6) Then he referred to the malicious schemes against Joseph and sang the praises of God's providence by which he vanquished those who quarreled with him: "Mightily were their shafts smashed, and the sinews of their arms undone by the hand of the Strength of Jacob. Thence comes the one who gave strength to Israel from the God of your father. My God helped you and blessed you with a blessing of heaven above and a blessing of the earth that contains all things. Because of a blessing of breasts and womb, a blessing of your father and your mother, you surpassed the blessings of immovable mountains and the desires of eternal mounds. They will be upon the head of Joseph and on the brow of the brothers he led."[7aaa] In all this he sang the God of his family, who made him stronger than the

---

6. Verse 49.21 is obscure. Speiser renders (p. 363) the MT: "Naphtali is a hind let loose / That brings forth lovely fawns." The LXX, relying on a pointing of the consonantal text different from that of the MT, reads "branch" ($\sigma\tau\acute{\epsilon}\lambda\epsilon\chi o\varsigma$) rather than "hind," and "bud" ($\gamma\epsilon\nu\nu\acute{\eta}\mu\alpha\tau\iota$) rather than "fawns."

7. Verse 49.26 exhibits textual difficulties in both the Hebrew and the LXX; *v.* Speiser on 49.26a.

185 πεπολεμηκότος ἀπέφηνεν ἀδελφοῦ καὶ τὸν υἱὸν ἄμαχον
ἔδειξεν, παρὰ τοσούτων ἀδελφῶν ἐπιβουλευθέντα. ταύτης δέ,
φησί, τῆς κηδεμονίας τετύχηκας, τῆς εἰς τοὺς γεγεννηκότας
θεραπείας μισθὸν κομισάμενος. τοῦτο γὰρ λέγει· *ἕνεκεν*
εὐλογίας μασθῶν καὶ μήτρας, εὐλογίας πατρός σου καὶ μητρός
190 *σου·* γηροκόμος γὰρ σπουδαῖος τοῦ πατρὸς ἐγεγόνει.ᵇᵇᵇ τὰ δὲ
εἰς αὐτὸν γεγενημένα κοινὰ αὐτοῦ τε καὶ τῆς μητρὸς εἶναί
φησιν· τῆς γὰρ αὐτῆς ἂν κἀκείνη τῆς κηδεμονίας ἀπήλαυσεν
εἰ μὴ θᾶττον ὑπεξῆλθε τὸν βίον.ᶜᶜᶜ εἶτα ἐπεύχεται αὐτῷ
περιφάνειαν ὥστε γενέσθαι αὐτὸν παρὰ πᾶσιν ἐπίσημον·
195 *ὑπερίσχυσας,* γάρ φησιν, *ὑπὲρ εὐλογίας ὀρέων μονίμων καὶ*
ἐπιθυμίας θινῶν αἰωνίων. ἔσονται ἐπὶ κεφαλῆς Ἰωσὴφ καὶ ἐπὶ
κορυφῆς ὧν ἡγήσατο ἀδελφῶν. τοὺς δὴ θῖνας ὁ Ἀκύλας
βουνοὺς ἡρμήνευσεν. ἐπειδὴ τοίνυν πόρρωθεν ὁρῶνται καὶ οἱ
βουνοὶ καὶ τὰ ὄρη, τούτοις παραπλησίως εὔχεται γνώριμον
200 αὐτὸν γενέσθαι καὶ πάντων περιφανέστατον.

(7) Τὸν δὲ Βενιαμὶν *λύκον ἅρπαγα* κέκληκε διὰ τὸ
συμβεβηκὸς πάθος τῇ τούτου φυλῇ. διὸ ἐπήγαγε· *τὸ πρωϊνὸν*
*ἔδεται ... καὶ εἰς τὸ ἑσπέρας διαδώσει τροφήν.*ᵈᵈᵈ ἐν γὰρ τῇ
πρώτῃ καὶ τῇ δευτέρᾳ συμπλοκῇ *νενικηκότες,*ᵉᵉᵉ ὕστερον
205 ἄρδην ἀπώλοντο, πλὴν ὀλίγων τινῶν ἄγαν εὐαριθμήτων,ᶠᶠᶠ οὓς
οἱ νενικηκότες οἰκτίραντες, δοῦναι μὲν αὐτοῖς γυναῖκας διὰ
τὸν ὅρκον ὑπείδοντο,ᵍᵍᵍ ἑτέρως δὲ αὐτοῖς τὸν γάμον
ἐμηχανήσαντο.ʰʰʰ εἰδέναι δὲ χρὴ ὥς τινες εἰς τὸν θεσπέσιον
Παῦλον τήνδε τὴν πρόρρησιν εἵλκυσαν. λύκου γὰρ δίκην
210 ἐλυμαίνετο τὴν ἐκκλησίαν, κατὰ τοὺς οἴκους εἰσπορευόμενος,ⁱⁱⁱ
ὕστερον δὲ τὴν πνευματικὴν τροφὴν τῇ οἰκουμένῃ διέδωκε.

Ταῦτα τοῦ Ἰακὼβ εἰρηκότος καὶ τὴν οἰκείαν τελευτὴν
μεμηνυκότος, ὁ συγγραφεὺς ἔφη, *καί, ἐξάρας τοὺς πόδας ἐπὶ*

---

bbb. *Cf.* Gn 45.9–11   ccc. Gn 35.16–19   ddd. Gn 49.27
eee. Jgs 19.19–25   fff. Jgs 19.29–48   ggg. Jgs 21.1   hhh. Jgs 21.15–24
iii. Acts 8.3

brother who quarreled with him, and showed his son to be invincible when so many of his brothers conspired against him. He declared, "You received this care as the recompense for your care of your parents"—this is the meaning of "Because of a blessing of breasts and womb, a blessing of your father and your mother"—for he was conscientious in caring for his elderly father.[bbb] He declared that what Joseph did for him he did also for his mother, as she would have enjoyed the same care if she had not previously departed this life.[ccc] He then prayed for fame for Joseph, that he become renowned throughout the whole world: "You surpassed the blessings of immovable mountains and the desires of eternal mounds. They will be upon the head of Joseph and on the brow of the brothers he led." Instead of "mounds" Aquila rendered "hills."[8] Since hills and mountains are visible from afar, Jacob prayed that Joseph would be well-known like them and more conspicuous than everyone else.

(7) He called Benjamin "a ravenous wolf" because of what happened to this tribe. Hence, he added, "He will eat in the morning and distribute his food for the evening."[ddd] Though victorious in the first and second engagements,[eee] they were subsequently wiped out, except for very few survivors.[fff] Though they took pity on the surviving Benjaminites, the victors were reluctant to give them wives on account of the ban,[ggg] and so they contrived a novel way for them to marry.[hhh] Now, you should know that some commentators have applied this prophecy to the divinely inspired Paul; he damaged the Church like a wolf, going from house to house,[iii] but later distributed spiritual nourishment to the whole world.[9]

According to the historian, after Jacob had made this speech and predicted his own death, "He lifted his feet onto the bed, expired,

8. Aquila substituted βουνός (hill) for θίς, a word that normally refers to a mound of sand or to the seashore.

9. This interpretation is first attested in Hippolytus (H. Achelis, *Hippolyt's Kleinere, etc.,* "Griechische Fragmente zur Genesis," #52). It was adopted by Cyril of Alexandria (*Glaph. Gen.* 7) and rejected by Diodore (Deconinck, frag. 59), who was probably Theodoret's source; *v.* Guinot, p. 764.

τὴν κλίνην, ἐξέλιπε καὶ προσετέθη πρὸς τὸν λαὸν αὐτοῦ.ʲʲʲ διὰ
215 δὲ τούτων τῶν λόγων ᾐνίξατο τὴν ἐλπίδα τῆς ἀναστάσεως· εἰ
γὰρ παντάπασι διεφθείροντο καὶ μὴ εἰς ἕτερον μετέβαινον
βίον, οὐκ ἂν εἶπε, προσετέθη πρὸς τὸν λαὸν αὐτοῦ. τοῦτο δὲ
καὶ πρὸς τὸν Ἀβραὰμ αὐτὸς ὁ τῶν ὅλων ἔφη Θεός· σὺ δὲ
ἀπελεύσῃ πρὸς τοὺς πατέρας σου ἐν εἰρήνῃ, τραφεὶς ἐν γήρει
220 καλῷ.ᵏᵏᵏ ἐντεῦθεν καὶ ὁ Κύριος τὴν τῶν σαδδουκαίων
ἀπιστίαν διήλεγξεν, εἰρηκώς, ὅτι δὲ ἐγείρονται οἱ νεκροί—ˡˡˡ
οὐκ ἀνέγνωτε, . . . ἐγὼ ὁ Θεὸς Ἀβραάμ, καὶ . . . Ἰσαάκ,
καὶ . . . Ἰακώβ; οὐκ ἔστιν ὁ Θεὸς Θεὸς νεκρῶν, ἀλλὰ ζώντων.ᵐᵐᵐ

jjj. Gn 49.33   kkk. Gn 15.15   lll. Lk 20.37   mmm. Mk 12.26

and was gathered to his people."[jjj] With this last clause he hinted at the hope of resurrection. After all, if they had disappeared without trace and not gone to another life, he would not have said, "He was gathered to his people." The God of the universe himself made the same statement to Abraham: "You will depart to your ancestors in peace, nourished to a fine old age."[kkk] Thus, refuting the unbelief of the Sadducees, the Lord said, "As to the resurrection of the dead,[lll] have you not read, 'I am the God of Abraham, Isaac, and Jacob'? God is not God of the dead, but of the living."[mmm]

QUAESTIONES IN EXODUM

I

Πῶς νοητέον τὸ χυδαῖοι ἐγένοντο;[a]

Οὐχ, ὥς τινες νενοήκασιν, ὑβριστικῶς αὐτὸ τέθεικεν, ἀλλὰ τὸ πλῆθος δεδήλωκεν· οὕτως, γάρ φησιν, ηὐξήθησαν ὡς κατὰ πάσης ἐκείνης ἐκχεθῆναι τῆς γῆς. οὕτω καὶ οἱ περὶ τὸν
5 Ἀκύλαν ἡρμήνευσαν. τοῦτο δὲ καὶ τὰ ἑξῆς δηλοῖ· ἐπλήθυνε..., γάρ φησιν, ἡ γῆ αὐτούς·[b] καὶ μετ' ὀλίγα, καθότι δὲ αὐτοὺς ἐταπείνουν, τοσοῦτον πλείους ἐγίνοντο καὶ ἴσχυον σφόδρα σφόδρα.[c]

II

Τί ἐστιν ἐπειδὴ ἐφοβοῦντο αἱ μαῖαι τὸν Θεόν, ἐποίησαν ἑαυταῖς οἰκίας;[a]

I A⁻⁶ [32], C, 7 9 10 31* 35 37 = 17 mss.

a. Ex 1.7   b. Ex 1.7   c. Ex 1.12

II A⁻⁶ [32], B, C, 7 9 10 17 31 35 37 = 20 mss.

a. Ex 1.21

ON EXODUS[1]

I

How are we to understand "They proved prolific"?[2a]
He did not employ the term as an insult, as some commentators
have understood it, but rather to indicate their vast numbers. His
meaning is that they grew so much that they spread throughout all
that land. This is how Aquila and his school rendered it. The sequel
also indicates this: "The land multiplied them";[b] and a little later,
"The more they oppressed them, the more numerous they became
and grew very greatly in strength."[c]

II

What is the meaning of "Because the midwives feared God, they
built themselves households"?[a]

1. Of Theodoret's Antiochene predecessors, Chrysostom has no commentary
on books subsequent to Genesis. For Theodore of Mopsuestia, though the Nestori-
an Ebedjesu ("early fourteenth century") mentions a three-volume commentary
on Genesis, the Syriac *Chronicle of Seert* ("perhaps of the first half of the thirteenth
century") speaks of a three-volume commentary on the Pentateuch; *v.* Devreesse,
Essai, notes 5f., pp. 4f. Devreesse apparently takes (p. 25) the notice in the *Chronicle*
as referring only to the work on Genesis. He has culled (pp. 25–27) from the *Catena Nikephori* (*CPG* #C2) three excerpts bearing on Ex 25, which he believes actually derive from a commentary on the Epistle to the Hebrews; *cf.* notes 35, 46 to the
"Introduction to Theodoret's Life and Works." For French translations and discussions of the catalogues of Ebedjesu and the *Chronicle of Seert, v.* J.M. Vosté, "La
chronologie de l'activité littéraire de Théodore de Mopsueste," *RB* 34 (1925), pp.
54–81, esp. pp. 57–61.
2. The adjective χυδαῖος, used in Ex 1.7 to mean "prolific," may also mean

Τοῦ Φαραὼ κελεύσαντος διαφθείρειν τὰ ἄρρενα, ἐκεῖναι δι'
εὐλάβειαν ὑπουργῆσαι τῷ τῆς παιδοκτονίας οὐκ ἠνέσχοντο
5 νόμῳ.[b] οὗ δὴ χάριν, αὐτὰς ὁ Θεὸς ἀμειβόμενος, ἀφθονίαν
αὐταῖς ἀγαθῶν ἐδωρήσατο.

III

Πόθεν ἔγνω τοῦ Φαραὼ ἡ θυγάτηρ ὅτι ἑβραῖον ἦν τὸ
παιδίον;[a]
Ἡ περιτομὴ τοῦτο δεδήλωκεν. ἐντεῦθεν δῆλον ὡς αἰγύπτιοι
κατ' ἐκεῖνον οὐ περιετέμνοντο τὸν καιρόν, ὕστερον δέ, τοὺς
5 ἑβραίους ζηλώσαντες, τὸν τῆς περιτομῆς ἠσπάσαντο νόμον.
ὅθεν καὶ διὰ Ἰερεμίου ἔφη ὁ τῶν ὅλων Θεός, ἐπισκέψομαι ἐπὶ
πάντας περιτεμνομένους ἀκροβυστίαν αὐτῶν· ἐπ'
Αἴγυπτον, . . . καὶ ἐπὶ υἱοὺς Ἐδώμ, καὶ τὰ ἑξῆς.[b]

IV

Διὰ τί ἀλλόφυλον γυναῖκα ἔγημεν ὁ Μωϋσῆς;[a]
Τύπος ἦν τοῦ δεσπότου Χριστοῦ, ὅς, ἐξ ἰουδαίων κατὰ
σάρκα βεβλαστηκώς, τὴν ἐξ ἐθνῶν ἐκκλησίαν νύμφην ἑαυτοῦ
προσηγόρευσεν.

---

b. Ex 1.16f.

III A^{-6} *[32]*, B, C^{-51}, 7 9 10 17 31 35 37 = 19 mss.
a. Ex 2.5f.   b. Jer 9.25f.

IV A^{-6} *[32]*, B, C, 7 9 10 17 35 37 = 19 mss.
a. Ex 2.21

Although Pharaoh ordered them to destroy the male children, their piety would not permit them to collaborate with the law of infanticide.[b] Hence, as a reward, God granted them many a blessing.

III

How did Pharaoh's daughter know that the child was a Hebrew?[a]

This was clear from his circumcision. Thus, we can deduce that, at that time, the Egyptians were not yet circumcised, although later, in emulation of the Hebrews, they embraced the law of circumcision. Hence, the God of the universe said through Jeremiah, "I shall call to account all those circumcised in their foreskin: Egypt and the sons of Edom" and so on.[1b]

IV

Why did Moses marry a foreign wife?[a]

He was a type of Christ the Lord, who, though a Jew by bodily descent, called the gentile Church his "bride."

"ordinary," "vulgar"; *v. LSJ sub uoce* II.2. As Guinot notes (p. 764), Theodoret rejects the interpretation of Clement of Alexandria, who, taking the term in this negative sense, had understood it to refer to the spiritual blindness of the Jews. *V. Strom.* 7.18.109.1 for his derisive rhyme Ἰουδαίων τῶν χυδαίων and *cf. Strom.* 7.16.100.4.

1. Theodoret declares also in Q. 69 on Gn that the Egyptians learned circumcision from the Jews. This practice was, however, widespread in the ancient Near East, excluding Mesopotamia; *v.* Speiser, pp. 126f.

V

Τινές φασιν ἄγγελον ὀφθῆναι τῷ Μωϋσῇ ἐν τῷ βάτῳ.

Ἡ ἀνάγνωσις τοῦ χωρίου τὸν ὀφθέντα δηλοῖ· ὤφθη . . . ,
γάρ φησιν, *αὐτῷ ἄγγελος Κυρίου ἐν φλογὶ πυρὸς . . . βάτου·*[a] *καὶ*
μετ᾽ ὀλίγα, *ὡς δὲ εἶδε Κύριος ὅτι προσάγει ἰδεῖν, ἐκάλεσεν*
5 *αὐτὸν Κύριος ἐκ τοῦ βάτου·*[b] *καὶ πάλιν μετὰ βραχέα, καὶ εἶπεν*
αὐτῷ, ἐγώ εἰμι ὁ Θεὸς . . . Ἀβραάμ, καὶ ὁ Θεὸς Ἰσαάκ, καὶ ὁ
Θεὸς Ἰακώβ·[c] *καὶ εὐθὺς ἐπήγαγεν, ἀπέστρεψε δὲ Μωϋσῆς τὸ*
πρόσωπον αὐτοῦ· ηὐλαβεῖτο γὰρ καταβλέψαι ἐνώπιον τοῦ
Θεοῦ·[d] *καὶ ἐπισυνῆψεν, ἰδὼν εἶδον τὴν κάκωσιν τοῦ λαοῦ μου,*
10 *τοῦ ἐν Αἰγύπτῳ, καὶ τῆς κραυγῆς αὐτῶν ἤκουσα, καὶ τὰ ἑξῆς·*[e]
καὶ αὖθις, ἐγώ εἰμι ὁ ὤν· . . . τάδε ἐρεῖς τοῖς υἱοῖς Ἰσραήλ· ὁ
ὢν ἀπέσταλκέ με πρὸς ὑμᾶς.[f] καὶ ὅλον δὲ τὸ χωρίον δείκνυσι
Θεὸν ὄντα τὸν ὀφθέντα.

Κέκληκε δὲ αὐτὸν καὶ *ἄγγελον* ἵνα γνῶμεν ὡς ὁ ὀφθεὶς οὐκ
15 ἔστιν ὁ Θεὸς καὶ πατήρ· τίνος γὰρ ἄγγελος ὁ πατήρ; ἀλλ᾽ ὁ
μονογενὴς υἱός, ὁ *μεγάλης βουλῆς ἄγγελος,*[g] ὁ τοῖς ἱεροῖς
μαθηταῖς εἰρηκώς, *πάντα ὅσα ἤκουσα παρὰ τοῦ πατρός μου*
δεδήλωκα ὑμῖν.[h] ὥσπερ δὲ τὸ *ἄγγελος* ὄνομα τέθεικεν, οὐχ
ὑπουργίαν τινὰ σημαίνων, ἀλλὰ τοῦ μονογενοῦς ἐμφαίνων τὸ
20 πρόσωπον, οὕτω πάλιν αὐτοῦ καὶ τὴν φύσιν καὶ τὴν ἐξουσίαν
|31 κηρύττει, λέγων αὐτὸν εἰρηκέναι, *ἐγώ εἰμι ὁ ὤν,* |*καὶ ἐγὼ ὁ*
Θεὸς . . . Ἀβραάμ, καὶ ὁ Θεὸς Ἰσαάκ, καὶ ὁ Θεὸς
Ἰακώβ . . . τοῦτό μοι . . . ὄνομα αἰώνιον καὶ μνημόσυνον γενεῶν
γενεαῖς.[i] ταῦτα δὲ καὶ τὴν θείαν οὐσίαν δηλοῖ καὶ τὸ αἰώνιον
25 καὶ τὸ ἀΐδιον δείκνυσιν.

---

v A⁻⁶ [32], B, 50, 7 9 10 17 31(inc.) 35 37 = 14 mss.

a. Ex 3.2   b. Ex 3.4   c. Ex 3.6   d. Ex 3.6   e. Ex 3.7   f. Ex 3.14
g. Is 9.6   h. Jn 15.15   i. Ex 3.14f.

v

Some commentators claim that an angel appeared to Moses in the burning bush.[1]

A reading of the text indicates who appeared. It says, "An angel of the Lord appeared in fiery flame issuing from the bush";[a] and shortly after, "When the Lord saw that he was approaching to see, the Lord called him from the bush";[b] and again a little later, "He said to him, I am the God of Abraham, the God of Isaac, and the God of Jacob."[c] The passage continues, "Moses averted his gaze, for he was afraid to look upon God";[d] and it adds, "I have indeed observed the abuse of my people in Egypt and heard their cry" and so on;[e] and again, "I am who am. You shall say this to the children of Israel: He who is has sent me to you."[f] The whole context shows that it was God who appeared to him.

Now, as he is also called "angel" we should realize that it was not God the Father who appeared to Moses. After all, is the Father anyone's messenger?[2] Rather, it was the only-begotten Son, "the angel of great counsel,"[g] he who said to the sacred disciples, "All I have heard from my Father I have revealed to you."[h] As Scripture uses the term "angel," not to suggest a subordinate minister, but to indicate the person of the Only-begotten, so it goes on to proclaim his nature and authority when it relates that he declared "I am who am," and "I am the God of Abraham, the God of Isaac, and the God of Jacob. This is my everlasting name and memorial for all generations."[i] This indicates his divinity and shows his everlasting eternity.

1. Guinot (p. 765). asks "Who are [these commentators]? Representatives of a Jewish exegesis or literalist exegetes like Theodore [of Mopsuestia]?"
2. *Cf. Q.* 90 on Gn and note 1.

VI

Τί δηλοῖ τὸ τὸν βάτον καίεσθαι καὶ μὴ κατακαίεσθαι;[a]

Τὴν τοῦ Θεοῦ δύναμιν καὶ φιλανθρωπίαν κηρύττει, ὅτι δή,
φρυγανώδη ὄντα, τὸ ἄσβεστον οὐκ ἀνήλισκε πῦρ. οἶμαι δὲ καὶ
ἕτερα διὰ τούτου παραδηλοῦσθαι· καὶ ὅτι ὁ Ἰσραήλ, ὑπὸ τῶν
5 αἰγυπτίων ἐπιβουλευόμενος, οὐκ ἀναλωθήσεται, ἀλλὰ κρείττων
ἔσται τῶν πολεμούντων, καὶ ὡς ὁ μονογενής, ἐνανθρωπήσας
καὶ παρθενικὴν οἰκήσας νηδύν, φυλάξει τὴν παρθενίαν
ἀκήρατον. φασὶ δέ τινες ἐν βάτῳ φανῆναι τὸν Θεόν, καὶ οὐκ
ἐν ἄλλῳ φυτῷ, διὰ τὸ μὴ δύνασθαί τινα ἐκ βάτου γλύψαι Θεόν·
10 εἰκὸς γὰρ ἦν ἰουδαίους καὶ τοῦτο τολμῆσαι εἴπερ ἐν ἄλλῳ
ὤφθη φυτῷ.

VII

Διὰ τί προσετάχθη ὁ Μωϋσῆς τὸ ὑπόδημα λῦσαι;[a]

Τινές φασιν ἵνα τὰς βιωτικὰς ἀπορρίψῃ μερίμνας, τὰς τῷ
θνητῷ βίῳ συνεζευγμένας· νεκρὰ γὰρ τῶν ὑποδημάτων τὰ
δέρματα· τινὲς δὲ ἵνα γυμνοῖς τοῖς ποσὶν ἁγιάσῃ τὴν γῆν.

---

vi A⁻⁶ *[32]*, B, C, 7 9 10 17 31 35 37 = 20 mss.

a. Ex 3.2

---

vii A⁻⁶ *[32]*, B, C, 7 9 10 17 31 35 37 = 20 mss.

l. 4. ἵνα γυμνοῖς τοῖς ποσὶν ἁγιάσῃ J.P. : ἵνα γυμνοῖς φασὶ τοῖς
ποσὶν ἁγιάσῃ Sir. Sch. : ἵνα γυμνοῖς, φησί, τοῖς ποσὶν ἁγιάσῃ F.M. I take
the verb indicating attribution (φησι) as an inept gloss. If F.M.'s note *ad loc.* is
reliable, the plural lacks all ms. support. The singular, of course, disagrees in
number with the preceding plural pronoun (τινὲς). Whether singular or plural,
it is oddly placed, and the transposed order of *C, 17 37* (ἵνα γυμνοῖς τοῖς
ποσὶν ἁγιάσῃ, φησί) suggests that its claim to a place in the text was
uncertain. *Cf.* the critical note for *Q.* 4 on Gn.

a. Ex 3.5

VI

What is the meaning of the verse "the bush was burning but not consumed?"[a]

The fact that the inextinguishable fire did not consume the dry wood proclaims God's power and loving-kindness. In my view, however, this suggests a number of other points as well: that Israel would not be consumed when subject to the schemes of the Egyptians but would prevail over its enemies, and that, when the Only-begotten became man and occupied the virgin's womb, he would preserve her maidenhood from defilement. Some commentators have claimed that God appeared in the bush rather than any other plant since no one can carve an image of God out of a bush. Indeed, the Jews probably would have attempted this if he had appeared in any other plant.

VII

Why was Moses ordered to take off his sandals?[a]

Some commentators have claimed he was to cast aside earthly cares linked to this mortal life, since the leather of sandals is dead. Others say he was to sanctify the ground with his bare feet. But I ac-

5 ἐγὼ δὲ οὐδέτερον τούτων προσίεμαι· πρῶτον μὲν γάρ, οὐδέπω
οὔτε ἀρχιερεὺς οὔτε προφήτης ἐκεχειροτόνητο· ἔπειτα δέ, τοῦ
Θεοῦ τὸν τόπον καθιερώσαντος καὶ τούτου χάριν ἅγιον
ὀνομάσαντος, περιττὸν οἶμαι λέγειν Μωϋσέα τοῖς ποσὶν
ἀγιάσαι τὸν τόπον.

10 Δύο τοίνυν ἡγοῦμαι διὰ τούτου δηλοῦσθαι· πρῶτον μὲν γὰρ
εὐλαβέστερον αὐτὸν τῷδε τῷ λόγῳ καθίστησιν ὥστε μετὰ
δέους τῶν προσταττομένων ἀκοῦσαι· ἔπειτα προπαιδεύεται
πῶς χρὴ τοὺς ἱερέας ἐν τῇ σκηνῇ λειτουργεῖν· γυμνοῖς γὰρ
κἀκεῖνοι ποσὶ τὰς λειτουργίας ἐπετέλουν καὶ τὰς θυσίας.[b]

VIII

Προειδὼς ὁ Θεὸς τοῦ Φαραὼ τὸ δυσπειθές, τί δή ποτε μὴ
ἐξ ἀρχῆς αὐτὸν ἐκόλασεν;

Ὅτι προῄδει δεδήλωκεν· *οἶδα, γάρ φησιν, ὅτι οὐ προήσεται
ὑμᾶς Φαραὼ βασιλεὺς Αἰγύπτου . . . εἰ μὴ μετὰ χειρὸς*
5 *κραταιᾶς. καὶ ἐκτείνας τὴν χεῖρα, πατάξω τοὺς αἰγυπτίους.*[a]
ἀλλ' ὅμως, ἀγαθὸς ὢν καὶ φιλάνθρωπος, κολάζειν ἐκ μόνης
προγνώσεως οὐκ ἀνέχεται, ἀλλ' ἀναμένει τῶν πραγμάτων τὸ
τέλος, καὶ δείκνυσιν ἅπασι τῆς τιμωρίας τὸ δίκαιον. ἄλλως τε
καὶ πολλῷ δικαιότερον τὸ τὴν ἐκείνου γυμνωθῆναι πονηρίαν
10 τοῦ τὸν Θεὸν ἀπηνῆ νομισθῆναι· εἰ γὰρ πρὸ τῶν ἐλέγχων
ἐκόλασεν, ἔδοξεν ἂν καὶ ὠμὸς εἶναι καὶ ἄδικος. νῦν δὲ καὶ τοῦ
Θεοῦ τὸ μακρόθυμον δέδεκται, κἀκείνου τὸ δυσσεβὲς καὶ
θηριῶδες ἐλήλεγκται.

---

b. *Cf.* Ex 30.19–21.

VIII A⁻⁶ *[32]*, B, C, 7 9 10 17 31 35 37 = 20 mss.
a. Ex 3.19f.

cept neither of these views. To begin with, no high priest or prophet had yet been appointed. Also, as God had consecrated the place and hence called it holy, I think it idle to claim that Moses sanctified the place with his feet.

In my view, this event indicates two things. First, God put him into a more reverent frame of mind, and Moses heeded his commands in fear. Next, he received prior instruction in how the priests ought to conduct worship in the tabernacle, as they also used to conduct rituals and sacrifices barefoot.[b]

VIII

Since God foresaw Pharaoh's disobedience, why did he not punish him from the outset?

That he knew in advance is indicated by "I know that Pharaoh king of Egypt will not let you go except with a mighty hand. I shall stretch out my hand and strike the Egyptians."[a] Yet, in his goodness and loving-kindness, he would not punish him solely on the basis of foreknowledge; instead he awaited the outcome of events and showed everyone the justice of his retribution. Above all, justice required that the Pharaoh's wickedness be laid bare rather than that God be thought harsh. If he had punished him before conviction, he would have seemed both cruel and unjust, while, this way, God's long-suffering was demonstrated and Pharaoh's impious ferocity exposed.

IX

Διὰ τί πρῶτον σημεῖον δέδωκε τῆς ῥάβδου τὴν εἰς ὄφιν μεταβολήν;[a]

Ἐπειδή, λογικῆς ὁ Φαραὼ φύσεως ὤν, ὠμότητι κατὰ τῶν ἑβραίων ἐχρήσατο καὶ τὸ θεοειδὲς θηριῶδες ἀπέφηνε, τὴν
5 ῥάβδον, δι' ἧς αὐτὸν ἐμαστίγωσεν, εἰς ὄφιν μεταβληθῆναι προσέταξεν· εἰς ἔλεγχον μὲν τῆς ἐκείνου θηριωδίας, ἔμφασιν δὲ τῆς δυσμενείας. καὶ γὰρ τῇ τοῦ ὄφεως ἀρᾷ καὶ τοῦτο προστέθεικεν· *ἔχθραν θήσω ἀνὰ μέσον σου καὶ ἀνὰ μέσον τῆς γυναικός, καὶ τὰ ἑξῆς.*[b]

ιχ A⁻⁶ *[32]*, B, C, *7 9 10 17 31 35 37* = 20 mss.

a. Ex 4.2–4   b. Gn 3.15

IX

Why did God give as his first sign the transformation of the rod into a serpent?[a]

Pharaoh, though endowed with human rationality, turned a God-given faculty into ferocity and behaved with savage cruelty towards the Hebrews. Therefore, God commanded that the rod, with which he scourged him, be turned into a serpent to reprove Pharaoh's ferocity and reveal his hostility. In fact, he had added to the curse of the serpent, "I shall put enmity between you and the woman" and so on.[b]

X

Ἡ λέπρωσις τῆς χειρὸς τί δηλοῖ;[a]

Ἐν εὐσεβείᾳ τραφέν, τὸ γένος τοῦ Ἰακὼβ εἰς τὴν Αἴγυπτον εἰσελήλυθεν ἀλλ' ἐκεῖ τῶν αἰγυπτίων μετέμαθε τὴν ἀσέβειαν, τῆς ἐκείνων δὲ δουλείας ἀπαλλαγείς, τὸν τῶν ὅλων ἐπέγνω
5 Θεόν. δεδήλωκε τοίνυν διὰ τῆς ἀλλοιώσεως τῆς χειρὸς τὴν λέπρωσιν αὐτῶν καὶ τὴν κάθαρσιν.

Πρὸς δὲ τούτοις καὶ ἕτερον ὁ δεσπότης ᾠκονόμει Θεός. ἐπειδὴ γὰρ ἤμελλε τὸν περὶ τῶν λεπρῶν τιθέναι νόμον καὶ ἀκαθάρτους τούτους προσαγορεύειν,[b] οὐδὲν δὲ τῶν ἀκουσίων
10 ἀκάθαρτον, ἕτερα δὲ διὰ τούτων οἰκονομῶν, τούτοις ἐχρήσατο τοῖς νόμοις, ἅπερ, ἐν ἐκείνοις γενόμενοι τοῖς χωρίοις, σὺν Θεῷ φάναι δηλώσομεν, ἐλέπρωσε τοῦ νομοθέτου τὴν χεῖρα, τοὺς τὰ τέλεια πεπαιδευμένους διδάσκων ὡς οὐδὲν τῶν τοιούτων ἀκάθαρτον· ἡ γὰρ τὰ θαύματα ἐκεῖνα ἐργασαμένη
15 δεξιά, λεπρὰ πρότερον γενομένη, ταῖς θεοσημείαις ὑπούργησε καὶ τὰ στοιχεῖα μετέβαλεν. τούτῳ δὲ καὶ τὸν νομοθέτην ἐπαίδευσεν μὴ μέγα φρονεῖν ἀλλ' εἰδέναι τὴν φύσιν, τῆς λεπρωθείσης ἀναμιμνησκόμενον δεξιᾶς.

---

x A⁻⁶ [32], B, C, 7 9 10 17 31 35 37 = 20 mss.

l. 10 ἕτερα δὲ a [32], 12, B, 51 53, 9 31, Pic. (Sch.) : ἕτερα Sir. Sch. F.M. = "As he was planning to establish a law about lepers and declare them 'unclean,' but there is nothing unclean where there is no act of will, he made use of these laws to effect other purposes of his own, as, with God's help, we shall indicate when we come to those passages. He made the lawgiver's hand leprous to teach the perfectly instructed that no such thing is unclean." The connective particle δέ is needed to bind ἕτερα ... τοῖς νόμοις to the conjunction ἐπειδὴ and divide it from the following main verb ἐλέπρωσε. The reading preferred by Sir., Sch., and F.M. separates ἕτερα, etc. from the conjunction ἐπειδὴ; requiring the initiation of a new sentence at ἐλέπρωσε, it creates a very unlikely asyndeton.

l. 16 τούτῳ δὲ J.P. : τοῦτο δὲ 2c [32], B, 10 17 : διὰ τοῦτο δὲ 35 = "On account of this, God also instructed the lawgiver" : διὰ τούτου δὲ 9 = "By means of this, God also instructed the lawgiver" : ἐκ τούτου δὲ 11, C, 37, Sir. Sch. = "From this point on, God also instructed the lawgiver" : τούτου δὲ F.M. Only the dative gives the appropriate sense; cf. Thdt., Dan. 5.9 (Τούτῳ δὲ καταπλήξας, etc.) and Q. 37.3 on Gn (τούτῳ μὲν ... μηχανώμενος).

a. Ex 4.6f.   b. Lv 13.9–11

X

What was the significance of the leprous hand?[a]

Jacob's family, raised in right religion, entered Egypt, where they learned the idolatry of the Egyptians, but when freed from slavery to the Egyptians, they acknowledged the God of the universe. Thus, through the change in his hand, he revealed their leprosy and their cleansing.

In addition, the Lord God had something else in mind. As he was planning to establish a law about lepers and declare them "unclean,"[b] but there is nothing unclean where there is no act of will, and he made use of these laws to effect other purposes of his own (as, with God's help, we shall indicate when we come to those passages), he made the lawgiver's hand leprous to teach the perfectly instructed that no such thing is unclean. Indeed, the right hand that worked those marvels ministered to the divine signs and wrought changes in the elements only after it had previously been leprous. In this way God also instructed the lawgiver not to become presumptuous, but to acknowledge his nature whenever he recalled that right hand covered in leprosy.

XI

Ὑπουργῷ κεχρημένος τῷ Μωϋσῇ τῶν ὅλων ὁ Κύριος, τί δή
ποτε ἰσχνόφωνον αὐτὸν διέπλασε καὶ βραδύγλωσσον;ᵃ
Ἐπειδὴ τοῦτο μᾶλλον τὴν δύναμιν ἐδείκνυ τὴν θείαν·
ὥσπερ γὰρ ἁλιέας,ᵇ καὶ τελώνας,ᶜ καὶ σκυτοτόμουςᵈ κήρυκας
5 ἀληθείας καὶ διδασκάλους εὐσεβείας ἐχειροτόνησεν, οὕτω διὰ
φωνῆς ἀσθενοῦς καὶ γλώσσης βραδείας κατήσχυνε τοὺς
αἰγυπτίων σοφούς.ᵉ

XII

Πῶς νοητέον τὸ ἐγώ ... σκληρυνῶ τὴν καρδίαν Φαραώ;ᵃ
(1) Μάλα ῥᾴδιον ἦν τῷ Θεῷ μετὰ τὴν πρώτην ἀπείθειαν
πανωλεθρίαν ἐπαγαγεῖν ἀλλ', ἀφράστῳ κεχρημένος μακροθυμίᾳ,
μετρίας αὐτῷ παιδείας ἐπήγαγε. ταῦτα δὲ ἀντίτυπον ἐποίει
5 τὴν ἐκείνου καρδίαν· οἰόμενος γὰρ μὴ δύνασθαι τὸν Θεὸν
μείζοσι χρήσασθαι τιμωρίαις, τῶν μετρίων κατεφρόνει
μαστίγων. καὶ ὅτι ταῦθ' οὕτως ἔχει ἡ ἱστορία διδάσκει·
πρῶτον μὲν γὰρ τῶν θείων ἐκείνων ἀκούσας ῥημάτων,
ἐξαπόστειλον τὸν λαόν μου ἵνα μοι λατρεύσωσιν ἐν τῇ ἐρήμῳ,ᵇ
10 ὑπολαβὼν ἔφη, τίς ἐστι Κύριος; οὐκ εἰσακούσομαι τῆς φωνῆς
αὐτοῦ· ... οὐκ οἶδα τὸν Κύριον καὶ τὸν Ἰσραὴλ οὐκ
ἐξαποστελῶ.ᶜ ἔπειτα δέ, τῆς ῥάβδου μεταβληθείσης εἰς ὄφιν,
φησὶν ἡ θεία γραφή, καὶ κατίσχυσεν ἡ καρδία Φαραώ, καὶ οὐκ
εἰσήκουσεν αὐτῶν καθάπερ ἐλάλησεν αὐτοῖς Κύριος·ᵈ καὶ εὐθὺς

xi A⁻⁶ *[32]*, B, C, 7 9 10 17 31* 35 37 = 20 mss.

a. Ex 4.10   b. Mt 4.18f.; Mk 1.16–20   c. Mt 9.9; Mk 2.14; Lk 5.27f.
d. Acts 18.3   e. Ex 4.10

xii A⁻⁶ *[32]*, B, C, 7 9 10 17 31*(inc.) 35 37 = 20 mss.

a. Ex 7.3   b. Ex 5.1   c. Ex 5.2   d. Ex 7.13

XI

Why did the Lord of the universe make Moses, his minister, stammering and slow of speech?[a]

Because this showed forth God's power all the more. Just as he appointed fishermen,[b] tax collectors,[c] and cobblers[d] heralds of truth and teachers of religion, so he confounded the Egyptian sages with a weak voice and a slow tongue.[e]

^e

XII

How should we understand, "I shall harden Pharaoh's heart"?[1a]

(1) It would have been an easy matter for God to destroy him after his first act of disobedience. Instead, in his ineffable long-suffering, God punished Pharaoh with but a moderate chastisement. Yet, this only made his heart obstinate. Thinking God could not apply heavier punishments, he scorned the moderate scourge. The sequence of events proves this. First, on hearing the divine words, "Let my people go so that they may worship me in the wilderness,"[b] he retorted, "Who is the Lord? I shall not heed his voice. I do not know the Lord and will not let Israel go."[c] Next, when the rod was changed into a serpent, holy Scripture says, "The heart of Pharaoh grew in strength, and he did not listen to them as the Lord had said to them";[d] and it continues, "The Lord said to Moses,

---

1. Schulze (PG, vol. 80, col. 233, note 66) complains of the length of this reply (*satis prolixa quidem est quaestio*), but Theodoret wishes to examine the implications for free will entailed by the scriptural statements deriving Pharaoh's obduracy from divine causation. This is an important moral principle, especially for an Antiochene; *v.* sec. 9 of the "Introduction to Theodoret' s Life and Works" and *cf.* J.N.D. Kelly, who attributes (*Early Christian Doctrines*, p. 373) to the Antiochenes "an intensified emphasis on individualism."

The Questions on Exodus

15 ἐπάγει, εἶπε δὲ Κύριος πρὸς Μωϋσῆν, βεβάρηται ἡ καρδία
Φαραὼ τοῦ μὴ ἐξαποστεῖλαι τὸν λαόν.ᵉ

(2) Ἀμφότερα δὲ σημαίνει τὸ τῆς γνώμης αὐθαίρετον· καὶ
τὸ κατίσχυσεν ἡ καρδία Φαραὼ καὶ τὸ βεβάρηται ἡ καρδία
Φαραώ. βαρύνεται μὲν γὰρ καρδία ὑπὸ πονηρίας καθελκομένη.

20 καὶ τοῦτο σαφῶς ἡμᾶς διδάσκει ὁ μακάριος Δαβίδ· αἱ ἀνομίαι
μου, γάρ φησιν, ὑπερῆραν τὴν κεφαλήν μου, ὡσεὶ φορτίον
βαρὺ ἐβαρύνθησαν ἐπ' ἐμέ.ᶠ καὶ ὁ Ζαχαρίας τὴν ἀνομίαν
ἐθεάσατο, μολίβδου τάλαντον ἐν τῷ στόματι φέρουσαν.ᵍ ἡ δέ
γε, ἀπονοίᾳ χρωμένη, κατισχύειν λέγεται ὡς ἀνθισταμένη τῷ

25 δεσπότῃ Θεῷ καὶ νικᾶν αὐτοῦ νεανιευομένη τὴν δύναμιν· ἡ
γὰρ εὐσεβὴς ὑποτάττεται κατὰ τὴν προφητικὴν παραίνεσιν,
τὴν λέγουσαν, ὑποτάγηθι τῷ Κυρίῳ καὶ ἱκέτευσον αὐτόν.ʰ ἡ δέ
γε ἀντίτυπος καὶ οἱονεὶ λιθίνη σκληρύνεται· ὅθεν ὁ τῶν ὅλων
‖31 Θεὸς διὰ τοῦ προφήτου Ἰεζεκιὴλ περὶ τῶν ἰουδαίων‖ ἔφη, καὶ

30 ἐκσπάσω τὴν καρδίαν τὴν λιθίνην ἐξ αὐτῶν.ⁱ διά τοι τοῦτο καὶ
ὁ μακάριος Μωϋσῆς, τὴν ἐπινίκιον ᾄδων ᾠδὴν περὶ τοῦ Φαραὼ
καὶ τῶν αἰγυπτίων, εἴρηκε, κατέδυσαν εἰς βυθὸν ὡσεὶ λίθος·ʲ
καὶ πάλιν, ἔδυσαν ὡσεὶ μόλιβδος ἐν ὕδατι σφοδρῷ.ᵏ ἐπειδὴ γὰρ
ἐβάρυναν αὐτῶν τὴν καρδίαν, ἔδυσαν ὡσεὶ μόλιβδος· ἐπειδὴ δὲ

35 καὶ ἐσκλήρυναν, κατέδυσαν εἰς βυθὸν ὡσεὶ λίθος. ὅτι δὲ ἡ
ἀντιτυπία τῆς καρδίας καὶ ἡ σκληρότης ὑφ' ἡμῶν αὐτῶν
γίνεται μάρτυς ὁ θεῖος ἀπόστολος λέγων, ἀγνοῶν ὅτι τὸ
χρηστὸν τοῦ Θεοῦ εἰς μετάνοιάν σε ἄγει; κατὰ δὲ τὴν
σκληρότητά σου καὶ ἀμετανόητον καρδίαν θησαυρίζεις σεαυτῷ

40 ὀργὴν ἐν ἡμέρᾳ ὀργῆς, καὶ ἀποκαλύψεως, καὶ δικαιοκρισίας τοῦ
Θεοῦ, ὃς ἀποδώσει ἑκάστῳ κατὰ τὰ ἔργα αὐτοῦ.ˡ

(3) Πρὸς δὲ τούτοις κἀκεῖνο σκοπητέον, ὡς εἰ φύσει
πονηρὸς ἦν ὁ Φαραώ, οὐκ ἂν αὐτοῦ τὴν γνώμην ἐνήλλαξε. νῦν
δὲ ὁρῶμεν ὑπὸ μὲν τῆς παιδείας αὐτὸν μαλαττόμενον, ὑπὸ δὲ

45 τῆς μακροθυμίας σκληρυνόμενον· παιδευόμενος γὰρ ἠντιβόλει

l. 34 αὐτῶν J.P. : ἑαυτῶν 11, c₁, 37, Sir. Sch. : αὐτῶν F.M.

e. Ex 7.14   f. Ps 38.4   g. Zec 5.7   h. Ps 37.7   i. Ezek 11.19   j. Ex 15.5
k. Ex 15.10   l. Rom 2.4–6

238

'Pharaoh's heart has been weighed down so that he will not let the people go.'"e

(2) Both expressions, "The heart of Pharaoh grew in strength" and "Pharaoh's heart has been weighed down," point to his free will. First, hearts that are weighed down are pulled down by wickedness, as the blessed David informs us in unequivocal terms: "My sins rose above my head; they bore down upon me like a heavy load."f And Zechariah had a vision of Iniquity bearing a talent of lead in her mouth.g Second, when the heart is in the grip of madness, it is said to grow in strength, as it sets itself in opposition to the Lord God and rebelliously seeks to prevail against him. While the devout heart subjects itself according to the prophet's exhortation, "Be subject to the Lord, and implore him,"h the resistant is hardened like stone. Hence, through the prophet Ezekiel, the God of the universe said of the Jews, "I shall pluck out their heart of stone."i For the same reason, the blessed Moses, in his victory song about Pharaoh and the Egyptians, declared, "They went down into the depths like a stone";j and again, "They sank like lead in churning water."k Since their hearts were weighed down, "they sank like lead," and since they were also hardened, "they went down into the depths like a stone." Now, the holy apostle offers confirmation that the resistance and hardness of heart originate in ourselves when he says, "Are you unaware that God's kindness leads you to repentance? In your hardness and impenitence of heart you are storing up wrath for yourself on the day of wrath and the revelation of the righteous judgment of God, who will repay each according to his deeds."l

(3) In addition, we should consider that if Pharaoh's evil had been rooted in his very constitution, he would not have changed his mind. In fact, we see him softened by correction but hardened by forbearance. When corrected, he appealed to the lawgiver and said,

τὸν νομοθέτην, *προσεύξασθε περὶ ἐμοῦ*[m] *λέγων·* καὶ πάλιν, ὁ
Κύριος δίκαιος, ἐγὼ δὲ καὶ ὁ λαός μου ἀσεβεῖς[n] τῆς δὲ
τιμωρίας παυομένης, ἐβαρύνετο, καὶ ἐσκληρύνετο, καὶ τοῖς
προστάγμασι τοῖς θείοις ἀντέλεγε. καὶ τῆς μὲν κυνομυίας
50 ἐπενεχθείσης, *ἐν Αἰγύπτῳ θῦσαι προσέταξε τῷ Θεῷ.*[o] τοῦ
θειοτάτου δὲ Μωϋσέως εἰρηκότος μὴ δύνασθαι τοῦτο δρᾶσαι
διὰ τοὺς αἰγυπτίους· *τὰ γὰρ ὑπ' ἐκείνων, φησί, θεοποιούμενα*
θύσομεν, καὶ καταλεύοντες ἡμᾶς ἀποκτενοῦσιν·[p] ἐπέτρεψεν
εἰς τὴν ἔρημον ἀπελθεῖν καὶ τὰς θυσίας ἐπιτελέσαι.[q] ἐπὶ
55 τούτοις τοῦ προφήτου προσευξαμένου καὶ τὴν κυνόμυιαν
ἀποφήναντος φροῦδον, *ἐβάρυνε, φησί, ... τὴν καρδίαν αὐτοῦ*
καὶ ἐπὶ τούτου τοῦ καιροῦ καὶ οὐκ ἠθέλησεν ἐξαποστεῖλαι τὸν
λαόν.[r] τοῦτο καὶ ἐπὶ τοῦ λοιμοῦ γεγένηται τῶν κτηνῶν· *εἶδε,*
φησί, Φαραὼ ὅτι οὐκ ἐτελεύτησεν ἀπὸ πάντων τῶν κτηνῶν
60 *τῶν υἱῶν Ἰσραὴλ οὐδὲ ἕν, καὶ ἐβαρύνθη ἡ καρδία Φαραώ, καὶ*
οὐκ ἐξαπέστειλε τὸν λαόν·[s] ἐν τούτοις ἅπασι δείξας τὸ τῆς
γνώμης αὐθαίρετον. καὶ διδάξας ὅπως αὐτοῖς ἐπηνέχθη τῶν
φλυκταινῶν τὸ πάθος,[t] καὶ ὅτι τοῖς φαρμάκοις ἡ νόσος
ἐπέσκηψε, *καὶ οὐκ ἠδύναντο οἱ φάρμακοι στῆναι ἐναντίον*
65 *Μωϋσῆ διὰ τὰ ἕλκη*[u] ἠσχύνοντο γὰρ καθηλκωμένοι καὶ σφίσιν
αὐτοῖς ἐπαμῦναι μὴ δυνάμενοι· ἐπήγαγε, καὶ
ἐσκλήρυνε ... Κύριος τὴν καρδίαν Φαραώ, καὶ οὐκ εἰσήκουσεν
αὐτῶν καθὰ συνέταξεν αὐτοῖς Κύριος.[v] καὶ μετ' ὀλίγα πρὸς
αὐτὸν ἔφη τὸν Φαραώ, *ἕνεκεν τούτου διετηρήθης, ἵνα*
70 *ἐνδείξωμαι ἐν σοὶ τὴν ἰσχύν μου, καὶ ὅπως διαγγελῇ τὸ ὄνομά*
μου ἐν πάσῃ τῇ γῇ.[w] καὶ αὖθις μετ' ὀλίγα καὶ ταῦτα ἔφη·
ἰδών..., γάρ φησι, Φαραὼ ὅτι πέπαυται ὁ ὑετός, καὶ ἡ
χάλαζα, καὶ αἱ φωναί, καὶ προσέθετο Φαραὼ τοῦ ἁμαρτάνειν·
καὶ ἐβάρυνε τὴν καρδίαν αὐτοῦ καὶ τῶν θεραπόντων αὐτοῦ, καὶ
75 *ἐσκληρύνθη ἡ καρδία Φαραώ, καὶ οὐκ ἐξαπέστειλε τοὺς υἱοὺς*
Ἰσραὴλ καθάπερ ἐλάλησε Κύριος τῷ Μωϋσῆ.[x] τὸ δὲ *καθάπερ*

m. Ex 8.8   n. Ex 9.27   o. Ex 8.24f.   p. Ex 8.26   q. Ex 8.28
r. Ex 8.32   s. Ex 9.7   t. Ex 9.8–10   u. Ex 9.8–11   v. Ex 9.12
w. Ex 9.16   x. Ex 9.34f.

"Pray for me";[m] and again, "The Lord is righteous, and I and my people impious."[n] But when the punishment ceased, he was weighed down and hardened and resisted the commands of God. Then, when the plague of dog flies was sent upon him, he ordered that sacrifices be offered to God within Egypt.[o] When the divinely inspired Moses replied that he could not offer these because of the Egyptians—"If we sacrifice creatures they regard as gods, they will stone us to death"[p]—he permitted them to withdraw into the desert and perform the sacrifices there.[q] Later, when, on these terms, the prophet prayed and brought an end to the plague of dog flies, as Scripture says, "he weighed down his heart this time as well and refused to let the people go."[r] This happened also in the pestilence of the cattle: "Pharaoh saw that none of all the cattle of the children of Israel had died, and the heart of Pharaoh was hardened, and he did not let the people go."[s] In all these cases he demonstrated his own freedom of will. Then relating how the scourge of boils was brought upon them and fell upon the sorcerers,[t] "and the sorcerers were unable to stand before Moses because of their sores"[u]—ashamed as they were of their ulcers and their inability to help themselves—Scripture adds, "The Lord hardened Pharaoh's heart, and he did not hearken to them as the Lord had ordained for them."[v] And shortly after, God said to Pharaoh, "This is why you have been spared: for me to demonstrate my power in you, and for my name to be proclaimed in all the earth."[w] Again, shortly after this, the text says, "Pharaoh saw that the rain, hail, and thunder had stopped, and Pharaoh went further in sinning; he weighed down his heart and that of his attendants. Pharaoh's heart was hardened, and he did not let the children of Israel go as the Lord had said to Moses."[x] The clause "as the Lord

ἐλάλησε τὴν πρόγνωσιν τοῦ Θεοῦ δηλοῖ ἀντὶ τοῦ· οὐδὲν
τούτων ἠγνόησεν ὁ τῶν ὅλων Θεὸς ἀλλ' ἐξ ἀρχῆς προείρηκε.

(4) Ταῦτα δὲ πάντα διεξῆλθον δεῖξαι βουλόμενος ὡς οὔτε
80 φύσεως ἦν ὁ Φαραὼ πονηρᾶς, οὔτε ὁ δεσπότης Θεὸς σκληρὰν
αὐτοῦ καὶ ἀντίτυπον τὴν γνώμην εἰργάσατο· ὁ γὰρ νῦν μὲν
εἰς τοῦτο ῥέπων, νῦν δὲ εἰς ἐκεῖνο, δείκνυσι τὸ τῆς γνώμης
αὐθαίρετον. ἵνα δὲ καὶ ἔκ τινος εἰκόνος τὸ ἀμφιβαλλόμενον
διαλύσω· ὁ ἥλιος τῇ τῆς θέρμης ἐνεργείᾳ τὸν μὲν κηρὸν
85 ὑγραίνει, τὸν δὲ πηλὸν ξηραίνει καὶ τὸν μὲν μαλάττει, τὸν δὲ
σκληρύνει. ὥσπερ τοίνυν οὗτος τῇ ἐνεργείᾳ τῇ μιᾷ τὰ ἐναντία
|31 ποιεῖ, οὕτω τῇ τοῦ Θεοῦ τῶν ὅλων μακροθυμίᾳ Ιοἱ μὲν
ὠφέλειαν, οἱ δὲ βλάβην καρποῦνται· καὶ οἱ μὲν μαλάττονται,
||31 οἱ δὲ σκληρύνονται.||

90 Τοῦτο καὶ ὁ Κύριος ἐν τοῖς ἱεροῖς εὐαγγελίοις δεδήλωκεν·
εἰς κρῖμα, γάρ φησιν, ἐγὼ εἰς τὸν κόσμον τοῦτον ἦλθον, ἵνα
οἱ μὴ βλέποντες βλέπωσι, καὶ οἱ βλέποντες τυφλοὶ γένωνται.[y]
τοῦτο δὲ οὐ τοῦ δεσπότου δηλοῖ τὸν σκοπόν· οὐδὲ γὰρ τούτου
χάριν ἐλήλυθεν, ἵνα τυφλοὺς ἀποφήνῃ τοὺς βλέποντας· ἀλλὰ
95 τὸ γεγενημένον δεδήλωκεν. αὐτὸς μὲν γὰρ βούλεται *πάντας*
ἀνθρώπους ... σωθῆναι καὶ εἰς ἐπίγνωσιν ἀληθείας ἐλθεῖν.[z]
ἐπειδὴ δὲ τὸ αὐθαίρετον ἔχει τῶν ἀνθρώπων ἡ φύσις, οἱ
μὲν πεπιστευκότες τῆς σωτηρίας ἀπήλαυσαν, οἱ δὲ
ἀπιστήσαντες πρόξενοι ἑαυτοῖς τῆς γεέννης γεγένηνται.
100 οὕτως ὁ Ἰούδας βλέπων· ἀπόστολος γὰρ ἦν· ὕστερον
ἐτυφλώθη, ὁ δὲ θεσπέσιος Παῦλος, τυφλὸς ὢν πρότερον,
ἀνέβλεψεν ὕστερον.[aa] οὕτω διὰ τῆς τοῦ σωτῆρος ἐπιφανείας
ἐτυφλώθησαν μὲν τῶν ἰουδαίων οἱ πλεῖστοι, ἀνέβλεψαν δὲ τὰ
ἔθνη. οὐ μήν, ἐπειδή τινες ἔμελλον ἀπιστήσειν, ἐχρῆν μὴ
105 γενέσθαι τὴν κατὰ σάρκα τοῦ σωτῆρος ἡμῶν οἰκονομίαν·
τοῦτο γὰρ ἀπεστέρει τὴν οἰκουμένην τῆς σωτηρίας. οὕτω καὶ
ὁ θειότατος ἔφη Συμεών, *ἰδοὺ οὗτος κεῖται εἰς πτῶσιν καὶ*

y. Jn 9.39   z. 1Tm 2.4   aa. Acts 9.18

had said" reveals God's foreknowledge. It amounts to saying that the God of the universe had not been ignorant of any of this but had foretold it from the outset.

(4) The purpose of my narrative recital has been to bring out that Pharaoh was not constitutionally evil, and that it was not the Lord God who caused his will to be hardened and resistant. His moving first in this direction then in that highlights his freedom of will. Let me clarify the issue with a simile. The sun with its heat melts wax but dries mud: softening one and hardening the other. As the same heat produces opposite effects, so from God's loving-kindness some reap benefit, others harm; some are softened, others hardened.

The Lord himself revealed this in the sacred Gospels: "I have come into this world for judgment, so that those who do not may see, and those who see may become blind."[y] Now, this does not suggest the Lord's intention—he did not come with the purpose of blinding those with sight—but reveals what actually happened.[2] For "it is his wish that everyone be saved and come to the knowledge of the truth."[z] But since human beings are naturally endowed with free will, the believers enjoyed salvation while the unbelievers bore the responsibility for bringing Hell upon themselves. Thus, Judas, who had sight as an apostle, was later blinded, whereas Paul, the divinely inspired, though originally blind, later opened his eyes.[aa] With the coming of the Savior, most of the Jews were blinded, but the gentiles opened their eyes. The fact that some would not believe did not mean that the Incarnation of our Savior should not have taken place. That would have deprived the world of salvation. Thus, Simeon, the most holy, said, "Lo, this one is destined for the fall

2. One may debate the appositeness of the dominical saying, which itself quotes Is 12.40. As R.E. Brown observes (p. 376), "the line of distinction between the result of Jesus' ministry and its purpose is not drawn sharply because of the oversimplified outlook which attributes everything that happens to God's purpose." This, of course, is precisely Theodoret's concern.

ἀνάστασιν πολλῶν ἐν τῷ Ἰσραὴλ καὶ εἰς σημεῖον
ἀντιλεγόμενον.[bb]

110 Κἀκεῖνο μέντοι εἰδέναι χρή, ὡς τὸν παρόντα βίον ὁ τῶν
ὅλων Θεὸς στάδιον τοῖς ἀνθρώποις ἀπέφηνεν ἵν', ἐν τούτῳ
ἀγωνιζόμενοι, δηλώσωσι τὸν οἰκεῖον σκοπόν. ἐν δέ γε τῷ
μέλλοντι, τὴν δικαίαν ποιούμενος κρίσιν, τοὺς μὲν ὡς
νικηφόρους ἀγωνιστὰς στεφανώσει,[cc] τοὺς δὲ κολάσει ὡς τῆς
115 κακίας ἐργάτας γεγενημένους.[dd] ἐπειδὴ δὲ οὐχ ἅπαντες τῷ
μέλλοντι πιστεύουσι βίῳ, μάλα σοφῶς ὁ τῶν ὅλων Θεὸς καὶ
κολάζει τινὰς ἐν τῷδε τῷ βίῳ πονηρίᾳ συνεζηκότας καὶ αὖ
πάλιν ἄλλους ἀνακηρύττει εὐσεβείας πεφροντικότας ὡς
μάλιστα. τούτου χάριν ὁ θεῖος ἀπόστολος τινὰς μὲν *σκεύη*
120 *ὀργῆς*, τινὰς δὲ *σκεύη ἐλέους* ὠνόμασεν,[ee] ἐπειδὴ δι' ἐκείνων
μὲν δῆλος γίνεται κολάζων ἐνδίκως ὁ δεσπότης Θεός, διὰ δὲ
τούτων ἐπιμελείας παντοδαπῆς ἀξιῶν καὶ προμηθείας τοὺς
τῆς ἀρετῆς ἀθλητάς.

(5) Ἴδοι δ' ἄν τις καὶ τῶν σωμάτων τοὺς ἰατροὺς τομαῖς
125 καὶ καυτῆρσι χρωμένους, καὶ τοὺς κεκρυμμένους χυμοὺς καὶ
χαλεπὴν τὴν νόσον ἐργαζομένους ἀναμοχλεύοντας καὶ
ἐξάγοντας, καὶ τὰ λανθάνοντα πάθη δῆλα ποιοῦντας. οὕτως
καὶ ὁ τῶν ὅλων Θεὸς τῶν λογισμῶν τὴν πονηρίαν ταῖς
παιδείαις γυμνοῖ· τοῦτο γὰρ καὶ ἐν τῷ Δευτερονομίῳ πρὸς τὸν
130 Ἰσραὴλ ἔφη· *καὶ μνησθήσῃ πᾶσαν τὴν ὁδόν, ἣν ἤγαγέ σε*
Κύριος ὁ Θεός σου τεσσαρακοστὸν ἔτος ἐν τῇ ἐρήμῳ,
ὅπως ... κακώσῃ σε, καὶ πειράσῃ σε, καὶ διαγνωσθῇ τὰ ἐν τῇ
καρδίᾳ σου· εἰ φυλάξῃ τὰς ἐντολὰς αὐτοῦ, ἢ οὔ. καὶ ἐκάκωσέ
σε καὶ ἐλιμαγχόνησέ σε, καὶ τὰ ἑξῆς.[ff]

135 Καθάπερ δὲ πάλιν οἱ ἰατροὶ τοὺς ἀνηκέστως διακειμένους,
πολλῶν παρόντων, τέμνουσιν, οὐκ ἐκείνοις τοσοῦτον
ἐπικουροῦντες· ἴσασι γὰρ αὐτῶν τὴν νόσον ἀνίατον· ἀλλὰ
τοὺς φοιτητὰς τὸν τῆς ἰατρείας διδάσκοντες τρόπον, οὕτω

---

bb. Lk 2.34   cc. *Cf.* 1Cor 9.25; 2Tm 4.7f.   dd. Lk 13.27   ee. Rom 9.22f.
ff. Dt 8.2f.

and rise of many in Israel and for a sign that will be contradicted."[bb]

Of course, we should also realize that the God of the universe constituted the present life as a race for human beings so that each might reveal his goal in the course of the contest. In the future life he will render righteous judgment and crown some as victorious athletes[cc] and punish others as workers of iniquity.[dd] Now, since there are those who do not believe in the life to come, even in the course of this present life, the God of the universe, in his great wisdom, punishes some for their wickedness and celebrates others for their great devotion to religion. Thus, the holy apostle calls some people "vessels of wrath" and others "vessels of mercy,"[3ee] since, in the case of the former, the Lord God is seen to punish justly and, in the latter, to accord the athletes of virtue every sort of providential care.

(5) We have all observed bodily surgeons using surgery and cautery to draw up and let out the hidden humors that cause severe illness and to bring to light concealed ailments. So the God of the universe by his chastisements lays bare the wickedness of our thoughts. In the book of Deuteronomy he declared to Israel, "You shall remember all the way the Lord your God led you for forty years in the wilderness so as to afflict and test you and discover what was in your heart, whether you would keep his commandments or not. He afflicted you and exposed you to hunger" and so on.[ff]

Indeed, as surgeons will conduct operations on the incurably ill before a large audience, not so much to help the sick—for they know that the illness is incurable—as to teach their pupils the doctor's craft, so too God inflicted every sort of punishment on Pharaoh as

3. In Rom 9.22f. Paul cites Pharaoh to illustrate his thesis of the gratuity of divine mercy. Again, this is at odds with Theodoret's argument; cf. R.C. Hill, "Theodoret Wrestling with Romans."

καὶ τὸν Φαραώ, ὠμοτάτῃ καὶ θηριώδει χρησάμενον γνώμῃ,
140 ταῖς παντοδαπαῖς τιμωρίαις ὑπέβαλεν ὁ Θεός, πάντας ὡς
ἐπίπαν διδάσκων ἀνθρώπους ὡς αὐτὸς ἰθύνει τὴν κτίσιν· καὶ
τοῖς μὲν ἀδικουμένοις ἐπαμύνει δικαίως, κολάζει δὲ τοὺς
ἀδικοῦντας ἐν δίκῃ· τοῦτο γὰρ καὶ πρὸς αὐτὸν ἔφη τὸν
Φαραώ· *ἕνεκεν τούτου διετηρήθης, ἵνα ἐνδείξωμαι ἐν σοὶ τὴν*
145 *ἰσχύν μου, καὶ ὅπως διαγγελῇ τὸ ὄνομά μου ἐν πάσῃ τῇ γῇ.*[gg]
ὅτι δὲ πάντοσε διέδραμε τῶν πεπραγμένων ἡ μνήμη μαρτυρεῖ
μὲν Ῥαὰβ ἡ πόρνη λέγουσα τοῖς κατασκόποις ὅτι, *ὁ φόβος*
ὑμῶν καὶ ὁ τρόμος ὑμῶν ἐπέπεσεν ἐφ' ἡμᾶς· ἠκούσαμεν γὰρ
ὅπως κατεξήρανε Κύριος ὁ Θεὸς ὑμῶν τὴν ἐρυθρὰν θάλασσαν
150 *πρὸ προσώπου ὑμῶν·*[hh] μαρτυροῦσι δὲ καὶ οἱ ἀλλόφυλοι
πόρρωθεν τὴν κιβωτὸν θεασάμενοι καὶ βοήσαντες, *οὐαὶ ἡμῖν,*
ἀλλόφυλοι, . . . οὗτος ὁ Θεός, ὁ πατάξας τὴν Αἴγυπτον.[ii]

XIII

Διὰ τί δὲ συνεχώρησεν ταῦτα παθεῖν τὸν λαὸν ὁ Θεός;
Ἵνα, μὴ μόνον τοὺς αἰγυπτίους, ἀλλὰ καὶ τοὺς ἐκείνων
μισήσωσι θεούς, ὡς τοιαῦτα παρ' αὐτῶν πεπονθότες, καὶ ἵνα
συντόμως ὑπακούσωσιν, ἐξελθεῖν κελευόμενοι. εἰ γάρ, καὶ
5 τούτων οὕτω γεγενημένων, ἀνεμιμνήσκοντο τῆς ἐν Αἰγύπτῳ
τρυφῆς καὶ πολλάκις ἐπειράθησαν ἀναστρέψαι, τίς ἂν αὐτοὺς
ἔπεισε καταλιπεῖν τὴν Αἴγυπτον, μηδὲν παρ' αὐτῶν
πεπονθότας δεινόν;

gg. Ex 9.16   hh. Jos 2.9f.   ii. 1Sm 4.8

XIII A⁻⁶ [32], B, C, 7 9 10 17 31 35 37 = 20 mss.

he pursued his cruel and savage will in order to teach people everywhere that it is he who governs creation, who justly assists the wronged and takes righteous vengeance on those who do wrong. As he said to Pharaoh, "This is why you have been spared: for me to demonstrate my power in you, and for my name to be proclaimed in all the earth."[gg] Evidence that a report of these events circulated everywhere is provided by Rahab the prostitute, who told the spies, "Fear of you and dread of you has fallen on us, for we have heard how the Lord your God dried up the Red Sea before you."[hh] The Philistines also confirmed this, when, upon seeing the ark from afar, they cried out, "Woe is us, Philistines, this is the God who smote Egypt."[ii]

XIII

Why did God allow the people to endure these sufferings?

So they would hate the Egyptians and their gods for inflicting such sufferings upon them, and so they would not delay in obeying the command to leave. After all, if even despite their sufferings, they remembered the luxury of Egypt and often tried to turn back, who could have convinced them to leave if they had endured no harsh treatment from the Egyptians?

XIV

Διὰ τί ἠβουλήθη ὁ ἄγγελος ἀνελεῖν τὸν Μωϋσῆν;[a]

Ἡ γυνὴ μὲν ἐτόπασε διὰ τὸ θάτερον τῶν παιδίων μὴ
περιτμηθῆναι κατὰ τὸν τῶν ἑβραίων νόμον· παραυτίκα γοῦν
αὐτῷ τὴν περιτομὴν προσενήνοχε· τινὲς δέ φασιν, ἐπειδή,

5 πεμφθεὶς ἐπ' ἐλευθερίᾳ τῶν ὁμοφύλων, κοινωνὸν εἶχε τῆς ὁδοῦ
τὴν ὁμόζυγα. οὓς ἐχρῆν συνιδεῖν ὅτι, πεῖσαι τὸν κηδεστὴν
βουλόμενος ὡς οὐ καταφρονήσει τῆς γυναικὸς οὐδὲ ἑτέραν
αὐτῆς προτιμήσει, λαβεῖν αὐτὴν ἠναγκάσθη, ἀλλ' οὐ
καταφρονητικῶς διακονῶν τῷ θείῳ προστάγματι. αὐτίκα γοῦν

10 λαβὼν τὴν ἀφορμὴν τοῦ ἀγγέλου, τὴν γυναῖκα πρὸς τοὺς
οἰκείους ἀναστρέψαι προσέταξε. καὶ ὅτι τοῦτό ἐστιν ἀληθὲς ἡ
ἱστορία διδάσκει. μετὰ γὰρ τὴν ἔξοδον, τὴν ἐξ Αἰγύπτου,
διαβάντων αὐτῶν τὴν θάλατταν καὶ εἰς τὸ Σίναιον
παραγενομένων ὄρος, ἀφίκετο σὺν τῇ γυναικὶ πρὸς αὐτὸν ὁ

15 κηδεστής. λέγει δὲ οὕτως ἡ ἱστορία· *ἔλαβε δὲ Ἰοθὼρ ὁ*
γαμβρὸς Μωϋσῆ Σεπφώραν τὴν γυναῖκα Μωϋσῆ μετὰ τὴν
ἄφεσιν αὐτῆς καὶ τοὺς δύο υἱοὺς αὐτοῦ . . . καὶ ἦλθε . . . πρὸς
Μωϋσῆν εἰς τὴν ἔρημον.[b]

Τοιγάρτοι ἄλλο τι κατασκευάζων, ὁ ἄγγελος ἔδειξε τὴν
20 ῥομφαίαν γυμνήν. ἐπειδὴ γὰρ ὁ μέγας Μωϋσῆς ἐδεδίει τὸν
Φαραὼ καὶ πολλάκις τοῦτο τὸ δέος ἐδήλωσε, *νῦν μὲν λέγων,*
τίς εἰμι ἐγὼ ὅτι πορεύσομαι πρὸς Φαραὼ βασιλέα Αἰγύπτου;[c]
νῦν δέ, προχείρισαι ἄλλον δυνάμενον ὃν ἐξαποστελεῖς·[d] καὶ
πάλιν, ἰσχνόφωνος καὶ βραδύγλωσσος ἐγώ εἰμι,[e] ἀπειλεῖ αὐτῷ

25 τιμωρίαν ὁ ἄγγελος, φόβῳ φόβον ἐξελαύνων, τῷ μείζονι τὸν
ἐλάττονα, μονονουχὶ λέγων διὰ τῆς γεγυμνωμένης ῥομφαίας,
εἰ τὸν Φαραὼ δέδοικας, μᾶλλον δεῖσον ἐμέ, τὸν καὶ ἀοράτως
σοι τὴν πληγὴν ἐπενεγκεῖν δυνάμενον.

---

xiv A⁻⁶ [32], B, C, 7 9 10 17 31 35 37 = 20 mss.

a. Ex 4.24   b. Ex 18.2–5   c. Ex 3.11   d. Ex 4.13   e. Ex 4.10

XIV

Why did the angel want to kill Moses?[a]

His wife supposed it was because one of their two sons had not been circumcised according to the law of the Hebrews, for she circumcised him then and there. But some commentators have claimed that it was because Moses, who was sent on the mission of liberating his kinsmen, had his wife accompany him on the way. But they should have seen that, in his wish to convince his father-in-law that he would not despise his wife or prefer someone else to her, he was obliged to take her along and that this was no indication of contempt for the divine command. In any case, he immediately took occasion from the angel's visit to order his wife to return to her own people. The truth of this inference is proven by subsequent events. After the exodus from Egypt, when they had crossed the Red Sea and reached Mount Sinai, his father-in-law came to him with his wife. The sacred history reads as follows: "Moses' father-in-law Jethro brought Moses' wife Zipporah after her dismissal and his two sons and came to Moses in the wilderness."[1b]

The angel had a further purpose in unsheathing his sword. The great Moses was afraid of Pharaoh and often betrayed that fear as when he asked, "Who am I to go to Pharaoh king of Egypt?"[c] and when he said, "Appoint someone competent whom you will send";[d] and again, "I have a weak voice and a slow tongue."[e] So by threatening him with punishment, the angel drove out one fear with another, the lesser with the greater. Baring his sword, he seemed to say, "If you are afraid of Pharaoh, you should fear me all the more, because I can strike you even when you cannot see me."

1. As R.J. Clifford suggests, Ex 4.24–26 may derive from "an old story of a night demon fooled by the blood from someone other than the intended victim." In the MT, it is the Lord himself who attacks Moses, and Zipporah saves her husband by anointing his penis—euphemistically referred to as "his feet"—with the blood of

XV

Τί ἐστι τὸ ὄνομά μου Κύριος οὐκ ἐδήλωσα αὐτοῖς;[a]

Διδάσκει πόσης αὐτὸν καὶ τιμῆς καὶ εὐμενείας ἠξίωσεν· ὃ
γὰρ τοῖς πατριάρχαις οὐκ ἐδήλωσεν ὄνομα, τοῦτο αὐτῷ δῆλον
ἐποίησεν· ἔφη γὰρ πρὸς αὐτόν, ἐγώ εἰμι ὁ ὤν.[b] τοῦτο δὲ παρ'
5 ἑβραίοις ἄφραστον ὀνομάζεται· ἀπείρηται γὰρ αὐτοῖς τοῦτο
διὰ τῆς γλώττης προφέρειν. γράφεται δὲ διὰ τῶν τεσσάρων
στοιχείων· διὸ καὶ τετράγραμμον αὐτὸ λέγουσι. τοῦτο καὶ τῷ
πετάλῳ ἐπεγέγραπτο τῷ χρυσῷ, ὃ τῷ μετώπῳ τοῦ ἀρχιερέως
ἐπετίθετο, τῇ ταινίᾳ τῆς κεφαλῆς προσδεσμούμενον.[c] καλοῦσι
10 δὲ αὐτὸ σαμαρεῖται μὲν Ἰαβέ, ἰουδαῖοι δὲ Ἰά.

XVI

Τί δή ποτε τῆς τοῦ Ἀαρὼν γυναικός, οὐ τὸν πατέρα μόνον,
ἀλλὰ καὶ τὸν ἀδελφὸν δῆλον ἡμῖν πεποίηκεν;[a]

Τῆς βασιλικῆς καὶ τῆς ἱερατικῆς φυλῆς τὴν ἐπιμιξίαν
διδάσκει· ὁ γὰρ Ναασσῶν υἱὸς τοῦ Ἀμιναδάβ, ὁ δὲ Ἀμιναδὰβ
5 τοῦ Ἀράμ, ὁ δὲ Ἀρὰμ τοῦ Ἐσρών, ὁ δὲ Ἐσρὼν τοῦ Φαρές, ὁ
δὲ Φαρὲς τοῦ Ἰούδα.[b] αὐτὸς δὲ ὁ Ναασσῶν φύλαρχος ἦν τοῦ
Ἰούδα·[c] ἐκ τῆς τούτων συγγενείας ὁ Κύριος κατὰ σάρκα
γεγέννηται. οὐ μάτην τοίνυν τῆς βασιλικῆς καὶ τῆς ἱερατικῆς
φυλῆς τὴν ἐπιμιξίαν ἐδίδαξεν, ἀλλὰ δεικνὺς ὡς ὁ δεσπότης
10 Χριστὸς ἐξ ἀμφοτέρων ἐβλάστησεν, ὁ βασιλεὺς καὶ ἱερεὺς
κατὰ τὸ ἀνθρώπινον χρηματίσας.

xv A⁻⁶ [32], B, C, 7 9 10 17 31* 35 37 = 20 mss.
a. Ex 6.3   b. Ex 3.14   c. Ex 28.36–38

xvi A⁻⁶ [32], B, C, 7 9 10 17 31 35 37 = 20 mss.
a. Ex 6.23   b. Ru 4.18–20   c. Nm 7.12

XV

What is the meaning of "My name 'Lord' I did not make known to them"?[a]

This conveys the great honor and kindness with which God treated Moses. Declaring, "I am who am,"[b] he disclosed to Moses the name he had never revealed to the patriarchs. Among the Hebrews this is known as the unspoken name; they are forbidden to utter it aloud. It is written in four consonants, and so they speak of it as the "Tetragrammaton." This name was also inscribed on a plate of gold worn on the forehead of the high priest and bound to his head with a fillet.[c] The Samaritans call it "Iabe," the Jews "Ia."

XVI

Why are we told the name of not only the father, but also the brother, of Aaron's wife?[a]

This informs us of the intermarriage of the royal and priestly tribes: Nahshon was the son of Amminadab, Amminadab of Ram, Ram of Hezron, Hezron of Perez, and Perez of Judah.[b] Thus, this Nahshon was the head of the family of Judah.[c] It was from their clan that the Lord drew his bodily descent. So there was good reason to point out the intermarriage of the royal and the priestly tribes; he wanted to bring out that Christ the Lord, styled king and priest according to his humanity, was descended from both.[1]

---

their son's foreskin. In the LXX, the Lord is replaced by an angel, and the story concentrates on the circumcision of Moses' son.

---

1. Theodoret here combines information drawn from Ex 6.23 and Ru 4.18–22. The first informs us that Elisheba, the wife of Aaron, the original high priest, was daughter of Amminadab and sister of Nahshon; the second traces the line from Perez to David.

XVII

Πῶς ἐγένετο τοῦ Ἀαρὼν θεὸς ὁ Μωϋσῆς;[a]

῎Ωσπερ ὁ Θεὸς προσέταττε τῷ Μωϋσῇ, οὕτως πάλιν ὁ Μωϋσῆς τῷ Ἀαρών· διὸ δὴ καὶ *προφήτης* ὁ Ἀαρὼν προσηγορεύθη τοῦ Μωϋσέως.

XVIII

Τί δή ποτε συνεχώρησεν ὁ Θεὸς τοῖς φαρμάκοις ταὐτὰ δρᾶσαι τῷ Μωϋσῇ;

Εἰσί τινες καὶ νῦν τῶν δυσσεβείᾳ συζώντων, οἵ φασι γοητείᾳ τεθαυματουργηκέναι τὸν θεσπέσιον Μωϋσῆν. τούτου
5 χάριν ἐνδέδωκε ὁ Θεὸς τοῖς φαρμάκοις ἔνια δρᾶσαι, ἵνα δειχθῇ τὸ διάφορον· μετέβαλον μὲν γὰρ αὐτοὶ τὰς ῥάβδους εἰς ὄφεις, ἀλλ' ἡ Μωϋσέως ῥάβδος τὰς ἐκείνων κατέπιεν·[a] καὶ μετέβαλον εἰς αἷμα τὸ ὕδωρ κἀκεῖνοι[b] ἀλλ' εἰς τὴν προτέραν ἐπαναγαγεῖν τὸ ὕδωρ οὐκ ἴσχυσαν φύσιν· καὶ τοὺς βατράχους
10 ἐξήγαγον·[c] οὐ μὴν καὶ ἀπαλλάξαι αὐτῶν τὰς τῶν αἰγυπτίων ἠδυνήθησαν οἰκίας.

Καὶ εἰς μὲν τὸ παιδεύειν τοὺς αἰγυπτίους καὶ τοῖς φαρμάκοις ἐνεργεῖν ἐνεδίδου, εἰς δὲ τὸ παύειν τὴν τιμωρίαν οὐκέτι. ἐπειδὴ γάρ, ὑπὸ τοῦ Θεοῦ κολαζόμενος, τῶν αἰγυπτίων
15 ὁ βασιλεὺς οὐκ ἠρκεῖτο ταῖς θεηλάτοις πληγαῖς ἀλλὰ καὶ τοῖς φαρμάκοις αὔξειν τὴν τιμωρίαν ἐκέλευσεν, καὶ διὰ τούτων

---

xvii A⁻⁶ *[32]*, B, C, 7 9 10 17 31 35 37 = 20 mss.

l. 1 Ἀαρὼν *Sir. Sch. F.M.* : Φαραὼ *2c*, 5, B, C, 9 31 35 37 = "In what sense did Moses become God to Pharaoh?"

a. Ex 7.1

---

xviii A⁻⁶ *[32]*, B, C, 7 9 10 17 31 35 37 = 20 mss.

a. Ex 7.11f.   b. Ex 7.22   c. Ex 8.7

XVII

In what sense did Moses become God to Aaron?[1a]
God gave orders to Moses, and Moses to Aaron. Hence, Aaron was even called Moses' "prophet."

XVIII

Why did God permit the sorcerers to work the same miracles as Moses?

Even today, there are pagans who claim that Moses, the divinely inspired, performed miracles by magic. But God allowed the sorcerers to work some miracles, precisely so that he might demonstrate the difference. While they also changed their rods into serpents, Moses' rod swallowed theirs.[a] While they also changed the water into blood,[b] they were unable to restore it to its original state. They brought forth the frogs[c] but could not rid the Egyptians' houses of them.

Furthermore, in order to chastise the Egyptians, he allowed the sorcerers to perform wonders but not to stop the punishment. Since the king of the Egyptians, when punished by God, was not content with the plagues sent from heaven but ordered his sorcerers to increase the punishment, God punished him through their actions as

---

1. Ex 7.1 speaks rather of Moses having been God to Pharaoh and of Aaron as Moses' prophet. In fact, the majority of the manuscripts of the *Quaest. in oct.* read "Pharaoh" for "Aaron"; *v.* the critical note. As Schulze points out (note 80, col. 244), Theodoret himself certainly reads the correct "Pharaoh" in his commentary on Ps. 112.7f. (LXX) = 113.7f. (MT).

αὐτὸν ἐκόλαζεν ὁ Θεός, μονονουχὶ λέγων, ἐπειδὴ τέρπῃ
κολαζόμενος, καὶ διὰ τῶν ἐμῶν θεραπόντων παιδεύω καὶ διὰ
τῶν σῶν σε κολάζω.

20   Ἰδὼν δὲ αὐτὸν πλέον σκληρυνόμενον,[d] ἐκώλυσε τὴν ἐκείνων
ἐνέργειαν, καὶ οἱ τὸ μεῖζον ζῷον ἐξαγαγόντες, τὸν βάτραχον,
τὸν σκνῖπα τὸν σμικρότατον ἐξαγαγεῖν οὐκ ἴσχυσαν[e] ἀλλὰ
δάκτυλον Θεοῦ τὴν πληγὴν προσηγόρευσαν.[f] τὰς μέντοι
φλυκταίνας καὶ τοῖς ἐκείνων ἐπήνεγκε σώμασιν[g] ἵνα καὶ αὐτοὶ
25 μάθωσι καὶ ὁ ἀνόητος αὐτῶν βασιλεὺς ὡς, οὐ μόνον ἐπέχειν
οὐ δύνανται τὰς θεηλάτους πληγάς, ἀλλὰ καὶ αὐτοὶ
συντιμωροῦνται τοῖς ἄλλοις. ἀναιδείας τοίνυν τὸ λέγειν
μαγγανείᾳ τινὶ τεθαυματουργηκέναι τὸν Μωϋσῆν, τῶν μάγων
βοώντων ὅτι θείας ἦν δυνάμεως τὰ σημεῖα. εἰ γὰρ φαντασία
30 ἦν τὸ παρ' αὐτοῦ δρώμενον, ἔδει κἀκείνους φαντάσαι καὶ τὸν
ὁμότεχνον διελέγξαι. νῦν δὲ διαρρήδην βοῶσι, δάκτυλος Θεοῦ
ἐστι τοῦτο.[h]

XIX

Τί δή ποτε πρώτην αὐτοῖς τὴν τοῦ ὕδατος ἐπάγει πληγήν;[a]
    Πρῶτον ἐπειδὴ μέγα ἐφρόνουν ἐπὶ τῷ ποταμῷ καὶ θεὸν
τοῦτον ἐνόμιζον, τὴν τῶν νεφῶν αὐτοῖς παρέχοντα χρείαν.
ἔπειτα καὶ διὰ τὰ βρέφη τῶν ἰουδαίων, τὰ τούτῳ
5 παραπεμφθέντα·[b] μεταβληθεὶς γὰρ εἰς αἷμα, τῆς γεγενημένης
κατηγορεῖ παιδοκτονίας. τούτου χάριν καὶ τοὺς βατράχους
ἀνέβλυσε τὰ ὕδατα[c] ἀντὶ τῶν ἐν ἐκείνοις ἀποπνιγέντων
ἀναδοθέντας παιδίων· μιμεῖται γάρ πως τὰ βρέφη τοὺς
βατράχους βαδίζοντα. μηδέπω γὰρ τοῖς ποσὶ μόνοις
10 κεχρῆσθαι δυνάμενα, ταῖς χερσὶν ἐπαμύνει τῇ τῶν ποδῶν

---

d. Ex 8.15   e. Ex 8.18   f. Ex 8.19   g. Ex 9.11   h. Ex 8.19

XIX A⁻⁶ [32], B, c, 50, 7 9 10 17 31 35 37 = 17 mss.

a. Ex 7.20f.   b. Ex 1.22   c. Ex 8.6

well. It was as if he said, "Since you enjoy being punished, I chastise you through my attendants and punish you through your own."

But when God saw that Pharaoh was hardened all the more,[d] he called a halt to their activity, and those who had brought forth the larger creature, the frog, were now unable to bring forth the smallest, the gnat,[e] but called the plague "the finger of God."[f] He also inflicted sores on their bodies[g] to teach them and their foolish king that they were unable to check the plagues sent from heaven and were condemned to share the punishment with everyone else. Therefore, only a shameless audacity could maintain that Moses worked wonders by magical trickery when the magicians themselves cried out that the signs were produced by divine power. If his deeds had amounted to no more than an illusion, they would have created the same illusion and unmasked their fellow practitioner. Instead, they cried out, "This is the finger of God."[1h]

XIX

Why did he strike them first with the plague of the water?[a]

First, because they gloried in the river and thought it a god, since it made up for their lack of rainfall. Next, because of the Jews' infants who had been thrown into it,[b] for when it turned into blood, it accused them of the crime of infanticide. For the same reason, the waters gushed forth frogs in place of the children,[c] who had been drowned in them. In their movements, infants to some extent resemble frogs, since, unable to rely solely on their feet, they use their hands to aid the weakness of their feet. The land stank of the

1. Perhaps Theodoret devotes this long discussion to the competition between Moses and the Egyptian sorcerers to exploit a sensational story. Guinot, however, suggests (p. 768) that Theodoret may be implicitly warning his flock against magic, either by defending Moses against pagan accusations of sorcery or by denying that Moses might supply an example for those who would wish to justify their own interest in magic.

ἀσθενείᾳ. προσώζεσε δὲ ἐκ τῶν βατράχων ἡ γῆ,[d] ἐπειδὴ
προσώζεσαν καὶ ἐσάπησαν τῶν αἰγυπτίων οἱ μώλωπες ἐκ τῆς
παμπόλλης πονηρίας.[e]

XX

Εἰ ὅλον τὸ ὕδωρ εἰς αἷμα μετεβλήθη, πῶς ἐποίησαν οἱ
ἐπαοιδοὶ τῶν αἰγυπτίων ταῖς φαρμακείαις αὐτῶν ὡσαύτως;[a]
  Ἐπέλαζεν αὐτοῖς καὶ ἡ θάλαττα, τὸ δὲ πότιμον ὕδωρ εἰς
αἷμα μετεβλήθη μόνον. ἠδύναντο τοίνυν μετακομίσαι
5 θαλάττιον ὕδωρ εἰς τὰ βασίλεια καὶ μεταβαλεῖν εἰς τὴν τοῦ
αἵματος χροιάν, τοῦ Θεοῦ δηλονότι συγχωροῦντος αὐτοῖς
ἐνεργεῖν δι' ἃς εἰρήκαμεν αἰτίας.
  Ἐπισημήνασθαι μέντοι καὶ τοῦτο δεῖ, ὡς τοὺς μὲν
βατράχους ἐκ τῶν ὑδάτων ἐξήγαγε,[b] τοὺς δὲ σκνῖπας ἐκ τοῦ
10 χώματος,[c] τὴν δὲ κυνόμυιαν ὅθεν ἠθέλησεν[d] ἵνα μάθωσιν ὡς
ῥάδιον τῷ Θεῷ, καὶ δίχα γῆς καὶ δίχα ὑδάτων, παράγειν ἃ
βούλεται. τούτου χάριν καὶ προλέγει τὰς τιμωρίας,[e] ἵνα μὴ
ἀπὸ ταὐτομάτου ταῦτα συμβαίνειν τοπάσωσιν, ἀλλὰ γνῶσιν
θεηλάτους εἶναι πληγάς.

XXI

Τί δή ποτε, μέλλων ἐπιφέρειν τὴν χάλαζαν, παρηγγύησεν
αὐτοῖς εἰς τοὺς οἴκους τὰ κτήνη συναγαγεῖν;[a]
  Φιλάνθρωπος ὤν, ὁ δεσπότης ἐλέῳ τὰς τιμωρίας

---

d. Ex 8.14   e. Ps 38.5

---

xx A⁻⁶ *[32]*, B, C, 7 9 10 17 31 35 37 = 20 mss.

a. Ex 7.22   b. Ex 8.6   c. Ex 8.17   d. Ex 8.24   e. Ex. 7.17; 8.2–4, 21–23

---

xxi A⁻⁶ *[32]*, B, C, 7 9 10 17 31 35 37 = 20 mss.

a. Ex 9.19

frogs,[d] because the Egyptians' "welts stank and festered" from their numerous iniquities.[e]

XX

If all the water was changed into blood, how did the Egyptian wizards produce the same effect with their charms?[a]

They were near the sea, and only the fresh water had been changed into blood. So, with God allowing them to act for the reasons already mentioned, they must have been able to bring seawater into the palace and change it to the color of blood.

We should also point out that while he produced the frogs from the waters,[b] and the gnats from the dust,[c] he produced the dog fly from wherever he chose,[d] so the Egyptians might learn how easy it was for God to bring forth whatever he wanted, even without land or water. He also foretold each punishment[e] so they would not imagine these things were happening of themselves but realize they were plagues sent from heaven.

XXI

Why did he urge them to round up their cattle into their houses when he was about to send down the hail?[a]

As the Lord is benevolent, he tempered retribution with mercy,

κεράννυσιν. ἄλλως τε καὶ ᾔδει τινὰς ἀξίους φειδοῦς· τοῦτο
5 γὰρ καὶ ἡ θεία διδάσκει γραφή· *ὁ φοβούμενος, γάρ φησι, τὸ*
ῥῆμα Κυρίου τῶν θεραπόντων Φαραὼ συνήγαγε τὰ κτήνη
αὐτοῦ εἰς τοὺς οἴκους· ὃς δὲ οὐ προσέσχε τῇ διανοίᾳ εἰς τὸ
ῥῆμα Κυρίου ἀφῆκε τὰ κτήνη ἐν τοῖς πεδίοις.[b]

Τὴν δὲ χάλαζαν καὶ τοὺς σκηπτοὺς αὐτοῖς ἐπενήνοχε,[c]
10 δεικνὺς ὡς αὐτός ἐστι τῶν στοιχείων ἁπάντων δεσπότης.
ἐπειδὴ γὰρ καὶ αἰγύπτιοι καὶ ἕλληνες ἐνόμιζον τοὺς μὲν
οὐρανίους, τοὺς δὲ ἐπιγείους, τοὺς δὲ ὑποχθονίους εἶναι
θεούς, καὶ τοὺς μὲν τῆς γῆς, τοὺς δὲ τῆς θαλάττης
δεσπόζειν, καὶ τοὺς μὲν τῶν ὀρέων, τοὺς δὲ τῶν πεδίων ἔχειν
15 τὴν ἐξουσίαν· διὸ καὶ οἱ σύροι ἔλεγον, *Θεὸς ὀρέων ὁ Θεὸς*
Ἰσραὴλ καὶ οὐ Θεὸς κοιλάδων·[d] ἀναγκαίως ἄγαν ὁ τῶν ὅλων
Θεός, οὐ μόνον αὐτοὺς διὰ τοῦ ποταμοῦ καὶ τῆς γῆς, ἀλλὰ
καὶ διὰ τοῦ ἀέρος καὶ τῆς θαλάττης ἐπαίδευσε καὶ οὐρανόθεν
αὐτοῖς κεραυνοὺς ἐπαφῆκε, διδάσκων ὡς αὐτός ἐστι τῶν ὅλων
20 ποιητὴς καὶ δεσπότης. τοῦτο γὰρ καὶ ὁ μακάριος εἴρηκε
Μωϋσῆς πρὸς αὐτόν· *ἵνα γνῷς ὅτι τοῦ Κυρίου ἡ γῆ, καὶ σύ,*
καὶ οἱ θεράποντές σου.[e]

XXII

Διὰ τί τὰ τῶν αἰγυπτίων ἀνεῖλε πρωτότοκα;[a]

Ἐπειδὴ πρωτόγονον ὄντα τοῦ Θεοῦ τὸν Ἰσραὴλ ἄγαν
σκληρῶς ἐκεῖνος ἐδουλαγώγει· τοῦτο γὰρ καὶ αὐτὸς εἴρηκεν ὁ
δεσπότης Θεός· *υἱὸς πρωτόγονός μου Ἰσραήλ*·[b] μάλα δικαίως
5 τὰ τῶν αἰγυπτίων πρωτότοκα θανάτῳ παρέπεμψεν.

Ἰστέον μέντοι ὡς ὁ πρωτόγονος καὶ ἀδελφοὺς ἔχει· ὁ γὰρ
πρωτόγονος ἢ πρωτότοκος πολλῶν ἐστι πρῶτος. γινωσκέτω

---

b. Ex 9.20f.   c. Ex 9.23f.   d. 1Kgs 21.23   e. Ex 9.29f.

xxii A⁻⁶ [32], B, C, 7 9 10 17 31 35 37 = 20 mss.

a. Ex 12.29   b. Ex 4.22

especially since he knew that some people were deserving of com-
passion. Indeed, holy Scripture informs us that "Pharaoh's attendants who feared the word of the Lord rounded up their cattle into
their houses, but whoever paid no heed to the word of the Lord left
his cattle in the fields."[b]

He brought down on them hail and thunderbolts[c] to show that
he is the Lord of all the elements. Since both the Egyptians and the
Greeks divided their gods into those of heaven, earth, and the un-
derworld and believed that some had charge of the earth and others
of the sea, that some had power over the mountains and others over
the plains—hence, the Syrians said "The god of Israel is a god of the
mountains, not a god of the valleys"[d]—it was absolutely necessary
for the God of the universe to instruct them not only through the
river and the earth, but also the sky and the sea. He cast on them
thunderbolts from heaven to teach them that he is the Creator and
Lord of all things. This is precisely what the blessed Moses said to
Pharaoh: "So you may know that the earth, you, and your attendants all belong to the Lord."[e]

XXII

Why did he kill the firstborn of the Egyptians?[a]

Since Pharaoh was subjecting Israel, God's firstborn, to such
harsh slavery—as you recall, the Lord God himself had said, "Israel
is my firstborn son"[b]—God quite justly gave the firstborn of the
Egyptians over to death.

Of course, you should understand that the first in line has brothers, as the first in line, or firstborn, is the first of many. So Israel

τοίνυν ὁ Ἰσραὴλ ὡς πρῶτος μὲν τοῦ Θεοῦ λαὸς ἐχρημάτισε,
πεπιστευκότα δὲ τὰ ἔθνη, οὐ μόνον τῆς σωτηρίας τετύχηκεν,
10 ἀλλὰ καὶ τῶν πρωτοτοκίων ἀπήλαυσε· *λαός, γάρ φησι, λαοῦ*
ὑπερέξει, καὶ ὁ μείζων δουλεύσει τῷ ἐλάσσονι.[c]

XXIII

Αἰτιῶνταί τινες τὸ προστεταχέναι τὸν Θεὸν τοῖς ἑβραίοις
αἰτῆσαι τοὺς αἰγυπτίους σκεύη χρυσᾶ καὶ ἀργυρᾶ καὶ ἐσθῆτα
καὶ σκυλεῦσαι τοὺς αἰγυπτίους· οὕτω γὰρ ὁ Σύμμαχος τὸ
σκευάσασθαι ἡρμήνευσεν.[a]

5 Πολὺν ἐν Αἰγύπτῳ χρόνον ὑπέμεινεν ὁ λαὸς πλινθουργῶν,
καὶ τειχοποιῶν, καὶ πόλεις οἰκοδομῶν. ἠβουλήθη τοίνυν μισθὸν
αὐτοὺς τῶν πόνων λαβεῖν ὁ δεσπότης Θεός· διὸ δὴ καὶ ταῦτα
δρᾶσαι προσέταξε. καὶ μηδεὶς ἄδικον νομιζέτω, τοῦ Φαραὼ
τὸν λαὸν ἠδικηκότος, τοὺς αἰγυπτίους τὸν μισθὸν
10 εἰσπραχθῆναι· ἐκοινώνουν γὰρ κἀκεῖνοι τῆς ἀδικίας,
μιμούμενοι τὴν τοῦ βασιλέως ὠμότητα.

XXIV

Διὰ τί φεύγουσιν ἐπιτελέσαι προσέταξε τὴν τοῦ Πάσχα
ἑορτήν;[a]

c. Gn 25.23

---

xxiii A^{-6} *[32], B, C, 7 9 10 17 31 35 37* = 20 mss.

l. 4 σκευάσασθαι Sir. Sch. F.M. : συσκευάσασθαι *7 9* = "*Symmachus who*
rendered 'plunder' rather than 'pack up'" : σκυλεύσασθαι *35* = "*Symmachus who*
rendered 'plunder' rather than 'plunder'"

a. Ex 12.36

---

xxiv A^{-6} *[32], B, C, 7 9 10 17 31 35 37* = 20 mss.

a. Ex 12.1–20

should recognize that it was styled God's first people, but that the gentiles not only gained salvation through faith but also succeeded to the rights of the firstborn. As Scripture says, "A people will surpass a people, and the elder will serve the younger."[c]

XXIII

There are those who find fault with God's command that the Hebrews ask the Egyptians for gold and silver vessels and clothing and plunder the Egyptians. That is the translation of Symmachus, who rendered "plunder" rather than "prepare."[1a]

The people spent a long time in Egypt making bricks, erecting walls, and building cities. Since the Lord God wanted them to receive some recompense for their labors, he ordered them to do this. No one should think it unfair that, though it was Pharaoh who wronged the people, payment was required of the Egyptians. They had also participated in this injustice by imitating the cruelty of their king.[2]

XXIV

Why did he command them to celebrate the paschal feast as they were fleeing from Egypt?[a]

1. According to Fernández Marcos and Sáenz-Badillos, Theodoret read σκευάσασθαι (to prepare) in Ex 12.36. If so, this would have been a corruption of συσκευάζω (to pack up), which appears in some manuscripts of the LXX at 3.22, a verse echoed by 12.36; *v.* J.W. Wevers and U. Quast, *ad loc.* This latter verb, a form of which appears in two manuscripts of our text, was itself a false reading for σκυλεύω (to despoil, to plunder). Though a form of σκυλεύω does appear in one ms. of the *Quaest.*, it seems most likely that Theodoret, puzzled by the inappropriate σκευάσασθαι, found the obviously meaningful σκυλεῦσαι in the translation of Symmachus; *cf.* the critical note.

2. The gnostics and Marcion had raised this objection against the justice of the God of the Old Testament. Theodoret's response follows those previously offered

The Questions on Exodus

(1) Ἀείμνηστον ἠβουλήθη φυλαχθῆναι τῆς σωτηρίας τὴν
μνήμην. διά τοι τοῦτο καὶ νομοθετῶν ἔλεγεν, ἐὰν ἐρωτήσῃ σε
5 ὁ υἱός σου..., λέγων, τί ἐστιν τὸ Πάσχα; ἐρεῖς ὅτι, ἐν τῇ
σήμερον ἡμέρᾳ ἐξήγαγε τοὺς πατέρας ἡμῶν Κύριος ὁ Θεὸς ἐκ
γῆς Αἰγύπτου καὶ ἐρρύσατο τὰ πρωτότοκα ἡμῶν ἡνίκα ὁ
ὀλοθρεύων ἐπάταξε τὰ πρωτότοκα τῶν αἰγυπτίων.[b] τούτου
χάριν παρακελεύεται ταύτην ἐπιτελοῦντας τὴν ἑορτὴν τῆς
10 ὁδοιπορίας περικεῖσθαι τὸ σχῆμα· ἔστωσαν, γάρ φησιν, αἱ
ὀσφύες ὑμῶν περιεζωσμέναι, καὶ τὰ ὑποδήματα ὑμῶν ἐν τοῖς
ποσὶν ὑμῶν, καὶ αἱ βακτηρίαι ὑμῶν ἐν ταῖς χερσὶν ὑμῶν, καὶ
ἔδεσθε αὐτὸ μετὰ σπουδῆς. Πάσχα ἐστὶ Κυρίου.[c]

Τὸ δὲ Πάσχα ὁ μὲν Φίλων ἡρμήνευσε διαβατήρια,[d] ὁ δὲ
15 Ἰώσηπος ὑπερβασία,[e] ὁ δὲ Σύμμαχος ὑπερβάσεις, ὁ δὲ
Θεοδοτίων φασέχ, αὐτὴν τὴν ἑβραίαν φωνὴν τεθεικώς.
σημαίνει δὲ τὸ ὄνομα τῶν ἑβραίων πρωτοτόκων τὴν σωτηρίαν·
παρεκελεύσατο γὰρ δέσμην ὑσσώπου λαβεῖν καί, τῷ αἵματι
τοῦ θυομένου προβάτου ἐμβάψαντας, τοὺς σταθμοὺς ἐπιχρίσαι
20 καὶ τὴν φλιὰν ἵν', ὅταν εἰσέλθῃ ὁ ὀλοθρεύων πατάξαι τὰ
πρωτότοκα τῶν αἰγυπτίων, ἰδὼν τὸ αἷμα, ὑπερβῇ τῶν ἑβραίων
τὰς οἰκίας—[f] οὐκ ἐπειδὴ τοιούτων ἐδεῖτο σημείων ἡ ἀσώματος
φύσις, ἀλλ' ὅτι διὰ τοῦ συμβόλου κἀκείνους ἔδει μαθεῖν τὴν
τοῦ Θεοῦ κηδεμονίαν, καὶ ἡμᾶς, τοὺς τὸν ἄμωμον ἀμνὸν
25 θύοντας, γνῶναι προδιαγραφέντα τὸν τύπον.

(2) Κελεύει τοίνυν αὐτοῖς λαβεῖν, οὐ μόνον ἐκ τῶν προβάτων
ἄρνας ἐνιαυσίους, ἀλλὰ καὶ ἐκ τῶν αἰγῶν ἐρίφους, οὐχ ἵνα
κατὰ ταὐτὸν τοῦτον κἀκεῖνον θύσωσιν, ἀλλ' ἵνα ὁ μὲν πρόβατον
ἔχων τοῦτο θύσῃ, ὁ δὲ σπανίζων προβάτου τὸν ἔριφον.[g]
30 παρεγγυᾷ δὲ τοῦτο λαβεῖν τῇ δεκάτῃ τοῦ πρώτου μηνός,[h] ἵν'

---

b. Dt 6.20–22   c. Ex 12.11   d. Ph., *Spec.* 2.145   e. Ios., *A.I.* 2.313
f. Ex 12.22f.   g. Ex 12.5   h. Ex 12.3

(1) He wanted the memory of their salvation to be preserved forever. Therefore, as he delivered the law, he commanded, "When your son asks you, 'What is the Pasch?' you shall say, 'On this day the Lord God brought our fathers out of the land of Egypt and rescued our firstborn when the destroyer struck the firstborn of the Egyptians.'"[b] This is why he commands those celebrating this feast to dress as if they were going on a journey: "Have your loins girt, your sandals on your feet, your staffs in your hands, and eat it in haste, for it is the Lord's Pasch."[c]

Philo rendered the term "Pasch" as "offerings made at a border-crossing,"[d] Josephus as "going beyond,"[e] Symmachus as "goings beyond," while Theodotion, simply transliterated the Hebrew word as "Phasech." The term signifies the salvation of the Hebrews' firstborn.[1] God commanded them to take a bunch of hyssop, dip it in the blood of a sheep that was being slaughtered, and smear the doorposts and lintel, so that when the destroyer came to strike the firstborn of the Egyptians, he would see the blood and pass by the houses of the Hebrews.[f] Not that an incorporeal being had need of signs. Rather, through this symbol they were to learn of God's providence, and we, who offer in sacrifice the blameless lamb, were to learn the type in which he is foreshadowed.

(2) Now, he commanded them to take not only yearling lambs from the sheep but also kids from the goats—not that they were to slaughter both together. Rather, those who had a sheep were to slaughter a sheep and those who had no sheep were to slaughter a kid.[g] He commanded them to take the animal on the tenth day of the first month[h] so as to have it ready before the feast and to slaugh-

---

by Irenaeus (*Haer.* 4.30.1f.), Clement of Alexandria (*Str.* 1.23.157.2–4), Tertullian (*Marc.* 2.20.1–4), and Chrysostom (*Iud.* 5.5). All these Christian exegetes follow a line of apologetic laid out by Philo (*De uita Mosis* 1.25.141); *v.* Guinot, p. 768 and R. Braun, pp. 225–27.

---

1. To explain the significance of the Passover for Jews and Christians, Theodo-

The Questions on Exodus

εὐτρεπίσῃ πρὸ τῆς ἑορτῆς, τῇ δὲ τεσσαρεσκαιδεκάτῃ πρὸς
ἑσπέραν τυθῆναι·[i] κατὰ ταύτην γὰρ τὴν ἑσπέραν καὶ ὁ
δεσπότης Χριστὸς παρεδόθη τοῖς ἰουδαίοις.[j] μετὰ πικρίδων δὲ
αὐτὸ βρωθῆναι προσέταξεν εἰς ἀνάμνησιν τῆς ἐν Αἰγύπτῳ
35 πικροτάτης ζωῆς καὶ τῆς χαλεπωτάτης δουλείας.[k] διὰ δὲ τῶν
ἀζύμων ἐμφαίνει, οὐ μόνον τῆς ὁδοιπορίας τὸ σύντονον καὶ τὸ
τῆς τροφῆς αὐτοσχέδιον, ἀλλὰ καὶ ὅτι προσήκει μηδὲ ἴχνος
τῆς αἰγυπτιακῆς ἐπιφέρεσθαι πολιτείας· οὕτω γὰρ καὶ ὁ
Κύριος ἐν τοῖς εὐαγγελίοις ἡρμήνευσε, *προσέχετε, λέγων, ἀπὸ*
40 *τῆς ζύμης τῶν γραμματέων καὶ φαρισαίων*.[l] ἐκέλευσε δὲ καὶ
τοὺς ἀρκοῦντας εἰς ἐδωδὴν προβάτου κατὰ ταὐτὸν θῦσαι τὸ
Πάσχα, φιλαδελφίαν αὐτοὺς ἐκπαιδεύων καὶ τὸν εἰς τοὺς
πένητας ἔλεον.[m] διὰ τοῦτο παρακελεύεται καὶ τὰ περιττεύοντα
τῶν κρεῶν κατακαίεσθαι καὶ εἰς τὴν ὑστεραίαν μὴ
45 φυλάττεσθαι, ταύτῃ καταναγκάζων αὐτοὺς καλεῖν τοὺς
δεομένους εἰς κοινωνίαν τῆς ἑορτῆς.[n]

Ταῦτα δὲ πάντα τῶν ἡμετέρων ἐστὶ μυστηρίων αἰνίγματα·
χρίομεν γὰρ καὶ ἡμεῖς τῷ αἵματι τοῦ ἡμετέρου ἀμνοῦ, οὐ
μόνον τὴν φλιάν, ἀλλὰ καὶ τοὺς δύο σταθμούς· κατὰ μὲν τὸ
50 ὁρώμενον τὴν γλῶτταν καὶ τὰ χείλη καθαίροντές τε καὶ
ἁγιάζοντες, κατὰ δὲ τὸ νοούμενον, ἀντὶ μὲν φλιᾶς τὸ
λογικόν, ἀντὶ δὲ τῶν δύο σταθμῶν τὸ θυμοειδὲς καὶ τὸ
ἐπιθυμητικόν.[o]

(3) Ἁρμόττει δὲ ἡμῖν καὶ τὸ μήτε ὠμὰ μήτε ἑψημένα

---

i. Ex 12.6   j. Mt 26.17; Mk 14.12   k. Ex 12.8   l. Mt 16.6   m. Ex 12.4
n. Ex 12.10   o. Cf. Pl., *Rep.* 441c–443b.

ter it on the fourteenth day towards evening,[i] as that was the evening on which Christ the Lord was handed over to the Jews.[2j] He bade it be eaten with bitter herbs in memory of their bitter life and harsh slavery in Egypt.[k] By the unleavened bread he indicated not only the haste of their departure and their rough and ready fare but also that they were not to take away with them even a trace of Egyptian ways. In the Gospels, the Lord himself interpreted this command when he said, "Be on guard against the leaven of the scribes and Pharisees."[3l] He also enjoined that a number sufficient for consumption of a sheep slaughter the paschal victim together, the intention being to teach them brotherly love and pity for the poor.[m] For the same reason he commanded that any leftover meat be burned, not kept for the day after, thus obliging them to invite the needy to share the feast.[n]

Now, all these requirements are obscure types of our Eucharist. We also anoint with the blood of our lamb, not only the lintel but also the two posts. At the visible level, we purify and sanctify our tongue and lips, and at the spiritual level, the rational faculty, represented by the lintel, and the principle of high spirit and the appetitive faculty,[o] represented by the two posts.

(3) The requirement to eat it, not raw or boiled, but roasted in

----

ret tries to uncover the etymology of the Hebrew word *Pesach* by referring to a range of Jewish authorities, who, as he discovers, differ considerably. He does not seem aware of the popular and unscientific Hebrew etymology deriving the name from the verb *psh* "to jump" or "pass by," which appears in Ex 12.13, 23, 27, where it is said that the Lord "passes over" the houses of the Hebrews on the night when he slays the firstborn of the Egyptians. For a brief discussion of modern attempts to derive the name from Akkadian and Egyptian stems, *v.* J.J. Castelot and A. Cody, "Religious Institutions of Israel," sec. 76.127.

2. In the synoptic Gospels, the Last Supper occurs on Passover. In the Gospel of John, however, the death of "the lamb of God" occurs on Passover, the Supper on the evening before (13.1); *v.* D.J. Harrington, "Mark," on 14.12–16.

3. Theodoret offers a version of this dominical saying, which differs from both

55 ἐσθίειν ἀλλὰ ὀπτὰ πυρί·ᴾ οὔτε γὰρ μόνῳ τῷ γράμματι
προσβλέπομεν ἀλλὰ τὴν διάνοιαν ἐρευνῶμεν. οὔτε μὴν
ἀνθρωπίνους λογισμοὺς τοῖς θείοις ἐπεισάγομεν λογίοις·
τοῦτο γὰρ καὶ Ἡσαΐας τινῶν κατηγόρησεν, ὡς ἀναμιγνύντων
ὕδατι τὸν οἶνον·�q ἀλλὰ μόνῳ χρώμεθα τῷ θείῳ πυρί, τῇ τοῦ
60 ἁγίου πνεύματος χάριτι. τὸ δὲ μὴ καταλιπεῖν τῶν κρεῶν εἰς
τὴν ὑστεραίαν οὕτω νοοῦμεν, ὅτι ὁ μέλλων βίος τῶν συμβόλων
οὐ δεῖται· αὐτὰ γὰρ ὁρῶμεν ἐν ἐκείνῳ τὰ πράγματα. τὰ δὲ
ὀστᾶ τοῦ προβάτου συντρίβουσιν οἱ κακῶς τὰ θεῖα νοοῦντες
λόγιαʳ καὶ εἰς τὴν οἰκείαν αὐτὰ πειρώμενοι μεταφέρειν
65 ἀσέβειαν.

Τὸ δέ, μὴ μόνον ἐκ προβάτων, ἀλλὰ καὶ ἐξ ἐρίφων
λαμβάνειν τὴν θείαν πάλιν κηρύττει φιλανθρωπίαν· οὐ γὰρ
μόνον ὑπὲρ δικαίων, ἀλλὰ καὶ ὑπὲρ ἁμαρτωλῶν, ὁ δεσπότης
Χριστὸς τὸ σωτήριον ὑπομεμένηκε πάθος.ˢ οὕτω δὲ νοεῖν
70 αὐτὸς ἡμᾶς ἐξεπαίδευσεν· ἀμνοῖς μὲν γὰρ τὸν τῶν ἁγίων
ἀπείκασε σύλλογον, τὸν δὲ τῶν οὐ τοιούτων ἐρίφοις·ᵗ ἔριφον
γὰρ ὑπὲρ ἁμαρτίας ὁ νόμος προσφέρειν ἐκέλευσε.ᵘ καὶ τῶν
θείων δὲ μυστηρίων οἱ μεταλαμβάνοντες, οἱ μὲν ὡς προβάτου
μεταλαμβάνουσιν, ἅτε δὴ τελείαν τὴν ἀρετὴν κεκτημένοι, οἱ
75 δὲ ὡς ἐρίφου, διὰ μετανοίας ἐξαλείφοντες τὰς τῶν
ἁμαρτημάτων κηλῖδας. οὕτω καὶ ὁ σωτὴρ ἡμῶν, οὐκ ἐκ σιτίνων
μόνον, ἀλλὰ καὶ ἐκ κριθίνων ἄρτων τοὺς συνεληλυθότας
διέθρεψε.ᵛ

Καὶ ἡμῖν δὲ ὁ δεσπότης ἐκέλευσεν ἔχειν τὰς ὀσφύας
80 περιεζωσμένας, καὶ τοὺς πόδας ὑποδεδεμένους, καὶ τοὺς
λύχνους καιομένους ὡς οἰκέτας δεσπότην προσμένοντας.ʷ ἀλλ'
ἑβραῖοι μὲν ὡς αἰγυπτίων ἀπαλλαττόμενοι καὶ εἰς τὴν
χαναναίαν γῆν εἰσαγόμενοι τοῦτο εἶχον τὸ σχῆμα, ἡμεῖς δε
ὡς ἐντεῦθεν εἰς ἕτερον μεθιστάμενοι βίον. διὰ τοῦτο καὶ ἡμῖν
85 ὁ θεῖος παρακελεύεται Παῦλος, βοῶν, *ἐκκαθάρατε τὴν παλαιὰν*
ζύμην ἵνα ἦτε νέον φύραμα καθώς ἐστε ἄζυμοι· καὶ ἐπήγαγε,

---

p. Ex 12.9   q. Is 1.22   r. Ex 12.46   s. Cf. Lk 5.32.   t. Mt 25.32
u. *V., e.g.,* Lv 4.23, 28; 5.6; 9.3, 15; 16.15–28.   v. Jn 6.9   w. Lk 12.35f.

fire also applies to us.[p] After all, we do not limit our attention to the bare letter of Scripture but also scrutinize the sense. Nor do we add human arguments to the divine prophecies, for which Isaiah blamed some people, as though "mixing wine with water."[q] Instead, we apply only the divine fire, the grace of the Spirit. We understand the requirement not to leave any meat for the next day in the sense that the life to come has no need of symbols; there we shall see things as they are. Those who break the bones of the sheep are those who misinterpret the divine prophecies[r] in an attempt to accommodate them to their own heretical notions.

Furthermore, the requirement to choose a victim not only from the sheep but also from the kids proclaims God's loving-kindness. Christ the Lord underwent his saving passion not only for the righteous but also for sinners, as he taught us to understand.[s] He compared the company of saints to the lambs and that of sinners to the kids,[t] since the Law ordained the offering of a kid for sin.[u] And those who participate in the sacred Eucharist are of two classes: those who may be said to partake of a lamb, since they possess perfect virtue, and those who may be said to partake of a kid, since they wipe away the stain of sin through repentance. Thus, our Savior nourished the crowd with barley, as well as wheaten, loaves.[v]

The Lord also ordered us to have our loins girt, our feet shod, and lamps lit, like servants awaiting their master.[w] This is how the Hebrews were dressed when they were being freed from Egypt and led into the land of Canaan, but we are traveling from this to the other life. Hence, St. Paul cries out instructing us, "Clean out the old leaven so you may be a new batch, as you really are unleavened"; and he went on, "for Christ our paschal lamb has been sacrificed"; and he added, "so that we may celebrate, not with old leaven nor

---

those found in the NT: Mt 16.6, which mentions the Pharisees and the Sadducees, and Lk 12.1, which names only the former; *cf.* note 1 to *Q.* 55 on Ex.

καὶ γὰρ τὸ Πάσχα ἡμῶν ὑπὲρ ἡμῶν ἐτύθη Χριστός· καὶ
προστέθεικεν, ὥστε ἑορτάζωμεν, μὴ ἐν ζύμῃ παλαιᾷ μηδὲ ἐν
ζύμῃ κακίας καὶ πονηρίας, ἀλλ' ἐν ἀζύμοις εἰλικρινείας καὶ
90 ἀληθείας.ˣ

(4) Ἄνωθεν δὲ προμεμήνυκε τὴν τῶν ἐθνῶν σωτηρίαν ὁ τῶν
ὅλων Θεός· καὶ γὰρ τοὺς προσηλύτους μεταλαγχάνειν τοῦ
Πάσχα προσέταξε. γειώραν γὰρ τὸν προσήλυτον προσηγόρευσε
καὶ ἰσονομίας αὐτῷ μετέδωκεν· ἔσται, γάρ φησιν, ὡς ... ὁ
95 αὐτόχθων τῆς γῆς.ʸ καὶ τὸ ἐν οἰκίᾳ μιᾷ βρωθήσεταιᶻ
φυλάττουσιν οἱ πιστοί, ἐν μόνῃ τῇ τοῦ Θεοῦ ἐκκλησίᾳ τῶν
θείων μεταλαμβάνοντες μυστηρίων, τὰς δὲ τῶν αἱρετικῶν
συναγωγὰς βδελυττόμενοι.

Τὰ μέντοι πρωτότοκα καὶ τῶν βοῶν καὶ τῶν προβάτων
100 προσφέρεσθαι νενομοθέτηκεν ὁ δεσπότης Θεός, τῆς τῶν
πρωτοτόκων αὐτῶν σωτηρίας ἀναμιμνήσκων· οὐδὲ γὰρ αὐτὸς
τῶν θυμάτων ἐδεῖτο ἀλλὰ τὴν ἐκείνων ὠφέλειαν
ἐπραγματεύετο· τοῦτο γὰρ καὶ αὐτὸς ὁ νόμος δηλοῖ·
ἐὰν ... ἐρωτήσῃ σε ὁ υἱός σου ..., λέγων, τί ἐστι τοῦτο; καὶ
105 ἐρεῖς πρὸς αὐτόν ὅτι, ἐν χειρὶ κραταιᾷ ἐξήγαγεν ἡμᾶς Κύριος
ἐκ γῆς Αἰγύπτου, ἐξ οἴκου δουλείας. ἡνίκα δὲ ἐσκλήρυνε
Φαραὼ ἐξαποστεῖλαι ἡμᾶς, ἀπέκτεινε Κύριος πᾶν πρωτότοκον
ἐν γῇ Αἰγύπτῳ ἀπὸ πρωτοτόκου ἀνθρώπου ἕως πρωτοτόκων
κτηνῶν. διὰ τοῦτο ἐγὼ θύω τῷ Κυρίῳ πᾶν διανοῖγον μήτραν,
110 τὰ ἀρσενικά, καὶ πᾶν πρωτότοκον τῶν υἱῶν μου λυτρώσομαι.
καὶ ἔσται εἰς σημεῖον ἐπὶ τῆς χειρός σου καὶ ἀσάλευτον πρὸ
ὀφθαλμῶν σου· ἐν γὰρ χειρὶ κραταιᾷ ἐξήγαγέ σε Κύριος ἐξ
Αἰγύπτου.ᵃᵃ τοιγάρτοι τούτων ἕκαστον, οὐ τῆς τοῦ Θεοῦ
χρείας ἕνεκεν, ἀλλὰ τῆς τοῦ λαοῦ ἐγίνετο ὠφελείας.

---

x. 1Cor 5.7f.   y. Ex 12.48   z. Ex 12.46   aa. Ex 13.14–16

with the leaven of malice and wickedness, but with the unleavened bread of sincerity and truth."ˣ

(4) Long ago, the God of the universe foretold the salvation of the nations, when he directed that proselytes participate in the Pasch. He designated the proselyte by the name "sojourner" and gave him equality of rights: "He will be like one born in the land."ʸ As to the requirement, "It will be eaten in one house,"ᶻ this is observed by the faithful, who partake of the sacred Eucharist only in God's Church and abhor the assemblies of heretics.[4]

When the Lord God legislated for the offering of the firstborn of oxen and sheep, he called to mind the salvation of the firstborn of the Hebrews. In no need of sacrificial victims himself, he was working their salvation, as the Law itself indicates: "If your son asks you, 'What does this mean?' you shall say to him, 'With a mighty hand the Lord brought us out of the land of Egypt, out of the house of slavery. When Pharaoh stubbornly refused to let us go, the Lord killed every firstborn in Egypt, from the firstborn of man to the firstborn of cattle. Therefore, I sacrifice to the Lord every male that opens the womb, but every firstborn of my sons I shall redeem. It will serve as a sign on your hand and a lasting reminder before your eyes, for with a mighty hand the Lord led you out of Egypt.'"ᵃᵃ In conclusion, every facet of this rite was meant to serve, not any need of God's, but the salvation of his people.[5]

4. Theodoret has developed an elaborate parallel between the original Passover and the liturgy of the Eucharist as a Passover meal; for him the former offers only "obscure figures" (αἰνίγματα), the latter, the reality foreshadowed by the figures.

5. Here Theodoret returns to the original point of the question, the reason for the Passover celebration, which he has answered at the two levels of literal and allegorical exegesis. The question-answer genre allows him to address his own theological and exegetical concerns.

XXV

Τινές φασιν εἰς δώδεκα διαιρέσεις διαιρεθῆναι τὴν
θάλατταν καὶ ἑκάστην φυλὴν καθ' ἑαυτὴν διαβῆναι καὶ τοῦτο
νομίζουσι τὸν μακάριον εἰρηκέναι Δαβίδ· *τῷ καταδιελόντι τὴν*
ἐρυθρὰν θάλασσαν εἰς διαιρέσεις.[a]

5 Ἐγὼ δὲ διχῇ νομίζω τμηθῆναι τὸ πέλαγος· τοῦτο γὰρ καὶ ἡ
θεία διδάσκει γραφή· *τὸ δὲ ὕδωρ αὐτοῖς τεῖχος ἐκ δεξιῶν καὶ*
τεῖχος ἐξ εὐωνύμων·[b] τὴν δὲ ὁδὸν εὐρεῖαν γενέσθαι,
σύμμετρον τῷ πλήθει τῶν παριόντων· *ὡδήγησε,* γάρ φησιν,
αὐτοὺς ἐν ἀβύσσῳ ὡς ἐν ἐρήμῳ.[c] τοῦτο δὲ τῆς ὁδοῦ τὴν
10 εὐρυχωρίαν δηλοῖ. οὐδὲ ἐκεῖνος μέντοι ὁ λόγος τῷ τῆς
εὐσεβείας λυμαίνεται λόγῳ· καὶ τοῦτο γὰρ κἀκεῖνο τῆς θείας
ἔργον θαυματουργίας. χρὴ μέντοι ἀκολουθεῖν τῇ τῆς θείας
γραφῆς ἀληθείᾳ. τῇ δὲ δι' ὕδατος πανωλεθρίᾳ τὸν Φαραὼ
πανστρατιᾷ παραδέδωκεν ὁ δικαιότατος δικαστής, ἐπειδήπερ
15 δι' ὕδατος ἀνεῖλε τῶν ἑβραίων τὰ βρέφη.[d]

XXVI

Ὁποῖον ἦν τὸ ξύλον τὸ γλυκᾶναν ἐν τῇ Μερρᾷ τὸ ὕδωρ;[a]
Περιττὸν καὶ ἀνόητον τὸ τὰ σεσιγημένα ζητεῖν. ἀρκεῖ δὲ
ἡμῖν μαθεῖν ὡς διὰ τοῦ ξύλου τὸ πικρὸν ὕδωρ εἰς γλυκεῖαν
μετεβλήθη ποιότητα· καὶ τοῦτο γὰρ τὴν ἡμετέραν προδηλοῖ

---

xxv A⁻⁶ [32], B, C, 7 9 10 17 31 35 37 = 20 mss.

a. Ps 136.13   b. Ex 14.22   c. Ps 106.9   d. Ex 1.22; 14.28

xxvi A⁻⁶ [32], B, C, 7 9 10 17 31 35 37 = 20 mss.

a. Ex 15.23–25

XXV

Some commentators have claimed that the sea was divided into twelve parts, and each tribe took its own path, and they believe that this is the meaning of David's: "[Give thanks to him] who divided the Red Sea into parts."[a]

My position is that the sea was divided in half. As holy Scripture teaches us: "The water formed a wall to the right of them and a wall to the left."[b] And I believe the way was made wide enough to accommodate the vast number of people making the crossing. Indicating the breadth of the path, Scripture says, "He guided them in the deep, as in the wilderness."[c] The other explanation, however, does not undermine orthodoxy; both the one and the other would be a divine miracle. Nevertheless, we should adhere to the facts of holy Scripture.[1] It was with perfect justice, that the judge consigned Pharaoh and all his host to destruction by water, because Pharaoh had used water to kill the babies of the Hebrews.[d]

XXVI

What kind of wood sweetened the water of Marah?[a]

It is pointless and foolish to inquire into unspoken secrets. It is sufficient for us to learn that, through the wood, the bitter quality of the water was transformed into sweetness. This was an early revela-

---

1. In his commentary on Ps 135.13 (= 136.13 MT), where he had rejected the possibility of multiple crossings as a "tale invented by Jews" ('Ιουδαϊκοῖς ... μύθοις), Theodoret had based his understanding of the event, as here, on Ex 14.22. That Jewish tradition arose because of the plural form of the Hebrew noun "parts," which Dahood (on Ps 136.13) regards as a corruption of an original dual meaning "in half"; in support of this view, he cites the phrase "through the middle" in the following verse. In his *hom. in Ex.* (5.5), Origen had treated this ancient tradition as worthy of consideration, and Chrysostom, who may have been Theodoret's source, endorsed it in sec. 2 of his *Exp. in Ps.* 135.

5 σωτηρίαν· τὸ γὰρ σωτήριον τοῦ σταυροῦ ξύλον τὴν πικρὰν τῶν
ἐθνῶν ἐγλύκανε θάλατταν.

XXVII

Πῶς νοητέον τὸ ὑπὸ τοῦ ἀποστόλου εἰρημένον· *πάντες εἰς*
τὸν Μωϋσῆν ἐβαπτίσθησαν ἐν τῇ νεφέλῃ καὶ ἐν τῇ
θαλάσσῃ ... καὶ πάντες τὸ αὐτὸ πόμα πνευματικὸν ἔπιον·
ἔπινον γὰρ ἐκ πνευματικῆς ἀκολουθούσης πέτρας. ἡ δὲ πέτρα
5 *ἦν ὁ Χριστός;*[a]

Τύπος ἦν τῶν νέων τὰ παλαιά· καὶ σκιὰ μὲν ὁ νόμος
Μωϋσέως, σῶμα δὲ ἡ χάρις. ἐπειδὴ τοίνυν ἐδίωκον τοὺς
ἑβραίους αἰγύπτιοι, διαβάντες δὲ τὴν ἐρυθρὰν θάλατταν, οἱ
ἑβραῖοι τῆς πικρᾶς τῶν αἰγυπτίων ἀπηλλάγησαν δεσποτείας,[b]
10 τύπον ἔχει τῆς κολυμβήθρας ἡ θάλαττα, ἡ δὲ νεφέλη τοῦ
πνεύματος,[c] ὁ δὲ Μωϋσῆς τοῦ σωτῆρος Χριστοῦ, τοῦ σταυροῦ
δὲ ἡ ῥάβδος,[d] τοῦ διαβόλου ὁ Φαραώ, τῶν δαιμόνων οἱ
αἰγύπτιοι,[e] τὸ δὲ μάννα τῆς θείας τροφῆς,[f] τὸ δὲ τῆς πέτρας
ὕδωρ τοῦ σωτηρίου αἵματος.[g] ὥσπερ γὰρ ἐκεῖνοι, μετὰ τὸ
15 διαβῆναι τὴν ἐρυθρὰν θάλασσαν, καὶ τῆς ξένης τροφῆς καὶ
τοῦ παραδόξου ἀπήλαυσαν νάματος, οὕτως ἡμεῖς, μετὰ τὸ
σωτήριον βάπτισμα, τῶν θείων μεταλαμβάνομεν μυστηρίων.

---

xxvii A⁻⁶ *[32]*, B, C⁻⁵², 7 9 10 17 31* 35 37 = 19 mss.

a. 1Cor 10.2, 4   b. Ex 14.22   c. Ex 14.19f.   d. Ex 14.16   e. Ex 14.5–9
f. Ex 16.14f.   g. Ex 17.6

tion of our salvation, of the saving wood of the cross that sweetened the bitter sea of the nations.[1]

XXVII

How should we understand the apostle's statement: "All were baptized into Moses in the cloud and in the sea; all drank the same spiritual drink, for they drank from the spiritual rock that followed them, and the rock was Christ"?[a]

The old was a type of the new, the Law of Moses a shadow, grace the body. As the Egyptians pursued the Hebrews, and, by crossing the Red Sea, the Hebrews were freed from the harsh domination of the Egyptians,[b] the sea represents, in typological terms, the baptismal font, the cloud the Spirit,[c] Moses Christ the Savior, the rod the cross,[d] Pharaoh the devil, the Egyptians the demons,[e] the manna the divine nourishment,[f] and the water from the rock the saving blood.[g] After the crossing of the Red Sea, the ancients enjoyed the novel food and miraculous spring; just so, after saving baptism, we partake of the sacred Eucharist.[1]

1. In a commentary of Ex 15.23–25, the reader might hope to find an exposition of the name "Marah" (= "bitter" in Hebrew) or a discussion of the murmuring of the people. Instead Theodoret focuses only on the wood, for which he offers an allegorical interpretation. Again, his exegetical choice is governed by his christology.

1. In 1Cor 10.2–4, Paul provides Theodoret with justification for seeing in the OT types of NT, especially sacramental, realities. Neither in his commentary on Paul nor in the *Quaest. in oct.* does Theodoret discuss the later Jewish notion of the moving, rock-shaped well, for which *v.* E.E. Ellis, "A Note," pp. 53–56.

XXVIII

Διὰ τί ἡ πέτρα Χριστὸς ὠνομάσθη;[a]

Ὡς τύπος γενομένη τοῦ δεσπότου Χριστοῦ. οὕτω καὶ ἡ θάλαττα βάπτισμα προσηγορεύθη καίτοι οὐδενὸς ἐν αὐτῇ βαπτισθέντος· κεκονιαμένος γὰρ μᾶλλον αὐτὴν ἢ διάβροχος
5 διῆλθεν ὁ Ἰσραήλ.

XXIX

||37   Διὰ τί ἄρτον ἀγγέλων τὸ μάννα προσηγόρευσεν|| ὁ προφήτης Δαβίδ;[a]

Ὡς ἀγγέλων τῇ τούτου δωρεᾷ διακεκονηκότων· ἡ γὰρ ἀσώματος φύσις οὐ δεῖται τροφῆς. οὕτως ἄρτος οὐρανοῦ
|37   5   προσηγορεύθη, ἐπειδὴ ἄνωθεν κατηνέχθη, οὐκ ἐξ αὐτοῦ τοῦ οὐρανοῦ, ἀλλ' ἐκ τοῦ ἀέρος. οὕτω καὶ πετεινὰ οὐρανοῦ προσηγόρευται τὰ τὸν ἀέρα διαπερῶντα.

XXX

Διὰ τί μάννα ἐκλήθη;[a]

Εὐθὺς αὐτὸ θεασάμενοι, ἀλλήλους ἠρώτων, τί τοῦτο; ἐπέθεσαν τοίνυν αὐτῷ προσηγορίαν τί τοῦτο· τοῦτο γὰρ

xxviii A^{-6} [32], B, C, 7 9 10 17 31 35 37 = 20 mss.
a. 1Cor 10.4

xxix A^{-6} [32], B, C, 7 9 10 17 31 35 37(inc.) = 20 mss.
a. Ps 78.25

xxx A^{-6} [32], B, C, 7 9 10 17 31 35 37 = 20 mss.
a. Ex 16.31

XXVIII

Why was the rock called "Christ"?[a]

Because it proved a type of Christ the Lord. Likewise, the sea was given the name "baptism," though no one was baptized in it, for in the crossing, Israel was covered in dust, not water.[1]

XXIX

Why did the prophet David call the manna "the bread of an-gels"?[a]

Because the gift of manna was conferred through the ministry of angels. Incorporeal beings, of course, have no need of food. Like-wise, it was called "the bread of heaven,"[1] since it was brought down from on high—not from heaven itself but from the sky. Similarly, the creatures that fly across the sky are called "birds of heaven."

XXX

Why was it called "manna"?[a]

As soon as they saw it, they asked each other, "What is it?" So they named it "What is it?" the meaning of *manna*. As we learn from sa-

---

1. Theodoret combines a typological approach with a literalistic reading of the text.

---

1. Surprisingly, Theodoret's replies to this and the next question contain no ref-erence to the Eucharist.

ἑρμηνεύει τὸ *μάννα*. τοῦτο δὲ καὶ ἡ ἱστορία διδάσκει·

5 *ἰδόντες* ..., *γάρ* φησιν, *οἱ υἱοὶ Ἰσραήλ, εἶπον ἕτερος τῷ*
ἑτέρῳ, τί ἐστι τοῦτο; οὐ γὰρ ᾔδεσαν τί ἦν·[b] ἐγένετο τοίνυν ἡ
ἐρώτησις ὄνομα. τὸ δὲ *ὡς ἐγκρὶς ἐν μέλιτι*[c] ὁ Σύμμαχος οὕτως
ἡρμήνευσεν· *ὡς ἄμυλος ἐν μέλιτι.*

Τὸ δὲ *γόμορ* μέτρον ἦν ἑβραϊκόν.[d] διδάσκει δὲ ὁ νομοθέτης
10 ὅτι *τὸ δέκατον ἦν τῶν τριῶν μέτρων*[e] ὡς δὲ Ἰώσηπος ἔφη,
τρεῖς ἥμισυ κοτύλας ἀττικὰς ἔχει.[f]

XXXI

Διὰ τί τὸ καταλειφθὲν εἰς τὴν ὑστεραίαν τοῦ *μάννα*
διεφθάρη;[a]

Ἐπειδὴ νόμου παράβασις ἦν. διδάσκων γὰρ αὐτοὺς τῶν
φροντίδων ἐλεύθερον βίον, ὑπέσχετο καθ' ἑκάστην αὐτοῖς
5 ἡμέραν παρέχειν τὴν ἀναγκαίαν τροφήν.[b] ἐκεῖνοι δὲ
ἀπιστήσαντες, μέρος τι τοῦ συλλεγέντος εἰς τὴν ὑστεραίαν
ἐφύλαξαν. διὰ τοῦτο ἐπώζεσεν. ὅτι γὰρ οὐ τῆς τοῦ *μάννα*
φύσεως ἦν τὸ πάθος μαρτυρεῖ τὸ σάββατον, ἐν ᾧ ἀλώβητον
διετηρήθη τὸ τῇ παρασκευῇ συλλεγέν·[c] μαρτυρεῖ δὲ καὶ τὸ ἐν
10 τῇ κιβωτῷ ἐπὶ πολλαῖς διαφυλαχθὲν γενεαῖς.[d]

XXXII

Διὰ τί ἐν τοῖς σάββασιν οὐ παρέσχε τὸ *μάννα*;[a]
Ἐπειδὴ μόνοις αὐτοῖς τοῦ σαββάτου τὴν ἀργίαν

b. Ex 16.15   c. Ex 16.31   d. Ex 16.16   e. Ex 16.36   f. Ios., *A.I.* 3.142

---

xxxi A^{-6} *[32]*, B, C, 7 9 10 17 31 35 37 = 20 mss.

a. Ex 16.19   b. Ex 16.16   c. Ex 16.19–24   d. Ex 16.33f.

---

xxxii A^{-6} *[32]*, B, C, 7 9 10 17 31 35 37 = 20 mss.

a. Ex 16.27

cred history, "When the children of Israel saw it, one said to the other, 'What is it?' since they did not know what it was."[1b] So the question became the name. Symmachus rendered the phrase "like pastry made with honey"[c] as "like a cake of fine meal made with honey."

The homer was a Hebrew measure.[d] As the lawgiver explains, "It was the tenth part of three measures,"[e] whereas, according to Josephus, "it contained three and a half Attic cups."[f]

XXXI

Why did any manna left over for the next day spoil?[a]

Because this was a transgression of the law. You see, to teach them about a life free from daily concerns, he promised to provide them with the food necessary for each day.[b] But, in their lack of faith, they kept part of what they had gathered for the next day, and as a result it went bad. The Sabbath provides proof that the trouble was not inherent in the nature of the manna, because, on that day, manna gathered the day before remained fresh.[c] And this is confirmed by the manna that was preserved in the ark for many generations.[d]

XXXII

Why did he provide no manna on the Sabbaths?[a]
Since he established the law of inactivity on the Sabbath for them

---

1. This popular etymology, attested also in Jos., *A.J.* 3.32, is not, in fact, accurate, since the correct Hebrew would be *mâ hû*. The term is actually derived from the name of a tamarisk indigenous to Palestine and the Sinai; *v.* R.J. Clifford, on Ex 16.13–30.

ἐνομοθέτησεν, ἔργῳ αὐτοὺς ἐδίδαξε φυλάττειν τὴν ἐντολήν.[b]
τὸν δὲ τῆς φύσεως οὐκ ἐκώλυσε δρόμον· ἀνίσχει γὰρ ἥλιος καὶ
5 σελήνη ὡσαύτως καὶ τὰ νέφη τὸν ὑετὸν ὠδίνει, καὶ ἄνεμοι
πνέουσι, καὶ γυναῖκες τίκτουσι καὶ τῶν ἀλόγων τὰ γένη.

XXXIII

Ποίοις ὅπλοις ἐχρῶντο, τῷ Ἀμαλὴκ πολεμοῦντες;[a]
Τῶν αἰγυπτίων ὑποβρυχίων γεγενημένων, ἐξεβράσθη αὐτῶν
εἰς τὴν ἠϊόνα μετὰ τῶν ὅπλων τὰ σώματα.[b] ταῦτα
σκυλεύσαντες, ἐχρῶντο τούτοις ἐν τοῖς πολέμοις.

XXXIV

Διὰ τί, τῶν Μωϋσέως χειρῶν ἐκτεταμένων, ἐνίκα Ἰσραήλ,
καθιεμένων δέ, ἡττᾶτο;[a]
Τοῦ σταυρωθέντος ὑπὲρ ἡμῶν ἐπλήρου τὸν τύπον, ἐκτείνων
τὰς χεῖρας. ἐδείχθη τοίνυν καὶ ἐν τῷ τύπῳ τῆς ἀληθείας ἡ
5 δύναμις· ὥσπερ γὰρ τοῦ θεράποντος τὰς χεῖρας ἐκτείνοντος,
ἔπεσεν Ἀμαλήκ, οὕτως τοῦ δεσπότου τὰς χεῖρας ἐκτείναντος,
κατελύθη τοῦ διαβόλου τὸ στῖφος. καὶ ἐν ἐκείνῳ δὲ τῷ πολέμῳ
ὁ τοῦ σωτῆρος ἡμῶν ὁμώνυμος τὸ τρόπαιον ἔστησε, τότε
ταύτην τὴν προσηγορίαν λαβὼν καὶ τοῖς λογάσι χρησάμενος
10 συνεργοῖς[b] ὡς ὁ δεσπότης Χριστὸς ὑπουργοῖς τοῖς ἱεροῖς
ἀποστόλοις.

b. Ex 20.8–10

---

xxxiii A⁻⁶ [32], B, C, 7 9 10 17 31 35 37 = 20 mss.
a. Ex 17.8–10   b. Ex 14.30

---

xxxiv A⁻⁶ [32], B, C, 7 9 10 17 35 37 = 19 mss.
a. Ex 17.11   b. Ex 17.8–13

alone, this was a way to instruct them to observe his command.[b] On the other hand, he did not halt the course of nature: the sun and moon rise, the clouds bring forth rain, the winds blow, and women and the different species of animals give birth on the Sabbath.

XXXIII

What weapons did they use to fight against Amalek?[1a]

When the Egyptians were drowned, their bodies were cast up on the shore with their weapons.[b] They plundered these and used them in warfare.

XXXIV

Why was Israel victorious when Moses stretched out his hands, but defeated when he let them drop?[a]

When Moses stretched out his hands, he represented a type of him who was crucified for us; the power of the reality was demonstrated even in the type. As Amalek fell when the servant stretched out his hands, so the devil's column was routed when the Lord stretched out his. And, in that battle, he who bore our Savior's name first took that name when he set up the trophy and employed some picked men as his helpers,[b] as Christ the Lord employed the sacred apostles as his lieutenants.[1]

1. Here is another merely inquisitive question possessing none of the typological interest of the next item. Theodoret delays comment on the provocation of God and the miracle of water flowing from the rock (Ex 17.1–7) until he comes to the doublet at Nm 20.2–13 (*Q.* 37 on Nm); *cf Q.* 5 on Dt.

1. In Ex 17.8–16 Joshua and his chosen men rout Amalek. "Joshua" is the same name as "Jesus"; in the LXX and the NT both are spelled Ἰησοῦς. The term τρό-παιον (trophy) is very frequently applied to the cross and death of Christ; *v. PGL, sub. uoc.* 1. For similar uses of this noun as the direct object of the verb ἵστημι (to set up): *cf.* Chrys., *hom.* 85.1 (*al.* 84.1) *in Ioh.:* [some say that Christ] ἔνθα ὁ θάνα-τος ἐβασίλευσεν, ἐκεῖ καὶ τὸ τρόπαιον στῆσαι (*i.e.,* on Calvary).

The Questions on Exodus

XXXV

Τί ἐστιν ἔσεσθέ μοι λαὸς περιούσιος ἀπὸ πάντων τῶν
ἐθνῶν· ἐμὴ γάρ ἐστι πᾶσα ἡ γῆ;[a]

Πάντων εἰμί, φησί, ποιητὴς καὶ δεσπότης καὶ πάντων ὡς
ποιητὴς προμηθοῦμαι, ὑμᾶς δὲ οἷόν τινα λαὸν ἐξαίρετον
5 ἐμαυτῷ ἀφιέρωσα. τοῦτο γὰρ ἐπήγαγεν· ὑμεῖς δὲ ἔσεσθέ μοι
εἰς βασίλειον ἱεράτευμα..., ἔθνος ἅγιον.[b] ὥσπερ γὰρ τοὺς
λευίτας, ἰσραηλίτας ὄντας, τῶν ἄλλων φυλῶν προτετίμηκε καὶ
εἰς τὴν θείαν ἀφώρισε λειτουργίαν,[c] οὐ τῶν ἄλλων ἀμελῶν,
ἀλλὰ διὰ τούτων τὴν ἐκείνων ποιούμενος ἐπιμέλειαν, οὕτω τὸ
10 τοῦ Ἀβραάμ, καὶ Ἰσαάκ, καὶ Ἰακὼβ ἐξελέξατο σπέρμα· πρῶτον
ἐπειδὴ ἐξ αὐτῶν ἤμελλε κατὰ σάρκα βλαστάνειν ὁ δεσπότης
Χριστός· ἔπειτα διὰ τῶν εἰς τούτους γινομένων τὴν οἰκείαν
ἐπιδεικνὺς δύναμιν καὶ πάντας διδάσκων ἀνθρώπους τὴν τῆς
θεογνωσίας ὁδόν. τούτων μέντοι εἰρημένων, ἀπεκρίθη... πᾶς ὁ
15 λαὸς... καὶ εἶπε, πάντα ὅσα εἶπεν ὁ Θεὸς ποιήσομεν καὶ
ἀκουσόμεθα.[d] αὕτη δὲ ἡ τοῦ λαοῦ συνθήκη ὑπογραφῇ τινι ἔοικε
γραμματίου. ὅθεν τὴν οἰκείαν παραβάντες ὁμολογίαν, ταῖς
τῆς νομοθεσίας ἀραῖς ὑπεβλήθησαν,[e] ὧν τοὺς εἰς αὐτὸν
πεπιστευκότας ὁ δεσπότης Χριστὸς ἠλευθέρωσε· Χριστός, γάρ
20 φησιν, ἐξηγόρασεν ἡμᾶς ἐκ τῆς κατάρας τοῦ νόμου, γενόμενος
ὑπὲρ ἡμῶν κατάρα.[f] τὸ μέντοι περιούσιος, ἐξαίρετος ὁ
Σύμμαχος ἡρμήνευσεν.

xxxv A⁻⁶ [32], B, C⁻⁵¹, 7 9 10 17 31 35 37 = 19 mss.

a. Ex 19.5   b. Ex 19.6   c. Nm 3.5–13   d. Ex 19.8   e. Dt 28.15–68
f. Gal 3.13

XXXV

What is the meaning of "You will be my special people out of all the nations, for all the earth is mine"?[a]

He means, "I am Creator and Lord of the universe, and, as Creator, I care for everything, but you I have consecrated to myself as a chosen people." In fact, he went on, "You will be my royal priesthood, my holy nation."[1b] In other words, as he honored the Levites —though they were Israelites like the rest—over the other tribes, and consecrated them to the divine worship[c] without neglecting, but actually showing care for, the others through the Levites, so he chose the offspring of Abraham, Isaac, and Jacob. First, because Christ the Lord would draw his descent from them according to the flesh. Next, to give evidence of his power through the acts he performed for them and to teach all men the way of the knowledge of God. Indeed, when God had made this promise, "All the people replied and declared, 'We shall do and heed everything God has said.'"[d] Now, this agreement of the people resembled a signature to a contract. Hence, when they broke their own agreement, they became liable to the curses prescribed by the Law,[e] from which Christ the Lord freed those who believe in him: "Christ redeemed us from the curse of the Law by becoming a curse for us."[f] Instead of "special" Symmachus rendered "chosen."

1. In this interpretation of Ex 19.5f. Theodoret anticipates the conclusions of modern scholarship. Noting the problematic movement of thought from choice of the people to mention of priesthood, he concludes the text must imply that the choice of the line of Abraham from all other peoples resembled the privileged position of the Levites among the other tribes; cf. R.J. Clifford *ad loc.*

XXXVI

Τί δή ποτε, οὐ μόνον ἁγνισθῆναι, ἀλλὰ καὶ πλῦναι τὰ
ἱμάτια προσετάχθησαν ἡνίκα τὸν νόμον ἐδέχοντο;[a]

Διὰ τῶν σωματικῶν αὐτοὺς ἐπὶ τὰ πνευματικὰ ποδηγεῖ, καὶ
δέος ἐντίθησι, καὶ εὐλαβεστέρους ποιεῖ· ἐλογίζοντο γὰρ ἐκ
5 τούτων ὡς πολλῷ μᾶλλον τὴν διάνοιαν καθαρεύειν προσήκει.
διά τοι τοῦτο καὶ σαλπίγγων φωναί, καὶ κτύποι βροντῶν, καὶ
γνόφος, καὶ θύελλα, καὶ πῦρ ἐν τῇ τοῦ ὄρους ἀκρωρείᾳ, καὶ
κάπνος ἄφραστος ἐκπεμπόμενος[b] ἵνα διὰ τούτων ἁπάντων τὴν
λιθίνην αὐτῶν καταμαλάξῃ καρδίαν.[c] ἐπειδὴ γὰρ τὰς μὲν τοῖς
10 αἰγυπτίοις ἐπενεχθείσας ἐθεάσαντο τιμωρίας, αὐτοὶ δὲ πεῖραν
τῆς παιδείας οὐκ ἔλαβον, διὰ τούτων δεδίττεται οἷα δὴ
παῖδας, ὥστε, μὴ μόνον ἀγαπᾶν διὰ τὰς ἀρρήτους εὐεργεσίας,
ἀλλὰ καὶ δεδιέναι διὰ τὰς τιμωρίας. τούτου χάριν καὶ περὶ
τῶν ἱερέων ἔφη, *οἱ ἱερεῖς, οἱ ἐγγίζοντες Κυρίῳ τῷ Θεῷ,*
15 *ἁγιασθήτωσαν μή ποτε ἀπαλλάξῃ ἀπ' αὐτῶν Κύριος.*[d] ἐπειδὴ
γὰρ εἰκὸς ἦν αὐτοὺς θαρρεῖν, ἅτε δὴ τὴν θείαν λειτουργίαν
πεπιστευμένους, διδάσκει ὡς διαφερόντως τοὺς λειτουργεῖν
τῷ Θεῷ προτεταγμένους ὑπερτέρους εἶναι τῶν γηΐνων
προσήκει.

---

xxxvi A⁻⁶ *[32]*, B, C⁻⁵¹, *7 9 10 17 31 35 37* = 19 mss.

a. Ex 19.10   b. Ex 19.18f.   c. Ezek 11.19   d. Ex 19.22

XXXVI

Why were they ordered, not just to sanctify themselves, but also to wash their garments when they were about to receive the Law?[a]

Through the bodily, he guided them to the spiritual, realities. He also instilled fear and put them into a more reverent frame of mind. In fact, they deduced from these instructions the much greater importance of purity of mind. The trumpet blasts, thunder claps, darkness, hurricane, the fire on the top of the mountain, and the marvelous cloud of smoke[b] were surely all means of softening their "stony heart."[c] Since they had observed the punishments inflicted on the Egyptians without themselves undergoing the experience of correction, he used these portents to terrify them like children, the result being that they not only loved him for his ineffable favors but also feared him for his punishments. Therefore, he also said in regard to the priests, "Let the priests approaching the Lord God sanctify themselves lest the Lord destroy any of them."[d] In other words, since their commission to perform the divine service was probably encouraging an attitude of overconfidence, he taught those appointed to conduct the worship of God that they should stand out by their superiority to earthly concerns.

XXXVII

Πῶς νοητέον τὸ οὐκ ἔσονταί σοι θεοὶ ἕτεροι πλὴν ἐμοῦ;[a]

Οἱ μίαν οὐσίαν τῆς τριάδος ὁμολογοῦντες φυλάττουσι τὸν
νόμον τῆς θείας φωνῆς· ἄλλο γάρ τι παρὰ τὴν θείαν φύσιν
θεοποιεῖν οὐκ ἀνέχονται. οἱ δὲ τὴν Ἀρείου καὶ Εὐνομίου
5 περικείμενοι λώβην τὸν θεῖον νόμον ἄντικρυς παραβαίνουσιν,
Θεὸν μὲν τὸν υἱὸν ὁμολογοῦντες, κτιστὸν δὲ ἀποκαλοῦντες
καὶ τῆς θείας οὐσίας ἀλλότριον. τοῦ γὰρ Θεοῦ λέγοντος, οὐκ
ἔσονταί σοι θεοὶ ἕτεροι πλὴν ἐμοῦ, οὗτοι ἕτερον Θεὸν
ἐπεισάγουσιν.

XXXVIII

Εἴδωλον καὶ *ὁμοίωμα*[a] ποίαν ἔχει διαφοράν;

Τὸ εἴδωλον οὐδεμίαν ὑπόστασιν ἔχει, τὸ δὲ ὁμοίωμα τινός
ἐστιν ἴνδαλμα καὶ ἀπείκασμα. ἐπειδὴ τοίνυν ἕλληνες
ἀναπλάττουσι τὰς οὐχ ὑφεστώσας μορφάς· σφίγγας, καὶ
5 τρίτωνας, καὶ κενταύρους· καὶ αἰγύπτιοι κυνοπροσώπους καὶ
βουκεφάλους, εἴδωλα καλεῖ τὰ τῶν οὐχ ὑφεστώτων μιμήματα,
ὁμοιώματα δὲ τὰ τῶν ὑφεστώτων εἰκάσματα οἷον ἡλίου καὶ
σελήνης, ἀστέρων, ἀνθρώπων, θηρίων, ἑρπετῶν, καὶ τῶν
τούτοις παραπλησίων. τούτοις κελεύει μήτε προσκυνεῖν μήτε
10 λατρεύειν.[b] οὐχ ἁπλῶς δὲ ἀπαγορεύει ἀμφότερα ἀλλ', ἐπειδὴ
συμβαίνει τινὰς προσκυνῆσαι μὲν διὰ φόβον ἀνθρώπινον οὐ
μὴν καὶ λατρεῦσαι κατὰ ψυχήν, ἐδίδαξεν ὡς ἑκάτερον ἀσεβές.

---

xxxvii A⁻⁶ [32], B, C, 7 9 10 17 31* 35 37 = 20 mss.
a. Ex 20.3

---

xxxviii A⁻⁶ [32], B, C, 7 9 10 17 31 35 37 = 20 mss.
a. Ex 20.4   b. Ex 20.5

XXXVII

How are we to understand the verse "You shall have no other gods but me"?[a]

Those who confess the oneness of being of the Trinity observe this law of God's utterance. They refuse to make a god of anything but divinity. By contrast, those infected with the ailment of Arius and Eunomius blatantly transgress the Law of God when they confess the Son to be God, but degrade him by calling him a creature and divorced from the divine being. Though God says, "You shall have no other gods but me," they introduce a second God.[1]

XXXVIII

What is the difference between "an idol" and "a likeness"?[a]

An idol has no reality behind it, while a likeness is an image and representation of someone or something. So since the Greeks mold forms of non-existent beings, such as sphinxes, tritons, and centaurs, and the Egyptians dog-faced and bull-headed beings, he referred by "idols" to representations of the non-existent. By "likenesses" he meant images of things that do exist, like the sun and moon, the stars, human beings, animals, reptiles, and the like. He forbade them to bow down to or worship these,[b] each prohibition being based on good reason. Since people sometimes bow down out of human respect without actually offering worship in their heart, he taught that both actions are idolatrous.[1]

1. Theodoret pays no attention to the opening statement of antecedent divine beneficence in 20.2, which provides the basis for the commands that follow; *cf.* Clifford on 20.2–6. He sees the first commandment (20.3) as infringed rather by Arians and Eunomians than by Jews.

1. With typical Antiochene precision (ἀκρίβεια), Theodoret notes the occur-

XXXIX

Τὸ Θεὸς ζηλωτὴς τί ἐστιν;[a]

Ὁ νόμος τάξιν ἐπέχει ἀνδρός, ὁ δὲ λαὸς γυναικός, καὶ
τοῦτο ἡμᾶς ἐδίδαξεν ὁ δεσπότης Θεός, διὰ μὲν Ἡσαΐου
λέγων, ποῖον τοῦτο τὸ βιβλίον τοῦ ἀποστασίου τῆς μητρὸς
5 ὑμῶν·[b] διὰ δὲ Ἱερεμίου, καθὼς ἀθετεῖ γυνὴ εἰς τὸν συνόντα
αὐτῇ, οὕτως ἠθέτησεν εἰς ἐμὲ ὁ οἶκος Ἰσραὴλ καὶ ὁ οἶκος
Ἰούδα, λέγει Κύριος·[c] καὶ πάλιν, ἐὰν ἀποστείλῃ ἀνὴρ τὴν
γυναῖκα αὐτοῦ, καὶ πορευθεῖσα ... γένηται ἀνδρὶ ἑτέρῳ, μὴ
ἀνακάμπτουσα ἀνακάμψει πρὸς αὐτὸν ἔτι; οὐ μιαινομένη
10 μιανθήσεται ἡ γυνὴ ἐκείνη· σὺ δὲ ἐξεπόρνευσας εἰς ποιμένας
πολλούς, καὶ ἀνέκαμπτες πρός με· λέγει Κύριος·[d] καὶ ὁ
ἀπόστολος δέ φησιν, ὅτι ὁ νόμος κυριεύει τοῦ ἀνθρώπου ἐφ'
ὅσον χρόνον ζῇ· ἡ γὰρ ὕπανδρος γυνὴ τῷ ζῶντι ἀνδρὶ δέδεται
νόμῳ· ἐὰν δὲ ἀποθάνῃ ὁ ἀνήρ, κατήργηται ἀπὸ τοῦ νόμου τοῦ
15 ἀνδρὸς ... τοῦ μὴ εἶναι αὐτὴν μοιχαλίδα, γενομένην ἀνδρὶ
ἑτέρῳ. οὕτως καὶ ὑμεῖς ἐθανατώθητε τῷ νόμῳ διὰ τοῦ σώματος
τοῦ Χριστοῦ εἰς τὸ γενέσθαι ὑμᾶς ἑτέρῳ, τῷ ἐκ νεκρῶν
ἐγερθέντι.[e] τούτου χάριν Θεὸν ζηλωτὴν ἑαυτὸν ὀνομάζει, τοῖς
ἀνθρωπίνοις μὲν κεχρημένος ὀνόμασι, δεδιττόμενος δὲ αὐτοὺς
20 καὶ σωφρονεῖν ἀναγκάζων· ὥσπερ γὰρ ἀνὴρ ῥάθυμον ἔχων
γυναῖκα παραινῶν αὐτῇ λέγει, ζηλότυπός εἰμι, οὐ δύναμαι
βλέπειν σε ἄλλῳ προσδιαλεγομένην ἀνδρί, οὕτως ὁ δεσπότης
Θεός, τῆς δεισιδαιμονίας αὐτοὺς ἀπαλλάξαι βουλόμενος, οὐ
μόνον ζηλωτὴν ἑαυτόν, ἀλλὰ καὶ πῦρ καταναλίσκον[f] ἐκάλεσεν.

25 Ὅτι δὲ φιλοστοργίας ὁ τοιοῦτος ζῆλος, αὐτὸς τοῦτο
δεδήλωκεν ὁ Θεὸς διὰ τοῦ Ἰεζεκιὴλ εἰπών, διὰ τοῦτο
ἀποστήσεται ὁ ζῆλός μου ἀπὸ σοῦ,[g] τουτέστιν, ὅτε ἠγάπων,

---

xxxix A^{-6} *[32]*, B, C^{-52}, 7 9 10 17 31 35 37 = 19 mss.

a. Ex 20.5   b. Is 50.1   c. Jer 3.20 (LXX var.)   d. Jer 3.1 (LXX)
e. Rom 7.1–4   f. Dt 9.3   g. Ezek 16.42

XXXIX

What does "a jealous God" mean?[a]

The Law has the role of husband, and the people that of wife, as the Lord God taught us when he said through Isaiah, "What is this bill of divorce of your mother?";[b] and through Jeremiah, "As a wife breaks faith with her partner, so the house of Israel and the house of Judah have broken faith with me, says the Lord";[c] and again, "If a husband sends his wife away, and she goes off to another husband, will she really return to him again? Will not that wife be defiled for good? But you have prostituted yourself with many shepherds, and you now return to me? says the Lord."[d] And the apostle says, "The Law is binding on a person only so long as he lives; for example, the wife is bound by law to her husband as long as he live, but if her husband die, she is discharged from the law concerning her husband, so that she is not an adulteress if she marry another husband. Likewise you, too, have died to the Law through the body of Christ so as to belong to another, who has risen from the dead."[e] God calls himself "a jealous God," using a human expression to put fear into them and compel them to live chastely. As a husband with a frivolous wife puts her on notice saying, "I am jealous and cannot bear to see you talking to another man," so the Lord God, wanting to rid them of superstition, called himself "jealous" and even "a consuming fire."[f]

Now, God himself indicated that jealousy arises from affection when he declared through Ezekiel, "Therefore, my jealousy will turn away from you."[g] That is, "When I loved you, I showed my jealousy,

---

rence of pairs of terms and shows that each member of the apparent duplication possesses a meaning of its own; *v.* sec. 4 of the "Introduction to Theodoret' s Life and Works."

ἐχρώμην τῷ ζήλῳ· ἀπωσάμενος δέ σε, καὶ τὸν ζῆλον ἔσβεσα.
τοῦτο καὶ δι' ἑτέρου προφήτου δεδήλωκεν· *οὐκ ἐπισκέψομαι*
30 *ἐπὶ τὰς θυγατέρας ὑμῶν ὅταν πορνεύσωσι καὶ ἐπὶ τὰς νύμφας*
ὑμῶν ὅταν μοιχεύσωσιν.[h] ἀγάπης τοίνυν ὁ ζῆλος δηλωτικός.

XL

Πῶς τὸ δίκαιον σώζεται, τῶν παίδων ὑπὲρ τῶν πατέρων
κολαζομένων;[a]

(1) Μείζους αἱ ἀπειλαὶ τῶν κολάσεων παρὰ τῷ δεσπότῃ
Θεῷ. καὶ τοῦτο ῥάδιον μαθεῖν παρὰ τῆς θείας γραφῆς· *πᾶς,*
5 *γάρ φησιν, ἀπερίτμητος ἄρσην, ὃς οὐ περιτμηθήσεται ... τῇ*
ἡμέρᾳ τῇ ὀγδόῃ, ἐξολοθρευθήσεται.[b] ἀλλ' ἔστιν εὑρεῖν τοὺς
μὲν περιτετμημένους ἐν τῇ ἐρήμῳ διαφόρως ἀναιρεθέντας,
τοὺς δὲ ἀπεριτμήτους μεμενηκότας τῆς τῶν προγόνων
ἐπαγγελίας τετυχηκότας· τούτους γὰρ ἐν Γαλγάλοις Ἰησοῦς
10 περιέτεμεν.[c] οὕτω ταῖς ἐχούσαις ζύμην οἰκίαις πανωλεθρίαν
ἠπείλησεν[d] ἀλλ' οὐκ ἐπήγαγε τὴν τιμωρίαν κατὰ τὴν ἀπειλήν.

Καὶ ἐνταῦθα τοίνυν, ὡς φιλόπαιδας καὶ φιλοπαιδίας
πεφροντικότας δεδίττεται ταῖς ἀπειλαῖς καί φησιν, *ἀποδιδοὺς*
ἁμαρτίας πατέρων ἐπὶ τέκνα ἐπὶ τρίτην καὶ τετάρτην γενεὰν
15 *τοῖς μισοῦσί με.*[e] ὅτι γὰρ γυμνῷ προσέχειν τῷ γράμματι
δυσσεβὲς αὐτὸς ὁ Θεὸς διδάσκει, τἀναντία νομοθετῶν· *οὐκ*
ἀποθανοῦνται, γάρ φησι, παῖδες ὑπὲρ πατέρων, οὐδὲ πατέρες
ὑπὲρ παίδων, ἀλλ' ἕκαστος ἐν τῇ ἁμαρτίᾳ αὐτοῦ ἀποθανεῖται[f]
καὶ διὰ τοῦ προφήτου Ἰεζεκιήλ φησι, *τίς ὑμῖν ἡ παραβολὴ*
20 *αὕτη ... λεγόντων, οἱ πατέρες ἔφαγον ὄμφακα, καὶ οἱ ὀδόντες*
τῶν τέκνων ᾐμωδίασαν; ζῶ ἐγώ, λέγει Κύριος, εἰ ἔσται ... ἡ

---

h. Hos 4.14

xl A⁻⁶ *[32]*, B, C, 4*(inc.)* 7 9 10 17 35 37 = 20 mss.

a. Ex 20.5   b. Gn 17.14   c. Jos 5.2–9   d. Ex 12.15, 19   e. Ex 20.5
f. Dt 24.16

but when I rejected you, I quenched my jealousy."[1] He conveyed the same idea through another prophet as well: "I shall not call your daughters to account for their prostitution, or your daughters-in-law for their adultery."[h] Jealousy, then, is indicative of love.

XL

How is justice preserved if children are punished for their parents?[a]

(1) With the Lord God, threats exceed punishments. It is an easy matter to prove this from holy Scripture: "Every uncircumcised male not circumcised on the eighth day will be destroyed,"[b] it says, yet note that in the wilderness it was the circumcised who were singled out for destruction while the uncircumcised received the fulfilment of the promise made to their ancestors. It was these that Joshua circumcised at Gilgal.[c] Similarly, he threatened destruction on any household that had leaven[d] but never proceeded to impose the punishment according to his threat.

In this case, he uses threats to put fear into people who loved children and large families, when he says, "I bring the sins of the parents upon the children to the third and fourth generation of those who hate me."[e] God himself teaches us that it is irreligious to focus on the face value of the text when he requires the opposite: "Children will not die for parents, nor parents for children; rather, each will die for his own sin."[f] And through the prophet Ezekiel he says, "What do you mean by the proverb, "The parents ate sour grapes, and the children's teeth are set on edge? As I live, says the

---

1. Theodoret had offered the same interpretation of Ezek 16.42 in his commentary on Ezekiel, composed some twenty-five years earlier.

παραβολὴ αὕτη·ᵍ ἀλλὰ τῶν φαγόντων τὸν ὄμφακα
αἱμωδιάσουσιν οἱ ὀδόντες,ʰ ὅτι πᾶσαι αἱ ψυχαὶ ἐμαί εἰσι·ⁱ καὶ
τὰ ἑξῆς δὲ τὴν αὐτὴν ἔχει διάνοιαν.

25   (2) Ἐγὼ δὲ οἶμαι μᾶλλον τὴν θείαν φιλανθρωπίαν ἐμφαίνειν
τὴν ἀπειλήν. πρόσκειται γὰρ τοῖς μισοῦσί με· τουτέστι,
μακροθυμῶ τοῖς πατράσιν ἡμαρτηκόσι, μακροθυμῶ καὶ παισίν·
εἰ δὲ οἱ ἔκγονοι καὶ οἱ ἀπόγονοι τὴν τῶν πατέρων καὶ
προγόνων ζηλώσαιεν πονηρίαν, ἐπάξω τὴν τιμωρίαν. ἡ δὲ τῶν
30   προγόνων εὐσέβεια μέχρι πολλοῦ τῷ γένει προξενήσει τὴν
σωτηρίαν· ποιῶν, γάρ φησιν, ἔλεον εἰς χιλιάδας καὶ μυριάδας
τοῖς ἀγαπῶσί με καὶ τοῖς φυλάττουσι τὰ προστάγματά μου.ʲ

Εὔροι δ' ἄν τις κἂν τῇ ἱστορίᾳ τὴν τῶν θείων λογίων
ἀλήθειαν· πέμπτη...γὰρ γενεᾷ, φησίν, ἀνέβησαν οἱ υἱοὶ
35   Ἰσραὴλ ἐξ...Αἰγύπτου.ᵏ ἀλλὰ τοῖς τῶν αἰγυπτίων ἐν Αἰγύπτῳ
|4   δεδουλευκότες θεοῖς, οὐ|κ ἔτισαν δίκας οὔτε οἱ πατέρες
αὐτῶν, οὔτε οἱ προπάτορες αὐτῶν. αὐτοὶ δέ, ζηλώσαντες τὴν
ἐκείνων ἀσέβειαν, ἐκολάσθησαν, ὡς μετὰ τοσαύτην εὐεργεσίαν
καὶ τὰ μυρία θαύματα τὴν ἀσέβειαν οὐκ ἐκπτύσαντες. οἱ δὲ
40   τούτων παῖδες, τὸν σωτῆρα Θεὸν ἠγαπηκότες, τῆς προγονικῆς
ἀπήλαυσαν ὑποσχέσεως. καὶ ὁρῶμεν τὸ ἀψευδὲς τῆς πρὸς
τοὺς πατριάρχας γεγενημένης ἐπαγγελίας· τὰ γὰρ ἔθνη διὰ
τοῦ σπέρματος Ἀβραὰμ τῆς εὐλογίας τετύχηκεν.ˡ

Ἐπειδὴ τοίνυν τὸν μόσχον ἤμελλον προσκυνεῖν, τὴν
45   τιμωρίαν προσαπειλεῖ.

g. Ezek 18.2f.   h. Jer 38.30 (LXX)   i. Ezek 18.4   j. Ex 20.6 (LXX var.)
k. Ex 13.18   l. Gn 12.3

Lord, this proverb will no more apply;[g] rather those who eat the sour grapes will have their teeth set on edge,[h] because all souls are mine";[i] the rest has the same sense.[1]

(2) In my view the threat actually has the effect of highlighting divine loving-kindness. Indeed, following this threat we find the phrase: "of those who hate me." That is, "I show long-suffering to parents who sin, and I show loving-kindness also to their children, but if their offspring and their descendants emulate the wickedness of their parents and forebears, I shall inflict punishment." In contrast, the piety of forebears will bring about salvation for many a generation, for God says, "I show mercy to thousands and tens of thousands of those who love me and keep my commandments."[2j]

The events of sacred history prove the dependability of the divine prophecy. "In the fifth generation," it says, "the children of Israel went up from Egypt."[k] While they were in Egypt, neither their fathers nor their forefathers paid the penalty for their slavish subjection to the Egyptian gods, but this generation was punished for emulating their idolatry, since even after they had experienced so much kindness and countless marvels, they did not reject the idolatry of their forebears. But their children, who loved God their Savior, came into the enjoyment of the promise made to their ancestors. And we witness the reliability of the promise made to the patriarchs, for the nations have attained the blessing through the offspring of Abraham.[l]

And a further point—he also threatened them, since they were just about to adore the calf.

---

1. Always anxious to resolve an apparent contradiction in the Bible, Theodoret cites Dt 24.16 and a form of Ezek 18.2–4 much influenced by Jer. 38.30 to claim that the literal sense (γυμνὸν γράμμα) is not a sure guide to the real meaning of Scripture.

2. In the Göttingen edition of the Septuagint, J.W. Wevers and U. Quast relegate the reading καὶ μυριάδας ("tens of thousands," Ex 20.6) to the *apparatus criticus;* it is attested only here by Theodoret and in the thirty-fifth of the *Interrogationes et Responsiones* (*Questions and Answers*) attributed to Anastasius Sinaita, the seventh-century theologian and abbot of the monastery of St. Catherine on Mt. Sinai; *v.* PG, vol. 89, col. 576.

XLI

Τί ἐστιν *οὐ λήψῃ τὸ ὄνομα Κυρίου τοῦ Θεοῦ σου ἐπὶ*
ματαίῳ;[a]

Τινές φασιν ἀπαγορεύειν τὸ ἐπιθεῖναι τοῖς ματαίοις,
|6 τουτέστι τοῖς εἰδώλοις, τὴν τοῦ Θεοῦ Ιπροσηγορίαν, τινὲς δὲ
5 τὸ ὀμωμοκότα ψεύσασθαι. ἐγὼ δὲ οἶμαι τὸν θεῖον
παρακελεύεσθαι νόμον δίχα διδασκαλίας, ἢ προσευχῆς, ἢ
ἀναγκαίας τινὸς χρείας, τὴν θείαν μὴ προφέρειν προσηγορίαν·
καὶ γὰρ εἰώθασί τινες, καὶ παίζοντες καὶ γελῶντες, προφέρειν
ὡς ἔτυχε διὰ τῆς γλώττης τὸ σεβάσμιον ὄνομα. τοῦτο οἶμαι
10 τὸν θεῖον νόμον ἀπαγορεύειν. εἰ γὰρ τὴν πολυτελεστέραν
ἐσθῆτα ταῖς ἑορταῖς φυλάττειν εἰώθασιν οἱ πολλοί, πολλῷ
μᾶλλον τὸ θεῖον ὄνομα προσευχαῖς καὶ διδασκαλίαις ἀφιεροῦν
δίκαιον.

XLII

Διὰ τί τὸ σάββατον τῇ ἀργίᾳ τετίμηκεν;[a]

Φιλανθρωπίαν τὸν λαὸν ἐξεπαίδευσεν. ἐπήγαγε γὰρ *ἵνα*
ἀναπαύσηται ὁ παῖς σου, καὶ ἡ παιδίσκη σου,[b] *ὁ βοῦς σου, καὶ*
τὸ ὑποζύγιόν σου, καὶ πᾶν κτῆνός σου, καὶ ὁ προσήλυτος, ὁ
5 *παροικῶν ἐν σοί.*[c]

xli 2c 6(inc.) [32], 5, a₂, B, C, 4 7 9 10 17 31 35 37 = 22 mss.
a. Ex 20.7

xlii A [32], B, C, 4 7 9 10 17 31 35 37 = 22 mss.
a. Ex 20.8–10   b. Dt 5.14   c. Ex 20.10

XLI

What is the meaning of "You shall not take the name of the Lord your God in vain"?[a]

Some commentators have claimed that the prohibition concerns giving empty objects—namely, idols—the name of God; others, the swearing of false oaths.[1] My own view is that the Law of God forbids invoking the divine name outside of teaching or prayer or apart from some urgent need. There are those, in fact, who are in the habit of uttering the august name quite casually, even when joking and jesting. I think this is what God's Law forbids. After all, if it is a general custom to keep one's finer attire for festivals, it is far more important to reserve the divine name for prayer and teaching.

XLII

Why did he dignify the Sabbath with rest?[a]

To teach the people a lesson in loving-kindness. As he went on to say, "so that your servant and maidservant,[b] your ox, your beast of burden, and all your cattle, and the alien dwelling among you may take their rest."[c]

1. The latter view is endorsed by R.J. Clifford (on 20.7): "The prohibition seems to be against the false use of an oath in legal proceedings rather than a general lack of reverence for the name." A bishop is naturally concerned with profanity in ordinary discourse.

XLIII

Καὶ διὰ τί μὴ ἐν ἄλλῃ ἡμέρᾳ τοῦτο γενέσθαι προσέταξεν;
Τοῦτο ἄν τις εἴποι καὶ περὶ ἄλλης ἡμέρας· τί δή ποτε
ταύτην ἐξελέξατο καὶ οὐχ ἑτέραν; εἶχε δὲ ὅμως αὕτη λόγον
τινὰ πεῖσαι δυνάμενον τὴν ἰουδαίων ὠμότητα· τῷ τὸν τῶν
5 ὅλων Θεὸν ἐν ἓξ ἡμέραις τὰ πάντα δημιουργῆσαι, ἐν δὲ τῇ
ἑβδόμῃ μηδὲν μὲν ποιῆσαι, εὐλογίᾳ δὲ ταύτην τιμῆσαι. τοῦτο
γὰρ καὶ ἐπήγαγεν ὅτι, ἐν ... *ἓξ ἡμέραις ἐποίησε Κύριος ὁ*
Θεός σου τὸν οὐρανόν, καὶ τὴν γῆν, καὶ τὴν θάλασσαν, καὶ
πάντα τὰ ἐν αὐτοῖς· καὶ κατέπαυσε τῇ ἡμέρᾳ τῇ
10 *ἑβδόμῃ ... καὶ ἡγίασεν αὐτήν.*[a]

XLIV

Τί ἐστιν ἐὰν δὲ θυσιαστήριον ἐκ λίθων ποιῇς μοι, οὐκ
οἰκοδομήσεις αὐτοὺς τμητούς· τὸ γὰρ ἐγχειρίδιόν σου
ἐπιβέβληκας ἐπ' αὐτό, καὶ μεμίανται;[a]
Ὅτι σιδήρῳ ἐχρῶντο καὶ οἱ τὰ ξύλα τῆς σκηνῆς
5 τεκτηνάμενοι καὶ οἱ τὸν χρυσόν, καὶ τὸν ἄργυρον, καὶ τὸν
χαλκὸν ἐργασάμενοι οὐδένα ἀντερεῖν οἶμαι. ὅτι δὲ καὶ οἱ
ἱερεῖς ταῖς μαχαίραις ἱέρευον τὰς θυσίας, καὶ ἀπέδερον, καὶ

---

xLIII A [32], B, C⁻⁵², 4 7 9 10 17 31 35 37 = 21 mss.

l. 2 εἴποι B, 4 17: εἶπε Sir. Sch. F.M. = "You would have raised the same
question about any other day." Thdt. is here expressing, not a contrary-to-fact
notion, but one of conditioned futurity; *cf.* the precisely similar construction in
Q. 35 on Gn (Τοῦτο ἄν τις εἴποι καὶ περὶ τοῦ ἀνθρώπου). The aorist
indicative is merely an error of etacism (*cf.* the critical note on ᾠκοδομῆσθαι in
Q. 59 on Gn).

a. Ex 20.11 (LXX var.)

---

xLIV A [32], B, C, 4 7 9 10 17 31 35 37 = 22 mss.

a. Ex 20.25

XLIII

Why not require this for some other day?

You could raise the same question about any other day: why he chose that day and not another. Nevertheless, this day did offer a reason sufficient to overcome the harshness of the Jews: the fact that the God of the universe created everything in six days but did nothing on the seventh, which he dignified with a blessing. As he went on to say, "In six days the Lord your God made heaven and earth, the sea, and all that is in them, but he rested on the seventh day and hallowed it."[a]

XLIV

What is the meaning of "If you make me an altar of stones, you shall not build it of hewn stones, for if you put a tool to it, they are defiled"?[a]

I believe no one will deny that the carpenters of the tabernacle and the gold-, silver-, and bronze-smiths used iron. And I believe it is also beyond question that the priests used knives to slaughter, skin, and divide the sacrificial victims. Therefore, the question is, if

ἔτεμνον, ἀναμφίλεκτον εἶναι οἶμαι καὶ τοῦτο. ζητητέον
τοίνυν πῶς ταῦτα μὲν ὁ σίδηρος οὐκ ἐμίαινε, τοὺς δὲ τμητοὺς
10 ἐμίαινε λίθους. τοιγάρτοι δῆλόν ἐστιν ὡς ἄλλα δι' ἄλλων
κατασκευάζει. ἐπειδὴ γὰρ ἐν τῇ ἐρήμῳ τεσσαράκοντα
διετέλεσαν ἔτη, συνεχῶς ἀπαίροντες καὶ τοὺς τόπους
ἀμείβοντες, ἀπαγορεύει ἐκ λίθων εἰργασμένων οἰκοδομεῖσθαι
θυσιαστήρια ἵνα μή, τούτων τὴν γῆν τὴν ἐπηγγελμένην
15 ἀπειληφότων, ἐν τοῖς θυσιαστηρίοις τούτοις οἱ πλησιόχωροι
τὰς τῶν δαιμόνων θυσίας ἐπιτελέσωσι. διὰ τοῦτο προσέταξεν
ἢ ἐκ γῆς ἢ ἐξ αὐτοφυῶν λίθων ταῦτα κατασκευάζεσθαι,
ἐπειδήπερ ἑκάτερον εὐδιάλυτον. ὅτι δέ, μετὰ τὴν τοῦ ναοῦ
κατασκευήν, οὐκ ἐξῆν ἐν ἑτέρῳ θύειν αὐτὸς ὁ νόμος διδάσκει.
20 εἰ δὲ θύειν ἔξω τοῦ ναοῦ ὁ νόμος ἀπεῖργε,[b] καὶ τὸ
θυσιαστήριον οἰκοδομεῖν ὡσαύτως ἐκώλυσεν. αὐτίκα γοῦν εἰς
ἔλεγχον τῶν ἀσεβούντων Ἠλίας, ὁ πάνυ, προσενεγκεῖν ἐν τῷ
Καρμήλῳ θυσίαν ἀναγκασθείς, ἰσαρίθμους τῶν φυλῶν
αὐτοφυεῖς συνέθηκε λίθους καὶ ἐπὶ τούτων τὴν θυσίαν
25 προσήνεγκεν ὥστε τὴν οἰκοδομίαν εὐθὺς διαλυθῆναι, καὶ
μηδένα ἕτερον ἐν ἐκείνῳ τῷ χωρίῳ θυσίαν προσενεγκεῖν.[c]

XLV

Διὰ τί τοῦ ἑβραίου, τοῦ τὴν ἐλευθερίαν δέξασθαι μὴ
βουλομένου, διατρηθῆναι τὸ ὠτίον προσέταξεν;[a]

Πάντων αὐτοὺς προτιμᾶν τὴν ἐλευθερίαν διδάσκει. τὸν
τοίνυν, ταύτης οὐκ ἀντεχόμενον, ἀλλὰ τὴν δουλείαν
5 ἀσπαζόμενον εἰς αἰσχύνην τοῦτο λαβεῖν τὸ σημεῖον

---

b. Dt 12.13f.   c. 1Kgs 18.31f.

---

xlv A [32], B, C, 4 7 9 10 17 31 35 37 = 22 mss.
a. Ex 21.5f.

iron did not defile these things, how did it defile the hewn stones? We conclude that God has different things built with different instruments. Since they spent forty years in the wilderness, constantly breaking camp and moving on, he forbade them to construct altars of worked stone, so that when they had received the promised land, the neighboring peoples would not use those altars to perform sacrifices to demons. Therefore, he commanded the altars be built of earth or natural stone, since these are both easily taken down. Now, the Law itself relates that, after the building of the Temple, they were not allowed to sacrifice anywhere else. As the Law forbade sacrifice outside the Temple,[b] it likewise prohibited the construction of an altar.[1] At any rate, it was in criticism of idolaters that, when constrained to offer sacrifice on Carmel, the great Elijah brought together as many natural stones as there were tribes and offered his sacrifice on those stones so that immediately afterward the structure could be taken down, and no one else would be able to offer sacrifice there.[c]

XLV

Why did he enjoin the piercing of the ear of the Hebrew who did not want freedom?[1a]

To teach them to esteem freedom above everything else. He prescribed this sign of shame for those who did not cling to freedom but embraced slavery. Further, the sign indicated obedience through

1. Believing that Moses had composed the Pentateuch, Theodoret proceeds to explain what he takes to be a usage of the wilderness period in the light of the law of Dt 12.13f., prescribing one central place of worship. Likewise, he apparently finds in the story of Elijah and the priests of Baal a confirmation of his conclusion that Hebrew worship had been centralized since the days of the Exodus.

1. Though he has passed over the last seven commandments of the Decalogue, Theodoret pauses to discuss this intriguing passage.

παρακελεύεται. πρὸς δὲ τούτῳ καὶ ὑπακοὴν διὰ τῆς ἀκοῆς τὸ σημεῖον ἐμφαίνει, καὶ τὸ παρὰ τὴν θύραν τὸ μὴ ἐξεῖναι προβαίνειν, οὐκ ἐπιτρέποντος τοῦ δεσπότου.

XLVI

Διὰ τί πρόσκειται *καὶ δουλεύσει αὐτῷ εἰς τὸν αἰῶνα,*[a] δήλης οὔσης τῆς ἀνθρωπίνης ζωῆς;

Ἐντεῦθεν δῆλον ὡς οὐ πανταχοῦ ὁ αἰὼν τοῦ ἀπείρου δηλωτικὸς ἀλλ' ἔστιν ὅτε καὶ ὡρισμένου χρόνου σημαντικός.
5 οὕτω καὶ ὁ μακάριος λέγει Δαβίδ, *ὁ αἰὼν ἡμῶν εἰς φωτισμὸν τοῦ προσώπου σου·*[b] τὸν δὲ ἀνθρώπινον οὕτως ὠνόμασε βίον.

XLVII

Τὸν ἀκουσίως πεφονευκότα διὰ τί φεύγειν παρακελεύεται;[a]

Τὴν φονικὴν αὐτῶν ἰατρεύων γνώμην καὶ διδάσκων ὡς, εἰ τὸ παρὰ γνώμην ἀνελεῖν ἔνοχον τῇ τιμωρίᾳ ποιεῖ, πολλῷ μᾶλλον τὸ γνώμῃ φονεύειν κολάσεως ἄξιον. πρὸς δὲ τούτῳ καὶ
5 τοὺς τέμνοντας ξύλα καὶ τοὺς ἀκοντίζοντας λίθους προμηθεστέρους ἐργάζεται καὶ μέντοι καὶ τοὺς ἄλλο τι τοιοῦτο δρῶντας παρασκευάζει δεδιέναι καὶ τρέμειν ἵνα μὴ παρὰ γνώμην τινὰ τῶν πελαζόντων ἢ πόρρωθεν ὄντων πημαίνωσι. χαλινοῖ δὲ καὶ τὸν τῶν συγγενῶν τοῦ
10 πεφονευμένου θυμὸν τῇ τοῦ πεφονευκότος φυγῇ.

---

xlvi A [32], B, C, 4 7 9 10 17 31 35 37 = 22 mss.

a. Ex 21.6   b. Ps 89.8 (LXX)

---

xlvii A [32], B, c, 50 53, 4 7 9 10 17 31 35 37 = 20 mss.

a. Ex 21.13

the organ of hearing, while the provision "at the door" referred to the prohibition against stepping outside without the master's permission.

XLVI

What is the reason for the addition, "He will serve him forever,"[a] when it clearly means just the length of a human life?

From this passage we may conclude that the term "ever," "age," does not always indicate eternity but sometimes signifies a limited amount of time. Likewise, when the blessed David says, "Our age in the light of your countenance,"[b] he uses "age" to denote the span of a human life.[1]

XLVII

Why did he enjoin flight for those who had committed involuntary manslaughter?[a]

To cure their homicidal inclinations and to convey the lesson that if he punished even involuntary manslaughter, deliberate killing would be much more deserving of punishment.[1] Furthermore, he put those hewing wood and casting stones on their guard and made those engaged in similar occupations tremble in fear that they might involuntarily injure someone close by or far away. Then, with the flight of the killer, he put a check on the anger of the relatives of the man who was slain.

1. Theodoret tries to explain the meaning of the term αἰών ("age") in Ex 21.6 by citing what he here seems to regard as a parallel usage in Ps 89.8 (LXX): ὁ αἰὼν ἡμῶν εἰς φωτισμὸν προσώπου σου. Yet when expounding that verse in his commentary on the Psalms, he had tacitly acknowledged that it is very hard to elicit real sense from the LXX version and had cited Symmachus' rendition, which, though it much better represents the Hebrew, does not contain the word αἰών.

1. Theodoret's answer to this question takes no notice of Ex 2.11–15, where Moses "looked this way and that" (*NRSV*) before deliberately killing the Egyptian.

XLVIII

Τί ἐστιν *ἐξεικονισμένον;*[a]

Φασί, τοῦ σώματος ἐν τῇ μήτρᾳ τελείου διαπλασθέντος, τότε ψυχοῦσθαι τὸ ἔμβρυον· καὶ γὰρ τοῦ Ἀδὰμ τὸ σῶμα πρότερον ὁ ποιητὴς διαπλάσας, οὕτως ἐνεφύσησε τὴν ψυχήν.[b]
5 κελεύει τοίνυν ὁ νομοθέτης, γυναικὸς ἐγκύμονος ἀμβλωσάσης ἐν μάχῃ, εἰ μὲν ἐξεικονισμένον ἐξέλθοι τὸ βρέφος, τουτέστι μεμορφωμένον, *φόνον* τὸ πρᾶγμα καλεῖσθαι καὶ τὴν ἴσην ὑπέχειν τιμωρίαν τὸν δεδρακότα· εἰ δὲ μὴ ἐξέλθοι μεμορφωμένον, μὴ λογίζεσθαι φόνον, ἐπειδήπερ οὐδέπω
10 ψυχωθὲν ἐξημβλώθη, ἀλλὰ ζημίαν τίνειν τὸν αἴτιον.

XLIX

Διὰ τί τὸν κερατιστὴν ταῦρον ἀναιρεῖσθαι κελεύει;[a]

Καὶ διὰ τῶν ἀλόγων παιδεύων τοὺς λογικοὺς ἡλίκον ὁ φόνος κακόν.

---

xlviii A *[32]*, B, C⁻⁵¹, 4 7 9 10 17 31 35 37 = 21 mss.

a. Ex 21.22   b. Gn 2.7

---

xlix A *[32]*, B, C⁻⁵¹, 4 7 9 10 17 31 35 37 = 22 mss.

a. Ex 21.28

XLVIII

What is the meaning of "with human features"?[a]

It is the general opinion that life is communicated to the fetus when its body is fully formed in the womb. Thus, right after forming Adam's body, the Creator breathed life into him.[b] So, in the case of a pregnant woman who suffers miscarriage in the course of a fight, the lawgiver ordains that if the infant comes out with human features—that is, fully formed—the case is to be considered murder, and the guilty party must pay with his own life. But if it comes out before it is fully formed, the case is not to be considered murder, since the miscarriage occurred before the animation of the child. Nonetheless, the party responsible is to make recompense.

XLIX

Why does he command the killing of a bull that gores?[a]

To use the brute beasts to teach rational people the enormity of homicide.

L

Διὰ τί ὁ μόσχον κεκλοφὼς πενταπλάσια ἐκτίνειν
ἐκελεύσθη, ὁ δὲ πρόβατον τετραπλάσια;[a]
Ὅτι τὰ μείζονα τῶν ἁμαρτημάτων μειζόνων ἄξια
τιμημάτων. οὕτω καὶ ὁ Κύριος ἐδίδαξεν· ᾧ μέν, γάρ φησι,
5 πολὺ δοθήσεται, πολὺ καὶ ἀπαιτήσουσι παρ' αὐτοῦ.[b]

LI

Πῶς νοητέον τὸ *θεοὺς οὐ κακολογήσεις;*[a]
Τοὺς κριτὰς ὀνομάζει *θεούς,* ὡς κατὰ μίμησιν τοῦ τῶν ὅλων
Θεοῦ κρίνειν πεπιστευμένους. τοῦτο σαφέστερον ἐδίδαξεν ὁ
προφήτης Δαβίδ· εἰπὼν γάρ, *ὁ Θεὸς ἔστη ἐν συναγωγῇ θεῶν,*
5 *ἐν μέσῳ δὲ θεοὺς διακρίνει,* ἐπήγαγεν, *ἕως πότε κρίνετε*
ἀδικίαν καὶ πρόσωπα ἁμαρτωλῶν λαμβάνετε;... κρίνατε
ὀρφανῷ καὶ πτωχῷ, ταπεινὸν καὶ πένητα δικαιώσατε. ἐξέλεσθε
πένητα καὶ πτωχόν, ἐκ χειρὸς ἁμαρτωλοῦ ῥύσασθε αὐτόν· εἶτα
κατηγορῶν προστέθεικεν, *οὐκ ἔγνωσαν οὐδὲ συνῆκαν, ἐν*
10 *σκότει διαπορεύονται·*[b] ἐπιδείκνυσι δὲ καὶ τὴν οἰκείαν
φιλοτιμίαν· *ἐγώ,* γάρ φησιν, *εἶπον, θεοί ἐστε καὶ υἱοὶ ὑψίστου*
πάντες. ὑμεῖς δὲ ὡς ἄνθρωποι ἀποθνήσκετε καὶ ὡς εἷς τῶν
ἀρχόντων πίπτετε·[c] οὕτω καὶ ἐνταῦθα, *θεοὺς οὐ κακολογήσεις*
καὶ ἄρχοντα τοῦ λαοῦ σου οὐκ ἐρεῖς κακῶς.

ʟ A [32], B, C, 4 7 9 10 17 31 35 37 = 22 mss.
a. Ex 22.1   b. Lk 12.48

ʟɪ A [32], B, c, 50 53, 4 7 9 10 17 31 35 37 = 20 mss.
a. Ex 22.28   b. Ps 82.1–5   c. Ps 82.6f.

L

Why is the thief of a calf commanded to repay fivefold, but the thief of a sheep fourfold?[a]

Because greater sins deserve greater penalties. The Lord himself gave similar instructions: "Of the person to whom much will be given much will also be required."[b]

LI

How are we to understand the verse "You shall not revile gods"?[a]

By "gods" he meant judges, since they are commissioned to judge in imitation of the God of the universe. The prophet David taught the same thing more explicitly. After declaring, "God has taken his place in an assembly of gods," he went on, "How long will you deliver unjust judgments and take the part of sinners? Judge in favor of orphan and poor; give justice to the lowly and needy. Rescue the needy and poor; deliver him from the hands of the sinner." Then by way of accusation he added, "They did not know, nor did they understand; they walk in darkness."[b] God also showed his own generosity with "I said, you are gods, and all of you children of the Most High. But as men you die, and as one of the rulers you fall."[c] Likewise here, too, "You shall not revile gods or malign a leader of your people."[1]

---

1. Had Theodoret been able to read the Hebrew, he would have seen that in Ex 22.28 the term ʿelohim (God) had been wrongly rendered in the plural by the LXX. Lacking this linguistic expertise, he sought clarification of the plural θεούς (gods) by reference to what he mistakenly imagined to be a parallel usage in Ps. 82, where God is presented as presiding over the council of the gods of the nations. In his commentary on Ps. 82.1, Theodoret had cited Ex 22.28 to show that both passages deal with judges.

LII

Τίνος ἔνεκεν θηριάλωτα κρέα ἐσθίειν ἀπαγορεύει;[a]

Λογικωτέραν αὐτοὺς διδάσκει ζωὴν καὶ μηδὲν ἔχειν
θηριῶδες παρεγγυᾷ. τὰ γὰρ θηρία οὐ θύει πρότερον, εἶθ' οὕτως
ἐσθίει. διὰ τοῦτο μετ' ὀλίγα καὶ τῶν ἐχθρῶν ἐπιμελεῖσθαι
5 κελεύει, καὶ τοῦ δυσμενῶς διακειμένου τὸν βοῦν πλανώμενον
μὴ παρορᾶν, ἀλλ' ἐπιστρέφειν εἰς τὴν τοῦ δυσμενοῦς οἰκίαν,
καὶ τὸ ὑποζύγιον πεπτωκὸς ἀνιστᾶν, καὶ ταῖς τοιαύταις
εὐεργεσίαις τὰς καταλλαγὰς μηχανᾶσθαι.[b] διδάσκει δὲ διὰ
τούτων ὡς εἷς παλαιᾶς καὶ καινῆς διαθήκης νομοθέτης, καὶ ὁ
10 τοῦτον δεδωκὼς τὸν νόμον καὶ τὸν εὐαγγελικὸν ἐδωρήσατο.

LIII

Τί ἐστιν *οὐκ ὀφθήσῃ ἐνώπιον Κυρίου τοῦ Θεοῦ σου κενός;*[a]

Ἀπιὼν προσκυνῆσαι τῷ δεσπότῃ Θεῷ, τὰ δυνατά σοι
πρόσφερε δῶρα. ἡμᾶς δὲ ὁ λόγος διδάσκει εἰ μὲν χρήματα
ἔχοιμεν, μετὰ τῆς τῶν πενήτων θεραπείας προσεύχεσθαι τῷ
5 Θεῷ· εἰ δὲ τὸν ἀκτήμονα προαιρούμεθα βίον, μὴ κενὴν ἔχειν
τῶν ἀγαθῶν τὴν ψυχήν, ἀλλ' ἔχουσαν τὸν πλοῦτον τῆς ἀρετῆς.

LII A [32], B, C, 4 7 9 10 17 31 35 37 = 22 mss.
a. Ex 22.31   b. Ex 23.4f.

LIII A [32], B, C, 4 7 9 10 17 31 35 37 = 22 mss.
a. Ex 23.15 (LXX var.)

LII

Why did he forbid them to eat the meat of beasts killed by wild animals?[a]

To teach them a more rational life and urge them to eschew the savagery of animals. Wild animals do not wait to offer their prey in sacrifice before they eat it. Hence, a little later, he also commands them to exert themselves on behalf of their enemies: not to ignore their adversary's ox when it is straying but to lead it back to the adversary's house, to raise up the ass that has fallen, and to effect reconciliation with this kind of good deeds.[1b] Now, in all these regulations, he teaches that there is one Lawgiver of Old and New Testaments, that he who gave the Law bestowed also the law of the Gospels.

LIII

What is the meaning of "You shall not appear before the Lord your God empty-handed"?[a]

When you go to worship the Lord God, offer gifts in accordance with your means. This verse teaches us, if we have money, to pray to God with the care of the needy, or, if we opt for a life of poverty, to approach God with a soul that is not empty of good things but wealthy in virtue.

---

1. Theodoret does not refer to the parallel passage Lv 17.14–16, which indicates the central concern of Ex 22.31, *i.e.*, that the life blood of the animal be offered to God; *v.* R.J. Faley, on Lv 17.1–16. Instead, he applies a spiritual exegesis that permits him to discover in this verse a general prescription of the civilized behavior described in 23.4f., which command considerate treatment of livestock belonging to one's enemy. Thus, he can claim that the prohibition of Ex 22.31 evinces the mercy of the gospel law and is, therefore, indicative of the unity of the two Testaments.

LIV

Ποία ἐστὶν ἑορτὴ ἡ *τοῦ θερισμοῦ τῶν πρωτογενημάτων, καὶ*
ποία ἑορτὴ τῆς συντελείας ἐπ' ἐξόδῳ τοῦ ἐνιαυτοῦ;[a]
Ἑορτὴν τῶν πρωτογενημάτων τὴν Πεντηκοστὴν καλεῖ,
ἑορτὴν δὲ συντελείας ἐπ' ἐξόδῳ τοῦ ἐνιαυτοῦ τὴν τῆς

5 Σκηνοπηγίας. καὶ τοῦτο διδάσκων, ἐπήγαγε, *τρεῖς καιροὺς τοῦ*
ἐνιαυτοῦ ὀφθήσεται πᾶν ἀρσενικόν σου ἐνώπιον Κυρίου τοῦ
Θεοῦ σου,[b] τουτέστι τῇ ἑορτῇ τοῦ Πάσχα, καὶ τῇ
Πεντηκοστῇ, καὶ τῇ Σκηνοπηγίᾳ. ἀναμιμνήσκει δὲ τὸ μὲν
Πάσχα τῆς ἐξόδου τῆς ἐξ Αἰγύπτου καὶ τῆς παρασχεθείσης

10 ἐλευθερίας, ἡ δὲ Πεντηκοστὴ τῆς εἰς τὴν γῆν τῆς ἐπαγγελίας
εἰσόδου· ἐκεῖ γὰρ σπείροντες, τὰς ἀπαρχὰς τῶν γενημάτων
προσέφερον· ἐν γὰρ τῇ ἐρήμῳ τὸν ἄσπορον καὶ ἀνήροτον
ἤσθιον ἄρτον.[c] ἡ δὲ Σκηνοπηγία τὴν ἐν ἐρήμῳ διαγωγὴν
ὑπογράφει· ἐν σκηναῖς γὰρ οἰκοῦντες τεσσαράκοντα

15 διετέλεσαν ἔτη.[d] ἐν ταύταις ταῖς ἑορταῖς συντρέχειν εἰς τὸν
θεῖον νεὼ παρεγγύησεν ἵνα καὶ τῶν θείων ἀναμιμνήσκωνται
δωρεῶν, καὶ εἰς ὁμόνοιαν καὶ φιλίαν συνάπτωνται, καί,
φιλεορτασταὶ ὄντες, μὴ περὶ τὰ τεμένη τῶν δαιμόνων
τρυφῶσιν, ἀλλ' ἐν τῷ ναῷ τοῦ πεποιηκότος καὶ τὰ ἀγαθὰ

20 χορηγοῦντος τῆς ἑορταστικῆς ἀπολαύωσιν εὐωχίας.

LIV A *[32]*, B*, C, 4 7 9 10 17* 31 35 37 = 22 mss.

a. Ex 23.16   b. Ex 23.17   c. Ex 16.13–15   d. *Cf.* Nm 33.38.

LIV

What were "the festival of the harvest of first-fruits" and "the festival of completion at the end of the year"?[a]

By "festival of the first-fruits" he referred to Pentecost and by "festival of completion at the end of the year" to Tabernacles. In the same provision, he added: "Three times in the year, all your males shall appear before the Lord your God,"[b] namely, Passover, Pentecost, and Tabernacles. Passover recalls the exodus from Egypt and the granting of freedom, Pentecost the entrance into the promised land, where they sowed crops and made offerings of their first-fruits, for, in the wilderness, they ate food that came without sowing or tilling.[c] Tabernacles represents their time in the wilderness, where they spent forty years living in tents.[d] He commanded them to repair to the temple of God on these festivals so they would remember the gifts they had received from him and unite in harmony and friendship. Thus, being great lovers of festivals, they would not revel in the demons' shrines but celebrate their holiday feasts in the temple of the God who had created them and blessed them with these good things.

LV

Τί ἐστιν *οὐ θύσεις ἐπὶ ζύμη αἷμα θυσιάσματός μου;*[a]

Ἀζύμους ἄρτους τῷ θυσιαστηρίῳ προσέφερον·[b] ζυμίτας δὲ ἀπαγορεύει προσφέρειν, διὰ τῶν αἰσθητῶν διδάσκων τὰ νοητά. ἐπειδὴ γὰρ ὁ ἄζυμος ἄρτος αὐτοσχέδιός ἐστιν, ὁ δὲ ζυμίτης

5 ἔχει τι τῆς ζύμης τῆς παλαιᾶς,[c] ἀπαγορεύει ὁ νόμος μηδὲν τοῖς θείοις τῆς αἰγυπτιακῆς ἀναμιγνύναι διδασκαλίας. οὕτω καὶ ὁ Κύριος τοῖς ἱεροῖς ἔλεγε μαθηταῖς, *προσέχετε ἀπὸ τῆς ζύμης τῶν γραμματέων καὶ φαρισαίων.*[d]

LVI

Πῶς νοητέον τὸ *οὐχ ἑψήσεις ἄρνα ἐν γάλακτι μητρὸς αὐτοῦ;*[a]

Πολλάκις ἔφην ὅτι διὰ πάντων αὐτοὺς φιλανθρωπίαν διδάσκει. τινὲς οὖν φασιν ἀπαγορεύειν τὸν νόμον τὸ

5 εὐθυγενὲς ἐσθίειν, τινὲς δὲ τῷ μητρῴῳ γάλακτι μὴ συνεψεῖν· τρόπον γάρ τινα καὶ τὴν μητέρα συνεψεῖ· ἀπαγορεύει δὲ καὶ τῷ Θεῷ προσφέρειν κατὰ ταὐτὸν μητέρα καὶ τὸ τεχθὲν ἐξ αὐτῆς. καὶ αὐτοῖς δὲ παρεκελεύσατο στρουθῶν εὑρηκόσι νεοττίαν μὴ συνθηρεύειν τοῖς νεοττοῖς τὴν μητέρα· τοῦτο

10 γάρ ἐστιν ἐξαλεῖψαι τῶν ὀρνέων τὸ γένος.[b]

LV A [32], B, c, 52 53, 4 7 9 10 17 31 35 37 = 20 mss.

a. Ex 23.18   b. Lv 2.4f.   c. 1Cor 5.7   d. Mt 16.6

LVI A [32], B, c, 4 7 9 10 17 31 35 37 = 22 mss.

a. Ex 23.19   b. Dt 22.6f.

LV

What is the meaning of "You shall not offer the blood of my sacrifice with leaven"?[a]

It was their practice to offer unleavened loaves on the altar,[b] and he forbade the offering of leavened, thus conveying spiritual, by means of material, realities. Since the unleavened is natural while leavened bread contains some of the old leaven,[c] the Law forbade the adulteration of the sacrificial offerings with anything derived from Egyptian religion. Thus, the Lord himself warned his holy disciples: "Be on guard against the leaven of the scribes and Pharisees."[1d]

LVI

How are we to understand the verse "You shall not boil a lamb in its mother's milk"?[a]

As I have often remarked, he employed every means to teach them benevolence. Some commentators have claimed that this law forbids the eating of a newborn creature, others the boiling of the newborn in its mother's milk, since this is, in a sense, to boil the mother along with her lamb, and he thus forbade them to offer God a mother and her offspring at the same time. He also enjoined that, on finding a swallow's nest, they were not to take the mother with the chicks, since this would wipe out the whole stock of birds.[1b]

---

1. On Theodoret's version of this dominical saying *v.* note 3 to *Q.* 24 on Ex.

---

1. The prohibition of Ex 23.19 is found also at 34.26 and Dt 14.21. In all these passages the LXX offers "lamb" rather than the "kid" of the MT.

LVII

Πῶς νοητέον τὸν ἀριθμὸν τῶν ἡμερῶν σου ἀναπληρώσω;ᵃ

Τὴν ὡρισμένην φησὶ τοῖς ἀνθρώποις ζωήν, τουτέστιν εἰς γῆρας μακρὸν ἐλθεῖν σε παρασκευάσω.

LVIII

Τί ἐστιν ἀποστελῶ τὰς σφηκίας προτέρας σου;ᵃ

Ὡς τοῖς αἰγυπτίοις βατράχουςᵇ καὶ σκνῖπαςᶜ καὶ κυνόμυιανᵈ ἔπεμψεν, οὕτω τοῖς χαναναίοις καὶ τοῖς ἄλλοις ἔθνεσι τὰς σφηκίας. τοῦτο δὲ δηλοῖ τὴν ὑπερβάλλουσαν

5 δύναμιν τοῦ Θεοῦ· ὅτι, καὶ διὰ τῶν σμικρῶν ζῳυφίων, καὶ τοῖς οἰκείοις ἐπικουρεῖ καὶ τοῖς ἐναντίοις ἐπάγει τὸν ὄλεθρον. τοῦτο καὶ διὰ τοῦ μακαρίου λέγει Δαβίδ, Ἰσραὴλ ταῖς ὁδοῖς μου εἰ ἐπορεύθη, ἐν τῷ μηδενὶ ἂν τοὺς ἐχθροὺς αὐτῶν ἐταπείνωσαᵉ ἀντὶ τοῦ· εὐπετῶς ἂν μάλα καὶ ῥαδίως τοὺς

10 πολεμοῦντας αὐτοῖς ἐξωλόθρευσα.

LVII A *[32]*, B, C⁻⁵¹, *4 7 9 10 17 31 35 37* = 21 mss.

a. Ex 23.26

LVIII A *[32]*, B, C⁻⁵¹, *4 7 9 10 17 31 35 37* = 21 mss.

l. 10 πολεμοῦντας αὐτοῖς *J.P.* : πολεμοῦντας αὐτοὺς *Sir. Sch. F.M.* = "I would have made short work of those who were making war." In this context, one would expect the pronoun to refer to those fought against, not those fighting; cf. Thdt., *Ps.* 16.8 (τοὺς πολεμοῦντας αὐτῷ) and *Ezech.* 30.4f. (Ἀσσυρίων καὶ Χαλδαίων πολεμούντων αὐτοῖς). It is just possible that Thdt. here joins πολεμέω to an accusative direct object rather than a dative complement, and Sir. and Sch. print αὐτοὺς πολεμοῦντας (= fighting against them) in his comment on Mi 4.1–3 (PG, vol. 81, col. 1761 A). Yet this seems dubious, since elsewhere Thdt. restricts πολεμέω + acc. pronouns to forms of ἐγώ and σύ.

a. Ex 23.28   b. Ex 8.6   c. Ex 8.17   d. Ex 8.24   e. Ps 81.13f.

LVII

How are we to understand, "I shall fill out the number of your days"?[a]

He means the span of life set for human beings, in other words: "I shall cause you to live to a great old age."

LVIII

What is the meaning of "I shall send wasps before you"? [1a]

As he had sent frogs,[b] gnats,[c] and dog flies[d] on the Egyptians, so he sent wasps on the Canaanites and the other nations. This indicates the surpassing power of God: that even with such tiny creatures he lends assistance to his own and brings ruin on their adversaries. As he declared through the blessed David, "If Israel had travelled in my ways, I would have brought their foes down with a mere nothing,"[e] that is: "I would have made short work of those who warred against them."

1. It is, in fact, the LXX that offers "wasp" (σφηκία) for the obscure Hebrew term rendered as "pestilence" or "hornets" in the NRSV.

LIX

Πῶς ἐπαγγειλάμενος ὁ Θεὸς μέχρι τοῦ Εὐφράτου ποταμοῦ παραδώσειν αὐτοῖς τὴν γῆν,ª οὐκ ἐπλήρωσε τὴν ὑπόσχεσιν;

Διὰ Ἱερεμίου τοῦ προφήτου τοῦτο σαφέστερον πεποίηκεν ὁ Θεός· πέρας, γάρ φησι, λαλήσω ἐπὶ ἔθνος καὶ ... βασιλείαν
5 τοῦ οἰκοδομεῖν καὶ ... καταφυτεύειν·ᵇ καὶ ἔσται ἐάν, στραφὲν τὸ ἔθνος ἐκεῖνο ποιήσῃ πονηρά, οὐ μὴ ἐπαγάγω ἐπ' αὐτῷ πάντα τὰ ἀγαθὰ ὅσα ἐλάλησα, καὶ τὰ ἑξῆς.ᶜ εἰσήγαγε τοίνυν αὐτοὺς ὁ Θεὸς εἰς ἣν ἐπηγγείλατο γῆν. ἐπειδὴ δὲ φυλάξαι τὸν θεῖον οὐκ ἠβουλήθησαν νόμον, οὐ πᾶσαν αὐτοῖς παρέδωκεν
10 ἀλλ' εἴασέ τινας διηνεκῶς αὐτοῖς πολεμοῦντας ἵνα πολεμούμενοι τὴν θείαν αἰτῶσι βοήθειαν, καὶ τοῦτο διαφερόντως ἡ τῶν κριτῶν ἱστορία διδάσκει. Δαβὶδ μέντοι τῷ βασιλεῖ καὶ τούτους ὑπέταξε· καὶ γὰρ οἱ ἀλλόφυλοι φόρους ἐδίδοσαν,ᵈ καὶ Συρία Δαμασκοῦ, καὶ Συρία Σουβᾶ.ᵉ καὶ Σολομῶν
15 δέ, ἕως ηὐσέβει, ταύτην εἶχε τὴν δυναστείαν· ἀποκλίνας δὲ εἰς ἀσέβειαν, τῆς ἐξουσίας ἐξέπεσε.ᶠ καὶ τούτοις δὲ δώσειν ἐπηγγείλατο τὰς ἐντολὰς καὶ τὸν νόμον φυλάττουσιν.

LX

Τὴν σκηνὴν τί δή ποτε προσέταξεν ὁ Θεὸς γενέσθαι;

(1) Αὐτὸς ὁ δεσπότης Θεὸς τὴν αἰτίαν δεδήλωκεν· ἔφη δὲ οὕτω· καὶ ποιήσεις μοι ἁγίασμα, καὶ ὀφθήσομαι ἐν ὑμῖν. καὶ ποιήσεις κατὰ πάντα ὅσα ἐγὼ δείκνυμί σοι ἐν τῷ ὄρει, τὸ

LIX A [32], B, C⁻⁵¹, 4 7 9 10 17 31 35 37 = 21 mss.

a. Ex 23.31   b. Jer 18.9   c. Cf. Jer 18.10.   d. 2Sm 8.1   e. 2Sm 8.6
f. 1Kgs 11.1–40

LX A [32], B, C⁻⁵¹, 4 7 9 10 17 31 35 37 = 21 mss.

LIX

How is it that, after promising to give them the land as far as the Euphrates River,[a] God failed to fulfil his promise?

God made this clearer through the prophet Jeremiah: "I shall declare a decision for a nation or kingdom, to build and plant;[b] and if that nation turn to do evil, I shall not bring upon it all the good things I said," and so on.[1c] So God brought them into the promised land, but, since they refused to keep his Law, he did not give them all the land but permitted other peoples to wage constant war on them, so that, when under attack, they would beg for his help. It is particularly the biblical book of Judges that teaches us this. Nonetheless, he subjected these peoples to King David. The Philistines paid tribute[d] along with Syria of Damascus and Syria of Zobah,[e] and Solomon held this empire as long as he lived a pious life. But when he slipped into idolatry, he lost his power.[f] God's promise of this gift was contingent upon their observance of the commandments and the Law.

LX

Why did God command the construction of the tabernacle?[1]

(1) The Lord God explained the reason himself when he declared: "You shall make me a sanctuary, and I shall appear among you. You shall make it according to all the details I show you on the mountain, according to the model of the tabernacle and the model

---

1. The word πέρας, here rendered "decision," very frequently means "limit" or "boundary"; *v. LSJ, sub uoce,* I.

---

1. Theodoret has so much to say on the tabernacle, its design and furnishings,

5 παράδειγμα τῆς σκηνῆς καὶ τὸ παράδειγμα τῶν σκευῶν αὐτῆς.ᵃ
ἐπειδὴ γὰρ ἐν τῷ Σινᾶ ὄρει τὸν νόμον ἐδεδώκει, εἰκὸς δὲ ἦν
τινας ὑποτοπῆσαι περιγεγράφθαι τὸ θεῖον, ἐκέλευσε γενέσθαι
σκηνὴν ἵν᾽, ἐκεῖθεν τὴν οἰκείαν ποιούμενος ἐπιφάνειαν,
ἐκπαιδεύῃ τὸν λαὸν τὴν εὐσέβειαν. ὥσπερ γάρ, τὴν
10 ἐπηγγελμένην αὐτῶν ἀπειληφότων γῆν, νεὼν γενέσθαι
προσέταξεᵇ καὶ τὰς θείας ἐκεῖ γίνεσθαι λειτουργίας
ἐνομοθέτησεν ἵνα μή, ἀδεῶς τοῦτο δρῶντες, τῇ τῶν ἀλιτηρίων
δαιμόνων περιπέσωσι πλάνῃ, οὕτως ὁδοιποροῦσι καὶ τὴν
ἔρημον διαβαίνουσι σκηνὴν ποιῆσαι προσέταξε, μεταβῆναι καὶ
15 αὐτὴν δυναμένην, ἵνα καὶ τὰς προσευχὰς καὶ τὰς ἱερουργίας
ἐν ταύτῃ προσφέρωσι. καὶ ταῦτα δὲ τῆς αὐτῶν ἕνεκα
γεγένηται χρείας. ἐπειδὴ γάρ, ἐν τῷ ὄρει τοῦ μεγάλου
Μωϋσέως πλείους διατρίψαντος ἡμέρας,ᶜ πρὸς τὸν Ἀαρὼν
ἔφασαν, ποίησον ἡμῖν θεούς, οἳ προπορεύσονται ἡμῶν,ᵈ καί,
20 τὴν εἰκόνα τοῦ μόσχου κατασκευάσαντες, ἐβόων χορεύοντες,
οὗτοι οἱ θεοί σου, Ἰσραήλ, οἱ ἐξαγαγόντες σε ἐκ γῆς
Αἰγύπτου,ᵉ τὴν σκηνὴν ταύτην γενέσθαι προσέταξεν ὁ Θεὸς
καὶ ἀπαιρόντων ἡγεῖσθαι νενομοθέτηκε καὶ αὐλιζομένων
ἵστασθαι ὥστε καὶ τοὺς ἱερέας ἐν αὐτῇ τὰς θυσίας ἐπιτελεῖν.
25   (2) Εἶχε δὲ αὐτὴ τῆς κτίσεως τὴν εἰκόνα. ὥσπερ γὰρ τὸν
οὐρανὸν καὶ τὴν γῆν δημιουργήσας, ὁ δεσπότης Θεὸς μέσον
πάλιν ἐξέτεινε τὸ στερέωμα καὶ διώρισε τὰ ὑπερῷα τῶν κάτω,ᶠ
οὕτω μίαν μὲν γενέσθαι προσέταξε τὴν σκηνήν, τριάκοντα μὲν
πήχεων τὸ μῆκος δέκα δὲ τὸ εὖρος ἔχουσαν, ἐν μέσῳ δὲ τὸ

a. Ex 25.8f.   b. 2Sm 7.13; 1Kgs 5.5   c. Ex 24.18   d. Ex 32.1   e. Ex 32.4
f. Gn 1.7

314

of all its furnishings."ᵃ You see, since he had given the Law on Mount Sinai, and there were probably those who had come to imagine that the divine nature was circumscribed, he ordered the construction of the tabernacle in which to reveal himself and instruct his people in right religion. When they had taken possession of the promised land, he commanded the building of the templeᵇ and prescribed the performance of the divine service there so that they would not fall victim to the deception of sinful demons by failing to worship with due reverence. Likewise, he bade them construct a tabernacle that could be moved when they were travelling across the desert so that they could offer prayers and worship in it. This was meant to meet their needs: After Moses, that great man, had spent many days on the mountain,ᶜ they said to Aaron, "Make us gods to go before us,"ᵈ and they made an image of the calf, danced, and cried out, "These are your gods, Israel, who brought you out of the land of Egypt,"ᵉ so God commanded the construction of this tabernacle and prescribed that it go before them when they were on the move and stop when they made camp so that the priests might perform the sacrifices in it.

(2) The tabernacle was a representation of creation.² When he created heaven and earth, the Lord God stretched a firmament in the midst and separated things above from things below.ᶠ Just so, he ordered the building of one tabernacle, thirty cubits long and ten

----

and the accoutrements of the priests, that it looks as if he used this question as an opportunity to produce an essay on the religious institutions of the Jews. It is puzzling that he should devote so much attention to Ex 25–28, since he makes so little effort to find in the various elements of the description reference to Christ or Christian liturgy. While he makes two quick allusions to their use in Hebrews 9 and 6, and two further typological comments meant to highlight the superiority of Christian to Jewish worship, he does not touch on the christological significance of the mercy seat, to which he had devoted a beautiful development in his comment on Rom 3.25; *cf.* his treatment of the manna in *Qq.* 29–32, where he never once mentions Christ or the Eucharist.

2. In his discussion of chh. 25–28, Theodoret may have drawn on Theodore of Mopsuestia's treatment of the topic, fragments of which have been preserved in

30 καταπέτασμα διατείνας, ἐν τύπῳ τοῦ στερεώματος διχῇ
διεῖλεν αὐτήν, καὶ τὸ μὲν παρὰ τὴν θύραν μέρος ἐκάλεσεν
ἅγια, τὸ δὲ τοῦ καταπετάσματος ἔνδον ἅγια ἁγίων ὠνόμασε.ᵍ
καὶ ὥσπερ λέγει Δαβίδ, ὁ οὐρανὸς τοῦ οὐρανοῦ τῷ Κυρίῳ, τὴν
δὲ γῆν ἔδωκε τοῖς υἱοῖς τῶν ἀνθρώπων,ʰ οὕτως ἔξω μὲν τοῦ
35 καταπετάσματος εἰσιτητὸς ἦν τοῖς ἱερεῦσι, τὰ δὲ ἔνδον
ἄψαυστα ἦν καὶ ἄδυτα καὶ ἀνάκτορα· τὸν ἀρχιερέα γὰρ μόνον
ἅπαξ τοῦ ἔτους νόμος ἦν εἰσιέναι.ⁱ ἦν δὲ ἐκεῖ τὰ τῶν
χερουβὶμ εἰκάσματα,ʲ τύπον τῶν ἀσωμάτων δυνάμεων ἔχοντα·
ἐν μέσῳ δὲ τούτων ἡ κιβωτὸς ἔκειτο, τὰς πλάκας ἔχουσα τοῦ
40 νόμου,ᵏ καὶ τὴν στάμνον τοῦ μάννα, καὶ τὴν ῥάβδον Ἀαρὼν
τὴν βλαστήσασαν.ˡ ἐπέκειτο δὲ ταύτῃ τὸ ἱλαστήριον, ταῖς
πτέρυξι τῶν χερουβὶμ σκιαζόμενον·ᵐ ἐν τούτῳ δὲ ὁ τῶν ὅλων
Θεὸς τὴν οἰκείαν ἐπιφάνειαν ἐποιεῖτο. ἐπειδὴ γὰρ ἡ θεία
φύσις ἀνείδεός τε καὶ ἀσχημάτιστος ἀόρατός τε καὶ
45 ἀπερίληπτος, καὶ τῆς τοιαύτης οὐσίας εἰκόνα τεκτήνασθαι
παντάπασι τῶν ἀδυνάτων, τὰ σύμβολα τῶν μεγίστων αὐτοῦ
δωρεῶν ἔνδον κεῖσθαι προσέταξεν. αἱ μὲν γὰρ πλάκες τὴν
νομοθεσίαν ἐδήλουν, τὴν δὲ ἱερωσύνην ἡ ῥάβδος, τὸ δὲ μάννα
τὴν ἐν ἐρήμῳ τροφὴν καὶ τὸν ἀχειροποίητον ἄρτον· τὸ δέ γε
50 ἱλαστήριον τῆς προφητείας σύμβολον ἦν· ἐκεῖθεν γὰρ αἱ
προρρήσεις ἐγίνοντο.ⁿ ὥσπερ γὰρ ἐκ μεγέθους καὶ καλλονῆς
κτισμάτων ἀναλόγως ὁ γενεσιουργὸς αὐτῶν θεωρεῖται,ᵒ οὕτω
διὰ τούτων ὁ μεγαλόδωρος ἐγνωρίζετο.

(3) Τὰ μὲν οὖν ἔνδον τῆς σκηνῆς τῶν ἐπουρανίων εἶχε τὸν
55 τύπον· διὸ καὶ ἅγια τῶν ἁγίων ὠνόμαστο. καὶ ὅτι τοῦτο

---

l. 30 καταπέτασμα 5, C⁻⁵¹, 35 37, Sir. Sch. : παραπέτασμα Pic. (Sch.) F.M.
In the twenty-nine other places where Thdt. uses καταπέτασμα, it always refers
to the veil of the temple. In the nine other places where Thdt. uses
παραπέτασμα, it is associated with the καταπέτασμα of the temple only in
one passage of the *Eran*. (*Dial*. 1, p. 76).
l. 32 καταπετάσματος a [32] , C⁻⁵¹, 37, Sir. Sch. : παραπετάσματος F.M.

g. Ex 26.33   h. Ps 115.16   i. Lv 16.34   j. Ex 25.18–20   k. Ex 25.21; 1Kgs 8.9
l. Ex 16.32–34; Nm 17.10f.; Heb 9.4   m. Ex 25.20   n. V., *e.g.*, Jgs 20.26–28
o. Wis 13.5

cubits wide, and in the middle he stretched the veil, which, as an image of the firmament, divided the tent in two. He called the part by the door "the holy place" and named the part behind the veil "the Holy of Holies."[g] As David declares, "The heaven of heaven is the Lord's, but the earth he has given to the sons of men."[h] Thus, the priests were permitted to enter the area outside the veil, but the area inside was inviolable, inaccessible, and sacred. By law the high priest alone entered just once a year.[i] Inside were the likenesses of the cherubim[j] presenting an image of incorporeal powers; between the cherubim was placed the ark containing the tablets of the Law,[k] the jar of manna, and Aaron's sprouting rod.[l] The mercy seat was placed on top of the ark, overshadowed by the wings of the cherubim,[m] and on it the God of the universe revealed himself. Since the divine nature is without form or shape, invisible, and incomprehensible, and it is utterly impossible to devise an image of such a being, he commanded symbols of his greatest gifts be placed there: the tablets representing the giving of the Law, the rod the priesthood, the manna the nourishment in the wilderness and the bread not made by human hands. The mercy seat was a symbol of prophecy, since predictions were made there.[n] Just as "the Creator is to some extent discerned from the magnitude and beauty of the creation,"[o] so the generous giver was made known in these gifts.[3]

(3) The area inside the tabernacle presented an image of heaven and hence was called the "Holy of Holies." The inspired apostle tes-

---

the *catena Nikephori; v.* note 1 to *Q.* 1. Theodore, for example, had argued that the tabernacle represented creation; *v.* Devreesse, pp. 26f.

3. Theodoret rarely cites the Wisdom of Solomon; *cf.* his comment on Ps 29.5f. LXX (30.4f. MT).

ἀληθὲς μάρτυς ὁ θεῖος ἀπόστολος, οὑτωσὶ λέγων· οὐ γὰρ εἰς
χειροποίητα ἅγια εἰσῆλθεν ὁ Χριστός, ἀντίτυπα τῶν ἀληθινῶν,
ἀλλ' εἰς αὐτὸν τὸν οὐρανὸν νῦν ἐμφανισθῆναι τῷ προσώπῳ τοῦ
Θεοῦ ὑπὲρ ἡμῶν·ᵖ καὶ πάλιν περὶ τῆς θείας ἐλπίδος
60 διαλεγόμενος, καὶ ταῦτα προστέθεικεν· ἣν ὡς ἄγκυραν
ἔχομεν...ἀσφαλῆ, τε καὶ βεβαίαν, καὶ εἰσερχομένην εἰς τὸ
ἐσώτερον τοῦ καταπετάσματος, ὅπου πρόδρομος ὑπὲρ ἡμῶν
εἰσῆλθεν Ἰησοῦς, γενόμενος ἀρχιερεὺς κατὰ τὴν τάξιν
Μελχισεδέκ.�q
65 Οὐκοῦν τὰ μὲν ἔνδον τοῦ καταπετάσματος τὴν τῶν
ἐπουρανίων εἶχεν εἰκόνα, τὰ δὲ ἐκτὸς τῶν ἐπιγείων· διὸ καὶ
τοῖς ἱερεῦσι διηνεκῶς ἦν βατά. εἶχε δὲ ταῦτα λυχνίαν μὲν ἐν
τῷ νοτίῳ μέρει κειμένην ἑπτάκαυλον,ʳ ἰσαρίθμους ἔχουσαν
λύχνους ἐπικειμένους·ˢ ἐδήλουν δὲ οὗτοι τῶν ἡμερῶν τῆς
70 ἑβδομάδος τὸν ἀριθμόν· τράπεζαν δὲ ἐν τῷ βορείῳ χρυσῆν,ᵗ ἐφ'
ἧς ἄρτους προκεῖσθαι προσέταξε δυοκαίδεκα καὶ φιάλας
χρυσᾶς πλήρεις λιβανωτοῦ καὶ ἁλῶν.ᵘ ἐν δὲ τῷ μέσῳ τῆς τε
λυχνίας καὶ τῆς τραπέζης χρυσοῦν ἔκειτο θυμιατήριον.ᵛ ταῦτα
δὲ ἦν αἰνίγματα τῶν ἀπὸ γῆς τοῖς ἀνθρώποις δεδωρημένων
75 καρπῶν. πρὸ δὲ τῆς σκηνῆς ἔξω τὸ χαλκοῦν ἦν θυσιαστήριον,
τὸ τὰ προσφερόμενα δεχόμενον θύματα.ʷ δηλοῖ δὲ τοῦτο
περιττὰ εἶναι ταῦτα καὶ μὴ ἀρεστὰ τῷ τῶν ὅλων Θεῷ. ὅθεν
ἐπιτελεῖσθαι μὲν αὐτὰ συνεχώρησε διὰ τὴν ἰουδαίων
ἀσθένειαν, ἔξω δὲ τῆς σκηνῆς ἱερουργεῖσθαι προσέταξεν, ὡς
80 τοῖς ἔνδον οὐκ ἀναγκαῖα. ἡμεῖς δὲ τὴν τοῖς ἔνδον
ἀπονεμηθεῖσαν λειτουργίαν ἐπιτελοῦμεν· θυμίαμα γάρ, καὶ
λυχνιαῖον φῶς προσφέρομεν τῷ Θεῷ, καὶ τὴν μυστικὴν τῆς
ἁγίας τραπέζης ἱερουργίαν.
(4) Ὅτι δὲ τριάκοντα πήχεων ἦν τὸ μῆκος τῆς σκηνῆς, καὶ
85 δέκα τὸ εὖρος καταμαθεῖν εὐπετές· εἴκοσι γὰρ σανίδας εἶχε
τὸ νότιον μέρος,ˣ καὶ τοσαύτας τὸ βόρειον·ʸ σανίδας γὰρ τοὺς
στύλους ὠνόμασαν οἱ ἄλλοι ἑρμηνευταί· ἑκάστης δὲ σανίδος

p. Heb 9.24   q. Heb 6.19f.   r. Ex 26.35   s. Ex 25.37   t. Ex 26.35
u. Ex 25.29f.   v. Ex 30.6   w. Ex 27.1–8   x. Ex 26.18   y. Ex 26.20

tifies to the truth of this when he says, "Christ did not enter a sanctuary made by human hands, a mere copy of the true one, but into heaven itself, and so he has now appeared in the presence of God on our behalf";[p] and again in speaking of hope in God he added, "We have this sure and steadfast anchor, a hope that enters behind the curtain, where, on our behalf, entered the forerunner, Jesus, who became a high priest according to the order of Melchizedek."[q]

So, what was inside the curtain presented an image of heavenly realities and what was outside of earthly, and hence the latter was constantly accessible to the priests. The area outside the curtain contained a seven-stemmed lampstand.[r] Situated on the south side, it bore seven lamps[s] indicative of the number of days of the week.[4] On the north side there was a golden table,[t] on which he commanded to be set out twelve loaves as well as golden bowls full of incense and salt.[u] In between the lampstand and the table was a golden incense altar.[v] These things were suggestive of the produce of the earth granted to mankind. Outside, in front of the tabernacle, there was an altar of bronze for the offering of sacrifice.[w] This suggests that these sacrifices were futile, not acceptable to the God of the universe; he allowed the performance of these rites as a concession to the limitations of the Jews but ordered them to be celebrated outside the tabernacle, as they were not essential for what was within. We, on the other hand, celebrate a liturgy corresponding to what is within, when we offer God incense, the light of lamps, and the eucharistic liturgy of the holy table.[5]

(4) Now, we can easily reckon the length of the tabernacle as thirty cubits and the width as ten. The south side had twenty planks,[x] and the north likewise.[y] "Planks" is the term the other translators

4. Neither here nor in his comment on Zec 3.9 does Theodoret explain that the number seven symbolizes completeness; *v.* J.L. McKenzie, "Seven," p. 794.

5. Here is a rare remark of a sacramental nature. Contrasting the offerings of

πῆχυν ἐχούσης καὶ ἥμισυ πήχεως, τριάκοντα πήχεις αἱ εἴκοσι
σανίδες ἐπλήρουν.ᶻ οὕτω πάλιν τὸ πρὸς δυσμὰς ἀποβλέπον ἐξ
90 εἶχε σανίδας τὸ αὐτὸ μέτρον ἐχούσας, καὶ δύο γωνίαις.
δώδεκα οὖν πήχεις ἐκ τούτων συναγόμενοι, οἱ μὲν δέκα τὸ
ἔνδον εὖρος ἐπλήρουν, οἱ δὲ ἄλλοι δύο τῶν ἑκατέρωθεν
πλευρῶν τὰς ἁρμονίας ἐδέχοντο.ᵃᵃ ἐκ μέντοι τοῦ ἑῴου μέρους
τὴν θύραν γενέσθαι προσέταξεν ἵνα, καὶ αὐτὸς ἀνίσχων, ὁ
95 ἥλιος οἱόν τινα προσκύνησιν προσφέρῃ τοῖς προπυλαίοις,
εὐθὺς ἐκεῖσε τὰς ἀκτῖνας ἐκπέμπων, καὶ οἱ τῷ θεῷ μόνῳ
λατρεύειν προστεταγμένοιᵇᵇ ὄπισθεν τὸν ἥλιον ἔχωσι, πρὸς
τὴν σκηνὴν τετραμμένοι καί, μὴ τοῦτον, ἀλλὰ τὸν τούτου
ποιητὴν προσκυνῶσι. δρυφάκτῳ τοίνυν ἡ σκηνὴ προσέῳκει,
100 σανίδας ἔχουσα πάντοθεν συνηρμοσμένας ἀλλήλαις. εἶχον δὲ
καὶ τὰς βάσεις ἀργυρᾶς καὶ τὰς κεφαλίδας ὡσαύτως,ᶜᶜ καὶ
αὐταὶ δὲ καὶ ἔνδοθεν καὶ ἔξωθεν ἦσαν ἠλειμμέναι χρυσῷ.ᵈᵈ τὸν
δὲ ὄροφον εἶχεν ἐξ ὑφασμάτων ποικίλων ἐκ διαφόρων
κατεσκευασμένων χρωμάτων. τὸ μὲν γὰρ ἦν ἁλουργόν, τὸ δὲ
105 ῥοδοειδὲς ἢ κοκκοβαφές, τὸ δὲ ὑακίνθῳ προσεοικός·ᵉᵉ ἡ δὲ
βύσσος τὴν λευκὴν εἶχε χροιάν. καὶ ταῦτα δὲ τῶν τεσσάρων
ἦν στοιχείων αἰνίγματα· ὁ μὲν γὰρ ὑάκινθος τῷ ἀέρι
προσέοικε, τὸ δὲ ῥοδοειδὲς ἢ κοκκοβαφὲς τῷ πυρί, τὸ δὲ
ἁλουργὸν μηνύει τὴν θάλατταν· ἐκείνη γὰρ τρέφει τὴν κόχλον,
110 ἐξ ἧς τὸ τοιοῦτον γίνεται χρῶμα· ἡ δὲ βύσσος τὴν γῆν· ἐκ
ταύτης γὰρ φύεσθαι λέγεται. καὶ δέρρεις δὲ εἶχε τριχίνας
ἐπικειμένας καὶ μέντοι καὶ διφθέρας ποικίλας ὥστε καὶ τὸν
ὑετὸν ἀπείργειν καὶ τὸν φλογμόν.ᶠᶠ

ll. 109f. τὴν κόχλον ἐξ ἧς *a [32], 14, c⁻¹⁵, 9 37* : τὸν κόχλον ἐξ οὗ *53, 4,
Sir. Sch.* : τὸν κόχλον ἐξ ἧς *F.M.* The feminine article is required by the
following relative pronoun; for the use of κόχλος in the feminine gender, cf.
Bas., *Hex.* 7.6; *Hom. in diuites* 4, and Gr. Nyss., *Placill.*, p. 487, l. 3. While τὸν
κόχλον ἐξ οὗ, though grammatically correct, would be the easier reading, the
combination of the masculine antecedent with the feminine relative pronoun
would be a solecism difficult to attribute to Thdt.

z. Ex 26.16   aa. Ex 26.22f.   bb. Ex 20.1–3   cc. Ex 27.17
dd. Ex 26.29   ee. Ex 26.14   ff. Ex 26.7, 14

used in place of "pillars."[6] Given that each plank was a cubit and a half wide, the twenty planks made up thirty cubits.[z] Similarly, the side facing west had six planks of the same dimensions and two on the corners, so of the twelve cubits that these amount to, ten was the breadth inside, and the remaining two were devoted to the joins from either side.[aa] He commanded the door be set on the eastern side so that the sun might, so to speak, itself offer adoration by directing its rays to the vestibule at the moment of its rising, while those ordered to serve God alone[bb] would be turned towards the tabernacle and have the sun at their backs and thus adore, not the sun, but its maker. So the tabernacle was like a railing, with planks on all sides fitted to one another. These also had silver bases and silver capitals[cc] and were gilded on both sides.[dd] They had a ceiling made of various woven fabrics of a number of colors: purple, roseate or scarlet, and a bluish color.[ee] The linen was white. These were suggestive of the four elements. The blue resembled sky, the roseate or scarlet fire; the purple recalled the sea, which nourishes the shellfish from which that color is produced, and the linen earth, from which it is said to grow. In addition, it was covered by hairy skins as well as tanned skins of various colors that kept off the rain and intense heat.[ff]

----

the lampstand, showbread, and incense, which were made inside the tabernacle, to the animal sacrifices that took place outside, Theodoret draws a typological connection between the former and the Christian liturgy in order to highlight the superiority of the Christian Eucharist to the bloody sacrifices of the ancient Hebrews. Note that, earlier in his reply, he had spoken carelessly of the priests offering sacrifices within the tabernacle (ὥστε καὶ τοὺς ἱερέας ἐν αὐτῇ τὰς θυσίας ἐπιτελεῖν).

6. The *apparatus criticus* to Ex 26.15 in the Göttingen Septuagint (*v.* J.W. Wevers and U. Quast) confirms Theodoret's report.

(5) Καὶ τοῖς ἱερεῦσι δὲ παντοδαπὸν περιτέθεικε κόσμον,
115 τὸν μὲν λαὸν καταπλήττοντα τῷ διαφόρῳ τοῦ σχήματος,
αὐτοὺς δὲ τοὺς ἱερέας διδάσκοντα ὅπως χρὴ τὴν ψυχὴν
ὡραΐζειν καὶ τὸν τῆς ἀρετῆς αὐτῇ κόσμον περιτιθέναι.
ὑποδύτην δὲ καλεῖ τὸν ἐνδότερον χιτωνίσκον, *ἐπενδύτην* δὲ
τὸν χιτῶνα τὸν ἔξωθεν. ὑακίνθινον δὲ τοῦτον γενέσθαι
120 προσέταξε καὶ *ποδήρη* προσηγόρευσεν, ὡς μέχρις ἄκρων
διήκοντα τῶν ποδῶν.[gg] ἀπήρτησε δὲ τούτου καὶ κώδωνας
χρυσοῦς καὶ ῥοΐσκους ἵνα, εἰς τὸ ἄδυτον καὶ ἀνάκτορον τῆς
σκηνῆς εἰσιὼν καὶ τὴν ἐκ τούτων ἀποτελουμένην ἠχὴν
εἰσδεχόμενος, μετὰ δέους τὴν λειτουργίαν ἐπιτελῇ, εἰς
125 μνήμην λαμβάνων τὸν ταῦτα προστεταχότα καὶ τὴν
προσφερομένην ἱερουργίαν δεχόμενον.[hh] διά τοι τοῦτο καὶ τοῦ
ἀέρος ὁ ποδήρης εἶχε τὸ χρῶμα· ὑακίνθινος γὰρ ἦν ὡς ἄν, καὶ
εἰς τοῦτον ἀφορῶν, μετάρσιος γένηται. ἐπέκειτο δὲ τῇ
κεφαλῇ κίδαρις, τὸν οὐρανὸν μιμουμένη.[ii] ἐκάλυπτε δὲ καὶ
130 ταινία τὸ μέτωπον, ἣν *μίτραν* εἶπον οἱ ἑβδομήκοντα. εἶχε δὲ
ἐν μέσῳ πέταλον αὕτη χρυσοῦν, ἐγγεγραμμένον ἔχον τοῦ
Θεοῦ τὸ ἄφραστον ὄνομα, ὃ καλοῦσιν ἑβραῖοι *τετράγραμμον*.[jj]
εὐλάβειαν δὲ τὸν λαὸν ἐκπαιδεύων, ὁ δεσπότης Θεὸς δι'
αἰνίγματος τοῦτο δεδήλωκεν· ἐπιγράψεις γὰρ αὐτῷ, φησίν,
135 *ἁγίασμα Κυρίου*.[kk] ἐκέλευσε δὲ αὐτῷ καὶ ἐφεστρίδα γενέσθαι,
ἣν οἱ ἑβδομήκοντα *ἐπωμίδα* ἐκάλεσαν,[ll] ἐν δὲ ταῖς βασιλείαις
εὑρίσκομεν *ἐφοὺδ* αὐτὴν κατὰ τὴν τῶν ἑβραίων γλῶτταν
ὠνομασμένην.[mm] αὕτη εἶχεν ἐφ' ἑκάτερου μὲν ὤμου δύο λίθους
πολυτελεῖς ἔχοντας τῶν φυλῶν τὰς προσηγορίας
140 ἐγγεγραμμένας,[nn] ἐν δὲ τῷ στήθει τὸ καλούμενον *λόγιον* τὴν
λογικὴν συγκαλύπτον καρδίαν. εἶχε δὲ καὶ τοῦτο δυοκαίδεκα
λίθους προσηρμοσμένους διάφορον ἔχοντας χροιάν·[oo] διὰ δὲ
τούτων ἐδηλοῦτο, πολέμου συγκροτηθέντος, ἢ νίκη ἢ ἧττα. καὶ
τοῦτο τῶν βασιλειῶν ἡ ἱστορία διδάσκει· ἐπιστρατευσάντων

gg. Ex 28.4, 31   hh. Ex 28.33–35   ii. Ex 28.4, 37   jj. Ex 28.36–38
kk. Ex 28.32   ll. Ex 28.6–8   mm. 1Sm 2.18; 14.3; 22.18   nn. Ex 28.9–12
oo. Ex 28.15–21

(5) He also clad the priests in the most comely attire to impress the people with their extraordinary appearance and teach the priests how to beautify the soul and bedeck it with the adornment of virtue. By "undergarment" he referred to the inner, and by "outer garment" to the outer, tunic. He commanded the latter be blue in color and called it "full length," because it reached to the top of the feet.[gg] To this he attached golden bells and pomegranates so that, on entering the unapproachable precincts and hearing the sound issuing from these, Aaron might celebrate the rite with reverence and call to mind him who had commanded these things and who was to receive the worship being offered.[hh] The outer garment had the color of the sky, blue, so that when he looked upon it, he might be elevated above this world. On his head was a turban in imitation of the sky.[ii] His forehead was covered by a headband, which the Seventy called a "head-dress"; in the middle it had a golden plate inscribed with the name of God that is not pronounced, which the Hebrews call "the Tetragrammaton."[7][jj] This was to teach the people reverence as the Lord God revealed in riddling manner: "You shall inscribe on it 'the holiness of the Lord.'"[kk] He also commanded there be made for Aaron an upper garment, which the Seventy called "the shoulder cape"[ll] though in First Samuel[8] we find it given the Hebrew name "ephod."[9][mm] It had two precious stones, one on each shoulder, inscribed with the names of the tribes[nn] and on the breast, what was called the "declaration" covering the heart, the seat of reason. This had fitted to it twelve stones of different colors,[oo] by means of which, as we learn from First Samuel, the issue of victory or defeat

7. *Cf.* Q. 15.
8. In the LXX, the books of Samuel and Kings are enumerated as the four books of "The Reigns" (αἱ βασιλεῖαι).
9. The ephod, a close-fitting waistcoat with shoulder straps, is referred to by the LXX as ἐπωμίς in Ex, but as ἐφούδ / ἐφώδ in 1Sm; *v.* the apparatus of ancient sources.

145 γὰρ τῶν ἀλλοφύλων τῷ Ἰσραήλ, οὐ πρότερον ἐτόλμησεν ὁ
Σαοὺλ παρατάξασθαι ἕως εἶδε τὰ τῆς νίκης μηνύματα·
προσάγαγε, γάρ φησι, τὸ ἐφούδ^{pp} εἶτα τὴν νίκην μαθών,
ἐπήγαγε, συνάγαγε τὸ ἐφούδ^{qq} καὶ οὕτως ἐξώπλισε τὸν λαόν.
διὰ τοῦτο εἰρηκὼς ὁ τῶν ὅλων Θεός, *καὶ ἐπιθήσεις τὸ λόγιον*
150 *τῆς κρίσεως ἐπὶ τὸ στῆθος Ἀαρὼν καὶ συνάψεις αὐτὸ... πρὸς*
τὴν ἐπωμίδα,^{rr} *ἐπήγαγε, καὶ ἐπιθήσεις αὐτῷ... τὴν δήλωσιν*
καὶ τὴν ἀλήθειαν.^{ss} *καὶ δήλωσιν* μὲν ἐκάλεσε τὰ ἐκεῖθεν
μηνύματα, *ἀλήθειαν* δὲ τῶν μηνυμάτων τὸ ἀψευδές.

155 (6) Ἰστέον μέντοι, ὡς παχυτέροις οὖσι τοῖς τηνικαῦτα καὶ
τῶν νοητῶν ἐφίκεσθαι μὴ δυναμένοις, διὰ τῶν σωματικῶν
συμβόλων τὴν ὠφέλειαν ὁ πάνσοφος δεσπότης ἐπραγματεύετο.
ἡμεῖς δὲ νοοῦμεν διὰ μὲν τοῦ λογίου τὴν θεωρίαν τῶν νοητῶν,
διὰ δὲ τῆς ἐπωμίδος τὴν ἐργασίαν τῆς ἀρετῆς, καὶ τὴν τοῦ
160 λογίου καὶ τῆς ἐπωμίδος ἁρμονίαν τε καὶ συνάφειαν εἰς τὴν
τῆς πίστεως καὶ τῆς ἀγαθῆς πράξεως λαμβάνομεν συμφωνίαν·
τὸ δὲ πρώτην ἐπιτίθεσθαι τὴν ἐπωμίδα, εἶθ' οὕτω ταύτῃ τὸ
λόγιον συνάπτεσθαι τὸ τὴν ἀγαθὴν πρᾶξιν ὑποβάθραν εἶναι
τῆς θεωρίας.

pp. 1Sm 14.18   qq. 1Sm 14.19 (LXX var.)   rr. Ex 29.5 (LXX var.)
ss. Ex 28.30

was revealed in the waging of war. When the Philistines were attacking Israel, Saul did not dare engage them until he saw the tokens of victory: "Bring forward the ephod,"[pp] he said. On learning that he would be victorious, he proceeded, "Withdraw the ephod"[qq] and then called the people to arms. Hence, after saying, "You shall put the declaration of judgment on the breast of Aaron and attach it to the shoulder cape,"[rr] the God of the universe proceeded, "and you shall put on it 'the demonstration' and 'the truth,'"[ss] by "demonstration" meaning the tokens it contained, and by "truth" the reliability of those tokens.[10]

(6) Now, you should realize that, since the people of that time were quite materialistic and incapable of attaining to spiritual realities, the Lord, in his great wisdom, devised a way of helping them through physical symbols.[11] We, on the contrary, understand by the declaration contemplation of the intelligible, and by the shoulder cape the practice of virtue. We take the close fit of the declaration and the shoulder cape as the harmony of faith and virtuous behavior and understand the prior donning of the shoulder cape and the subsequent clasping to it of the declaration to signify that virtuous behavior is the foundation of contemplation.

10. Theodoret tries to clarify the description of the ephod in Ex 28 by reference to 1Sm 14.18f., where the LXX twice reads "ephod" but the MT "ark." He understands those verses to indicate that Saul employed the ephod as an oracle to determine whether the ensuing encounter with the Philistines would lead to his victory or defeat. This is also the interpretation of the Greek offered by H.W. Hertzberg (on 1Sm 14.16–18), who, however, warns against too easy acceptance of the widely held belief that the LXX here offers a text closer to the original Hebrew than the MT. For the breastpiece of judgment worn by Aaron, with its Urim and Thummim (rendered in Greek as δήλωσιν = demonstration and ἀλήθειαν = truth; v. Ex 28.26 LXX), and displayed at important moments of judgment, the LXX uses the term λογεῖον, represented in the text of Theodoret by the closely related form λόγιον. Due to the stem it shares with λόγος, "reason" or "word," λογεῖον is rendered *rationale* in the Vulgate, but the context of Exodus indicates that the "declaration" was actually an oracle, which is the meaning ordinarily borne by Theodoret's λόγιον; v. *LSJ, ad voc.*

11. In his "Quotations of Theodoret's *De sancta et vivifica Trinitate*," part of his project of detecting Theodoret's influence in the work of later authors, I. Pásztori-Kupán points out (pp. 488f.) that this sentence appears in the *Catena on Luke* composed by Nicetas of Heraclcia.

LXI

Διὰ τί οἱ ἱερεῖς, τοῖς ἱερείοις τὰς χεῖρας ἐπιτιθέντες, οὕτως ἱέρευον;ᵃ

Οὐ πᾶσι τοῖς ἱερείοις, ἀλλὰ τοῖς ὑπὲρ αὐτῶν προσφερομένοις καὶ μάλιστα τοῖς ὑπὲρ ἁμαρτίας. τοῖς δὲ
5 ἄλλοις αὐτοὶ τὰς χεῖρας ἐπετίθεσαν οἱ προσφέροντες. ἦν δὲ τοῦτο σύμβολον τοῦ τὸ ἱερεῖον τὸν τόπον πληροῦν τοῦ προσφέροντος, τὴν ὑπὲρ αὐτοῦ δεχόμενον σφαγήν.

Ἐπισημήνασθαι δὲ προσήκει ὡς ὑπὲρ τοῦ ἀρχιερέως προσεφέρετο μόσχος,ᵇ ὑπὲρ δὲ παντὸς τοῦ λαοῦ πάλιν
10 μόσχος,ᶜ ὑπὲρ δὲ τοῦ ἄρχοντος χίμαρος,ᵈ ὑπὲρ ἑκάστου δὲ ἀνδρὸς χίμαρα·ᵉ πρόσφορον γὰρ τῷ μὲν ἄρχοντι τὸ ἄρρεν, τῷ δὲ ἀρχομένῳ τὸ θῆλυ, ἐπειδὴ καὶ τὴν γυναῖκα τῷ Ἀδὰμ ἐξ ἀρχῆς ὑπέταξεν ὁ Θεός.ᶠ

Ὁ δὲ μόσχος, ὁ περὶ ἁμαρτίας θυόμενος, ἔξω τῆς
15 παρεμβολῆς κατεκαίετο.ᵍ τούτου χάριν καὶ ὁ δεσπότης Χριστός, ἥ φησιν ὁ θεῖος ἀπόστολος, *ἔξω τῆς πύλης ἔπαθεν*ʰ καὶ τῷ τύπῳ τὴν ἀλήθειαν ἐπιτέθεικε.

Τῷ δὲ θυσιαστηρίῳ προσεφέρετο τὸ ἐπίπλουν. τοῦτο γὰρ λέγει *τὸ στέαρ τὸ ἐπι . . . κοιλίας, καὶ οἱ δύο νεφροί, καὶ τὸ*
20 *στέαρ τὸ ἐπ' αὐτῶν, καὶ ὁ τοῦ ἥπατος λοβός,*ⁱ ὅπερ οἱ ἄλλοι ἑρμηνευταὶ *περιττὸν* προσηγόρευσαν. αἰνίγματα δὲ ταῦτα τῶν ἐν ἡμῖν παθημάτων· τὸ μὲν γὰρ στέαρ, τὸ τὴν κοιλίαν καλύπτον, σημαίνει τῆς γαστριμαργίας τὴν νόσον, οἱ δὲ νεφροὶ τὰς ὑπογαστρίους ἡδονάς, ὁ δὲ λοβὸς τοῦ ἥπατος τὸ

ʟxɪ A [32], B, C, 4 7 9 10 17 31 35 37 = 22 mss.

l. 20 ὅπερ *Sir. Sch. F.M.* : ὄνπερ 7 9 = "*The membrane enclosing the entrails was offered on the altar, for this is the meaning of 'the fat on the belly, the two kidneys and the fat on them, and the lobe of the liver,' which the other translators called 'the remainder.'*" Cf. Wevers and Quast, *ap. crit.* on Ex 29.13.

a. Ex 29.10, 15, 19   b. Lv 4.3–12   c. Lv 4.13–21   d. Lv 3.22–26
e. Lv 4.27–31   f. Gn 3.16   g. Ex 29.14   h. Heb 13.12   i. Ex 29.13

LXI

Why did the priests lay their hands on the victims before sacrificing them?[a]

The priests did not lay their hands on all the victims, but only on those they offered for themselves, especially the sin offerings. In other cases, the person offering the sacrifice put his hands on the victim. This was a sign that the victim took the place of the offerer by undergoing death for him.

We should note that a calf was offered for the high priest,[b] a calf likewise for all the people,[c] a he-goat for the ruler,[d] and a she-goat for each man.[e] It was appropriate, you see, that a male be offered for the ruler, but a female for the ruled, since God at the outset subjected the woman to Adam.[1f]

Now, the calf sacrificed for sin was burned outside the camp.[g] Therefore, as the holy apostle says, Christ the Lord also "suffered outside the gate."[2h] He, thus, provided the fulfilment of the type.

The membrane enclosing the entrails, which the other translators called "the remainder," was offered on the altar, for this is the meaning of "the fat on the belly, the two kidneys and the fat on them, and the lobe of the liver."[i] These details are obscure references to our passions.[3] The fat covering the belly signifies the vice of gluttony, the kidneys sexual pleasures, the lobe of the liver anger, because the liver is linked to the gall bladder, containing the bile. He

1. Theodoret supplements his exposition of the offerings made by the priests with reference to Lv 4.22–31, where different sin offerings are prescribed for rulers and common people, and refers to Gn 2f. for proof that woman is subject to man; *cf.* note 7 to Q. 20 on Gn.

2. Again, the christological interpretation is brief; Theodoret's interest is in the OT ritual itself.

3. The respondent now goes beyond the limits of the question to offer a moral interpretation of the sacrifice of consecration.

25 θυμοειδές· ἐκείνῳ γὰρ συνῆπται τὸ χοληδόχον ἀγγεῖον. ταῦτα
δὲ καθιεροῦν κελεύει καὶ οἱονεὶ νεκρὰς αὐτῶν ἀποφαίνειν τὰς
πονηρὰς ἐνεργείας.

Τοῦ δὲ τῆς τελειώσεως κριοῦ τὸν βραχίονα τὸν δεξιὸν
προσενεγκεῖν διηγόρευσε,ʲ τὴν πρακτικὴν ἀρετὴν δεξιὰν οὖσαν
30 καὶ ἀρίστην τῷ Θεῷ προσφέρειν κελεύων. ὁ δὲ ἄρτος, καὶ τὸ
λάγανον,ᵏ καὶ ἡ τοῦ οἴνου σπονδὴˡ τοὺς ἀπὸ γῆς φυομένους
δηλοῦσι καρπούς, ὧν τὰς ἀπαρχὰς προσφέρειν ὅσιον τῷ Θεῷ.

LXII

Τί ἐστιν εἰς ὀσμὴν εὐωδίας ... κάρπωμά ἐστι Κυρίῳ;ᵃ

Διὰ τῶν ἀνθρωπίνων τὰ θεῖα διδάσκει. ἐπειδὴ γὰρ ἡμεῖς
ταῖς εὐοσμίαις τερπόμεθα, τὴν κατὰ νόμον γενομένην
ἱερουργίαν ὀσμὴν εὐωδίας ὠνόμασεν. ὅτι γὰρ οὐ δεῖ γυμνῷ
5 προσέχειν τῷ γράμματι καὶ ἡ τοῦ Θεοῦ φύσις διδάσκει·
ἀσώματος γάρ· καὶ ἡ δυσοσμία τῶν καιομένων ὀστῶν· τί γὰρ
ἐκείνων ἐστὶ δυσωδέστερον; οἱ μέντοι ἄλλοι ἑρμηνευταὶ
εὐαρεστήσεως ἀντὶ εὐωδίας τεθείκασιν.

LXIII

Τίνος χάριν ἐξ ἑκάστης θυσίας ὑπὲρ σωτηρίας
προσφερομένης τὸν ἱερέα λαμβάνειν τὸν βραχίονα τὸν δεξιὸν
καὶ τὸ στηθύνιον διηγόρευσεν;ᵃ

j. Ex 29.22–25   k. Ex 29.23   l. Ex 29.40

ʟxɪɪ *A [32], B, C⁻⁵⁰, 4 7 9 10 17 31 35 37* = 21 mss.

a. Ex 29.25

ʟxɪɪɪ *A [32], B, C, 4 7 9 10 17 31* 35 37* = 22 mss.

a. Ex 29.26–28

commanded them to sacrifice these things and, as it were, put their wicked inclinations to death.

In prescribing the offering of the right shoulder of the ram of consecration,[j] he commanded us to bring to God virtue active in deed, a virtue right and proper, the best kind of virtue. The bread, cake,[k] and libation of wine[l] represent the crops that grow from the earth; it is a religious act to offer the first-fruits of these to God.

LXII

What is the meaning of "It is an offering to the Lord for a sweet odor"?[1a]

Through things human he gives instruction in things divine. Since we like sweet fragrances, he called worship according to the Law "a sweet odor." Yet we learn that one should not heed the bare letter if we consider God's nature, which is incorporeal, and the foul smell of burning bones. After all, what could be more malodorous? For "sweet," in fact, the other translators put "acceptable."

LXIII

Why did he order the priest to take the right shoulder and breast of each victim offered for salvation?[a]

1. This translation represents the truncated version of the second half of Ex 29.25 that Theodoret read in his Bible, and which appears also in the Samaritan Pentateuch. In the more widely attested LXX form of this verse ἔναντι κυρίου (before the Lord) follows εὐωδίας (a sweet odor) and is understood as the end of one clause, while κάρπωμα (an offering) is taken as the beginning of another: "[you will offer them upon the altar of burnt offering] as a sweet odor before the Lord; it is an offering to the Lord." One could introduce a stop before κάρπωμά also in Theodoret's text, but, given his habit of citing single sense units in the

Διὰ τοῦ στηθυνίου τὸ λογικὸν καὶ τὸ θεωρητικὸν ἀπαιτεῖ
5 τὸν ἱερέα· κάλυμμα γὰρ τὸ στηθύνιον τῆς καρδίας· διὰ δὲ τοῦ
δεξιοῦ βραχίονος, τὴν πρᾶξιν τὴν δεξιάν· οὐκ ἀρκεῖ γὰρ ἡ
πίστις εἰς σωτηρίαν ἀλλὰ δεῖται τῶν ἔργων εἰς τελειότητα.

LXIV

Τί ἐστι τὸ εἴν;[a]

Μέτρον ἑβραϊκὸν οἴνου καὶ ἐλαίου. δέχεται δέ, ὥς φησιν
Ἰώσηπος, δύο χόας ἀττικούς.[b] πιστευτέον δὲ ἐν τούτοις αὐτῷ,
ἀκριβῶς τοῦ ἔθνους τὰ μέτρα ἐπισταμένῳ.

LXV

Περὶ τῶν σαββάτων νομοθετῶν, ἔφη, ἔστι γὰρ σημεῖον ἐν
ἐμοὶ καὶ τοῖς υἱοῖς Ἰσραὴλ εἰς τὰς γενεὰς ὑμῶν.[a] πῶς οὖν
τοῦτο νοήσομεν;

Ὥσπερ, τῷ Ἀβραὰμ τὴν περιτομὴν διδούς, ἔφη, καὶ ἔσται
5 εἰς σημεῖον ... ἀνὰ μέσον ἐμοῦ καὶ ὑμῶν,[b] οὕτω, καὶ περὶ τοῦ
σαββάτου νομοθετῶν, ἔφη, ἔστι γὰρ σημεῖον ἐν ἐμοὶ καὶ
τοῖς υἱοῖς Ἰσραὴλ εἰς τὰς γενεὰς ὑμῶν.[c] τὸ γὰρ καινὸν τῆς
πολιτείας ἀεὶ τοῦ νομοθέτου τὴν μνήμην ἀνθεῖν παρεσκεύαζε
καὶ τῶν ἐθνῶν τῶν ἄλλων ἐχώριζε. καθάπερ γὰρ τὰς ποίμνας

LXIV A [32], B, C⁻⁵¹, 4 7 9 10 17 31 35 37 = 21 mss.

a. Ex 29.40   b. Ios., A.I. 3.234

LXV A [32], B, C, 4 7 9 10 17 31 35 37 = 22 mss.

ll. 1f. ἐν ἐμοὶ c⁻⁸, 50, 9 31 35 : ἐμοὶ Sir. Sch. F.M. Cf. Wevers and Quast, *ap.
crit.* on Ex 31.13.
l. 6 ἐν ἐμοὶ F.M. : ἐμοὶ [32], 5, 8, 51, Sir. Sch.
l. 7 τοῖς υἱοῖς A [32], cₚ, 7 10, Sir. Sch. : ἐν τοῖς υἱοῖς F.M.

a. Ex 31.13 (LXX var.)   b. Gn 17.11   c. Ex 31.13 (LXX var.)

By mention of the breast, he required of the priest the exercise of reason and contemplation—the breast enclosing the heart—and by mention of the right shoulder, right actions, for faith does not suffice for salvation but requires works for perfection.[1]

LXIV

What is a hin?[a]

A Hebrew measure of wine and oil. According to Josephus, it holds "two Attic pints."[b] He is to be trusted in these matters, as he had precise knowledge of the measures used by his people.[1]

LXV

Laying down the law regarding the Sabbath, he said, "It is a sign between me and the children of Israel for your generations."[a] How is this to be understood?

When he gave circumcision to Abraham, he said, "It will be a sign between me and you";[b] so also, in laying down the law regarding the Sabbath, he said, "It is a sign between me and the children of Israel for your generations."[c] This novelty in their way of life had the effect of keeping the memory of the Lawgiver always before them and marked them off from the other nations. The special features of the

----

questions, it looks more likely that he regarded all six words as constituting one sentence, as Sirmond, Schulze, and Fernández Marcos and Sáenz-Badillos have all punctuated; *v.* J.W. Wevers and U. Quast, *ap. crit. ad loc.*

---

1. *Cf.* sec. 9 of the "Introduction to Theodoret's Life and Works" and note 1 to *Q.* 12.

---

1. Theodoret carefully explains these details regarding the daily life of the ancient Hebrews. Here, as in *Q.* 30, he consults Josephus; in his earlier commentary on Ezekiel (on 4.11), he had consulted the Syriac version for a modern measurement equivalent to the hin.

10 καὶ τὰς ἀγέλας αἱ σφραγῖδες δηλοῦσι, οὕτω τὰ τῆς τῶν
ἑβραίων πολιτείας ἐξαίρετα καὶ τῶν ἄλλων αὐτοὺς διεῖργε καὶ
τῷ νομοθέτῃ προσεδρεύειν ἐδίδασκεν.

LXVI

Τί δή ποτε ὁ Ἀαρὼν τῷ λαῷ τὸν μόσχον διέγλυψεν;[a]
Τὸν σκοπὸν τοῦ γινομένου προσήκει ζητεῖν· οὕτω γὰρ
ἐξετάζοντες, εὑρήσομεν αὐτὸν οὐ παντάπασι συγγνώμης
ἐστερημένον. τοῦ γὰρ ἀδελφοῦ τεσσαράκοντα ἡμέρας
5 διατρίψαντος ἐν τῇ τοῦ ὄρους ἀκρονυχίᾳ,[b] καὶ τοῦ λαοῦ
λυττήσαντος καὶ εἰς τὴν Αἴγυπτον ἀναστρέψαι ὁρμήσαντος,[c]
πρῶτον μὲν ἐπειράθη λόγοις αὐτῶν τὴν ὁρμὴν χαλινῶσαι.
ἐπειδὴ δὲ ἀπειθοῦντας εἶδεν, ᾔτησε τῶν γυναικῶν τὰ χρυσία,[d]
πάθει πάθος ἀντιστρατεύσας, τὸ φιλόκοσμον καὶ
10 φιλοχρήματον τῇ τῆς δεισιδαιμονίας μανίᾳ, ἀλλ' οὐδὲ τοῦτο
τὸ μηχάνημα τὴν ἐκείνων ἔσβεσε λύτταν. ὅθεν ἠναγκάσθη
διαγλύψαι τὸν μόσχον καί, τοιούτῳ σκοπῷ χρησάμενος, τῆς
θείας ἐδεήθη φιλανθρωπίας ὥστε τὴν τιμωρίαν διαφυγεῖν. καὶ
τοῦτο Μωϋσῆς ὁ θειότατος ἐν τῷ Δευτερονομίῳ δεδήλωκεν·
15 ἐδεήθην, γάρ φησι, τοῦ Κυρίου περὶ Ἀαρὼν τοῦ ἀδελφοῦ μου,
καὶ οὐκ ἀπέθανεν.[e]

LXVI A *[32]*, B, C⁻⁵¹, 4 7 9 10 17 31 35 37 = 21 mss.

l. 12 τοιούτῳ σκοπῷ B, 50, 4 17 : τοιούτῳ δὲ σκοπῷ *Sir. Sch. F.M.* = "and
then, acting with this sort of intention, he was in need of God's loving kindness to
escape retribution." The consecutive δὲ would undermine the concessive force the
participle evidently bears in the context; *cf., e.g., Thdt., H. rel. pf.,* sec. 4 ('Ἀλλ'
ὅμως καὶ τοιούτους ἔχουσα τοὺς ἀντιπάλους ἡ τῶν ἁγίων τούτων
συμμορία ...οὕτω λαμπρὰν ἀνεδήσαντο νίκην).

a. Ex 32.4   b. Ex 24.18   c. *V., e.g.,* Ex 17.3   d. Ex 32.2   e. Dt 9.20

Hebrews' way of life set them aside from others and taught them to serve their Lawgiver much as branding identifies the owners of flocks and herds.

LXVI

Why did Aaron fashion the calf for the people?[a]

We should inquire into the purpose of his action. If we examine this carefully, we shall find it was not completely without excuse. His brother had spent forty days in the darkness of the mountain,[b] and the people were raving and bent on returning to Egypt.[c] First, he tried to curb their impulse with words. Then, when he saw they continued to rebel, he asked for the women's golden jewellery,[d] so as to set one passion against another, namely, their love for adornments and possessions against their crazed superstition. But not even this ruse quenched their frenzy. Hence, he was forced to make an image of the calf, and though he had acted with this sort of intention, he was in need of God's loving-kindness to escape retribution. That is what the divinely inspired Moses indicated in Deuteronomy: "I interceded with the Lord for my brother Aaron, and he did not die."[e]

LXVII

Πῶς νοητέον τὸ *καὶ νῦν ἔασόν με καί, θυμωθεὶς ὀργῇ εἰς
αὐτούς, ἐκτρίψω αὐτοὺς καὶ ποιήσω σε εἰς ἔθνος μέγα;*[a]

Καὶ τὸ ἀπαθὲς τοῦ Θεοῦ καὶ τὸ φιλάνθρωπον ὁ λόγος
δηλοῖ· ὁ γὰρ θυμῷ τι πράττων καὶ τοὺς παρακαλοῦντας
5 δυσχεραίνει. ὁ δὲ Θεὸς ἔφη, *ἔασόν με καί, θυμωθεὶς ὀργῇ εἰς
αὐτούς, ἐκτρίψω αὐτούς.* οὐδεὶς δὲ ἀναμένει τοὺς
παρακαλοῦντας, ἵνα ὀργισθῇ, ἀλλ' ἵνα παρακληθῇ· τὸ οὖν
ἔασόν με ἀντὶ τοῦ κώλυσόν με εἴρηκεν. ἐπειδὴ γὰρ ἠγνόει
Μωϋσῆς ὁ μέγας τὴν τοῦ λαοῦ παρανομίαν, καὶ ταύτην αὐτῷ
10 δεδήλωκεν ὁ Θεὸς καὶ εἰς πρεσβείαν διήγειρε. τὸ δὲ *ποιήσω
σε εἰς ἔθνος μέγα* τὰ ἡμέτερα προσημαίνει· ὅπερ γὰρ τότε οὐ
γέγονε μετὰ τὴν τοῦ σωτῆρος ἡμῶν ἐπιφάνειαν γέγονεν. ὁ
μέντοι νομοθέτης, καὶ ταῦτα τοῦ Θεοῦ ἀρκεῖν αὐτὸν εἰς τὴν
ὑπὲρ τοῦ λαοῦ πρεσβείαν εἰρηκότος, οὐχ ὑπέλαβεν ἱκανὸς
15 εἶναι παῦσαι τοῦ Θεοῦ τὴν ὀργήν. ὅθεν τῶν πατριαρχῶν τὰς
προσηγορίας ἀνθ' ἱκετηρίας προσήνεγκεν, καὶ τῶν πρὸς
ἐκείνους ὅρκων ἀνέμνησε, καὶ τὰς γεγενημένας συνθήκας
ἐμπεδωθῆναι ἱκέτευσεν.[b]

LXVIII

Διὰ τί τὰς πλάκας συνέτριψεν;[a]

Ἀνάξιον κρίνας τὸν λαὸν τῆς θείας νομοθεσίας. ἐπειδὴ γὰρ
προικῴων γραμματείων τύπον εἶχον αἱ πλάκες, ἡ δὲ νύμφη

ʟxvɪɪ A *[32]*, B, C, 4 7 9 10 17 31 35 37 = 22 mss.
a. Ex 32.10 b. Ex 32.13

ʟxvɪɪɪ A *[32]*, B, c, 50, 4 7 9 10 17 31 35 37 = 19 mss.
a. Ex 32.19

LXVII

How are we to understand the verse "Now let me be, and in my burning anger, I shall consume them and make of you a great nation"?[a]

This verse reveals both God's impassibility and his loving-kindness. Anyone who acts in anger also turns on those who try to calm him, whereas God said, "Let me be, and in my burning anger, I shall consume them."[1] Now, nobody waits for someone to rouse him to anger, but to be calmed. So his words "Let me be" meant, "Stop me." Since the mighty Moses was ignorant of the people's transgression, God communicated this to him and prompted him to intercession. But the statement "I shall make of you a great nation" foreshadows our situation; that is, what at that time did not occur took place after the coming of our Savior. Despite God's assurance that he was capable of interceding for the people, the lawgiver did not believe he was up to the task of quelling God's wrath. Hence, he cited the names of the patriarchs as an olive branch, reminded God of the oaths he had sworn to them, and begged him to confirm the covenants he had already made.[b]

LXVIII

Why did he smash the tablets?[a]

Because he judged the people unworthy of the God-given laws. As the tablets represented a kind of dowry agreement, and the bride

---

1. As in *Q.* 20.1 on Gn, Theodoret is concerned to explain the anthropomorphic language of the OT in a way that safeguards the divine transcendence; *v.* also Theodoret's explanation of the expression "God's back" (Ex 33.23) in *Q.* 68 and *cf. Q.* 70 on Gn.

πρὸ τῆς παστάδος εἰς μοιχείαν ἀπέκλινε, μάλα εἰκότως τὸ
5 προικῷον διέρρηξε γραμματεῖον.

'Επισημήνασθαι δὲ προσήκει ὡς, τότε μὲν δεξάμενος τὴν
ἱκετείαν, ὁ τῶν ὅλων Θεὸς ἀνεβάλετο τὴν τιμωρίαν·
προστέθεικε δέ, ᾗ δ' ἂν ἡμέρᾳ ἐπισκέπτωμαι, ἐπάξω ἐπ'
αὐτοὺς πᾶσαν τὴν ἁμαρτίαν αὐτῶν.ᵇ ἔοικε δὲ τοῦτο τοῖς ὑπὸ
10 τοῦ ἀποστόλου εἰρημένοις· ἀγνοῶν ὅτι τὸ χρηστὸν τοῦ Θεοῦ
εἰς μετάνοιάν σε ἄγει; κατὰ δὲ τὴν σκληρότητά σου καὶ
ἀμετανόητον καρδίαν θησαυρίζεις σεαυτῷ ὀργὴν ἐν ἡμέρᾳ
ὀργῆς, καὶ ἀποκαλύψεως, καὶ δικαιοκρισίας τοῦ Θεοῦ, ὃς
ἀποδώσει ἑκάστῳ κατὰ τὰ ἔργα αὐτοῦ.ᶜ

15 Ὁ μέντοι νομοθέτης ἀκούσας ὡς οὐκ ἀνέξεται συνεῖναι
αὐτοῖς ὁ τῶν ὅλων Θεὸς διὰ τὸ σκληρὸν αὐτῶν καὶ ἀντίτυπον
ἀλλ' ἄγγελον αὐτοῖς ἐπιστήσει,ᵈ ᾔτησε μὲν γνῶναι τίς ὁ τὴν
κηδεμονίαν αὐτῶν πιστευθείς, ἠντιβόλησε δέ, μὴ δοῦναι
αὐτοῖς ὁμόδουλον ἡγεμόνα, ἀλλ' αὐτὸν αὐτῶν ἡγήσασθαι τὸν
20 δεσπότην.ᵉ ἐπειδὴ δὲ καὶ ταύτην ὑπέσχετο δώσειν αὐτῷ τὴν
χάριν ὁ ἀγαθὸς Θεός, ἔρωτι μεθύων ἐπαινουμένῳ, τῶν ὑπὲρ
ἄνθρωπον ἠράσθη καὶ τὴν ἀθέατον φύσιν ἰδεῖν ἐπεθύμησεν.
ἀλλὰ μεμάθηκεν ὡς ἐκείνην ἰδεῖν τὴν οὐσίαν ἀδύνατον·ᶠ Θεὸν
γὰρ οὐδεὶς ἑώρακε πώποτε,ᵍ κατὰ τὴν τοῦ Κυρίου φωνήν. τὰς
25 δὲ θείας οἰκονομίας τε καὶ ἐνεργείας· οὕτω γὰρ προσήκει
νοεῖν τοῦ Θεοῦ τὰ ὀπίσθια·ʰ θεωρῆσαι δυνατὸν τοῖς κατὰ
Μωϋσέα τελείοις τὴν ἀρετήν, καὶ οὐδὲ τούτοις ὡς ἔτυχεν,
ἀλλ' εἰς τὴν πέτραν ὑπ' αὐτοῦ τοῦ Θεοῦ τεθειμένοις·ⁱ
σημαίνει δὲ αὕτη τῆς πίστεως τὸ στερρὸν καὶ ἀκράδαντον·
30 καὶ διὰ τῆς ὀπῆς τῆς πέτρας· δηλοῖ δὲ αὕτη τὸν τῆς πίστεως
ὀφθαλμὸν θεωροῦντα τὰ τοῖς αἰσθητοῖς ὀφθαλμοῖς ἀνέφικτα
καὶ ἀθέατα.

---

b. Ex 32.34   c. Rom 2.4–6   d. Ex 33.2f.   e. Ex 33.12–16
f. Ex 33.18–20   g. Jn 1.18   h. Ex 33.23   i. Ex 33.21f.

had lapsed into adultery right on the threshold of the bridal chamber, he was entirely justified in tearing up the agreement.[1]

Now, we should also note that, when he accepted Moses' petition, the God of the universe postponed retribution but went on to say, "On the day I call them to account, I shall punish them for all their sin."[b] This is similar to the words of the apostle: "Are you unaware that God's kindness leads you to repentance? In your hardness and impenitence of heart you are storing up wrath for yourself on the day of wrath and the revelation of the righteous judgment of God, who will repay each according to his deeds."[c]

But when he heard that, on account of their obstinate hardheartedness, God refused to consort with them but would send them an angel,[d] the lawgiver asked to be told who was to be entrusted with their care and begged that they be given no fellow slave as a leader, but that the Lord himself lead them.[e] Since the good Lord promised to grant him this favor as well, Moses became intoxicated with a commendable love, and, conceiving a desire for what is beyond a human being, longed to see him who is by nature invisible. He learned, however, that it is impossible to see that being[f]—"No one has ever seen God,"[g] as the Lord said—whereas to see the divine dispensations and actions (the true meaning of "God's back")[h] is possible for those perfect in virtue like Moses. But, even for them, this is not possible just anyhow, but only when they have been placed by God himself "on the rock"[i] (that is, in stability and constancy of faith), and only through "a cleft of the rock" (that is, with the eye of faith, which can discern things inaccessible and invisible to bodily eyes).

1. The analogy is Theodoret's own and serves to acquit Moses of the imputation of rash behavior. For Theodoret's ability to imitate biblical imagery, *v.* note 1 to Q. 86 on Gn.

LXIX

Τί σημαίνει τὸ κάλυμμα τὸ ἐπιτεθὲν τῷ προσώπῳ τοῦ νομοθέτου;[a]

Ἔχομεν τοῦ ἀποστόλου τὴν ἑρμηνείαν· μέχρι, γάρ φησι, τῆς σήμερον, ἡνίκα ἀναγινώσκεται Μωϋσῆς, κάλυμμα ἐπὶ τὴν
5 καρδίαν αὐτῶν κεῖται[b] μὴ ἀνακαλυπτόμενον, ὅτι ἐν Χριστῷ καταργεῖται[c] ἡνίκα δ' ἂν ἐπιστρέψῃ πρὸς Κύριον, περιαιρεῖται τὸ κάλυμμα.[d] ὥσπερ γὰρ τότε θείας ἐνεπλήσθη δόξης τοῦ νομοθέτου τὸ πρόσωπον, καὶ σέλας ἐκεῖθεν ὑπὲρ ἀστραπὴν ἐκπεμπόμενον ἀντιβλέπειν οὐκ εἴα τοὺς
10 ἐντυγχάνοντας ἀλλ' ἢ ἑτέρωσε τὰ πρόσωπα τρέπειν ἢ τοὺς ὀφθαλμοὺς μύειν ἠνάγκαζε· καὶ τούτου χάριν ἐχρῆτο τῷ προκαλύμματι, τῷ λαῷ διαλεγόμενος, πρὸς δὲ τὸν Θεὸν ἐπιστρέφων, γυμνὸν εἶχε τὸ πρόσωπον· οὕτως ἰουδαῖοι, τῷ τοῦ νόμου προσέχοντες γράμματι, τὴν μὲν δόξαν οὐχ ὁρῶσι,
15 μόνον δὲ τὸ κάλυμμα βλέπουσι· τῇ δὲ τοῦ παναγίου πνεύματος χάριτι προσιόντες, ἀπαλλάσσονται μὲν τοῦ προκαλύμματος, θεωροῦσι δὲ τὴν δόξαν, ἧς Μωϋσῆς

LXIX A [32], B, C, 4 7 9 10 17 31* 35 37 = 22 mss.

l. 4 ἀναγινώσκεται J.P. : ἀναγινώσκηται Sir. Sch. F.M. Sir. and Sch. attribute to Thdt. one more citation of 2Cor 3.15 (*Epp. Paul. ad loc.*) in which ἡνίκα is followed by the subjunctive without ἄν, and both print ἡνίκα …ἔλθωσιν in his comment on Ez 33.33 (*Ezech. ad loc.*). Nonetheless, given the rarity of this anomalous construction (only two other cases among the 212 appearances of ἡνίκα in the works of our author; v. the *TLG*) and the evidence of the mss. which agree, apparently without exception, in offering the indicative in the two other quotations of this verse in the *Quaest. in oct.* (v. Q. 43 on Dt and pf. *Qq. on Jos*), it seems likely that the indicative should be read here as well; the subjunctive in this passage and in the comment on 2Cor 3.15 may be due to a careless attempt at regularization or mere etacism. Yet the subjunctive with ἄν is read by Sir. and Sch. in Thdt.'s quotation of 2Cor 3.15 in his comment on Rom 5.14, and the omission of ἄν both in Q. 69 on Ex and in the comment on 2Cor 3.15 may be nothing more than an error of haplography.

a. Ex 34.33–35   b. 2Cor 3.15   c. 2Cor 3.14   d. 2Cor 3.16

LXIX

What is the meaning of the veil placed on the face of the law-giver?[a]

We have the apostle's interpretation: "To this day, as Moses is read out, there lies over their heart a veil[b] that is not lifted, but which is set aside by Christ.[c] When one turns to the Lord, the veil is lifted."[d] At that time, the lawgiver's face was filled with divine glory, and the ray issuing from it, brighter than lightning, would not permit anyone who conversed with Moses to look at him but forced them to turn away their faces or close their eyes. Hence, his having recourse to a veil when talking to the people, whereas, when turning to God, he kept his face uncovered. Just so, by focusing on the letter of the Law, the Jews see not the glory but look only upon the veil. Those, on the other hand, who have access to the grace of the most Holy Spirit are rid of the veil and gaze upon the glory with which Moses was filled. As St. Paul says, "All of us with face unveiled reflect, as in a mirror, the glory of the Lord and are being transformed into the same image from one degree of glory to another, for this comes

ἐνεπλήσθη. τοῦτο γὰρ καὶ ὁ μακάριος λέγει Παῦλος· *ἡμεῖς δὲ*
πάντες ἀνακεκαλυμμένῳ προσώπῳ τὴν δόξαν Κυρίου
20 *κατοπτριζόμενοι, τὴν αὐτὴν εἰκόνα μεταμορφούμεθα ἀπὸ*
*δόξης εἰς δόξαν, καθάπερ ἀπὸ Κυρίου πνεύματος.*ᵉ ὥσπερ γὰρ
τὰ διειδῆ κάτοπτρα τῶν εἰσορώντων τοὺς τύπους ἐκμάττεται,
οὕτως αἱ καθαραὶ καρδίαι τοῦ Θεοῦ τὴν δόξαν εἰσδέχονται·
διὸ δὴ καὶ ὁ Κύριος ἔφη, *μακάριοι οἱ καθαροὶ τῇ καρδίᾳ, ὅτι*
25 *αὐτοὶ τὸν Θεὸν ὄψονται.*ᶠ καὶ ὥσπερ ὁ Ἰούδας, τὸν διάβολον
εἰσδεξάμενος, τὴν ἐκείνου πονηρίαν ἐτύπωσεν ἐν ἑαυτῷ,
οὕτως ὁ τῇ θείᾳ χάριτι προσιὼν ταῖς ἐκεῖθεν φερομέναις
μαρμαρυγαῖς καταυγάζεται. οὕτως ὁ ἐν σκότῳ καθήμενος
σκοτοειδὴς γίνεται, ὁ δὲ ἐν ἡλίῳ ἡλιοειδὴς καὶ φωτοειδής.
30 οὕτως ὁ τῷ Θεῷ προσεδρεύων θεοειδεῖς δέχεται χαρακτῆρας.

LXX

Πόθεν εἶχον *τὰ ξύλα τὰ ἄσηπτα;*ᵃ

Σανίδες ἦσαν δεκαπήχεις·ᵇ εἰκὸς τοίνυν ταύτας ἐσχηκέναι
τοὺς εὐπορωτέρους ἐξ Αἰγύπτου μετενεγκόντας ἡνίκα ἐκεῖθεν
ἐξῆλθον. τοὺς δὲ πολυτιμήτους λίθους, καὶ τὸν χρυσόν, καὶ
5 τὸν ἄργυρον, καὶ τὸν χαλκὸν παρ' αἰγυπτίων λαβόντες,
ἀπῆραν· κατὰ γὰρ τὴν θείαν ἐντολήν, *ᾔτησε γυνὴ παρὰ*
γείτονος καὶ συσκήνου αὐτῆς σκεύη ἀργυρᾶ καὶ χρυσᾶ καὶ
*ἱματισμὸν . . . καὶ ἐσκύλευσαν τοὺς αἰγυπτίους.*ᶜ διὸ δὴ καὶ τὰ
προσφερόμενα *ἀπαρχὰς* προσηγόρευσεν ὁ τῶν ὅλων Θεὸς ὡς
10 ἀκροθίνια σκύλων.ᵈ

---

e. 2Cor 3.18   f. Mt 5.8

lxx A [32], B, C, 4 7 9 10 17 31 35 37 = 22 mss.

a. Ex 35.24   b. Ex 26.16   c. Ex 3.22   d. Ex 35.5

from the Lord, the Spirit."[e] Just as a clear mirror reproduces the image of one who looks into it, so a pure heart takes into itself the glory of God. Hence, the Lord said, "Blessed are the pure in heart, for they will see God."[f] As Judas received the devil into himself and gave shape to the wickedness of the devil in his own person, so he who approaches divine grace reflects its splendor. As the face of a man sitting in darkness becomes dark, while the face of a man sitting in sunlight becomes beaming and bright, so he who sits next to God acquires the features of God.

LXX

How were they in possession of incorruptible wood?[1a]

The planks were ten cubits long,[b] so it is likely that the more affluent people took them along when they were departing from Egypt. When they left, they took from the Egyptians precious stones, gold, silver, and bronze as they were commanded by God: "A woman asked her neighbor and her housemate for silver and gold vessels and clothing, and they despoiled the Egyptians."[c] Hence, the God of the universe referred to these offerings as "first-fruits," since they were the first pickings of booty.[d]

---

1. The Greek ἄσηπτα, representing the Hebrew word for "acacia," may also mean "incorruptible," the sense in which Theodoret here understands the term. It is unclear whether the question regards the marvelous incorruptibility of the wood or the availability, in the wilderness, of any wood at all.

LXXI

Ποίου χαρίσματος οἱ περὶ τὸν Βεσελεὴλ ἔτυχον;[a]
Σοφίας ἀρχιτεκτονικῆς. ἔστι γὰρ σοφία ὑφαντική, καὶ
σοφία γεωργική, καὶ σοφία ἰατρική. ἕκαστον δὲ τούτων δῶρον
Θεοῦ, εἰς χρῆσιν τοῖς ἀνθρώποις δεδωρημένον.

LXXII

Διὰ τί τῇ νουμηνίᾳ τοῦ πρώτου μηνὸς στῆσαι τὴν σκηνὴν
προσέταξεν ὁ Θεός;[a]
Ἐπειδὴ κατὰ τοῦτον τὸν καιρὸν τὴν κτίσιν ἐδημιούργησε.
καὶ μαρτυρεῖ τῷδε τῷ λόγῳ τῶν δένδρων ἡ βλάστησις·
5 *βλαστησάτω, γάρ φησιν, ἡ γῆ βοτάνην χόρτου, σπεῖρον*
σπέρμα κατὰ γένος καὶ καθ' ὁμοιότητα καὶ ξύλον κάρπιμον,
ποιοῦν καρπόν, οὗ τὸ σπέρμα αὐτοῦ ἐν αὐτῷ εἰς ὁμοιότητα
κατὰ γένος ἐπὶ τῆς γῆς·[b] ἀρχομένου δὲ τοῦ ἔαρος, καὶ οἱ
λειμῶνες ἀνθοῦσι, καὶ κυμαίνει τὰ λήϊα, καὶ τὰ δένδρα φύει
10 καρπόν. διά τοι τοῦτο καὶ τὸν Ἰσραὴλ κατὰ τουτονὶ τὸν
καιρὸν ἠλευθέρωσε τῆς αἰγυπτίων δουλείας,[c] καὶ τῇ ἁγίᾳ
παρθένῳ Γαβριὴλ ὁ ἀρχάγγελος ἐκόμισε τῶν παραδόξων ὠδίνων
τὰ εὐαγγέλια.[d] κατὰ τοῦτον τὸν καιρὸν καὶ ὁ δεσπότης
Χριστὸς τὸ σωτήριον ὑπέμεινε πάθος.[e] μάλα τοίνυν εἰκότως τῇ
15 μίᾳ τοῦ πρώτου μηνὸς στῆναι τὴν σκηνὴν ὁ τῶν ὅλων
δεσπότης Θεὸς προσέταξε καὶ ὅτι τοῦ κόσμου παντὸς
ἐκτύπωμα ἦν, καὶ ἵνα εὐτρεπίσῃ πρὸς τὴν τοῦ Πάσχα ἑορτήν,

LXXI A [32], B, C, 4 7 9 10 17 31 35 37 = 22 mss.
a. Ex 35.30–36.2

LXXII A [32], B, c, 50* 51 52 53, 4 7 9 10 17 31* 35 37 = 22 mss.
a Ex 40.1f.   b Gn 1.11 (LXX var.)   c Ex 12.1f.   d Lk 1.26   e Mk 14.12

LXXI

What gift were Bezalel and his men given?[a]

Skill in construction. There is a skill of weaving, a skill of agriculture, and a skill of medicine—each a gift of God bestowed for the use of humanity.

LXXII

Why did God command Moses to erect the tabernacle on the first day of the first month?[a]

Because that was when he created the world. The sprouting of the trees confirms my statement: "Let the earth produce green vegetation, scattering seed according to its kind and likeness, and fruit-bearing trees producing fruit that contains its seed in it for a likeness according to each kind on the earth."[b] At the beginning of spring, the meadows blossom, the wheat waves in the breeze, and the trees bear fruit. Therefore, it was at this time that he freed Israel from slavery to the Egyptians,[c] and the archangel Gabriel brought to the holy Virgin the good news of a miraculous birth.[d] At this time also, Christ the Lord underwent the saving passion.[e] It was entirely appropriate for the Lord God of the universe to order the erection of the tabernacle on the first day of the first month, because it was both a representation of the whole world and a reminder for the

ἦν πρώτην ἐπιτελεῖν νόμος ἦν ἰουδαίοις.ᶠ τότε δὲ καὶ πρῶτον
ταύτην ἔμελλον ἑορτάζειν τὴν ἑορτὴν ἐν τῇ ἐρήμῳ· δεύτερον
20 γὰρ ἦν ἔτος μετὰ τὴν τῆς δουλείας ἀπαλλαγήν.ᵍ

f Ex 12.1–20   g Ex 40.17

people to prepare for the feast of the Passover, the first feast whose celebration was enjoined upon the Jews by the Law.[1f] At that time they were due to have the first celebration of this feast in the wilderness, for a year had passed since their liberation from slavery.[g]

---

1. Theodoret finds four justifications for the date prescribed in Ex 40.2: (1) the indication he discovers in Gn 1.11 that creation occurred in the spring of the first year; (2) the observance of Passover in the month of Nisan, the first month of the Israelite calendar, which fell during our March and April (v. J.L. McKenzie, "Nisan," p. 618); (3) the spring-time date of the Annunciation, which he probably deduces from the liturgical celebration of the birth of Christ nine months later, though Lk 1.21 explicitly dates the Annunciation to the sixth, rather than the first, month; (4) the coincidence of the Passion with the Passover.

Support for the
LIBRARY OF EARLY CHRISTIANITY
from the following donors is gratefully acknowledged

The Annenberg Foundation
Ave Maria School of Law
Christopher A. Beeley
The Gladys Krieble Delmas Foundation
Mr. and Mrs. Peter Flanigan/New York Community Trust
Herrick Jackson and Polly Jackson/The Connemara Fund
Rev. Richard T. Lawrence
The National Endowment for the Humanities
Mr. and Mrs. Michael Novak
Dr. and Mrs. Paul S. Russell
Mark Ryland
Sacred Heart School of Theology
The Cynthia L. and William E. Simon Foundation
The Strake Foundation

Michael J. Aquilina Jr.
Rev. William R. Deutsch
Rev. Gerard H. Ettlinger, S.J.
Everett Ferguson
Rose A. Frascello
Michael Gaddis
Craig L. Hanson
Rev. Stanley S. Harakas
Walter Harrelson
Daniel and Ann James
Joel D. Kalvesmaki
Adam Kamesar
Paul R. Kuhn

Henry Ciemniecki Lang, Ph.D.
Johan Leemans
Rev. Joseph T. Lienhard, S.J.
Samuel J. Mikolaski
Michael Mintz
Susan E. Myers
Rev. Karen L. Onesti
Rev. Dr. L. G. Patterson
Claudia Rapp
Michael Slusser
Louis Swift
Dr. Karen Jo Torjesen
Efthalia Makris Walsh, Ph.D.

Robert Wilde